MW00603737

EVERY MAN DID HIS DUTY

CONTENTS

FOREWORD

THE CIVIL WAR WAS THE SINGLE most important event in American history. It shook the foundations of the Constitution and the union of states, challenged America's self-image as a progressive and growing nation, and was a turning point in the Industrial Revolution. The war killed three-quarters of a million citizens and touched every household. The young state of Minnesota saw tragic civil strife at home when the Dakota War emptied half the state and killed more of its civilians than the Civil War did its soldiers on the battlefield. The 24,000 Minnesotans who served on campaigns in the East, the Deep South, and Dakota Territory left an enviable record of hardship, heroics, and triumph. But none surpassed the sacrifice of the state's first volunteers. Their iconic charge at Gettysburg symbolizes a devotion to the cause that has become legendary.

But why the continuing fascination with the First Minnesota when so many other of the state's youths were equally heroic? The regiment was the very first to be volunteered in April 1861 and soon suffered a higher percentage of casualties than any other federal unit at the war's first big battle, Bull Run. As the only Minnesota regiment to serve in the East through the entire war, it gained the attention of the East Coast press, which dominated national news. Fighting there in the war's best-known battles, the First earned a solid record surpassed by few units. Indeed, they carried the reputation of their state on their sleeves more than any other of Minnesota's twenty-one Civil War military organizations. And twenty horrific minutes on July 2, 1863, at Gettysburg Pennsylvania crowned them with the laurels of heroic and patriotic martyrs.

Author Wayne Jorgenson was captivated by the legend of the First Minnesota some forty years ago when he helped found the *re-created* First Minnesota reenactment unit. He marched and camped with similar-minded amateur historians in parades, movies, community festivals, and battle reenactments to get a firsthand, if safe and temporary, feel for a Civil War soldier's life. Over the years he has painstakingly assembled the largest collection of original First Minnesota artifacts through carefully nurtured contacts, perusal of dealer catalogs and auctions, and not a little serendipity. He now eagerly shares the resources of that collection with scholars and museums.

But in Jorgenson's focus on the regiment, he soon came to awe the men who made it. These men were New England bluebloods, transplanted Maine lumbermen, native Minnesotans born in a tipi or a military outpost, recent immigrants from Europe, former legislators or soldiers, and not a few teenagers who lied about their age in order to enlist. They were the first to rush to join up, quickly filling hundred-man companies raised from the new villages and farms along the Mississippi, St. Croix, and Minnesota rivers.

The new recruits were led by a succession of experienced or career soldiers, each of whom earned a general's star by promotion or brevet largely through the exploits of the men they commanded. The volunteers rivaled regulars in their drill and bearing, while the casualties they suffered at Bull Run, on the Peninsula Campaign, and at Antietam and elsewhere proved their eagerness to fight. But as experienced veterans at Gettysburg, their willing sacrifice in the face of assured death or injury proved them even more.

These individuals who collectively decided to charge were the ones who prompted Jorgenson to write this book. He has painstakingly re-created their stories from county histories, family records, 1860s letters and diaries, census records, and newspaper accounts. On numerous trips to the National Archives, he perused hundreds of service records and pension files. Eventually, he helped produce the most complete website for any Civil War regiment, with personal biographies of well over a thousand men who served with the First and photographs of a quarter of them. This book contains a selection of those biographies and photos in order to help readers understand this unique group of Minnesotans.

Sgt. George Buckman wrote a final entry in his

diary as he mustered out of the First Minnesota: "The past seems like a dream. Three years of active service in Va., Md. and Penna., and a citizen again. Truly I have something to remember. The terrible battlefield, the dusty weary march, the long nights when on pickets in storm and cold—can I forget?" Jorgenson's compelling stories will help modern readers never forget the men of the First Minnesota.

The story of the First Regiment of Minnesota Volunteer Infantry is a fine source of inspiration today. What kind of men, especially young men with all of life before them, would hold love of country, belief in a righteous cause, and personal and collective honor so highly that they would willingly sacrifice their lives? They were indeed exceptional. Their story needs to be told again and again!

Stephen E. Osman
Senior Historian,
Minnesota Historical Society
(Retired)
May 2012

PREFACE

FOR OVER 150 YEARS both professional and lay historians have been captivated by the Civil War, and they have written thousands of books about its battles and the regiments that fought in them. The First Regiment of Minnesota Volunteer Infantry was one such unit, and several fine books have been written about it and its outstanding record of service during the war, particularly at the Battle of Gettysburg.

Theirs was the first volunteer regiment tendered to President Lincoln at the outbreak of the war, and they served from April 29, 1861, until they were mustered out on May 5, 1864, at the expiration of their three-year term of enlistment. Some of the men went on to serve out their enlistment in the successor unit, the First Battalion of Minnesota Infantry, which was mustered out at the end of the war on June 25, 1865.

Most deservedly, the First Minnesota received many honors for its service to the cause. The regiment's men had a reputation for being physically strong and mentally determined and knowing how to shoot a rifle. Yet this regiment was made up of common men who, like anyone, had strengths and weaknesses. Many were farmers or lumberjacks who by such lifestyle were comfortable being outside and in a rugged environment. Living on the frontier, many had to learn to shoot to both protect themselves and provide food for the table.

At the beginning of the war, approximately one thousand men were brought together to form the regiment. Many were transplants from eastern states, but many others were recent immigrants from countries like Norway, Sweden, Ireland, Germany, France, and Switzerland. Many spoke their native language better than they did English. More than one soldier wrote home about hearing another language being spoken among a cluster of men in their tents at night.

Pinpointing why these men fought so well and earned the respect of other states' units might start with their origins and the hardships they endured emigrating from other countries. These men appreciated their newfound freedom and the opportunities available to them in this new land. A pioneering spirit lifted the state, and people were excited about the future. And these men were used to the rugged life required to develop their new home. That strength and rugged individualism served them well during the war. When the nation that had offered them opportunity and freedom was threatened, many rose up to fight for themselves and their newly adopted country. Few believed it would take long to put down the rebellious Southerners. Few of the Minnesotans, if any, could imagine how this insurrection, begun in South Carolina, would change their lives and those of every person in the nation.

The trials and tribulations they experienced over the next three years would leave all who survived changed for life. Some would be maimed physically; others, emotionally. But one thing became clear: these men of differing backgrounds were comrades in arms, and their friendships bound them together for the rest of their lives. No matter what they did for a living after the war and no matter where they were living, they shared a common bond.

This book is not a history of the regiment, which has been done very well already. This is a study of and tribute to the individual men. For the most part, I have organized the men by company. By presenting their stories in this way, I hope you will get to know them in the smaller groups that were their families in the field. I also have chosen to present only the stories of men for whom I have found a photograph. My hope is that by seeing them and reading their stories you will feel like you have gotten to know them a little better. When you have finished the book, I hope you will say a silent thank you to these men for what they undertook so many years ago and, by doing so, thank every service person who has risen to the call of their country when they were needed.

In 1890 a board of commissioners appointed by the state legislature published a two-volume work entitled *Minnesota in the Civil and Indian Wars*. It contains the rosters and a brief history of every Minnesota regiment in the war. *The History of the First*

Minnesota Infantry, published in 1916, has been the basis for our knowledge about the unit and was compiled from notes and records of many of the survivors. Almost ninety years later, in 1993, Richard Moe added an updated history entitled *The Last Full Measure*. His thorough research brought many interesting stories to light. For *No More Gallant a Deed,* published in 2001, Steven Keillor edited the memoirs of Sgt. James Wright of Company F. This wonderfully written book is an excellent presentation of the life of a soldier as seen through his own eyes. In the early 1900s, Sgt. Wright was encouraged by his comrades to write the history of their company, and over several years he did so, sending the finished manuscript to a newspaper editor in Red Wing. Unfortunately, the editor did nothing with it until years later he sent it to the Minnesota Historical Society, where it lay unappreciated in their archives. Keillor found it, skillfully edited the work, and made this marvelous story available to the world. In 2002, Brian Leehan published the definitive study of the First Minnesota at Gettysburg, entitled *Pale Horse at Plum Run*. These books cumulatively comprise a wealth of knowledge about the regiment. In this book I have tried to add a personal touch by sharing photographs of the men and stories that help us get a feel for their character. Some stories are from the books previously mentioned, and some have since surfaced from other sources.

Finally, I would like to acknowledge that even with twenty years of research and data gathering, once this book has gone to print new facts will arise. Some will refute what I have thought to be the case. Others simply will add to what is known. That is the way it will always be. I have tried my best to do justice to these men, and I apologize for any errors that will show up over time. I hope you enjoy the journey through this book. Come meet some of the men of the First Regiment of Minnesota Volunteer Infantry.

Wayne D. Jorgenson

ACKNOWLEDGMENTS

No book like this can be put together without the help of other people, and I would like to thank a few that have been particularly important for this one.

Stephen Osman is my oldest friend in terms of a shared Civil War passion and thirst for knowledge. We met in the summer of 1973 and, along with a few others, formed a Civil War reenactment group, the First Regiment of Minnesota Volunteer Infantry, named after the most famous regiment to serve from Minnesota. Because of the regiment's history of sacrifice, we always held ours as a position of responsibility and took pride in always "doing it right." Steve started reenacting while still in high school. After his graduation from St. Olaf College, he worked for the Minnesota Historical Society, and his intimate knowledge of the Civil War made him the perfect candidate to work at and eventually run the society's Ft. Snelling historic site. He has been a continual source of inspiration in writing this book and in my collecting Civil War artifacts related to the First Minnesota.

Several years ago, Chuck Barden, who initially created the First Minnesota website, showed me what he was doing. I fell in love with it and soon began to contribute my research and writing. I am proud of its use by teachers and students in studying Minnesota's role in the Civil War. Descendants of these soldiers have learned about their ancestors, and many have also offered information that has helped round out the soldiers' stories. Over the past twenty years, thousands of hours have gone into the website's creation, growth, and improvement, and I hope it will be available as a resource for years to come. My thanks go to Chuck for starting this process. Without him the site would not be what it is (www.1stminnesota.net).

Several years ago, Ewald Hausdorf, military attaché at the Austrian embassy in Washington, DC, sent an email asking if I would like the website translated into German. He wrote that many Germans would enjoy reading the site. I was impressed by his offer but believed it too big a task for anyone to take on. I asked, however, if he could suggest a translator for a diary I possessed that was written in Old German, and as luck would have it, both Ewald and his wife, Maria, were raised speaking Old German. I sent them the diary, written by Pvt. Balthasar Best (Co. K), and over a period of months, they translated it. Thus began a friendship that has lasted many years. I stayed with them while researching at the National Archives in Washington, DC, and they have been to our home in Minnesota. Together, we gave a presentation for the townspeople of Traer, Iowa, where Best lived and ran a hotel after the war.

Roger Norland has spent hundreds of hours at the microfilm library of the Minnesota Historical Society, searching through newspapers and copying articles relating to the First Minnesota and its men. The letters he found, sent home by soldiers and then published in local papers, have been a great source of information.

Jonathan Webb Diess has spent countless hours at the National Archives in Washington, DC, where his full-time job is researching military records for people throughout the world. I have enjoyed my many trips and hours spent at the archives, and he has always made that time even better by finding new tidbits of useable information. Jon proudly notes that he can trace his family tree back to several men who served in the Civil War, including Pvt. Lester Webb of Company F.

Michael Cunningham has built an excellent collection of First Minnesota artifacts over the years and has been a good source of information on the men.

Perry Tholl and Jeff Williamson have spent a lot of time researching the First Minnesota at the Minnesota Historical Society and have been kind enough to share their wealth of knowledge.

Brent Peterson, curator of the Washington County Historical Society, has helped greatly with my research on the men from Stillwater who comprised most of Company B.

Darryl and Diane Sannes have been dedicated to the history of the men who served from the Brooklyn

Center/Osseo area northwest of Minneapolis. They aided me as I began to add the final touches to the book.

The Minnesota Historical Society has been the repository of our state's history for over 150 years. The society's staff is dedicated to both preserving and exhibiting documents and artifacts that record the history of the state and the people who have lived within its boundaries, and they do a superb job. Ft. Snelling, the society's largest historic site, is a living history exhibit, having been many Minnesota soldiers' point of entry into the Civil War and the wars that followed.

I thank Ben Saltzman, a professional photographer who, with the aid of his artistic wife, Judy, brought to life many of the artifacts seen in this book.

I would like to take a moment to acknowledge all the wonderful friends I have made over the years through my association with the First Minnesota reenactment unit. Begun in 1973, it quickly became regarded as one of the finest and most authentic of the reenactment units in the field. We took pride in representing the men of the Old First and enjoyed camping and reenacting battles with other authentic units who had that same pride in what they were doing and representing. We camped together, acted as extras in a few movies, and "drank from the same canteen," as the veterans used to say. Knowing that I cannot name all, I will mention a few of the many who have been important friends over the years: Terry Clymer, Bill Dalin, Chuck Fouzie (a World War II POW), John Grossman, John Guthmann, John Hackett, Gene Henrickson, George Johnson, Jim Moffett, John Murdock, Stephen Osman, Bruce and Bernie Paulson, Steve Rogosheske, and Bob Snoufer.

Over the years many other people, including descendants of the veterans, have added to this work, and I give them my sincere thanks.

My thanks go to book designer and project manager Wendy Holdman and my editor, Mike Hanson, for their hard work and dedication.

Finally, I want to thank my wife, Carol, who has patiently and lovingly tolerated my thousands of hours spent in front of the computer. She also worked on cleaning up many of the pictures you see in this book. Without her support this book could not have been realized. I cannot thank her enough or adequately express my appreciation and love for who she is and what she has meant to me through all these years.

About the Photographs

Having come to america from France in the 1840s, photography was still in its infancy when the Civil War began. Most people did not own photographic equipment, so portraits had to be taken at a photographer's studio. It took several seconds to get enough light into the camera to produce a high-quality picture (oftentimes, a hidden brace would be used to hold subjects' necks straight and prevent movement while the picture was being taken). These necessarily long exposures explain the unsmiling faces commonly seen in photography and typical of the photographs in this book.

Four types of technology were available to the 1860s photographer. Invented in France around 1838–39, the daguerreotype was the first commercially successful photographic process. Commonly referred to as *dags,* they predominated from 1839 to the mid-1850s. Produced in the camera by exposure onto either a silver plate or a silver-covered copper plate, daguerreotypes can be easily identified by their mirror-like reflections. Though not reflective on the printed page, the picture of Dr. Jacob Stewart as a militia soldier in the 1850s provides an example (see p. 57).

In the 1850s the newer ambrotype process rose in popularity. A negative image was developed on clear glass, and when a black cloth or other dark backing was placed behind it, the result was a clear positive image. Since ambrotypes were glass, it was necessary to house them in a hard case for protection. Examples include the images of Pvt. Charles Baker and Pvt. Adelbert Bryant on the next page.

Somewhat concurrently with and eventually eclipsing ambrotypes, another new photographic technique began to catch on in the late 1850s. The image was produced on a thin iron plate using an underexposed negative image. The use of an underexposed image allowed for a shorter exposure time, which was a boon to portraiture. At first known as *ferrotypes* or *malainotypes,* these new creations quickly came to be called *tintypes.* Though still needing a case, tintypes were more durable than either daguerreotypes or ambrotypes. They also could be produced more cheaply. Tintypes were popular into the late 1800s but could not compete with paper photography as it developed.

The *carte de visite* (visiting card) was created in 1854 by Parisian photographer André-Adolphe-Eugène Disdéri and was the cheapest of the four photographic processes. Using a single glass negative, multiple copies of an image could be printed onto thin sheets of paper treated with albumen, a chemical found in egg whites. These prints were then neatly cut and pasted onto stiff, thick paper that resembled thin pieces of cardboard.

Shortly after the beginning of the war, photographers began taking their equipment to their clients in the field. They set up their studios in tents, where they took soldiers' likenesses, processed the photographs, and delivered them to the soldiers soon after.

These photographs were exchanged with or given to comrades as a remembrance of someone with whom they had served, and they were lightweight and easily mailed to loved ones back home. This form of photography quickly became the most popular for the Civil War soldier.

In the fall of 1861, the men of the First Minnesota were issued their first dress uniforms. The uniform consisted of a nine-button dark-blue frock coat, sky-blue wool pants, and a stiff black felt Hardee hat with a black ostrich plume. On each shoulder of the frock coat was attached a brass shoulder scale. The shoulder scales consisted of a series of brass plates, or scales, articulated together. These pieces were held together by another piece of brass wrapped around the outer edge, which created a smooth look and feel. The shoulder scales were copied from French dress uniforms. In theory, they were designed to fend off saber blows from oncom-

ing cavalry, but that event seldom if ever happened. If anything, the sun's reflection off the bright, polished brass served more to draw the attention of enemy riflemen than to protect soldiers from harm. Thus, early in the war the soldiers learned to discard their scales or to wear them only when required: during dress parades or when on provost guard detail. Part of the shoulder scale looked somewhat like fish scales, and thus, veteran troops mockingly referred to new troops who marched into camp or battle proudly wearing their shiny, new uniforms as "fresh fish."

The following is a sample of pictures taken by the men at the time they received their dress uniforms. The similar backdrop and style of posing show that many men went to the same photographer. One can imagine them walking together to the photographer's tent and waiting and watching from the side while a friend posed for his picture.

Some photographers used a U.S. flag for a backdrop in their tents. From left to right is Pvt. Charles Baker (Co. D), Pvt. Adelbert Bryant (Co. D) (inscribed on the inside of this ambrotype's case is, "Received Dec 3, 1861, Adelbert Bryant, Age 22 years"), Pvt. Ed Bassett (Co. G), Pvt. Adin Laflin (Co. D), and Pvt. William Roe (Co. I).

These photographs were processed in the hard-paper carte de visite format. These two soldiers from Company K went to a photographer's tent, where a dark cloth was used for a background. On the left is Pvt. Balthasar Best, and on the right, Pvt. William Abell.

"Please rest your elbow on the table next to your hat." From left to right above is Cpl. Henry Van Vorhes (Co. B), Pvt. Dietrich Vogelsang (Co. A), and Pvt. William Worthington (Co. I). Cpl. Charles Steen (Co. A) is at the left.

"Or if you didn't bring a hat, just rest your arm on the table." Pictured here is Pvt. George Sawyer (Co. G).

Hat Brass

Later in the war, as the rules on uniforms and dress relaxed somewhat, some enlisted men started wearing more comfortable hats. Some decorated their hats with letters and numbers, usually made of stamped brass, which designated their units. Here are three examples of head gear and decoration done by men of the First Minnesota in the 1863–64 time period.

Charles Boardman (Co. K) had this picture taken while recovering in Philadelphia from a wound received at Fredericksburg. He has discarded the regular-issue forage cap and decorated his floppy "slouch hat."

This unidentified soldier has placed a similar marking on his forage cap. The picture was also taken in Philadelphia, where many men were sent to recover from their Gettysburg wounds. He appears to be from company B or D.

Seen here in 1864, Emil Graf (Co. B) added a large corps badge and regimental markings to his forage cap.

A Brief History of the First Regiment of Minnesota Volunteer Infantry

IN 1819 THE U.S. GOVERNMENT authorized the establishment of a military outpost at the meeting point of the Minnesota and Mississippi rivers in an effort to secure the country's westwardly expanding border. Initially named Fort St. Anthony, after the nearby waterfall, the fort had its name changed in 1824 to honor its first commandant, Col. Josiah Snelling. Between 1828 and 1848, settlements developed along the Mississippi and St. Croix rivers—St. Paul, St. Anthony, and Stillwater—and in 1849, with a population of about 4,500, Minnesota Territory was established. In 1853, President Pierce appointed thirty-seven-year-old Willis Gorman the first territorial governor. Gorman was a lawyer who had fought in the U.S.–Mexican War as an officer in an Indiana regiment. Gorman would go on to play a prominent role during the Civil War as the first of five colonels who commanded the First Minnesota.

Col. Josiah Snelling

During the territorial period, logging and grain milling were the primary industries, but by the late 1850s, the state had become fundamentally agricultural. As the Ojibwe and the Dakota ceded more land to European settlers the state's population mushroomed from just 6,077 people in 1850 to 172,023 in 1860. Unfortunately, little of the money paid for the land actually made its way to the tribes themselves.

Many of the new settlers were from northern European countries such as England, Ireland, Norway, Sweden, Germany, France, and Switzerland. Most were farmers seeking new land, and many saw settling in Minnesota as their chance at a good life. The land was a virtual Garden of Eden for those who had fled poverty and hunger in their former homelands. Now, they could own land, raise and support a family, and be a part of the growth of this new frontier. As settlements began to spring up throughout the territory, the excitement was palpable. Almost every ten miles a small settlement would appear—a comfortable day's roundtrip for a farmer tending business in a neighboring town.

On May 11, 1858, Minnesota became the thirty-second state admitted to the Union. It was a difficult year for Minnesota, as a land speculation bubble burst and the ensuing financial panic forced several banks to close their doors. That same year in Wright County, just west of Minneapolis, Henry A. Wallace was murdered, and his neighbor Oscar Jackson was indicted. Jackson went to trial in St. Paul in 1859 and was found not guilty. The residents of Wright County were outraged. Jackson would have been wise to leave the state, but instead, upon his release on April 21, he returned to his home in Rockford Township and was lynched by his fellow citizens in a ruckus that became known, somewhat overdramatically, as the Wright County War.

The local sheriff did little either to prevent the hanging or to bring the lynchers to trial, and the general lawlessness led Governor Sibley to order the state's

Farmers use an Esterly reaper in St. Paul in 1860

militia units to the county to stabilize the area, which was quickly done. Tempers cooled, and people returned to their daily lives. The units sent by Sibley included the Pioneer Guard, the Stillwater Guard, and the City Guard of St. Paul.[1] When the Civil War began, many men from these units were early enlistees and formed the core of the First Minnesota.

At 4:30 A.M. on April 12, 1861, angry Southern citizens bombarded Ft. Sumter, located on a small island in the harbor of Charleston, South Carolina. The federal government was unprepared for war. At the time, the U.S. Army comprised 16,000 men, most of whom were stationed on the western frontier. Supporting the regular army were various state militia groups, but their training and discipline were questionable at best. Under the old militia law of 1795, Congress was able, through the president, to increase the army and call up state militias. Showing their roots in the Revolutionary War experience, the militias could be called up for a term of service no longer than three months. With that as his guideline, President Lincoln sent a message to Secretary of War Simon Cameron authorizing him to recruit an army of 75,000 men for the specified three-month period to put down this uprising.

On Sunday morning, April 14, Governor Ramsey happened to be in Washington, DC, and visited his friend Simon Cameron to pay his respects. He found Cameron in his coat and hat, ready to leave to see the president. After a brief discussion of what had transpired at Ft. Sumter and what the president was requesting, Ramsey quickly volunteered 1,000 men from the state of Minnesota for the cause. Cameron said, "Sit down and place in writing the tender you have made, as I am now on my way to the president's mansion." Governor Ramsey sat down and wrote out his offer. He handed the paper to Secretary Cameron,

Driving logs in 1860

The Minnesota State Capitol in St. Paul in 1860

who folded the paper, put it in his pocket, and headed off to see the president. Thus, Minnesota gained the claim of being the first state to volunteer men for service in the Civil War.

On April 15, President Lincoln called forth the militia, and the tender was accepted. Governor Ramsey immediately telegraphed Lieutenant Governor Ignatius Donnelly the following:

Issue proclamation in my name calling for volunteers under a requisition of the President of the United States for one regiment of infantry from Minnesota, to report at St Paul forthwith.

For the next four years, the men of the state rallied to their country's call. No other northern state provided a higher percentage of men to the Union's cause. About half the state's eligible male population entered the service in one of the state's twenty-two military units.

Adjutant General Acker immediately went to work

Seen here in August 1859 are three civilian military companies in Monticello during what came to be called the Wright County War: the Pioneer Guard *(left)*, the Stillwater Guard *(center)*, and the City Guard of St. Paul *(right)*.

Governor Alexander Ramsey in 1860

Greenwald. A message had been sent from St. Paul to Willis Gorman, who was then a judge and was, on that date, holding court in Anoka. Upon reading the message, he adjourned court, announced what had happened at Ft. Sumter, and asked for volunteers from among the citizens of Anoka. That evening, a meeting was held, and several men stepped forward to stamp out this treason.

Aaron Greenwald was the first to volunteer and later claimed to be the first man to volunteer for the Union cause. That same evening, however, a recruiting rally was also held at the St. Paul armory, where the Pioneer Guard held their meetings. At the end of the rally, Josias King ran forward to be the first to put his name down. Both he and Greenwald served in the regiment together, and both laid claim to being the first man to volunteer. Greenwald died at Gettysburg, and thus, almost by default, the title and credit for this distinction went to Josias King.

Acker arranged to have the volunteers meet at Ft. Snelling. The government had stopped using the fort several years prior and had sold the property. A farmer had purchased the land and was using the grounds as grazing land for his animals. Acker arranged to bring it back into service and have supplies sent to the fort to equip and feed the troops. Quickly, groups of men formed and headed to Ft. Snelling to join the army, including several students from Hamline University in Red Wing who had enlisted together and formed the core of what would become Company F.

The population of Minneapolis at the time of the

raising a regiment comprising ten companies of about one hundred men each. Theoretically, Minnesota had eight militia units in the state, which were there to protect the civilians from harm should any trouble develop with the native Indian population. The hope was that they would be the nucleus of some of the ten companies recruited.

Patriotic recruiting rallies occurred throughout the state, and many men were proud to step up and be one of the first to volunteer. One such man was Aaron

In 1858, seeking to preserve history, ambrotype pictures were taken of the members of Minnesota's first state legislature. In April 1861, as recruiting rallies were held, four of these men rose to the call. Others would follow and join later regiments. From left to right is John Chase of St. Vincent (Co. E), Dr. John LeBlond of Brownsville (surgeon), Lewis McKune of Morristown (Co. G), and Anson Northrup of Swan River (wagon master).

In 1860 the state fair was held on the grounds of Ft. Snelling. At the time the picture was taken, Senator Cassius M. Clay was delivering an address to the crowd. Little did these visitors know that within a year these peaceful grounds would become a recruiting depot used to send Minnesota's sons and loved ones off to war.

1860 census was just 2,564. Across the river was St. Anthony, with a larger population of 3,258. Despite the cities' relatively small size, their militia units became the core of two companies, each comprising close to one hundred men. Minneapolis' militia formed Company D, and St. Anthony's, the St. Anthony Zouaves, became Company E. Taking so many men from these small populations had an impact. In St. Anthony the owner of the St. Charles Hotel, Anson Northrup, announced that since all the able-bodied male employees "to the number of seven" had enlisted, the hotel would "probably be closed in a few days." Northrup intended to serve with his two sons in Company E, but as the regiment was taking shape, he was given a greater responsibility and appointed the wagon master of the regiment.

Adjutant General Acker actively recruited a company of men on his own. Once the needed men had been raised and his primary duty accomplished, he resigned his position as adjutant general and joined the regiment. In the tradition of the militia units, the men elected their company officers, whereas the regiment's three senior field officers were appointed by the governor. Acker was voted captain, and his group became Company C of the new regiment.

Ft. Snelling, located on the banks of the Mississippi River, served as the staging place for all of the troops Minnesota contributed to the Civil War.

By April 29, 1861, just two weeks after the shelling of Ft. Sumter, enough men had arrived to muster ten companies into the service of the U.S. government. They were thenceforth known as the First Regiment of Minnesota Volunteer Infantry. Governor Ramsey appointed Willis Gorman colonel of the regiment. Forty-six years old, he was a medium-sized man with dark hair and a mustache that was starting to gray. A U.S.–Mexican War veteran, he was a fine, soldierly looking man with a strong, clear voice easily heard and felt, and as the men soon learned, he was an expert in the classical use of cuss words. He was a strict disciplinarian and drilled the men constantly. Though they complained at times, later in the war many acknowledged that this early training helped them to survive and to gain the distinction and respect accorded them as one of the best units in the Union army.

The companies chose their names and were assigned letters based on their acceptance by the state. The names and dates of acceptance are as follows:

Co. A, Pioneer Guard, St. Paul, April 19
Co. B, Stillwater Guard, Stillwater, April 20
Co. C, St. Paul Volunteers, St. Paul, April 22
Co. D, Lincoln Guards, Minneapolis, April 23
Co. E, St. Anthony Zouaves, St. Anthony, April 24
Co. F, Goodhue County Volunteers, Red Wing, April 25
Co. G, Faribault Guards, Faribault, April 25
Co. H, Dakota County Volunteers, Hastings, April 26
Co. I, Wabasha Volunteers, Wabasha, April 26
Co. K, Winona Volunteers, Winona, April 26

The state arsenal had some muskets, which were distributed along with some leather gear, also known as *accoutrements*. Though uniforms were available for the officers, the men continued to wear their civilian clothes, as there were not enough uniforms for all one thousand newly enlisted men. Since logging was a major industry in the state, an ample supply of lumbermen's clothes was available. The clothes were ordered, and soon, the men found themselves clothed in black felt hats, dark pants, and overshirts of various colors, though red seemed to predominate. The men of Company K received new handmade gray uniforms from the women of Winona, which were gladly accepted. Frank Mead described the uniforms as being more white than gray, which can be seen in George Burgess' photograph (see p. 219). The Winona men

proudly wore these uniforms until the Battle of Bull Run, where the prevalence of Confederate gray caused a problem in identifying friend from foe.

On Thursday, May 8, 1861, the ladies of St. Anthony and Minneapolis treated the men of the First to a gala feast at the fort. At three o'clock, the entire regiment was drawn up in a hollow square formation to witness the presentation of flags by the ladies of the two cities to Minneapolis' Company D and St. Anthony's Company E.

At about this time, the government changed their call from an enlistment of ninety days to one of three years—or less if it took less time to suppress the rebellion. The men were asked to reenlist for the three years. Some had families that would suffer without their support for that long. Others felt they needed to be back for the fall harvest. In the end 619 men reenlisted for the three years, and several hundred declined and returned home.

By May 10, recruiting was begun to refill the ranks. Many of the regiment's officers were sent back out into the state to fill the vacancies. While recruiting, Col. Gorman received an invitation from the ladies of St. Anthony and Minneapolis to a picnic for the soldiers, which was to be held on Nicollet Island, located on the Mississippi River between their two communities. Thinking the event would be enjoyable for the men and the march to and from the island good exercise, he agreed. On Tuesday morning, May 21, 1861, eight companies marched out of the Ft. Snelling gate and headed to Minneapolis.

Once there, the troops took turns crossing the recently constructed suspension bridge. A photographer set up his camera and took what has turned out to be a historic picture—an ambrotype of the men of Company D. With 2nd Lt. DeWitt Smith standing in command at their front, the photographer took a picture.

As mentioned, Col. Gorman was a stickler for drill, and though the men complained, the constant attention paid to learning the drill and knowing how to maneuver on the battlefield benefited them time and time again throughout their service. According to one member of the regiment, a typical day was as follows:

5 AM	Reveille
6 AM	Sick Call
7 AM	Breakfast (coffee, good bread, butter, cold beef hash and boiled murphies)
7:30 AM	Guard Mount
8–10 AM	Company Drill

Taken at about the time it opened in 1855, this sixth-plate daguerreotype view shows the first permanent span across the Mississippi River. After the men of Company D had their picture taken, they crossed this bridge from Minneapolis, in the foreground, to Nicollet Island, on the far side, and to the picnic that awaited them.

10–11 AM	Battalion Parade
1 PM	Dinner
2–4 PM	Company Drill
4–6 PM	Battalion Parade
6 PM	Supper
7 PM	Dress parade
9 PM	Roll Call—tattoo
9:30 PM	Lights Out

[The term *murphies* is a reference to a common Irish food—boiled potatoes.]

A story is recorded that indicates other photographs may have been taken of the regiment in its early existence. Unfortunately, none seem to have been preserved. The event occurred in June, just before the regiment left for the East. The following excerpt is from *Crusader and Feminist: Letters of Jane Grey Swisshelm, 1858–1865*:

About 2 o'clock, Col. Gorman's great war horse was led up to the door of headquarters, and three men succeeded in getting the saddle on him. Was there to be a drill? Nobody knew. The band drew up at the headquarters, and rolled out great strain of martial music, swelling up to the clouds in a grand symphony, and carrying the souls of the listeners so far upward that the bodies appeared loth to stay pinned to the solid Earth.

This photograph was taken in front of the commandant's house at Ft. Snelling, probably in May 1861. From left to right are Lt. Col. Stephen Miller (in front of the flag), Sgt. Howard Stansbury (holding the flag), Col. Willis Gorman (sash across chest), Maj. William Dike, Lt. and Adj. William B. Leach, Lt. and Quartermaster Mark Downie, Pvt. Edgar L. Sproat, Senator Morton S. Wilkinson, Lt. Sanders (mustering officer), and John B. Sanborn (white pants and vest), who served as the state's adjutant general. Standing in the center of the crowd, behind and between Dike and Leach, can be seen the tall Capt. William Colvill. The identifications were made by William Leach in 1897 for the *Minneapolis Times* when he lent the picture for publication. At the time, he was the last survivor of the men identified in it.

Presently Col. Miller comes hurrying up. They are to proceed to the parade ground, and his horse is away to be shod. Maybe Major Dyke's in the same case, as a noble animal is un-hitched from a visitor's buggy, and prepared for his use—Soon they all mustered on the parade ground—Col. Miller on a fine grey, borrowed to take Fanny's place. By slow degrees it became known that the object of the muster was to permit an artist to take Photographic views of the regiment. These were taken first in line-of-battle order, or standing side by side two deep, one rank behind the other. Col. Gorman and staff in the centre, and behind far enough to command a view of the entire line. Col. Miller to his right and Major Dyke to the left. The standard bearer, young Strawsberry [Howard Stansbury], a slight, fiery youth, held aloft the magnificent flag presented by Mrs. Ramsey and the ladies of St. Paul. It is of heavy silk, dark blue, the Min-

nesota coat of arms exquisitely painted in the centre on one side and a Union motto on the other and edged in heavy gold fringe. This is the parade flag. The battle flag is the National ensign of rich silk. A second picture was taken, every company standing in single file, one behind the other, about twenty rods apart.—Col. Gorman and staff in the centre, between the lines, Col. Miller near the front and Major Dyke in the rear. They presented a fine appearance. The two rear companies under Major Dyke had been uniformed at Fort Ridgely in the U.S. uniform of dark blue frock coats with brass shoulder pieces. The others were all in bright red shirts with dark blue pants like the others. Col. Gorman's horse is a superb and ponderous bright bay, a gift from the people of St. Paul. The Col. rides well, so does Major Dyke, who is a large and portly man; but Col. Miller is much the best rider of the three, mounts with the utmost ease and looks exceedingly well on horse-back. The arms of the men were highly polished and they handle their guns with great precision.—The few maneuvers they performed in getting into line and changing form were done promptly and without the slightest confusion. From this parade they were dismissed until the dress parade at six in the evening. There appeared to be thousands of visitors on the ground. They were from all parts of the State. So a large proportion of both officers and privates had friends to attend to as well as packing to do.

Several national flags were presented to the companies by the residents of their cities of origin. Winona's Company K presented their flag of stars and stripes to the regiment as its first national color. It was carried in the Battle of Bull Run and was so shot up during the battle that it was retired, sent to St. Paul, and deposited in the capitol.

At five o'clock on the morning of June 22, 1861, the men marched out of Ft. Snelling down to the wharf at the base of the fort, where they boarded two steamers, the *Northern Belle* and the *War Eagle,* and headed down the Mississippi River on the start of their three-year adventure.

It appears that the regiment left with four companies wearing federal blue uniforms (companies A, B, E, and G), one wearing gray uniforms (Company K), and the remaining five (companies C, D, F, H, and I) wearing red shirts and black pants and hats. It appears that the newly uniformed soldiers brought along their red shirts and black pants, as well. In a letter to Governor Ramsey dated July 30, 1861, Col. Gorman notes that prior to Bull Run, nine companies put on their red shirts and black pants and went into the battle looking alike. He writes:

> When we left Alexandria for the battlefield those companies of my Regiment who were provided with fine clothes, had them boxed up & stored in Alexandria for safekeeping & donned their old *Minnesota uniform* & in the battle field covered themselves with Glory. A heavy cloth uniform (such as the regulations require) in summer, if the men were compelled to wear them on drill & parade would be a most intolerable nuisance.

The single exception were the men of Company K, who chose to proudly wear their gray uniforms. As mentioned, Bull Run was the first and last battle in which those uniforms were worn.

The *War Eagle,* seen here in 1865, was one of two paddle-wheelers that carried the First Minnesota troops from Ft. Snelling to La Crosse, Wisconsin. From there the men boarded a train and headed east.

About their clothes and the Battle of Bull Run, historian William Watts Folwell writes, "Their picturesque attire—red flannel shirts, black trousers and slouch hats, however, made them too fair a mark for rebel rifles." After the battle the men straggled back to Centerville and, from there, to Washington, DC. Those who had them put on the federal blue, and those who didn't wished they could be found, for their Minnesota uniforms were not strong enough for the rigorous use of a soldier and were falling apart. The men of those companies that had not been issued regulation uniforms complained, as they were soon reduced to wearing rags. Eventually, the uniforms arrived, and the soldier's life of drilling, drilling, and more drilling under the command of Col. Gorman continued in earnest.

Approximately 1,242 men served in the regiment during its three-year term of enlistment.[2] The youngest was William "Billy" Nixon, who served as the drummer for Company A. He was fourteen years, one month, and two days old when he enlisted. The oldest was probably William Gordon, who was somewhere between fifty-eight and sixty-one when he enlisted.

Most of the men were born in the United States, but many were of northern European ancestry. Of those who served and whose ancestry is known, about 10 percent was born in either Germany or Prussia. Company A alone had twenty-nine men born in Ger-

many. During their leisure time, soldiers would often gather to comfortably speak in their native languages. A soldier walking the campground at night could have passed by crowded tents and heard animated conversations in German, Norwegian, or Swedish. Most of the nineteen recorded Swiss volunteers came from the Stillwater community and served in Company B.

At least eight hundred of the men were born in the United States. Maine was an important contributor to Minnesota, both as settlers and as troops for the new regiment. Approximately 10 percent of the regiment was born or raised in the wooded state of Maine. Several were born in eastern Canada and moved to Maine with their families when they were young children. These families settled in the same area and likely later traveled together to Minnesota. For example, five men in the regiment could trace their roots back to Calais, Maine. Elvin and Jonas Hill (Co. E) and George Boyd (Co. I) were born in New Brunswick, Canada, but spent their childhoods across the river in Calais. Both families moved from Maine to Minnesota in 1855. The two other men from Calais were Henry McAllister (Co. D) and Henry O'Brien (Co. E). As was common, a family or two would move west to start a new life and then send word home if the land was fertile and plentiful. The good news would motivate other families from the same area to join their former neighbors. This may have been the case with the men from Calais.

While at Camp Stone near Edwards Ferry during the winter of 1861–62, six officers posed for this picture. They are, from left to right, Capt. Wilson Farrell (Co. C), 1st Lt. Samuel Raguet (Co. C), Capt. Louis Muller (Co. E), Lt. Charles Zierenberg (Co. A), and Capt. Henry Coates (Co. A). Seated is Capt. Mark Downie (Co. B), who was six feet three inches tall and, if standing, would have towered over the others.

The winter quarters camp of the First Minnesota near Edwards Ferry, known as Camp Stone, during the winter of 1861–62

Many of the men from New England made a living in the lumber industry and settled around Minneapolis, St. Anthony, and St. Paul on the Mississippi. Some also settled in the Stillwater area, located on the St. Croix. They worked in the vast woodlands surrounding these growing settlements, cutting down trees, floating logs downstream to the sawmills, and cutting logs into boards. These were industrious men whose days were filled with hard work and long hours. When the call for volunteers came, the men from Maine were especially noticeable. In Company D they represented twenty-three of the ninety-nine volunteers, and in Company E, they made up thirty-one of the ninety-one volunteers.

Throughout the war the First Minnesota earned a reputation for unfailing accountability—not only in battle but also in daily work details. When on May 27, 1862, the Army of the Potomac needed a bridge to span the Chickahominy River, the army's command turned to the First Minnesota to build it, and they did, using their own skills and without the help of the engineering corps personnel. The men studied the river and devised a plan for the methodical construction of a bridge that would hold up to the heavy weight of an army's wagons and horses. Capt. Mark Downie (Co. B) suggested using the long grapevines plentifully found in the trees to bind the logs, and after the bridge was constructed, it became known as the Grapevine Bridge. The First Minnesota's was the only bridge that held against the rising, rushing water and allowed the surrounded federal troops to move back safely across the river when the army was attacked four days later. The other bridges simply washed away.

On February 5, 1888, years after the war, a Massachusetts newspaper reported a speech Gen. Charles Devans gave about his old regiment, the Fifteenth Massachusetts. In his speech he mentioned the First Minnesota:

> I remember when my regiment and one from Minnesota were ordered to build a road and I found that the Minnesota regiment, composed as it was in the main part of men accustomed to wielding an axe, were doing more wood chopping in one day than my regiment was in two. I entered into a compact with them, and instead of alternately doing guard duty my men did guard duty all the time and the Minnesota men did the chopping.

In speaking of the way these Minnesota men fell trees, he said that they were

> a regiment of large men, who swung the axe breast high, and cut the trees nearly through and left them standing just ready to fall. They would begin on one side and work their [way] thus through a lot and on reaching the other side, would fall the outer trees inward. These would communicate their fall to the adjoining trees

This was the only bridge to hold up against the rising water of the Chickahominy River as the Union army made its retreat. The portion of the bridge crossing the main stream was constructed by the men of the First Minnesota, who used local grapevines to lash various timbers together. Some of the approaches and corduroy work was done by other units. Seen here is a group from the Fifth New Hampshire Infantry doing some of that finishing work and maintenance after the area had once again been secured and the Rebels had left the area.

and so on, the whole forest falling together. The First Minnesota were great fighters as well as choppers.[3]

Like almost every regiment that formed early in the war, the First Minnesota was made up of men who felt a strong sense of patriotism. These men had left homes in the East or resettled from countries far away, all with the hope of starting a better life and with an appreciation for having the opportunity to do so. They felt that any attempt at tearing down a government that had given them this opportunity was not right. Out of a sense of loyalty, these men rose to defend their government and the freedoms it provided. They were men like Benjamin Staples (Co. E), a farmer from

St. Joseph. At noon one day, as he plowed his field, he heard the news of the firing on Ft. Sumter and the government's call for troops to put down the insurrection. Staples literally left his plow in the field and traveled to Ft. Snelling to enlist.

In June 1861, as the regiment passed through Chicago on their way east, the *Chicago Tribune* praised these frontiersmen: "There are few regiments we have ever seen that can compare to the brawn and muscle with these Minnesotians, used to the axe, the rifle, the oar and the setting pole. They are unquestionably the finest body of troops that has yet appeared in our streets."

Then suddenly, the war ceased being a lark and became nasty business. One day short of a month after the regiment left Ft. Snelling, they marched onto the fields of Manassas, Virginia, and received their baptism by fire, and American history was forever changed. The First Minnesota was among few regiments to retire the field in good order, though they did not walk away unharmed. In this disaster for the Union army, the regiment lost 42 men killed, 108 wounded, and 30 captured, representing around 20 percent of the regiment's men that were engaged. They did their job, though, and they did not run. This sterling conduct became the regiment's hallmark, and so the men of the First Minnesota earned the respect of their commanding generals.

At Savage Station, one of the Seven Days' Battles, the regiment lost forty-eight men killed or wounded when they were ordered to act as the rear guard while the Army of the Potomac retreated across the James River. At Antietam they lost 147 more. And at Gettysburg, of the men ordered into the regiment's legendary charge on July 2, 1863, 82 percent was reported either killed or wounded. They saved the center of the Union line, but at great cost. Gen. Hancock knew the likely enormity of their sacrifice when he ordered the charge, and the men knew it, too. But not a man wavered. They performed their duty as they had in every prior engagement, and they did so with a courage that commanded the esteem of all witnesses.

The men leavened their reliability and esteemworthy conduct with a sense of humor that found expression despite war and its sufferings. On March 11, 1862, the First Minnesota was on the move in Virginia and approached the Confederate-sympathizing town of Berryville, with Sgt. Myron Shepard proudly carrying the Stars and Stripes. After meeting limited resistance, they occupied the town and made camp on its outer edge. At least twenty-five men had worked as printers prior to the war, and these men had formed a printers association, the First Minnesota Typographical Society (Sam Stebbins of Company K, who had worked at the *Winona Republican,* was elected its secretary). These men of the printer's trade rarely turned down an opportunity once presented. As 1st Sgt. James Wright, of Company F, later noted:

There was a paper published at this place called the "Berryville Conservator," and a portion of the paper had been set up before arrival, but the editor and his help had "skedaddled" along with the soldiers. The printers in the regiment—among them Company F's contingent was prominent—managed to get into the office of the "secesh sheet," changed the name of the paper to that of "The First Minnesota" and its policy to one of radical support of the Union cause. A paper was set up, struck off, and ready for distribution before morning, when it found ready sale around the camps.

Seven men proudly placed their names on the paper. They were Ed A. Stevens (Co. B), Ole Nelson (Co. A), Frank Mead (Co. H), Thomas H. Pressnell (Co. C), Charles S. Drake (Co. A), Julian Kendall (Co. H), and Henry W. Lindergreen (Co. H).

Years later, Tom Pressnell related the story as follows:

In the spring of 1862, when Gen. Banks crossed the Potomac at Harper's Ferry for the purpose of reconnoitering down the Shenandoah, the whole army went as far as Charlestown and then the brigade commanded by Gen. Willis Gorman, the

These were four of the seven printers who put out the *Berryville Conservator. From left to right,* Frank Mead, Thomas Pressnell, Julian Kendall, and Henry Lindergreen.

first colonel of the First Minnesota was detailed over to Berryville to occupy the turnpike road which runs from Winchester to Snicker's Gap. Our brigade consisting of the First Minnesota, the Fifteenth Massachusetts, Thirty-fourth and Eighty-second New York, entered the village just before dark and soon disposed the small body of cavalry stationed there.

The men bivouacked in the roads near the village and to prevent pillaging in the town Gen. Gorman immediately placed a number of safe guards all through the streets. One of these guards was placed in front of the office of the Berryville Conservator, the village newspaper. In our regiment there were a number of printers who had formed an association called the Typographical Fraternity of the First Minnesota, which was very prominent in the social affairs of the regiment.

The first night we were in town I had a camp leave of absence, and going down the streets of the village noticed the printing office, and the idea struck me that it would be a good thing for the boys of the association to take possession and issue a paper provided we could get permission of the proper authorities. I eluded the guard in front of the shop and entered by the way of one of the windows. It was one of the best equipped little printing offices I had ever seen, and I found that the outside page of the next issue of the paper had already been printed and lay on the "bank." Everything was in good shape, and I concluded to get the rest of the boys together and get out a paper.

I left the office and soon met Ed A. Stevens, now a resident of Minneapolis, and Frank J. Mead, now editorial writer on the New York Post and they agreed to go into the deal with me. We went to the general's headquarters and soon had an order to take possession of the printing office and go ahead getting out the paper. We asked Ole Nelson, Charles S. Drake and Julian J. Kendall, who are now dead, and Henry W. Lindergreen, who is now a publisher in Ohio, to assist us, and soon took over the whole plant.

As our time was somewhat limited, we used the outside part of the edition, which had already been printed for the Conserva-

tor and printed the first edition of the "First Minnesota" on the other side. The next morning they were distributed among the soldiers and brought all kinds from 5 cents to a dollar each. As the command was required to remain another day we issued a half sheet edition on March 12, the first one having been printed on March 11. On March 13 we started work on another, but orders came to march and we returned to Charlestown.[4]

The First Minnesota participated in all the major engagements of the Army of the Potomac and did so with honor to themselves and their state. Antietam, Chancellorsville, Fredericksburg, and Gettysburg were monumental tests of the armies of both the North and the South.

At the First Battle of Bull Run, the First Minnesota fell in at 2:00 A.M. and marched out four hours later. The regiment was ordered to support Robert Ricketts' battery in an attack on Henry House Hill. There, they met the Thirty-Third Virginia. Thinking they were Yankees, Col. Gorman ordered his men to hold fire. Exploiting Gorman's misapprehension, the Rebels sent a deadly volley into the ranks of the First, and the war was on. That day, the Union and Confederate troops waged battle back and forth over the same ground, and Ricketts' battery was lost and recaptured several times before finally falling to the Rebels. During the battle a Confederate cavalry unit sliced through the regiment's line, splitting it in two. Companies A and F had led the attack and were separated from the rest of the regiment, being pushed to the right of the battery. After discovering that they were isolated, Lt. Col. Miller ordered the two companies left under his command to retreat. The regiment then covered the western flank of the Union retreat. The First Minnesota was one of the last regiments to leave the battlefield and suffered the highest casualties of any Northern regiment.

By the Battle of Antietam in September 1862, the regiment, which had started 1,000 strong, had just 435 men in the line. During the battle the First served on the extreme right of the leading brigade (commanded by now Brig. Gen. Willis Gorman) as Maj. Gen. John Sedgwick's division charged through the West Woods. Bursting through the far side of the woods, the column was exposed to heavy fire from both flanks. Being on the right flank, the First suffered less than those regiments on the left. Casualties in the action that

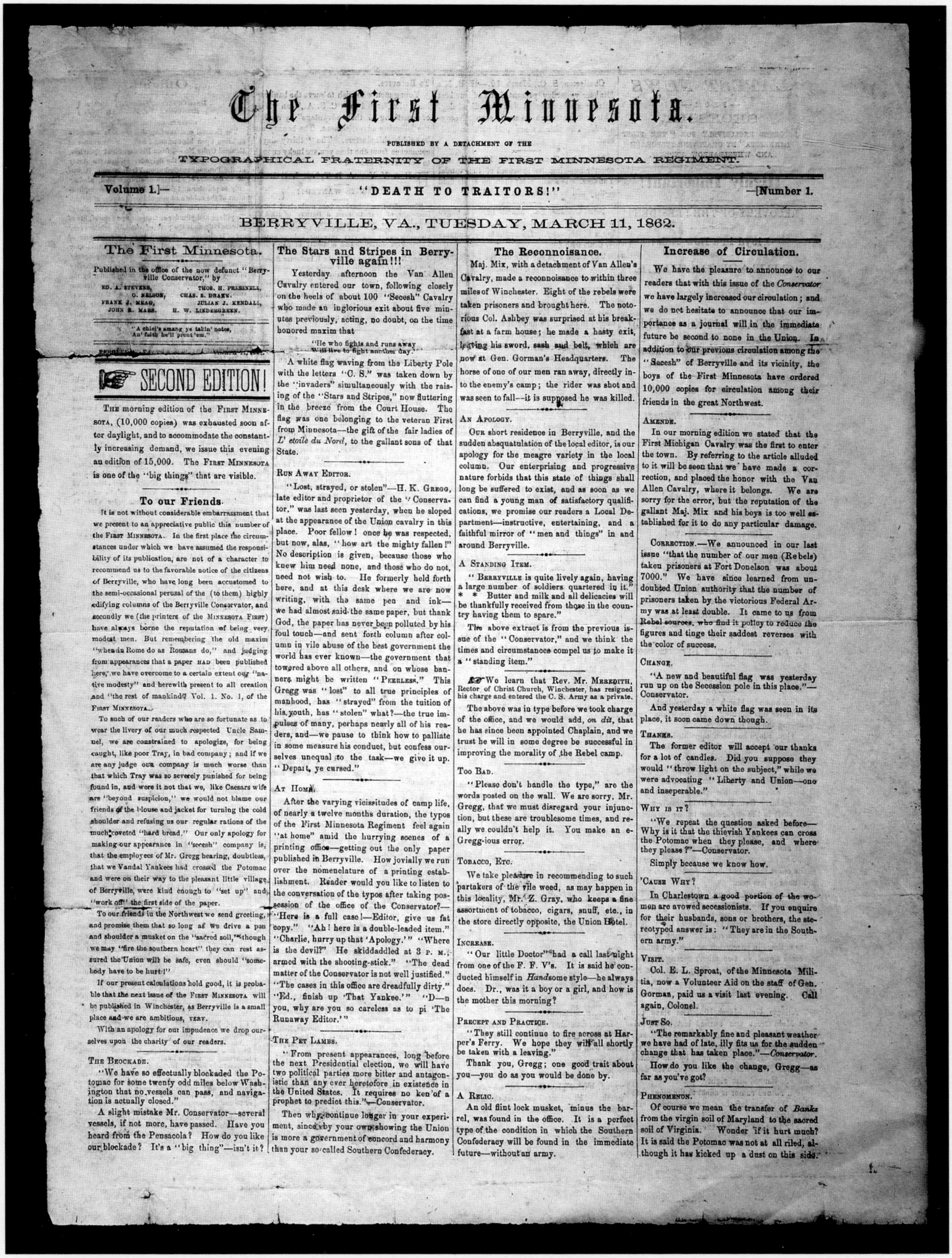

The First Minnesota.

PUBLISHED BY A DETACHMENT OF THE
TYPOGRAPHICAL FRATERNITY OF THE FIRST MINNESOTA REGIMENT.

Volume 1.]— "DEATH TO TRAITORS!" —[Number 1.

BERRYVILLE, VA., TUESDAY, MARCH 11, 1862.

The First Minnesota.

Published in the office of the now defunct "Berryville Conservator," by

ED. A. STEVENS, THOS. H. PRESSNELL,
O. NELSON, CHAS. E. DRAKE.
FRANK J. MEAD, JULIAN J. KENDALL,
JOHN R. MARS. H. W. LINDERGREEN.

"A chiel's amang ye takin' notes,
An' faith he'll prent 'em."

SECOND EDITION!

THE morning edition of the FIRST MINNESOTA, (10,000 copies) was exhausted soon after daylight, and to accommodate the constantly increasing demand, we issue this evening an edition of 15,000. The FIRST MINNESOTA is one of the "big things" that are visible.

To our Friends.

It is not without considerable embarrassment that we present to an appreciative public this number of the FIRST MINNESOTA. In the first place the circumstances under which we have assumed the responsibility of its publication, are not of a character to recommend us to the favorable notice of the citizens of Berryville, who have long been accustomed to the semi-occasional perusal of the (to them) highly edifying columns of the Berryville Conservator, and secondly we (the printers of the MINNESOTA FIRST) have always borne the reputation of being very modest men. But remembering the old maxim "when in Rome do as Romans do," and judging from appearances that a paper HAD been published here, we have overcome to a certain extent our "native modesty" and herewith present to all creation and "the rest of mankind" Vol. 1. No. 1, of the FIRST MINNESOTA.

To such of our readers who are so fortunate as to wear the livery of our much respected Uncle Samuel, we are constrained to apologize, for being caught, like poor Tray, in bad company; and if we are any judge our company is much worse than that which Tray was so severely punished for being found in, and were it not that we, like Caesars wife are "beyond suspicion," we would not blame our friends of the blouse and jacket for turning the cold shoulder and refusing us our regular rations of the much-coveted "hard bread." Our only apology for making our appearance in "secesh" company is, that the employees of Mr. Gregg hearing, doubtless, that we Vandal Yankees had crossed the Potomac and were on their way to the pleasant little village of Berryville, were kind enough to "set up" and "work off" the first side of the paper.

To our friends in the Northwest we send greeting, and promise them that so long as we drive a pen and shoulder a musket on the "sacred soil," though we may "fire the southern heart" they can rest assured the Union will be safe, even should "somebody have to be hurt!"

If our present calculations hold good, it is probable that the next issue of the FIRST MINNESOTA will be published in Winchester, as Berryville is a small place and we are ambitious, VERY.

With an apology for our impudence we drop ourselves upon the charity of our readers.

THE BLOCKADE.

"We have so effectually blockaded the Potomac for some twenty odd miles below Washington that no vessels can pass, and navigation is actually closed."

A slight mistake Mr. Conservator—several vessels, if not more, have passed. Have you heard from the Pensacola? How do you like our blockade? It's a "big thing"—isn't it?

The Stars and Stripes in Berryville again!!!

Yesterday afternoon the Van Allen Cavalry entered our town, following closely on the heels of about 100 "Secesh" Cavalry who made an inglorious exit about five minutes previously, acting, no doubt, on the time honored maxim that

"He who fights and runs away
Will live to fight another day."

A white flag waving from the Liberty Pole with the letters "C. S." was taken down by the "invaders" simultaneously with the raising of the "Stars and Stripes," now fluttering in the breeze from the Court House. The flag was one belonging to the veteran First from Minnesota—the gift of the fair ladies of *L' etoile du Nord*, to the gallant sons of that State.

RUN AWAY EDITOR.

"Lost, strayed, or stolen"—H. K. GREGG, late editor and proprietor of the "Conservator," was last seen yesterday, when he sloped at the appearance of the Union cavalry in this place. Poor fellow! once he was respected, but now, alas, "how art the mighty fallen!" No description is given, because those who knew him need none, and those who do not, need not wish to. He formerly held forth here, and at this desk where we are now writing, with the same pen and ink—we had almost said the same paper, but thank God, the paper has never been polluted by his foul touch—and sent forth column after column in vile abuse of the best government the world has ever known—the government that towered above all others, and on whose banners might be written "PEERLESS." This Gregg was "lost" to all true principles of manhood, has "strayed" from the tuition of his youth, has "stolen" what?—the true impulses of many, perhaps nearly all of his readers, and—we pause to think how to palliate in some measure his conduct, but confess ourselves unequal to the task—we give it up. "Depart, ye cursed."

AT HOME.

After the varying vicissitudes of camp life, of nearly a twelve months duration, the typos of the First Minnesota Regiment feel again "at home" amid the hurrying scenes of a printing office—getting out the only paper published in Berryville. How jovially we run over the nomenclature of a printing establishment. Reader would you like to listen to the conversation of the typos after taking possession of the office of the Conservator?—"Here is a full case!—Editor, give us fat copy." "Ah! here is a double-leaded item." "Charlie, hurry up that 'Apology.'" "Where is the devil?" He skiddaddled at 3 P. M., armed with the shooting-stick." "The dead matter of the Conservator is not well justified." "The cases in this office are dreadfully dirty." "Ed., finish up 'That Yankee.'" "D—n you, why are you so careless as to pi 'The Runaway Editor.'"

THE PET LAMBS.

"From present appearances, long before the next Presidential election, we will have two political parties more bitter and antagonistic than any ever heretofore in existence in the United States. It requires no ken of a prophet to predict this."—Conservator.

Then why continue longer in your experiment, since by your own showing the Union is more a government of concord and harmony than your so-called Southern Confederacy.

The Reconnoisance.

Maj. Mix, with a detachment of Van Allen's Cavalry, made a reconnoisance to within three miles of Winchester. Eight of the rebels were taken prisoners and brought here. The notorious Col. Ashbey was surprised at his breakfast at a farm house; he made a hasty exit, leaving his sword, sash and belt, which are now at Gen. Gorman's Headquarters. The horse of one of our men ran away, directly into the enemy's camp; the rider was shot and was seen to fall—it is supposed he was killed.

AN APOLOGY.

OUR short residence in Berryville, and the sudden absquatulation of the local editor, is our apology for the meagre variety in the local column. Our enterprising and progressive nature forbids that this state of things shall long be suffered to exist, and as soon as we can find a young man of satisfactory qualifications, we promise our readers a Local Department—instructive, entertaining, and a faithful mirror of "men and things" in and around Berryville.

A STANDING ITEM.

"BERRYVILLE is quite lively again, having a large number of soldiers quartered in it." * * Butter and milk and all delicacies will be thankfully received from those in the country having them to spare."

The above extract is from the previous issue of the "Conservator," and we think the times and circumstances compel us to make it a "standing item."

☞ We learn that Rev. Mr. MEREDITH, Rector of Christ Church, Winchester, has resigned his charge and entered the C. S. Army as a private.

The above was in type before we took charge of the office, and we would add, *on dit*, that he has since been appointed Chaplain, and we trust he will in some degree be successful in improving the morality of the Rebel camp.

TOO BAD.

"Please don't handle the type," are the words posted on the wall. We are sorry, Mr. Gregg, that we must disregard your injunction, but these are troublesome times, and really we couldn't help it. You make an e-Gregg-ious error.

TOBACCO, ETC.

We take pleasure in recommending to such partakers of the vile weed, as may happen in this locality, Mr. Z. Gray, who keeps a fine assortment of tobacco, cigars, snuff, etc., in the store directly opposite, the Union Hotel.

INCREASE.

"Our little Doctor" had a call last night from one of the F. F. V's. It is said he conducted himself in *Hand*some style—he always does. Dr., was it a boy or a girl, and how is the mother this morning?

PRECEPT AND PRACTICE.

"They still continue to fire across at Harper's Ferry. We hope they will all shortly be taken with a leaving."

Thank you, Gregg; one good trait about you—you do as you would be done by.

A RELIC.

An old flint lock musket, minus the barrel, was found in the office. It is a perfect type of the condition in which the Southern Confederacy will be found in the immediate future—without an army.

Increase of Circulation.

We have the pleasure to announce to our readers that with this issue of the *Conservator* we have largely increased our circulation; and we do not hesitate to announce that our importance as a journal will in the immediate future be second to none in the Union. In addition to our previous circulation among the "Secesh" of Berryville and its vicinity, the boys of the First Minnesota have ordered 10,000 copies for circulation among their friends in the great Northwest.

AMENDE.

In our morning edition we stated that the First Michigan Cavalry was the first to enter the town. By referring to the article alluded to it will be seen that we have made a correction, and placed the honor with the Van Allen Cavalry, where it belongs. We are sorry for the error, but the reputation of the gallant Maj. Mix and his boys is too well established for it to do any particular damage.

CORRECTION.—We announced in our last issue "that the number of our men (Rebels) taken prisoners at Fort Donelson was about 7000." We have since learned from undoubted Union authority that the number of prisoners taken by the victorious Federal Army was at least double. It came to us from Rebel sources, who find it policy to reduce the figures and tinge their saddest reverses with the color of success.

CHANGE.

"A new and beautiful flag was yesterday run up on the Secession pole in this place."—Conservator.

And yesterday a white flag was seen in its place, it soon came down though.

THANKS.

The former editor will accept our thanks for a lot of candles. Did you suppose they would "throw light on the subject," while we were advocating "Liberty and Union—one and inseperable."

WHY IS IT?

"We repeat the question asked before—Why is it that the thievish Yankees can cross the Potomac when they please, and where they please?"—Conservator.

Simply because we know how.

'CAUSE WHY?

In Charlestown a good portion of the women are avowed secessionists. If you enquire for their husbands, sons or brothers, the stereotyped answer is: "They are in the Southern army."

VISIT.

Col. E. L. Sproat, of the Minnesota Militia, now a Volunteer Aid on the staff of Gen. Gorman, paid us a visit last evening. Call again, Colonel.

JUST SO.

"The remarkably fine and pleasant weather we have had of late, illy fits us for the sudden change that has taken place."—*Conservator*.

How do you like the change, Gregg—as far as you've got?

PHENOMENON.

Of course we mean the transfer of *Banks* from the virgin soil of Maryland to the sacred soil of Virginia. Wonder if it hurt much? It is said the Potomac was not at all riled, although it has kicked up a dust on this side.

This second edition of the *Berryville Conservator* was printed on the evening of March 11, 1862.

The right column is a spoof on their sutler, Oscar King. A sutler, or traveling storekeeper, offered those little items that made a soldier's life more tolerable

day were fifteen killed, seventy-nine wounded, and twenty-one missing. Unlike other regiments, the First departed from the field in good military order, returning fire as it retreated. Color Sgt. Samuel Bloomer was left behind, though, wounded in the knee. A Confederate sergeant found him and mercifully hid him behind a pile of wood, thus protecting him from incoming shell bursts. The injured Bloomer was later brought back to the regiment but had to have his leg amputated and was later discharged for disability.

At Fredericksburg, Maj. Gen. Ambrose Burnside foolishly ordered an uphill frontal assault over a long, unprotected field against Confederates strongly positioned behind a stone wall on the hilltop known as Marye's Heights. Regiment after regiment fell under the withering fire. Brig. Gen. Alfred Sully, who commanded the First, saw the idiocy in this decision and ordered the regiment to help protect the right flank of the Union lines rather than take its turn moving uphill to certain death. Though the men came under artillery fire in this new position, they were relieved to avoid the pointless charge on Marye's Heights. On the evening of December 14, 1862, they secured a forward picket post and dug in. The next day, they took fire in this position, including enfilading artillery fire that sent the three regiments on their right to the rear.

Chancellorsville (May 1–3) was the Army of the Potomac's first major battle in 1863. Lt. Hezekiah Bruce led a group of twenty-five volunteers in a stealth movement across the river. When the request for volunteers was made, emphasis was placed on how dangerous the mission was expected to be, that failure was likely, and that it was entirely possible that not a man would return alive. In spite of this, Bruce and more enlisted men than were needed volunteered. At first it was thought that more than one officer was needed, but when Lt. Bruce volunteered, Gen. Sedgwick's aide, who had brought the request, said, "Who is that young man?"

"Lieutenant Bruce," was the reply.

"Well, if it is Bruce, he will be as good as three," he said, and Lt. Bruce took charge of the detail by himself. They succeeded in clearing the way across the river and spent the day in advance of Gen. Sedgwick's command as skirmishers, charging the Rebels' works and taking over two hundred prisoners.

The Battle of Gettysburg was the site of the regiment's most valiant and crucial stand. During the second day of battle, on July 2, 1863, the Confederates broke through Maj. Gen. Daniel Sickles' position. After a failed attempt at rallying Sickles' men, Maj. Gen. Winfield S. Hancock ordered the First, which was being held in reserve nearby, to counterattack and fill the gap in the Union line until reinforcements could arrive. Prior to the attack, three companies, C, F, and L (the Second Company of Minnesota Sharpshooters), totaling some 73 men, had been detached. The remaining eight companies comprised approximately 271 men. The men plainly saw the superiority of the opposing force, and knowing what was needed and its cost, the small group attacked. In about twenty minutes of the most deadly fire the regiment ever faced, 215 men were either killed or wounded. Theirs was the highest-percentage loss of any Union regiment during the Civil War.

In August the still small band of men who made up the regiment was sent to New York to help suppress the draft riots that had been occurring in parts of the city. On August 28, 1863, while it marched through Brooklyn, a woman who had seen the First Minnesota at Ft. Snelling in the spring of 1861 watched the diminished regiment. As she relates in a September 9, 1863, letter to the *Minnesota Pioneer*:

As I saw this little fragment of the once splendid Minnesota First march by me, carrying their stained and tattered flag, scarcely a shred of which is left, except the design close by the staff, and take their places in line of battle just as they stood on that bright morning more than two years ago at Fort Snelling, when so many of us were there and heard General Gorman's last directions and Mr. Neill's prayer previous to their breaking camp and embarking for the war, and their glorious destiny, I absolutely shivered with emotion. There the brave fellows stood, a grand shadow of the regiment which Fort Snelling knew. Their bronzed faces looked so composed and serious. There was a history written on every one of them. I never felt so much like falling down and doing reverence to any living men. The music of the band, as the men went steadily through the changes of the drill was very sweet, but it seemed to me all the while like a dirge for the fallen.

Over their three years of service, each battle took its toll. Between battle injuries, disease, and the wear and tear of the soldier's life, the ranks thinned month by month. The total strength of the regiment when mustered in was 1,023 men. During its three years of service, 219 more men were brought in as replacements.

When mustered out, only 16 officers and 309 enlisted men remained.

A farewell banquet for the regiment was held in Washington, DC, on Sunday, February 7, 1864. The next day, the men boarded a train and headed back to Minnesota. In the spring of 1864, as the regiment was preparing to be mustered out, preparations for a new regiment were being made to replace the old First. Only a few men opted to reenlist, however. Since the regiment would be made up of mostly new men and was going to be much smaller (300 men) than a normal 1,000-man regiment, the unit was required to take on a new name, and thus, they became known as the First Battalion of Minnesota Infantry.

Once formed, the battalion headed east comprised of new recruits, the men who had reenlisted, and dozens of men who had enlisted for three years and served in the First but who still owed the government time on that three-year commitment. The battalion lost several men at the Battle of Petersburg, including Color Sgt. William Irvine. In June the battalion was ordered to Tennessee, where it became part of Brig. Gen. Henry Morrow's Army of the Tennessee. A month later, on July 15, 1865, the battalion was mustered out at Jeffersonville, Indiana, and the men returned to their homes.

When their record was written, of the approximately 1,242 men who served in the "Old First," 125 had suffered death on the battlefield and another 30 had died of disease or accident. The number of wounded was approximately 500. In percentage of total enrollment killed during the war, the First Minnesota ranked twenty-third out of 2,047 federal regiments. It also never lost a color nor turned its back on a foe.

The regiment's history continues through the Minnesota Army National Guard, First Brigade Combat Team, Thirty-Fourth Infantry Division. Today, their national flag bears the battle ribbons of Bull Run, Antietam, Fredericksburg, Chancellorsville, Gettysburg, and others won so many years ago by the men of the First Minnesota. The men of the First took pride in doing things well and in doing them because it was the right thing to do. At Gettysburg not a man wavered. They knew their duty, and they acted in the service of a tradition that has been a source of pride for the thousands of men and women who have since served their country under their banner.

Regimental Battles and Other Significant Dates

April 28, 1861: The volunteers are mustered into the service.

May 22, 1861: After a second round of recruiting to replace the original volunteers who would not reenlist for three years, the new recruits are mustered in, bringing the strength back to about one thousand men.

June 22, 1861: The First leaves for Washington, DC, arriving at midnight on June 26.

July 21, 1861: The regiment fights its first battle, at Bull Run. They perform well and are one of the last units to leave the field, thus beginning their reputation as a hard-fighting unit.

August 16, 1861: The regiment moves to Camp Stone near Edwards Ferry.

October 21–22, 1861: At the Battle of Ball's Bluff, the First makes a crossing and is lightly engaged at Edwards Ferry but is removed from the main fighting by several miles.

February 26, 1862: The regiment moves their camp to Harpers Ferry.

March 7–12, 1862: The first marches, with only token resistance, to the Rebel town of Berryville, where the printers of the unit print a regimental edition of the *Berryville Conservator.*

March 27, 1862: The regiment boards transports for the Virginia Peninsula. Their tents are left behind and do not catch up to them until April 18.

April 5–May 4, 1862: During the Siege of Yorktown, uncomfortable in incessant rain and without tents, the regiment performs various duties and is often called out on false alarms at night.

May 6, 1862: The regiment moves by transports to West Point, Virginia.

May 25, 1862: Camp is set up near the Chickahominy River, and four days later, the Grapevine Bridge is built.

May 31–June 1, 1862: At the Battle of Fair Oaks, the regiment is sent in as reinforcements. Companies H, K, and D engage the extreme left of the enemy while the remainder of the unit delivers an enfilading fire.

June 1862: The regiment is camped near Fair Oaks (Camp Sully).

June 29, 1862: At the Battle of Savage Station, the First defends the Union's left flank, almost as an independent unit, and does not leave the field until 10:00 P.M. Color Sgt. George Burgess is killed.

June 30, 1862: At the Battle of White Oak Swamp (Glendale), the regiment crosses White Oak Swamp in the early morning, leaving the wounded behind, and marches to Brackett's Ford and then to Glendale, where it fights until midnight. At Malvern Hill the next day, the First is present but does not fight.

July 2–August 4, 1862: The First is camped at Harrison's Landing. President Lincoln visits on July 9.

August 25–28, 1862: They return to Alexandria on transports.

August 28–September 2, 1862: The First marches hard to cover the Union's retreat in the wake of Second Bull Run, covering sixty-five miles, often under fire, in four days. On September 2, Confederate attacks are repulsed at Vienna and Flint Hill, and that night, the regiment is mistakenly attacked by Union cavalry.

September 17, 1862: After the Battle of Antietam, one of the fiercest battles of the war, the field is literally covered with bodies of the dead and wounded. Pvt. George H. Smith (Co. D) may have described it best when he said, "You could walk from here to Osseo [a town near his home in Minnesota] and never touch the ground." He later added, "No one should ever have to witness such acts." The regiment remains camped on the stinking field, doing burial duty, until September 22, when they move to Bolivar Heights overlooking Harpers Ferry.

October 9–24, 1862: Recruiting of volunteers by regular army units is authorized, and almost one hundred men of the First are transferred to the regulars.

October 30, 1862: The First moves to Stafford Hills near Falmouth.

December 11–15, 1862: At the Battle of Fredericksburg, Gen. Burnside makes a major error in sending his army in an uphill attack against an entrenched enemy, but Gen. Sully protects his former regiment from certain death by ordering them to another part of the field.

December 16–June 15, 1863: The regiment spends seven months in winter quarters and through the spring near Falmouth, Virginia.

May 3–5, 1863: At the Battle of Chancellorsville, Gen. Lee takes a risk by dividing his army in two, and by doing so, he beats a substantially larger Union army. Lee's reputation is heightened, and Gen. Hooker is removed from the command of the Army of the Potomac. Lee loses his best general, however, when Gen. Stonewall Jackson is shot by one of his own pickets as Jackson and his escort reenter the Confederate lines after performing some nighttime reconnaissance.

June 15–June 30, 1863: The First marches in dust and heat to Uniontown, Pennsylvania. On June 25 it is attacked by J. E. B. Stuart's cavalry at Haymarket. On June 29, Col. Colvill is arrested for allowing the men to cross a stream over a fallen tree trunk. The march from Fredericksburg to Gettysburg takes fourteen days—eleven traveling days averaging over fourteen miles a day. By the time the men reach the small town, they are exhausted.

July 2–3, 1863: The Battle of Gettysburg is considered the turning point of the war. The First Minnesota plays a key role in the Union's victory and the beginning of the end for the South.

July 24, 1863: The First fights in the Battle of Kelly's Farm.

August 15–September 6, 1863: The First is transported to New York City to keep order after the draft riots. The regiment camps near Somerville Ford on the Rapidan River until October 6. There, they vote in the Minnesota state elections.

October 14, 1863: At the Battle of Bristoe Station, after a march to Robinson's Tavern, the regiment is ordered early in the morning to deploy as skirmishers and, on a signal, to lead an attack on Confederate entrenchments at the crest of a rising slope. After waiting all day for the signal, the attack is called off, much to the relief of all.

December 1863–February 1864: The First spends the winter near the courthouse in Culpepper, Virginia.

February 6, 1864: The regiment is honored at a banquet held at the National Hotel in Washington, DC, attended by Vice President Hamlin and Secretary of War Stanton. The following day the regiment departs for home.

February 15, 1864: Thirty-day furloughs are given after a gala reception in St. Paul.

April 28, 1864: The regiment's final parade is held at Ft. Snelling. They have completed their three-year enlistment.

May 3–5, 1864: The veterans of the First Minnesota are mustered out of the service.

May 5, 1864: Fifty-eight veterans, seventy men who had enlisted in early 1864, and eighty-nine new recruits form two companies that become the First Battalion of Minnesota Infantry.

September 29, 1864: At the Battle of Petersburg, many men are either killed or captured and imprisoned.

April 9, 1865: The battalion is on picket at the time of Lee's surrender at Appomattox, and Confederates come in to surrender in large numbers.

July 15, 1865: The battalion is mustered out of the service, and the veterans then try to return to civilian life.

THE BATTLE OF GETTYSBURG

THE FIRST MINNESOTA ARRIVED at the Gettysburg field in the early morning of the battle's second day. As the men tried to build fires to brew some coffee several assignments thinned their ranks. Company C was detailed as the provost guard at Gen. Gibbon's Second Corps headquarters. The Second Company of Minnesota Sharpshooters, which was periodically attached to the regiment, was detailed to support Kirby's artillery battery. After those units left, Sgt. Buckman of Company G was ordered to organize a twenty-man detail and report to the surgeon at the Second Corps' hospital to help with the wounded that were sure to arrive as the day's battle wore on. After two years of hard fighting, each company was diminished. Once nearly one-hundred-men strong, most companies now counted from twenty to perhaps forty men in their ranks, and these three detachments further depleted the regiment's strength.

A Critical Moment at the Battle Gettysburg, Seven O'clock P. M. Jul 2, 1863. This drawing was done by Josias King (Co. A) after the war. He was not at the battle and must have consulted with his comrades who were. It shows eight companies in line with Gen. Hancock, accompanied by a single aide, talking with Col. Colvill and giving him the order to advance against the enemy.

The Second Corps had been placed in the center of the Union line, and the First Minnesota was stationed on Cemetery Hill in support of a battery of the Fourth U.S. Artillery. Capt. Christopher Heffelfinger later wrote in his memoirs:

> Generally the infantry troops that are chosen for the support of batteries are selected from those that are regarded by the general as the most reliable, tried and experienced. The First Regiment was chosen in this and various other battles for special duty, as it was the oldest three-year regiment in the service, and was known to have extended experience in military training and in battle, thoroughly disciplined and thoroughly organized.

The First's position was about one hundred yards south of the small two-room whitewashed farmhouse owned by Mrs. Leister that served as General Meade's headquarters during the battle. As the regiment watched the battle unfold from their reserve position they began to receive harassing fire from off to their left front. It was thought that perhaps a line of skirmishers or some sharpshooters had reached the cover of some bushes and fences across the hollow and that they should be looked after. Col. Colvill sent 1st Lt. Ball and Company F to take care of the problem. They stepped out from their position on the far right of the line, crossed in front of the regiment, and headed off in the direction of Little Round Top.

It is worth taking a moment to understand how companies were positioned in a line of battle. The tradition was to place the companies in line based on when the captain had received his commission, with the most senior on the far right and the second-most senior on the far left. The seniority numbering was, from left to right, 2nd, 7th, 10th, 5th, 8th, the color guard, 3rd, 9th, 4th, 6th, 1st. Early in the war when a new captain was appointed, some companies would then change to a new position in the line as their captain moved up in seniority. This caused confusion, as men were not always able to form up quickly in the same position in line. This scheme was changed in September 1862, when each company's position in their regimental line was made permanent regardless of its commander's seniority.[1] Based on this rule, I believe that the formation of the First Minnesota in a line of battle would have been H, D, K, G, A, color guard, I, E,

B, C, F. Company C had been detailed for provost duty earlier that morning. When Company F was sent off to the left as skirmishers, five companies remained on the left of the color guard, and three, on the right. It would be reasonable to assume that the color guard shifted down by one company to put it back in the middle. In my opinion the companies of the First Minnesota on July 2, 1863, were aligned as follows (also included are my estimates of the number of men in each company):

H	D	K	G	Color Guard	A	I	E	B
(18)	(35)	(33)	(36)	(4)	(38)	(33)	(36)	(34)
				Staff and Field Officers				
				(4)				

The commonly understood number of men in the charge is 262, and 215 were either killed or wounded, for a casualty rate of 82 percent. Research since indicates that a few more than 262 may have been in the charge, but because many men were detailed for service elsewhere, the exact number is hard to determine. Men were detailed to serve at many places. Some were at the division headquarters serving as clerks. Some served as teamsters driving in the division's wagon train. Some were driving ambulances under the command of Lt. Jasper Searles of the First Minnesota. That morning, twenty-one men were pulled away to serve at the Second Corps' field hospital. In the field the musicians were moved to the rear and held in reserve to act as stretcher-bearers after the fighting was over. Additionally, a few men probably were holding the officers' horses. The author's best estimate for the number of men in the charge is closer to 271.

The men stood behind a slight rise in the terrain and could discern the shifts in battle only through the intensity of musket fire and the direction of its sound. They were then ordered forward until they stood at the top of the rise. Here, they watched the battle in the famous peach orchard, half a mile to their front. They saw Sickles' men give way before the heavier forces of Longstreet and Hill, rallying at times but, at length, breaking into utter disorder. And back Sickles' men came, past the First's position to their rear, followed by the enemy. Most soldiers would have run at the sight of the Confederate's overwhelming advance. In a few moments those eager Southern soldiers would be sweeping over the Minnesota soldiers, but as desperate as the situation was, the men of the First stood firm.

At that moment Gen. Hancock rode up accompanied

by a single aide, and the general made a vain attempt at rallying Sickles' frightened and retreating forces. Reserves were on their way but could not reach this critical position in time unless the enemy was stopped. The general surmised that a few minutes' delay of the enemy's advance might be enough. Quickly leaving Sickles' fugitives, Gen. Hancock galloped to the First's position.

Looking first at the enemy and then at the line of men, he shouted, "My God, are these all the men we have here?"

"The First Minnesota," Col. Colvill replied proudly.

Turning to Colvill, he gave the order, "Advance, colonel, and take those colors."[2]

Every man in the depleted regiment must have realized his awful fate. Though the charge meant destruction for the handful of Minnesota heroes, Hancock knew that if it was successful, they would save not only the position on Cemetery Hill but possibly the entire battlefield. The regiment was to be sacrificed for a few moments' time.

The color guard stepped forward, and the rest of the regiment dressed on it, forming a line of battle. Col. Colvill gave the order, "Forward, double-quick," and the Minnesota soldiers swept down the slope. The enemy line's concentrated fire bombarded them, and brave fellows fell at every stride. Double-quick turned into hell bent as the soldiers ran down the hill, speed giving their only hope of surviving the awful storm of lead.

"Charge!" shouted Colvill as they came within fifty yards of the first line. The men dropped their gun barrels into their left hands in the charge bayonets position and dashed forward. The Confederate line was slightly disorganized from trying to cross a little brook. Seeing the mass of charging bayonets coming at them, the first line broke and rushed back through the second, causing confusion in the third and fourth and, thus, stopping the Confederate advance. The First then finally opened fire, taking advantage of the brook's low banks and shrubs for cover. As they continued to be torn to shreds by the Rebels' bullets the men reloaded and fired again and again. The thick smoke of burned gunpowder from both sides gave some cover, as did dusk's settling darkness. They held the Confederates at bay until the reserves appeared on the ridge, and that fresh force pushed the exhausted enemy back into the darkness to the lines on Seminary Ridge. The charge had temporarily paralyzed a Rebel line stunned by the Minnesotan's ferocious onslaught. If the larger Confederate force had found the will to rally and countercharge, the small regiment would have been crushed, and the position would have been lost. But one little regiment, in the face of two larger Rebel forces, saved it.

The sacrifice was, however, terrible. Brave Col. Colvill had been wounded twice and would be lame for the rest of his life. Maj. Downie and Lt. Col. Adams, each wounded three times, also lay somewhere on the battlefield. Rebel bullets and artillery shell fragments had cut down almost everyone. Initially, as the darkness turned to night, only forty-seven men returned to the top of the slope and answered roll call. Gradually, a few other walking wounded worked their way back to the top of the hill—the regiment a mere shadow of its former self.

After the attack the dazed and exhausted men reflected on what had just happened. Where were all their comrades of just a few minutes earlier? Most lay bleeding back down on the slope. Many were dead or dying. Was this small group all that was left? As nightfall set in, though completely spent, they staggered back down the bloody incline. Thoughts of tomorrow's battle were of no concern; they wanted to find their friends and brothers and help as best they could. Then, they needed to sleep.

As Gen. Winfield Scott Hancock writes about ordering the charge:

> I had no alternative but to order the regiment in. We had no force on hand to meet the sudden emergency. Troops had been ordered up and were coming on the run, but I saw that in some way five minutes must be gained or we were lost. It was fortunate that I found there so grand a body of men as the First Minnesota. I knew they must lose heavily and it caused me pain to give the order for them to advance, but I would have done it [even] if I had known every man would be killed. It was a sacrifice that must be made. The superb gallantry of those men saved our line from being broken. No soldiers on any field, in this or any other country, ever displayed grander heroism.

One hundred years later, Bruce Catton wrote in *Glory Road*:

> The whole war had suddenly come to a focus in this smoky hollow, with a few score westerners

This is the flag of the Twenty-Eighth Virginia Infantry captured by Pvt. Marshall Sherman (Co. C) on July 3, 1863, at the end of the fighting known as Pickett's Charge.

trading their lives for the time the army needed. . . . They had not captured the flag that Hancock had asked them to capture, but they still had their own flag and a great name.

Lt. Col. Joseph B. Mitchell in *Decisive Battles of the Civil War* states: "There is no other unit in the history of warfare that ever made such a charge and then stood its ground sustaining such losses."

On July 3 the First found itself on the receiving end of Pickett's Charge. Company F had rejoined the regiment in the morning before the artillery barrage, and Company C had been dismissed as provost guard and rejoined the regiment after the barrage had ended and as the fight was taking place. Of that fierce fight, Alf Carpenter of Company K writes:

For two hours we had fought desperately. Our muskets became so heated we could no longer handle them. We dropped them and picked up those of the wounded. Our cartridges gave out. We rifled the boxes of the dead. Artillerymen from the disabled pieces in our rear sprang forward, and seizing guns and cartridges of the wounded, fought by our side as infantrymen. Many of the men became deaf and did not recover their hearing for a day or two. It was a grand and terrible scene.

During the fight a bullet pierced color-bearer Henry Dehn's finger, taking it off and shattering the flagpole. Cpl. Henry O'Brien grabbed the stub of the pole that held the regiment's flag and carried it into the fray, spurring the men to follow him and protect the colors. As they charged into the Confederate hoard chaos ensued. When ammunition ran out, the men threw stones. Hand-to-hand combat was to the death. The regiment faced another fifty-five casualties, twenty-three of whom either were killed that day or later died of their wounds. Pvt. Marshall Sherman of Company C did, though, capture the Twenty-Eighth Virginia's colors. Both O'Brien and Sherman were awarded the Medal of Honor for their bravery during the fight.

The First Minnesota's total casualties during the two-day struggle were 5 officers and 47 enlisted men killed and 13 officers and 162 enlisted men wounded, for a total of 226 casualties out of 330 engaged, or 70 percent.

On the morning of July 4, after the battle had ended and the Southern army had retreated, Capt. Henry Coates was in command of a regiment that consisted of 8 officers and 91 enlisted men under arms. A month later, he wrote an official report of the battle and eloquently summarized the regiment's role in the last line: "Every man in the regiment did his whole duty. The accompanying list of the killed and wounded shows the severity of our loss."

Participants in the July 2 Charge

Officers

Col. Colvill stood behind the color guard. Lt. Col. Adams was behind the center companies, on the right wing. Maj. Downie was in the corresponding position on the left wing. Adams and Downie were fifteen paces behind the file closers (sergeants or corporals), and Colvill was thirty paces behind. This position allowed the senior officers to see what was happening with the regiment and issue appropriate orders during the battle. In the brutal enfilade that erupted from the Confederate rifled muskets for those fifteen to twenty minutes, almost every Minnesotan received an unwelcomed gift from the South.

Col. William Colvill was wounded twice, in the shoulder and in the ankle.

Lt. Col. Charles P. Adams was wounded three times, in the chest, the hip, and a leg.

Maj. Mark Downie was wounded three times, in the chest, a foot, and an arm.

Lt. and Adj. John Peller's left arm was shattered.

Color Guard

The color guard stood at the regiment's center. Though each man was assigned to a specific company, when acting as the color guard they were their own small unit. Theirs was a position of certain peril. Three of the four men in the color guard on July 2 were wounded. The fourth, John Dehn, carried the color off the field only to be wounded the next day during Pickett's Charge.

Sgt. Ellet P. Perkins (Co. D), wounded, leg
Cpl. Thomas B. Nason (Co A), wounded, arm, chest
Cpl. John B. Stevens (Co B), wounded, chest
Cpl. John Dehn (Co. A), wounded July 3, wrist, amputated

Musicians

The musicians were usually held in reserve to act as stretcher-bearers when needed after the fighting had ended.

Musician William Nixon (Co. A)
Musician Andrew Connolly (Co. B)
Musician Lucius Ford (Co. E)
Musician Charles W. Merritt (Co. F)
Regimental Bugler Ezra Haskins (Co. G)
Musician Edgar Tiffany (Co. G)
Musician Carl Carlson (Co. I)
Musician Erick Iverson (Co. K)

Orderlies

Orderlies, also called officers' servants, may have held the senior officers' horses to the rear and behind the hill where the regiment was positioned.

Pvt. Ed Needham (Co. G), held Lt. Col. Adams' horse
Pvt. Milton Bevans (Co. F), Col. Colvill's orderly, may have held Colvill's horse
It is not known who may have held Maj. Downie's horse.

Company A

Company A was one of the center companies, located next to the color guard. This position placed Capt. Coates close to Col. Colvill during the charge. It was Coates to whom Colvill spoke after he was severely wounded and lay on the ground.

Capt. Henry C. Coates
1st Lt. Charles Edward Davis
2nd Lt. August Kruger
1st Sgt. Charles Steen, wounded, thigh
Sgt. James C. Farwell
Sgt. Charles Hausdorf, wounded, leg
Sgt. Henry Wright, died of wounds July 6, head
Sgt. William H. Dooley, wounded July 3, arm
Cpl. Timothy Crawley, died of wounds July 20, leg
Cpl. Julius Edler, killed in action
Cpl. James N. Keyes, killed in action
Cpl. Stephen Lyons, wounded thigh
Cpl. Peter Marks, died of wounds July 23, ankle

Pvt. Lucius Adams, wounded, foot
Pvt. Clark Brandt, wounded, knee
Pvt. George B. Clark
Pvt. Michael Devlin, wounded July 3, arm
Pvt. Charles S. Drake wounded July 3, arm
Pvt. Daniel Farquhar, wounded, leg, ankle
Pvt. John Farquhar, wounded July 3, thigh
Pvt. Jacob Feger
Pvt. Frederick Geiser, wounded, side
Pvt. Frederick Glave, died of wounds July 10, knee
Pvt. John Hauser, killed in action
Pvt. Harrison Lyons
Pvt. Maxwell A. McLane
Pvt. William F. Miller, killed in action
Pvt. Rascellas Mowry, wounded, side
Pvt. Charles Muller, wounded, thigh
Pvt. Henry Nickel, died of wounds August 19, leg
Pvt. Samuel J. Pitkin
Pvt. Benjamin F. Sanders, wounded, hips, captured
Pvt. William Schmidter
Pvt. Joseph Schmucker, killed in action
Pvt. Hans M. Simonson, wounded, leg
Pvt. Joseph Theim, wounded, hip (slight)
Pvt. Warren Wagner, died of wounds July 6, back
Pvt. John Wilson, killed in action

Company B

The men of Company B were positioned on the far right of the regiment. The right side came in closest contact with the enemy from both the front and the flank. Only half a dozen men were not hit.

Capt. Thomas Sinclair, wounded, chest
2nd Lt. William M. May, wounded, leg
1st Sgt. David Lord, wounded, shoulder
Sgt. Frederick Crome, wounded, arm, amputated
Sgt. John Densmore (Co. B), wounded, jaw, chest,
    leg, thumb
Sgt. Samuel B. Nickerson, killed in action
Sgt. George Oliver, wounded, chest
Cpl. Patrick Fallihee
Cpl. Adolphus C. Hospes
Cpl. Edwin P. Welles, wounded, leg
Pvt. John Anderson, wounded, unknown
Pvt. George Arnold, wounded, shoulder, leg
Pvt. William H. Aucker, wounded, hip, abdomen
Pvt. William F. Bates, killed in action
Pvt. Frederick L. Bernds
Pvt. Rufus G. Blanchard, wounded July 3, side

Pvt. Albert Caplazi, wounded, thigh, foot
Pvt. Bartholomew Carrieget, wounded, thigh
Pvt. Moritz W. Erhardt, wounded, ankle
Pvt. Peter Everson, wounded, jaw
Pvt. Charles H. Gove, died of wounds July 30,
    spine, shoulder
Pvt. Charles Hamann, wounded, head, hand
Pvt. Martin J. Henry, wounded, back
Pvt. David Johnson, wounded, knee
Pvt. Augustus Koenig, died of wounds July 30
Pvt. Adam Marty, wounded, thigh
Pvt. Fridolin (Fred) Marty, wounded, hand
Pvt. Freeman McKusick
Pvt. Erick Nystedt, wounded, thigh
Pvt. Andrew Quist, wounded, thigh, hand
Pvt. John P. Schoenbeck, wounded, hand, thigh
Pvt. Albert Sebers (Sieber), wounded, head, leg
Pvt. Joseph Tanner, wounded July 3, shoulder
Pvt. Ole Thompson, died of wounds August 8,
    arm, amputated

Company D

Company D was the second company in from the regiment's far-left flank. It faced fire from the front and from the left as the Confederate forces started to envelope the regiment before the retreat up the slope. Cpl. Ed Walker said that of the thirty-five men in the fight, six were killed and eighteen were wounded, several slightly but the majority severely.

Capt. (1st Lt.) Christopher B. Hefflefinger, chest
    (slight)
2nd Lt. Charles H. Mason, died of wounds August
    18, hand
1st Sgt. Raymond J. Parker
Sgt. Horace Martin
Sgt. John W. Plummer
Sgt. Calvin D. Robinson, wounded (slight)
Cpl. James Bryant, wounded, thigh
Cpl. George Grandy, died of wounds July 4, chest
Cpl. William N. Irvine
Cpl. Jacob Kouts, wounded, elbow
Cpl. Joseph Smithyman, wounded, lung
Cpl. Edward Walker
Pvt. William R. Allen, died of wounds July 18,
    abdomen
Pvt. Archibald Curtis
Pvt. Charles E. Baker, killed in action
Pvt. George W. Bartlett, wounded, thigh

Pvt. Cyrus Eddy
Pvt. Ami Fergusen
Pvt. John O. French
Pvt. Charles W. Geer, wounded, shoulder
Pvt. Lewis B. Geer wounded, leg, lung, hand
Pvt. August A. Goeppinger, wounded, foot, hand
Pvt. Alonzo C. Hayden, killed in action, head
Pvt. Archibald Howe, wounded, hip
Pvt. Charles W. Hughes
Pvt. Irving (Ervin) Lawrence, died of wounds
    July 7
Pvt. Benjamin F. Noel, wounded, leg
Pvt. Marcus Past, died of wounds July 6, chest
Pvt. Joseph H. Prime, killed in action
Pvt. Charles H. Rines, wounded, side
Pvt. Frank Rollins, killed in action
Pvt. William C. Smith, wounded, shoulder
Pvt. Daniel Sullivan, wounded, heel
Pvt. James W. Walsh, wounded, back

Pvt. John W. Davis, killed in action
Pvt. Hiram Drake, wounded, foot
Pvt. Henry I. Fisher, wounded, heel
Pvt. Norman Fowler, killed in action
Pvt. William W. Goundry
Pvt. Elvin Hill
Pvt. Jonas R. Hill, wounded, both legs
Pvt. William W. Holden, wounded leg
Pvt. Israel Jackins, killed in action
Pvt. Ernest R. Jefferson, wounded, leg, amputated
Pvt. William Losee, wounded, chest
Pvt. John McKenzie, died of wounds August 4
Pvt. Vincent Middlestad, wounded, foot
Pvt. Adam C. Stites, wounded, head
Pvt. Isaac L. Taylor, killed in action
Pvt. Daniel H. Waite, wounded, leg
Pvt. Elijah Weaver, wounded, neck
Pvt. Peter Welin, died of wounds July 30, leg,
    amputated

Company E

According to Sgt. Henry Taylor, "Company E went in with thirty-six men, including two commissioned officers, three sergeants, six corporals and twenty-seven privates. After the 'charge,' we were one sergeant, two corporals (one of them slightly wounded) and five privates!" Note the five sets of brothers who served together.

Capt. Louis Muller, killed in action, head
1st Lt. David B. Demerest, died of wounds July 30,
    hip
1st Sgt. Joseph Trevor, killed in action
Sgt. Samuel Stites, wounded, arm
Sgt. Patrick Henry Taylor
Cpl. Edward A. Austin, wounded (slight)
Cpl. Henry C. Bradley, wounded, ankle
Cpl. James S. Brower, wounded (slight)
Cpl. Henry O'Brien, wounded, side, wounded
    July 3, head, hand
Cpl. Benjamin F. Staples, wounded, leg
Cpl. Mathew F. Taylor, wounded, chest
Pvt. Daniel Adams
Pvt. George M. Adams, wounded, shoulder
Pvt. William Henry Bassett, wounded, arm, thigh
Pvt. Amos O. Berry, wounded, leg
Pvt. Charles A. Berry, wounded, toe
Pvt. William E. Cundy
Pvt. John Curry (Currie), wounded, shoulder

Company G

Company G was positioned second to the left of the color guard, between companies A and K. Ed Needham was not in the charge. He was Lt. Col. Adams' orderly. When the officers dismounted for battle, the orderly took the officer's horse and held it in a position in the rear of the regiment.

Capt. Nathan S. Messick, killed in action July 3,
    neck
2nd Lt. James DeGray, wounded, head
1st Sgt. Henry Clay Whitney
Sgt. Philo Hall, wounded, unknown
Sgt. Charles C. Parker
Sgt. Edward Tuman
Cpl. Phineas L. Dunham, died of wounds July 17,
    thigh
Cpl. Anthony Jones, wounded July 3, head (slight)
Cpl. George P. Sawyer, killed in action
Cpl. John Strothman, killed in action
Pvt. Adam J. Areman, wounded, shoulder
Pvt. Dana S. Barton, wounded, chest
Pvt. Edward Bassett
Pvt. William W. Brown, wounded, ankle
Pvt. James Carney, wounded, hip
Pvt. William G. Coen, wounded, hip
Pvt. Charles C. Davis, wounded knee
Pvt. Anthony W. Ernst, died of wounds August 5,
    shoulder

Pvt. Jerome Farnsworth, died of wounds July 27, thigh, amputated
Pvt. John Gatzke, wounded, thigh
Pvt. Jonathan Goodrich, wounded, leg
Pvt. George J. Hopkins, wounded, hip, wrist, thigh
Pvt. Caleb B. Jackson
Pvt. William A. Joy
Pvt. Samuel Lilly, wounded, back
Pvt. George Magee, wounded, chest
Pvt. William Meyers (Myers)
Pvt. Ludwell Mosher, wounded, hip, wrist, thigh
Pvt. James L. Nichols
Pvt. William M. Ramsey
Pvt. Walter Reed, wounded, July 3
Pvt. John M. Rhorer, wounded, shoulder
Pvt. Benjamin Roberts
Pvt. Joseph Sisler, killed in action
Pvt. George Thom
Pvt. George A. Williams

Company H

Small but tough, Company H stood on the regiment's far left. Once one hundred strong, it now numbered closer to just twenty men in the field. They suffered a withering fire, and only a handful made it back to where they had started.

1st Lt. Martin Maginnis
1st Sgt. James Akers, killed in action
Sgt. Frederick Diehr, died of wounds July 21, lung, side
Sgt. William Henry Wikoff, killed in action, heart
Cpl. Edward Wood, wounded, unknown
Pvt. George W. Bradbury, wounded, shoulder
Pvt. Mortimer Canfield
Pvt. John F. Clausen, wounded, chest
Pvt. Samuel S. Cronkite, wounded, head
Pvt. John H. Docken, wounded July 3, arm
Pvt. Kellian Drondt, wounded, head
Pvt. John H. Essency, killed in action
Pvt. Thomas Galvin, wounded, arm
Pvt. Ransom Harmon
Pvt. Reinhalt Hess, wounded, head (slight)
Pvt. John Nelson
Pvt. Peter Peterson
Pvt. J. Benjamin Smith, wounded, unknown

Company I

Company I was second to the right of the color guard. The right side of the regiment received tremendous fire from the front and side with devastating effect. After the battle Pvt. Ed Soper counted only eleven men who were still able to answer roll call.

1st Lt. George Boyd, wounded, leg, thigh
2nd Lt. Waldo Farrar, killed in action
1st Sgt. James M. O'Neale, wounded, unknown
Sgt. Oliver M. Knight, wounded, arm
Sgt. William K. Richards, wounded, leg
Sgt. William J. Roe, died of wounds April 1, 1864, leg
Sgt. Oscar Woodward, killed in action
Cpl. Anson Hayden
Cpl. Herman Lawson, wounded July 3, thumb
Cpl. Ernst L. F. Miller, wounded, thigh
Cpl. George Millikin, wounded, leg, amputated
Cpl. William N. Peck, wounded, leg, amputated
Pvt. Henry Abbott, wounded, leg
Pvt. John Churchill
Pvt. Jeremiah Donovan, wounded, wrist
Pvt. Philander Ellis, killed in action, head
Pvt. Jacob F. Freeze, died of wounds August 2, heel
Pvt. Joseph Frey, killed in action
Pvt. Edward P. Hale, died of wounds, hip, leg
Pvt. William D. Howell, wounded, hand
Pvt. Daniel Hutchins, wounded
Pvt. Benjamin Jackson, wounded, leg
Pvt. Charles F. Mason, wounded, leg
Pvt. Edwin Paul, died of wounds, leg, amputated
Pvt. William B. Philbrook, wounded, thigh
Pvt. Edward B. Price
Pvt. Herman Rabaca, wounded
Pvt. Edmund Soper
Pvt. Omar Sutcliff, wounded, thumb
Pvt. Daniel Weaver, wounded, knee
Pvt. Wilbur F. Wellman, died of wounds, leg, amputated
Pvt. Henry Widger, wounded, hip, leg
Pvt. Byron Welch, killed in action

Company K

Company K stood on the left of the line of battle, between companies D and G.

Capt. Joseph Periam, died of wounds July 7, head
2nd Lt. William Lochren
1st Sgt. Mathew Marvin, wounded, foot
Sgt. Levi Allred
Sgt. Alfred P. Carpenter, wounded, foot
Cpl. John Einfeldt, wounded, shoulder (slight)
Cpl. Leslie P. Gore, killed in action
Cpl. Timothy Keiley, wounded, thigh, calf
Cpl. Stephen Martin
Cpl. Charles F. North, wounded (slight)
Cpl. William G. Sargeant
Cpl. Randolf Wright, died of wounds, July 3
Pvt. Charles Behr, wounded, chest, head
Pvt. Balthasar Best
Pvt. Joseph C. Chandler, wounded, knee
Pvt. Chester Durfee, wounded, calf
Pvt. Israel Durr, died of wounds July 3, lung
Pvt. Joseph S. Eaton, wounded, thigh, calf
Pvt. Charles Ely, wounded, chest
Pvt. Jacob Geistreiter, killed in action
Pvt. Charles Goddard, wounded, shoulder, thigh
Pvt. Lewis Hanson, wounded, calf
Pvt. Joseph S. Hill
Pvt. William Kinyon, wounded, knee
Pvt. Alonzo Pickle, wounded, leg
Pvt. Franklin Sheeks
Pvt. Augustus H. Smith, killed in action
Pvt. David Taylor, killed in action
Pvt. Samuel S. Tenny, wounded, leg
Pvt. James Towner, wounded (slight)
Pvt. Peter Vosz, died of wounds July 3, bowels
Pvt. Henry C. Winters, killed in action
Pvt. Randolph Wright, killed in action

Soldiers with Unverified Whereabouts

The author has not been able to verify the whereabouts of about eight men in these companies and a half dozen in companies C and F at the time of the July 2 charge. They may have been in the charge, absent sick, or detailed elsewhere in the Gettysburg area, as were many of the regiment's men at that time. Subsequent research may shed light on additional men having been in the charge or perhaps some whose names should be removed from the list.

Companies Not in the July 2 Charge
Company C

On July 2, 1863, the company was detached to serve as provost guard at Gen. Gibbon's headquarters. Col. William Colvill later wrote that they wore their full-dress uniform, including Hardee hats with feathers. The rest of the regiment had discarded these uniforms for quite some time and went into battle wearing the standard four-button fatigue blouse and slouch hats. Colvill described Capt. Farrell and his men as follows: "His Company 'C' was particularly noted for discipline, drill and fine appearance. He was a favorite at Div, Hdqtrs., being a strict disciplinarian and being very systematic, prompt and accurate in a business way."

On the morning of July 3, Gen. Meade informed Gen. Gibbon that Meade felt the thrust of the expected attack would be at the center of the Union line along Cemetery Hill. Meade suggested that all spare men be directed at that point. Gibbon turned to Capt. Wilson Farrell and directed him to take his company back to the line, which he did. Though they avoided casualties on July 2, they suffered considerably on July 3. The company arrived on the field as Pickett's Charge was taking place. As he led his men to where the rest of the First Minnesota was fighting Capt. Farrell was wounded. He died just after noon on the next day.

Capt. Wilson B. Farrell, killed in action, July 3
1st Lt. William Harmon, wounded, slight, July 3
1st Sgt. Henry H. Howard, wounded, arm, July 3
Sgt. Andrew Krueger (Kreger), wounded, thigh, July 3
Sgt. Wade Lufkin, killed in action, July 3
Sgt. Robert P. Owen
Sgt. Chesley B. Tirrell
Musician Henry Fifield
Cpl. John W. Coles
Cpl. Aaron Greenwald, killed in action, July 3
Cpl. Charles J. Hotchkiss
Cpl. Joseph McDonald
Cpl. Thomas H. Pressnell
Cpl. Gideon Squires, wounded, arm, July 3
Cpl. Reuben Westlake
Pvt. John D. Abell
Pvt. Minor Atherton, wounded, both legs, July 3
Pvt. Henry W. Boyce
Pvt. William A. Brack

Pvt. Henry J. W. Brown

Pvt. George W. Buck

Pvt. George Burt

Pvt. Daniel Clancey, wounded, shoulder, July 3

Pvt. Charles I. Clark

Pvt. Jeremiah Collins

Pvt. William Coombs

Pvt. Charles Dorathy

Pvt. Rufus Eastman

Pvt. Henry Ellingson

Pvt. John Ellsworth, wounded, July 3, died of
wounds July 20

Pvt. Benjamin F. Finical

Pvt. Jacob George

Pvt. Henry (Harry) Ghostley

Pvt. James Gilman

Pvt. Julius Harvey

Pvt. Faxon Hayford, wounded, leg, July 3

Pvt. Herman Klein

Pvt. Sigismond Kramer

Pvt. Maurice Leonard, wounded, slight, July 3

Pvt. John Lindberg

Pvt. John Longquist

Pvt. David McLean

Pvt. George Mortimer

Pvt. Wilhelm Onerman

Pvt. Turner Pribble

Pvt. John Sernan

Pvt. Marshall Sherman

Pvt. George Sias

Pvt. Julius Smith (Schmidt)

Company F

As the regiment stood in reserve before the charge Confederate sharpshooters fired at the regiment from their left. Col. Colvill ordered 1st Lt. John Ball to take Company F to the left flank and relieve the pressure being applied. Thus, Company F was not in the charge. It did receive casualties in its own fighting that day and on July 3 during Pickett's Charge.

1st Lt. John Ball

1st Sgt. James Wright, wounded, July 3

Sgt. Jefferson Benner

Sgt. Henry T. Childs

Sgt. Philip Hamlin, killed in action, July 3

Cpl. Marion Abbott, wounded, right arm,
shattered, July 2

Cpl. Enos Grow

Cpl. Leonard J. Squires, killed in action, July 3

Pvt. James F. Bachelor, wounded, shot in foot,
July 2

Pvt. Horatio N. Barber, wounded, back, July 3

Pvt. Charles Berdan

Pvt. Daniel Bond

Pvt. Hezekiah Bond

Pvt. Cyris Bondurant, wounded, right thigh and
hip, July 3

Pvt. Calvin Clark

Pvt. Almeron Davis, wounded, right hand, July 3

Pvt. Jonas P. Davis

Pvt. Ole Gilberson

Pvt. Romulus E. Jacobs, wounded, shoulder, July 3

Pvt. Levi King, wounded, shot through the face,
July 2

Pvt. Edmund F. Parker, wounded

Pvt. Thomas Peterson

Pvt. Josiah Richardson

Pvt. James W. Imeson

Pvt. Henry Burgetorf, wounded, back, July 3,
detached with Cushing's Battery, wounded,
back

Pvt. Artemus Decker, wounded, knee, July 3,
detached with Cushing's Battery, wounded,
knee

Pvt. Charles Hubbs, wounded, wrist, July 3,
detached with Cushing's Battery, wounded,
wrist

Company L

At the time of Gettysburg, Company L was part of Berdan's Sharpshooters. It was stationed at a different part of the battlefield, detailed to support Battery I of the First U.S. Artillery. It saw action as it protected the battery until the close of the battle.

Sgt. George Buckman and the Twenty-Man Detail

George R. Buckman (b. December 23, 1832; d. April 17, 1899) was born at Crown Point in Essex County, New York, and moved to Winona, Minnesota, in 1855. Two years later, he settled in St. Mary, a small community in Waseca County, where he worked as a carpenter. St. Mary got a post office in 1856 and was organized as a township in 1858. In the winter of 1857–58, the citizens organized a literary society, held some rousing debates, and read a paper each week titled the *St. Mary*

Sgt. George Buckman led a twenty-man detail to serve at the Second Corps' hospital at Rock Creek, a mile behind the front lines at Gettysburg.

Literary Union, edited by G. R. Buckman. The town continued to develop until the Civil War, when most of its men enlisted and for all practical purposes it ceased to exist. Buckman was twenty-eight when he enlisted and was placed in Company G.

At midnight on July 1, 1863, Sgt. Buckman was detailed to take twenty men from the First Minnesota to Surgeon General Hammond's headquarters. Buckman took his detail to a newly established field hospital behind Little Round Top, where he and his men lay down to sleep briefly until dawn awoke them. Here, they tended to the wounded during the fighting of July 2. They remained there until that night, when the field hospital was moved about a mile away to a location on the Jacob Schwartz farm along Rock Creek. Buckman and his detail stayed with the wounded for over five weeks, until the last ones were finally moved to the large field hospital known as Camp Letterman or sent to hospitals in Philadelphia and elsewhere. He kept a diary, which describes an aspect of the battle seldom discussed. In it, he tells of his work at the field hospital and some of his postwar recollections. Note how the

focus changes from a humorous look at the plight of the soldier to the weary anguish felt after the battle.

July 1st. Broke camp at 8 am, passing through Uniontown, turned to the right, going in a N. East direction across Big Pipe Creek and going into camp about noon near Taneytown. . . . Went into camp about three miles from Gettysburg and formed a line of battle. The roads passed over during the day were bad from late rains and blistered feet added to my discomfort. After the line was formed a search was made for water to make coffee. It was found after a tedious tramp and preparations at once made for a royal supper which consisted of hard tack in addition to the coffee. The hard tack was considered to be very choice as it came from a box marked 2,000 B.C. This was interpreted by the boys to mean 2,000 years before Christ. Indeed its appearance confirmed the interpretation. But I digress from my coffee. It is doing nicely but as it commenced to boil the orderly came along with orders to move. The line had to be changed. Over went the coffee & my expectations with it. Well the line is reformed and a new cup of solace prepared. It is almost ready when that confounded orderly shows up again and I am detailed with twenty men and ordered to report to Surg. Genl. Hammond's Hdqrs. That fixed the coffee business, and if I remember correctly, my temper too. It was now twelve o'clock. I got my detail together and started out to find the Surgeon Genls. Hdqrs. It was a foggy dismal night and after wandering around for some time at last found Hdqrs. and reported. "All right," said the Genl. "Lie down and make yourselves comfortable." Comfortable! Gracious me. Wet grass for a bed and a delicious hard tack thrown in. I unslung my knapsack for a pillow, unrolled my blanket and rolled up in it, and slept all unconscious of the impending morrow until the guns at the first streak of daylight awoke the echoes of the morning. My detail under the guidance of a staff officer led the advance of the 2nd Corps. Genl. Hancock was at the head of the column which entered the field about half way between the Gettysburg cemetery and Little Round Top. The line of battle was formed there and several hours were spent in preparation. Immediately after the formation of the line we were ordered to the Hospital which had been located just south of the road in the rear of Little Round Top. The ground selected was an orchard which extended on the south to a log house near a fine spring of water. In the northwest corner of the enclosure was a barn, and between that and the road a stone wall. We stacked guns and awaited the developments. Heavy skirmishing and cannonading soon commenced and by the middle of the afternoon the battle began in earnest. From the crackling of musketry it increased to a roar of thunder augmented by the artillery fire and exploding shells. The earth fairly shook with the concussion, not only for the moment but for two solid hours. The field to the right of the hospital looked as though a hurricane was passing over it. Solid shot that struck the ground in front of our line ricochet and plowed great furrows in the earth to our right.

Wounded men began to pour into the hospital, hobbling along, using their muskets for walking sticks, while the more seriously hurt were brought in on stretchers, mangled and torn, bleeding, groaning, dying. Everything in our power was done to relieve the suffering. What could we do except to bring them water and receive their last messages to friends at home. When the attack upon Round Top was made the shell and musket balls poured into our hospital from a new direction. The wounded in the barn were frantic to be removed fearing they would be burned alive if it should take fire from the shelling. I removed them with the assistance of some of the detail. Among the wounded in the barn was the Col. of the 14th Ala., a Confederate.

It soon became evident that we must get away from that locality and we pressed every man into the service who had one hand to use and could walk. Holes were knocked in ambulances as they were being filled. Pandemonium reigned. I ran over a stretcher with one leg knocked off which I took and looking about to see who I would take first discovered my comrade L. J. Mosher lying on his back with the hot sun pouring into his face, badly wounded. He greeted me with a welcome I shall never forget.

The wounded were all moved back about a mile to Rock Creek during the night. A large

Badly injured during the fighting on July 2, Pvt. Ludwell Mosher was found at the field hospital by George Buckman as the sergeant was helping to remove the wounded to a safer location.

number of the wounded died in the orchard. The number of wounded increased materially on the following day. We were short of rations, tents and blankets. Many of the wounded were uncared for several days and exposed to a drenching rain in the night of the 3rd. We were in a deplorable condition without supplies and scant medical attendance. Nearly four thousand men, many entirely helpless lay scattered over the ground, Union and Confederate intermingled.

On July 4 Buckman wrote:

The wounded continue to be brought in. Some are dreadfully mangled and suffering excruciating pain. It is truly heart rending to witness the condition in which men are in when brought from the field to the hospital covered with blood and dirt and without care or attention. The matter of hospital tents means or means of alleviating the suffering seems to have been entirely neglected. Language fails to describe the scene. Surgeons are busy with amputations.

The Second Corps' hospital at Rock Creek

One young fellow, a Confederate, was taken up in the arms of one of the surgeons and carried to the amputation table, pleading all the way to have the surgeon save him. Putting his arms around his neck and telling him of his home, his mother, and his sister that he wanted to see again. His appeal was so pathetic and earnest that I could not endure it and turned away. The poor lad did not survive.

On the 6th of July we received a supply of hospital necessities and the situation began to be improved. The wounded still continued to be brought in. After being ordered by the surgeon in charge I went over the hospital ground and picked up hands, feet, legs and arms enough to make as high as a common table and then buried them. But the most sickening duty was yet to come. In spite of all we could do many of the dead were left unburied for three and four days. We had great difficulty in finding spades and shovels to work with but the dead must be buried. I took four men out of my detail one afternoon and went just across the creek and buried forty five men.

Previous to our going over the creek some of the hospital men had dug a trench over there about fifty feet in length and about eighteen inches deep in which had been placed as near as I can recollect about forty men for burial. They had not been covered. Alongside had been placed the bodies we were to inter, bloated, blackened and greatly decomposed. We considered the question for a few minutes as to the best way to proceed. We had an abundance of resolution but our stomachs offered a strong protest. Ignoring everything we commenced our labor by excavating by the side of the first man. When done we laid the corpse over and proceed to dig the next, throwing the earth over the first man and so for a few times when the stench became so unbearable that we were obliged to adopt different tactics. I returned to the hospital steward and procured some brandy in which we washed our faces. Took a swallow inside. All are unanimous that we could not continue the excavation. Four of us then placed ourselves by the side of a body, drew a long breath and carried it over, and deposited it upon the corpse already in the trench, and ran hastily away to breath. In this manner we completed our task and covered the bodies with earth.

On the 7th the Sanitary Commission arrived with wagon loads of supplies and immediately oranges, lemons, clean clothes and a great many delicacies sorely needed. The situation of the hospital at that time was deplorable in the extreme. I cannot describe—there is no language that can describe—no pen picture, or work painting that can or ever will illustrate the scenes that transpired in the 2nd Army Corps hospital at Gettysburg. The wounded numbered three thousand, a large number being Confederate. The heavy downpour of rain added to the misery. The wounded of the enemy presented a pitiable sight on the morning of the 8th as they lay shivering in the rain. We could not do much though ever so willing for the reason that we had nothing to do with. Many died during the storm of last night. The creek overflowed its banks and washed away several wounded and dead. I pulled one man out of the creek, who belonged to the 106th Pa.

It is difficult to imagine the condition of the 2nd Corps hospital for the weeks after the battle. Equally difficult is the horror that must have gone through the soldiers' minds as they lay helpless and wounded after battle only to feel the water swirling around them and carrying them off as the creek overflowed its banks. The able saved many of those who couldn't move, but some were lost to the flooded creek.

As the days went on some men regained strength, and others failed. The following men of the First Minnesota died at the Second Corps' hospital during this period, as reported by Sgt. Buckman:

Pvt. Peter Vosz (Co. K), shot through bowels
Pvt. Israel Durr (Co. K), shot through lung
Capt. Wilson Farrell (Co. C), shot through chest and bowels
Capt. Joseph Periam (Co. K), shot to head
Cpl. Aaron Greenwald (Co. C), shot through lungs
Pvt. Marcus Past (Co. K), shot through breast
Sgt. Henry Wright (Co. A), shot to head
Pvt. Russell Allen (Co. E), shot through bowels
Cpl. Phineas Dunham (Co. G), shot through left thigh and testicle
Pvt. Edwin Paul (Co. I), left leg amputated below knee
Pvt. John Ellsworth (Co. C), right leg amputated above knee

Pvt. Clark Brandt (Co. A), right leg amputated above knee
Cpl. Timothy Crawley (Co. A), shot through left leg above knee
Sgt. Frederick Diehr (Co. H), shot through the lung
Sgt. Aaron Greenwald (Co. C), shot through lung
Cpl. Peter Marks (Co. A), right foot amputated
Cpl. William Peck (Co. I), shot through left leg below knee, leg amputated
Pvt. Peter Welin (Co. E), shot in ankle, suffered through two amputations

Later in life, Buckman maintained that being detailed on the night before the second day's battle saved his life. He commented that the slaughter the regiment endured on July 2 was "an excellent opportunity of having to wear a wooden arm or being knocked into eternity." Looking back on his Gettysburg experience, he wrote, "I never will complain again happen what may. I was very much out of temper when I had to spill my coffee a second time and to go out in the darkness and mist, weary and foot sore, to hunt up headquarters but the sequel taught me a lesson."

To see how difficult the situation and, by modern standards, ineffective the care was at the Second Corps' field hospital, one only needs to look at those who were later buried at the Gettysburg Cemetery. Of the fifty-six First Minnesota men buried there, thirteen died after having a leg amputated, and twelve died between July 20 and August 10. Undoubtedly, most of the men died from infections caused by unclean conditions. The danger of germs was not widely understood until after the Civil War, and many doctors unknowingly passed on infections from one wounded soldier to another. The glories of fighting for one's beliefs and of victory in battle often get emphasis in military histories and in the larger world. More could be placed, however, on the cost in suffering for those who were wounded—some for the rest of their lives and some only briefly until they met their end.

On August 12, 1863, after caring for the wounded for five weeks, Sgt. Buckman and twenty-seven other Minnesotans left Gettysburg for Baltimore and eventually rejoined the regiment in Washington, DC. These men included members of his detail, as well as some wounded who could return to the regiment. Years after the war, Buckman wrote of his experiences, "The past seems like a dream. Three years of active service in Va.

Sgt. Henry Wright was wounded at Gettysburg on July 3 during the repulse of Pickett's Charge. He lingered for three days, dying on July 6. This temporary grave marker was carved from what appears to be a hardtack box. Sgt. Buckman noted in his diary on August 8, 1863, that he and his men "spent the day painting Hd Boards." This is very likely one of the headboards that they made that day.

Md. and Penna., and a citizen again. Truly I have something to remember. The terrible battlefield, the dusty weary march, the long nights when on pickets in storm and cold—can I forget?"

In 1897 a monument was dedicated to the First Minnesota at the Gettysburg National Battlefield Park. A large brass plaque on the monument bears the following inscription:

On the afternoon of July 2, 1863 Sickles' Third Corps, having advanced from this line to the Emmitsburg Road, eight companies of the First Minnesota Regiment, numbering 262 men were sent to this place to support a battery upon Sickles repulse. As his men were passing here in confused retreat, two Confederate brigades in pursuit were crossing the swale. To gain time to bring up the reserves & save this position, Gen Hancock in person ordered the eight companies to charge the rapidly advancing enemy. The order was instantly repeated by Col Wm. Colvill. And the charge as instantly made down the slope at full speed through the concentrated fire of the two brigades breaking with the bayonet the enemy's front line as it was crossing the small brook in the low ground there the remnant of the eight companies, nearly surrounded by the enemy held its entire force at bay for a considerable time & till it retired on the approach of the reserve the charge successfully accomplished its object. It saved this position & probably the battlefield. The loss of the eight companies in the charge was 215 killed & wounded. More than 83% percent. 47 men were still in line & no man missing. In self-sacrificing desperate valor this charge has no parallel in any war. Among the severely wounded were Col Wm. Colvill, Lt. Col Chas P Adams & Maj. Mark W. Downie. Among the killed Capt. Joseph Periam, Capt. Louis Muller & Lt Waldo Farrar. The next day the regiment participated in repelling Pickett's charge losing 17 more men killed & wounded.

I believe the following men made up most of Sgt. Buckman's twenty-man detail:

Pvt. John H. Alpers (Co. A)
Pvt. John Sonderman (Co. A)
Pvt. John S. Goff (Co. B)
Pvt. Henry Goodman (Co. B)
Pvt. Lafayette Snow (Co. B)
Pvt. Adin Laflin (Co. D)
Pvt. George Fuller (Co. D)
Pvt. Daniel Legg (Co. D)
Pvt. Paul Nelson (Co. F)
Pvt. Jefferson Baker (Co. G)
Pvt. Charles Benson (Co. G)
Pvt. Walter Sastrow (Co. H)
Pvt. John Shafer (Co. H)
Pvt. Carl Carlson (Co. I)
Pvt. George Keeler (Co. I)
Pvt. John Abell (Co. K)
Pvt. Henry Boyson (Co. K)

Pvt. Charles Benson of Company G (*left*), a member of the twenty-man detail, and his Second Corps badge (*right*)

Pvt. Adin Laflin served as part of the 20 man detail at the 2nd Corps Hospital at Rock Creek. He is seen here in a picture which was hand tinted at the time it was taken. He is wearing a red shirt and the uniform of the common soldier, a wool four button jacket or "blouse" and sky blue wool pants. The same uniform was worn summer or winter.

FIELD AND STAFF OFFICERS

FIVE MEN HAD THE HONOR of leading the First Minnesota during its three-year term of service. The first three had experience in the U.S.–Mexican War: Willis Gorman, Napoleon J. T. Dana, and Alfred Sully. The last two, George Morgan and William Colvill, rose from the ranks to command the unit. All five were promoted to the rank of brigadier general during their service, Colvill by brevet. Both Dana and Sully were brevetted major generals. Gorman was a strict disciplinarian, and at the beginning of the war, though the men complained, this was exactly what they needed to stay alive. Both Gorman and Sully were known for their liberal use of profanity, whereas Colvill was a more mild-mannered though still effective leader. All led their men well, and all were, in turn, loved and respected by those men.

Willis A. Gorman

b. January 12, 1816; d. May 20, 1876

Born near Flemingsburg, Kentucky, Willis Gorman graduated from law school at the University of Indiana. In 1835 he moved to Bloomington, Indiana, and in January 1836 married Martha Stone. In 1837 and 1838, he worked as a clerk at the state senate, and being a popular young lawyer, at twenty-three he won a seat in the state legislature. There, he served five or six terms, until the outbreak of the U.S.–Mexican War.

During the U.S.–Mexican War, he entered military service as a private in the Third Indiana Voluntary Infantry. Before leaving for the war, the men elected their officers and chose Gorman as their major. He served with credit in Gen. Zachary Taylor's campaign. In May 1847, when the regiment's one-year enlistment was up, he enlisted again and was unanimously chosen to be the colonel of the Fourth Indiana. He served with distinction in Gen. Winfield Scott's campaign that captured Mexico City and, thus, ended the war. Gorman was cited for bravery under fire.

Returning to Indiana in August 1849, he was elected to the U.S. House of Representatives, where he served two terms. In May 1853, he was appointed governor of Minnesota Territory by President Pierce and held office four years. He moved his family to St. Paul and resided there for the rest of his life.

Gorman was a member of Minnesota's constitutional convention in 1857. In public office as well as private practice, he acquired a reputation for sterling, unbending integrity and for being one of the most effective orators in the country. His voice was said to be a model of flexibility and power.

A pronounced Union man, at the outbreak of the Civil War he tendered his services and was commissioned colonel of the First Minnesota. He was indefatigable in drilling and preparing it for service. Brave in action and, at times, rough in manner, he always manifested the utmost pride in and love for his regiment. His generous commendations to the men for their conduct as a regiment built and fostered the regiment's pride and esprit de corps. The regiment's success might not have been so great without Col. Gorman.

He and Martha had five children. The oldest, Richard D. Gorman, served under his father for a time as an enlisted man in the First Minnesota, until he accepted an officer's commission in another regiment. Another son, James, served as an adjutant on his father's staff once he became a general. Martha died in Indiana on March 1, 1864. She had been temporarily living with her family while her husband was serving in the army.

Years later, one of the men in his command described Gorman as follows:

> He had the real democratic inspiration that one man is just as good as another except when the entanglement of untoward social conditions changed their attitude toward each other. The colonel had the qualities necessary to make clear that this change of conditions had taken place and that it was now necessary that some should command and others obey, some lead and others follow. His tact was tireless, his profanity voluminous and resounding, but artistic. It did not take the enlisted men long to learn that his bark was worse than his bite and so it

was not infrequent for some of them to violate some pet regulation of the commanding officer "just to hear the old man swear."

The War Department quickly realized the need for high-quality leaders. For the superb way the First Minnesota handled itself at Bull Run and its orderly retreat, Gorman drew much acclaim and was promoted to brigadier general on October 2, 1861. He took command of the First Brigade, Second Division, of the Second Army Corps—of which the First Minnesota was a part. The men missed their leader, but the regimental pride he instilled continued even after he left the regiment—perhaps best exemplified during the charge at Gettysburg. The mutual high regard existing between him and the men of the regiment continued after the war. He regularly attended their annual reunions and was always honored, up until his death in 1876.

James Wright of Company F relates the story of an altercation between the colonel and a private while the regiment was boarding a transport ship. Gorman told the drunken private to make way, and the soldier cracked that if the colonel hadn't held such a high rank, he wouldn't talk so bravely. This defiance proved too much for the bellicose Gorman, and he pounced on the private with little ceremony and proceeded to beat the man until the soldier cried, "I give up!" Then, the colonel dusted himself off, bowed to the onlookers, and walked away. The soldier was never tried for insubordination.

Known for his strong language and no-nonsense demeanor, Gorman had little time for anything he considered unimportant to the tasks at hand—commanding his soldiers wisely and winning a war. The January 21, 1862, *Stillwater Messenger* recounts a story from the regiment's time in winter quarters at Camp Stone before Gorman was promoted and left the regiment.

> The New York 39th and Minnesota First are near neighbors on the Potomac. The Chaplain of the 39th is a Baptist, and one day called on Col. G. to talk about the religious interest of his men. He was politely received and beckoned to a seat on a chest.
>
> "Colonel," said he, "you have a crack regiment—one of the best regiments in the army."
>
> "That's so." said the Colonel.
>
> "Do you think you pay sufficient attention to the religious instruction of your men?" said the 39th.

The St. Paul law office of Willis Gorman in 1870

"Chaplain Neil attends to that branch of the service, Sir—hard to beat, sir—good talker—devotedly pious, sir!" replied the Colonel.

After a moment of reflection the chaplain replied—"A lively interest has been awakened in the 39th; the Lord has blessed the labors of his servants, and I have already baptized ten men."

"Is that so? Honor bright, now." Asked the Colonel

"Yes, Sir, ten of them."

"Sergeant!" said the Colonel to Orderly Sproat, "detail fifteen crack men for immediate baptism. The Minnesota First s—b—can't be beat by any d—d regiment in the service!"

The chaplain withdrew, and the Colonel resumed his writing.

Gorman proved a creative and effective leader who also had a sense of humor when needed. On June 10, 1862, at Fair Oaks, a heavy rain fell. The mud was ankle deep, and the men were somewhat demoralized. In the afternoon a Rebel artillery battery began showering the Union troops with several rounds of shells.

Gen. Gorman's headquarters was located between the Union artillery and the horses, and one shell landed shy of his tent but did not explode. He said, "Bring it here. Let's see if there is a message in it for me." After it was opened, he wrote a note and put it into the shell. Then, he sent it up to the Union battery and asked them to send it back with his compliments.

In November 1862, Gorman was transferred to command the District of Arkansas from its headquarters in Helena. On May 5, 1864, he resigned due to ill health. He was mustered out of service in Arkansas on the same day his men from the First Minnesota were being mustered out back in Minnesota at Ft. Snelling.

After the war he returned to St. Paul and his law practice. On April 27, 1865, Gorman married Emily Newington; they had no children. In April 1869, he was elected St. Paul's city attorney, and he was re-elected several times. He died in St. Paul on May 20, 1876. Being one of the most respected men to serve in the First Minnesota, when he died many men of the regiment expressed their care and love for their leader. His body was buried in his family plot in Oakland Cemetery in St. Paul.

Napoleon Jackson Tecumseh Dana

b. April 15, 1822; d. July 15, 1905

If ever a man bore a name that foretold his future career, it was Napoleon Jackson Tecumseh Dana. This eventual soldier and future business executive was born at the military post of Ft. Sullivan, located in Eastport, Maine. His father, Nathaniel Giddings Dana, was an army officer, and his grandfather had been an officer in the navy during the American Revolution. On his mother's side he descended from Woodbury Langdon, a member of the Continental Congress. His name undoubtedly came from his military father's respect for three great leaders who were in current news when the baby was born.

Dana graduated from West Point on July 1, 1842, and was commissioned a second lieutenant in the U.S. Army's Seventh Infantry Regiment. He married Susan (Sue) Lewis Martin Sandford in June 1844. She and Dana had three children, born between 1845 and 1851. He served with his regiment in Louisiana and Mississippi until August 1845 and then in the U.S.–Mexican War from 1845 to 1848. He was promoted to first lieutenant on February 16, 1847, and was appointed cap-

tain and assistant quartermaster on March 13, 1848. On April 18, 1847, at the Battle of Cerro Gordo, he was severely wounded while storming the entrenchments on Telegraph Hill. He was left for dead on the battlefield until picked up by a burial party thirty-six hours later.

After his injury he was absent sick and then placed on recruiting service until March 1849. Dana was stationed at Ft. Snelling from 1848 to 1849 and, again, in 1853. While at Ft. Snelling, he became familiar with business conditions in Minnesota, and in 1855 he resigned from the army and established a banking business in St. Paul as a member of the firm Dana and Borup. He also served as a brigadier general of the Minnesota militia from 1857 to 1861.

He entered the volunteer army on October 10, 1861, and was appointed the colonel of the First Minnesota, replacing Willis Gorman. Within a few days Dana took the regiment into action at Ball's Bluff. He left the regiment the following winter when he was promoted to the rank of brigadier general on February 3, 1862. He was put in command of the Third Brigade in the Second Army Corps' Second Division during the Peninsula Campaign. On September 17, 1862, at Antietam, he received a gunshot wound in his left leg. The ball entered his calf and traveled forward and inward, lodging near the surface of his shin, one and a half inches below the knee. Though painful, the wound was not dangerous. He was, however, disabled for many months.

As the war progressed, Dana held several different and notable commands. He was promoted to major general on March 1, 1863, and was tasked with the defense of Philadelphia from June 16 to August 27, 1863. He then served in the Department of the Gulf in Texas and commanded the Second Division of the Thirteenth Army Corps from September 28 to October 26, 1863, and then with the entire Thirteenth Army Corps from December 1863 to January 1864. Other commands included the District of Vicksburg, from August 17 to October 30, 1864; the Sixteenth Army Corps and the districts of West Tennessee and Vicksburg, in November 1864; and the Department of the Mississippi from December 1864 to May 27, 1865, when he resigned from military service.

After the war he worked for five years as a general agent of the Russian-American Company. Thereafter, he was an executive for several railroads, notably the Chicago, Burlington and Quincy, and the deputy commissioner of pensions in Washington, DC, from 1895 to 1897. He died in Portsmouth, New Hampshire, on July 15, 1905.

Alfred Sully as a cadet at West Point

being commissioned brigadier general on September 26, 1862. His Civil War service included numerous military actions, including Yorktown, West Point, Fair Oaks, Peach Orchard, Savage Station, Glendale, Malvern Hill, Second Bull Run, Antietam, Fredericksburg (where he was slightly wounded in the leg), and Chancellorsville.

At the Battle of Fredericksburg in December 1862, the regiment was, at one point, under particularly heavy fire from the enemy. As other regiments gave way and threatened the collapse of the entire Union flank the First Minnesota held its ground. Noting their tenacity, Second Division commander Brig. Gen. O. O. Howard is said to have exclaimed to the commander of his First Brigade, "Sully, your First Minnesota does not run!" To this, Gen. Sully replied with firm pride, "The First Minnesota never runs."

Sully garnered even greater esteem for his role in the Indian Wars. Around the time of Chancellorsville, he was assigned to serve under Gen. John Pope (whom he loathed). As a response to the Dakota War in Minnesota, Sully was appointed by Pope to command the Northwest Indian Expedition, with the intent of

Alfred Sully

b. May 20, 1821; d. April 27, 1879

Alfred Sully was the son of the famous American painter Thomas Sully. After his graduation from West Point in 1841, 2nd Lt. Sully took part in the Florida Seminole Wars. He then saw action during the U.S.–Mexican War, including the Siege of Vera Cruz, where he landed on March 9, 1847. Two days later, he was promoted to first lieutenant. He also served on frontier duty at a number of widely disparate points, being promoted to captain during his service in California in 1852. Sully served under Gen. Harvey in the 1855–56 campaigns in the Dakotas and stayed with Harvey on the frontier until the Civil War began.

At the outbreak of the Civil War, as a major in the U.S. Army, he secured St. Joseph, Missouri, for the Union in the absence of the incompetent Gen. John Fremont. He was appointed colonel of the First Minnesota on March 4, 1862, replacing N. J. T. Dana. Having served in Minnesota throughout the 1850s, he had connections with the governors and great affection for the state, which helped him secure his commission. He was not, however, with the regiment for long,

Gen. Sully and his staff are pictured during the Northwest Indian Expedition of 1863. *From left to right,* Capt. John Pell; 1st Lt. Andrew Levering (standing); and Lt. Josias King. All were officers in the First Minnesota detached to serve for a time with Sully.

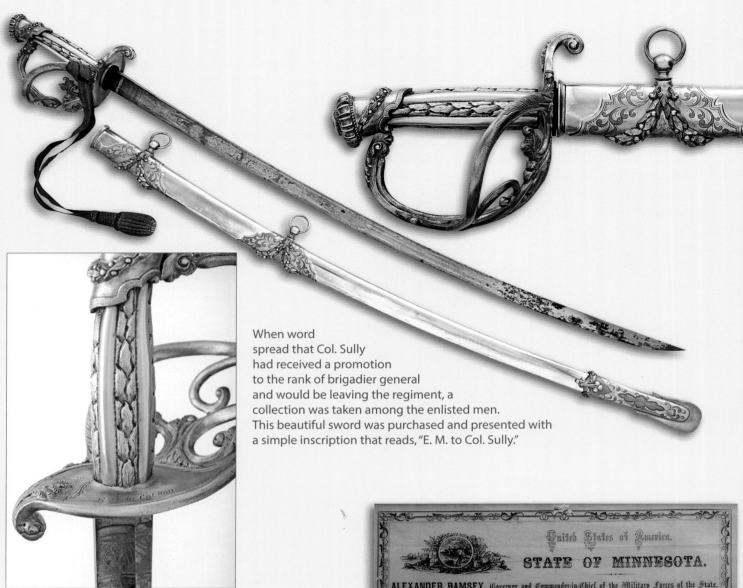

When word spread that Col. Sully had received a promotion to the rank of brigadier general and would be leaving the regiment, a collection was taken among the enlisted men. This beautiful sword was purchased and presented with a simple inscription that reads, "E. M. to Col. Sully."

suppressing any further Native hostilities. During this campaign Sully brought in Josias King and others from the First Minnesota to serve on his staff.

After the war Sully was made commander of the departments of Kansas, Dakota, and Montana. During this time he also investigated the Fetterman Massacre. Coincidentally, one of the officers killed during the massacre, 2nd Lt. Horatio Bingham, served under Sully in the First Minnesota, as a sergeant in Company K.

As a lieutenant colonel of the regular army, he led the Seventh Cavalry against the Cheyenne and, while doing so, butted heads with Lt. Col. George Armstrong Custer, an officer junior to him in length of service. By crossing swords with Custer, he came into ill favor with generals Sheridan and Sherman, the latter being the greatest power in the post–Civil War army. Sully was relieved of his position by Gen. Sheridan, with the

This eleven-by-fourteen-inch document is the commission signed by Governor Alexander Ramsey appointing Alfred Sully to the position of colonel of the First Minnesota.

concurrence of Gen. Sherman. Custer took control of the Seventh Cavalry and proceeded to attack too many "renegades" at the Little Bighorn. Sully correctly predicted that Custer would "come to no good." The rest of that story is history.

George N. Morgan

b. September 7, 1825; d. July 24, 1866

George Morgan was born in Masina, St. Lawrence County, New York. He married Delia E. Warner on December 9, 1852, and moved to St. Catherines in Canada, near Niagara Falls. In June 1856 the couple moved to Minnesota, living for a few months in Lakeland and then in St. Paul until June 1857, when they moved to St. Anthony. Near St. Anthony Falls, Morgan and his partner built the town's first foundry and machine shop, under the name of Scott and Morgan. His business prospered, and he participated in St. Anthony's civic life. He was also considered a gifted coronet player.

George N. Morgan

This sword was carried by Morgan throughout the war. The enthusiastic townspeople of St. Anthony presented it to him in 1861. The inscription reads, "Presented by the citizens of St. Anthony, June, 1861; G. N. Morgan; Major 1st Regt Min." The sword is engraved with the rank of major, not captain, which would have been correct. The sword also has faint engravings of the sixteen battles in which he participated while with the First Minnesota: Bull Run, Nelson's Farm, Edwards' Ferry, Malvern Hill, Yorktown, South Mountain, West Point, Sharpsburg, Fair Oaks, Antietam, Orchard Station, Charlestown, Savage Station, Ashby's Gap, White Oak Swamp, and Fredericksburg.

This painting, known as an *escutcheon,* measures twenty-three by thirty inches and is in superb condition. These paintings were popular after the war. For a fee an artist would paint the wartime story of a soldier in this standard format. It lists his various ranks, his service record, and the battles in which he was involved. The following sad notation graces the base of the painting: "Died July 24, 1866."

Col. Morgan reviewing the troops of the Veteran Reserve Corps at Ft Snelling in 1864

William Colvill Jr.

While living in St. Anthony, he joined the private militia unit known as the Minnesota Militia, which became the St. Anthony Zouaves, working his way to captain. When the war began, the men unanimously voted to volunteer for the Union. They elected Morgan their captain and became the nucleus of Company E. He was promoted to major on October 22, 1861, to lieutenant colonel on August 28, 1862, and to colonel on September 26, 1862. He participated in all the regiment's battles, up to Chancellorsville.

Morgan's health suffered from the rigorous field duty, and he resigned on May 5, 1863, returning to Minnesota. He was appointed major of the Second Veteran Reserve Corps in June and stationed at Ft. Snelling, where he remained in command of the post for three months. In September 1863 he was ordered to Louisville, where on his arrival he was commissioned colonel of the Second Veteran Reserves. That fall, he and his command brought five hundred prisoners to the Northern prisons without the loss of a single man. He was then stationed at the barracks in Detroit for about one year, returning to Ft. Snelling in December 1864, where he remained until June 30, 1865.

On March 13, 1865, he was commissioned brevet brigadier general by President Lincoln for gallant and meritorious service during the war. Weakened and exhausted by his service, he died of tuberculosis at his home in Minneapolis on July 24, 1866, at the age of forty-one, just three weeks after being mustered out of government service.

William Colvill Jr.

b. April 5, 1830; d. June 12, 1905

Born in Forestville, New York, William Colvill studied law at Forestville and Buffalo and was admitted to the bar in 1851. In 1854 he moved to Cannon Falls, Minnesota, and claimed a tract of land, upon which part of the city now stands. He opened a law office in Red Wing in 1854 and in 1855 established the *Red Wing Sentinel*, a Democratic newspaper. When the war broke out, the thirty-one-year-old Colvill was the first man from Goodhue County to volunteer and was elected captain by the men who would become the core of Company F. He was well loved by his men. As James Wright, who served as first sergeant in Company F, writes of him, "To sum up his characteristics, he was a large-bodied, big-hearted, fair-minded, a real man, loyal to his friends and country, a comrade and a patriot."

At the time of the regiment's first fight, the First Battle of Bull Run, Colvill was the captain of Company F. During the battle the regiment was sent onto the field to support Rickett's artillery battery, and while engaged with the enemy, the regiment was split in two when the battery rapidly moved through them, causing a loss in the regiment's fighting efficiency. In

1877 Colvill's writings about his war experiences were published for the regimental reunion:

We gaily file across the pike, our banners—each company has one—fluttering. The chaplain [Rev. Edward Neill] rushes to the front, tears the fence away to let us through, and commences his speech. Each company as it passes picks up the sense of it. It is "to remember Minnesota, whose honor is in our keeping." It is appreciated and our eyes gleam an answer. In the field across the pike we for the first time draw the enemy's fire.

We cross the creek, file into the field towards the designated position. . . . Rickett unlimbers his first gun to the front, fires one shot, and in answer the enemy concentrate the fire of their two batteries upon him. In an instant his guns are horseless and most of his men killed or wounded. We on the right, still firing into the woods, hear a tremendous volley to the left and looking that way see where the guns stood in sight a moment ago a great mass of gray. They have come out of the woods—but a few rods to march—and with Union colors at their head, came up to the guns and fired almost in the faces of our center companies—till then in doubt whether they are friends or not. That fire caused awful destruction. One third or the four center companies were laid prostrate [it was probably during this volley that Capt. Lewis McKune of Company G was shot through the heart and, though carried to the rear, died soon thereafter]. . . .

As I look over the lines of Company F at the enemy, someone touches my right shoulder, and looking up there is a horseman in gray. We have many regiments dressed in gray and I think nothing of it, but he says, "Why do you fire on your friends?" "Where do you belong?" "Second Mississippi Brigade." "We are the First Minnesota." The officer dismounts and is sent under guard [Pvt. Javan Irvine (Co. A)] to the Brooklyn Zouves.

Eventually, the battle turned in the South's favor. The First Minnesota made an orderly retreat and was one of the last units to leave the field. During the retreat Capt. Colvill, through his quick thinking and reflex, dodged death and left the enemy a little dumbfounded. Colvill later noted:

Capt. Pell was also "rallying" with the greatest vigor some distance down to the left, and we observed the colors of his company [Co. I] and called the bearer to us, and advanced it toward the wood, getting in line for a moment and pushing the enemy back. The color bearer, Sergeant Knight, behaved most gallantly . . . before we realized it our men were mostly gone, and the Colonel [Gorman] with reluctance fell back with the flag. . . . The wounded, alarmed at the idea of being left, calling for aid. With a few words of assurance they are quieted. Happening at this point to catch a view of our old position at the toll gate, there appeared a large column of men, vast numbers apparently pushing up from the ford. At the same time a squadron of cavalry is gaily trotting across the valley from that direction. The impression received was that we were to make another and decisive advance. Getting back to the road along the line of the wood, this cavalry had then halted, and while I was trying to make out the movements of our large column at the toll gate, quick as a flash about turned this cavalry and off they gallop. Stupidly gaping after them, I was aroused by the sound of footsteps, and looking around saw a platoon front of the enemy, marching double quick and within a few feet distance. This startled me out suddenly as a partridge and my movement startled them as much. Instinctively I started for the slope of the hillside towards the creek and diagonally from the road. It was but a few rods, but that distance was never made more quickly by a race horse. You should have seen me with a secesh smooth bore on my shoulder, a large artillery sword in my hand, make my long shanks spin.

There was no sign of fatigue, although before I considered myself just about used up. Turning my head when about half way to the bank—the platoon was in the act of wheeling around the corner of the wood towards me; a step or two farther—I heard the chuck of the muskets brought briskly to the palm of the hand, and then with a mighty leap and feet thrown out I landed on my back with head crouched downwards, just below the top of the bank, at the same instant, through the space I filled when they pulled the trigger, buzzed a hundred bullets. You should have seen the surprise—the actual astonishment in their faces as, springing up, I rushed down to and up the creek, out of the fire behind the bank.

Having escaped death by a hundred bullets, he found some Union soldiers stooping to get a drink of water. They crossed the creek and eventually came upon a house full of wounded soldiers. Some of them turned out to be men of the First Minnesota, including part of the color guard, who had possession of the regimental colors. Colvill and his men made it back to the Union lines and lived to fight another day.

During his service Colvill was wounded several times, the first time being on Monday, June 30, 1862, at the Battle of White Oak Swamp (also known as Glendale). Phil Hamlin of Company F wrote home describing the incident:

> When we reached the rear of our reserves, we halted, threw off our knapsacks and advanced in battle line with loud cheers. We finally halted in a ravine at the edge of the woods, the field being in our rear and a knoll in front of us and, beyond the knoll, our troops in action. This was about 5 PM. We had not been in this position long before we began to receive scattering shots by one of which Captain Colville was wounded in the shoulder and compelled to leave the field. On being hit he said to those men near him "Say nothing about it" and picking up his sword walked away.

His wound was serious, however. He was sent to a hospital in Baltimore to recover and did not return to the company until a month later on August 31, 1862.

Capt. William Colvill, early in the war, circa 1861–62

On August 28, 1862, Colvill was promoted to the rank of major. On September 16, 1862, Lt. Col. Stephen Miller received a commission as colonel of the Seventh Minnesota Infantry and returned to the state. Upon his resignation, Colvill was promoted to lieutenant colonel. On May 6, 1863, Colvill became the fifth and final colonel of the regiment.

On June 25, 1863, Col. Colvill was leading his men through the mud and rain near Haymarket, Virginia. Confederate general Jeb Stuart spotted Hancock's Second Corps wagon train and decided to attack it with his horse artillery. Colvill was riding a beautiful horse, recently sent to him by well-wishers in Minnesota.

Col. Colvill's sword

It was shot from beneath him by a piece of artillery shell. As the horse went down, Colvill was sure-footed enough to jump away and not get pinned underneath. The horse could not be saved, so he immediately ordered it put out of its misery. He gave the bridle to his orderly, Milt Bevans, and asked him to find him another horse. Then, he picked up the saddle by the stirrup straps, threw it over his shoulder, looked back at the men, and with a twisted smile said, "Forward"—of course, the men did not let him carry the saddle for long. Within an hour Bevans appeared with a very ordinary-looking horse, and Colvill was back in the saddle. He then rode to his place in line as if nothing had happened.

Colvill was wounded twice at Gettysburg. When the First Minnesota made its charge on July 2, he was positioned behind the regiment in the center. Lt. Col. Adams was on the right, and Maj. Downie was on the left. Colvill was shot in the right shoulder and the right ankle. These wounds permanently maimed him, requiring him to walk with a cane for the rest of his life.

In a letter written some years later, Colvill describes the action at the time he was wounded:

I was immediately behind the colors. . . . I saw a number of our men lying as they had fallen. . . . Then came a shock like a sledge hammer on my backbone between my shoulders. It turned me partly around and made me "see stars." I suppose it was a piece of shell. Just then I perceived Captain Coates, who said, "Colonel, are you badly hurt?" I said, "I don't know. Take care of the men." Just then I was putting my foot on the ground; there was a smart pang through it. It gave way and falling to the ground I saw just beside me a gully not more than two feet wide and less in depth.

As I struck the ground I rolled over into it and listened among other things to the bullets zipping along the ground and thought how fortunate for me was the fact of the gully. I need not describe the rest of it. I saw it grow dark and then it became quiet. I saw the stars shining overhead. Presently I heard voices of our men. The boys were looking up the dead and the wounded. I heard some of them talking with the wounded and in one case where their search had found a comrade they were taking his last words for his home and family.

Col. Adams and Major Downie must have

been struck down about the same instant as myself, it was just a moment before I had noticed them each in his place. My first wound, the blow to my back bone, was caused by a minnie ball which penetrated at the top of the right arm, passed under the shoulder blade, struck the back bone, and lodged in the flesh about the middle of the shoulder blade. It was extracted one week afterward. The wound to the foot was from a ball also from the right, striking the right foot at the ankle joint, crushing that and smashing up the joint which, with the ball, was extracted two weeks afterward.

Sgt. Henry Taylor helped carry the colonel to a large stone barn to the rear of the Union lines that was being used as a field hospital. Though critically wounded, Colvill was left to lie on the ground with no protection from the rain, which began to fall in torrents that evening. Although he suffered intensely, he did not complain but rather kept inquiring as to the care of his men, saying that they should be treated first. In the words of Charles Hubbs, "He was ever brave, gentle, kind and tolerant." Colvill was then moved to the Second Corps' hospital at Rock Creek. Sgt. George Buckman's twenty-man detail undoubtedly gave their colonel the best care they could. That said, the field hospital was still an unclean place, filled with men who were dying daily.

Attempts were made to find shelter in local homes for all wounded officers bearing the rank of colonel and above. On July 28 Buckman noted, "Colonel Colvill is doing very well, he has been carried to Gettisburg [sic] today on a stretcher to a more comfortable quarters." Colvill was taken to the Pierce home, located at 303 Baltimore Street on the corner of Baltimore and Breckenridge. He was carried on a stretcher to a second-floor bedroom overlooking Baltimore Street. Because of his size, eight men from Buckman's detail were required to carry him up the narrow, angled stairway. His orderly, Pvt. Milt Bevans, remained by his side and continued to act as his personal nurse, and on August 5, Pvt. Walter Reed was also detailed to assist the colonel. Tillie Pierce, then fifteen years old, later recounted the colonel's stay at their home:

A few days after the battle, several soldiers came to our house and asked mother if she would allow them to bring their wounded Colonel to the place, provided they would send two nurses along to help him wait on him, saying they would like to have him kept in a private house.

As we had a suitable room she consented.

The wounded officer was carried to the house on a litter, and was suffering greatly. After they got him up stairs, and were about placing him on the bed, it was found to be too short, so that the foot-board had to be taken off and an extension added. The Colonel was a very tall man and of fine proportions.

He had been severely wounded in the right ankle and shoulder, the latter wound extending to his spine. The surgeons at first wanted to amputate his foot, saying it was necessary in order to save his life; but the Colonel objected and said if his foot must go he would go too.

Mother waited on him constantly, and the nurses could not have been more devoted.

He was highly esteemed by all his men, many of whom visited him at the house, and even wept over him in his suffering and helplessness. They always spoke of him as one of the bravest men in the army.

Before long his sister came, who with tender care and cheering words, no doubt hastened his recovery.

Several months elapsed before he was able to be removed; when, on a pair of crutches, he left for his home in St. Paul. As he was leaving the house he could hardly express fully, his thanks and appreciation of our kindness; and on parting kissed us all, though he were bidding us farewell to his own kith and kin. We, on our part, felt as though one of our own family were leaving. He promised that whenever able he would come back to see us.

About three years after the battle, I was standing on the front pavement one day, when a carriage suddenly stopped at the front door. A gentleman alighted, came up to me, shook hands, and kissed me without saying a word. I knew it was the Colonel by his tall, manly form.

We were all glad to meet each other again, and we earnestly desired him to stay. He however, said his time was limited, and friends were waiting in the carriage to go over the battlefield. So we were forced to again say farewell.

When Colonel Colvill and his attendants left our house, one of the men who had been nurs-ing him, presented me with a gun and bayonet, saying: "I bought it with my own money, and I give it to you; and if any one comes after it, and wants to take it from you, just tell them that the gun was bought and paid for by the soldier who gave it to you."

From Gettysburg Colvill was sent to a hospital in Harrisburg, Pennsylvania. He did not see the men of his regiment again until February 1864, when they were ready to be sent home and mustered out. In his memoirs 1st Sgt. James Wright (Co. F) writes about the love the men had for their colonel and about a banquet held for them in Washington, DC, the night before they departed for home:

The return of Col Colvill to the regiment for the first time since Gettysburg was one of the events of the evening. Most men in his condition would have felt it impossible to be present. He could not walk or stand and was carried in by two of the stalwart members of the regiment, Captain Tom Sinclair and Sergeant Johnny Merritt. His entrance into the banquet hall was unexpected, and when he was brought in, there was a spontaneous outburst of shouting and cheering, which showed the feelings of the men toward him. He was the original captain of Company F and had won his way to command of the regiment.

After the First was discharged in 1864, Colvill returned to Minnesota, edited the *Red Wing Republican* until January 1865, and then took a seat in the legislature, to which he had been elected the previous autumn.

Immediately after the adjournment of the legislature, he received an appointment as colonel of the First Minnesota Heavy Artillery, which was stationed in Chattanooga. He accepted and, on paper, was its commander from February 25 to April 26, 1865. Owing to his wounds, he was, however, never able to serve with the battery. On May 6, 1865, he received a brevet commission as brigadier general, undoubtedly for his gallantry at Gettysburg. He was mustered out of service in July 1865 and returned to his home in Red Wing.

Though now crippled for life, Colvill was described as a man of commanding appearance. On his six-feet-five-inch frame he maintained a full beard and liked to

In 1884, out of love and respect for their final commander, the veterans of the First Minnesota presented this gold Second Corps badge to Colvill. The attaching pin has broken off, but the following engraving can plainly be seen: "Col. Wm Colvill; 1st Regt; Minn Vols; 1884."

wear a Prince Albert–style long coat. Colvill was a member of the A. E. Welch GAR Post #75 in Red Wing and was a frequent visitor at the First Minnesota's reunions.

Colvill served as a state legislator from 1865 to 1866 and as the state's attorney general from 1866 to 1868. Afterward, he returned to his law practice in Red Wing. He also served in the Minnesota House of Representatives in 1878 and, from 1887 to 1891, as register of the Duluth Land Office. While living in Duluth, he became acquainted with the North Shore of Cook County on several visits to the area.

In April 1893, Colvill and his wife, Elizabeth, boarded the *Dixon* and traveled upriver to the shoreline seven miles north of Grand Marais. There, they staked out a homestead of 167 acres. The land lay east of a small creek that would soon be named in honor of Judge George Durfee of Grand Marais. Judge Durfee had served in the First Minnesota (Co. K) under Col. Colvill, and while living in Duluth, Colvill became good friends with both George and his brother Chester, another First Minnesota vet. Eventually, other people settled in the area, and the small community came to be called Colvill. Colvill always maintained a home in Red Wing,

This ribbon was given to each of the veterans who attended the June 13, 1905, reunion at the soldiers' home in Minneapolis. That year, they planned to honor the man who had led them at Gettysburg and had his picture and the date of the reunion worked into the ribbon. Col. Colvill arrived at the home and was looking forward to the reunion the next day. Unfortunately, he passed away while sleeping that night, so the date on the ribbon is both a date of celebration and the remembrance date of his death.

but he spent his summers at his Cook County homestead until 1900.

On June 12, 1905, he left his farm in Red Wing and traveled to the soldiers' home in Minneapolis, looking forward to the reunion being held the next day. He visited until eleven that evening with many of his old comrades living at the home, including Freeman L. McKusick, who was the adjutant of the soldiers' home. When Colvill went to bed, he said goodnight to McKusick and that he felt sure of a good night's rest. McKusick slept in the adjoining room and left the door between the rooms open. He heard nothing during the night, and shortly after six in the morning, McKusick went to call on the colonel. Entering the room, he spoke to his friend but got no answer. Approaching the colonel, he was startled by his pallor and upon closer inspection discovered that he was dead. The body of the colonel lay naturally on its left side, with the left hand under the cheek. His features were calm. The old soldier had evidently gone to a peaceful sleep, never to return. He was seventy-five years old.

William and Elizabeth lay beside each other underneath a statue dedicated to the colonel in the Cannon Falls Community Cemetery. The monument was dedicated on July 28, 1928, and along with many remaining veterans of the First Minnesota, Governor Christianson, President Coolidge, and twenty thousand other dignitaries attended.

Lt. Colonel Stephen Miller

Stephen Miller

b. January 7, 1816; d. August 18, 1881

Born in Perry, Cumberland County, Pennsylvania, Stephen Miller learned the milling business after leaving school. In 1837 he became a forwarding and commission merchant in Harrisburg, and in 1839 he married Margaret Funk of Dauphin County. They raised three sons and had one daughter, who died in infancy. Miller, an ardent old-line Whig, was elected probate officer of Dauphin County in 1849, a position he held until 1855. From 1853 to 1855, he also edited the *Telegraph,* an influential Whig paper in Harrisburg. In 1855 he was appointed flour inspector of Philadelphia and continued in that position for three years. In 1858, for his health, he moved his family to Minnesota. They moved to St. Cloud, where he ran a mercantile business with Henry Swisshelm, who had come from Pittsburg in 1856. In 1860 he was elected delegate at large to the national Republican convention in Chicago that nominated Lincoln for president.

At the outbreak of the war, he and his son Wesley enlisted as privates in the newly forming First Minnesota. Governor Ramsey and Miller had been good friends back in Pennsylvania, and knowing Miller as he did—as well as his recruiting efforts and general fitness—Ramsey lifted his forty-five-year-old friend from private to lieutenant colonel of the First. In August, Wesley Miller received an appointment as a second lieutenant in the Seventh U.S. Infantry. He later died at Gettysburg on July 2, 1863, while serving with the Seventh. Stephen and Margaret's second son, Stephen C. Miller, enlisted as a private in the Sixth Minnesota and, as a reward for good service, rose to the position of commissary of subsistence, with the rank of captain, while serving with Gen. Frederick Steele in Arkansas.

Miller faithfully served the First during his sixteen-month tenure as its lieutenant colonel. At the First Battle of Bull Run, he commanded the regiment's right wing, and as one member reported of his courage:

> It is simple justice to mention the brave conduct of our officers. Lieut. Col. Miller and Major Dike dismounted and were found in the thickest of the fight. Our Lieutenant Messick, regardless of the storm of deadly hail, did his best to rally the men until the last.

He also fought with the men of the First at Yorktown, West Point, Fair Oaks, Peach Orchard, Savage Station, White Oak Swamp, and Malvern Hill. During these several engagements, the regiment lost ninety-one men killed, wounded, and missing. On July 2, 1862, he commanded the rear guard on the retreat to Harrison's Landing, and on September 15, 1862, he commanded the reserve at the Battle of South Mountain.

Ill for much of the winter of 1861–62 and into the spring, Miller was away from the regiment for many months and unable to act as second in command. This was unfortunate given the regiment's frequent turnover of colonels. Miller hoped for the colonel's commission, but given his health and absence, perhaps he expected too much. Having been repeatedly passed over, Miller reached out to his political friends in both Washington and Minnesota and secured an appointment to lead a new regiment. On September 16, 1862, the day after the Battle of South Mountain and the day before Antietam, he resigned from the First in order to accept an appointment as colonel of the Seventh Minnesota. The effective date of his resignation was August 24, 1862, but the order from Gen. Halleck had been slow to reach him. He wanted to stay and fight with the First in the upcoming battle, but Gen. Sedgwick refused, telling him that he was no longer a soldier in the regiment and had not been for some time.

Of his departure, Lt. William Lochren (Co. K) later wrote:

> Here our brave Lieut. Col. Stephen Miller left us, on receipt of his commission as colonel of the Seventh Minnesota regiment. Without military training previous to the organization of our regiment, his bravery was conspicuous on every battlefield, and endeared him to the men, who parted with him with sincere regret.

Miller served with the Seventh on the Minnesota frontier during the Dakota War of 1862. He commanded the troops at Camp Lincoln near Mankato, which housed 303 Dakota men who had been sentenced to death. President Lincoln commuted the sentences of 264 of the men, and one was granted a last-minute reprieve. Gen. Sibley placed Col. Miller in charge of the execution of the 38 remaining men, who were hung on December 26, 1862, the largest mass execution in U.S. history.

Miller was promoted to brigadier general on November 6, 1863. In 1863 he was also elected governor of Minnesota, after which he resigned his commission and returned to the state. He served as governor from January 1864 to January 1866.

From 1871 to 1878, he lived in Windom, Minnesota, and was employed as a field agent for the St. Paul and Sioux City Railroad. Afterward, he moved to Worthington. On August 18, 1881, he died of mortification (gangrene) that had started in his left foot. He was sixty-five years old. Miller was a Mason, and members from many lodges attended his funeral. He was buried in the Worthington Cemetery east of town. During his busy life Stephen Miller had been a railroad superintendent, merchant, editor, soldier, and legislator.

Rev. Edward Duffield Neill
b. August 9, 1823; d. September 26, 1893

Born in Philadelphia, Edward Neill studied theology at the University of Pennsylvania and Amherst College, from which he graduated in 1842. At his own request, he was transferred by the Presbyterian Church to St. Paul in 1849 and served from 1849 to 1860 as a minister at the House of Hope Church. In 1858 Rev. Neill was appointed the superintendent of public instruction for the State of Minnesota, and soon after, he resigned from the ministry and served as chancellor of the University of Minnesota, from 1858 to 1861. Neill had married Nancy Hall on October 4, 1847, at Snow Hill, Vermont, and they had five children prior to the war, daughter, Minnesota, and sons Samuel, Henry, Edward, and John.

When the call for troops came, he volunteered as chaplain of the First Minnesota. On June 22, 1861, the thirty-seven-year-old Rev. Neill conducted religious services for the men of the First at Ft. Snelling. Afterward, the men marched through the gates of the fort to the streets of St. Paul, stopping at the steps of

Rev. Edward Duffield Neill

Neill returned to Minnesota and served as president of Macalester College in 1873. From 1884 until his death in 1893, he served there as a professor of history, literature, and political economy. He was also secretary of the Minnesota Historical Society from 1851 to 1863, even while the war was raging. An educated man, he authored many books, including *The History of Minnesota* in 1858, which was reprinted in 1882. He also wrote *The History of Hennepin County* in 1881, which includes an autobiographical sketch. He was instrumental in the erection of Christ Church, located on Hennepin Avenue in Minneapolis, and served as its minister for many years. Clergyman, educator, and historian Rev. Edward Neill died in St. Paul on September 26, 1893. He was seventy years old. He was buried in Oakland Cemetery in St. Paul.

Regimental Medical Staff

Every regiment was given medical care by a surgeon and an assistant surgeon, who quickly became two of the most indispensable people in any regiment. When formed, the First Minnesota was ably cared for by doctors Jacob Stewart and Charles Le Boutillier. Doctors Daniel Hand, William Morton, John LeBlond, Edmund Pugsley, and Peter Gabrielson also saw to the care of the men of the First Minnesota during its three years of active service. Hospital stewards oftentimes were enlisted men chosen to assist the regimental surgeons. They served both in the field and as nurses in military hospitals.

Dr. Jacob H. Stewart
b. January 15, 1829; d. August 25, 1884

Jacob Stewart was born in Claremont, New York, and at an early age he and his parents moved to Peekskill. He attended Yale and, after leaving, decided upon the profession of surgeon. He entered the University of New York, graduating in 1851. He returned to Peekskill, where he practiced until 1855. In May 1855, he came to St. Paul, where in 1856 he was appointed physician of Ramsey County. He married Katherine Sweeny of Philadelphia on October 1, 1857. Returning to Minnesota, Dr. Stewart served as a state senator from 1858 to 1859. The year before, he had been appointed surgeon general of Minnesota and served from 1857 to 1863.

In June 1861, Dr. Stewart resigned his position as

the state capitol. Here, they were presented with a flag from the women of St. Paul.

Chaplain Neill served the men from Bull Run through Malvern Hill. He left the regiment on July 13, 1862, when he was appointed the U.S. hospital chaplain, serving at the Philadelphia-area military hospitals. Neill was a political ally of Governor Ramsey, and the hospital appointment was arranged through the governor's influence.

In January 1864 President Lincoln appointed Neill as one of his two private secretaries. As the president's secretary, he opened and arranged his correspondence and signed land grants for the president, among other things. After Lincoln's assassination he stayed on and served as secretary to President Johnson. He remained in that position until he was appointed by President Grant, in 1869, as U.S. consul to Ireland, a post he held from 1869 to 1870, at which time he resigned from governmental service.

Dr. Jacob H. Stewart

surgeon general of the state and accepted a commission as chief surgeon of the First Minnesota, and Dr. Charles Le Boutillier of Minneapolis was appointed assistant surgeon.

At Bull Run several regimental surgeons established a field hospital near the Sudley Church. When the First Minnesota and the rest of the regiment retreated, they decided to stay and care for the wounded. As Dr. Stewart tells the story:

Having sent forward the assistants and ambulances, there being as yet no duty for me to perform, I went upon the battle field, and was immediately in the rear of my regiment when it first came under and returned fire.

The first man of our regiment brought to me wounded had his arm nearly shot off, and I took him in an ambulance and went with him to the Church Hospital and before I got his arm dressed the wounded were poured in thick upon me, until I had all and more than I could attend to, especially as no temporary dressings had been applied to the men on the field.

While working among my wounded—there being at that time over fifty brave Minnesotans

stretched bleeding and ghastly upon the grass under the trees of the beautiful grove wherein the Hospital was located, a mounted officer of Gen. McDowell's staff suddenly rode to the door of the church and loudly cried out to us; "We're whipped to death—a retreat has been ordered—retreat immediately!"

At this moment this was the condition of things at the Church: There were in it, or lying immediately around it, on the grass, nearly five hundred wounded soldiers, nearly four hundred of whom were our own men—all moaning and groaning with pain—some calling for "water!" "water!" "just one drop of cold water!" others, "Oh Doctor, come stop this bleeding, or I'll bleed to death!"—"for God's sake, Doctor, come take off this arm," or "this leg," or "take out this ball," & etc.

When the officer was heard by them ordering the Surgeons and Hospital attendants to "retreat" along with the army, I was in the midst of our Minnesota boys, attending to them, and the poor fellows cried out to me, "If you are going to leave us, kill us first, the enemy will bayonet us as they did the wounded before," (referring to the skirmish of the 18th) and "Don't let us live to be butchered by them;" while some of the enemy's wounded, mainly Alabamians and Carolinians, also begged "For God's sake don't leave us to die, without our wounds dressed."

I replied to our Minnesota boys, that "I disbelieved the reports that the enemy bayoneted the wounded, and that in no event would I leave them, or obey the order to retreat—this they might rely upon."

Having thus calmed them somewhat, I went into the Church and got together with the other Surgeons, about twenty five in all, and a brief consultation was had as to what we should do; when all but five or six concluded to run, and some of them forthwith went off at a double quick without so much as taking their instruments.

For myself I feel no regret that I deemed it my duty to be one of the few who deliberately stayed rather than of the many who saved themselves from imprisonment . . .

Between six and seven o'clock the enemy at length appeared . . . . I was outside the church

This daguerreotype was taken circa 1850–55. It shows a young Dr. Stewart wearing the militia uniform of the Eighteenth New York State Militia.

on my knees, extracting a Minnie ball from the head of an Alabamian, when a squad of cavalry rode up to the church. It was commanded by Lieut. Cummings, of Col. Stuart's Virginia Cavalry who, leaning from his horse and placing a pistol at my head, and cocking it with a sort of disagreeable "click" said: "I demand you to surrender."

I had just cut down to the ball and felt indignant at his treatment, especially as he saw me engaged so busily. I drew my head out of the range of his pistol, and said to him sharply: "Use a little more care in the handling of that article, as my experience the last few hours makes me extremely sensitive to the even careless use of firearms." He retorted, "God d—n your soul, answer me more civilly or I will put a bullet through your head!" This piece of agreeable information accompanied by his very prepossessing appearance and amiable manner, induced me to request him politely, to defer that little operation until I had completed mine—my language being, "Just wait sir, first, until I extract this bullet out of this patient's head, as he is one of your own men, of the Alabama Fourth."

He immediately replied, "I beg your pardon," and did manage to wait until I had extracted the ball. In a few seconds I had the Minnie in my hand, and the Lieutenant then very politely asked me to "give my word of honor not to escape." I replied, "I have voluntarily remained to take care of the wounded, and of course will not leave them," and I so pledged myself. . . .

. . . In the afternoon of Monday we were notified by Col. Stuart, of the Virginia Cavalry, that the orders from headquarters were to take us to General Beauregard, at Manassas Junction . . . .

Our course of travel lay over the battle field, and on the road leading from it. As long as daylight permitted us to see, which was until we were within three miles or so of Manassas, we noticed that the dead of the enemy, men and horses, were continually scattered, and yet unburied. . . .

. . . We were told that two of our wounded men were picked up, and were in one of the lumber wagons; from which we heard them ordered to be transferred to a covered ambulance behind us, and taken along with us to the Junction; but we did not see them, not being allowed to get out of our vehicle.

We reached Manassas about ten o'clock. . . . We were next shown into a small neighboring barn, where in the midst of wounded and dying Confederates, . . . we laid down on the barn floor, on which was a slight sprinkling of hay, and without blankets or covering of any kind, our clothes all wet through, slept or tried to sleep until morning. . . .

In the morning, on going from the barn over to Beauregard's headquarters, I passed in the barn yard, the four wheeled ambulance which had accompanied us from the battle field the night before. Observing that two men were lying in it, I looked in curiously to see who they were when, to my astonishment, I found them to be two of our own "boys"—Private Cannon of Company I, (the same whose wounded leg Capt. Pell; when ordered so peremptorily to retreat, stopped behind to bind up before he left him), and Corporal Pierson of Company B, of Stillwater, who had received two balls through his right thigh, fracturing the bone. The astonishment of the poor fellows even surpassed

This photo of Sudley Church was taken well after the First Battle of Bull Run. It was here that doctors Stewart and LeBoutillier tended to the wounded soldiers, including many from Minnesota.

my own, for they did not imagine that I was within fifty miles of them; and the joy of all three of us meeting cannot be adequately expressed. They had lain out in the rain on the field all Sunday night, and managed to crawl during Monday between two and three miles from where they fell, towards Manassas, to the spot where the rebels had picked them up. They were the same two men we heard ordered to be transferred to the ambulance on our night journey; in which they were compelled to sleep all night, having their blankets to cover them. I immediately procured

These epaulette's were worn by Dr. Stewart on his dress uniform.

This sash was worn by Dr. Stewart during his service. Whereas most officers were noted by the maroon-colored sash wrapped around their waists, officers in the medical corps wore bright-green sashes that differentiated them from combat officers.

their removal to a Confederate hospital, where I dressed their wounds, and left them again until I saw them at a hospital in Richmond, some two weeks afterwards; Cannon had nearly recovered, and Pierson doing as well as could be expected of a man with a fractured thigh.

We were then returned to our hospital at the battlefield, our return being made in a more comfortable vehicle and by a different route from that by which we had come. Upon our arrival we were distressed to find that during our absence of about 24 hours only, nearly 20 of our men had died, some of whom would almost certainly have been saved if the surgeons had not been removed so long away from them; and this melancholy fact confirmed us that we had pursued the true path of duty in subscribing to the only course by which we were still allowed to give those who yet remained alive the benefit of all the skill and nursing that we could bestow. This we continued to do for some two weeks longer, when the Confederates deemed them sufficiently recovered to be removed to Richmond. . . .

William Lochren later noted of their act of bravery at that first battle and thereafter:

They remained in attendance upon the wounded on the field when they might have escaped with the retreating troops, and were detained as prisoners. Their skillful care of our wounded doubtless saved many lives and alleviated in many ways the condition of their wounded comrades.

Doctors Stewart and Le Boutillier were released by the rebels and eventually returned to St. Paul. Dr. Le Boutillier became a surgeon for the 9th Minnesota Infantry and died in 1863, while in the service. Dr. Stewart worked at Fort Snelling, mustering in troops for Minnesota's other regiments.

After the war Dr. Stewart was elected mayor of St. Paul four times. He was elected to Congress and served in the U.S. House of Representatives from 1877 to 1879. In 1880 he became the surgeon general of Minnesota. He died in St. Paul in 1884 at the age of fifty-five. He was buried in Oakland Cemetery.

Dr. Daniel Hand

b. August 18, 1834; d. June 1, 1889

After the Battle of Bull Run and the capture of the surgeons, the state moved to fill their vacant positions. One of the men recruited was Dr. Daniel Hand of St. Paul. He was appointed assistant surgeon and immediately headed east to assume his duties. He did excellent work.

At the Battle of Fair Oaks, the surgeons worked feverishly to care for both sides' wounded, and at one point Chaplain Neill explained to Dr. Hand that a Rebel officer whose face was bloodied needed attention. Upon washing his face, the doctor discovered Gen. J. Johnston Pettigrew was in his care, with a wound on the side of his head and a hurt shoulder. Dr. Hand treated him, Pettigrew walked to the rear, and they never saw each other again.

On May 16, 1863, while on a brief journey up the Petersburg Railroad bed with another officer and two orderlies, his party was ambushed by a party of Mississippi riflemen. When ordered to halt, Dr. Hand galloped away. His horse did not run thirty feet before falling dead, shot through the neck. Dr. Hand sprawled over the horse's head and tumbled to the ground. As he tried to rise one of the Mississippians knocked him out with a musket. He knew nothing until he found himself being dragged in a great hurry into a swamp. As he came to his senses the men holding him told him to keep still and asked if he could ride. Responding that he could, they put him on one of the orderly's horses and rapidly made their way through the woods.

An entire North Carolina regiment was camped within one hundred yards of where Dr. Hand and the group had emerged and been captured. The party traveled through bushes most of the night, and at daylight they crossed the Black Water River and were in a Confederate camp. From there, they moved a few miles downriver to the camp of Gen. Jenkins. Dr. Hand and the other captive officer were then sent to Weldon, North Carolina, and put on a train for Petersburg. It was, in his words, "a tough place," and he was happy to be put on a train bound for Richmond. He later retold what happened next:

> Here my good luck came in, for there were some ladies in the car, and their curiosity being excited by seeing two Yankee officers, they sent a young artillery officer who was with them to ask who we were. When I told him I was from Minnesota, he said, "Do you know my uncle, Colonel Sully?" When he found the relation I had held to Colonel Sully he was very gracious, and promised to see that we were sent out by the first exchange boat that came up. I suppose that was all talk, but the next day after we were lodged in Libby Prison a guard called out that I was wanted at General Winder's office. On being conducted there I found the nephew of Colonel Sully, Lieutenant Wheeler, of South Carolina, had brought me a towel, tooth-brush, and comb, and a bottle of applejack; and he said he had seen Colonel Ould, the commissioner of exchange, and my name and that of my friend were down for the first boat.
>
> Our life in the prison was not hard. I was in a room on the second floor with one hundred and seventy six other officers, and we were so crowded we all had to go to bed at once, as we covered the floor completely.

Fortunately, Dr. Hand was involved in a prisoner exchange on May 24 and returned to the Union lines at City Point, Virginia. During the Battle of Gettysburg, he lay sick in a New Jersey hospital and felt bad about not being there to help the men. Two weeks later, he visited many of the men in their Baltimore hospitals.

When Dr. Hand returned, he was placed in charge of the Union hospitals in North Carolina. Working out of Foster General Hospital in New Bern, he helped combat a small pox epidemic in New Bern and an outbreak of yellow fever in Wilmington. In November 1864 he was brevetted lieutenant colonel of volunteers for meritorious service during the war, particularly for his skill, energy, and fidelity while medical director of the military district of North Carolina. On November 8 he himself contracted yellow fever, which resulted in a bacterial infection known as *pyelitis*.

He was promoted to colonel of volunteers in March 1865 for meritorious service during the war. He was compelled, however, to return to the North for two months' sick leave, and then returned to duty May 1865. He again fell ill and once more took sick leave for two months, until September 1865. He continued to have spells of illness until he was mustered out of the service at Raleigh, North Carolina, on December 13, 1865. After the war he returned to his practice in St. Paul. He was a founder of the Minnesota Medical Society and served as a professor of surgery at the University of Minnesota from 1882 to 1887. He died in 1889 from complications resulting from his yellow fever exposure during the war.

Cyrus Adrian Brooks

b. January 29, 1842; d. March 27, 1928

Cyrus Brooks was named after his father, Rev. Cyrus Brooks, who was a Methodist minister. The younger Brooks studied at Hamline University in Red Wing and, upon graduation, planned on entering the ministry. He was twenty-two years old when he was mustered and subsequently detailed as a hospital steward for the regiment.

Dr. Daniel Hand tells of the young steward's role in their grim sleeping accommodations after the Battle of Fair Oaks:

> All that afternoon the surgeon's knife flashed lively, and arms and legs and thighs were sacrificed, but not without thoughtful care. Whenever there was a possible chance to save a limb a council of us all was called to decide; and as surgeon in charge of the hospital I was held responsible for what was done. . . . By night all

Cyrus Adrian Brooks

James Kirkman

b. January 17, 1824; d. September 6, 1866

James Kirkman was a veteran of the U.S.–Mexican War, having served when he was twenty-four. During the Battle of Cerro Gordo, he helped carry his wounded captain and future First Minnesota colonel N. J. T. Dana from the battlefield. Kirkman served five years and was discharged on November 21, 1851.

He was thirty-seven when he enlisted to put down the rebellion in the South. He was placed in Company I and is recorded as being five feet eight inches tall, with a ruddy complexion, blue eyes, and dark hair. Two weeks later, he was detailed to serve as the regiment's hospital steward.

During his service he wrote letters home that were published in the *Wabasha County Herald.* On March 11, 1862, he sent home from Berryville, Virginia, the following letter:

Friend Stevens:

The brigades of Gens. Gorman and Burns, which compose Gen. Sedgwick's Division, took possession of Bolivar Heights on the 1st of March,

was quiet and we were tired out. All tried to get some sleep. It was late in the night before my own cares allowed me to rest, and then, where should I lie down? A cold wind was blowing, and we shivered in our scanty clothing. Every foot of sheltered ground was covered with sleeping men, but near the operating-table, which was under a tree in the house-yard, there lay a long row of dead soldiers. My faithful steward, Cyrus Brooks, a detailed man from the First Minnesota, suggested we make a wind-break by piling them up against the remnants of a fence. We did so, and then lying down behind them, we slept soundly until morning.

On June 12, 1863, Brooks was discharged from the First Minnesota and promoted to a position as hospital steward in the U.S. Army. Thus, he was probably not with the regiment at Gettysburg. On December 12, 1864, he was commissioned into the field and staff of the Tenth Minnesota Infantry as assistant surgeon. He was mustered out on August 19, 1865, at Ft. Snelling. After the war he became a minister, like his father. He lived a long life, served many parishes, and died in Leadville, Colorado, on March 27, 1928, at the age of eighty-six.

James Kirkman

where we established a general hospital, where all the sick of the division is to be left. On the 7th of March we took Charlestown, Va., a town of about three thousand inhabitants, where we remained until the 10th inst., when we took up the line of march for Berryville, a distance of 12 miles, where we arrived at 3 P.M., and routed about three hundred rebels, taking 6 prisoners. . . .

Gen. Gorman took the Berryville Conservator, the only paper and press in the town. The editor left with one side of the paper struck off, and the typos of the 1st Minnesota Regiment are now striking off the other side, a copy of which I hereby send to you. . . .

It was very cold last night. We dare not keep fires, and our thin shoddy blankets, without tents did not protect us much against the cold and wind. The 1st Minnesota is in high repute, and is the leading regiment; being in the advance with Rickett's battery. The duty is very hard, but the men do not grumble.

Yours,
James Kirkman

On July 2, 1862, the *Wabasha Herald* published his thoughts following the Battle of Fair Oaks:

After battle, persons connected with the Hospital Department have no time to write, and but little time to sleep. This has been the case with me up to this time. . . . A battle is nothing; the field afterwards is the horror of all horrors. As we had not much to do in our regiment, I went on the field to help Surgeon Morton, and for three days and three nights, we worked dressing wounds, amputating, and giving water to the dying.

Shortly before this report was published, Kirkman was discharged from the First Minnesota. He worked briefly as a clerk in the War Department, until he received an appointment as sutler to the Sixty-Ninth New York Infantry. Each regiment was allowed one sutler, who was, effectively, a traveling seller of non-military personal goods, including food items like canned peaches and sardines, writing paper, pencils, pens, and other personal items. Kirkman's last service was with the Sixth U.S. Cavalry. He died of cholera at Onion Creek, Texas, on September 6, 1866, while still in the service. He was a veteran or two wars and, unfortunately, dead by the age of forty.

COMPANY A
THE PIONEER GUARD (ST. PAUL)

I N 1856 THE PIONEER GUARD was formed to defend the citizens of St. Paul against potential Indian hostilities. As one of the most prominent of Minnesota's seven militia organizations, its men had their own uniforms and drilled with some regularity. The unit comprised about forty members when the war began. After Lincoln's call for volunteers, a rally was held in St. Paul on the evening of April 16, and at its conclusion Josias King, a member of the guard, raced forward to sign his name to the enlistment paper and, in so doing, became a claimant to the title of first man to join the Union cause.

Several other members also volunteered, though not everyone rushed to the call, given the gravity of the decision. The choice to leave a family unprotected and travel somewhere far-off was not an easy one. Many thought they would be back by fall, but being gone even that long required some thought and quick planning. Single men were less burdened by concern, however, and many who served in the First Minnesota were young and unmarried. For them adventure held more allure, and fewer strings tied them to home.

Company designations were issued as men tendered their service at Ft. Snelling. Being a capital city militia, as well as counting the first man to join the Union cause a member, it perhaps was only natural that the Pioneer Guard formed the core of Company A.

A composite picture of the members of the Pioneer Guard in 1858.

These nine members of the Pioneer Guard also served in the First Minnesota. Though they came from many professions, most were single. They are, *left to right,* Henry Coates (printer, single), Richard Gorman (student, single), Javin Irvine (plasterer, married), Charles H. King (law student, single), Josias King (surveyor, married), Andrew Levering (land speculator, single), Samuel Raguet (grocer, single), Edgar Sproat (clerk, single), and Charles Zierenberg (lawyer, single). All served in Company A, except Gorman (Co. I) and Raguet (Co. C). Seven of the nine rose to become officers during their service.

Future railroad executive and empire builder James J. Hill wanted to serve in the guard but did not pass the physical. Though he was not able to serve with his friends, he always championed them, and after the war he was a loyal friend and, as founder of the Great Northern Railroad, helped the veterans whenever he could. *Left,* Hill as a member of the guard. *Right,* Hill in the 1870s.

First Lt. Josias King sometime after January 21, 1863, when he received his promotion

Josias Ridgate King

b. February 21, 1832; d. February 19, 1916

Josias King was born in Washington, DC, to a father active in capital politics and a devout Catholic family. He gained his first taste of independence at fourteen when, in 1847, he joined a crew surveying the relatively new state of Florida. He returned to Washington in 1850 and decided to pursue a career in the military, enrolling at Georgetown University and hoping to gain admission to West Point. Six months after he began his studies, however, he heard about the California gold rush, and without hesitation the eighteen-year-old left school and, thanks to family money, sailed for California. He traveled by way of Cape Horn and was detained at the Straits of Magellan until 1851, where he hunted ostrich and llama in Patagonia and Tierra del Fuego.

When he arrived at California, he made for Bodega Bay and, with several others, began growing a crop of potatoes. They planted seven acres and, at the end of three months, sold their crop for $5,000. He and his friends then purchased pack mules and miners' outfits and headed for the gold fields. He found some gold but not enough, so his stay in the mines was a short one.

After this stint as a gold miner, King worked as a surveyor, tried gold mining again, chased a Mexican bandit name Joaquin, and surveyed yet again before returning to Washington, DC, in 1855. Using his political connections, his father saw to Josias' appointment, in 1857, as assistant to the surveyor general of Minnesota. Around that time, he also married Louisa Meeks, and between 1857 and 1869, they had eight children.

On April 15, 1861, Governor Ramsey tasked Lieutenant Governor Donnelly with raising a thousand-man regiment. Donnelly convened a meeting of the Pioneer Guard at the St. Paul Armory. Their captain, A. T. Chamblin, related the situation to the attendees, and after several patriotic speeches, he moved to pass around the sign-up book. However, King, who had joined the guards shortly after arriving in St. Paul, reportedly bounded onto the stage and signed it first. One version has him declaring, "Here's another for the war!" while another has him exclaiming, "I'll be the first to sign!" He later claimed to be the first volunteer for the Union cause. Aaron Greenwald (Co. C) made this claim, as well, having been first to volunteer at a meeting in Anoka. Greenwald died at Gettysburg, however, so he was unable to defend his claim after the war, and thus, the honor has generally gone to King.

Company A was commanded by Capt. Alexander Wilkin, who had called that first recruitment meeting. Perhaps because of his enthusiasm, King was appointed to the rank of first sergeant, also known as the orderly sergeant. On September 18, 1861, he was discharged to receive a commission as second lieutenant when Captain Wilkin left for the Second Minnesota, and all company officers were moved up one rank. On July 10, 1862, King was made adjutant of the regiment and served as such until January 14, 1863.

He participated in the battles of Bull Run and Edwards Ferry, the Siege of Yorktown, the action at West Point, the battles of Seven Pines, Fair Oaks, Peach Orchard, Savage Station, White Oak Swamp, Glendale, First and Second Malvern Hill, Vienna, South Mountain, and Antietam, the action at Charlestown, and the battles of Fredericksburg and Chancellorsville. He had a horse shot out from under him at Charlestown.

In September 1862, Lt. Col. Stephen Miller received an appointment to become colonel of the Seventh Minnesota and resigned his commission in the First Minnesota. His promotion caused more upward movement

This picture of a dapper Lt. Josias King wearing a winter overcoat was taken at Mathew Brady's studio in New York City.

in the officers' ranks and some transfers between companies. At this time, 2nd Lt. King was temporarily detailed to Company F, and on January 21, 1863, he was promoted to first lieutenant of Company G.

In mid-1863 he was assigned, for a short time, to Gen. Sully's staff and accompanied him in the Indian campaign on the upper Missouri River and was, thus, not with the First at Gettysburg. He did fight with Sully against the Sioux at the battles of Whitestone Hill and Taka-on-Koutay in Dakota Territory.

After Gettysburg had decimated the regiment's officers, several men were promoted to fill the vacancies. On September 14, 1863, King was transferred back to the First Minnesota to become the first lieutenant of Company A. He again was promoted, on October 19, 1863, to captain of Company G. King was wounded at Savage Station. On May 5, 1864, he was mustered out with the regiment.

His military career was not over, however. He received an appointment as lieutenant colonel of U.S.

volunteers and was later mustered out of the volunteer service in 1865. On May 26, 1866, he received a commission and entered the service as a second lieutenant in the Second U.S. Infantry. Since the postwar U.S. Army was much smaller, many men who had held high rank during the war and continued their military service were brought in at a lower rank.

He had hoped to spend the rest of his life in the military, but in 1870 his wife, Louisa, became seriously ill. Since her doctors believed a cooler climate would improve her health, King resigned from the military in 1871, and they moved back to St. Paul, where for a time he once again worked as a surveyor. He had one last fling with the military when he was appointed inspector general of the Minnesota National Guard. During his brief tenure he effected a number of improvements and afterward became known as the father of the Minnesota National Guard.

Javan Irvine
b. April 3, 1831; d. January 20, 1904

Thirty years old when the war began, Javan Irvine was a member of the Pioneer Guard. Though records show he officially joined the First Minnesota on September 3, 1861, he was with the regiment from April 29 to May 15, before the War Department changed the term of service from ninety day to three years. Irvine, who was married, did not immediately reenlist. Sometime after the regiment left for the East, however, Irvine traveled to visit his brother-in-law, John Halstead, who was single and had reenlisted. He arrived a few days before the First Battle of Bull Run. Chaplain Edward Neill records in his journal that when the action began, Irvine, in his civilian clothes, took a musket and joined Halstead and the other men of Company A.

After the battle Irvine wrote to his wife of his actions:

At about eleven o'clock we halted in a ravine, to give the men an opportunity to fill their canteens with water. At this time the fighting had become pretty general, and the roar of the artillery and the rattle of musketry were heard only about a mile distant.

We did not remain long in the field where we were stationed, before the order came to advance, which we did through the woods at the double-quick up to where the conflict was raging. Here we halted in the edge of the woods,

Javan Irvine

in the presence of the dead and wounded, who were lying all around us, until about 5,000 troops filed past us to take their position.

As they passed the general officers and staff they cheered in the wildest and most enthusiastic manner. After they had passed, we took our position in the open field in sight of the enemy's batteries. We were soon ordered to advance from this position and file around to the left, for the purpose of outflanking and taking them. While doing this the cannonballs and bomb-shells flew around us thick and fast. . . . We ran down a hill and crossed a small stream. I, being a little in advance, stopped to pick a few blackberries to quench my thirst while the regiment came up. We soon came to a road where we were met by an aid to the commanding officer, who desired us to follow him and take up a position where he could get no other troops to stand. We told him we would follow him, and he gave us a position to the left of the battery and directly opposite it. Here we formed a line of battle, with a strip of woods between us and about four thousand secessionists. We had

just formed when we were ordered to kneel and fire upon the rebels, who were advancing under cover of the woods. We fired two volleys through the woods, when we were ordered to rally in the woods in our rear, which all did except the first platoon of our own company, who did not hear the order and stood their ground. The rebels soon came out from their shelter between us and their battery. Colonel Gorman mistook them for friends and told the men to cease firing upon them, although they had three secession flags flying directly in front of their advancing columns. This threw our men into confusion, some declaring they were friends, others that they were enemies. I called to our boys to give it to them, and fired away myself as rapidly as possible. The rebels themselves mistook us for Georgia troops, and waved their hands at us to cease firing. I had just loaded to give them another charge when a lieutenant-colonel of a Mississippi regiment rode between us, waving his hand for us to stop firing. I rushed up to him and asked if he was a secessionist. He said "he was a Mississippian." I presented my bayonet to his breast and commanded him to surrender, which he did after some hesitation. I ordered him to dismount, and led him and his horse from the field, in the meantime disarming him of his sword and pistols. I led him off about two miles and placed him in charge of a lieutenant, with an escort of cavalry; to be taken to General McDowell. . . . I retained his pistol but sent his sword with him.

Irvine's time with the First Minnesota was relatively short. For his gallant and meritorious conduct, Irvine received a commission in the Thirteenth U.S. Infantry, leaving the First on December 2, 1861. He was commissioned as a first lieutenant in the Thirteenth on December 23, 1861. In 1862 he served as an adjutant at the military prison at Alton, Illinois, and was regimental quartermaster at Newport Barracks, Kentucky, from November 1, 1862, until March 1865. Irvine continued his military service after the war, traveling for years from post to post across the United States.

When stationed as a caption at Ft. Sully in Dakota Territory, the fort's officers matched hunting dogs with those of Gen. Custer. Belonging to the Hunting Club of the Twenty-Second Infantry, foxhounds and some fleet purebred English greyhounds added excitement to the officers' hunting of wolves, rabbits, and antelope, and within a few years the pack had increased to twenty-five dogs. The officers who owned them were very proud and loved to watch them race. In May 1873 Gen. Custer, in command of the Seventh Cavalry and on his way to Ft. Abraham Lincoln, camped for several days about four miles south of Ft. Sully. Irvine relates how the fine greyhounds belonging to Custer—whose speed and prowess the general had praised in *Galaxy* magazine—were outdone in a race by Ft. Sully's hounds. Irvine reports with pride that "during the straight chase our slowest dog kept ahead of General Custer's fastest."

Hunting had its dangers, however. In 1872 Capt. Irvine left alone on horseback with his hounds, and a few miles from the fort, he encountered an Indian who said he was trying to locate some stray ponies. Irvine recognized the man as one he had seen before and considered him to be friendly. He pulled a revolver out of his pocket, however, fired four bullets at the captain, hitting him once, and then quickly fled. The bullet had lodged itself under Irvine's scalp. He made it back to the fort, where the post surgeon removed the bullet. Irvine did hunt again a month later, but this time he took some friends, and they remained alert, though nothing happened.

After being assigned to posts at New Orleans, Detroit, and New York, Irvine closed out the last years of his military life on the western frontier. His last assignment, in May 1891, was at Ft. Lincoln in North Dakota. There, he was promoted to major and then retired. He was sixty years old and had spent thirty years in the military. Irvine died in Los Angeles on January 20, 1904, and was buried in Evergreen Cemetery. He was seventy-two years old.

Charles Muller

b. March 14, 1832; d. April 5, 1925

Charles Muller was born in the Alsace-Lorraine region of France and came to America in 1852, moving to Minnesota on May 11, 1856. The spring of 1861 found him working at a stone quarry and living in Shakopee. He was the third man to enlist at the recruiting rally in St. Paul. According to records, the twenty-nine-year-old was five feet eight and five-eighths inches tall and had a fair complexion, hazel-colored eyes, and dark-brown hair.

Charles Muller

Muller's English was not solid, as can be seen in his recollection of being wounded during the July 2 charge at Gettysburg. Muller fired his first round as he reached the bottom of the slope, and he recalls what happened next:

> I stood bihind a Brush and reloded my Gun and as I was redy to fire I just stept to the right of the brush when a [Confederate] coller sargent cam up on the other sid of the Brush and called for the other to folow him and just as [he] dit so and move his flag I held my gun up to him and fired wen the pure man fell down then I begin to see for my friends but most of them have gone or were shot down then I started to run out of it to but wen I got out on the fild the enemis flanks had so mush advanced that the[y] wer only about 50 yards apart and I had to go trouht ther and just as [I] went trought that point a man from my left dit rais his gun and point at me and fired and hit me in my right tigh but as it hapen did not Brok my boon so I Kupt on running up to the open fild in a ziksak way.

Muller eventually made it back to Cemetery Ridge and met up with what was left of the regiment. His captain, Henry Coates, asked Pvt. Jacob Feger, also of Company A, to help Muller get back to the field hospital in the rear. Once there, Muller sat on a rock and cut away the blood-soaked leg of his pants. Feger brought him a pail of water and a small, fifteen-inch piece of cloth, which was all that he could find. In the dark of the night, Muller washed and bandaged his own wound.

The field hospital had been established near a low stone fence that ran along the Baltimore Turnpike. Across the road was a clover field. As he recalls, on July 3

> in the afternoon some 20 or 30 ambulances cum up . . . with orders to clear our hospital out as fast as posible because the Eneme is consentrating its artilery to fire in that direction. I shuld think the ambulances dit tak 35 or 40 man in the first load and the[y] just started when the[y] becan to troe shell and ball in our direction and in a bout ½ hour that clover fild on the other sid of Baltimor Turnpike dit look as if it had bin plouhd.

Later, he learned about the day's fighting and the repulse of Pickett's Charge: "That same Evening som of our wounded cam in and [told] us how the day went, and said, Boys today we paid the Rebels back for wat they have done to us yesterday."

Muller eventually transferred to the Broad Street General Hospital in Philadelphia and was mustered out with the regiment on May 5, 1864. He went on to live a long life and attended many reunions with his comrades. On April 5, 1925, he died at his home in St. Paul at the age of ninety-three. He was buried at Elmhurst Cemetery in St. Paul.

John Peller

b. February 5, 1830; d. September 6, 1878

John Peller was born in Heidelberg, Germany, and likely arrived in America as a young boy. By his excellent penmanship and command of English, one could expect that he was educated in the United States. He came to Cannon City (now Cannon Falls) in 1855 and moved to Hastings in 1859. He worked as a merchant with Thorne, Norrish & Co until the beginning of the war, when he went to St. Paul to enlist.

John Peller

He was thirty-one when he enlisted and stood five feet eight and a half inches tall. He had blue eyes, brown hair, and a fair complexion. John was a very competent soldier. The company muster roll for October 1, 1861, has him listed as the company's second sergeant. Later, he was promoted to sergeant major of the regiment, and on July 19, 1862, he was discharged to receive a commission as second lieutenant of Company A. On January 13, 1863, he was promoted to first lieutenant and adjutant of the regiment. As adjutant he was responsible for the regiment's official correspondence and monthly muster rolls. His experience as a merchant served him well here, and the regiment's documents show his clear and careful penmanship.

Peller participated with the regiment on July 2 and, like the other senior officers, fell to the ground with a severe wound. A minié ball fractured his left arm, three inches below the shoulder. He lay on the field until after dark, when Dr. LeBlond found him, bandaged his wound, and sent him to the Leitner house, where a regimental hospital had been set up. Later, he was admitted to the hospital put up within the Gettysburg Lutheran Theological Seminary. From there, he was sent to the Armory Square General Hospital in Baltimore. His wound was severe, and he recovered slowly. The bullet had created a deep hole and greatly damaged his muscles. For the rest of his life, he suffered a partial paralysis of the third and fourth fingers of his left hand. On October 2, 1863, while in Baltimore, he wrote the following thoughts in a letter to Lt. William Lochren, who had taken his place as the regiment's adjutant and who had written the field report on its casualties at Gettysburg:

> It will be sometime yet before I get able for duty; my arm is doing very well at present and the Surgeon says that I will have the full use of it again, but that it may require probably a couple of months to get sufficiently strong for service. As soon as I am sufficiently recovered to travel, which will probably take three weeks yet, I intend to make a trip to Minnesota. I am very tired of this place, the want of all acquaintances here making it dull and lonesome for me.
>
> Dr. Morton is the only one I know here and he is busy most [of] the time. He came here about a fortnight ago, having received the appointment as Surgeon from the Department here and being placed in charge of the Convalescent & Stragglers Camps in this city. There are about 30 men of our Regt in the hospitals here, of whom nearly one half are again fit for duty but cannot get away from here. I hope Major Downie will succeed in getting an officer to fetch them back to the Regt.

Peller was still unfit for duty in December 1863. As mentioned in his letter, he briefly returned home to Hastings. In January he headed back east and on the fifteenth arrived at the First Minnesota's camp. Within a month the regiment was given its farewell banquet in Washington, DC, and returned to Ft. Snelling. He was discharged with the other men on May 4, 1864. That year, Governor Stephen Miller, who had served with Peller as the regiment's lieutenant colonel, appointed him adjutant general of the state.

In 1865 he returned to Hastings and became a partner in a dry goods store. He was active in his community, serving as an alderman, the secretary of the Oakwood Cemetery, and the director of the Hastings Library Association. The men of the First began to hold reunions shortly after the war, and on June 17, 1869, at their reunion in White Bear Lake, he was elected vice president of the First Minnesota Association.

On September 5, 1878, Peller left Nick Horn's tavern, where he enjoyed playing cards in his free time. Between eleven o'clock and midnight, he was seen by E. L. Rice, a night watchman. Peller lived above his store, and Rice observed him talking to his dog, entering his building, and lighting an upstairs lamp. Later, at about three o'clock in the morning, Rice walked with a policeman by the name of Black to the First National Bank building and saw a light carried from one of Peller's front rooms to the other. Peller often read or wrote late into the night, and Rice thought nothing of it. He also thought Peller may have been a little intoxicated that evening. The next morning, town officials came to his store and left a message that he had been selected as a member of the greeting committee for President Hayes' arrival. He could not be found, and they assumed he had gone to the state fair in St. Paul.

When he did not show up for the Sunday event, they began a search, and on Monday word came that a body had been found in the Mississippi River at Diamond Bluff, some ten to thirteen miles downstream. Though a bullet was lodged in the rib cage, an autopsy determined drowning to be the cause of death. The body was identified as Peller's by the color of the hair and goatee and the old wound on the arm; the body was otherwise unrecognizable.

The coroner ruled Peller's death a suicide, concluding that he first shot himself before falling into the river. Some unusual circumstances hint, however, at the possibility of foul play. His key was found in his safe, and both it and the back door were slightly ajar. No money was missing, but both of his revolvers were gone. He may have been confronting a thief when Rice saw the light in his window at three o'clock. Perhaps, he pulled a gun on this possible intruder, who then fled and whom Peller then chased. Perhaps, somewhere near the river, the robber turned and fired at Peller, hitting him and causing him to fall into the water. Of course, this scenario is the product of speculation.

Peller was forty-eight when he died. He was buried in Oakwood Cemetery, and during his funeral procession the Great Western Band played. When created, the GAR post in Hastings was named in his honor.

Augustus Ludwig Dietrich Vogelsang

b. May 26, 1826; d. July 21, 1885

Dietrich Vogelsang was born in Minden, Germany. He immigrated to America and settled in Detroit. On November 18, 1849, he married Sophia Fuss. He was twenty-three, and she was twenty-two. They were living in St. Paul when the war began, and he, now thirty-one years old, enlisted.

On September 17, 1862, he was seriously wounded in his left thigh at the Battle of Antietam. The wound required his leg's amputation above the knee, and he was discharged for medical disability on November 30, 1862.

After his discharge he struggled with both illness and its remedies. His amputation did not heal well, and gangrene set in at his stump. He returned to Detroit, which he considered both his home and the place he wanted to die. The pain increased greatly, as did his dependency on morphine to control it. On January 24, 1863, another amputation farther up the leg was required. The amputation saved his life, but he suffered for years, becoming ever-more dependent on morphine, which in turn ate away at his mind. He died on July 21, 1885, at the age of fifty-nine.

Samuel Pitkin

b. August 9, 1837; d. February 9, 1904

Ohioan Samuel Pitkin was twenty-three when he was mustered into Company A on May 18, 1861. He was with the regiment at Gettysburg and participated in their July 2 charge. He was one of the few to return from the fight unwounded.

Saul, as he was known, was stabbed in his side by a bayonet during the hand-to-hand fighting at Bristoe Station. Cpl. William Shaw, who served in Company B of the Nineteenth Maine, wrote the following in a letter to his mother, dated April 5, 1864:

Just as the battle of Bristow was beginning, the First Minnesota was deployed as skirmishers, and when they were driven in, one of them fell, shot through the fleshy part of the leg. It was not a dangerous wound but he could not walk. So he crawled into a hollow between two knolls to shelter him from the passing bullets and lay there on his back waiting for something to turn up to better his position. It was but a few moments before the Rebel Line came along, and as he was not more than 100 yards in front of us, their line was badly broken when they got to him. One of their soldiers seeing that he was not dead, stepped up to him and attempted to pin him to the ground with his bayonet, but the fellow seeing his inten-

tions knocked the gun to one side with his hand, but it took affect in his side & went through into the ground. Just then a Rebel Officer halloed to him, the Rebel, and told him not to do that, but he paid no attention to it, and said he was bound to finish one damned Yankee, and was about making another thrust at him when a Minnie ball [probably from the 19th Maine] struck him in the head, and he fell dead, without finishing his intended work. After the fight was over some of the Minn boys went out and got their comrade and brought him in, and last that I heard of him was that he was nearly well. The wound in his side was fairly slight from the bayonet only just went beneath the skin. The First Minnesota at that time belonged to this Brigade.

Pitkin was taken off the field by Harrison Lyons and other men from the regiment and placed in an ambulance. He was sent to a hospital in Alexandria, Virginia, known as McKim's Mansion. The bayonet wound caused a rupture in his abdomen. He spent the rest of his service in the hospital, until he was mustered out of the service at Ft. Snelling on May 5, 1864. Though he recovered, he was troubled by the hernia for the rest of his life.

COMPANY B
THE STILLWATER GUARD

B Y 1861 STILLWATER, ONE OF MINNESOTA'S oldest settlements, was a busy town heavily focused on harvesting the surrounding abundant forests— besides being home to a large Swiss community, many strong woodsmen from Maine had found this area a good place to make a living. The town's lumbermen felled trees from nearby forests, floated logs down the St. Croix, and milled them in town.

The Stillwater Guard was created, like several other state militias, to defend against possible attack by Indians. Many members of the guard were the nucleus of Company B. These men often shared similar ethnic backgrounds, held occupations in the lumber industry, and became a tight-knit group. When the First Minnesota was formed, Company B comprised forty-seven men who had been born in America and fifty-five who were foreign born. Of those fifty-five, fifteen were born in Switzerland, eleven in Sweden, and seventeen in either Prussia or Germany. After the war many men returned to Stillwater to stay.

Picturesque Stillwater on the western bank of the St. Croix River.

Mark Downie

b. March 15, 1836; d. November 12, 1879

Leaving Ireland in 1832, Mark Downie's parents settled in Canada, and he was born in Chatham, New Brunswick. When he was nineteen, the family moved to Stillwater, where Downie found work as a bookkeeper and a cashier at a bank. He was a tall man, standing six feet two and three-quarters inches tall.

A member of the Stillwater Guard, he was among the core of men who formed Company B, and on April 29, 1861, when the regiment was organized, he was made, perhaps because of his bookkeeping skills, the regimental quartermaster. On July 16, 1861, after Capt. Carlisle Bromley resigned, Downie received a commission as captain of Company B. At the First Battle of Bull Run, he was wounded in the chest by a piece of shell. Though it caused him problems later in life, at the time the wound was thought only slight, and he soon returned to duty. The men liked their captain, and though Sgt. Myron Shepard noted negatively in his diary that Downie's tent was the site of late-night gambling and drinking, Shepard still liked the captain.

During a series of hard-fought engagements near Richmond, Virginia, Gen. George McClellan found it nearly impossible to extricate his army from a dangerous position. His retreat having been cut off by Gen. Lee, the army's only means of escape seemed to be by constructing a few bridges across the Chickahominy

Capt. Mark Downie

River in a single day. The Union's engineers reported, however, that it could not be done. Gen. Sully sent for Capt. Downie, who was lying in his tent prostrate with fever. Upon hearing what was needed, he replied,

Prior to the war, Ed Stevens had worked for the town newspaper, the *Stillwater Messenger*. After joining the First Minnesota, he reported home on the men and the war's progression. In a December 18, 1862, letter, he tells the following funny and somewhat amazing story about several young men of Company B at the Battle of Fredericksburg:

A very large number have been struck by spent balls, stones, splinters, etc., but their injuries are so slight that they are all on duty again. Shells sometimes play queer freaks. For proof of this witness the following, which occurred a few days ago in Company B. John B. Stevens—who has risen from the ranks to a corporalship—noticed a small rifle shell, nearly spent, come ricocheting toward him, and leaned to one side just in time for the shell to pass his shoulder. The shell struck the pack of Charley Gove, knocking him down and spilling sundry bottles of catsup, etc., which he had rolled in his blankets, all over our good friend Fallahee. Not yet satisfied, the shell struck a fence, and glancing, struck Sebers in the stomach, knocking him down also, when it fell to the ground in the midst of the company without bursting. Had it burst, many of company B would not have lived to tell the tale.

"General, find me a thousand lumbermen from the northwest, and the bridge will be built." The men of the First went to work and built the storied Grapevine Bridge, and the army made its escape. The bridge forever was a source of pride for the men of the regiment, theirs being the only one not destroyed by the Chickahominy when the rushing river overflowed its banks.

As mentioned, at the time Downie suffered from a wasting fever—the product of dysentery—and after the retreat, on June 9, 1862, he was admitted to the U.S. Army's general hospital in New Haven, Connecticut. He was furloughed on August 22, 1862, and returned to Ft. Snelling, taking over ordnance duties at the fort. He oversaw the storing of arms and ammunition in the fort's old Round Tower prior to their being issued to new regiments. His health did improve, and he was ordered back to the First, returning to his men in February 1863.

Promoted to the rank of major on May 6, 1863, he was third in command of the regiment at Gettysburg. On July 2 he was positioned behind the regiment on the left. Col. Colvill held the center, and Lt. Col. Adams, the right. In the mad rush to stop the Rebels, regimental structure blurred. Colvill fell, and Adams took command. When he too went down, Downie briefly commanded the regiment as it melted under heavy enemy fire. His moment ended within seconds as he fell with two wounds in his right arm, a bullet through his left foot, and a shell wound to his chest. His arm received the worst of it, with one minié ball entering his middle upper arm, breaking the bone near the shoulder, and another hitting him just above the elbow. Unable to move as the regiment retreated back up the slope, Downie lay within yards of the Rebels. Union reinforcements arrived, however, and the Confederates withdrew. He received no further injury but was not rescued until after dark.

Dr. LeBlond attended Downie and removed several pieces of bone from his broken arm. He remained at the Second Corps' field hospital at Rock Creek for a while. Because of his wounds' seriousness, the surgeons recommended amputating his arm, but he refused. He then spent the next month and a half in army hospitals, followed by six weeks recovering in Minnesota. He spent two weeks in St. Paul, where his sister, Ellen, nursed him. He then returned to his home in Stillwater for about a month.

Three months after the battle, on October 4, 1863, Maj. Downie returned to the regiment and assumed its command. Of all the officers wounded at Gettys-

Maj. Mark Downie

burg, he and Thomas Sinclair were the first to return to duty. He enhanced his military reputation by skillfully handling the First Minnesota as a skirmish line at the Battle of Bristoe Station later that month.

In May 1864, when the First Minnesota was consolidated into a battalion, Downie did not reenlist, instead returning to Stillwater.

His time in the service was not, however, over. He received a commission from the governor and joined the First Battalion of Minnesota Infantry on April 6, 1865, as its commander with the rank of lieutenant colonel. He and the battalion were mustered out three months later on July 14, 1865. Downie returned to Stillwater, where he lived for five years.

He never fully recovered from his war wounds, and they led to his early death. His right arm was virtually useless, and eventually, he could not use it to hold a pen or even feed himself. The wound to his foot also was troublesome and resulted in a limp. As a civilian, Downie was content enough as a merchant and bookkeeper, until his health broke and he relied more on his pension. Hoping that a warmer climate would improve his health, he moved to Fernandina, Florida, in 1870.

Though he was a man who had fought for the North,

he earned the respect of his Florida neighbors by showing friendship and sympathy for the poor and suffering. During an 1871 yellow fever epidemic in Cedar Key, he nursed the sick, fed the poor, and buried the dead, expending all his strength and money on their behalf. The six weeks' incessant labor further weakened his body, from which he never fully recovered.

Owing to the mild climate and loving care from his wife, his life was extended a few years, but his life's wounds and exertions caught up with him when he was still young. He developed pneumonia and died on November 12, 1879, at the age of forty-three.

Adam Marty

b. August 2, 1837; d. February 7, 1923

Adam Marty was born in Engi, Glarus, Switzerland. Leaving his family behind, Adam's father, Sebastian Marti, immigrated to America in 1839 and settled in Stillwater in 1845. There, he worked as a cook at John McKusik's sawmill and, later, began farming. In 1843, when Marty was six years old, his mother died, and he was placed in the care of his aunt and uncle.

In 1846 Adam; his aunt and uncle; his brother, Fridolin; and his cousins Sam Bloomer and Jacob Marti immigrated to America, settling in St. Louis, where the young men worked in an arsenal making cartridges for the U.S.–Mexican War. (His older cousin Jacob enlisted and fought in the war, and later, he moved to Minnesota and served in the Fifth Minnesota Infantry during the Civil War.) In 1849 the family moved to Stillwater, and like his father, Adam worked for McKusik, though only for one year. He then lived with his father on the farm. In 1856 Adam began working as a house painter, which he continued until his enlistment in the First Minnesota.

A member of the Stillwater Guard, he enlisted on April 29, 1861. When mustered, he was recorded as standing five feet seven inches tall and having a ruddy complexion, blue eyes, and brown hair. On October 10, 1861, he wrote the following to a Mr. H. A. Jackman in Stillwater and explained his reasons for enlisting:

I have done nothing more than that duty which I owe to my adopted country, which has sheltered me when young and given me all those liberties and privileges which I enjoy and which are dear to every Foreigner as well as Americans, for they having lived under the iron rule

Adam Marty

of European Monarchys can appreciate them and it becomes every one of them to fight for her in this her most dire extremity, and freely bleed and even die for her if need be. Who would not fight for such a country, such blessings and such privileges! I trust there are few that would not.

At Gettysburg, Marty was shot in his right thigh, and he spent the next eight months recovering at Broad Street Hospital in Philadelphia. During his recovery he wrote to his cousin Sam Bloomer back in Stillwater. Bloomer was the color sergeant for the First at Antietam, where he was severely wounded and subsequently lost a leg to the surgeon's knife. The letter is dated February 2, 1864, and refers to a picture not seen here:

Enclosed I send you a picture I had taken down to Falmouth yesterday. It was a very poor production for the artist was a botch, his chemicals poor, his machines out of order and a one horse concern generally but I presume good enough for his soldiers. I sat three times and this was the best of the three. There was such a crowd there that they did not take much pains but took them as fast as they could. I was so mad about it when I got home that I thought at first I would not send it but on thinking over it last night I concluded to send it anyhow thinking it might please you better than none at all as it at least resembles me some and will show you my conditions.

Marty was released from the Philadelphia hospital on April 29, 1864. He immediately headed home and was mustered out with the regiment on May 5, 1864. He then returned to Stillwater, where he got work as a sign and carriage painter.

He married in 1869, but unfortunately, his wife and child died in childbirth in 1870. In 1884 he married Augusta Burrow, and they raised four children.

Marty helped form the first fire department in Stillwater. He was also active in the First Minnesota Association and other veterans' organizations. He joined Stillwater's Muller GAR Post #14 in 1875 and was elected post commander for six terms. In 1881 he

Marty in the uniform of a Stillwater fireman

was elected department commander for the State of Minnesota and was elected Washington County sheriff in 1890, holding the office two terms. He was one of the last members of the Last Man's Club (see the chapter's last section). Marty died in St. Paul at the home of his daughter on February 7, 1923. He was buried at Fairview Cemetery in Stillwater near his cousin Sam.

Adam Marty kept a small red book, which he called the "Muster Out Roll of Company B." In it he recorded the passing of each comrade. Some thoughtful person recorded Marty's own death in 1923. Seen here is a cabinet photo of him, circa 1881, wearing his GAR state commander's badge for the Department of Minnesota.

John S. May

b. 1839; d. November 27, 1895

John May was born in Allegheny County, near Pittsburgh, Pennsylvania. He was twenty-two and living in Stillwater when he was mustered into service on April 29, 1861. May stood five feet eleven inches tall and had a light complexion, brown hair, and blue eyes. He was promoted to corporal during his service and was mustered out on May 5, 1864, having been fortunate never to have been wounded.

On March 24, 1864, he reenlisted as a corporal in Company A of the First Battalion. At Petersburg, on June 22, 1864, he was captured, along with several other former men of the First Minnesota, while trying to save the guns of McKnight's Tenth New York Battery. Others captured at the time included George B. Clark (Co. A) and Daniel Perkins (Co. C). May first was taken to Libby Prison and then to Belle Isle Prison. From there, he was sent to Andersonville, where he remained until about February 1865. He was then sent to a prison at Wilmington, North Carolina. Government records state that he escaped on February 23, 1865. Back with the Union, he was taken to College Green

Barracks in Annapolis on March 5, and on March 8 he was sent west to Benton Barracks, Missouri, arriving on March 14. From there, he received a furlough and returned to Stillwater, where he received medical treatment. His imprisonment weakened and emaciated him, and he suffered from diarrhea and piles. He returned to his unit on April 3, 1865, and was mustered out as a sergeant on July 14, 1865, at Jeffersonville, Indiana, along with the rest of the men of the battalion.

The following is an account of May's escape as reported on March 28, 1865, in the *Stillwater Messenger*:

> Sergeant John May, a former resident of this city, a veteran of Company B, and at present a member of Company A, First Battalion, was captured by the rebels in an engagement near Petersburg, VA., on the 22nd day of June last. He made his escape by jumping from the cars, while being transferred from Florence to Salisbury, NC via Wilmington.
>
> He was taken prisoner, as stated above, with 1,600 of our men and taken into Petersburg that night. They removed to Libby Prison the next day, where they remained two days, long enough to be closely searched, by an officer connected with the prison, who took from them money, pocket-knives, valuables of every kind. . . .
>
> The search was conducted in the basement, and John being luckily located on the third floor, received timely notice of the manner in which the examination was conducted. . . . Mr. May had skein or two of what is known as patent linen thread, and undoing the skeins, and rolling up his money—about forty dollars—in as small a package as possible, wound his thread carefully around it, and stuck his needles carelessly around it, and when the officer, in turning his pockets wrong side out, saw the skein, he remarked that it was d—d nice looking thread, but put it back into the pocket, very much to the relief of the owner. The prisoners were taken to Belle Island, where they remained almost ten days, and were then transferred to Camp Sumter, at Andersonville, Ga. . . .
>
> The Sergeant relates the following incident, which occurred on the march between Lynchburg and Danville. They had halted at a little town for a few moments to procure water,

when a great crowd assembled to gaze upon the extraordinary sight—many of them having never seen a live Yankee—and of course, the darkies were out in full force. The sergeant overheard the following remark, "Wy, lor a massa, dese men look jis like de rebs; got no horns at all!"

At Camp Sumter, in Andersonville, the prisoners were divided into detachments of 300 men each with a Sergeant for each detachment, called a Hundred-Sergeant, whose business it was to call the roll every morning, and form his men in line, for the purpose of receiving rations. These detachments numbered about 112, making the number of prisoners between 33,000 and 35,000.

The rations here consisted of nearly one quart of corn meal, about a quarter of a pound of bacon, and at rare intervals—once or twice a week—half a pint of beans.

The stockade in which they were confined was made by placing logs over twenty feet long in an upright position. About fifteen feet from this, on the inside, a row of posts was set, about four feet high, with poles nailed along the top, which was called the "Dead Line."

A stream of water ran directly thro' the camp, and of course was crossed in two places by this "dead line," and the Sergeant says he has often seen men, who came down to the stream to get water near the prescribed boundary, while stooping to dip water with their cups, fall from weakness and exhaustion, and accidentally falling with a few inches of their bodies exposed beyond the pole would be shot dead where they fell. He once saw a man shot dead by the guard who was scuffling with a comrade, and happened to fall under the pole which constituted the "dead line." On one occasion of this kind, he overheard the author of the dastardly deed hail a comrade with, "I say Bill, I've got a thirty days furlough, now shore; for I've jist shot my regular Yank." . . .

The date of Mr. May's arrival was the 10th of July—and on the day following he witnessed the execution of six of our men, who were hung in the camp. The particulars of this sad affair have been published in all the papers. These six were the ringleaders of a band of hardened, blood-thirsty wretches who system-

atically plundered their comrades throughout the camp, and when resistance was shown, the poor fellow was beaten to death with clubs and buried beneath the tents of the murderers. After this dreadful example, comparative order and quiet reigned. . . .

Mr. May remained in this den of horrors for two months and five days and was then—Sept 15 [the date should be February 15]—started for Salisbury, N.C. via Wilmington. . . .

On the 18th he started on a train for Salisbury, and that night, when about 65 miles out of Wilmington, he resolved to make one desperate attempt to escape. The guard at the door of the car had fallen asleep, with his loaded musket across the doorway, and John, taking down his haversack, containing about a quart of corn meal, stepped over the prostrate guard, and after satisfying himself that he was really asleep, crept stealthily to the edge of the platform, peered out into the gloomy night, and made the bold leap. The train was moving at the rate of twelve miles an hour, and in the language of the Irishman, the next thing he knew, he didn't know anything. He lay stunned and senseless for a time, but on recovering, found that no bones were broken, though he was not in the best condition for traveling. The train was out of hearing so he was obliged to guess which direction to take in order to reach Wilmington, but fortunately took the right course, and at daylight turned off the railroad, and finding a secure retreat in the thick bushes, slept soundly through the entire day, resuming his journey the next night. On the third night he came upon rebel pickets, but discovering them by their fires, and having ascertained from friendly negroes that there was a dirt road a short distance from the railroad, running parallel with it, he struck through the swamps and bushes and gained it safely. Here he was continually obliged to make short detours to avoid citizens and soldiers who were fleeing from Wilmington.

On the fourth night he came to the Cape Fear River, ten miles from Wilmington and knew that if he could get across that he was safe. The river at that point is one fourth of a mile in width, with a swift current. His meal was gone, but he invariably found negroes friendly, cheerfully dividing their scanty stores of food with him, and gladly piloting him on his way, and pointing out the proper course to take to avoid the rebel pickets.

Stopping at a negro shanty he found an old negro woman, who quickly prepared some food for him, and while partaking of their humble fare noticed a negro man sitting in one corner with bowed head, and who appeared much dejected. On inquiry, he ascertained that the darkey had just heard of the determination of the rebel government to arm the Negros to fight the Yankees. "But," said he with terrible earnestness "dis chile neber shoots one of you Yankees."

John proposed to him to find some means for crossing the river and assured him that as soon as he was safe on the other side he would be a free man. This was about 10 o'clock at night, and the negro started out to reconnoiter, but returned at 2 o'clock, sorrowfully declaring that he could find no boat, and that the ferry, a short distance above, was strongly guarded by rebels. John proposed to "appropriate" a couple of "Massa's" horses and swim them across, but the darkey was confident no horse could accomplish such a feat. Upon John suggesting to him that perhaps some dug-out or trough of some kind might be found capable of floating them across the darkey replied that there was a watering trough at the barn, about ten feet long, but too heavy for them to "tote." But when John inquired why not take a horse from the stable and drag it down to the river, the negro threw up his hands, leaped into the air, and fairly screamed with delight. This plan was quickly put into execution, but when about thirty rods from the shore the horse sank in the mud and could go no farther. Tying the horse to a tree, they rolled the trough the whole distance to the river bank. It was an exceedingly difficult and hazardous undertaking to paddle such a craft across the rapid stream; but freedom was too nigh and too many formidable dangers had been encountered and overcome to think of faltering now. John found that his experience in riding logs and navigating all sorts of crafts on the Minnesota streams, was of use to him in this emergency, and he "made the riffle" in safety. The negro being familiar

with all the roads, they had no difficulty in reaching our lines at Wilmington. He arrived there the 23d of February, having been just five days and nights getting through. His weight at the time was 106 pounds. He was immediately furloughed for thirty days, and arrived home last week.

John May was discharged on July 14, 1865, and returned to Stillwater. He died there on November 27, 1895, from the diseases he had contracted while in Confederate prisons. He was fifty-seven years old.

Freeman Louis McKusick
b. August 14, 1841; d. November 18, 1912

Freeman McKusick was born in Baring, Maine, and was nineteen years old and working in the lumber business when the war began. Entering the service on May 20, 1861, he stood about five feet ten inches tall and had a fair complexion, brown hair, and gray eyes.

Though McKusick was one of the fortunate few to escape injury at Gettysburg, in the fall of 1863 he suffered from the malarial conditions in the low, swampy land occupied by the Union army along the Rapidan

Freeman Louis McKusick

River in Virginia. Developing what was called "fever and the ague," on October 3 he was sent to Mount Pleasant Hospital in Washington, DC, where he remained until the end of December.

He returned home on furlough to recover and later rejoined the regiment in Washington on February 1, 1864, just as the regiment prepared to return home and be mustered out of the service. On February 23, 1864, the *Stillwater Messenger* heralded his return with the following announcement:

> FREEMAN MCKUSICK of company B, First regiment, just returned, brought back the same musket he took with him from the Armory here nearly three years ago. It is numbered eleven, and is the only one left of the forty muskets which originally belonged to the old Stillwater Guard. It was carried by Col. Thomas while he was a member of the Guards.

McKusick was very active in the First Minnesota Association. He spent the last years of his life at the soldiers' home in Minneapolis and served as its adjutant. He was the man who found that William Colvill had died in his sleep during the night of June 12, 1905. On November 18, 1912, while standing on a bridge at the home, McKusik suffered a heart attack and died. He was seventy-one years old. He was buried at Fairview Cemetery in his hometown of Stillwater.

Albert Sieber

b. February 27, 1842; d. February 19, 1907

Born in Mingolsheim, Germany, Albert Sieber was barely a year old when his father died. His mother, Katherina, and six older siblings immigrated to the United States in 1849, living briefly in Lancaster, Pennsylvania, before settling near the Conestoga River. After marrying an enterprising young man named Henry Oswald, Albert's older sister Theresa and her new husband moved to Minneapolis, where he ran a saloon across the river at St. Anthony. Shortly thereafter, Katherina packed up and, with her twelve-year-old son, Albert, moved to live with the newlyweds.

As a teenager, Sieber worked as a teamster, hauling logs to the mills and taking lumber to the docks. When the war broke out, the eighteen-year-old teamster chafed at the bit to join the fray, but his mother disapproved, at least of immediate enlistment. How-

Albert Sieber

ever, she agreed to let him join when he turned nineteen and on March 4, 1862, the first possible day after his birthday, she wrote a note of approval. He enlisted and was mustered into the service.

He signed his enlistment form as Albert Sebers, though the family name seemed to have always been Sieber. During the war he went by Sebers but, afterward, was known as Al Sieber. At five feet ten and a half inches, he was two inches taller than the average Civil War soldier. He had dark eyes, dark hair, and a fair complexion. He enlisted in Minneapolis but gave Stillwater as his residence, which may have been where he was working at the time.

When he joined, he was already an expert shot with a rifle, but he and the other recruits were given little time to drill. They were quickly shipped east and joined the regiment during the Siege of Yorktown. Sieber participated in the battles at Fair Oaks, Antietam, Fredericksburg, Chancellorsville, and Gettysburg.

He was seriously wounded during the July 2 charge at Gettysburg. A piece of artillery shell smashed into the right side of his head, and as he fell a minié ball pierced his right leg, just above the ankle, and traveled up his calf to his knee. After the battle he was sent to the makeshift Second Corps field hospital at Rock Creek, where he remained for several days. An army

This cabinet photo probably dates from the 1880s or 1890s. On the left is Al Sieber, wearing his winter overcoat. It was probably taken during the winter of 1863–64. On the right, likely, is his sister Theresa. Her clothing is not from the 1860s, thus indicating the two pictures were taken at different times and put together years later as a precious memory. Sieber was, by the 1870s, living in Arizona. Theresa and the rest of his relatives remained in the Minnesota area. Though he wrote periodically, he seldom visited them.

surgeon removed the minié ball. The artillery shell had fractured his skull, the fragment having broken off a piece of his facial bone on the right side. Some brain tissue also was lost.

On July 10, 1863, he was admitted to York U.S. Army Hospital in Pennsylvania, also known as the Little York Hospital. On August 30 he was admitted to the army hospital at Fairfax Seminary near Alexandria, Virginia, and then on September 5, he was briefly admitted to Bellevue Hospital in New York, only to be returned to duty five days later. He spent the next three months in convalescence camp and never returned to active duty with the regiment.

On December 24, 1863, he was transferred to the 145th Company, First Battalion, Invalid Corps. On February 23, 1864, he was reported as recovering in the convalescent camp in Alexandria, Virginia. In May 1864, while the First Minnesota was being discharged back in Minnesota, Sieber was still recovering near Washington. Though he had been transferred to the Veteran Reserve Corps (VRC), record of it must not have reached Minnesota. His record showed that he still owed some time on his three-year enlistment, so even though he was not present, he was transferred, on paper, to the First Battalion and carried on the roll of Company B until it was mustered out at Jeffersonville, Indiana, on July 14, 1865.

On December 14, 1864, during his service with the VRC, Sieber was promoted to corporal. In later years he confessed that he had been "too full of the devil—played too many pranks" to ever get promoted while with the First, but he felt that to be a member of the regiment was to be an "elite soldier." Sieber finished his service in Company K of the First Regiment of the VRC, serving as a guard at the prisoner-of-war camp

at Elmira, New York. The war ended, and Sieber was discharged at Elmira on November 14, 1865.

He tried living in Minneapolis right after the war. On October 6, 1866, at the age of twenty-three, he filed a claim for an invalid's pension as a result of his Gettysburg wounds. He was a young but hardened Civil War veteran, and like many men who had served in the war, he was changed and could not return to civilian life. So he left Minnesota and headed west. First, he moved to California, where he worked as a cowboy in San Bernardino. In 1867 he prospected for silver in Nevada, and in 1868 he headed to Arizona and remained there for the rest of his life.

Early in his time in Arizona, he managed a ranch in Prescott and helped to defend it against periodic attacks by local Apache. While there, he developed the ability to follow tracks and hunt down an enemy. He was naturally gifted and, before long, became a local legend. Running across the rough Arizona terrain, he could keep up with and catch just about anything or anybody. By 1871 he was well known enough that Gen. George Crook hired him as the army's chief of scouts in that area, putting him in charge of eighty Yavapai-Apache scouts.

Gen. Crook, who was commander of the Department of Arizona from 1871 to 1875 and again in the 1880s, discovered what none of his predecessors had learned: only Apaches could catch Apaches. Thereafter, he relied heavily on Apaches both as scouts and as fighting men under civilian scouts, a practice Gen. Philip Sheridan in Washington, DC, frowned upon because it reflected poorly on the cavalry. The detachments sent after hostile Apaches typically were a combination of Apache scouts and U.S. troops. Crook advised recruiting the "wildest" Apaches as scouts, for they enjoyed battle and knew their kindred's hiding places, as well. Such Apaches, often enemies one day and scouts for the cavalry the next, required unusual men to control them and ensure their loyalty. Crook was fortunate in being able to hire some excellent white scouts to manage the Apaches, of which the very best was Al Sieber.

During his time in the government's service, Sieber also tried prospecting. In 1876 he saw the potential for gold in an area northwest of Camp Verde and staked his first claim. When word got out about his mining claims, other people followed. A settlement developed, and it was named Jerome, after one of its early financial backers. Sieber was restless, though, and unfortunately, not finding quick success, he sold the rights to his stake. Eventually, rich veins of copper, gold, zinc, and lead were discovered. One mine, the United Verde Mine, eventually produced in excess of $1 billion in copper, gold, zinc, and lead during its decades of active use. Of course, Sieber never benefited from it.

Sieber became a hardened Indian scout and fighter. He was a professional, though, and always held to a code of ethics. His ability to control the fiercest Apaches and to use them effectively as scouts against renegade Apaches indeed was extraordinary. When asked to explain the secret of his success in managing the Apache scouts, he replied, "I do not deceive them

In 1877, Sieber sat for this picture at Camp Verde in Arizona.

but always tell them the truth. When I tell them I am going to kill them, I do it, and when I tell them I am their friend, they know it."[1] For the next few years, Sieber was involved in most of the major engagements during Crook's campaign against the Tonto Apache Indians. Later, he occasionally was sent into Mexico as a spy and participated in a major expedition that Crook led into the Sierra Madre against the Chiricahua Apache who were led by Geronimo. Sieber became known as "the paleface who knew no fear."

In 1881, he took under his wing a young White Mountain Apache who became known as the Apache Kid. For several years the Kid worked with Sieber and his scouts, thriving under Sieber's guidance and greatly respecting his mentor. However, six years later, in April 1887, life took a turn for the worse. One day, Sieber left the San Carlos Reservation on business and put the Kid in charge of maintaining law and order. One night, the Kid got drunk with some

Al Sieber in 1874

Taken in 1878, Sieber is seen in the center of his Apache scouts, who are posing with their trapdoor Springfield rifles. They did effective service with Gen. Crooks.

of his scout friends and killed an Apache involved in a family feud with the Kid. Then they fled the reservation. Knowing that Sieber would and could hunt them down, on June 1 they returned to the reservation to face the consequences for what they'd done. They dismounted at his tent and, holding the horses' reins and the arms, waited while word was sent for Sieber to come. During this time other Indian scouts started to form a crowd, many carrying weapons. Leaving the agency building seventy-five yards away, Sieber, an officer named Pierce, and two interpreters, all unarmed, headed for the tent. Sieber gruffly told the Kid to surrender his arms and those of his companions. This was done, and the arms were placed on the table in front of the tent. Lt. Pierce ordered the Indians to report to the guardhouse to be put under arrest. This peaceful surrender was about to wrap up when some hothead in the crowd started shooting. In seconds firing

erupted. One Indian grabbed his carbine off the table, but Sieber kicked it out of his hands and jumped into his tent to arm himself. As he came back out the opening, a scout named Curley fired a .45–70 slug, which hit Sieber in the left foot.[2] The Kid and his friends ran away, and a troop of the Fourth Cavalry was quickly sent after them. Hearing about the incident, Gen. Miles traveled to San Carlos to see what could be done, declaring that Sieber "was the most self-contained and most fearless Indian scout in the service." The Kid and his friends ran for twenty-four days, killing settler Mike Grace in the process, until they were surprised high in the Rincon Mountains by U.S. troops, who captured their horses and supplies. On June 25 the Kid surrendered to authorities but subsequently escaped. A reward was posted, and he was hunted. One person claimed to have wounded him, but the Kid was never found. He may have escaped to Mexico or perhaps died alone in the Arizona desert.

During the surgery on Sieber's leg, five inches of his tibia were removed. Small parts of his leg bone ulcerated through the wound for years afterward. His left leg ended up three inches shorter than his right, and he was doomed to be lame for the rest of his life.

Sieber tried to continue his life as he had known it, but times were changing. Three years later, a new Indian agent arrived at the reservation. This agent had a history of exploiting his charges, a history he continued with the Apaches at San Carlos. Sieber argued against his poor treatment of the Apaches but was unable to convince the military authorities of the agent's treachery. In December 1890, the agent succeeded in getting Sieber fired as chief of scouts, and thus, his twenty-year career as a scout, Indian fighter, and reservation law officer came to an end. He was now forty-

Al Sieber is standing on the right with his Yavapai-Apache scouts.

The military campaign against Geronimo was led by Gen. George Cook, seen here with his scouts, cooks, and wagon drivers. He is seated in front of the middle tent wearing a white hat and a light-colored jacket. Seated fifth from the left in a white shirt and white hat is Tom Horn. Standing ninth from the right in a dark shirt, suspenders, and a wide-brimmed light-colored hat is Al Sieber. This picture was taken in 1886 by photographer C. S. Fly of Tombstone, Arizona. Fly's shop in Tombstone was located next to the OK Corral, scene of the famous shootout on October 26, 1881, that pitted three Earp brothers and Doc Holliday against Billy Clanton and Tom and Frank McLaury.

Sieber is shown here on crutches after having been shot in the leg. The caption reads, "Al Sieber, Deputy US Marshall & Chief of Scouts, A.T."

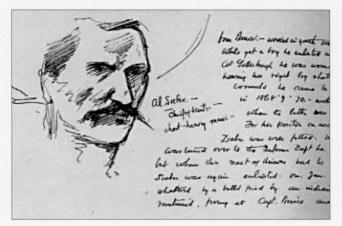

Frederick Remington created this sketch of Al Sieber, calling him "Chief of Scouts."

seven and on his own again. From that time on, he prospected and took odd jobs, but nothing contained the fame or excitement he had known.

Years later, on February 2, 1906, Sieber saw Dr. R. F. Palmer in order to have a medical form filled out that he needed for his military pension. Dr. Palmer's examination describes the toll Sieber's rugged lifestyle had taken over the years:

Mr. Seiber is a man of 62 years, 198 lbs, 5.11½ ft. He presents the following wounds and scars:

Head, . . . a depression which will admit the tip of a finger. Said to have been caused by a shell wound at Gettysburg, July 2nd 1863.

Right leg, . . . at about middle of leg is a circular scar 1 inch in diameter. Another scar

Sieber's last picture was taken in 1906, at the age of sixty-three, one year before his death.

between the knee cap and head of fibula, oval in form, 1 ¾ in long. Said to be entrance and exit of bullet received at Gettysburg July 2nd 1863.

Hernia . . . said to have been from riding a bucking horse issued by Quartermaster at Fort Wallapai 9/20/1872.

Left leg is 3 inches shorter than right . . . Said to have been received at San Carlos June 1st 1887. 5 in of tibia said to have been removed at the time and many small pieces have ulcerated through at various times since.

Mr. Sieber complains of constant pain in right knee cap, more severe in winter time and during sudden changes of temperature and moisture.

Sieber's final job was supervising a group of Apache during the construction of a road leading to the Roosevelt Dam, which was being created about seventy-six miles northeast of Phoenix. On February 19, 1907, his crew was trying to dislodge and remove a huge boulder perhaps fifteen feet high and wide. The afternoon was waning, and they were having trouble finishing the day's tasks. Now using a cane, Sieber limped over and walked around the back side of the boulder to see what was causing the problem. What happened next is not clear. He may have reached under the boulder to dislodge something, or perhaps, one of his workers leaned on the rock. In any event, the boulder rolled, and he was immediately crushed. Al Sieber was dead at the age of sixty-three. Sieber's body was buried in the Odd Fellows section high on the hill of the Globe Cemetery in Globe, Arizona.

Sieber had never married—his lifestyle certainly was not conducive to it. Back in Minnesota, Adam Marty, a comrade from Company B, kept a record of the company members' death dates. When he recorded Sieber's death, he made a notation, part of which sums up the life of this rugged individual: "Capt of scouts under Crook in Arizona."

Thomas Sinclair

b. 1832; d. May 18, 1875

Irishman Thomas Sinclair worked as a stonemason, and when he went to war, he left behind a wife and two children. He had married Elmira Butler on August 20, 1854, in Stillwater. Their son, Robert, was born on July 28, 1858, and their daughter, Mary, was born on

Thomas Sinclair

May 26, 1861, one month after he had enlisted and was mustered into the service.

On April 29, 1861, he was mustered in as a sergeant in Company B. His record indicates that he was a good soldier. On January 3, 1863, he was promoted to second lieutenant, which was retroactively dated back to November 18, 1861. At the same time, he also was promoted to first lieutenant, this one dated to September 1862. The backdating indicates he assumed these ranks in the field but was not formally promoted until that January date. He was last promoted on May 7, 1863, rising to captain of Company B and replacing Mark Downie, who was promoted to major on the same day.

Sinclair was wounded four times during the war. At Antietam on May 17, 1862, he was shot in the right leg below the knee. At Fredericksburg he was shot in the left shoulder, dislocating the shoulder and breaking the bone. On July 2 at Gettysburg, Sinclair was charging toward the Plum Run ravine when he was hit in the breast by a spent minié ball. Though spent, it was strong enough to break the breast bone. The ball lodged in his breast near the pit of his stomach. Pvt. Joseph Tenner was just a few feet from him when Sinclair was hit. Tenner was wounded the next day when he was shot in the shoulder during the repulse of Pickett's Charge.

Sinclair's wound at Gettysburg required his hospitalization, and he and Maj. Downie, who was similarly recovering, returned to the regiment on Sunday, October 4, 1863, at which time Downie took command. Though he stayed with the regiment, Sinclair developed a severe cough as a result of his chest wound, and his physical condition weakened considerably.

He was wounded for a fourth and final time at Bristoe Station on October 14, 1863, when he was shot in the left arm. Sinclair was mustered out with the regiment at Ft. Snelling on May 5, 1864.

After the war he returned to Stillwater, where he continued to suffer from his severe cough. By 1874 his health had completely broken down from tuberculosis (consumption), and he was confined to his home. He died in Stillwater on May 18, 1875. He was about forty-three years old.

The Last Man's Club

On July 21, 1867, thirty-four surviving members of Company B formed the Last Man's Club, the first of its kind in the nation. The club met at the Sawyer House in Stillwater at 102 Second Street North (now the Lowell Inn). Each year, the members gathered to remember the past and pay tribute to those who had "crossed

The Sawyer House in Stillwater

the river," the chairs of the departed draped in black. A bottle of wine, donated by the father of Adolphus Hospes, stood as centerpiece at their table, the contents being the last man's prize. Each year, the number dwindled, and the gathering became less joyful, and in 1928 the three remaining members disbanded their increasingly grim club. Member Charles Lockwood advised some of the people in attendance, "Don't ever start a club like this again." Lockwood died on October 4, 1935, the last survivor. The charter members and their eventual dates of death are as follows:

Henry C. Van Vorhes (3/28/1888)
William A. Morgan (9/7/1888)
Alonzo Capron (10/2/1889)
William Turich (11/2/1889)
John P. Schoenbeck (2/3/1892)
Albert Caplazi (11/2/1892)
John S. May (10/2/1895)
Joseph A. Tenner (1/3/1902)
George C. McNeal (11/3/1902)
Patrick Fallihee (6/4/1907)
James Cleary (3/4/1909)
Harlow McIntyre (8/10/1909)
Morris Erhardt (12/7/1909)
William Aucker (4/7/1910)
George Oliver (1/19/1911)
Adolphus Hospes (8/2/1911)
Freeman McKusick (11/8/1912)
Samuel Johnson (1/4/1913)
William May (2/3/1914)
Oscar VanKuster (3/7/1914)
Andrew Peterson (3/4/1915)
Rudus Blanchard (6/4/1915)
Samuel Bloomer (10/14/1917)
Henry Goodman (10/7/1918)
William F. Schroeder (7/7/1920)
Myron Shepard (7/9/1920)
Edward Stevens (8/8/1920)
Jacob Gruseman (9/4/1920)
William Kelly (10/7/1920)
Adam Marty (2/7/1923)
Emil Graf (3/4/1926)
John Goff (8/27/1929)
Peter Hall (4/18/1930)
Charles Lockwood (10/4/1935)

LAST MAN—Charles M. Lockwood, last member of the Last Man's Club, brings to a close existence of this famous Civil War organization, formed 45 years ago by survivors of Co. B, First Minnesota Volunteer Infantry. He is shown at the head of the banquet table, surrounded by vacant chairs set for departed comrades, at the final meeting of the club in Stillwater Monday.

In 1930 Charles Lockwood toasted his fallen comrades for the last time. On the wall behind him can be seen the flag of Company B, presented to them in 1861 and carried at the beginning of the war.

This is the bottle that held the wine brought out each year that the Last Man's Club met. It was housed in the beautiful wooden cask seen here, which had the Second Corps' emblem placed in its cover.

COMPANY C
THE ST. PAUL VOLUNTEERS

WHEN THE WAR BROKE OUT, St. Paul was the largest city in the state, as well as its capital, and it provided two companies for the First Minnesota. William Acker, the adjutant general of the state, took charge of arranging for the recruitment of the men for the regiment and helped form Company C.

Seen here in 1857, St. Paul was still laying out streets and creating itself on the western frontier. This picture shows the intersection of Fifth and Wabasha. Construction of the Cathedral of St. Paul can be seen in the center.

By 1860 the town had grown considerably and used the river as a lifeline for commerce. This photograph of the lower levee was taken from a spot called Dayton's Bluff.

William Henry Acker

b. December 5, 1833; d. April 7, 1862

William Acker was born in Clyde, Wayne County, New York. His family moved to Michigan when he was three years old, and in the spring of 1854, they came to St. Paul, where his sister resided. Her husband, Edmund Rice, had a law office, which Acker joined for about one year. Afterward, for about two years, he held the position of bookkeeper in the banking house of Marshall and Company.

Early on, Acker developed a decided taste for military life and devoted much of his leisure time to studying works on military science. In 1856 he took an active part in organizing the Minnesota Pioneer Guards, the first uniformed military company in Minnesota. His diligent efforts expanded four loose quasi-military groups into eight structured militia units. Three of them formed the core of three companies in the First: the Pioneer Guard, the Stillwater Guard, and the St. Anthony Zouaves. In the original agreement to form this company, his name stands first on the list. On March 19, 1860, Governor Ramsey, appreciating Acker's military talent, commissioned him adjutant general of the state.

Acker was a friend and confidant of Col. Elmer Ellsworth. They visited each other when opportunity offered and corresponded regularly. Ellsworth confided to Acker his plans for the formation of a national guard composed of branch companies in all parts of the Union, forming together into one grand organization ready at a moment's warning to respond to the call of the government whenever its integrity might be threatened. Because of the war and Ellsworth's early death, his grand concept went unrealized, though it became the eventual basis for our modern National Guard.

Acker played a prominent role during the Minnesota political campaign of 1860. He was a captain in the St. Paul Company of Wide Awakes, which though not a military organization had some military features. The opposite political party had a similar organization, called the Little Giants. These two groups, having their counterparts in nearly every city and town in the free states, counted many young men as members. They familiarized themselves with rudimentary military training, which proved useful when the war began.

When word of Ft. Sumter's bombardment was received, as well as word from Governor Ramsey in Washington, DC, Acker ordered the formation of the First Minnesota. While performing his duties as adjutant general, he raised a company for the regiment, resigned his position with the state, and then accepted a commission as the company's captain. The various companies met at Ft. Snelling on April 28.

On July 21, 1861, he led Company C into their first battle, at Bull Run. Early in the battle he was in the foremost of the advance upon the enemy when buckshot struck the visor of his cap and, glancing, grazed his forehead over the right eye. He fell unconscious but awoke after being taken up by some of his men. The wound, though painful, was not serious. He remained with the regiment and was among the last to leave the field.

As Chaplain Neill reports, he found Acker at a makeshift field hospital that had been set up at the Sudley Church:

> Captain Acker of St Paul, slightly wounded
> in the eye, was lying on the church floor near
> the pulpit. As the groans of those mortally
> wounded were dreadful, he walked out to the
> open air leaning on my arm. As I sat with him
> near a tree, I noticed my trunk containing my

entire wardrobe not far distant, also those of Doctors Stewart and Le Boutillier, all of which became spoils of the enemy. . . . Captain Acker, fearing capture, told me he would like to find our regiment. Taking my arm, we walked down to the ford, not far from the church, and there Colonel Gorman, with such officers and soldiers as he could find, had returned towards Centerville. Meeting Gates Gibbs, a son of Justice Gibbs of St Paul, and one of my Sunday school scholars when I preached in the First Presbyterian Church, driving an empty ambulance, I placed therein Captain Acker.[1]

Acker made it back to camp and escaped capture. He quarreled with Col. Gorman over an unknown topic, and their argument resulted in Capt. Acker's resignation. His gallantry at Bull Run was, however, so conspicuous and noted in Washington that he received a captaincy in the regular army.

He left the First Minnesota on August 8, 1861, and accepted a commission as the captain of Company C in the Sixteenth U.S. Infantry. Initially, he was placed on recruiting duty and ordered to St. Paul. From there he was sent to St. Peter and then to Watertown, Wisconsin. He found recruiting duty irksome, and finally after repeated requests, he was permitted to join his regiment at Munfordville, Kentucky. From then on, he shared with his men the discomforts of camp life, the dangers of picket duty, and the long and arduous marches over horrible roads in Kentucky and Tennessee, made to reinforce Gen. Grant at Pittsburgh Landing, also known as Shiloh.

During the fighting at Shiloh, the men of the regiment were exhausted, and many dropped out along the route. Most hung together, though, and, on the evening of the first day's fight, April 6, 1862, made it to the opposite side of the river, about twelve miles below the landing. There, they stood in the rain until about 4:00 A.M., when they embarked on steamboats for the scene of the conflict. Arriving there at about 6:00 A.M., they disembarked and prepared to participate in the bloody work of that memorable day.

That morning, Captain Acker had dressed in full uniform, and when urged by a friend to change—to at least put on a private's blouse so that he would not be such a target—he replied, "No! If I am to die, I will die with my harness on!" Scarcely had the regiment formed in line—in fact, he was just bringing his company into position—when a Rebel sharpshooter sin-

gled him out. The Rebel discharged his rifle, sending a bullet into Acker's forehead, near his Bull Run wound, killing him almost instantly.

William Acker had been a highly respected citizen of St. Paul, and his death made the front page of the *Minnesota Pioneer*. His body was buried on the battlefield near the Old Shiloh Church, but his remains subsequently were removed by his father and deposited in Oakland Cemetery in St. Paul. After the war the Grand Army of the Republic's (GAR) posts were named in honor of men who had served honorably. One of the first posts in Minnesota was St. Paul's GAR Post #21, and after some discussion, members unanimously chose to name it the William H. Acker Post.

Charles Ichabod Clark
b. July 26, 1831; d. June 18, 1864

Born in Wolfeboro, New Hampshire, Charles Clark and his family moved to Anoka in the mid-1850s, where he found work as a painter. A bachelor, Clark volunteered and was mustered into Company C on June 22, 1861. A month later, as he was about to turn thirty and while fighting in the First Battle of Bull Run, he was wounded, unable to get off the field, and subsequently captured. He finally rejoined his regiment on December 22, 1862, at its camp at Falmouth, Virginia.

After his prisoner exchange, he spent some time with his parents. While at home, he spoke with the editor of the local paper, the *Anoka Star*. After recounting the perils he had escaped, he said, "I have been in many places from which I never expected to come out alive, and though I may have felt fear, I never for one moment lost courage or self possession."

Clark served with many men from the Anoka–Champlin area in Company C. Sewall Waterhouse, James Groat, Aaron Greenwald, Charles Mason, and Turner Pribble were familiar faces. Sewall Waterhouse, a teacher from Anoka, died at Bull Run. In 1862 Groat left the regiment for the cavalry. Mason and Greenwald both died of wounds at Gettysburg. At the time the regiment was mustered out on May 5, 1864, Clark still had six weeks left on his three-year term of enlistment. He and others who had joined after May 1861 were transferred to the First Battalion of Minnesota Infantry. Of their original group, only Pribble was left to join Clark in the battalion. The loss of so many friends was something that bothered Clark but which he accepted as a reality of war.

Charles Ichabod Clark

His letters show he was barely literate but a friendly fellow with a good sense of humor. In 1864 he wrote a letter that succinctly addressed the feel of returning to action once again: "Herd bulets whisl and sen powder burn so yu se we ar bak hom agin."

At the Battle of Petersburg on June 18, 1864, the battalion was sent forward as skirmishers. The fighting lasted from 5:00 P.M. until 10:00 P.M. By the end of the day, it had captured and held the Rebel trenches. During this skirmish, as the men took the trenches, Clark was killed. He was buried at Petersburg. Later, his body was reinterred at a cemetery in Wolfeboro.

In 1904 Thomas Pressnell, a sergeant in Company C, told the following story of Clark's last days on earth. (In the story Clark's middle initial is wrong. Pressnell also states that Clark died of his wounds in October 1864, though other records indicate he died the day of the battle.)

In decorating the graves on Memorial Day of old soldiers who died in battle, the average person little thinks what a small circumstance might have kept among the living the man to whom he is doing the honor. A movement of the head, stooping over to adjust a belt or shoe,

or a step to the side—any of these slight incidents might have kept the man from the bullet's path and preserved his life.

Never was this more forcibly impressed upon my mind than at the battle of Petersburg, Virginia, on June 18, 1864. . . . One of the most promising young men of our regiment, and one to whom I had taken a liking was, Charles R Clark, of Lake City, Minn. He was a brave young fellow, and faithfully served his country from the beginning of the war. He fought in the first battle of Bull Run, and was wounded there. Before entering the battle of Petersburg I assigned Clarke to detail duty, which would keep him pretty much to the rear, and in a position much less dangerous than in the front ranks of fighting men. His term of enlistment expired on June 22, only four more days, so that in view of his past service, he was certainly entitled to some consideration.

Clarke asked if it was his turn to go on detail. It was not, and I told him so, adding that it was the expressed desire of the man whose turn it was that his place should be taken by Clarke. But Clarke would not hear of this arrangement. He said he would not go on detail until his turn, even though his term expired the next day. And he didn't. He was in the thickest of the fight, brave and daring as ever. He was shot, and died of the wound the following October. A bullet struck him in the center of the forehead. If he had gone on detail he would probably have been among the living today. Any one of a score of things might have caused him to jerk his head from in front of that little chunk of lead.

The *Anoka Star* recorded the following in his obituary, printed on July 2, 1864:

Of the many who have fallen in battle none will be more generally missed in the community, and few will be more deeply mourned than the gallant soldier who fell at the assault upon Petersburg. His native wit, humor, cheerfulness of disposition, and kindness and gentleness of manner made him a favorite with all, while his superior mental and moral endowments endeared him to the few who knew him intimately.

Wilson Bernard Farrell

b. August 26, 1829; d. July 4, 1863

Wilson Farrell was born in Cincinnati. His father died while Wilson was quite young. Farrell was apprenticed to a tradesman in Cincinnati, but not liking the business, he moved southwest about thirty miles to Vevay, Indiana.

Farrell was sixteen when the U.S.–Mexican War broke out, and he promptly enlisted. On January 22, 1846, he became a private in Company B of the Third Indiana Infantry, commanded by Capt. Willis Gorman, who afterward was promoted to major. Farrell was with his regiment in all its battles, except Buena Vista, when he was quite sick and in the hospital. He was discharged for disability on February 3, 1847. Coincidentally, fifteen years later, Gorman again would be Farrell's commanding officer—this time in the First Minnesota and a different war.

Upon his discharge in 1847, Farrell returned to Indiana and moved across the river to Covington, Kentucky, where he commanded a volunteer company of militia. He also was for a long time employed as a bookkeeper in a mercantile house in Cincinnati.

He moved to Minnesota in 1856. After residing in the southern part of the state for some time, he moved to St. Paul, where he was soon employed as a bookkeeper by Borup and Oates. He remained in this position until receiving an appointment as clerk in the surveyor general's office in St. Paul. Farrell became a member of the Odd Fellows Lodge and a volunteer fireman with the Minnehaha Engine Company.

He was thirty-one when news of the attack on Ft. Sumter arrived. Immediately upon the first call for volunteers, he assisted James Acker and Samuel Raguet in raising a company of men. He was elected by the men to be their first lieutenant. On August 8, 1861, when Acker was discharged to accept a commission in the U.S. Army, Farrell became the captain of Company C. Regarding Farrell, Col. Colvill later said, "He always distinguished himself. His Company C was particularly noted for discipline, drill and fine appearance. He was a favorite at Div. Hd. Qtrs., being a strict disciplinarian and having a very systematic, prompt accurate business way."

On July 2, 1863, at Gettysburg, Capt. Farrell and his Company C were detached from the regiment, serving as provost guard at division headquarters. Having earned the respect of the generals at division headquarters, the company had acted in this capacity for many months. While acting as provost guard, the men wore the full-dress uniform, consisting of the nine-button frock coat and a stiff black model 1858 Hardee hat. As a rule, the men of the regiment did not wear the dress uniform, preferring a slouch hat (a floppy hat with a wraparound brim) and the four-button sack coat, also called a blouse. Having been detailed as provost guard, Company C did not participate in the July 2 charge.

On the morning of the next day, Gen. Meade told Gen. Gibbon that when the Rebels attacked, he thought it would be at Gibbon's front. Meade told Gibbon that he wanted all the provost guard to be relieved and sent back to the regiment to add as much manpower as possible should a fight occur. Lt. Frank Haskell of Gibbon's staff later recalled:

> General Gibbons called up Captain Wilson Farrell, 1st Minnesota, who commanded the provost guard of his division, and directed him for that day to rejoin his regiment. "Very well, sir" said the Captain as he touched his hat and turned away. He was a quiet, excellent gentleman and a thorough soldier. I knew him well and esteemed him. I never saw him again.[2]

As Lt. William Harmon of Company C remembers Farrell's death:

We all lay low while the artillery duel lasted. When it was over, Captain Farrell ordered me to form the company and added that he would take command himself, something he rarely did. We had hardly begun to advance when he was killed. Just as we were going into action, I caught sight of Heffelfinger, so it happened by chance that we fought near the rest of the First Minnesota, though we had not been with them during the battle.[3]

Every indication points to Company C not joining the repulse of Pickett's Charge until it was well under way. More than one source indicates Farrell was hit while advancing with his company into the fight near the Confederate target, the copse of trees on Cemetery Ridge. This could have been after the regiment

had taken its first shots and then shifted to its right and toward the trees.

Maj. Edward Rice of the Nineteenth Massachusetts was a friend of Farrell's and wrote about the part his regiment and the Forty-Second New York played in repelling Pickett's Charge and of the captain's death:

Our two regiments were ordered forward to the clump of trees: The advance was rapidly thinned by the hostile fire on the flank and in the clump of trees as we came to the line. Captain Farrell, of the First Minnesota, with the company, came in on my left. As we greeted each other, he received his death wound and fell in front of his men, who now began firing.

Lt. Harmon's full account of Farrell's death was reported in the *St. Paul Daily Press* on July 26, 1863:

On the 3d inst., all provost guards were ordered to the front, and thus the guard of which the late Captain Farrell was in command was engaged with the enemy . . . the Captain was one of the first to receive a wound. He was wounded in the breast, when he said to me, "Lieutenant, take command of the company, for I am wounded." Immediately after, and even before he had turned to go to the rear, he received a mortal wound from a minnie ball through the bowels. When he fell, I detailed two men to carry him to the rear. He was put in an ambulance and conveyed to the corps hospital, about two and a half miles from the field. The hospital was an orchard with mother earth for a bed and the canopy of heaven for a covering. Here he died at 12:30 P.M. on the 4th of July. A member of the company remained with him and administered to his wants till the last.

It was utterly impossible to procure even boards with which to make a box, but he was buried in his blanket under the branches of an apple tree. A head board made from a piece of cracker box, engraved with a jack knife by the drummer boy of his company [Henry Fifield], bears his name, rank, and regiment.

Captain Wilson B. Farrell was a good soldier and efficient officer, and in his death his country as well as his friends has sustained a great loss. He was held in high esteem by his brother officers. . . .

This photograph is believed to be of Capt. Wilson Farrell. It was taken from an album that also contained a carte de visite of Lt. Mark Hoyt of Company F. Both men were from St. Paul and may have been friends.

Aaron Greenwald

b. December 6, 1832; d. July 5, 1863

Aaron Greenwald was born in Pennsylvania and died in the same state thirty years later. He moved to Minnesota in about 1854, eventually settling in Anoka, where he found work as a miller in one of the local flour mills. He married the Irish-born Ann Sweeney on December 15, 1858, and they had two sons, born in 1859 and 1860.

When news of the war arrived on April 15, 1861, a message was sent to Willis Gorman, who was holding court in Anoka. Upon its receipt Gorman adjourned court, went outside, and announced what had happened. A meeting was called to sign volunteers to the Union cause, and the twenty-eight-year-old Greenwald was the first to sign up. Some claimed that Greenwald volunteered in the afternoon, when Gorman first made the announcement outside the courthouse. Others stated that the volunteering occurred that night at a recruiting rally.

He was mustered and placed as a corporal in Company C on April 29, 1861. He stood five feet eight and a half inches and had a fair complexion, blue eyes, and light-colored hair. On November 17, 1861, he was promoted to the rank of regimental quartermaster sergeant. Though it has never been stated, this position may have been given out of gratitude by the former Judge Gorman, now commander of the regiment, in recognition of Greenwald's patriotic rush forward to be the first to volunteer. Sometime later, however, Greenwald resigned the position and was transferred back to Company C.

He was a corporal at the time the regiment marched into Gettysburg. On July 3, however, Company C was brought in to shore up the Union line, and during the battle Greenwald was mortally wounded. One account states that he was lying down "after a charge," which would explain the path of the musket ball that killed him; the ball entered his head and lodged in his shoulder. He was not immediately found by his comrades but lay unprotected on the field all night, along with the other dead and dying.

On Saturday, July 4, he was found and brought to the field hospital. He died the next day. Greenwald was buried on the battlefield along with his many other fallen comrades. Nineteen days later, his father arrived to take the body of his son home. Greenwald was put to his final rest at the Jerusalem Union Church Cemetery in Wernersville, Berks County, Pennsylvania.

The epitaph on his gravestone reveals much about his Pennsylvanian German background, including a different spelling of his name. It reads:

> In memory or Aaren Greenewalt
> Son of DANIEL AND MARIA GREENEWALT
> Born on 2 December 1832
> He was a Soldier in the Army of Potomac
> 2 years 3 month and in 9 battles
> He was mortally wounded in the head
> by a musket ball, on 3 July
> Died on 5 of July 1863
> Aged 30 years 7 Month 3 Days
> He left a Widow and 2 sons

After the war local historian A. M. Goodrich wrote a history of Anoka County and defended Aaron Greenwald as the first man to volunteer for the Union:

> Immediately after his inauguration, President
> Lincoln called a conference of the governors of
> the loyal states to consult upon the measures to
> be taken for the preservation of the Union, and
> when the news of the firing of Fort Sumter was

received, Governor Ramsey was in Washington. The president decided to issue a call for 75,000 troops. Governor Ramsey immediately made an offer of a regiment of Minnesota men, which was promptly accepted, and he telegraphed to Lieutenant Governor Ignatius Donnelly and also to former Governor Willis A. Gorman, the substance of his offer. Gorman, who was a Mexican War veteran, was in Anoka attending the session of the district court, which was being held in the Shuler building.

When the telegram reached St Anthony it was placed in the hands of a messenger who carried it with all speed to Anoka. A recess of court was taken at 11 A.M.

Gorman addressed the assembled people and called for volunteers. Aaron Greenwald was the first to record his name, and in all probability he was the first man in America to volunteer for the defense of the Union under the President's call. James W. Groat and five others were enrolled at the same time. Josias R. King and others signed a similar paper agreeing to enlist, at a meeting in St. Paul on the evening of the same day.

Josias King also held claim to being the first man to volunteer for the Union, having run forward at the meeting in St. Paul. King survived the war, however, and Greenwald did not. Thus, Aaron was not around to defend his case, and King's claim was left to stand by most people.

William Harmon

b. June 28, 1835; d. October 28, 1903

William Harmon was born in Lee, Maine, the son of Allen and Charlotte Harmon and the oldest of nine children. He received an education through the sixth grade. In the summer of 1850, the family immigrated to Minnesota, making the trip from Chicago on wagons pulled by oxen and settling in St. Anthony, where his father operated a boardinghouse. Though only fifteen years old, Harmon got a job driving a stagecoach from St. Paul to Stillwater, for which he was paid sixteen dollars a month. Late in the fall of 1851, his father moved the family from St. Anthony and made a claim "out on the territorial road," now known as Hennepin Avenue. Allen Harmon dealt in real estate,

William Harmon

and today, the street next to Hennepin is known as Harmon Place.

In 1852 William took a job with a steamboat company and, by 1857, was able to purchase his own steamboat, the *H. M. Rice,* at a cost of $21,000. He was the boat's captain and did a profitable business as the boat plied its way between Minneapolis and St. Cloud to the northwest.

Though business was very good, when the war broke out, twenty-five-year-old Harmon dropped everything to respond to President Lincoln's call for troops. He attended a recruiting rally in Minneapolis on April 18, 1861, and his signature is third on the list. He was mustered and placed in Company D on April 29, 1861. On May 15 he was made the company's fourth sergeant and was later promoted to first sergeant. On September 13, 1862, he was discharged to accept a commission as the company's second lieutenant. Harmon was a good friend of Christopher Heffelfinger's, the captain of Company D.

In January 1863, Company C was posted as the provost guard at Second Division headquarters, and on March 26, 1863, Harmon was transferred to Company C to become its first lieutenant. He and the company were the provost guard at division headquarters at the time of the charge on July 2, 1863. The next day, the company received orders to return to the front,

This photograph was taken at the headquarters of the Second Brigade, Second Division, Second Army Corps in Culpepper, Virginia, in December 1863. The flag flying in the foreground bares the Second Division's emblem, a white trefoil on a dark-blue background. Harmon had been appointed provost marshal of Gen. Webb's brigade. Harmon can be seen standing in the center of the picture wearing light pants with an open coat, facing the viewer's right and holding something in his hands.

and they arrived in time to participate in the repulse of Pickett's Charge. During the fight Capt. Farrell was killed, and shortly after his death, Lt. Harmon was slightly wounded while in command of the company. Harmon was discharged in St. Paul with the regiment on May 5, 1864, at the expiration of its three-year enlistment.

After the war he worked in the Pennsylvania oil fields, spent some time in Washington, DC, and then returned to Minnesota. He was appointed second lieutenant in the Eighteenth U.S. Infantry on July 21, 1866. He transferred to the Thirty-Sixth U.S. Infantry on September 21, 1866, and was promoted to first lieutenant on November 14, 1867. During this time he commanded troops protecting the engineer corps surveying the Union Pacific Railroad in Wyoming.

In 1869 1st Lt. Harmon was stationed as a commissary officer at the Grand River Indian Agency, located at the junction of the Missouri and Grand rivers in Dakota Territory. In August, Harmon and a few of his men found themselves barricaded in their office, surrounded by many angry Lakota. Fortunately for Harmon and his men, a respected full-blooded Lakota woman named Matilda Picotte Galpin (aka Eagle Woman That All Look At) came to their rescue.

"Shame on you cowards!" she scolded. "To come here, five thousand of you to slaughter a half dozen white men. . . ."

Galpin saved their lives, and during the ordeal, Harmon met Galpin's daughter, Zoe "Lulu" Picotte. Lulu's father was a French-Canadian fur trader who ensured that his daughter was schooled in languages and the arts at a Catholic convent school. She was refined, beautiful, and talented. Harmon conducted a whirlwind courtship, and they were married on June 25, 1870. Rather than risk receiving a regimental assignment that might pit him against Lulu's Lakota relatives, Harmon resigned from the service effective December 31, 1870. He immediately picked up a job as a trading post agent at Grand River.

William and Lulu's first son, Leo, was born at the agency on October 31, 1871. The next year, Harmon was transferred to Ft. Rice as the post trader. Their second son, Milan, was born at Ft. Rice. Between 1875 and 1880, Harmon was post trader at Ft. Abraham Lincoln. At the time the fort was commanded by Col. Custer, and thus, Harmon was working at the fort when Custer rode out to meet the Sioux at the Little Bighorn in 1876. Leaving the trading post business in 1880, Harmon and his family moved to Bismarck in northern Dakota Territory, where he engaged in the real estate business. Their fourth son, Joseph, was born in Bismarck in 1882.

In the summer of 1881, Sitting Bull and his followers had surrendered in Canada and were being returned to the Dakota agencies via steamboat. The steamboat *General Sherman* with its human cargo stopped in Bismarck on the morning of August 1, 1881. On board, Sitting Bull, who was from the Hunkpapa tribe, specifically asked to see Lulu Harmon, the daughter of his respected friend Matilda Galpin, who was also Hunkpapa. Harmon brought his wife on board, and she visited with Sitting Bull, speaking in their native Lakota.

In 1884 Harmon and his family moved to Miles City, Montana, where he purchased a general store and established a two-thousand-head cattle company in a southeastern portion of the state known as Ekalaka. He became a merchant in Miles City. His stationary was printed, "William Harmon, Wholesale and retail dealer in Groceries, Provisions, Crockery and Glassware." He also was known to be a livestock man and a banker while he lived in Miles City, as well as to do contract work in Dakota Territory for the government.

Theodore Roosevelt attended the Stock Growers Convention in Miles City in 1885 and was a guest at the Harmon home. Years later, in 1898, when Harmon's son Leo and his new bride were on their honeymoon, they stopped at the White House to see the president. Roosevelt welcomed them warmly and said, "Your father was a fighter, and I always admired him."

Charles Savage, a comrade from his days in the First Minnesota, also moved to Miles City. In 1887 they traveled together to attend the dedication of the First Minnesota monument at Gettysburg. William O'Brien, another comrade from the First, had become the editor of his own newspaper. After the reunion he wrote, "Comrade William Harmon came from Miles City, Montana and has no reason to regret it. The boys were all glad to see him. Holds his own fairly—a little gray and step not quite so steady."

Lulu died in Miles City in 1895. In his later years, Harmon was very sick. In 1901 he moved to the sol-diers' home in Milwaukee. This move allowed him to get the care he needed and to be near his son Leo, who was about thirty and lived nearby. William Harmon died at the home on October 28, 1903. He was sixty-seven years old. He was buried in Miles City beside his wife and their two sons, Elmer and Milan, who had predeceased him.

The following account was written on July 30, 1897, upon the return of the veterans from the dedication of the First Minnesota monument. It was published in the *Minneapolis Journal.*

Co. C. at Gettysburg
Capt. Wm. Harmon Gives a Bit of Unpublished History.
GEN. MEADE KNEW ALL LEE'S PLANS
and Anticipated Them With the Forces at His Command—Longstreet's Error.

From time to time after the lapse of a third of a century, important details and personal reminiscences of the battles of the civil war get into print for the first time. It is the Journal's good fortune to be able to publish today a story of Gettysburg that has not hitherto been used, a story that is interesting because it explains the movement that Longstreet made for an advance of his skirmishers preparatory to a counter assault after Pickett's charge.

"I have never told this story for publication before," said Captain William Harmon, company C, First Minnesota, now of Miles City, Mont., "but on this occasion of the old regiment's reunion for the dedication of the monument it is possibly of some interest."

"As first lieutenant of Company C, which was the provost guard of the second division of the second corps, General Gibbon's division, I was at the division headquarters on the forenoon of the third day's fight at Gettysburg. About noon General Meade, commander-in-chief, General Hancock, corps commander, and General Gibbon, division commander, came to our headquarters for lunch. The mess chest was taken from the mess wagon and the three generals sat down together to eat and discuss the battle. I was standing nearby and heard all their conversation. In the course of it General Meade said to the others:"

'Lee has concentrated his 160 guns in his center and will soon open fire on our center.

Our artillery will answer, and for a while there will be a grand artillery duel. After it is over, Lee having massed his infantry will attack our center in force. There will be close and desperate fighting, so desperate that every available man must be used. General Gibbon, see that your provost guards are sent to the front after the artillery cease firing.'

"At the conclusion of this accurate prediction of what Lee would do, General Gibbon turned to me and said,"

'Do you hear that Harmon?'

'Yes,' I answered.

'Well, see that your company is there.'

"Almost at this moment Lee fired his two signal guns for the action to commence. One of the shells decapitated Gibbon's orderly, frightened the mess wagon horses so that they overturned the wagon; and the three generals scurried away from the spot where the fire was centered. In a minute it was a very center of death and destruction. We all lay low while the artillery duel lasted. When it was over, Captain Farrell ordered me to form the company and adding that he would take command himself, something he rarely did. We had hardly begun to advance when he was killed. Just as we were going into action, I caught sight of Heffelfinger, so it happened by chance that we fought near the rest of the First Minnesota, though we had not been with them during the battle. I was struck in the belt by a bullet, but in the excitement didn't feel my hurt enough to keep still and getting up went into the melee with the rest of the company."

"Say! but there was fighting for you. If men ever become devils that was one of the times. We were crazy with the excitement of the fight. We just rushed in like wild beasts. Men swore and cursed and struggled and fought, grappled in hand-to-hand fight, threw stones, clubbed their muskets, kicked, yelled and hurrahed. But it was over in no time. Marshall Sherman captured a flag, and as our line of bayonets swept over the ground the rebs threw down their arms. I remember that a confederate officer—who had come up at the head of Pickett's charge—gathered himself up as our men swept by and coolly remarked, 'You have done it this time.'

"Well, then, when the rebs were throwing down their arms and surrendering by the thousands, General Hayes rode along the line swearing like a pirate, as the best men sometimes will in battle. He was trailing a confederate flag in the dust behind his horse and shouting,"

'Stop firing you—fools; don't you know enough to stop firing; it's all over—stop! stop! stop!'

"Then our company was ordered to the front to pick up the straggling prisoners. We advanced clear to the Emmetsburg road, gathering up the defeated men and sending them to the rear. I remember that one confederate private tried to get me to overlook a slightly wounded officer. A little later a straggler lying in a fence corner drew a bead on me, and was about to shoot, when I covered him with my revolver and told him to drop his gun. He did, too, and it was all I could do to keep the boys from killing him."[4]

This belt and buckle were worn by Harmon during the war.

Charles H. Mason

b. 1836; d. August 18, 1863

Charles Mason lived in Anoka and was twenty-five years old when he was mustered and placed in Company D. He was promoted to corporal and then sergeant, and later, when 2nd Lt. Seth Hammond of Company D resigned from the service, Mason replaced him as Company D's second lieutenant. Mason was transferred to Company C on September 27, 1862, as its second lieutenant, replacing William Larned, who had transferred to the signal corps.

Mason applied for a leave of absence on February 13, 1863, to buy the appropriate "uniform of an officer." His photograph, taken in New York City, shows him proudly wearing that new uniform.

Mason was wounded in the hand at the Battle of Gettysburg and was sent to a hospital in Harrisburg, Pennsylvania. The following letter was written by a nurse, Marian Verbeke, whom he met while in the hospital. It is addressed to DeWitt Smith (the captain of Company D) and his family. Smith had been seriously wounded in the hip at Antietam and was sent to a hospital in Harrisburg, where his wife, Melissa, and son, Eugene, came from Minnesota to nurse him back to good health. She had become acquainted with the Smith family while they were in Harrisburg.

My dear friend,

I went to Chestnut Street last Saturday and found a Lieut there very ill and asked him what Regt. he belonged to, he replied the 1st Minnesota. I then spoke of Capt Smith, he said he was Capt of the same Company.

Yesterday he sent me word he would like to see me. When I went down he asked me to write you. His name is Charles A. Mason. He is wounded in the left hand the thumb is off and the hand very much shattered. It commenced festering some days ago and he asked to have it lanced. Dr. Dick refused so to do. He made the request several times and still was refused. Finally he asked to see Dr Wilson our Surgeon General. When he came he expressed surprise that it had not been opened. He immediately lanced it in several places, now it seems to be better and he thinks he will recover speedily. He has rheumatism also. Yesterday he was better than two days before. He said he was a Corporal while you was with the Company and he was under the impression that you thought that he thought that you promoted others when you might have promoted him. He says such was not the case and asked me to tell you so. He sends his love to yourself and family and asked me to tell you to write to him soon. When you write direct to Chestnut Street Hospital or in my care and he will receive it.

I think the Lieut is a good deal worse than he thinks he is but he told me he did not want me to say that he would die for he would not.

I am very busy all of the time in one of the hospitals. We have twenty five men in my ward who are badly wounded and I have them all under my care at present. One man died. He was the first and only man who died since our hospital opened and he was in a dying condition when he was brought in. He lived but a very few hours after he came.

[Eugene,] please tell your father to write to Lieut Mason as soon as he can for I know he will be expecting a letter every day until he gets one. I will close with love to all.

Your true friend,
Marian Verbeke[5]

This letter was written on July 28, 1863. Unfortunately, Mason died on August 18, six weeks after being wounded at Gettysburg and just three weeks after the letter was written. It is not known if he ever received a return letter from his captain, but one would like to hope that he did.

Thomas Pressnell

b. February 8, 1843; d. December 1, 1915

Five weeks after his birth in Shipton, Oxfordshire, England, on March 14, 1843, Thomas Pressnell and his parents immigrated to America, leaving from Liverpool on April 1 and reaching the United States six weeks later. They settled in Monroe, Michigan, and from there moved to what is now Buffalo, New York. Tom's father died in 1848, and that year, his mother moved, eventually settling in Pittsfield, Illinois.

Pressnell's parents wanted him to be a doctor, like his father, but he aspired to either painting or printing as a profession. He went to work at a newspaper whose foreman was John G. Nicholay, who later became Lincoln's private secretary. In 1853 Tom was apprenticed to a publisher in Pittsfield who in 1855 sold his paper and moved to Stillwater, where he purchased a half interest in a paper. Pressnell followed him to Minnesota and worked for that newspaper until the war began. On March 12 and 13, 1862, while the First was on the move in Virginia, he was one of the soldiers to appropriate the *Berryville Conservator* for the Union cause.

He was mustered into service for three months on April 29, 1861, and is recorded as being five feet ten inches and having a fair complexion, blue eyes, and dark hair. When the term of enlistment was changed from three months to three years, Pressnell planned on reenrolling on May 11, but he fell ill and did not recover until July. When the regiment passed through St. Paul on its way east, he was still recovering and, contrary to his doctor's orders, went outside and watched it march through the city. Afterward, he relapsed and did not recover until August 1, so he returned to the Minnesota *Pioneer* and resumed his work as a printer.

Thomas Pressnell

On September 7, 1861, Lt. Samuel Raguet of Company C came to St. Paul with a recruiting party, and Pressnell attempted to reenlist. When he had volunteered in April, he claimed to be eighteen years old, but it had since come to light that he was underage. (I have a document in which Pressnell claims to have been born on February 8, 1843, which, if accurate, would make him eighteen when he tried to enlist. Perhaps, he did not know his own age; perhaps, my document is inaccurate.) Being underage, he needed his parents' consent to enlist, which was difficult to get—his father was dead, and his mother had moved back to England. Sam and Tom found a workaround, however. The lieutenant's father, Col. James Raguet, was appointed Tom's guardian by the Ramsey County probate court, and his new guardian quickly gave his permission. The next day, he resigned his position at the paper, which the editor told him would be waiting for him when he returned from the war.

Pressnell was promoted to corporal at the Battle of Antietam, on September 17, 1862, a difficult day for the Union. During the battle Gen. Sedgwick's division was thrown into nearly hopeless confusion, and Gen. Dana, the former colonel of the First, tried to maneuver hismen into a position to attack. During this action Dana was wounded in the leg. The Minnesotans were on the extreme right of the Union line. Col. Sully masterly maneuvered the men back, and they maintained an orderly withdrawal. As Pressnell recalls:

Owing to the cool head of Sully, the 1st Minnesota was the only organization in the division which maintained anything like organization, and when we were about half way up the slight rise of ground over which we were retreating the Colonel gave the order to face and fire, with the result that a solid volley from about 300 muskets poured into the following enemy and caused a quite appreciable check on their oncoming.[6]

Pressnell mistakenly concluded that the order to turn and fire was an order to stand and fight. As a result, he reloaded and fired a second round before he "discovered that the rest of the boys were several rods in my rear hastily retreating." Sully was so impressed that he later promoted Pressnell to corporal over the objections of Pressnell's company commander. "Had I realized that the boys turned back after they fired their volley, I would have been with them, and in the lead," he later confessed. "So that foolish act of mine, under excitement, but misconstrued by Sully as bravery, that gave me my start in the line of promotion."[7]

During the cold winter of 1862 at the Battle of Fredericksburg, the regiment was in a forward position in support of an artillery battery and under continual Rebel artillery fire. The next night, the men were sent out on picket duty and spent the night digging rifle pits into the cold, open plain. As Pressnell writes of his night:

After three hours of steady hard work on the trenches I was relieved about 2 o'clock for 2 hours rest. In groping around for a place to lie down I came upon a man covered by a large double blanket. Considering that this blanket was large enough to cover two comfortably, I crept in beside him and in 2 minutes was sound asleep. About 4 o'clock I was awakened by a subdued voice and ordered to "fall-in." Observing that my sleeping companion did not move I endeavored to wake him also, but there being no response to my kicks, I passed my hand over his face and thus discovered that I had been sleeping with a dead man.[8]

He was wounded several times. His right eye and face were burned by gunpowder at the Battle of Vienna on September 2, 1862, also called Flint Hill. At Antietam he was slightly wounded on his right wrist. While crossing a field during the Battle of Savage Station, he was painfully wounded in the left groin by a cannonball. Two of his comrades, William Black of St. Paul and Joe McDonald of St. Cloud, also were wounded by the cannon's shot. On August 14, 1864, at the Battle of Deep Bottom, he was slightly wounded on the right hand and was knocked over by a minié ball that hit him in the head. In addition, he was badly scratched on the head by a dose of buck and ball at Farmville, Virginia, on April 7, 1865.

After Flint Hill, Pressnell was confined at a hospital at Harpers Ferry, where he wore a patch over his inflamed and powder-burned eye. Eventually, Pressnell wanted to return to his regiment, but when refused by the doctors, he left of his own accord. He boarded a train bound for Washington with the idea of heading from there to the regiment at Falmouth. Once in Washington, he took some time to see the sights. He found himself near the steps of the White House when a guard stepped forward and challenged him, "What are you doing here?" Pressnell shot back, "Well, I came up to see Abraham Lincoln." In fact, the idea had not occurred to him until he blurted it out. He then continues his story:

But I had now said it. And to fail to at least make an effort would be ignominious retreat, so with quickened step I brushed past him and to the very door, which stood slightly ajar, when to my utmost surprise who should step out but President Lincoln himself, and extending his hand said; "Well here I am, my man, what can I do for you?" at the same time giving my hand a squeeze which I felt for days afterward. "Oh, nothing in particular, only that I was on my way to my regiment at the front I would like to be able to tell the boys that I had the pleasure of shaking hands with Abraham Lincoln." was my stammering answer, o which he said "Well, you can now do that, which is your regiment?" When I gave him the name he said "Why that is Gen. Gorman's old regiment" and complimented both the regiment and the General. He pulled the bandage down so he could see eye and remarked that you have a very bad eye, be careful with it. He then gave me another but less tightened shake by the hand and went back saying "Good bye, God bless you." with what I intended to be a withering look at the orderly who was still standing at "Attention" I proceeded to retrace my steps down the Av. And toward the Soldier's Rest where I was due to take the train in about an hour.[9]

Since Pressnell was with his company serving as provost guard, he did not participate in the July 2 charge at Gettysburg. When the company was ordered back into action the next day, he helped repel Pickett's Charge. After the war he wrote to a friend and discussed the battle; the letter was published in the *Duluth Weekly Herald* on March 3, 1890:

My dear Capt. Searles,

I have received your copy of your paper, "The First Minnesota Infantry" read before the Loyal Legion Jan 4. I must compliment you on your success in "boiling it down" so as to give such a complete, intelligent and satisfactory story of our campaign and battles in such a small space. In your account of the battle of Gettysburg I see you have alluded to myself in connection with the death of Gen Armistead. I have concluded to give you, to be used as you see fit, my recollections of his death and last moments:

After the battle was over, but while everything was confusion and excitement, I was returning from one of the wheat stacks to which I had assisted one of my comrades, toward the point occupied by Cushing's battery. I met a party carrying a wounded man in a blanket. I noticed that one of the party was wounded in the shoulder, so I stepped up and asked him to let me take his place. I immediately saw that the occupant of the blanket was a Confederate officer, and was informed that he was Gen Armistead. He seemed to be badly wounded in the head but was conscious and was talking, though rather incoherently. Among other things he asked was how Gen Hancock was, and on being told that he was wounded, said: "I am sorry; he is a grand man." I remember he said this: "We made a good fight, but lost; thank God Virginia did its duty." He had almost

lost consciousness and died within a very few minutes.

I have seen among published articles of Gen Armistead's death, a statement that he inquired for Gen Hancock and said: "Tell him that he was right and I was wrong." If he used that expression I did not hear it, and I do not believe he did. I have quoted his reference to Gen Hancock as nearly verbatim as possible. The theme of his expression seemed to be that the Virginians had done their duty, and his regret that they had lost. The South had at no time a more loyal or devoted soldier than Gen Armistead on his deathbed.

Yours truly,
T. H. Pressnell

Pressnell was one of the few who served in both the First Minnesota and the First Battalion. After the three-year term was up for the veterans of the First Minnesota, Pressnell was, on March 24, 1864, remustered as a veteran volunteer. On May 5, he was promoted to orderly sergeant of Company A. Pressnell was commissioned as a second lieutenant on December 26, 1864, to fill the hole created when Charles Parker was promoted, and he was promoted to first lieutenant on March 13, 1865, when Parker became the company's captain. Pressnell said that he closed his "fighting career" at Appomattox Courthouse on April 9, 1865. He was promoted to captain of Company B on April 24, 1865.

He served as provost marshal of the Provisional Division of the Army of the Tennessee from May 3 to July 15, 1865, when it was disbanded. This division comprised all the western regiments in the Army of the Potomac. The battalion traveled to Jeffersonville, Indiana, and on July 15, 1865, Pressnell and the battalion were mustered out and discharged from the service.

After the war he worked at the *Minnesota Pioneer* until 1867. He moved to several papers in Northfield and Stillwater and then back to St. Paul before moving north to Duluth. He worked for two newspapers and eventually ended up running the *Duluth Minnesotian*. Pressnell was seventy-two years old when he died in Duluth on December 10, 1915.

Pressnell's sister Nellie married one of his comrades in the First Minnesota, becoming the second wife of Sam Bloomer, who served as the regimental color-bearer from Company B. Nellie died on August 30, 1936, at the age of ninety.

Samuel Raguet

Samuel Raguet

b. August 25, 1837; d. August 4, 1867

Samuel Raguet was born in Zanesville, Ohio. When the war began, he was single, twenty-three years old, and working as a clerk in his father's grocery store in St. Paul. He had been a member of the Pioneer Guard. At six feet two and a half inches tall, with a fair complexion and dark hair, Raguet struck a commanding pose. When he enlisted, he was given a commission as the second lieutenant of Company C.

His cousin Henry Raguet, though also born in Ohio, opted to serve the Southern cause. He became a major in the Confederate army and was killed on March 28, 1862, in New Mexico at the Battle of Glorietta Pass.

Sam Raguet was wounded at Bull Run on July 29, 1861. Charles Hazlett mentions him in a letter home to Raguet's father:

> Dear Sir:
>
> I telegraphed you yesterday that Samuel was wounded by a buck shot in the neck. I procured the services of Zanesville, who extracted the ball. It was a very severe operation, but Sam stood in manfully. He is now doing very well. The shot entered the right side of his neck about three fourths of an inch below the ear, passing the jaw bone without injuring it, and around until it struck the bone in the back part of the neck. It made a very deep and severe looking wound. It did not pass through in the throat, however. The ball was completely flattened out against the bone. You need not give yourself uneasiness in regard to his not receiving the proper care and treatment. We have quite a number of patriotic Northern ladies who have come here as nurses. They are very kind; and you could not wish for better treatment than you would receive at their hands.
>
> Samuel walked nearly the whole distance from the battlefield to this city, arriving here about nine o'clock Monday morning. He was wounded in the second fire of the traitors, but remained on the field and fought manfully all day. His sword was broken in the first of the fight. He has a sword that he took from a "Secesh" cavalryman. He held his revolver

Second Lt. Raguet took this sword from the Confederate cavalryman he killed at Bull Run. The cavalryman probably was a member of the Fourth Virginia Cavalry, also known as the Black Horse Cavalry, which attacked the regiment and lost many men in doing so.

towards the above named traitor, and he fell, Sam having relieved him of the trouble of doing more damage.

There was such chaos after the fiasco at Bull Run that Raguet did indeed end up walking all the way back to Washington, DC, from the battlefield, arriving at about nine o'clock the next morning. He manfully withstood the difficult and painful operation that followed.

On August 8, 1861, he was transferred to Company I as its first lieutenant. Sometime later, he was transferred once again, this time to Company E. On July 15, 1862, he became the aide-de-camp to Gen. Willis Gorman. Raguet was discharged from the service on May 4, 1864. He died in St. Paul just three years later, on August 4, 1867. He was only thirty years old.

Marshall Sherman

b. 1823; d. April 19, 1896

Born in Burlington, Vermont, Marshall Sherman settled in St. Paul in 1849 and was working as a painter when the war began. He was mustered on April 29, 1861. He was thirty-seven years old, stood five feet six inches tall, and had a fair complexion, black eyes, and black hair.

Marshall Sherman's name goes down in the annals of First Minnesota history as the man who captured the battle flag of the Twenty-Eighth Virginia Infantry at Gettysburg on July 3 during Pickett's Charge. For his gallantry during the battle, he was awarded the Medal of Honor.

After his three-year enlistment, he was one of only a few veterans of the Old First to reenlist and helped form the nucleus of the First Battalion of Minnesota Infantry. On August 14, 1864, at the Battle of Deep Bottom in Virginia, he was shot in the left foot. The wound was severe, and the leg was amputated at Campbell Hospital. He was then sent to the Soldier's Rest General Hospital in Boston. He was fitted for and, on July 8, 1865, furnished with an artificial leg that had been made by Jewitt of Salem, Massachusetts. Sherman was declared unfit for service in the Veteran Reserve Corps and discharged for disability on July 25, 1865. The following is a brief excerpt from a St. Paul newspaper at the time:

Lost a Leg.—The State Agent for the relief of our soldiers in the hospitals at Washington writes that Marshall Sherman, of the First

Marshall Sherman

Marshall Sherman in civilian clothes showing his artificial leg, the price he paid for being wounded at Deep Bottom in 1864

Battalion, has had his leg amputated, and is doing well. Mr. Sherman is well known in St Paul. He was formerly a painter here.

Sherman returned to St. Paul and the life of a civilian crippled from the war, like thousands of other veterans. At first he worked as a painter and, later, went into the life insurance business. He died in St. Paul on April 19, 1896, at the age of seventy-three. He was buried in the Soldiers Rest area of Oakland Cemetery in St. Paul. His headstone denotes that he was a recipient of the Medal of Honor.

7

COMPANY D
THE LINCOLN GUARDS (MINNEAPOLIS)

O N APRIL 18, 1861, FIVE DAYS AFTER Rebel forces had forced the surrender of Ft. Sumter, a patriotic rally in support of the Union was held in
Minneapolis. Speeches were given, and men were recruited to volunteer.
H. R. Putnam helped to secure enlistments of many
of the members of Minneapolis' militia unit, known
as the Lincoln Guards. Though little is known of who
was in it, these men became the nucleus of Company
D. Many others also stepped forward and, by putting
their names on paper, stated that they would volunteer for the requested three months to serve their
country and help put down the insurrection.

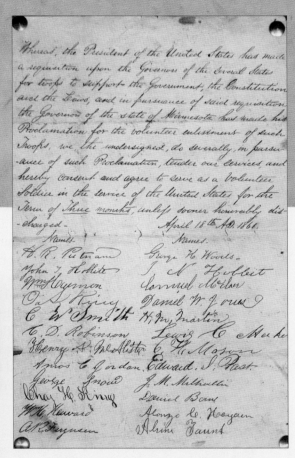

Pictured here is a portion of the document the
men signed. Some signatures are of men who
decided not to stay once the request was made
to volunteer for three years, but some are familiar,
including H. R. Putnam, William Harmon, Charles
Mason, and Daniel Bond.

This photograph was taken in 1857 from Second Avenue South and Washington Avenue, looking east toward St. Anthony Falls. In the foreground
is the office of the *Minnesota Democrat* newspaper. When this photo was
taken, Minneapolis was smaller than its neighbor across the river, the village of St. Anthony. In 1860 the combined population of the two cities was
around three thousand.

Charles E. Baker

b. circa 1842–43; d. July 2, 1863

In the 1850s Charles Baker's family moved from Utica, New York, to Barnesville in Clay County, Minnesota. By 1861 the family had grown to nine children, of which Charles was the second oldest. Family life for the Bakers was made hard by their father, William, who was an alcoholic and rendered nearly blind by bad liquor, and so support of the family fell to Charles and his brothers.

The nineteen-year-old Baker was working in the town of Rosemount when news of the war arrived. He said goodbye to his family and traveled to Ft. Snelling to enlist in the army. He was mustered on May 29, 1861.

This photograph of Baker was probably taken in late November 1861 while the regiment was in winter camp at Poolesville, Maryland, which they called Camp Stone. While there, the unit was issued new clothes, of which Sgt. James Wright of Company F writes:

> More clothing also came, and this time we drew overcoats and dress coats, and new hats with a feather on one side and a brass spread eagle on the other. There were also "shoulder scales" and some other redundant "brass work" which we transported for a time and then "chucked it overboard" on the Peninsula.

A photo of Pvt. Adelbert Bryant, also of Company D, shows him in the same style of new nine-button frock coat (see p. 109). It is dated December 3, 1861, and shows a similar photographer's studio background.

On July 2, 1863, the morning of his parent's twenty-third wedding anniversary, Baker stood shoulder to shoulder with his comrades and friends. He now knew these men well—men he could count on and men who could count on him. In front was the Confederate army, specifically the men of Gen. Wilcox's brigade, who greatly outnumbered the roughly 271 men in the ranks of the First Minnesota that day. One can only wonder at Baker's thoughts as he readied to charge. As the regiment stood in line and prepared to move down the slope toward Plum Run, Baker was shot and died instantly, among the first of many who sacrificed their lives in that charge.

Later, his body was identified, and he was buried on the slope where he was killed. By November, when the Gettysburg National Cemetery was dedicated, his body was moved to grave no. 10, section B, of the Minnesota plot. Today, he lies there along with over fifty of his comrades who also died at Gettysburg.

Baker used this stencil to mark his equipment and personal items.

Adelbert Bryant

b. February 9, 1841; d. February 21, 1901

Adelbert "Del" Bryant was born in Windsor, Maine. At the war's outbreak, he was working as a blacksmith at the Pickin's Blacksmith Shop in Monticello, Minnesota. The local paper reported the following action:

> As the whistle of the steamboat was heard last Monday and our volunteers were hurrying to get aboard, a young man, D. Bryant, of this place, who was engaged in Pickin's Blacksmith Shop, could withstand his patriotic feelings no longer, and dropping his sledge hammer he put for the boat, minus coat, carpet bag or any preparations, and manfully resisting the entreaties of his sisters and relatives he embarked in his countries cause.[1]

Bryant was mustered as a private in Company D on May 21, 1861. He was twenty-one years old, stood five feet nine inches tall, and had a light complexion, gray eyes, and brown hair. His photograph probably was taken, like Charles Baker's, while the regiment was in winter camp at Poolesville, Maryland. In late November the regiment was issued new nine-button frock coats and black Hardee hats with ostrich plumes. Many of the men went right to the photographer's

tent and had their pictures taken, sending them home with a letter. Inside the case that encloses Bryant's photograph is written, "Received Dec 3, 1861, Adelbert Bryant, Age 22 years." As mentioned, Charles Baker's picture (see p. 108) was taken with a similar backdrop and is dated on its reverse, "Dec, 1861."

Bryant participated in most of the regiment's battles, though he did not take part in the Seven Days' Battles in late June 1862. Around June 8, 1862, he had

This carte de visite is of Bryant as a second lieutenant in Hatch's battalion of cavalry. Bryant is on the left, and Capt. George Whitcomb of Company B is on the right.

contracted a severe cold—fever and ague—that rendered him unfit for duty. William Irvine mentions him in a letter written home on July 13, 1862. He writes, "Del was sick with the teams therefore was not in the fight. He has the fever and ague, shook a good deal but is better now; sits beside me now writing to his father. He is not very strong yet."

He was sent to the Second Corps' hospital at Bolivar Heights, Virginia, on October 30, 1862. On December 1, he was sent to the army's convalescent camp in Alexandria, Virginia. He was discharged for disability on January 28, 1863. The specific problem was listed as "Incipient Consumption with a deposit of tuberculosis in left lung."

He returned home to recover, and six months later, on July 2, 1863, enlisted in Hatch's Battalion, Minnesota Volunteer Cavalry, as a sergeant in Company B. Later, he was promoted to first sergeant and, on July 6, 1865, was commissioned as a second lieutenant in the company. He served in the unit from July 23, 1863, until discharged with the company on June 9, 1866.

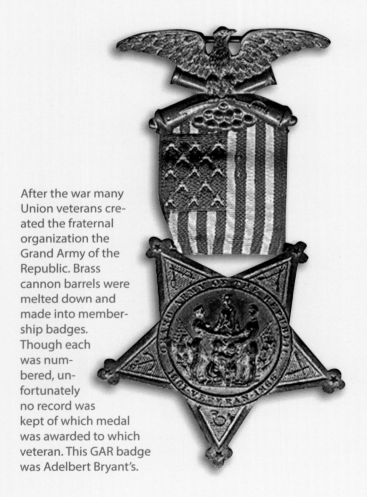

After the war many Union veterans created the fraternal organization the Grand Army of the Republic. Brass cannon barrels were melted down and made into membership badges. Though each was numbered, unfortunately no record was kept of which medal was awarded to which veteran. This GAR badge was Adelbert Bryant's.

Christopher B. Heffelfinger
b. January 13, 1834; d. November 7, 1915

Born in Cumberland County, Pennsylvania, Christopher Heffelfinger came to Minneapolis in 1857 and was working as a painter when the war broke out. Mustered in on April 29, 1861, he was made a sergeant, and in August after the First Battle of Bull Run, he was promoted to first sergeant. On November 27, 1861, Heffelfinger was promoted to second lieutenant, and on September 17, 1862, he was promoted to first lieutenant.

At Gettysburg, Heffelfinger commanded Company D and, during the July 2 charge, was one of the fortunate few to escape relatively unscathed. In the following excerpt from his wartime memoirs, he describes the position of his company once they had reached Plum Run and were receiving the worst of the enemy's fire:

In the charge the position of the enemy threw the right wing of the regiment closer to the enemy's line than the left wing; consequently this wing received the effects of the fire first and suffered a great loss.

Upon reaching the ravine, we halted and engaged the enemy in our immediate front; the right wing, being more crippled in the first firing than the left, retired a little in advance of the left; consequently, the left wing had more or less a flank fire from our right. At this time, or within a very few minutes, and while in this position, Company D lost three men killed and ten or twelve wounded. I received a slight wound, which was very painful, but not of a serious nature. While here, my attention was concentrated on the front, and I did not notice the colors go to the rear. Sergeant Martin called my attention to the fact that the right of the regiment was retiring. I immediately ordered my company to the rear and we fell back on a line with the battery.[2]

Company D lost three men killed in action that day and four who later died of wounds. The three men referred to in his story may be privates Charles Baker, Marcus Past, and Joseph Prime. A total of eighteen more were wounded.

Christopher Heffelfinger in his second lieutenant's uniform

During the fight a minié ball pierced Heffelfinger's coat and hit the top of the pocketbook he carried in his inside breast pocket. The ball broke the pencil on the inside cover, glanced off, and seared the skin of his chest, almost knocking him down. Had the book not been positioned in just the right spot, Heffelfinger would have been severely wounded or possibly killed. He carried the book with him through the rest of the war.

On July 25, 1863, he was promoted to the rank of captain of Company D, backdated to July 4. This last promotion helped fill the holes left by the many officers who had been killed or seriously wounded at Gettysburg. On December 20, 1863, while on leave, he married Mary E. Totten in Pittsburgh. She stayed in Pennsylvania while he returned to the war. He continued to serve with his unit until they were discharged in May 1864.

In 1865 he was tendered a commission as major of the First Minnesota Heavy Artillery by Governor Stephen Miller. He served with them in Chattanooga, Tennessee, from April to September. They then returned to Ft. Snelling and were discharged in October 1865.

Shortly after the war, the veterans of the First Minnesota began to hold annual reunions, and at the reunion held in White Bear Lake on June 17, 1869, he was elected president of the First Minnesota Association. He also was a member of the Minnesota Commandry of the Loyal Legion of the United States, a fraternal organization whose members had served as officers in the Union army. He was offered the commandership of the organization twice but refused because of defective hearing. He was made vice commander, however, which also placed him on the staff of the National Commandry of the Loyal Legion.

He was one of the commissioners of the project to erect a Minnesota monument on the field at Gettysburg commemorating the unparalleled charge of the Old First. He was there for its dedication in 1897, as well as in 1913 for the fiftieth reunion of the battle. Christopher Heffelfinger died on November 7, 1915, and was buried at Lakewood Cemetery in Minneapolis.

John Wesley Plummer

b. December 14, 1838; d. May 7, 1867

John Plummer was born in Lower Dublin Township, Pennsylvania. In 1853 his family moved to Brooklyn Township and established a farm. He was a quiet and unassuming man who attended Methodist school in 1856–57. He had excellent penmanship and was very articulate, as can be seen in his letters. He was working as a plasterer when the war began, and at the age of twenty-one, he enlisted. He was mustered on April 29, 1861, and during the course of his service, he was promoted to corporal, on May 11, 1862, and to sergeant on November 1, 1862.

At Gettysburg on July 2, 1863, the regiment stood in line and watched the Union troops of the Third Army Corps panic and run from the Confederates. Shortly after the battle, John recalled his thoughts in a long letter to his brother at home:

As I saw our men fall back, rally, and fall back again, skedaddlers rushing to the rear in squads, I never felt so bad in my life. I thought sure the day was gone for us, and felt that I would prefer to die there, rather than live and suffer the disgrace and humiliation a defeat of our army would entail on us, and if I ever offered a sincere

prayer in my life, it was then, that we might be saved from defeat. We all felt but resolved when our chance came to do our best to retrieve the fortunes of the day, hardly expecting to come out of the conflict unharmed.

His prayer was answered when moments later the unit rushed to fill the hole created by the retreating troops. History was in the making.

Our turn soon came. We were ordered forward against the enemy, who were then within musket range of us, and if any ever were willing and anxious to go forward into what we all could see was a deadly place, our boys were.

About the charge, he writes: "The bullets were coming like hailstones, and whittling our boys like grain before the sickle." During their fierce fighting, a time came when they had to withdraw to where they had started.

We dreaded to go back for the dangers of it, more than staying there. . . . We fell back, and it was then I had the first feeling of fear during the fight. I felt almost sure I would be hit, and I saw many wounded going back.[3]

Plummer, one of the few who made it back unharmed, survived the next day's battle, as well. On July 5, after having spent some time burying their dead, the First Minnesota and the Army of the Potomac left the battlefield and chased after Gen. Lee and his army, which had headed back to Virginia. In February the regiment returned to Minnesota, where Plummer and all the three-year veterans were mustered out of service on May 5, 1864.

On August 2, 1864, he enlisted and was mustered as a recruiting lieutenant for the Eleventh Minnesota. His job was to raise Company F by September 5 or his commission would be null and void. He raised the company and was promoted to captain on August 22. Once mustered, the regiment was sent to Gallatin, Tennessee. On November 23, 1864, he was transferred from command of his company and assigned to duty as provost marshal of the District of Tennessee in Nashville. He was mustered out of the service on June 26, 1865.

After the war Plummer served as clerk of the Hennepin County District Court. In 1867 he died from consumption (tuberculosis) while staying at his father's home. He was twenty-nine years old.

Henry Roscoe Putnam

b. January 21, 1832; d. February 12, 1872

In 1861 Henry Putnam was a twenty-nine-year-old carpenter living in Minneapolis. One of the first to volunteer, his name is first on the roll signed at the April 18, 1861, recruiting rally in Minneapolis. He also helped secure the enlistments of the Lincoln Guards, who became the nucleus of Company D, and they elected him their captain. Since he did not like being called Henry, the men called him Capt. Put, and his fellow officers called him HR.

On July 21, 1861, he was seriously wounded at the First Battle of Bull Run. In a letter printed in the *Minneapolis State Atlas* in August 1861, Pvt. Edward Past writes:

> We were drawn up in a line of battle. Shells were falling thick and fast. Our Captain Putnam gave the order to fire, which we did in one tremendous volley, pouring death and destruction into the ranks of the enemy. This we did

three times, when, overpowered by superior numbers, we were forced to fall back. Captain Putnam was shot down, a bullet striking him in the right arm near the shoulder joint. His wound was bandaged but our gallant Captain Put marched at the head of his company like a true soldier. He did not leave the field even though severely wounded. Had it not been for him I greatly fear our whole regiment would have sustained a much greater loss.

In a letter home John Hoblitt mentions the same incident:

> When Capt Putnam was shot the ball struck with such force as to knock him down. "O God!" exclaimed one of the boys, "our Captain is killed."
> "Go ahead boys" cried the Captain as he jumped to his feet. "I'll take care of myself!"

On August 8, 1861, Capt. Putnam resigned his commission in the First Minnesota in order to accept a commission as a captain in the Twelfth U.S. Infantry. He then served as the commanding officer at Ft. Sandy Hook in New York City. He played a major role in stopping the New York City draft riots in July 1863 and was described as a "gallant officer with cool courage."

Maj. Putnam after his service with the First Minnesota

He was promoted to major and aide-de-camp in the volunteer army on October 7, 1864. He was promoted to brevet major in the regular army on March 13, 1865, for "gallant and meritorious service during the riots in New York City in 1863." On March 26, 1865, he was promoted to brevet lieutenant colonel in the regular army for "faithful and meritorious service during operations against the city of Mobile, Alabama, and its defenses." He was honorably discharged from the volunteer army on July 20, 1865.

After the Civil War, Putnam stayed in the army, enlisting in the Twenty-First U.S. Infantry on September 21, 1866. In 1869 and 1870, he commanded several companies of men, including his brother, Capt. James Edward Putnam (also an officer in the Twelfth Infantry), and was ordered to rebuild Ft. Hall, near the town of Pocatello in Idaho Territory. A Mt. Putnam near Pocatello is named after the two Putnam brothers.

Due to ill health and at his own request, Maj. Putnam resigned his commission and was honorably discharged on November 23, 1870, his wound from Bull Run perhaps being a partial cause. He moved to Helena, Montana, to be closer to his family: his wife, three children, father, and mother. He died fifteen months later on February 12, 1872, at the age of forty.

DeWitt Clinton Smith

b. August 20, 1825; d. October 28, 1864

DeWitt Clinton Smith was born in Barre, New York, just a few miles from the Erie Canal. The canal was completed in 1825, the year of Smith's birth, and the governor at the time was DeWitt Clinton. Governor Clinton was one of the prime movers in getting the canal constructed, and undoubtedly, Smith was named after him.

In 1845 Smith moved to Adrian, Michigan, and on July 6, 1847, in Jackson Mills, he married Melissa R. Shepard, who also was from Barre. DeWitt and Melissa had a son, Eugene, born March 20, 1850. Later, while some of Smith's family were moving to Minnesota, he and Melissa decided to move to Roscoe, Illinois, instead. There, they taught school, Smith also acting as the principal. In October 1857 they joined Smith's family and moved to Osseo, where they bought a farm. In 1859 he was elected county commissioner of Brooklyn Township, and as a letter written on January 10, 1861, indicates, he was also appointed postmaster of Osseo.

When the war began, Smith was thirty-five years

DeWitt Clinton Smith

old. He enlisted in the First Minnesota and was commissioned as a lieutenant in Company D. On Thursday, May 8, 1861, the ladies of St. Anthony and Minneapolis presented flags to companies D (Minneapolis) and E (St. Anthony).

When the term of enlistment changed from ninety days to three years, Company D's ranks thinned substantially and Capt. Putnam and 1st Lt. George Woods went out on recruiting details, leaving 2nd Lt. Smith in charge. While they were out, Col. Gorman and the new soldiers received from the ladies of St. Anthony and Minneapolis an invitation to a picnic to be held on Nicollet Island. On Tuesday morning, May 21, 1861, eight companies marched out Ft. Snelling's gate and on to Minneapolis. Once there, the troops took turns crossing the recently constructed suspension bridge. A photographer set up his camera and took an ambrotype of the men of Company D, with Smith standing in command at their front. Smith purchased the picture and left it with his wife when he went east with the regiment.

Before leaving for the East, he wrote to his wife and encouraged her to bring the family for a photograph. He wrote, "Have the boys bring you down on Thursday to get the likenesses taken." The *St. Cloud Democrat* made the following notation on July 4, 1861:

On Friday afternoon all was bustle at Ft Snelling.—It was a pleasant and novel sight, the clean, white tents ranged in two streets, the back part of the tents in the two center rows coming close together.—To the right of the colonel's tent, and in range with it stood the Surgeon's tent.—Capt Acker and his two lieutenants Farrell and Ragent [Raguet] occupied the same tent, but Lieutenant [DeWitt C.] Smith, of Company D, had a separate tent to the left of Capt Putnam's as his wife and son were with him.

On June 22, 1861, the troops boarded two paddle wheelers, the *War Eagle* and the *Northern Belle*, and headed down the Mississippi, stopping at several cities along the way so that soldiers and loved ones could say good-bye.

Pvt. John Hoblitt mentions Smith in a letter, published in a Minneapolis newspaper after Bull Run, about officers' remaining calm and in command dur-

Second Lt. DeWitt Clinton Smith, his wife, Melissa, and his son, Eugene, taken in June 1861

Taken on May 21, 1861, this exquisite ambrotype is the earliest-known photograph of First Minnesota troops and the only picture known to exist that shows the new volunteers still dressed in civilian clothes, with some regulation uniforms mixed in. Also seen is the flag presented on May 8, 1861, by the ladies of Minneapolis to the men of Company D. The men hold Model 1855 Springfield Rifle-Muskets with bayonets. The men had been issued military leather gear, underwear, socks, and woolen overshirts purchased from a St. Paul wholesale supply house known as Culver and Farrington. The overshirts were cheap, ready-made clothing intended for the Indian trade. The shirts were of various colors, predominantly red. They had also been issued black felt hats, plus black and dark-blue pants that had been hastily sewn the week before to military specifications. Second Lt. DeWitt Smith stands in front of his company. He purchased the ambrotype and gave it to his wife.

Capt. Smith and his family in 1863 after their return to Minneapolis so that he could recover from his wound received at Antietam

ing battle: "Lieut. Smith of our company was decidedly the coolest man whom I saw in the fight. The men all declare that he is brave as brave can be." Smith was promoted to captain on August 8, 1861, to replace Henry Putnam, who received an appointment in the U.S. Infantry.

Having some trouble with asthma, Smith requested a furlough to Minnesota so that he could recover at home. The only remaining officer in the company was, however, Seth Harmon, who was already in Minnesota recovering from a rupture received at Bull Run. And he was finding reasons not to return as speedily as the colonel had ordered. On January 17, 1862, Smith finally got his furlough. He stopped in Michigan on his way home, where his wife and son lived during the war. On May 6, 1862, he returned to the regiment and again assumed command of the company. A strict officer, he created some enemies but soon proved a competent leader.

At the Battle of Antietam on September 17, 1862, a minié ball badly wounded his left hip, lodging in his pelvis, about three inches form his spine. Privates Dan Sullivan and Mark Past of Company D carried him off the field, and he was taken to a hospital in Hagerstown, Maryland, ten miles away. Surgeon Jacob Stewart of the First and other doctors attended to him, but the ball was never extracted. The surgeons told him that one of the nerves in his leg had been severed, produc-

ing a partial paralysis in his left leg, and he had to rest until a new one formed. For his few remaining years, even the slightest change in weather could cause him great discomfort.

Melissa and Eugene traveled east, staying to nurse him back to health. Eventually, the family returned to Minneapolis, where he is reported as recovering from at least January 22, 1863, to April 6, 1863. In August 1863 Smith transferred to Company G as its captain, but his wound continued to bother him. He resigned from the service on October 7, 1863.

Back home, he was appointed state librarian by his comrade and fellow officer Stephen Miller, who had been elected governor. This position did not last long, however, and shortly thereafter, Smith sought and received a position as a paymaster in the army and headed south once more. With Smith's departure, Governor Miller appointed Melissa Smith to replace her husband as state librarian. Smith was commissioned a major on February 23, 1864, and reported to a Maj. G. L. Febiger in St. Louis. He served in the pay district of Missouri and Tennessee from July 1864 until he was mortally wounded.

DeWitt Smith died on October 28, 1864, at Randolph, Tennessee, of wounds received in an attack by Confederate guerrillas while he was on the steamboat *Belle of St. Louis.* The guerrillas lured the boat to an advantageous point and attacked, and Smith died de-

This photograph of Maj. DeWitt Smith was taken sometime between the date of his commission, February 23, 1864, and his death on October 28, 1864.

fending it. His nephew, nineteen-year-old Andrew J. Smith, was serving as a clerk in the Paymaster's Department during the summer of 1864, most probably at Smith's request, and was on board the *Belle* when it was attacked. Thus, he was there when Smith was killed. His body was sent to Roscoe, Illinois, where he was buried in his father-in-law's family plot in the town cemetery.

The following report wonderfully details the attack in Tennessee and Smith's service to his country at the very end of his life:

Sir:

As the senior officer on board, under orders from headquarters, District of West Tennessee, I have the honor to submit the following as a report of the trip of the steamer Belle of St Louis, from Memphis, Tenn., to this place:

We left Memphis at or about 6 P.M. of the 27th instant with a large number of passengers, including several officers and about fifty discharged or furloughed soldiers. Of

this number six were paymasters returning to Saint Louis from payment of the troops in the field. They had with them, I was informed by one of the corps, about $40,000. The steamer reached Randolph, Tenn. about 12 o'clock of the same night, landed, and proceeded to take on board eight bales of cotton under permit of the military authorities at Memphis, the port from which the boat was cleared. The cotton belonged to one Harris, who was the first to leave the boat. He appeared to hasten at once to the top of the bank and immediately a party of armed rebels, numbering, I should think, at least fifty, rushed toward the boat, discharging their arms, and attempted to get on. Only six of them succeeded, as Capt. Alexander Zeigler, master, as soon as they were discovered, ordered that the steamer be backed into the stream, which was done, leaving the second clerk, Mr. George Atherton, and crew ashore. The rebels on board entered the engine room at once, ordered the engines to be reversed, and the boat run to the landing. By their knowledge of their duties and their coolness they succeeded in only complying with part of their orders, kept the boat at a sufficient distance from the shore to prevent others from getting on board. Defeated in their effort these rebels then attempted to reach the pilot and compel him to execute the orders they had given the engineers. By this time, the passengers had not only become thoroughly aroused, but most thoroughly panic-stricken. The appearance of the rebels in the cabin and their orders to surrender gave rise on the part of many to the belief that we were then past relief. The only arms on board were pistols in possession of the officers, and in many cases these were either with their baggage in the party's room or in unserviceable condition. My first effort upon observing the critical condition of affairs was to see that orders were given not to land the steamer under any circumstances, knowing that under way these rebels on board could easily be disposed of by superior numbers. Majors Smith and Beeler, paymasters, with their pistols, advanced to the forward part of the boat just as the men before mentioned were ascending to seize the pilot. Shots were at once exchanged and Major Smith severely wounded, from the effects of which he died on the evening of the succeeding day. Major Beeler received a severe wound in the breast, but continued to fight until he had killed one and mortally wounded another. He then was able to return to the cabin and lingered until about noon of the succeeding day. The rebels then observing their failure to capture the boat and being aware of their own danger, escaped by jumping overboard. I do not know whether they succeeded in reaching the shore or not. Mr. L. F. McGowan, paymaster's clerk, one of the engineers sick in his berth, and a negro were severely, though not fatally, wounded. Majors Smith and Beeler deserve great praise for their bravery and presence of mind. Both had previously served in the line of the army with commendable distinction.

The pilots, S. A. McPheeters, Lewis Moan, and assistant Charles Ziegler stood by the wheel and never flinched, though shots were repeatedly discharged at them. John McBride, engineer, and John Dorris and George Beebe, assistants, never left their posts, even while their lives were threatened. To all the officers of the boat, and these in particular, especial credit is due for the display of coolness and bravery, which saved the boat and passengers from capture. Permit me to say that no suspicion of collusion with the rebels, who were a portion of Forrest's command, rests upon Captain Zeigler or any officers of the steamer. The permit for the boat to land was seen by the Government aide on board, Mr. Peterson, who was left with the rebels, all were exonerated from blame.

The steamer arrived at Cairo on last evening without further molestation.

I have the honor to be, very respectfully, your obedient servant,
Colonel Loren Kent,
29th Illinois Infantry
Cairo, ILL., October 29, 1864[4]

Sometime after Smith's death, Melissa moved to Wisconsin with their son. On January 1, 1884, she married Lent B. Bradley of Beloit, Wisconsin. After his death she apparently moved back to Minnesota. As of January 2, 1903, she was seventy-five and living in the town of Benson in Swift County, Minnesota. She died in 1905 and was buried in Osseo, where she and DeWitt had begun their life in the state almost half a century earlier.

COMPANY E
THE ST. ANTHONY ZOUAVES

AT THE TIME OF THE CIVIL WAR, though smaller than St. Paul but larger than Minneapolis, St. Anthony boasted its own militia unit. Known as the St. Anthony Zouaves, they were perhaps more of a show than a formidable foe for any potential hostile Indians. Their uniform consisted of red Turkish pants, blue jackets, and a red fez, making as the *Minnesota Pioneer* recorded on April 14, 1861, "a blending of bright colors at once striking and pleasing." Men from this group formed the core of Company E.

The St. Anthony harness shop in which George Boyd worked prior to the war is the flat-roofed front farthest from the camera. Note the large boot outside, which advertises their leather trade. Straight down the street are the twin towers of the suspension bridge, with Minneapolis on the other side.

This is a daguerreotype of George and Nancy Boyd at some time prior to her death on February 17, 1857, while giving birth to their son, George.

George Boyd Jr.

b. 1831; d. August 21, 1879

George Boyd Jr. was born in St. Stephen, New Brunswick, Canada, and spent his childhood in Calais, Maine, becoming a U.S. citizen in 1853. He married Nancy Williams, also from Calais, and in about 1855, they moved to St. Anthony, where John Noble employed him as a harness maker. Incidentally, the law office next door belonged to William Lochren, with whom Boyd served in Company E. Along with his work in the harness shop, Boyd volunteered as the assistant foreman on Engine No. 1 in the fire department. On February 12, 1857, tragedy struck the family as Nancy died giving birth to their son, George Jr. She was buried in Beltrami Park in St. Anthony. In 1859, he gave his son to the care of a family member and moved in with Noble and George Pomeroy, who ran a store nearby and who also went on to serve as an officer in the regiment.

When war was declared, Boyd and Pomeroy immediately enlisted. Boyd is recorded as standing six feet one inch tall and having a fair complexion, brown

hair, and blue eyes. He was mustered in on April 29, 1861, as a sergeant in Company E and was promoted to first sergeant on October 22, 1861. From late August to early December 1862, Boyd was hospitalized for general disability and spent time in various army hospitals. He returned to duty on December 8, 1862. On April 15, 1863, while the regiment was in camp at Falmouth, Virginia, he was promoted to first lieutenant in Company I.

During the July 2 charge at Gettysburg, he was severely wounded in the right thigh.On July 18 he received a wounded furlough and returned to his native Calais to rest and recover. Two months later, on September 25, he received orders to report to the medical director in Georgetown, Maryland, and spent a week at Seminary Hospital. On October 1 he returned to the regiment. Though he served out his enlistment, his wound left him lame for the rest of his life. He was mustered out with the regiment on May 5, 1864.

Boyd reenlisted in Hatch's Battalion, Minnesota Volunteer Cavalry, on August 31, 1864, and was commissioned as the captain of Company E. With the battalion he served on the frontiers in western Minnesota and Dakota Territory.

In January 1866, toward the end of his military career, he returned to his childhood home of Calais and, on January 16, married his sister-in-law, Sarah A. Williams, Nancy's twenty-four-year-old sister. Boyd was mustered out of the service for the last time on May 1,

To the right is a silver-wired bullion corps badge the may have been worn by George Boyd on his hat. It is the only known example of a bullion corps badge worn by an officer of the First Minnesota. To the left is the Second Corps badge that Boyd wore during the war. It is simply marked, "Lieut G Boyd Jr, 1st Minn Vols."

1866. Afterward, George and Sarah moved to St. Anthony, where he ran a harness business.

Unfortunately, on August 21, 1879, just seven months after his son Samuel was born, George died. While in a skiff on the Mississippi River, just above St. Anthony Falls, crossing during a storm, he slipped while trying to disembark and drowned. His body went over the falls and was recovered several days later. George Edward Boyd, his twenty-two-year-old son from his first wife, purchased a plot for his father, lot no. 5, block 59, in St. Anthony's Maple Hill Cemetery. He then took care of Sarah and her chil-

dren, aged seven months to ten years. He comfortably provided for them and was always kind to the family. Reflecting on Boyd's death, Millard Davis, a friend who had known him for eight years, gave the following testimony:

That [Davis'] occupation is that of a lumberman; that he knew Capt Geo. Boyd for 8 years last past and knew that he was physically disabled on account of lameness etc. from the performance of ordinary manual labor: that on or about the 21st day of August 1879, to the personal

George Boyd sometime between April 15, 1863, when he promoted to first lieutenant, and July 2, 1863, when he was wounded at Gettysburg

This photograph, taken in Calais, Maine, may be from the time of Boyd's wedding on January 2, 1866.

knowledge of this deponent, said Capt. George Boyd Jr had been during said day on Nicollet Island on the Mississippi River in the city of Minneapolis, Minn, for the purpose of grinding axes, tools, etc. That at about six o'clock in the afternoon of said day, this deponent did then and there cross said river in a bateau for the purpose of taking said Capt George Boyd Jr across the stream to the opposite side and that while crossing said river, which had a swift and strong current, although the water was only six inches deep, said George Boyd Jr did then and there attempt to and did step out of the bateau, when owing to his lameness and physical disability he slipped and fell into the water and was drowned before assistance could be rendered.

William Lochren

b. April 3, 1832; d. January 27, 1912

William Lochren was born in Tyrone County, Ireland. His father died when he was a year old, and his mother found it necessary to immigrate to America with relatives in 1834 when he was two. His mother settled in Franklin County, Vermont, where they lived until 1850, when he moved to Auburn, Massachusetts. He worked as a farmer and mill hand in a sawmill, attending common schools and the academy at Auburn when he could afford it.

In 1854 he move back to Franklin County and began studying law. In 1856 he was admitted to the bar and moved to St. Anthony, Minnesota, where he set up practice. He was an active Democrat in pre- and post-war years and frequently corresponded with fellow officers John Chase (Co. H) and George Boyd (Co. E). With the exception of his war experiences, he lived in St. Anthony for the rest of his life.

The war broke out, and the young Irish-born man volunteered to defend his new country. Mustered on April 29, 1861, he was placed in Company E. Not long afterward, he was promoted to sergeant, and on September 22, 1862, he was discharged in order to accept a commission as second lieutenant of Company K. After Gettysburg, on July 3, 1863, he was made the first lieutenant of his old company, E. He replaced David Demerest, who had been severely wounded during the battle and subsequently died on July 30. From that time on, he also served as the regiment's adjutant.

Lochren stood with Company K when Gen. Han-

William Lochren

cock shouted, "Charge those lines!" As he writes of the moment, "Every man realized in an instant what the order meant, death or wounds to us all; the sacrifice of the regiment to gain a few minutes' time and save the position, and probably the battlefield. And every man saw and accepted the necessity for the sacrifice." Moments later, "it seemed as if every step was over some fallen comrade, yet no man waivers, every gap is closed up . . . the boys . . . with silent desperate, determination, step forward in unbroken line."

Chris Heffelfinger, a comrade in the First, later recalled about Lochren:

When the fall of Sumter, in April, 1861, first startled the nation with the sound of actual war, and Abraham Lincoln issued his first call for 75,000 three-months volunteers, William Lochren turned the key upon the doors of a lucrative law practice and gave himself to the service of his country. He enlisted in Company "E" (known as the St Anthony Company) of the First Minnesota Volunteers, I entering Company D, (known as the Lincoln Guards) the

Minneapolis company, and when the rebellion had assumed formidable proportions and the president issued a call for 250,000 three-years men Judge Lochren, with his company and regiment, were re-mustered in for three years or during the war.

At the first battle of Bull Run we were both together in front of Beauregard, and also through the historic peninsular campaign, and thereafter the campaign of Antietam, Fredericksburg, etc. He was always with his regiment in active service. From Falmouth, VA, in June, 1863, the regiment marched with the army to take its place on the noted Gettysburg campaign, Judge Lochren as second lieutenant of Company K and the writer as first lieutenant in command of Company D, were always near each other; in fact messed together the entire campaign. Both companies formed a part of the left wing of the regiment, Company D being at the left of Company K in the line of battle, bringing us within a few feet or yards of each other most of the time.

At Gettysburg, July 2, Lieutenant Lochren was in line of battle with his company when the command was given by Gen. Hancock to Col. Colvill, commanding the regiment, to charge the enemy, and I know from personal knowledge that Lieut. Lochren was present and in his place at the time the charge was ordered, and went into the charge with his company. In this charge, Capt. Periam, of Company K, was mortally wounded, and in the absence of any superior officer, Lieut. Lochren assumed command of his company. Prior to this charge, our regiment was supporting Battery C, 4th United States Artillery, but after the charge, between sunset and dark, we were ordered to join our brigade on a different part of the field. All the regimental officers being disabled, we were under the command of Capt. Messick, of Company G, senior officer remaining.

Our regiment participated in the great battle of July 3, in the repulse of Pickett's famous charge at the point well known as the "Clump of Trees," of the "High Water Mark of the Rebellion." On this day Capt. Messick and Capt. Farrell being both killed and all the field officers being killed or wounded, Lieut. Lochren was one of the five lieutenants, the only officers of the regiment left for duty, at the close of the third day, July 3.

The regimental adjutant, Peller, being wounded and disabled, Lieut. Lochren was appointed acting adjutant, and personally wrote the report of the battle of the regiment, which report is on file in the adjutant general's office of the state, in his own hand.

The rigors of war in the East and its wearing climate wore him down. The increased responsibilities of command and those of being the regimental adjutant also took their toll. Suffering from chronic bronchitis and a weak left ankle caused by a partial dislocation, his ill health forced him to resign from the service. On December 30, 1863, he received a certificate of disability.

After his discharge Lochren returned to St. Anthony and found he had to start his law practice from scratch, which he did. In 1868 he entered the political arena and was elected state senator from St. Anthony and served for two years, from 1869 to 1870. He became the Minneapolis city attorney in 1877 and 1878 and was elected judge of the Fourth Judicial District in 1881 and served for twelve years, from 1882 to 1893.

President Cleveland appointed him commissioner of pensions for all veterans, and from 1893 to 1896, he lived in Washington, DC. He ran for the U.S. Senate in 1896 but failed in his bid. On May 20, 1896, President Cleveland appointed him judge of the U.S. District Court for the State of Minnesota. He continued in this post until his retirement on July 11, 1908. William Lochren died at his home in St. Anthony on January 27, 1912. He was seventy-nine years old. His body was buried in Minneapolis' Lakewood Cemetery.

Anson Northrup

b. January 3, 1817; d. March 27, 1894

Anson Northrup, one of the most noteworthy characters on the rolls of Minnesota pioneers, was born in the Conewango Valley in Cattaraugus County, New York, in 1817. He married Betsy Jane Edwards on August 3, 1838, at Waterbury, New York. They moved to Morgan County, Illinois, in the spring of 1839. Over the years they had ten children. Two of his sons, Charles and George, also served in the First Minnesota during the war.

Anson was restless and energetic. In October 1840 he left for the northern wilds with a drove of twenty oxen

Anson Northrup

for the Falls of St. Croix and twenty more to be delivered to another camp near Chippewa Falls, Wisconsin. His was the first drove of oxen ever brought to the territory. They were to be used by the lumbermen to haul felled trees. It was a tough and rugged journey, but he accomplished his mission and then returned to Illinois.

He liked what he had seen the year before and in 1841 took a boat from St. Louis up the Mississippi to the end of the line, which was Prairie du Chien. In May 1844 he moved to what is now Stillwater and built a hotel, the first in town. He also bought 160 acres that now covers about half of the main city of Stillwater.

In 1849 he sold his interest there and built the American House in St. Paul. After it was opened, he sold it and moved to St. Anthony, where he erected the St. Charles Hotel, which he opened on July 4, 1851. After running it for two years, he rented it and engaged in other pursuits. In 1858 he served in the first state legislature. That same year, he visited the Pacific Coast, returning after an absence of four months. In 1858 he also bought the steamer the *Governor Ramsey*.

In 1811 a settlement was established in Winnipeg, Canada, and they relied on supplies brought via the Hudson Bay and the Hayes River. The short arctic sum-

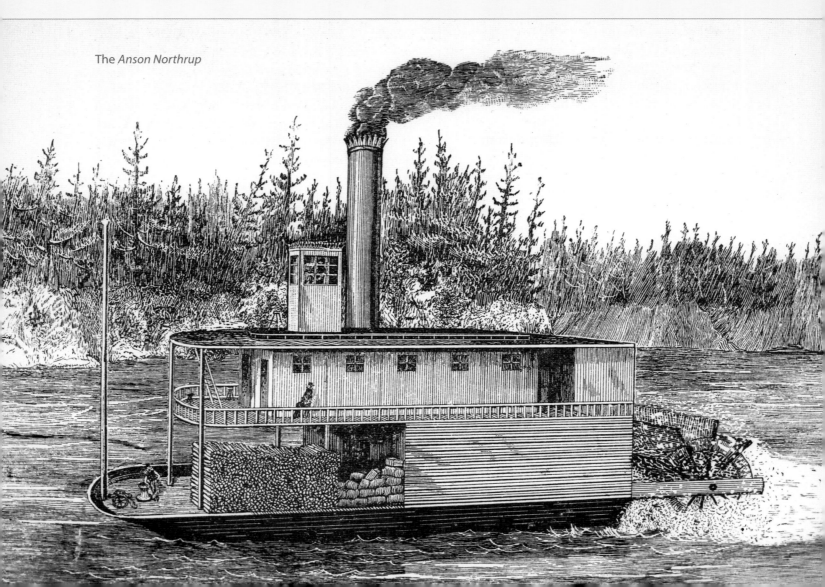

The *Anson Northrup*

mers often interfered, however, with the unloading of their needed cargo. Beginning with the Panic of 1857, St. Paul businesses were suffering from an economic depression. The Red River carts that transported goods between them and the Hudson Bay Company were very slow, and businessmen dreamed of finding a way to move their wares by water instead.

In late 1858 St. Paul's businessmen offered $1,000 to the first person who could launch a steamboat on the Red River. Anson, who had his steamboat on the Mississippi, agreed to try for the prize, but only if they raised it to $2,000. In January 1859 he and his men steamed the *Governor Ramsey* up the Crow River. When they could go no farther, they dismantled the boat and hauled it overland. Through bitter cold the men persevered and on April 1 arrived at the Red River. They spent six weeks reassembling the boat and cutting oak trees for planking for a new hull. Before launching it, they rechristened it the *Anson Northrup*. On June 5, 1859, the journey up the Red River began. They arrived at Ft. Garry in four days, and three days later, Anson and his boat headed back to Ft. Abercrombie with twenty passengers on board. Then, leaving his boat behind, he returned to St. Paul to claim his prize. Soon after, he sold the *Northrup* for $8,000.

At the outbreak of the rebellion, the forty-four-year-old Anson was running the prosperous St. Charles Hotel. Anson, as proprietor, made an announcement. He stated that due to the fact that *all* the able-bodied men in his employment, "to the number of seven," had "enlisted for the war," the hotel would "probably be closed for a few days."

Leaving the hotel behind, he and his sons, Charles and George, volunteered with the other men from St. Anthony. All were mustered as privates in Company E, though it appears he was never formally mustered into the service. Anson received an appointment to be the regiment's wagon master, providing prompt transportation of ammunition and supplies to strategic points, day in and day out. He was in charge of all the wagons, their cargo, and seeing that the men had supplies, tents, and all gear assigned to them when needed. He took the job seriously and was well liked by the men for his constant attention to their care.

Though he was not required to drill as often as most enlisted men, when it came time for their first battle, at Bull Run, Northrup made sure he was in the lines with the rest of the regiment. An August 22, 1862, newspaper reports Anson's minor confusion during the battle:

SURPRISED.—A Minnesota paper tells this story of the battle of Stone Bridge [Bull Run]: Adjutant General Sanborn relates that when the Minnesota regiment was drawn up in line of battle opposite the Mississippi regiment, our old friend, Anson Northup, was in the ranks, musket in hand. The regiment, practicing the Zouave drill, in which Northup was not very proficient, fell flat on the ground—"every man killed!" thought Northup; but, resolved to have another crack at the rebels, Northup re-loaded his musket, and just after he fired, up jumped his comrades and fired another round, as much to Northup's surprise, he said, as if many dead men had come out of their graves.[1]

The wagon master's role was crucial and demanding, and Northrup proved up to the task. In September 1861 he was appointed wagon master in Gen. Gorman's brigade, and in March 1862 he received a like position in Gen. Sedgwick's division. In June he was put in charge of all the wagon trains of Gen. Sumner's corps in the Army of the Potomac. During the Seven Days' Battles in June 1862, he had charge of the entire wagon train of the Second Army Corps and continued in that capacity during the Peninsula Campaign that summer. He remained in this position until the Dakota War began that August, when he obtained leave and hurried home to protect the home frontier.

The day following his arrival in Minneapolis, he received a commission as a captain from Governor Ramsey, with instructions to raise a company of mounted men. He was ordered to proceed with all speed to the relief of Ft. Ridgely, which the Dakota were besieging. Having the townspeople's confidence, Anson raised a company of ninety-six men in one day. At nine o'clock that evening, they marched for twenty-five miles, stopping at Shakopee and continuing on the next day to Ft. Ridgely. The entire march was made in three days, their ranks growing to 140 as they journeyed to their destination. They reached the beleaguered fort just at daylight, having marched all night. As one member of the group, A. Barnard, tells the story:

Early in the morning of the 27th the fort, a mile distant, became visible beyond and over the tops of trees bordering a deep wooded ravine. The national flag—the glorious stars and stripes—could be seen flying from the top of the staff. "Were our friends in the fort safe?" was the audible voice from every heart. A halt was ordered and a hurried counsel ensued. Antoine, the half breed, suggested that the Indians might have captured the fort and were now using the flag as a decoy to lead us into an ambush in the ravine which it was necessary for us to cross. While the signals from the fort that reached our eyes left painful doubts in the minds of some of the company, they also inspired hope and confidence in others. To relieve the suspense, Captain Northrup, Antoine, J. H. Thompson, Ed Nash and one or two others, dashed down the winding road into the gorge and after a few moments we saw them emerge safely upon the high prairie by the fort on the other side. As we followed, near the entrance to the ravine the bloated corpse of a man, dressed like a soldier, attracted our attention, and at the bottom by the brook was another similar in appearance.

Our coming was hailed by the inmates of the fort with the liveliest manifestations of joy and gratitude. For nearly nine days they had been closely imprisoned, the men constantly upon the alert, repelling in the meantime four attacks.

General Sibley arrived with infantry and mounted volunteers on the 28th. Captain Northrup and a few of his men went up the river in the direction of the Redwood Agency. They found and brought into the fort a German woman and seven children who were the only survivors of several large families. For eight days they had subsisted upon roots and berries gathered under the cover of darkness while they lay in hiding during the hours of sunlight. Having now accomplished the object for which we set out and seeing no prospect of a speedy move against the Indians, the pressure of home interests the faces of most of our party toward the Falls [St. Anthony], where they arrived in due time.

After the war Northrup ran the First National Hotel in Duluth for two years. He spent five years there, mainly contracting and jobbing for the Northern Pacific Railway. In 1874 he left Duluth, and after taking a short trip to Texas, he returned to St. Paul and remained until May 1880, when he moved to Ft. Snelling and opened a boardinghouse. Anson died in Minneapolis on March 27, 1894. He was seventy-seven years old. He was buried at Lakewood Cemetery. In the same area lies George, his son and comrade in the First.

Henry O'Brien
b. January 21, 1842; d. November 2, 1902

Henry O'Brien was born in Calais, Maine, and he and his family moved to St. Anthony in 1857. About four years later, on September 29, 1861, he was sworn into service at St. Anthony by Capt. Morgan, joining Company E. As early as that fall, the regiment was seeking to replace those lost by death or disability, and O'Brien was one of those replacement soldiers. He was nineteen years old and, according to records, stood five feet seven inches tall and possessed a light complexion, hazel eyes, and dark hair.

At Gettysburg, O'Brien, then a corporal, went above and beyond during both the July 2 charge and the repulse of Pickett's Charge, being awarded the Medal of Honor for his part in carrying the regiment's colors.

During the charge, while fighting at Plum Run, a Rebel soldier managed to wound O'Brien with his bayonet, though only slightly. As the regiment withdrew he noticed his comrade Ernest Jefferson drop to the ground after being shot in the leg. With no thought of his own injury, O'Brien picked up Jefferson and was carrying him to safety when a ball hit O'Brien's cartridge box plate, knocking them to the ground. Undaunted, O'Brien rose up and carried the wounded soldier to the rear without further mishap. After the battle Jefferson was taken to a field hospital. Though his leg was later amputated, he went on to live a long life and was always thankful for O'Brien's help that day. Though somewhat wounded himself, O'Brien stayed with the regiment and lined up with his comrades the next day.

During Pickett's Charge the Confederate forces were aimed at a group of trees located on Cemetery Ridge. The First Minnesota lay waiting behind a low fence to the left of the trees, putting them near the thick of things once again. During the firing between the advancing Rebels and the opposing Union line, Cpl. Dehn, the only member of the color guard left from the previous day's fight, was shot through the hand, forcing him to drop the colors. O'Brien picked up the flag, leapt over the fence, and charged the Confederates. The shot had broken the flagstaff in half, so it was difficult to hold. But hold it he did, and his comrades followed. Lt. Lochren was angry at first, blaming O'Brien for imperiling the regiment's flag, stained in blood the day before. But the effect of O'Brien's act "was electrical," Lochren later wrote. "Every man of the First Minnesota sprang to protect its flag, and the rest rushed with them upon the enemy."

Charging headlong onto the field, the Minnesotans encountered the Twenty-Eighth Virginia Infantry and engaged in fierce hand-to-hand combat. "If ever men became devils, that was one of those times," as Lt. William Harmon recalls. "We were crazy with the excitement of the fight. We rushed in like wild beasts. Men swore and cursed and struggled and fought, grappled in hand to hand fight, threw stones, clubbed their muskets, kicked, yelled and hurrahed!"

As 1st Sgt. James Wright (Co. F) writes about the incident:

Captain Messick was in command, and Corporal John Dehn carried the flag—he being the only one of the color guard of the day before able to be on his feet at the close of fighting the evening of the 2nd—a new detail being necessary. In the "mix-up" with Pickett's men he was shot through the hand, and the same shot splintered the flagstaff so that it broke in two pieces. Corporal Henry D. O'Brien then took the piece with the flag on and kept it until twice wounded, when it passed to the hands of Corporal William N Irvine, who carried it through the fighting. The flag of the 28th Virginia was captured by Marshall Sherman. A portion of this staff was used to replace the broken portion of ours. The splice made in the field by a little rough whittling and bound with a knapsack strap and was carried afterwards

until the regiment returned to Minnesota the next February.[2]

Marshall Sherman, a thirty-seven-year-old painter from St. Paul, who fought barefoot the last day at Gettysburg because his shoes had come apart, captured the flag of the Twenty-Eighth Virginia. Both he and O'Brien, who had been wounded again while carrying the flag, were years later awarded the Medal of Honor.

Pvt. Caleb Jackson of Company G also remembers O'Brien's valor that day:

When General Pickett made his famous charge his men succeeded in striking our line near a battery and close to our right flank and for a moment it seemed that we would be overwhelmed. At this critical time the last of our color guards was shot and the flag fell to the ground. Corporal Henry D. O'Brien, of Company E, though not a member of the color guard instantly seized it and waving it over his head rushed ahead of the Regiment and close up to the muzzles of the Confederate muskets. His example was quickly followed by the rest of the men and the Confederates were beaten back leaving the colors of the 28th Virginia with our command. Corporal O'Brien's action at that time was fearless and as daring as anything I saw during the war, and there is no doubt in my mind that it was one of the principal causes that led to the defeat of the Confederates at that point. I looked at his face and smiled as he broke off a piece of the shattered staff and threw it to the ground and marched on. He was struck in the head by a musket ball and although stunned by the force of the blow, he held to the colors until he was again struck in the left hand. This occurred at the moment of victory.[3]

After the great clash was over, the Union army took time to care for its wounded and bury its dead. O'Brien and many of the wounded men of the First Minnesota were sent to Chestnut Hill Hospital in Philadelphia.

When on May 5, 1864, the regiment was mustered out after their three years of service, Henry reenlisted in the First Battalion. On May 12, 1864, he was appointed second lieutenant in Company B and acting adjutant for the battalion. On August 14, 1864, at the Battle at Deep Bottom, he was shot in the right shoulder and lung, a portion of the minié ball passing through him. O'Brien was carried to safety by Alonzo Pickle.

He was not expected to survive but did. This wound in particular continued to bother him for many years afterward, reopening every year for nineteen years. Finally, he submitted to surgery, and twenty-two pieces of bone and a piece of bullet were removed.

O'Brien served for a while as first lieutenant and acting quartermaster and was promoted to captain of Company A on May 16, 1865, replacing James Farwell, who was mustered out. Some records indicate that O'Brien was promoted to major and adjutant at the end of the war. He was mustered out on July 14, 1865.

After the war he returned to St. Anthony. In 1872 William Lochren wrote a status report on some of the men to Mathew Marvin, and of O'Brien he wrote, "H D O'Brien lives here (Minneapolis)—married—Insurance agent." He was appointed postmaster in St. Anthony and served in that capacity for four years, until he moved to East St. Louis, Illinois.

There, at 421 Chestnut Street, Room 421, he edited and published the *Picket Guard,* a publication covering the interests of Civil War veterans. He also served as a government pension agent, helping his comrades file for and receive their pension benefits. He seemed to be a jack of all trades in this area, as evinced by an advertisement he ran: "Henry D O'Brien—Pension, Patents—Increase back pay, bounty caveats, copy writes, trademarks."

At some point he moved across the river to St. Louis. He was a member of the Ransom GAR Post in St. Louis and also a member of the Military Order of the Loyal Legion of the United States, a fraternal group like the GAR, but membership was only for men who had served as officers during the Civil War. Henry died of pneumonia in St. Louis on November 3, 1902. He was sixty-one years old.

The following are testimonials given about O'Brien's service when he was being considered for the Medal of Honor:

Duluth, Minn., Nov. 23, 1889.
Hon. Sect'y of War
Dear Sir:

I was present at the Battle of Gettysburg on the P.M. of July 2, '63, and took part in the charge made at the time the Confederates were driving back the Third Corps. Said charge was made in obedience to the command of General Hancock.

I lost my leg in that engagement, and while the enemy rained shot and shell over the open space between my regiment and their line, Comrade Henry D. O'Brien came to my relief and carried me to a place of safety.

His action at the time is deserving of commendation and was an exhibition of courage characteristic of the fearless soldier and devoted friend.

I have the honor to be your obedient servant,
Earnest R. Jefferson

Minneapolis, Minn, Dec. 28, 1889.
Hon. Sect'y of War
Dear Sir:

I was Captain of Co. "B" 1st Minn, Veteran Vol. Infty. and participated with my company in the battle of Deep Bottom, Va, on the 14th of August, 1864. On the P.M. of that day the organization to which I belonged was assigned to the extreme right of the line and ordered to charge the Confederate breastworks. Second Lieut. Henry D. O'Brien, of my company, acting adjutant, had been quite sick for some time and was excused from duty; but when the charge was to take place insisted on participating in it, notwithstanding the protests of his comrades. The assault was made and Lieut. O'Brien, whose assigned position was in the rear of the command, was shot through the right shoulder and lung, when 20 feet in advance of it, and close to the Confederate breastworks. He was carried to a ravine, where the line was reformed and then attacked by the enemy. He urged his comrades to hold the position which they did and a few moments afterwards he became unconscious through the loss of blood.

In my report of the battle I stated that he had been mortally wounded and I certainly had no reason to expect his recovery. His action on this occasion was commendable. He did more than his duty.

Yours respectfully,
E. P. Perkins,
Late Capt. Co B, 1st Minn. Vols.

Patrick Henry Taylor

b. August 3, 1838; d. December 20, 1907

Isaac Taylor

b. January 23, 1837, d. July 2, 1863

Both Isaac and Patrick Henry Taylor (known as Hank, Henry, and PH) were born in Rowe, Franklin County, Massachusetts. Isaac was the fifth and Henry the sixth in a family of twelve boys and girls. In 1840 the family moved to St. Lawrence County, New York, and in 1852, they moved to Prairie City, Illinois.

Henry both farmed and taught school until about 1859, when he moved to Morrison County, Minnesota. In 1860 he traveled to the Red River country of British Columbia and returned to Morrison County that fall, canoeing from the headwaters of the Mississippi River to Belle Prairie, a distance of about five hundred miles. There, he resumed teaching school. Belle Prairie's name was later changed to Little Falls.

In a childhood accident Henry had lost sight in one eye. Despite this handicap, he wanted to enlist and found an opportunity when he met Anson Northrup, who was on a recruiting mission looking to enlist men to fill the ranks of the First Minnesota. Taylor quickly signed up, packed his bags and headed to Ft. Snelling. He was mustered into Company E on May 26, 1861. He later wrote: "The spirit of patriotism prompted me to volunteer to go and fight for my country."

Isaac came up from Illinois to take his place as a teacher, and before long Isaac and their cousin Edward also felt the call. Isaac went to Ft. Snelling, enlisted on

Patrick Henry Taylor *(left)* and Isaac Taylor *(right)*

August 21, and was assigned to Company E. Cousin Edward followed a week later, enlisted on August 28, and was assigned to Company C. They and other recruits were then taken east to catch up with the regiment. Once there, they were formally mustered into service on September 21, 1861.

Henry was wounded in the left hand and wrist by a piece of artillery shell at the Battle of Bull Run. William Fullerton was a few feet from Henry when he was wounded and remembered that as the regiment retreated Henry used a handkerchief tied around his neck to create a sling to support his arm and wrist. The next day, July 22, the regiment marched in the rain from their camp in Alexandria to Washington, DC.

Confusion at Bull Run

From the August 6, 1861, *Stillwater Messenger*:

[Sergeant Benjamin F Staples], Company E, being cut off, mistook Mississippi Rifles for a Vermont regiment, ran toward them, and they took him prisoner. Some wanted to bayonet him on the spot, others to shoot him; but many said he was too brave a fellow to be dispatched so, and the majority prevailed. Just then a Michigan regiment charged them and they broke and fled like sheep to their batteries, and their prisoner stood still, and getting a gun, fired after them, and then joined again the loyal troops. This regiment in turn thought they had a rebel, and in took him prisoner and brought him in!

Upon arriving in Washington, they were quartered in a church provided by the efforts and influence of Senator William Windom. The wound was treated at the church, and it was noted that, when treated, a few small pieces of bone were taken out. After his wound had been dressed, he was sent to the hospital, where he remained for several weeks.

In the fall of 1861, the regiment marched from Washington, DC, to Camp Stone, their winter camp in Maryland. His wound left him disabled to the point of being frequently excused from drill and other duties. He did perform guard and other light duties as his turn came up for regular details made from the roster of the company. This weakness in his arm and inability to do heavy lifting continued throughout the rest of the war.

Henry was wounded once again at the Battle of Savage Station on June 29, 1862. A musket ball injured his left hand and index finger. He and his unwounded brother, Isaac, went to a field hospital, where they tended to their dying cousin, Edward. On June 30 the Confederates took Henry and Isaac prisoner, sending them first to Libby and then to Belle Isle prisons. They spent eleven weeks as prisoners before being paroled. Afterward, Henry was sent to Annapolis, where he remained in a convalescent camp a short time.

The following letter from Isaac to an unknown cousin tells of Edward's death, as well as their experiences as prisoners of war. In it one can sense his compassion:

Camp at Bolivar Heights, VA., Oct 19, 1862
Dear Cousin,
    I will tell you something of our fare as prisoners of war. . . .
    . . . We were formed in an open field and ordered to advance on the enemy. The shells sounded wickedly as they passed over our heads, and plowed up the earth around us. Now and then, a man would reel from the ranks and be borne to the rear. . . .
    Cousin Edward Taylor, my particular friend, fell mortally wounded. He called us to bear witness that he fell with his face to the foe. The fight continued till quite dark. During the night our forces, except a picket-guard, withdrew. Henry and I remained with Edward, and the other wounded of our regiment, giving them water, etc. as long as we dared to, and were about to move on and join the Regt. When the man whom

the Dr. had ordered to stay with the wounded "turned up" missing. The boys implored us to stay and not "leave them alone." We hesitated for we had no orders to stay. But the boys were suffering from thirst; they were lying on the ground in the open air, and it had already commenced to rain. Who would dress their wounds and take care of them on the morrow when the burning sun would pour his rays upon them? It took but a "jiffy" to twist Henry's gun into an unserviceable shape. I hated to destroy my gun which had been so true a friend, so I handed it over to a soldier who happened to be passing without one, and to work we went. We carried a portion of the wounded into a house nearby, and covered the rest with rubber blankets. From that time to the 25th of July we were constantly at work over the sick and wounded. Our patients appeared very grateful for services rendered. One young fellow of Baxter's Zouaves said he was going to have our names written in their family Bible.

After the battle of the 29th of June, we remained with the wounded at Savage Station about two weeks. Among the wounded that we had the care of were several Confederates. One young man from South Carolina Henry gave his canteen, which he seemed to prize very highly. We were obliged to work day and night, and then could only half take care of the wounded.

The Confederates treated us very kindly, and allowed us to go a mile or more into the country to buy food for our patients. Near the middle of July, we were removed with the wounded to Richmond in the cars. There the sick and wounded were crowded into filthy tobacco factories.

We did the best we could for them, but bandages were scarce and we had very little medicine. Most of them lay upon the hard floor with nothing but a single blanket under them. There, a great many died that might have lived could they have had proper care. The despondence of some, I think, assisted materially in carrying them off. I believe that many died not from wounds or sickness, but simply because their spirits drooped. We tried to revive their spirits in every possible way. They frequently asked us to read the Richmond papers to them and were particularly interested in anything that related to the "Yankee prisoners."

We were in the tobacco factory (prison No. 2) about two weeks when the sick and wounded were sent North, and the nurses to Belle Isle in James River at the upper end of the City. You never saw so happy a company as those sick and mutilated soldiers as we helped them into the ambulances. . . .

While on Belle Isle, we were kept on very short allowances and, in fact, nearly starved. I never knew what it was to suffer the pangs of hunger till I was a prisoner of war. We managed to get bread enough to keep body and soul together by selling our watches and other available property, and stealing what we could from the Sesesh commissary. When we went on the island, our ration of salt was one spoonful per week and very soon after, we could get none except on doctor's orders. We got hold of a paper containing the Dr's signature and with a little practice, Henry got so he could manufacture salt orders just as good as the original.

This device probably saved us from sickness, and certainly rendered our food somewhat palatable. You see what great crime hunger will drive a person to theft and forgery. But somehow, I don't feel much compunction of conscience. I suppose it is on account of the "demoralizing effects of the enemy."

Isaac L. Taylor

Henry was paroled on September 13, 1862, along with 1,000 other Union prisoners. Isaac and 1,050 men remained on the island with sadness in their hearts. The next morning brought good news, however, and they began their journey back home, as well. Their parole required an oath refusing to bear arms against the Confederate States of America. Within a short time, though, they were back in the ranks and found themselves once again facing the enemy.

By Gettysburg, Henry was twenty-four years old and a sergeant in Company E. On the night of July 1, the day before the First's charge at Plum Run, Henry wrote in his diary:

Wednesday, July 1st, 1863, bivouacked at 9:00 P.M. Made coffee; built barricade of fence rails and lay down to sleep. The full moon frequently showed itself through the clouds. My brother and I talk of the expected battle tomorrow and mutually agree

that should we survive this battle we may hope to see friends and home again.[4]

On July 2 Henry noted:

Aroused at 3 A.M. & ordered to pack up & at 4 A.M. move towards the battlefield where we arrive at 5–40 A.M. Order from Gen. Gibbon read to us in which he says this is to be the great battle of the war & that any soldier leaving the ranks without leave will be instantly put to death.

Skirmishing commences about 8 A.M. At 9–30 H. and I take a cup of coffee. At 3–15 P.M. our artillery opens on the left. 3–40 our infantry advance across plain. Rebel battery opens at 4 P.M.

Sometime later, the regiment was called to action. Both of the Taylor brothers went into the charge, but in the smoke and confusion of the fighting, they lost track of each other. After Col. Colvill and the other senior officers were wounded, Capt. Messick passed along word for the regiment to retire to the ridge. The right side of the regiment was most heavily engaged. The order to pull back had to be yelled several times before they responded and withdrew.

After the battle Henry helped carry Col. Colvill and other wounded comrades off the field. Still separated from his older brother, that night he wrote in his journal, "I helped our Colonel off the field but fail to find my brother who, I suppose, is killed. I rejoin the regiment and lie down in the moonlight, rather sorrowful. Where is Isaac?" Henry had looked for Isaac for more than an hour in the dark. Another soldier said he had seen Isaac near the end of the fight, while most of the others were withdrawing, still firing away at the Confederates, and smiling.

Early the next morning, at about 8:30 A.M., he got the news he feared. Lafayette Snow of Company B had found Isaac on the field and took Henry to where his brother lay. "I find my dear brother dead!" he wrote in his journal. "A shell struck him on top of his head and passed through his back, cutting his belt in two. The poor fellow did not know what hit him."

He retrieved Isaac's pocket watch for a keepsake and then wrapped his brother in the half tent soldiers carried to shelter themselves. With the help of privates William Cundy and James Brower, Taylor buried his brother. He put up a board on which he wrote:

I. L. Taylor, 1st Minn Vols.
1st Minn. Vols.
Buried at 10 O'clock A.M. of July 3d, 1863
By his brother
Sergt P. H. Taylor
Co. "E" 1st Minn. Vols.

On it he also inscribed:

No useless coffin enclosed his breast,
Nor in sheet nor shroud we bound him,
But he lay like a warrior taking his rest,
With his shelter tent around him.

Taylor later wrote in his journal, "As we laid him down, I remarked, 'Well Isaac, all I can give you is a soldier's grave.' . . . I was the only one to weep over his grave." His father, mother, and sisters were all at home and, like so many families during the war, unaware of the death of their loved one.

Henry was mustered out with the regiment at the end of their three-year enlistment. He engaged in civil pursuits for a while. Later in 1864, he received a commission as a lieutenant in Hancock's Veteran Corps, an organization of volunteers who had at least two years' military service remaining on their enlistment. He served with them until being mustered out as a second lieutenant of Company C on July 20, 1866.

Edward Taylor

b. 1837; d. June 29, 1862

Edward Taylor was born in Massachusetts and came to Minnesota in 1855, settling in Belle Prairie. Though better land could be found to the south and the west, Edward chose to stay near relatives in the area who had established a mission for the Ojibwe. He began to farm with Henry and Isaac Taylor's younger brother Jonathan. In 1858 or 1859, Edward married and had a daughter. When Henry moved to the area, he moved in with Edward and Jonathan.

A week after his cousin Isaac left to join Henry in the First Minnesota, Edward decided to do the same, though it meant leaving his wife and daughter. While his cousins served in Company E, Edward was placed in Company C. Edward was twenty-three years old. Mili-

Edward Taylor

tary records show little about Taylor as a person. His entry in the 1860 census, taken on June 11, recorded that he and his wife, Margaret, had a ten-month-old baby girl by the name of Lula. His cousin Isaac made several notations in his diary about Edward, one mentioning that they had played a game of chess.

In the late afternoon of June 29, 1862, at Savage Station, the First Minnesota was placed in a small field to slow the advancing Confederates. When the Rebels emerged from the woods, the Minnesotans opened fire and were fired upon in return. Here, Edward was hit in the head by a bullet. Still breathing, he was carried back to the field hospital, where he was found by his cousins. They did what they could, but Edward was only semiconscious. Isaac noted in his diary that Edward "died at about midnight, experiencing but little pain." On July 1, 1862, he was buried alongside Cpl. George L. Smith of Company C, who had died on June 30 from wounds received at the same battle.

COMPANY F
THE RED WING VOLUNTEERS
(AKA THE GOODHUE COUNTY
VOLUNTEERS)

THE PEOPLE OF RED WING were proud that their town was home to an institution of higher learning, Hamline University. When news of the attack on Ft. Sumter came, a recruiting rally was held in town, and several men from Hamline attended along with local farmers and merchants. This group called themselves the Goodhue County Volunteers and when mustered in became Company F. One out of every four men had been a student at Hamline.

In telling how they approached their first battle, at Bull Run, 1st Sgt. James Wright describes the character of the men of Company F:

Company F was not "spoiling for a fight" when it started for Bull Run or any other occasion, but it meant business, as it always did when confronting an enemy, and did its level best to make things interesting for its "friends, the enemy." It did not "move as steadily as if on parade" or "march undismayed in the face of batteries" or "smile at bursting shells"; but it did try to march wherever it was ordered; we were all more or less scared—and in my case it was more; we dodged the shell on the hillside

At the start of the war, Red Wing was a small, bustling town located on the Mississippi River.

both coming and returning; and all through the fight we fully realized that it was serious business, and I have no doubt we "looked it." In a word, we fully understood that life and limb were in danger, and the fact impressed itself upon us—much as it would on anyone under like circumstances.[1]

Hamline University

The following students from Hamline served in the First Minnesota. Many were discharged for disability during the war, and some transferred to other units and finished their service elsewhere. Only seven of the twenty-three mustered out with the regiment on May 5, 1864.

Abraham Baker, April 29, 1861, to May 5, 1864

Archibald Bamber, April 29, 1861, to May 5, 1864

Jefferson Benner, April 29, 1861, to May 5, 1864

William Bennett, April 29, 1861, to February 4, 1863, wounded at Savage Station

Charles Berdan, October 29, 1861, to November 17, 1864, wounded at Bristoe Station and Fredericksburg

Henry Bevans, April 29, 1861, to September 9, 1863, discharged for promotion

Milton Bevans, May 22, 1861, to May 5, 1864

Cyrus Brooks, May 22, 1861, to June 12, 1863, transferred to assistant surgeon, Tenth Minnesota

Edwin Cox, May 22, 1861, to September 17, 1862, killed in action at Antietam

Joseph Garrison, April 29, 1861, to August 10, 1862, died of wounds received at Bull Run

Charles Harris, April 29, 1861, to December 5, 1862, wounded at Bull Run

William Herbert, May 22, 1861, to December 19, 1863, wounded at Fredericksburg

Mark Hoyt, April 29, 1861, to July 18, 1862, died of consumption

Robert Leeson, April 29, 1861, to June 30, 1862, killed in action at Glendale

Martin Maginnis, April 29, 1861, to May 5, 1864

Frederick Miller, April 29, 1861, to December 28, 1863, promoted to first lieutenant, Sixty-Second U.S. Colored Troops

Paul Nelson, June 19, 1861, to July 4, 1864

Hiram Rush, April 29, 1861, to July 21, 1861, killed in action at Bull Run

John H. Smith, April 29, 1861, to October 2, 1861, discharged for disability

Merritt Standish, August 26, 1861, to October 26, 1862, transferred to the Fourth U.S. Cavalry

Elijah F. Thomas, April 29, 1861, to September 6, 1861, died of wounds received at Bull Run

Lester Webb, May 15, 1861, to October 24, 1862, wounded at Antietam

A. Edward Welch, April 29, 1861, to November 5, 1861, promoted to major, Fourth Minnesota, died of consumption

Edwin Oscar Williams, April 29, 1861, to October 24, 1862, transferred to the Fourth U.S. Cavalry

James Wright, April 29, 1861, to May 5, 1864, wounded at Bull Run and Gettysburg

From left to right is Charles Harris, Joseph Garrison, and William Bennett, with their female classmates Mary Gillette, Helen Sutherland, Ellen Gillette, and Sarah Pettibone.

William Bennett

Charles Berdan

Cyrus Brooks

Joseph Garrison

Charles Harris

Mark Hoyt

Martin Maginnis

Lester Webb

A. Edward Welch

James Wright

Charles North Harris

b. September 1842; d. March 7, 1902

Born in New York, Charles Harris and his family moved to Minnesota, settling in Richfield. Harris spent part of his youth in St. Anthony living with his uncle John W. North, a lawyer with whom he may have apprenticed, since he became a lawyer himself later in life. Like many men of Company F, he studied at Hamline University. He was considered a good student and a fine scholar with a keen interest in science and a passion for the classics. He often quoted favorite passages from memory.

He was said to stand straight as an arrow and have a stalwart frame, a firm, mild brow, and undaunted courage. When he was mustered in on April 29, 1861, his age was recorded as twenty-two, though he was actually twenty. He was appointed the company's fourth corporal and by July 1861 had been promoted to fifth sergeant.

No doubt Harris and his regiment went into their first battle, at Bull Run, with mixed emotions. Some thought of death; others, of quickly ending the rebellion. On July 8, 1861, shortly before the battle, Harris wrote the following correspondence, which was published in a Red Wing newspaper:

Ours is now the front regiment of the advance guard of the U.S. Army. Every man will do his duty, and we are sure of success. We represent Minnesota in the field, and she shall not want of character for military prowess by any failure of ours.

Sgt. James Wright, a friend in Company F, makes mention of Harris before the battle and of his unusual situation afterward:

Just when the coming light of day began to make things distinctly visible, while talking with Charley Harris, he was accosted by William A. Croffut, who was—or recently had been—connected with a Minneapolis paper, but who was there as a representative of some paper for the occasion. After an introduction, there was a short talk with Croffut, who questioned us as to the "state of our minds" at the near-approaching hour of battle. Neither of us could truthfully affirm that we were not somewhat disturbed as to our individual safety for the day—though we both tried to consider the matter hopefully and referred lightly to what might happen. We each left a message for our friends and, in case of "an accident" requested a complimentary obituary notice. After that we shook hands and parted. Charley got his obituary and—it was a little premature—lived to read it. A privilege granted to but a few.[2]

Harris was shot in the chest and left on the field when the regiment was forced to retreat. The bullet had shattered his shoulder, and his comrades thought he was dead. News of the battle and his death quickly was sent home. Arrangements were made, and soon after, Rev. Crary, the president of Hamline University, was preaching at a funeral in Harris' honor before a large audience in Richfield, where his parents and sisters grieved for their lost loved one.

While his funeral was being conducted and his loss mourned, Harris was actually a prisoner in Rebel hands. After being wounded, he had laid on the ground for many hours through that hot July day. He and other wounded men from Minnesota were taken prisoner by the Confederates and sent to a prison in Richmond, which just weeks before had been the Ligon and Company's tobacco warehouse. He was given care and after many days was paroled and sent north. He recovered, though his wound was severe, and he eventually was discharged for disability on December 5, 1862.

Wright later saw Harris after his discharge but before he had returned to Minnesota. As he writes:

Another event of the day gave me much personal pleasure. Sergeant Charles N Harris, who had been wounded and left at Bull Run, came out to see us. He had recovered (except for one arm which he never regained the use of), had been paroled, and sent home. He was now in Washington but had recently come from his home in Minnesota and brought us lots of home news. We had been classmates at school and very good friends since the first time we had met.

We sat on my rubber blanket in the shade of the tree, and he told me his experiences after he was wounded, his captivity, and release; and I recounted some of the experiences of the company since he had left it. We talked about the war that was desolating the land—speculated as to when and how it might end and what might be the future of the country and ourselves afterwards. It was not a cheerful outlook—any view we could take of it—but we were hopeful for brighter days.

Charley almost cried that he could no longer take an active part, and told me that it made him feel mean and selfish to think of trying to do anything for himself while the war continued and his old comrades were in it. He was still a member of the company, a prisoner on parole, and hoping that when exchanged he might get some appointment where he could be of service despite his useless arm—for it was certain that he could never handle a rifle.

We talked of our homes, of the old days at school (which, somehow, seemed so far back in our life), of schoolmates and mutual friends, until our feelings got pretty close to the surface. Then we clasped hands for a farewell that we felt might be final, as I knew we were to march in the morning. When the war was over, he had gone to Nevada, and he died in California about four years ago, but it never was our privilege to meet again.[3]

After the war Harris did move west. He became a lawyer like his uncle and was, for eight years, a district judge in Nevada. He was also considered a talented speaker and writer. He eventually moved to California and reportedly died in San Francisco on March 7, 1902.

Joseph Garrison

b. September 26, 1840; d. August 10, 1861

Mantorville resident Joseph Garrison, also a student at Hamline when the war began, was described as being well educated, refined, of excellent family, kind, deeply religious, and intensely patriotic. When news of Ft. Sumter's attack arrived, he wrote his parents in Mantorville seeking permission to join his fellow classmates in enlisting to put down the rebellion. At twenty years of age, he was old enough to enlist on his own, but as an only son, he felt he still needed their approval. While waiting for an answer, he said to one of his teachers, "I can never be content to stay here, and see my fellow students go out to defend our country. I am not worthy of my country if I will not fight for her. I can never hold up my head among men if I am not permitted to enlist." He headed home, obtained the consent and blessing of his parents, and then left for Ft. Snelling.

At Bull Run, Garrison was wounded, of which James Wright mentions in a letter to the *Red Wing Weekly Republican*:

Joseph P Garrison, brave boy, was shot through the hips early in the fight. He was close to me

and called me to him. I picked him up and carried him to the rear in the shade, and set him with his back to a tree. He asked me to load his gun and give it to him. I did so and gave him water. I asked him if he was prepared to die; he said he was and could die happy. When we left the field he was brought to the ambulance, but whether living or dead I do not know.

Garrison was actually captured along with many other men who had to be left on the field when the regiment retreated. As Charles Merritt, the drummer for Company F, relates:

I was captured at Bull Run the 1st. Four of us carried a comrade, Joseph Garrison, to Sudley Church and in consequence was picked up and was trotted off to Manassas. We slept on the sand that night surrounded by a cordon of guards who seemed to think a great deal of us—judging by their watchfulness. It rained hard during the night which by the way was very welcome and all the water we had was caught in a rubber blanket.

In the morning the Rebs threw some pieces of ham into the pen. Some were lucky to get some but I was not. We were put aboard box cars and shipped to Richmond where we arrived Tuesday night.[4]

Garrison was part of this group taken to Richmond and held in the warehouse turned prison with other captured men from the First. He died on August 10, 1861, of wounds received at the battle three weeks earlier.

Dr. Jacob H. Stewart, who was the regimental surgeon for the First Minnesota, wrote a letter to Garrison's mother on September 12, 1861. It was later published in the *Mantorville Press* on October 18, 1861.

I have received several letters from your friends asking information relative to your dear son, Joseph. I would have written to you before, but sent word to you by some gentleman who called on me, that he was dead, and now I have a moment's time to write you all the particulars of his death. I knew him well. He was one of my favorites in the Regiment and I can truly say that not one of all my brave boys who met death on that battlefield was so dear to me as Joseph Garrison;

his universal good humor, his constant attention to duty, his willingness to oblige, his bravery, attached all who knew him, closely to him.

As we were passing a branch of Bull Run, just on the verge of the battlefield, I stood near where I could say Good bye, to the brave ones, who must soon throw their lives in front of the enemy, feeling that many, alas, too many of them, would soon lie down to die, away from home and friends or be shattered by bullets of the rebels. Joseph saw me and giving me his hand said, "Good bye, Dr. I hope you and I will meet soon, in as good health as we now part." and pressing my hand, passed on as cheerful as if going to a dress parade instead of a battlefield; but he was determined to do his duty to his God and his country and do it cheerfully.

The next I saw of him was coming down from the field carried by his comrades, badly shot through the hip; the ball passing through the hip and remaining in the pelvis in the vicinity of the bladder so that it could not be reached or extracted without causing instant death. He was suffering great agony but in a short time I quieted him by chloroform and put him in the care of his friend Fred Miller, of Red Wing, who by the way, was with him to the very last breath. After a day or two he appeared quite comfortable and complained very little indeed and in a day or two after sat up a little and I hoped he might get along; but he very imprudently went downstairs, (he was occupying with the rest of the First Minnesotans, a second story of a wheelwright's shop) and in a few hours after he got back he complained again of the greatest agony and I was obliged to keep him under the influence of chloroform nearly twenty four hours. After that time he again became quiet and remained so until he left for Richmond, about two weeks after the battle.

When he was about to be removed, I fixed up a number of blankets in the ambulance and put him on them and gave him some morphine to take if his pain should recur on the way down to Manassas, ten miles [distant]. From there he was taken to Richmond by the cars.

I did not see him again until I saw him in the hospital at Richmond, nearly a week after he left Sudley Hospital, as the authorities would not allow me to visit my friends there until the day before I left. When I entered the building I was informed that he was dying. I hastened up stairs where he was lying and found our own men and surgeons standing at his bedside in the deepest of grief. I approached his bed and spoke to him, but he was too near Heaven to hear an earthly call; and in a few moments, while I was holding his hand, with a feint sob, his soul was safe in his savior's bosom. I was told that my time was up and left him with those who cared for him tenderly while living.[5]

Of the various reports, the following extract from a letter written on June 25, 1861, to Garrison's parents by James H. Croff of the Eleventh Massachusetts gives the best account of Joseph's last days and who he was as a person:

I was taken prisoner at the battle of Bull Run the 29th of July last. I was at the hospital at the moment of my capture assisting a wounded friend of mine. After the battle, I was placed in the same ward with Joseph to take what care could be taken of the poor, wounded soldiers. Joseph's wound was a very painful one, yet he bore it all with quiet resignation, conversing daily of his father, that he would miss him in harvest time, of his sister, how he would have to put forth great exertions to overtake her in the studies they were pursuing together when he left home. He hoped to recover and return home, until the third day before his death. It was then we had a serious talk of death and life beyond the grave; then, when he knew he could not live but a short time, he looked at me with a smiling face, saying, "It is hard to die so young; to leave all—parents, home friends, and my studies; but there is a better life beyond, and I am going home—my pain will end in Heaven."

After a few minutes, he added, "Jim, I want you, when you are released, to write home and tell my friends I died happy, feeling I fell in a good and just cause. My sister will miss me in her studies. It is very hard, but I die happy, for I shall go to the home of the blessed." I trust the impression I received there will never leave me. I, who had seldom thought of God's supremacy, could poorly appreciate such implicit trust; such a cheerful resigning of one's self unto Him, in whose hands all our lives are.

The next morning, when I relieved the night-watch, I noticed an unusual flush on his cheek; a wildness in the eye. Pain was fast doing the work of death on that blooming body. He recognized me with a smile and as I stooped to fan him, said, "Tell them I died happy, but I wanted to see them all; I hope to meet them all in Heaven."[6]

It is believed that Garrison was buried in or near the Shockoe Hill Cemetery just north of Richmond, as were the other Union prisoners who died there at that time. After the war, in 1866–67, their bodies were removed to the Richmond National Cemetery, where they rest today. There is no grave that bears his name. His remains are probably in one of the graves marked "Unknown."

William David Bennett
b. August 13, 1842; d. September 26, 1886

William Bennett was born in Livingston, Illinois, to Rev. George W. Bennett and Rachel (Wood) Bennett. The 1857 Minnesota Territorial Census reports that the family had moved to Mantorville in Dodge County, where George worked as a merchant and William worked with him.

In 1860 William was a student at Hamline, studying to become a minister, like his father. He was nineteen when he enlisted and, at some point, was promoted to the rank of corporal. He was wounded at Savage Station on June 29, 1862. On October 21, 1862, suffering from chronic diarrhea, he was admitted to the U.S. Army General Hospital, Camp A, in Frederick, Maryland. He did not sufficiently recover from this weakened condition and was discharged for disability on February 4, 1863.

Charles A. Berdan
b. October 27, 1840; d. May 12, 1914

Charles A. Berdan was born into a farming family near Cleveland, Ohio, and when he was sixteen, they moved to Hastings, Minnesota. Like many of his comrades, he was a student at Hamline University at the time the war broke out. When he enlisted on October 29, 1861, the regiment was already out east, Bull Run had been fought, and news of Joseph Garrison's death had probably been received back home. According to the records, Berdan was twenty-four years old, stood five feet eleven inches tall, and had a light complexion, hazel eyes, and auburn hair.

William David Bennett

Charles A. Berdan

In his memoirs 1st Sgt. James Wright mentions Berdan in a story of the Battle of Fredericksburg:

Our brigade had the right front of the troops that spread out into the city; the regiment covered the right of the brigade; and our company was deployed covering the right front and flank. . . . The pickets on the hillsides also had spells of firing at us that gave us an uncomfortable half hour or so occasionally. At such times we took to cover wherever we could find it, and, if they persisted, we watched for their smoke and tried to make them understand "it was a game which two could play."

At the first of these disturbances, I found shelter behind a small enclosure of brickwork three or four feet high and I think that it was Charley Berdan that was with me. We fired several times from behind this, and a number of bullets struck it. We did not know at the time that the protecting shelter marked the resting place of Mary Washington [the mother of George Washington]. And if we had, I have no doubt but we would have crouched down there just the same. It might have seemed a little lacking in respect for the dead to be "scrapping" with the descendants of her old neighbors over her grave, but, if she had been conscious that we were trying to preserve what her son had fought to establish, I doubt not that she would have willingly offered the protection we found there.[7]

Berdan was also at Gettysburg skirmishing to the left of the regiment on July 2 and in the thick of the fight on July 3 during Pickett's Charge

On October 14, 1863, Berdan was wounded at the Battle of Bristoe Station. The First Minnesota was the lead regiment for the Second Corps as it advanced toward the ruins of the Bristoe railroad station. They met enemy skirmishers and maneuvered to hold the high ground as long as they could. When the main body of the larger Confederate force advanced upon them, the men of the First had to make a hasty retreat amid heavy fire to a railroad grade downhill from them, where their comrades from the Nineteenth Maine waited to help defend the position. As Wright describes the situation:

Naturally we supposed that our line was behind the railroad grade. We had no notice of where they were and, as we ran, could not see a flag, a gun, or a black hat. I only recall seeing Andrew Bayer and Charley Berdan as we ran, and they were near me before we started. Reaching the railroad we tumbled into the excavation, scrambled up the embankment, and slid down the other side—among the men of the Nineteenth Maine. . . .

. . . Edrick Frary was hit in the hand and Berdan in the right arm. Berdan had previously had a bullet graze his neck and pass through his rubber blanket, which was rolled on top of his knapsack, and another had cut away part of his hat brim on the opposite side of his head.[8]

When treated for his wound, only a part of the bullet was removed, and the part that remained gave him pain for the rest of his life. On October 19, 1863, Berdan was treated at the Lincoln U.S. Army General Hospital in Washington, DC. He returned to duty on February 6, 1864, the same night the regiment enjoyed a banquet in their honor at the National Hotel in Washington.

When the regiment was mustered out in May 1864, his three-year term of enlistment was not yet over, so he was transferred to Company A of the First Battalion. He was discharged as a sergeant near Petersburg, Virginia, on November 17, 1864.

Brass corps badge worn by Charles Berdan during the war

Mark Anthony Hoyt

b. circa 1838–39; d. July 13, 1864

Another student at Hamline, Mark Hoyt was close to graduating when he enlisted and had been preparing to enter the ministry. He was a literate, well-read man with an excellent vocabulary. When, on April 29, 1861, the group became Company F of the First Minnesota, he was voted by the men to become their second lieutenant. He was married on June 13, 1861, prior to the regiment's heading east. In charge of a detail left behind in Washington to guard the regiment's camp and equipment, he did not participate in the Battle of Bull Run that following month.

On January 1, 1862, he was promoted to first lieutenant and also became the regimental quartermaster. The life of an officer can be a busy and sleep-depriving one, as can be seen in one of his journal entries from 1862:

> During the night—which was cold and stormy—our picket men stood close down to the water's brink where the conversation of the insurgents could easily be heard. No firing occurred until the break of day when the enemy undertook to drive in the pickets of the 15th

Mass. Regiment—which was stationed half a mile, or less, on our right. The engagement was a spirited one and several men were lost on both sides . . . our company, being relieved, returned to camp at "eight" this morning. After eating breakfast—prepared by Hank—I went into the timber to the little streamlet and bathed. Thence returned to quarters, rolled myself in my blankets and proceeded to make up for the countless privations of the preceding night. In about an hour was hastily routed from dreamland by water running into my ear. Jumped up and accused Hank of the mischief, but soon discerned his innocence in the storm which had opened a little "porthole" directly above my head. Attempted to sleep again but was soon roused by Sergeant Williams who wanted a "commission" present at the drawing of rations. No avoiding this—therefore I put my slumbers aside and proceeded to the Commissary's Apartment.[9]

Hoyt served until July 18, 1862, when he resigned and returned to Minnesota, suffering from rheumatism in the lower limbs and shoulders. In November 1863 he received an appointment to the Veteran Reserve Corps and went to Indianapolis. On December 9, 1863, he was assigned to duty as a first lieutenant in Company A of the Fifth Veteran Reserve Corp, stationed at Camp Morton.

On or about May 19, 1864, he returned to St. Paul. His rheumatism had developed into consumption, and Mark died in St. Paul on July 13, 1864, from what was termed *quick consumption*. He was buried in Oakland Cemetery. Unfortunately, his wife, Ella, died shortly thereafter, on October 10, 1865, leaving an orphaned daughter.

Charles Merritt

b. December 30, 1837; d. January 11, 1926

Charles Merritt moved to Minnesota in 1860 and, a year later, enlisted in Red Wing. He was twenty-three years old, stood five feet nine inches tall, and had a light complexion, dark hazel eyes, and light-colored hair. He must have had some musical talent, for he is listed on the muster roll as a musician and served as a drummer for the company. Though younger boys

Charles Merritt

often filled that role, several drummers in the First were over twenty years old.

He was slightly wounded in the regiment's first fight, at Bull Run. Toward the end of the battle, Merritt and three comrades carried Joseph Garrison to the shelter of the Sudley Church. Their kind action placed them, however, in a position to be captured by the Confederates. They spent their first night sleeping on the ground in the rain. The Rebels threw some ham into the crowd, but Charles unfortunately did not get any and thus went hungry.

The Union prisoners were loaded onto boxcars and shipped to Richmond, arriving on a Tuesday night, when they were forced to march through streets filled with jeering men, women, and children. Their journey ended at Libby Prison, and a few days later, he and some others were transferred to Castle Thunder. From there he was, on November 25, 1861, sent to a prison in Tuscaloosa, Alabama. He was returned to Richmond on December 31 and paroled at Washington, North Carolina, on May 28, 1862.

During the Civil War an honor system existed for prisoners that may be hard to imagine today. Early in

the war men were paroled and later formally exchanged for prisoners from the other side. During their parole soldiers pledged not to take up arms against their enemy until they were formally exchanged and, furthermore, were expected to report to wherever the exchange was to take place. Merritt's group of fellow parolees were taken to New York City and given passes to return home. After a time they were ordered to report to Benton Barracks, Missouri, which Merritt did in October 1862. He was formally exchanged, returned to the regiment at Falmouth, Virginia, and back on the muster roll of the First Minnesota by December 31, 1862.

Though Merritt was a musician, who were normally kept out of battle action, he appears to have been an active soldier, as well. He was in the thick of it at the Battle of Chancellorsville, where he volunteered to serve with Lt. Hezekiah Bruce in a difficult mission. At Gettysburg he was probably held in reserve with the other drummers, though he may have been serving in the ranks and moved off with Company F when they were detached as skirmishers.

On May 5, 1864, Merritt was discharged after fulfilling his three-year term of enlistment. Merritt's photograph was taken in St. Paul in 1864 while the unit was back home and awaiting their discharge.

Charles Merritt was one of the last survivors of the regiment, dying at his home on January 11, 1926, at the age of eighty-nine. He was buried in Woodlawn Cemetery in Winona, where several of his comrades from Company F had also been laid to rest, including John Ball, Charles Ely, Charles Goddard, and Mathew Marvin.

Abraham Edward Welch

b. August 16, 1839; d. February 1, 1864

Abraham Welch (known as Ed to his friends) was a twenty-two-year-old student ready to enter his junior year at Hamline when the war began. As was the custom early in the war, the men of Company F elected their officers, and Welch was voted first lieutenant.

During the Civil War, Southerners named battles after nearby towns or cities, whereas Northerners named them after rivers, creeks, or other landmarks. Hence, the first major battle can be called either Bull Run or First Manassas, depending on your point of view, North or South. At one point during this epic first confrontation, Welch was seen rallying his men and discharging his pistol at the enemy, declaring, "So

Abraham Edward Welch

Hubbs, C. S. Mills, C. W. Merritt, Hans Halstead and Henry Burtuff. I am here with nothing but a woolen shirt on, just as I went into the fight, and have to sleep on the bare floor, but this I do not mind. The confinement is very galling to me, but my care will be very light if I can only be assured you are well and not in a state of anxiety on my account. . . . The officers in charge here are gentlemen, and treat us as kindly as their orders will permit. Remember me to all my friends in Red Wing, and tell them that if all, or even a majority, had followed where Company F led, the field would have been ours. P. S. I was not wounded during the fight, except a bruise upon my hip from a spent ball, which only lamed me, and is no longer felt.

Within a few days of writing his father, Welch tried to escape. Two articles published in the *Richmond Dispatch* on August 15, 1861, tell the story:

AN ESCAPED PRISONER.—Rev. Newton Short, a Baptist clergyman, of Henrico, fell in yesterday with a suspicious looking military character on the Meadow Ridge, about six miles from Richmond. He said that he was going to Old Church to see a man named Carpenter, and as he was altogether out of the way for such a destination, and no such man as Carpenter was there, Mr. Short suspected that he was an escaped prisoner, and, after a little more questioning, accused him of it, which he stoutly denied, of course, but afterwards admitted that he was a Yankee Lieutenant, escaped from one of the tobacco factories on Main street. Mr. Short compelled him to return to town, and delivered him up to the proper authorities. The prisoner stated that a number of others had also escaped.

Later in the same paper:

Recaptured.—A Yankee officer, named Welch, who succeeded in escaping from Harwood's tobacco factory, a few days ago, by the rear, having eluded the guard and obtained access to the open air through the kitchen of the establishment, was captured yesterday by the Rev. Mr. Short, living six miles beyond Richmond, and returned to his old quarters. Welch had no

help me God, I will never run. I will die here." Welch went down with a bullet wound in his hip. After the battle twenty-five-year-old Pvt. Theodore Wood wrote:

Poor Ed Welch (our favorite) who was wounded in the hip by a musket ball, was the last to retreat. I saw him stand and drop three rebels in succession with his revolver. I don't know whether he is safe or not, for the last words I heard him say were that he wouldn't leave the field so long as his legs remained under him.

Captured by the Rebels, Welch was held in a Richmond prison, along with many other men from the First. The enlisted men were held at Ligon's tobacco warehouse, whereas the officers and NCOs were held in Harwood's tobacco warehouse on the adjacent corner. The enlisted men and officers were separated in a belief that it would reduce escape attempts. From one of these prisons, Welch wrote to his father on July 30, 1861, briefly describing the battle:

There are twenty-three here from the First Minnesota, besides some in the hospital. . . . From Company F there are E. F. Thomas, Charles

shoes on or shirt. His military dress coat being without buttons, had been tied up with strings. He professed to be making his way to Hanover Court House to collect a debt due by a man named Carpenter. He was at first directed how to proceed, but his appearance exciting suspicion, he was detained and brought to town.

Welch was sent to New Orleans with 250 other prisoners. On May 4, 1862, he was placed in confinement in the prison at Salisbury, North Carolina. He was paroled on August 17, 1862, at Aiken's Landing, Virginia, which had become the common place for the two opposing armies to exchange and release prisoners through parole.

Welch had actually been taken off the regimental rolls as of July 21, 1862. He returned to Minnesota to recover. His recovery was slow, though, and he remained in Minnesota for some time.

In the summer of 1862, Minnesota's Dakota people and the state came into conflict, resulting in what later came to be known as the Dakota War of 1862. When the first whites arrived in what would become Minnesota Territory, they found two tribal groups of Indians residing in the area. The Dakota people were called the Sioux by their enemies, the Ojibwe, and this name was adopted by French trappers. They lived primarily in the southern part of the territory. Those who called themselves Ojibwe (or Chippewa, an alternative and, in the United States, a more common Anglicization) lived more to the north.

In early September, the Third Minnesota arrived home after their surrender at Murfreesboro, Tennessee. The field officers remained imprisoned in the South, but the enlisted men were paroled and sent home. On September 4, 1862, with the conflict between the settlers and the Dakota beginning, Governor Ramsey gave Welch a commission as a major in the Fourth Minnesota Infantry. However, he appointed Welch to temporarily command the Third Minnesota and sent it and other units to fight against the Dakota. On September 23, 1862, he led the Third in a victory at the Battle of Wood Lake, though he was seriously wounded in the fight.

On December 20, 1862, after some time for recovery, he was formally mustered as a major in the Fourth Minnesota by Ft. Snelling's mustering officer during the Civil War, army captain A. D. Nelson. Welch was sent south to take his new position. He was wounded at the Battle of Vicksburg on May 21, 1863.

In September 1863 he was sent to the officers' hospital in Nashville, Tennessee. Having suffered from chronic diarrhea for six months, he was gravely ill and knew that he would never sufficiently recover to command again. On January 2, 1864, he submitted his resignation. On January 31, 1864, Lt. Col. John E. Touttellotte, Maj. Welch's commanding officer in the Fourth, described him as follows when addressing Welch's petition to resign:

> In regards to Major Welch, I wish to say that he has been in the service since April 25, 1861. He has been three times wounded, once very severely. He is an excellent soldier & a high minded gentleman. He is, if still alive, very sick in Hospital at Nashville. I would respectfully recommend the acceptance of his resignation as it appears that he will never again do service in the Field.

Unfortunately, Welch died of disease in Nashville on February 1, 1864. He served and fought bravely wherever he was sent, and he was dead at the age of twenty-four. The township of Grant in Goodhue County was settled in 1857, and in 1872 it was renamed Welch in honor of Abraham Edward Welch.

Hezekiah Bruce
b. November 4, 1832; d. April 24, 1911

Hezekiah Bruce was born in Faceton, Vermont. At the outbreak of the war, twenty-eight-year-old Hezekiah lived on a farm with his father, Horace, his older brother, George, and his younger brother, W. H. Bruce. When mustered into service, he was made the Company F's second sergeant. Bruce stood five feet ten inches tall and had a fair complexion, blue eyes, and brown hair. During his service he was promoted to first sergeant and, later, to second lieutenant.

At the Battle of Chancellorsville, 2nd Lt. Bruce led a small contingent from the First Minnesota who were involved in the capture of Marye's Heights during the battle's final stage. When the command requested volunteers, the mission's danger was emphasized and the statement made that failure was likely, that not a man might return alive. In spite of this peril, Bruce, as well as many privates—even more than was needed—volunteered. Out of these volunteers, twenty men were chosen. At first it was thought that more than one officer would be needed. When Hezekiah volun-

Hezekiah Bruce

teered, Gen. Sedgwick's aide, who had brought the request, asked, "Who is that young man?"

"Lieutenant Bruce," was the reply.

"Well, if it is Bruce, he will be as good as three," the aide affirmed, and Lt. Bruce took charge of the detail alone.

As Charles Merritt, who also served in Company F, tells the story:

On May 2nd, the regiment received marching orders and on arriving in front of Fredericksburg, twenty-five men were chosen from the regiment, one of whom was the writer, to help lay the pontoon bridge across the Rappahannock in front of the city. The opposite shores were lined with rifle pits filled with men and artillery in the rear. We were placed under the command of Lieut. Bruce of Company F, First regiment, a cool, level headed officer. His men knew they could depend on his cool judgment and courage which means much in a tight place. We worked our way down the river but for some reason were not fired upon. We lay there for some little time waiting orders. Meantime, Gen. Sedgwick with the sixth corps had crossed the river below the city and the enemy, except

a thin line in the pit, were withdrawn from our front. Then the pontoons were quickly laid and Bruce and his men charged across, capturing a number of prisoners that remained in the rifle pits. We were closely followed by Gibbon's division of the second corps. The balance of the day we were in the front ranks with Sedgwick's men when Mary's Heights were carried and the enemy driven out at the point of the bayonet, leaving large quantities of knapsacks and baggage that had been thrown off in the rear of their works. We were again deployed as skirmishers moving to the right towards the Rappahannock above the city. In the rifle pits on the side of the hill were squads of "Johnnies" who failed to get out in time. They surrendered and were sent to the rear.

I should have said that about twenty men were added to the skirmish line after the capture of the heights. During the day we captured something over two hundred men in small squads numbering from a half dozen to fifteen or twenty each. We had a sharp scrap with about twenty men lodged in an old log barn. When we had them nearly surrounded they attempted to get out, but our persuasive Springfield rifles dropped several of them and the rest surrendered. The wounded were obliged to leave. They were cared for later. One of the funny incidents was the capture of a redoubt or earth work, with two embrasures from which pointed two guns of large caliber. Bruce maneuvered for its capture without getting directly in front of the guns, and then charged the works. The guns proved to be stove pipes mounted on old wagon wheels. There were several "Johnnies" inside, but they made no show of fight and were disarmed and sent back. A little further on we captured a sergeant and a number of men that had been left on the picket line in the bend of the river above town. From this we moved on up the river with now and then a lively scrimmage with the enemy who supposed the battle line was close behind. But in fact, the commander had lost us. We went back towards Chancellorsville some two miles picking up small squads of prisoners, so that when we were recalled we had about seventy five victims.

In going back over the field the knapsacks of the "Johnnies" that were left were overhauled, the prisoners being allowed to take such articles as would be of use to them. Some good homemade stockings, I remember, were among the things the knapsacks contained. It was dark when we crossed the river. A drizzling rain had set in and wet, foot sore and weary we found the regiment about midnight and we were very glad to bunk down on a wet blanket.

Lieut. Bruce was brave, cool, calm, and one of the kindest of men. The boys all loved him.[10]

Col. Colvill also reports:

I cannot pass over the gallant conduct of twenty-five privates of the regiment under the command of Lieutenant Bruce of Co F, who volunteered upon the call of the general, to clear the way across the river at the point of the bayonet in case of opposition, as was expected should be offered to our passage, and who being then detached from the regiment, were deployed in front of General Sedgwick's command as skirmishers, and were among the first to enter the enemy's works, and continued the whole day in the advance, killing, wounding and taking numbers of the enemy, fortunately without the loss of a man on their part.

Hezekiah Bruce was with the regiment when it fought at Gettysburg. The battle left most officers either killed or wounded, so on September 26, 1863, he was promoted to first lieutenant of Company F, serving the rest of his enlistment as such. He was mustered out with the regiment on May 5, 1864.

Amos G. Scofield

b. 1837; d. August 18, 1861

Born in New York, Amos Scofield was named after his father, who moved the family to Illinois, where he died in 1844. His mother then moved the family to Wisconsin sometime between 1846 and 1850, and in the mid-1850s, when land became available for settlement, they finally settled on a farm near the small community of Roscoe in Goodhue County. Scofield was twenty-four when he was mustered on April 29, 1861. Capt. Colvill appointed him second corporal, a distinction showing he had some favor with the captain.

When the regiment went into its first battle, at Bull

Amos G. Scofield

Run, Company F was positioned on the regiment's far right and as it joined the action lost contact with all but Company A. Suddenly, the men faced soldiers in blue uniforms and dared not fire until they were recognized as friend or foe. Unfortunately, they were the latter, and as a stunning volley hit the line about six of the company fell. Scofield and the rest returned fire and advanced until forced back by a galling fire. As they retired, George McKinley and Joseph Garrison went down. Moments later, Scofield also fell when a bullet entered the left side of his head, just above the ear, exiting through his mouth and severely wounding him. Scofield's head was quickly bandaged, and friends laboriously hauled him to Sudley Springs, where a field hospital was being established. James Wright and others from Company F helped carry some of the wounded to safety. As Wright recalls:

A hospital had been located at the Sudley Church; an effort had been made to get the wounded there; and both surgeons—Stewart and LeBoutillier— were there. Some of the wounded were being assisted up the hill at the time, and I helped to carry Joe Garrison on a blanket a part of the way. At the same time, Corporal Schofield was being helped by some of the other of the company.

Scofield had the good fortune to be put into an ambulance and carried off the field to the Third Division's hospital in Alexandria. He languished, though, in the hot hospital, barely able to breathe, fighting fever and pain from the gaping wound. He lived only one more month and mercifully died August 18, 1861. His medical report tells of a side of warfare more tragic than any battlefield death. As it states:

Amos Scofield Co. F

Corporal Amos G. Scofield 1st Minnesota Volunteers was wounded at the battle of Bull Run, Virginia July 21, 1861 by a minnie ball which entered two inches behind the left mastoid process, and escaped at the mouth, fracturing the lower maxilla, and carrying away a portion of the primitive carotid and its branches from the left side. He was admitted to the 3rd division hospital, Alexandria, the next day; an aneurismal tumor had formed. The case did well, except that there was a hard circumscribed swelling behind the left ear. On August 4th, a hemorrhage occurred from the wound of entrance, which was controlled by a graduated compress, but which was gradually succeeded by a swelling which extended from the mastoid process to the clavicle and which was caused by the escape of blood into the tissues of the neck. Frequent hemorrhages occurred from the wound in the mouth, which could not be controlled but by compression on the left carotid. The compression on the veins of the neck induced great edematous swelling of the face, the left eye was closed, the tongue hung from the mouth, and articulation became impossible. The hemorrhage from the mouth returned about 5 AM on August 11th, compression was made over the carotid, when the patient appeared to have drawn into his glottis a clot of blood during an effort of inspiration, Apnoea ensued, followed in a few moments by death, his strength being entirely exhausted by his losses of blood and rest, and his continued suffering. At the autopsy the left side of the neck was found distended by effused blood. The internal carotid was uninjured, but the external was lost in the tumor, which seemed to be a true aneurism undergoing consolidation. Behind the larynx was found a quantity of dark fluid blood. In the right ventricle of the larynx was found a soft clot, which was the immediate cause of death, since it acted as a valve permitting of expiration, but prevented inspiration. Assistant Surgeon H. Lawrence Sheldon, USV decided against an operation, as he could not satisfy his mind as to the source of the hemorrhage. The pathological specimens, consisting of a part of the lower jaw and a portion of the primitive carotid and its branches exhibiting a tumor, were contributed to the Army Medical Museum, with a history of the case, by Assistant Surgeon William Thompson, U.S.A., and are numbered 4923 and 4925 of the Surgical Section.[11]

Scofield's body was laid to rest in Alexandria National Cemetery, section A, site 1089. His mother, Alvira, received a mother's pension of eight dollars a month to ease her loss. After the war a Grand Army of the Republic post was established in Zumbrota, near his homestead, and was named in his honor.

On October 14, 1861, following Scofield's death, his twenty-one-year-old younger brother, George, was mustered into the Fourth Minnesota. He was a member of the Fourth's color guard and carried the flag at Vicksburg. George was killed in action on December 8, 1863, at Murfreesboro, Tennessee.

John Ball

b. December 5, 1835; d. September 26, 1875

John Ball grew up in Rutland, New York, and came to Minnesota in 1853, settling in Winona. He worked as a surveyor and owned and operated an abstract company in town, drawing its first plat map. He was twenty-five years old when the war began, and on April 29, 1861, he was mustered in as the orderly sergeant, also known as the first sergeant, of Company K. This company was mostly made up of men from the Winona area.

Sgt. John Merritt of Company K mentions him when discussing the Battle of Bull Run:

I was a sergeant in Co. K, First Minnesota Volunteers. The regiment broke camp about 3 o'clock on the morning of Sunday, July 21, 1861. With a soldiers and three days rations, we realized before sunrise that it was going to be a hot day. . . . John Ball, the orderly sergeant of K Co., was sick and I was acting orderly sergeant. As sick as Ball was, he came onto the

John Ball

field, and I saw him standing near the regiment while we were engaged, with his arms folded, apparently the most unconcerned person of the lot; he was a brave and fearless man.

On November 15, 1861, while in camp at Poolesville, Maryland, Ball was discharged and commissioned a second lieutenant of the company. On July 17, 1862, at Harrison's Landing, he was promoted to first lieutenant. In September 1862, Lt. Col. Miller received an appointment as colonel of the Seventh Minnesota, causing several upward promotions within the officer corps, as well as transfers from one company to another. Ball was transferred from Company K to Company F to become its first lieutenant.

Just three months later, in December 1862, Capt. John McCallum of Company F was wounded in the foot at Fredericksburg and was sent to the hospital. During the following months, his wound did not heal well, and on May 6, 1863, he was transferred to the Veteran Reserve Corps, effectively putting 1st Lt. Ball in command of the company. He was formally pro-

moted to the rank of captain after Gettysburg, with his promotion being retroactively dated to May 6.

In the late afternoon of July 2, Company F was in line, waiting and watching the battle before them. The regiment received harassing fire from their left, and Col. Colvill ordered Lt. Ball to take Company F as skirmishers and handle the problem. Ball advanced his company a few paces and then moved off at a left oblique angle. They proceeded about two hundred yards to a rail fence and then followed it toward their target, eventually moving out of sight of the regiment.

As the afternoon wore on and evening approached, the haze of smoke covered the battlefield. The company engaged in a fight, and some men were wounded. In the distance Ball could see a large body of Confederates moving across the field in the direction of the regiment, probably the right side of Wilcox's brigade. He dispatched Pvt. Jonas Davis to find Col. Colvill, report the company's situation, and ask for instructions. Almost immediately, he noticed another large body of the enemy, which may have been part of Barksdale's brigade. Company F began firing into the right of their line and drew return fire.

Firing intensified on the left near Little Round Top and on the right, which was thought to be the First Minnesota engaged with the enemy Ball had just seen. He gave the order for his small band to fall back a short distance and continue firing. Fresh Union troops came over the ridge behind the company and moved forward into the battle. With that, Capt. Ball brought his men back to the ridge, where they rested and waited in reserve. He was anxious to learn about the status of the regiment and to get new orders from Col. Colvill. Pvt. Davis had not returned, so he sent Sgt. Philip Hamlin down the line to find the regiment.

By ten o'clock that night, neither man had returned. Weary and tired from the day's fierce fighting yet without orders to return, Ball had the men of Company F lay down to eat and sleep, as best they could, with their arms at their sides. About this time Sgt. Hamlin came back with the sad news that he had found only a few men of the regiment under the command of Capt. Messick, believing the rest killed or captured. Many of the men wanted to return to the regiment, which they estimated to be less than a quarter mile to the right. Though at first inclined to return, Ball had received orders from a higher-ranking officer to stay in place until morning, and that is what they were forced to do.

After receiving permission to return early the next

Commanding officers of the Eleventh Minnesota, *from left to right,* Lt. Col. John Ball, Col. James Gilfillan, Surgeon Henry McMahon, and Major Martin Maginnis

morning, Lt. Ball led Company F back to where they had left the regiment the day before. Moving down the line of weary, sleeping soldiers, he found Capt. Messick, who was now the ranking senior officer. Messick had only a handful of men left from the previous day's fighting who could shoulder a musket. Ball's group added about twenty more. The men helped their wounded comrades and prepared for the next Confederate attack. A few more from Company F were wounded when Pickett made his charge that afternoon.

On October 14, 1863, Ball was severely wounded at the Battle of Bristoe Station. He was sent to the hospital in Alexandria, Virginia, where he was expected to die. Surprisingly, he recovered but was, thereafter, always bothered with pain caused by the wound. Though faded and emaciated and having developed a slight cough, he returned to duty on January 19, 1864. Showing a strong will and determination, he served until the regiment was mustered out on May 5, 1864, at which time he returned to Winona.

Four months later, he accepted a commission as lieutenant colonel of the Eleventh Minnesota, to date from September 7, 1864, and then as colonel, to date from September 10. One of his best friends in the Old First, Martin Maginnis, was commissioned as the major of the Eleventh. Together, they traveled to Tennessee and their new command, where they cooked together and shared the same tent until the end of the war.

The following affidavit was written on June 10, 1890, by Maginnis for Ball's widow as she applied for her widow's pension. It mentions Ball's being wounded, that war was hell, and that surviving it was a challenge:

I knew said John Ball initially as a Sergeant, 1st & 2nd Lieut. and as Captain of said 1st Minn Vol Infty. I messed with him and was his tent mate for a great portion of the years of 62 & 63. I knew him to be of hardy, robust and enduring

John Ball as a lieutenant colonel in the Eleventh Minnesota
Volunteer Infantry Regiment

enemy, threw his revolver in their faces. That just as they broke and retreated before our fire, he was shot down, by my side, as we supposed mortally wounded—the ball passing through his groin and carrying away one of his testes. He came very close to death, but unexpectedly recovered and rejoined his regiment, though he never recovered his former vigor and superb health. I served with him until the regiment was re-organized.

In September 1864, we were respectively appointed as Lieut. Col & Major of the 11th Minnesota. We again went together to Tennessee. We messed and lived together and were in constant companionship until June 1865, when we were both mustered out.

I distinctly and positively assert that though zealous and active in duty he never recovered from his wound and that before our parting I felt that his constitution was irretrievably shattered. After this I met him on a number of occasions, at re-unions of the regiment and elsewhere up to the time of his death—and saw a great decline on each meeting—and heard his complaints that he never recovered his health. I believe that his death resulted from disease, induced by his wound and the hardship that he underwent. I repeat that when I first knew him he was in rugged health and capable of as much endurance and fatigue as any man in the service. He was a brave and gallant soldier. He endured constant service—was tried in many battles and was wounded under circumstances which won the praise of all witnesses.

constitution. He was capable of standing and did stand, with less trouble than others, the hard marches and battles in which the regiment was engaged—on the Peninsula, at Antietam, the battles on the Rappahannock and at Gettysburg. We were both in command of companies on the day of the battle of Bristoe Station. The regiment was deployed as skirmishers, for the Second Division of the Second Army Corps, commanded by Gen. G K Warren. We discovered a corps of the enemy endeavoring to advance and cut us off from the ford, near Bristoe. We gave the alarm and engaged the skirmishers of the enemy and held them until the 2nd Division 2nd Corps had time to form a line along the railroad embankment extending from the ford to the cut below Bristoe Station. Then, in obedience to orders, we fell back to the line of battle and that our companies were together. The enemy advanced in several charges upon the line and once seemed about to take the railroad—when among a few others, Capt. Ball, sprang in front of the line upon the embankment and firing all the shots from his revolver into the advancing

After the war he returned to Winona. He was married on December 27, 1865, and fathered three children over the next six years. He was elected a representative in the Minnesota state legislature in 1866 and later served as the Winona County treasurer. As Maginnis mentions, owing to the hardships of military service, his health never was very good. He was treated for a form of bronchitis, probably suffering from tuberculosis, and his health continued to deteriorate. He died on September 26, 1875, while visiting his hometown of Rutland, New York. His body was returned to Winona, where it was buried in Woodlawn Cemetery, the final resting place for several other men who had served in the First Minnesota.

Philip Rice Hamlin

b. May 24, 1839; d. July 3, 1863

In 1855 at the age of fifteen, Philip Hamlin came to Minnesota with his family and helped his father set up their new farm. Five years later, when war was declared, he joined Company F and was appointed a corporal. He survived the Battle of Bull Run and was soon after appointed a sergeant.

Hamlin got along well with his comrades, many of whom were his age and had been students at Hamline University. He was well educated and during his studies had developed a flair for writing. His letters home were often religious in nature, yet his commentaries on the military situation were surprisingly accurate. He considered the confidence in Gen. McClellan misplaced and the performance of regimental officers courageous but inexperienced.

His friends in the company included James Wright, another sergeant who also was a Methodist, and a close relationship soon developed. In his memoirs Wright notes:

Company F was not a "religious" company, but Company F—like every other company—had its little circle of praying men who used to gather at convenient times in some tent or under the trees for prayer. The real leader of these was big, manly Sergeant Philip Hamline. No man in the company but respected him and his sentiments, and he and his associates were always treated with all proper consideration by the other members of the company. There were many earnest, praying men in the regiment, and my guess is that about all of the men did some praying on special occasions.

Hamlin survived the battles of Savage Station and Antietam, and as the war dragged on, he struggled against a growing depression. In a letter to his younger brother, Charlie, he told him to look at the small details of life and to think of God. He finished the letter with a more permanent farewell to his brother: "You may someday hear that Philip is dead and know that I have fallen in battle and been buried in a strange land where you may never see me but hoping for better things, I bid you goodbye."

At Gettysburg, Hamlin and Company F had all they could handle. On the late afternoon of July 2, the company was detached to take out some Confederate sharpshooters. The company suffered five casualties. Capt. Ball sent a messenger back to find the regiment, and when he didn't return, Ball sent Hamlin, knowing that he could count on him. Late that night, he returned with the melancholy news of the regiment's fate. Many in Company F did not believe the situation could be that bad and went to sleep at their position on the field thinking the men would be found in the morning.

The next morning, Company F rejoined the regiment, learned the grim truth of the prior day, and began to build a barricade, anticipating a major frontal attack from the enemy. At one o'clock a terrific barrage began, which was followed by an assault by the cream of the Confederate army. Nine brigades of about 12,000 men made up the advance toward the First Minnesota and the center of the Union line. Hamlin waited with the others for the Rebels to come into range, and when they did, the entire regiment fired as one, visibly staggering their line, the survivors drifting to the left. Hamlin and the rest of his comrades did not wait for orders and bolted to the right to confront the enemy in the open. The flag of the First Minnesota was in the forefront, with Hamlin close at hand. Here, in the open, the flag went down, and moments later, Hamlin was hit in the neck, leg, and chest, dying instantly.

Men like Hamlin helped to carry the day for the Union. After the battle Sgt. Wright and his comrades managed to care for the dead and wounded before caring for themselves. Later in life, Wright wrote the following about the aftermath of the battle on the third:

> We now began to realize that we were getting hungry, and in the darkness we built little fires and made coffee. None of us knew where we were likely to be, or what the morrow would bring for us to do, and as we drank our coffee we decided to bury Hamlin that night. Search was made for a spade and after some time a shovel was found. With this a shallow trench was dug beside a walnut tree, near which he had been killed, struck by four bullets. His blanket and tent-cloth were spread in it. He was then laid upon them and covered with the remaining portions. Then those present knelt in silence about him, with uncovered heads. I do not recall that a word was spoken; but it was a sincere and reverential service fitting the time and the situation. Then we covered him over with dirt and stones we had thrown out of the trench and placed at his head a board, on which his name, company and regiment, had been marked.

Sgt. Wright later added:

> I feel that I ought not to pass on without a word about two members of Company F who gave that "last full measure of devotion" to their country of which Lincoln spoke at Gettysburg. I do not think it would have been possible to have taken two from the company who would have been so generally missed and so sincerely mourned. Big-chested, broad shouldered young fellows, almost if not quite six feet tall, they were a couple of splendid specimens of physical development. Neither had had much in the way of educational advantages, but both were well-endowed mentally. Their standing in the company as soldiers was first class. Men of proved courage and "plenty of sand"—to be depended upon anywhere and all of the time. As "non coms" they were a credit to themselves and the company—and a commission to either of them would have been worthily bestowed with no discredit to the State of Minnesota.

> I had no acquaintance with either until I met them as members of the company, but I judge their early life had been under very different environments. Squire was the older, 26 years, and he was not exactly a saint—as he sometimes asserted. He did not always refuse a drink. He would sometimes "set into a game" and use profanity, but these things were not of a degree to in any way interfere with his duties as a soldier.

> Hamline, in these things, was a strong contrast. He was in his 23rd year, was of a religious temperament, trained up in a good old-fashioned Methodist home, where the day began and ended with reading the Bible and prayers. He was always and everywhere an honest, earnest, consistent Christian man, whose open unostentatious, frank, manly and unobtrusive observance of what he considered his religious duties was well-known and respected by all who knew him.

Sgt. Wright wrote to Hamlin's father describing his last moments in as gentle a way as he could. If the Hamlin family took any comfort in the letter, it was short lived, for one year later their next oldest son, Jacob, died of wounds at Nashville. Hamlin's parents remained in New Haven, taking care of their remaining children, and when pensions became available for the mothers of deceased soldiers, Mrs. Hamlin applied for one. She received eight dollars a month for her loss, keeping the memory of her sons alive by rereading their letters. She died in 1882, and her husband, Rice Hamlin, followed her in 1887.

Philip's brother W. H. Hamlin kept his letters, as well as a tintype that was badly damaged by many years of poor storage (see p. 151). Hamlin's body was exhumed from the battlefield in October 1863 and interred in the Gettysburg National Cemetery, where today he rests alongside his comrades of the First Minnesota in section A, grave no. 10.

James Wright
b. November 27, 1840; d. August 25, 1936

James Wright's parents moved their family from Illinois to Minnesota in 1855, landing at Red Wing on April 22, 1855. They settled in an area called Spring Creek Valley, located about five miles from Red Wing. James recalled that he "was struck by Minnesota lightning in [his] boyhood days." The expression was both figurative and lit-

James Wright

erally true; his family's cabin was nearly destroyed by a lightning strike that killed two of his siblings, his oldest brother and his youngest sister.

After farming with his family for a while, he entered Hamline University. Wright left his studies to join the crusade against the Confederacy. After the attack on Ft. Sumter, he wrote that he felt this was an "affront to national dignity" and that "the only consistent attitude of a loyal man was with a rifle at his shoulder, and the only logical argument a bullet."

He joined the Goodhue Volunteers, which was composed almost entirely of single young men like himself. He was twenty-two years old at the time and stood five feet six inches tall. He had a dark complexion, hazel-colored eyes, and chestnut-colored hair. He was appointed a corporal in the company and, shortly thereafter, was promoted to fifth sergeant. Eventually, he was promoted to first sergeant, also known as the orderly sergeant.

After the regiment's first fight, at Bull Run, Wright wrote an article published in the Hastings newspaper, the *Weekly Republican*. In it he describes the battle:

The rebels had made a stand in front of the woods and batteries began to play upon us as we approached them. The cannon balls were shrieking over our heads, and the wicked shells went hissing by, striking in the ground, bursting, and throwing dirt and gravel in every direction. . . . It was somewhat startling but still interesting, to see the balls strike and go skipping along, making dust fly like a whirlwind. . . . Some of the balls flew so close we felt the air they set in motion. Some fell short and rolled under our feet. At this point we got under cover of a hill and marched up to the rebel lines. They sought the cover of the woods and trenches about their works.

When we again reached the rising ground we were subjected to a galling fire of shot and shell from the breastworks. We were now in an old field of open ground and the rebels in the brush. We fell on our faces close by the road awaiting their fire. It came quick and like a hailstorm, but mostly too high. We sprang up and gave them a quick response and kept firing, loading, lying on our backs and raising up on our knees to fire; we were greatly exposed, and they had the protection of the trees and trenches. Col. Franklin now ordered us to get under cover of the woods, by falling back to the rear and left, this we did and fought from behind the trees and fences. We then charged on them three times successively, driving them back into the woods behind their batteries, they as often rallied, compelling us to fall back with loss. They outnumbered us I think three to one, . . . But we kept up the fight, pouring in shot when they came out of the brush, compelling them to fall back, their loss as well as ours being great. The third time we crossed the ground it was strewn thickly with the dead. The attack had been made by the second Mississippi regiment, and they mistook us in the fight for a regiment of Alabamian's. One of their Colonels rode close up to us, and cried out, "don't fire on your own men for God's sake." Captain Colvill asked what regiment he belonged to. He said the 2nd Mississippi. Our captain leveled a revolver and ordered him to get off instantly. He obeyed and was sent to the rear (a coerced, subjected rebel,). . . . A company of black horse cavalry then came out in fine order and made a dash at our regiment, but we poured in a destructive fire that emptied the saddles faster than you could count; they came bravely on but could not stand our fire and had to run, what was left of them. . . .

. . . I will now try to give you a few particulars and incidents, as I know all my friends desire them. . . . Among those you know, first, is my best and nearest friend, C. N. Harris. He was shot in the breast, and died in a few minutes. He was cool and brave. When he fell he cried out, "God help me;" and as the blood spurted from his wound he said in broken sentences, "Write to my parents and sisters; tell them I died like a man, rallying the men to the charge; I glory in my death; I stood by the flag till shot down;" then he gasped, "I have a brother in heaven, I hope to be there soon." He motioned for water, drank a little, closed his eyes, and soon his manly bosom ceased to move.

Joseph P. Garrison, brave boy, was shot through the hips early in the fight. He was close to me and called me to him. I picked him up and carried him to the rear in the shade, and set him with his back to a tree. He asked me to load his gun and give it to him. I did so, and gave him water. I asked him if he felt prepared to die; he said he did and could die happy. When we left the field he was brought to the ambulance, but whether living or dead I do not know.

H. J. Rush was shot dead. I did not see him. . . . Corp. Scofield was shot through the head, just above and back of the ears, the ball entering the side of his head. . . . John Lee shot in the leg and I think afterwards bayoneted by a rebel on the field. . . . McKinley shot in the hips: I judge his wound proved fatal in a few hours.

. . . I cannot describe my feelings for those brave boys and their friends at home. Some of them imposed on me the painful task of writing to their friends of their death. It is a sad duty. We had met in times of peace in the school room and the lyceum, had mingled in society, together had endured the hardships and privations of the camp and campaign, trying to while away the dreary hours of the one by talking home and friends in the past, and cheering each other in the dangers of the other.

. . . When we received the first fire I felt a little "queer," my thoughts ran quicker, my mind was clearer, and my body felt lighter than it ever did before to my recollection. Just as I rose to fire the third shot, I felt something

and sat down suddenly without intending it. I sprang up again and Williams said, "Corporal Wright is shot," and asked me if I was. At first I told him that I was, then I thought I was not, at least not hurt. I could fight at any rate. On looking, I found the bottom of my shirt pocket torn off and the top of my pants gone. I afterwards found a small pocket glass had the edge shot off and a pocket memorandum had the corner cut off, while the medal that fastened my belt was bent into a very awkward shape. But for this bit of brass you would not receive this letter, and your correspondent would be with the killed or wounded. Late in the fight I had my musket knocked out of my hand by a piece of shell. I looked for it, and found it laying about six feet from me, too badly bent for straight shooting. I got a dead Vermonter's gun, but found my bullets would not fit, so I returned and got some of his, and found they answered the purpose very well.

There is a kind of intoxication in the sight of blood and the smell of powder, that gave me a strange excitement, and earnestness never felt before, and which I do not wish to feel again. The most surprising thing of all was the perfect obliviousness to the flight of time. . . . I was then aware of being feint, weak, and parched with a burning thirst, which I could not quench with a canteen of dirty water that I took from the stream as I came away. I had emptied my canteen, giving to the wounded in battle. The bullets had whistled so close, so loud and so long, that it seemed dull, as if something was lacking, when the firing ceased. The horrors of war cannot be described. I shall never forget the looks of some of the fellows I met at bayonet's point. The look of unutterable agony of some of the wounded, death stricken soldiers will haunt me to the grave, and their piercing cries will ring in my ears while I have an existence.

Wright, who was only twenty, also had a sense of humor that helped him get through the ugliness of war. About the Battle of Bull Run he also writes:

While lying on my right side—ramming a cartridge, which was lodged part way down the barrel—I had my feet crossed to hold the butt of the musket and my left knee bent—when a

James Wright as a captain in the First Battalion of Minnesota Infantry

bullet cut through my pants and across the inside of my left knee, but did no damage. It was a pretty close call for a leg.

At Gettysburg, Wright was slightly wounded in the face during the repulse of Pickett's Charge. In his memoirs he writes about the incident, which occurred as the regiment was shifting position:

When we were running to the right to close the break in the lines, it was a case of "get there" and each one was trying to make it as quickly as possible. There was not much regard for formation. I could only recall afterwards that Joe Richardson was just to my right and trying to talk as we ran. . . .

Just then I was conscious of coming in contact with something. I was partly turned aside, staggered, confused and half-blinded—but it was only for an instant. Then my vision cleared, and I "braced up" and ran on again. And my mind was so wholly taken up with what was before me that I thought no more about it.

. . . It was not until after the excitement of the moment had subsided, and we began to get together, that I observed that my neck and face were bleeding. I then found that the left shoulder, breast, and sleeve of my blouse were ornamented with shreds of lead and splinters of wood, and several of the latter were driven into the side of my face and neck.

Some of the larger pieces of lead had gone through my clothes, and one had lodged in the left shoulder, and another just below the collar bone. A more careful inspection showed that the splinters were of seasoned walnut. They must have come from a gun stock and the lead from a bullet that struck something harder at the same time. But I never knew whose gun or more about it. The splinters and lead were easily removed and, though sore and painful for a time, were not disabling or serious. But the whole affair shows the absorbing degree of the excitement under which we were acting.

Wright was discharged on May 5, 1864, and returned home to Red Wing. Records indicate that on March 8, 1865, he enlisted as a substitute for a man who was liable to be drafted. He was accepted that same day as an unassigned private. He was received into Hancock's First Veteran Reserve Corps at a draft rendezvous at Ft. Snelling on March 11. On March 24, however, he was discharged by order of the War Department so that he could accept a commission as first lieutenant of the First Battalion's Company E. He served for four months, during which time the war ended and President Lincoln was assassinated. Wright was mustered out as a captain with the battalion at Jeffersonville, Indiana, on July 14, 1865.

Wright was a prolific writer and left many accounts of his comrades' lives during the war. He later moved to Beverly, Massachusetts, and while corresponding with his comrades and visiting with them at the 1906 National GAR encampment in St. Paul, he was encouraged to write a history of Company F. From 1906 to 1911, he worked on what is today the finest known personal recollection of the men of the First Minnesota. Edited by Steven Keillor, it was published in 2001 as a book entitled *No More Gallant a Deed*.

James Wright was the last survivor of the First Minnesota, dying at his home on August 25, 1936. He was ninety-five years, eight months, and twenty-eight days old. His body was buried in Central Cemetery in Beverly.

Morton, the regimental surgeon, also wrote on the discharge that William was "incapable of performing the duties of a soldier because of old age (62 years) and debility."

William Gordon appears, then, to be the oldest man to serve in the First Minnesota. This claim of old age is supported by the 1860 Minnesota census. When it was taken, Gordon stated that he was then fifty-seven years old; his wife, Mary, was twenty-nine, and his three children at that time were four years, two years, and six months old. After his discharge in August 1862, he returned home to his family. Unfortunately, he died only eight months later in April 1863. He was buried in Oakwood Cemetery in Red Wing.

William Gordon

b. circa 1802; d. March 1863

In early 1861, Scottish-born William Gordon was working as a tailor in Red Wing and supporting a wife and three children. When he enlisted in the First Minnesota, he stated he was forty-three years old. Records indicate, however, that Gordon was born in about 1802, during President Thomas Jefferson's administration, which would have made Gordon about fifty-nine when he enlisted.

Gordon stood five feet six inches tall and had a light complexion, blue eyes, and gray hair. He was mustered in on April 29, 1861, and was placed in Company F, along with the other men from Red Wing. His photograph was taken late in October 1861, when the regiment was issued new dress uniforms. The men were in camp at Poolesville, Maryland, at the time and probably had their pictures taken there or in nearby Washington, DC.

In March 1862 Gordon became sick enough to be admitted to the hospital at Harrison's Landing, Virginia, and on August 20, 1862, he was discharged for disability. His discharge certificate states, "By reason of age, rheumatism and debility said soldier has been unable to do active duty for the past six months." Dr.

While William Gordon was probably the oldest man in the regiment, another, William "Billy" Nixon, was probably the youngest. Born on February 15, 1847, Nixon, who served as a drummer in Company A, was just fourteen years, two months, and five days old when he enlisted at the start of the war.

COMPANY G
THE FARIBAULT GUARDS

FARIBAULT WAS ESTABLISHED IN 1826 where Alexander Faribault built the largest of his six fur trading posts. The influx of settlers into the area's rich agricultural country began in about 1850. In 1859 the first Episcopal bishop in Minnesota, H. B. Whipple, made Faribault the headquarters of his Indian missions. During his forty years as bishop, Whipple's counsel was sought by Queen Victoria, as well as by many U.S. presidents.

The first war meeting in the county was held in Faribault at the Metropolitan Hall. At one point a long sheet of paper almost three feet long was brought out. At the top was printed the governor's call for volunteers to create a thousand-man regiment. Ninety-seven men stepped forward to sign, and a company was born.

Faribault in 1862

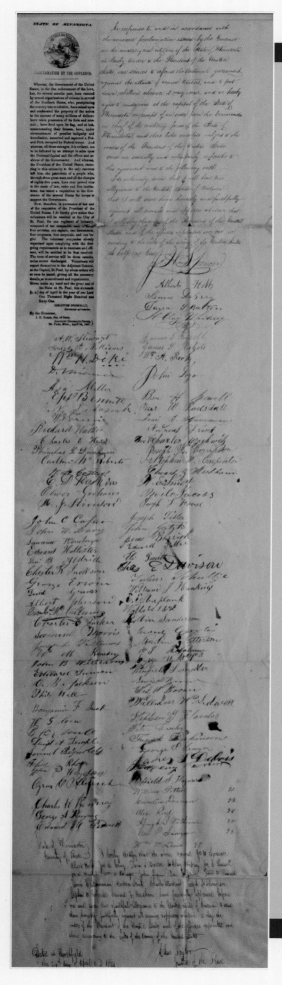

On March 22, 1865, Capt. Joseph Spencer sent the following letter to Governor Stephen Miller:

I have the honor to enclose a lithograph copy of the original enrollment list of Company "G" 1st Regiment Minnesota Volunteers. Inasmuch as this paper forms a part of the early history of the 1st Regiment and more especially the early military history of those who first entered the service from Rice Co. I would respectfully ask that this paper may be filed in the Adjutant Genl's office of the State of Minnesota with other papers pertaining to the organization of the Regiment. The original paper of which the enclosed is a lithograph was drawn up and the first name enrolled thereon, at Northfield Rice Co. on the 17th day of April 1861. Subsequent to the death of Capt. Nathan Messick at the battle of Gettysburg Pa. it was confided to my care by Lieut. James DeGray, the then commanding officer of the Company. As the paper had become somewhat mutilated I caused it to be lithographed with all its imperfections in order that the record might be kept. The paper is of peculiar interest to those who first tendered their services from the "North Star State" to defend the integrity of the nation's honor and should be carefully preserved as written evidence of the fervent patriotism and true sense of duty that prompted them to thus act in the early days of the war.

I am Sir, Very respectfully,
Your Obedient servent,
Jas, H.

This lengthy document is a lithograph of the paper signed by the patriotic volunteers at the Faribault recruiting rally. It measures 9½" × 34½".

Edward Bassett

b. December 21, 1841; d. April 9, 1897

Edward Bassett was born in Connecticut, and later, he and his family settled in Morristown in Rice County, Minnesota. He was nineteen when he was mustered into service on April 29, 1861, becoming a private in Company G. Bassett stood five feet seven and three-quarters inches tall, about average for most men who served in the Civil War. He had a fair complexion, gray eyes, and black hair.

On December 11, 1862, the First Minnesota participated in the Battle of Fredericksburg. The regiment was stationed on the right of the Union line, where they saw the fruitless assault on the Rebel position at Marye's Heights. The First was initially ordered into the attack. As Bassett writes of the event:

> The Genls done the ordering and the soldiers charged up the hill and tried to force the rebs from their position but it was of no use. They were shot down by the hundreds. There was some of the hardest fighting done that day that has been done during the war. Our regt. was ordered to charge but they were finally countermanded so we did not get into the hardest part of the fight. . . . The last day that we were on picket the

rebel sharpshooters kept us low all day. We had dug rifle pits during the night and we had to lay in them all day for every man that showed his head got a bullet after him. . . . The 127th Penn. Regt which was on our right run away & behaved disgracefully so that our flank was open to the enemy if they wished to make an attac. It left us in a very dangerous situation and it would have been easy for the enemy to have killed nearly all of us if they had dared to try it. . . . (I don't pretend to say that McClellan would have whipped the rebels here. But I ask, has Burnside?) Who shall be the next one to try them.[1]

Bassett survived the July 2 charge at Gettysburg and tells of his experience:

> July 2nd, we marched to the front where we lay quiet all the forenoon until almost dark. Then the Rebs drove our men back in the center and we were sent to their support. We charged down across a stubble field about thirty rods, and stopped in a ravine lined with brush and trees. The Rebs were about three to our one, and [had] gotten the first fire on us. The Gen. ordered us to retire, which we did, losing some over 200 killed and wounded in fifteen minutes. We rallied what was left on the same ground from which we started and were ready for another fight. . . .
>
> Wm. Ramsey, Cal Jackson and myself went down onto the field to do what we could for the wounded. As fast as the stretcher bearers and ambulances could be gotten they were borne from the field and taken to the Hospitals. Then we rejoined our Regt. and lay on our arms until morning.[2]

Gettysburg devastated the ranks of the regiment. In October, Bassett simply states, "Our company numbers seven men now in the field."

On October 14, 1863, he suffered a slight wound to his head at the Battle of Bristoe Station. A month later, the First was on the move again and engaged the Rebels at a place called Mine Run. Of this battle, Bassett writes:

> We lay there all day expecting they would open up on us, but they didn't. We were relieved at night and went to the rear. Thus we got out of another bad spot. I believe that if we had charged, as first ordered, not ten men of our

Regt. would have come out alive. It was one of the worst places I have seen. We were lucky. I shall never forget Nov. 30th, 1863.[3]

Bassett was mustered out with the regiment on May 5, 1864. Though he chose not to reenlist in the First Battalion, on February 21, 1865, he did enlist in the First Minnesota Heavy Artillery. Several men from his old unit were now in service with this unit. Bassett was promoted to sergeant four days after enlisting, undoubtedly because of his experience with Minnesota's other First. They were stationed in Tennessee, where they trained and performed guard duty until mustered out on September 27, 1865.

James DeGray

James DeGray

b. March 12, 1840; d. March 31, 1922

James DeGray was born in Huntington County in East Canada on March 12, 1840. He was twenty-one when he enlisted in Northfield, where he worked as an apprentice tinsmith. He stood five feet ten and one-quarter inches tall and had a sandy complexion, dark-gray eyes, and brown hair. He was placed in Company G and appointed a corporal. He was on detached service at Ft. Ridgely from April 29 to June 30, 1861, and appointed sergeant on July 17, 1862. On September 17, 1862, while at Antietam, he received a commission as second lieutenant of Company G.

At Gettysburg, 2nd Lt. DeGray was in command of his company when the order to charge the advancing Confederate line was given. During the charge a bullet pierced his hat and struck him in the forehead, cracking but not penetrating his skull, the bullet then exiting the left side of his hat. The wound left a permanent scar on his forehead—and managed to knock him senseless at the time.

This officer's slouch hat was worn by Capt. James DeGray (Co. F) when he received a gunshot wound to the head on July 2 at Gettysburg. Note the bullet hole in the center above the bugle insignia with a "1" inside it. This hat is the only known piece of First Minnesota headgear still in existence known to have been worn during the charge.

On July 28, 1863, he was admitted to a hospital for volunteer officers located in Washington, DC, receiving a thirty-day furlough on August 15, but two weeks later he was admitted to the U.S. Army's general hospital in Georgetown. On September 14 a doctor made a medical notation that reads, "Find him laboring under a gunshot wound of the cranium producing a fracture, and is unfit for duty."

Two weeks later, on October 1, DeGray was returned to duty, and soon after, on October 14, he was wounded again—this time at the Battle of Bristoe Station. On October 17 he was promoted to first lieutenant, backdated from July 2. His wound from Bristoe Station apparently continued to bother him, and he was discharged on March 15, 1864, to accept an appointment in the Nineteenth Veteran Reserve Corps. He served in the Nineteenth through the war's end and beyond, in companies C and I, and was discharged in Clinton, Louisiana, on January 1, 1868. While serving in Louisiana, he grew fond of the area and decided to live there after his discharge. James DeGray died in New Orleans on March 31, 1922, at the age of eighty-two.

Lewis McKune

b. July 22, 1821; d. July 21, 1861

Lewis McKune was born and raised on a farm near Meriden in Susquehanna County, Pennsylvania. On June 11, 1844, he married Laura Ett, and they farmed until 1846. When he was twenty-five, they headed west, settling in Illinois. In 1849, at the outbreak of the California gold rush, they headed west to seek their fortune, where he was reasonably successful in his mining operations, returning to Illinois about 1855. In 1856 he purchased an emigrant outfit and traveled by prairie schooner to Minnesota. He settled with his family in Blooming Grove in Waseca County. He had brought several horses, and breeding occupied much of his time. In 1857 he opened a store in Morristown, though he continued to live on his farm in Blooming Grove.

McKune was an ardent Republican and participated in the local political campaign of 1856. He also was a member of the state constitutional convention in 1857 and served as a state senator from 1857 to 1858. James Childs, who later wrote a history of Waseca County, got to know him during the political campaign of 1856 and describes him as follows, "He was a born hero, ready to stand by and fight for what he believed was right, regardless of personal ease, safety or financial sacrifice."

During the constitutional convention, the Republi-

Lewis McKune

cans, fearing the Kansas-style tricks of proslavery men, held several private caucuses to devise ways of preventing advantage being taken of them. Upon McKune's suggestion, the Republican members quietly took possession of the hall where the convention was to meet the next day. They remained there until noon and then, as the Democrats arrived, proceeded to organize the convention in opposition to them. The Democrats tried to counterorganize but immediately adjourned, leaving the hall to the Republicans. The state's constitution finally was submitted by two conventions, and a conference committee worked out the final version.

During this conference committee, St. Paul Democrat and future First Minnesota colonel Willis Gorman assaulted Republican Judge Thomas Wilson from Winona. Gorman was a large, powerful man, and Wilson was not only a small man but also in poor health. Incensed, McKune sought out Gorman and gave him a severe tongue lashing, informing Gorman that if he wished to whip a Republican, McKune was ready to receive the blows. At six feet five and a half inches tall, McKune was an imposing figure, and Gorman chose otherwise. Hopefully, when war came, they set aside their dislike for each other and united to defend their country.

Upon his return from the constitutional convention, the area's men were so well satisfied that they chose him as their first state senator. McKune served in the state legislature from December 1857 to August

1858, after which he devoted himself to his farm in Blooming Grove and his mercantile store in Morristown. He moved his family to Morristown, where he resided until 1861.

McKune was an ardent patriot, and in a conversation with his friend James Childs on the night of March 9, 1861, he talked about the war's inevitability. He declared not only that he would be involved but his premonition that he would die in the struggle and, thus, that he needed to make arrangements for his family. At the outbreak of the war, thirty-nine-year-old McKune volunteered as a private in the Faribault company and was elected by the men as their first lieutenant. When Capt. Dike was appointed to the rank of major in the regiment, McKune became the company's captain.

Unfortunately, Capt. McKune was mortally wounded in the unit's first battle, at Bull Run. At the start of the battle, with the enemy's first volley, he was shot through the heart. Pvt. William T. Mollison and another member of Company F carried him on their shoulders to the rear of the company, and McKune died soon thereafter.

Sergeant George Boyd states in a letter home that "Capt. McKune was shot down by my side, on the charge." Ed Stevens of Company B recalls, "Capt McKune, of Company G, was killed just after the first volley, while rallying his men for a charge. His last words which were addresses to his men while the bullets were fast flying around him, were, 'Rally men rally!'"

McKune would have been forty years old the next day. His body was carried off the field, and his sword, belt, and pistol were retrieved and sent to his family.

Nathan S. Messick

b. circa 1827; d. July 3, 1863

In 1850 New Jersey–born Nathan Messick and his wife, Amanda, were living in Noblesville, Ohio, where he worked as a shoemaker. At the time of the 1860 U.S. census, they had moved to Faribault and had four children, ages ten, seven, two, and one month. There, he continued in his profession as a shoemaker.

In April 1861 the thirty-four-year-old Messick volunteered to serve his country. He was recorded as being five feet eight and a half inches tall, with a dark complexion, hazel-colored eyes, and black hair. He left his wife and young family and rallied to the cause of suppressing the rebellion.

He was placed in Company G, and on April 29 the

Nathan S. Messick

men of the company chose Messick as their first lieutenant. He was promoted to captain on July 29, 1861, after the death of Capt. McKune at Bull Run. One member of the First mentions his and other officers' courage during the battle:

> It is simple justice to mention the brave conduct of our officers. Lieut. Col. Miller and Major Dike dismounted and were found in the thickest of the fight. Our Lieutenant Messick, regardless of the storm of deadly hail, did his best to rally the men until the last.
>
> Asa Miller, Millersburgh, who carried our Company Colors, was shot down, and our 1st Lieut. tore it from the staff and saved it. It was riddled with bullets.

Gettysburg was considered the high-water mark of the Confederacy's effort against the Union, being the site of their northernmost battle. The Rebels were turned back at the cost of many Union lives, including Nathan Messick's. Though still recovering in Washington, DC, John McCallum, Messick's former first lieutenant, wrote a letter to Amanda Messick detailing the captain's death.

> At daylight the enemy opened fire on our pickets. The regiment was instantly in line of

Capt. Nathan S. Messick

battle. Thus we remained until nearly noon, when once more the enemy opened—this time in earnest. Eighty pieces of cannon vomited shot and shell on our devoted division. Under this terrific artillery fire they advanced their infantry, driving our right flank and capturing the 4th regular battery, the horses of which had all been killed. Our brigade was then ordered to support the right. In the execution of this movement, Capt. Messick being in command of his own regiment and the 15th Mass. was instantly killed by a piece of shell striking him in the head near the right eye, going clear through and coming out back of the right ear. Thus perished the gallant Captain Messick.

George Williams of Company G, hearing of the fate of his Captain, went in pursuit of the body, and finding it, with the help of others, carried it to the rear, where he remained with it until three o'clock next morning, when an ambulance sent for the purpose by Lieut. Searles of Hastings, took it still farther to the rear. It being impossible to procure boards or nails the body was wrapped in a shelter tent, towels being put round the face to protect it; a grave was dug, and the burial service read by our Chaplain, Rev. Mr. Conwell; green boughs were laid over the remains, and the earth closed over all that was mortal of a born hero.

The site selected was in every way a fit resting place for the noble dead. A fine oak spreads its shadows like a pall over the spot which overlooks the field of our triumphs, and the place

where he fell. Loving hands carved his name on a board which is spiked to the tree, at whose roots he reposes.[4]

Ed Bassett of Company I also recalls Messick's death:

As soon as they came in range of our guns, we sent them our compliments in the shape of one ounce bullets. They came determined to drive us back, but when they were about half shot down, they commenced to retreat. We chased them and took many prisoners. . . . I passed the Captain just before he fell but did not know he was killed until after the fight. He was killed instantly, shot thru the head. After the fight I helped carry him off the field. One of the boys that had been cooking for him said that he would see that he was buried. He would also take care of his things.[5]

Bassett writes the following in a letter:

You ask about Captain Messick? I have no doubt that he did request that his body be sent home. He must have done it before he was hit, as he certainly didn't have a chance afterwards. I helped carry his body from the field, perhaps a half hour after the rebs were driven back. We took him back to the Field Hospital where his cook took charge, staying with him until an ambulance took him back to the General hospital. His sword and pocket book were taken from him within fifteen minutes after he fell. Who took them I do not know. There was perhaps $15 in it. There was a gold watch in his pocket, which belonged to Col. Adams, who was wounded the day before. It was returned to Col. Adams. I was not present when he was buried. . . . After we laid him down, I was looking at him for the last time, and thinking if there was anything more I could do, that would do any good. I asked Mr Williams, his cook, to take off his shoulder straps and send them to his wife, which he did. I am sorry that we could not save his sword, but in a battle like that there are lots of things one would like to do, but cannot. . . . He died at his post, doing his duty. Thousands fell that day the same way. Capt Messick died as he would wish to die, fighting for his country.

On July 4 Nathan Messick was buried on the Jacob Schwartz farm near Gettysburg. Ed Needham of Company G made a headboard to mark his gravesite. Later, the captain was reinterred in the National Cemetery at Gettysburg, along with many other Minnesota men who gave their last full measure on that battlefield. He is in the Minnesota area, section A, grave no. 4.

Edward Z. Needham
b. March 25, 1843; d. April 27, 1919

Edward Needham was born in Wales, Massachusetts, and in 1852 his family moved to Cleveland, where Ed received his childhood education. Seven years later, they moved again and, on May 11, 1859, established a farm in section 28 of Greenvale Township, near Northfield.

Enlisting in Northfield, he was mustered into the service at Ft. Snelling on April 29, 1861, and served as a private for three years. At the time of his enlistment, he was eighteen years old and stood five feet six inches tall. He had a fair complexion, gray eyes, and brown hair.

At the beginning of the war, many companies carried flags presented by the women of their cities, and Company G's was from the ladies of Faribault. Asa Miller carried Company G's flag at the Battle of Bull Run. Needham wrote the following story to his fiancée, Georgiana G. Holt:

Edward Z. Needham

Dear Georgia

When I first heard the fire I was bewildered for an instant, the roar was so terrific & consequently didn't drop as quick as the rest of our men did, but looked around to see what was going on. It did not take me long to find out & I drawed my gun up & was going to fire, when I remembered that we had strict orders not to fire till we had orders to do so. So I did not fire but laid down as quick as possible.

I heard somebody yell "fire" so I raised up & fired into the thicket & laid down & loaded as quick as possible & fired again. By this time the boys finding it too hot for them had all gone back over the knoll that I spoke about, but myself & a few others. I saw it was no use for me to stay there as it was sure death as it was a crossfire of our own men & the enemy so I got up to leave & had got a rod or so when I saw our flag bearer fall, a shot having broken his leg (The Asa

Miller that you spoke about had it.) He acted nobly. When he fell he raised the flag again & motioned to the boys to get it. I sprang forward & grabbed it & then retreated to the rest of the company where I found our Captain shot dead & some of the boys carrying him off. I followed our Lieutenant [Messick] back down into a hollow & left the flag & then we all rushed forward up onto the hill again & at the rebels.

When our company retreated they did not go together but every man for himself after the Capt. was shot so when we rushed at them we were all mixed up but they ran & we drove them back into the woods & then they stopped & peppered us & we retreated to an opposite hill. All this time the musket balls flew around us like hail, whistling as they passed something like a bee passing quickly by your head only louder and sharper. There was one continual hum they flew so thickly. The rebel batteries were throwing shot & shell (bomb shell) among us & every little while one would go by with a whish-shish-bang & explode making every[one] dodge that they went near. Our batteries run short of ammunition & some of them got taken.

Our whole force had to retreat & the enemy

chased us 5 or 6 miles. They had the advantage in every way & their ambuscades & masked batteries were very plenty. Another trick they played was they hoisted our flag & we thought they were friends & marched right up to join them & when we got within a few rods they fired whole volleys into us & put us into confusion before we had time to fire. . . .[6]

The *Faribault Central Republican* reported the event on August 7, 1861:

Our Company Flag

The presentation, of which to Company "G" we will not soon forget as I had occasioned before to remind, is preserved, but the particulars of its rescue I did not learn until recently. After the brave Miller was shot down, E. Z. Needham, of Northfield, took it and by command of our Lieutenant stood it by a tree, while he, Needham, made good use of his gun. The next that was seen of it, one of the company "B" had it, and E. Hollister took it from him, and was carrying it, when Lieut. Messick came up and told Hollister he would not be able to carry it through. Hollister replied that he would not leave it then, and was about to tear it from the staff, when the gallant Lieut said he would do it, and do it he did; and thus it was that our colors were saved, after having eight musket balls.

Needham survived the battle and later served as the orderly for Messick, who became captain of Company G after the death of Capt. McKune at Bull Run.

On June 30, 1862, during the Battle of Savage Station, Needham was standing next to Pvt. Jonathan Goodrich. Needham notes in his diary that a bullet had hit Goodrich's gun and then Needham's elbow. The bullet must have had little force left, however, because, as he notes, it did not hurt.

George Sawyer mentions his friend Needham in a letter to his sweetheart, Helen:

You asked what kind of boy Ed Needham is. He is as good hearted a one as ever lived and brave as a lion. There is not a better soldier in the Co. He fears no danger when in the performance of duty. Always cool and determined when on duty. He and I have been together several times on what were considered a little dangerous

[assignments]. He is always one of the first to volunteer for such duty. He is moral, but not religious. I like him well. I admire a brave man and a true soldier and he is such. He and [I] were mess mates most of the time from the first Bull Run till he went to cooking for the Lieut. last fall.[7]

Prior to the July 2 charge at Gettysburg, the officers dismounted and stood in their appropriate places with the regiment. The horses were moved to the right and rear of the regiment, just up the slope, and held as a group. Needham was detailed to hold the reins of Lt. Col. Adams' horse and missed the fateful charge, though he may have been able to watch his comrades from his position in the rear.

On July 3, however, Needham was involved in the repulse of Pickett's Charge. He had a piece of his blouse torn off by a shell but was not wounded. Capt. Messick, however, was killed during the battle. The next day, Needham took care of the wounded Lt. DeGray and made a headboard to mark the spot where the men had buried Capt. Messick. The following are excerpts from his diary:

Thursday July 2, 1863.
Col, Lieut Col & Major wounded. Marched onto the battlefield, they commenced shelling about noon skirmishing all the forenoon, 1st Minnesota went in on a charge about 5 o'clock. Lieut DeGray wounded, G P Sawyer killed. Total loss of co. 18 of Regt. 200. Was not in the ranks.

Friday, July 3, 1863.
Our arms gloriously victorious!!! Took care of Col Adams horse. Regt was engaged again in afternoon. Capt N. S. Messick killed by a piece of shell.—had my blouse sleeve cut by a piece of shell. Total loss of co G in both days, 4 killed & 27 wounded out of 37 men who went into the fight. Total loss of Regt 234 men out of 337 that went in. 64 killed.

Saturday, July 4, 1863.
Staid at 2nd Corps hospital & took care of DeGray. Helped George [Buckman] bury Capt. Messick, made him a head board. Rained. Took care of boys.

Sgt. George Buckman considered his friend a reliable and trusty soldier, fearless of danger and bold to an extreme. Buckman recollects Needham's daring at the Battle of Bristoe Station:

Ed was engaged with his company and regiment at the battle of Bristow Station, Va. During the engagement, several Confederate soldiers, to protect themselves from the withering fire of the Union troops, had crowded into a cellar under the rear of the brick building that was located directly in front of Company G and the rest of the regiment. When Ed noticed a Reb looking around the corner of the building, he asked Major Downie if he could go out and get them.

He said, "Two or three of you should go out."

George Williams and Jefferson Baker then went out with Ed. They went around the building to the right. Ed went to the left. On his side was an open cellar way and as he passed within twenty feet of it, he saw that it was full of aroused Rebs.

He brought his musket down and pointed it, through the cellar opening, at the Confederates inside. He then demanded their surrender. Though some were tempted to fire on him they were dissuaded by others in the group.

"Don't fire!" They hollered. "We surrender!"

Ed told them to throw down their guns and come out. They did and Ed brought 20 prisoners back to the regiment.

He then turned around and, with George Williams, went back for a Confederate horse he had seen tied to a tree beyond the back of the house. George stopped to help a wounded rebel who by the hand gestures appeared that he may have been another Odd Fellow, as was George. George got help for the Reb and then continued on.

They kept going across a narrow flat and then up a hill. As they got to the top the Union skirmish line from Owen's Brigade came up behind them. The Rebs began to fire and the men of the First returned the fire. Just then Ed saw two artillery pieces. He rushed ahead putting his gun on one he yelled, "Hurrah for Minnesota!"

Just back of the artillery they noticed a horse harnessed to a limber. Ed unhitched it and rode it back to their line. He brought it back successfully even though the skirmisher firing had intensified. Ed was always willing to

This picture of Ed Needham was taken sometime between October 16, 1863, when he was promoted to the rank of corporal, and May 5, 1864, when he was discharged.

volunteer, and did so on several occasions, performing hazardous duty. He was considered the daring spirit of the company.[8]

Two days later, on October 16, Needham was promoted to corporal. He served in nearly all of the regiment's battles. On February 2, 1864, Ed returned to Minnesota with Lt. James DeGray on recruiting duty. The day before, they had been in Washington, where they visited Col. Colvill. They also saw Drum Major Kittle, George Kenny, and Walter Reed. Needham had a lot of free time and spent much of it with Georgia in Northfield or its vicinity. He also did some work for family and friends.

When the regiment returned to Minnesota, an effort was made to induce the veterans to reenlist and form the successor unit to the First Minnesota. Needham made the following entries in his diary:

April 6, 1864—Adams promised me Comm Sergt position if—

April 7, 1864—Made up my mind not to reenlist. Wrote to Georgia.

Needham was mustered out as a corporal on May 5, 1864.

On December 19, 1864, seven months after being mustered out of the Old First, he enlisted as a substitute in Company B of the Eleventh Minnesota Infantry. During the Civil War when a man was drafted, he could hire someone else to serve in his place. Needham may have seen that the war was coming to a close and would not last much longer. Perhaps, he thought the money was worth the risk. In any event, he decided to rejoin the fray.

Before returning to the fight, however, he had one more thing to do. On Christmas Day 1864, he married Georgia. They were married in her parents' home in Greenvale, a small settlement near Northfield. Newly wed, he joined the Eleventh and served as a private until the war ended, being mustered out on June 26, 1865, in Gallatin, Tennessee.

Ed and Georgia farmed in Northfield and raised a family. In May 1870, when he moved his family to Farmington, he and his brother, A. L. Needham, bought a building on Elm Street, a twenty-by-sixty-foot foundry and machine shop. They employed two men and two horses in making farm implements, and in 1874, they put in a four-horsepower engine and made bobsleds and performed other light production.

The family lived in Farmington until 1902, when they moved to Spokane, Washington. Ed and Georgia both lived long lives. Georgia died on March 3, 1915,

and Ed died on April 27, 1919, at the age of seventy-six. They are both buried in Spokane.

A fiftieth-anniversary display of some of Ed Needham's gear, including Company G's flag, reads as follows:

> This flag was presented to Co. G First Minn. Vol. Inf. by the ladies of Faribault, Minn at the organization of the Co. It was carried into the 1st battle of Bull Run Va. on July 21st 1861, by Asa Miller of Millersburg who was killed at that time. It was then taken and carried by E. Z. Needham.
>
> After this battle no Company flags were allowed to be carried & it was sent back to Faribault. At a Regimental Reunion at Waseca after the war the members of the Co. present gave it to E. Z. Needham who as of June 28th 1903 still has it.[9]

Charles Parker

b. 1837; d. July 13, 1884

Born in Faribault, Charles Parker was living there and working as a millwright when the war began. He enlisted at the age of twenty-four. He stood six feet tall and had a light complexion, blue eyes, and dark-brown hair. Placed in Company G and appointed a sergeant, Parker was considered a strong and able-bodied soldier.

In June 1861, before the regiment was sent east, Company G spent a brief period at Ft. Ridgely in southwestern Minnesota. On June 20, while Parker was serving as sergeant of the guard, a drunken soldier became belligerent and unruly. While attempting to put him into a cell in the guardhouse, the soldier delivered a powerful blow to Charles' nose, smashing the bones and breaking it badly. He fell back from the blow and would have fallen to the floor had not another guard and member of the company, Ezra Haskins, caught him. The drunk was eventually subdued, but Parker never fully recovered from the blow. He suffered from nasal catarrh, an inflammation of the mucous membrane, for the rest of his life.[10]

After the Battle of Antietam in September 1862, he was sick in the hospital at Harpers Ferry for about four weeks. He was promoted to first sergeant of Company G on July 26, 1863.

Parker fought in all the regiment's battles. On May 12, 1864, he enlisted in the First Battalion and was commissioned as a second lieutenant in Company A.

This flag was carried by Company G and was given to Ed Needham after the war. One of Needham's descendants donated it to Oklahoma State University, where these photos were taken. Years later, other family members requested that it be returned, and today, its whereabouts is unknown.

Charles Parker

Parker constantly suffered from the nasal trouble, however, and was repeatedly advised by his fellow officers to leave the field and go to a hospital, but he persistently refused, saying that he would remain as long as he could stand up.

Parker and the battalion participated in the skirmishes at Deep Bottom, Virginia, on July 28 and 29, 1864. He then started back with the battalion toward Petersburg but was so sick on July 29 that he could not keep up. He rejoined them the next day and, although sick all the time, remained with them in the battles at Deep Bottom on August 14 and Ream's Station on August 25, 1864. Finally, around October 25, 1864, while the battalion was stationed at Ft. Rice near Petersburg, he was taken with a violent sickness that developed into inflammation of the lungs, and he was taken to the Second Division's field hospital. From there he was sent to the Second Army Corps' depot field hospital in City Point, Virginia, now diagnosed with pneumonia.

He returned to duty on November 30, 1864. Although not well, he returned to his command and was assigned to duty as acting quartermaster of the battalion because he was physically unfit for active duty. He was promoted to first lieutenant on December 26, 1864, to replace Chesley Terrill, who had been discharged.

Parker remained in the position of quartermaster until January 5, 1865, when he was sent to Minnesota on recruiting service. Charles E. Davis was also in St. Paul to recruit. He reported that at the time he arrived Parker was spitting up blood, suffering from nasal catarrh, and seriously ill with consumption (tuberculosis).

Parker returned to the battalion in May 1865. In the meantime, he had been promoted to captain of Company C, a new company, which had been organized and assigned to the battalion in April. He finally resigned his commission on June 15, 1865, being physically unable to continue in the service.

Thomas Pressnell and others refer to him positively, describing him as a diligent soldier. He is mentioned in an article published in the *Minnesota Pioneer* at the end of the war. Regarding his action at the Battle of Jerusalem Plank Road on June 22, 1864, Maj. Farwell writes:

> To the men for their coolness and gallant bearing under fire, too much praise cannot be awarded. We were so close to the enemy on the 22nd that revolvers were used freely. Lieut. Parker, with his, spoiled the evil intention of a rebel, who had deliberately aimed his Enfield at him, at a distance of thirty feet.

He died in 1884 at the age of forty-seven. When organized in 1894, the veterans of Verndale, Minnesota, where he lived for many years, named their GAR post after him.

Charles Parker after his promotion to first sergeant on July 26, 1863

George Sawyer

b. December 7, 1838; d. July 2, 1863

George Sawyer was born in Alexandria in Grafton County, New Hampshire. His father, Phineas, died in 1853, and sometime afterward, George, his mother, and at least one sister moved to Minnesota. In the spring of 1861, he was farming in Medford, Minnesota. When news of the war reached Minnesota, George was one of the men who first rose to the call. At the time he enlisted, he was twenty-two years old and five feet nine and one-quarter inches tall and had a light complexion, blue eyes, and dark-brown hair. During his service he wrote several letters to Helen Sanborn relating a soldier's daily life in the First Minnesota.

On May 30, 1862, he wrote a letter mentioning his work on the Grapevine Bridge. In it he also describes the sleeping accommodations of the enlisted man:

> Our little tents are very small and unhandy, there being hardly room to sit on the ground erect in them. Yet they are of great value to us. They protect us from a burning sun which would allow most of us had we not some protection. They shield us from the very heavy dews which fall here and are some protection from rain although a hard rain drives through them.[11]

Sawyer was promoted to corporal on October 29, 1862, and fought in all the regiment's battles, up to Gettysburg.

He was a very religious young man. In a letter dated March 24, 1863, he writes:

> When I enlisted I pledged all I had even to life if necessary to maintain this Government and thank God *I have never regretted the course I then took*. The cause of *Country* and of *Freedom* is the one nearest my heart and I believe I am if necessary willing to give my life for it.[12]

Unfortunately, his life was cut short during the July 2 charge at Gettysburg. He charged down the hill into the Rebel hoard but never made it back, one of the First's many casualties that day. He had died before reaching his twenty-fifth birthday.

On Christmas Day 1863, a comrade from Company G, Henry Clay Whitney, wrote to B. C. Sanborn about George's last moments:

> I was near George when he fell and he spoke to me and said he was mortally wounded. I do not remember but think he was at the head of the Co. when he fell. I do not know how long he lived as when I left him he still lived and [was] conscious and bore his fate with true Christian fortitude.
>
> He requested me to write to his friends and say to them "that he died with his faith in his god and his face to his Enemy." He also remembered your sister and sent his love to her in his dying moments.
>
> I understand that his remains have been taken up and [interred] in the National Cemetery near Gettysburg.
>
> With you I think Geo was a true noble and brave man. As a soldier he did his whole duty with a patriotic zeal and true devotion to his country's flag for which he fell. As a Christian and Moral Man he was respected by all.
>
> As a friend he was steadfast and true.[13]

President Lincoln dedicated the National Cemetery at Gettysburg in November 1863. Sawyer's body was recovered from its battlefield burial site and reinterred at the new cemetery. Later, his body was brought home to Medford for burial. Services were conducted at the Congregational church, and he was buried in Riverside Cemetery in Medford, which is located near Faribault.

George Alfonso Williams

b. January 15, 1836; d. April 21, 1909

Born in Ithaca, New York, George Williams came to Minnesota in 1855, settling in Faribault, where he enlisted. When he was mustered into the service on April 21, 1861, he was twenty-five years old and carried a large, strong six-foot-tall frame. He had a fair complexion, blue eyes, and auburn-colored hair. A month later, on May 29, 1861, he was appointed sergeant in Company G but was reduced to the ranks on December 17, at his own request.

At the Battle of Bull Run, Williams was struck in the back by a rail that had been cut to pieces by a piece of artillery solid shot. After the regiment began its retreat, he made his way back to Washington with the assistance of teamsters, who allowed him to ride part of the way on their wagon. Once back in Washington, Col. Gorman gave him a thirty-day pass to either enter a hospital or go home to recover. He chose home and traveled back to Ithaca, where he was treated by a doctor for his back pain and also for nephritis of the kidney and the bladder. Still unable to return to his regiment, his furlough was extended for another thirty days. During this time, on September 5, 1861, he was married to Charlotte Marion in Candor, New York. A daughter, Jennie, was born in 1864.

Sgt. Charles Davidson, also of Company G, mentions him in a letter sent home on October 8, 1861: "Sergeant Williams, who on account of sickness, went to Candor, N.Y., on leave, has recently returned to our company, restored to nearly his former health, after nearly two months of absence."

When he returned, he rejoined the regiment at Poolesville, Maryland, and served the balance of the spring of 1862 during the Peninsula Campaign in front of Yorktown and in the swamps of the Chickahominy River. During this time he contracted rheumatism and was treated by the regimental surgeons, doctors Morton and Le Blond, for both the injury to his back and the rheumatism.

On October 15, 1863, Williams was promoted to the rank of sergeant, a position that he accepted and fulfilled for the rest of his service. He was mustered out at Ft. Snelling on May 5, 1864. During his service this soldier participated in First and Second Bull Run, the battles of Williamsburg, Seven Pines, Fair Oaks, Peach Orchard, Savage Station, White Oak Swamp, Malvern Hill, First Fredericksburg, Chantilly, South Mountain, Antietam, and Gettysburg, the Mine Run Campaign, and innumerable skirmishes.

After being mustered out of the service, he immediately headed back east. From May 1864 until July 1865, he resided in Virginia and worked for the U.S. Sanitary Commission. When his work was finished, he moved back to his hometown of Ithaca and his wife for the months of July and August 1866. Unfortunately, Charlotte died on August 27, 1866.

Williams left New York and resided briefly in Indianapolis. He may have then moved back to Faribault for a while. He later stated that he moved to the town of Tremont in Jackson County, Wisconsin, in 1868.

On August 22, 1870, he was married to Caroline Miller in an Episcopal wedding in Faribault. The Williams moved to Tremont, where their son was born. They lived there until 1883, when they moved to La Crosse, Wisconsin, where Williams worked as a foreman on a logging crew. Later, when he could no longer do that work, he made a living as a painter.

Their last move was to Los Angeles. On February 24, 1900, he entered the soldiers' home in Sawtelle, which is today a part of Los Angeles. He died of pneumonia on April 21, 1909, and was buried in the national cemetery next to the home—section 16, row A, number 7. He was seventy-three years old.

COMPANY H
THE DAKOTA COUNTY VOLUNTEERS

HASTINGS IN DAKOTA COUNTY was the first stop when heading down the Mississippi from Ft. Snelling. At the beginning of the war, many men from the Hastings area rallied to the cause, as did those in nearby river towns of Red Wing (Co. F), Lake City (Co. I), and Winona (Co K). Being a smaller community, however, it did not raise as many men, and thus, many volunteers from other parts of the state were placed in Company H to fill its ranks.

Hastings before the Civil War

and Lincoln's call for troops, he volunteered and, on April 30, 1861, was mustered into service. The men of Company H elected him their captain. He stood six feet one inch tall and had dark hair. He was a striking figure of a soldier. One month later, both John Mars and Frank Mead joined the regiment.

Over the course of the war, Adams was wounded many times. The first was at Bull Run, where he was hit by an artillery shell in his left thigh and received a slight head wound from a minié ball. During the battle he also had his pistol knocked from his hand by a musket ball. (On a side note, while leading charges against the enemy, he reportedly would shout, "Honor to whom honor is due!")

At Malvern Hill on July 1, 1862, he was injured a second time. The regiment was quickly running downhill into a heavy forest, and while running, he tangled his feet in a bush or briar and fell hard, straining his groin, resulting in a hernia on his left side. He continued through the battle, and the army moved to Harrison's Landing the following day. There, the swelling confined him to his bed for ten days, and while so confined, he was attacked with malarial and swamp fever. He was sent to the general hospital in Harrison's

Charles Powell Adams

b. March 3, 1831; d. November 2, 1893

Born in Rainsburg, Pennsylvania, Charles Adams graduated from Cincinnati's Ohio Medical College in 1851. Afterward, he married Mary Florence Buxton, and they had a daughter, Flora, in 1853. Adams and his family moved to Minnesota in 1854, settling in Hastings, where he set up a medical practice. He quickly rose to prominence within the town, serving in the territorial legislature in 1857. In 1856, Charles and Mary had another child, their son, William, but sadly, Mary died in October 1858.

In addition to his medical practice, Adams began publishing a newspaper in December 1859, the *Hastings Democrat*. A year later, on December 8, 1860, he sold the paper to John Mars, who was one of his printers. Frank Mead was another of the printers at the paper. When the war began, both men volunteered and served under Adams in Company H.

Earlier that year, Adams had married Mary C. Hover. She brought into their home her mother and a daughter by a previous marriage, who was working as a dressmaker. They had one other boarder, Frank Mead.

When Adams heard of the shelling of Ft. Sumter

This picture of Adams was taken while back home in Minnesota and after his May 6, 1864, promotion to the rank of lieutenant colonel.

Landing and, from there, to Hygeia Hospital in Fortress Monroe, where he remained for some time. He returned to the regiment two days before the Battle of South Mountain.

Adams was wounded at Antietam when a bullet grazed his left shoulder, and he reinjured himself when he fell from his horse near Falmouth, Virginia. On February 9, 1863, he was sent to the Army Hospital for Volunteer Officers in Washington, DC, where his hernia was treated. He spent two weeks recovering and then returned to the regiment.

During his career with the First Minnesota, Adams worked his way up the ranks. Starting as the captain of Company H, he was promoted to major on September 26, 1862, after Antietam. He made lieutenant colonel on May 6, 1863, and was second in command when the First made its July 2 charge at Gettysburg.

That day, Adams was positioned behind the regiment on the right. Col. Colvill was in the center, and Maj. Downie was on the left. In the mad rush to stop the Rebels, command of the regiment quickly changed hands. When Colvill fell, Adams took command, and when he too went down, Downie commanded. Shortly thereafter, Downie also fell wounded.

Adams was shot twice in his left leg and once in his chest. A minié ball entered his left breast, passed through his left lung, fractured the lower portion of his scapula, and exited near his spine. The bullet decimated his left lung, requiring more work from his right lung for the rest of his life. Creating the upper wound in his left leg, a ball entered his left groin, passed obliquely backward and downward through his thigh, and exited his posterior a few inches below the hip joint. During the minié ball's flight, it struck his femur, injuring but not breaking it. The second ball that hit his leg may have been the last of the three shots that took him down. It entered the lower third of his thigh from the rear, passing obliquely inward and downward and lodging about two inches above the knee joint. It remained with him for the rest of his life.

As darkness set, the remnants of the regiment searched the field for survivors. Adams' wounds were judged mortal, and he was left on the field. In the morning, however, he was still alive, so he was taken to the rear, where doctors had more wounded than they could handle. Once again, he was judged too far gone and was left outside to die while other wounded were treated. Partially protected from the strong thunder

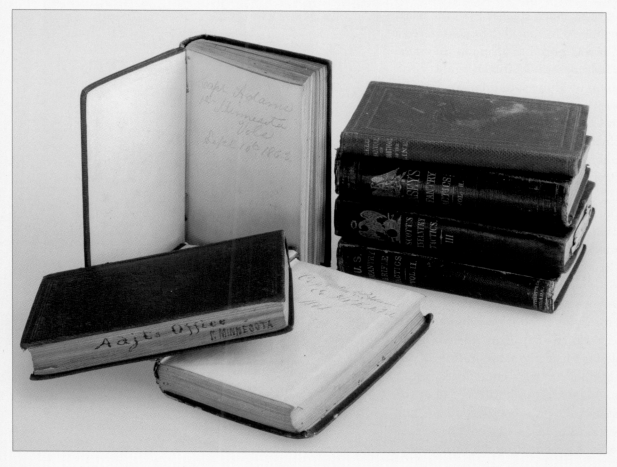

Charles Powell Adams began his service as a captain in Company H and rose to the rank of lieutenant colonel of the regiment. As an officer moved up in rank he needed to know more complicated drills. Whereas a captain needed to know how to maneuver his company, a major or lieutenant colonel needed to know how to move a regiment or even a battalion. As Adams moved up in rank he acquired more manuals and dated them. These are the manuals he carried and used throughout the war.

showers that came that evening, he refused to die and eventually received medical attention.

Adams spent some time at the Gettysburg hospital and, then, returned to Minnesota on September 1, 1863, to finish his recovery. On November 24 he was sent to Washington and was treated at the hospital for volunteer officers, where he had been earlier that year. He returned to the regiment on Saturday, December 12. Writing in his diary on December 13, 1863, Sgt. George Buckman made the following notation:

> Lt. Col. Adams took command of the Regiment. He has not recovered from his wounds which he received at the battle of Gettysburg. He has no use of his left lung and walks lame from a musket ball in his knee. Had 7 rounds. It is surprising to see how he lived.

The First returned to Minnesota in late February 1864, and he was mustered out with the regiment on May 5, 1864.

When a new fighting unit to replace the First Minnesota was being formed, Adams vied for its command. He tried to recruit veterans of the First, but only fifty-eight enlisted. The unit was comprised of, for the most part, new men and was much smaller than the usual thousand-man regiment. Too small to be considered a proper regiment, it was forced to abandon the name First Regiment of Minnesota Volunteer Infantry and adopt First Battalion of Minnesota Infantry. Further weakening his position, Adams was unpopular with many of the men and, apparently, with a few of the higher-ups, and thus, he was not offered the command of the new battalion. So he decided not to reenlist. He returned to Hastings, and the battalion went east without him.

Two months later, on July 15, 1864, however, he received a commission as a major in Hatch's Battalion, Minnesota Volunteer Cavalry, which he accepted. He was promoted to lieutenant colonel of the battalion on September 5, 1864. Frank Mead, who had worked as his printer, and Adams were good friends. Mead had been discharged for disability, but he volunteered to serve with Adams in Hatch's Battalion. Adams was no doubt responsible for Mead's promotion from a private in the First Minnesota to a second lieutenant in Hatch's Battalion. Adams served until the end of the war and was mustered out with the battalion on June 5, 1866. On June 22, 1867, he was given a brevet, or honorary, promotion to colonel for faithful service during the war and a brevet promotion to brigadier general for meritorious service.

He returned to Hastings, where he was elected mayor in 1872. He also served as a state senator from 1879 to 1881. His marriage to Mary ended in divorce on October 18, 1873, and five weeks later, on November 29, 1873, he married Mary Sophia Pettibone in Vermillion. Later in life, necessitated by his wartime injuries, especially the unremoved bullet in his left leg, Adams used a cane to steady his walk. He died of cancer on November 2, 1893. He was sixty-two years old. He was buried at Lakeside Cemetery in Hastings.

Joshua Dyer

b. October 8, 1834; d. March 29, 1865

Joshua Dyer was twenty-two when he enlisted, mustering into Company H on November 5, 1861. He was promoted to corporal in July 1862 and to sergeant in November 1863. On March 18, 1862, he was sent to a hospital, where he remained until September 1863, thus missing Gettysburg. In February 1864, the regi-

Joshua Dyer

ment headed back to Minnesota to be mustered out. On February 17, 1864, Dyer married Lucy Charlotte Mosher in Argyle, Wisconsin, where she remained when he returned to duty. Since Dyer enlisted six months after the First had formed, he still had time on his enlistment, so he transferred to the First Battalion on March 31, 1864, as a sergeant in Company B.

On June 28, 1864, at the Battle of Petersburg, he went missing and was presumed dead by his comrades. He actually had been captured, however, along with twenty other men from the regiment. He was sent to Andersonville, arriving around July 13. There, he found William Haskin, who had served in the Second Minnesota and known Joshua since his family arrived in Minnesota in the fall of 1855. Haskin had been captured at Chickamauga. On September 10, 1864, he and Dyer were sent to Charleston and, from there, were moved to a prison in Florence, South Carolina, and then to one in Wilmington, North Carolina. As part of a prisoner exchange, Joshua was prepared for release on February 28, 1865. On March 4 Haskin helped load Dyer, who fell ill while suffering through Confederate detention, into an ambulance headed to the hospital in Wilmington.

On March 28, 1865, Dyer was placed on the steamer *General Lyon,* a ship ferrying released prisoners to New York City. Unfortunately, on March 29 the ship set fire and sank off the coast of Cape Hatteras, North Carolina. All aboard drowned. After having survived the hazards of war and prison, he tragically died at sea, and his comrades, who had assumed him dead at Petersburg, never did see him again.

Frank Mead

b. February 13, 1839; d. November 29, 1908

Born in Greensburg, Indiana, Frand Mead moved to Lewiston near St. Paul in 1854. In 1858 Mead moved to Hastings, where he worked as a printer for the *Hastings Democrat.* He lived with the paper's owner, future lieutenant colonel Charles Adams. Mead was working at the paper when the war broke out. (He was one of the seven men who printed the *Berryville Conservator* on March 11.) Calling themselves the Dakota County Volunteers, Mead and several men enlisted, and on May 24, 1861, they were mustered into service and placed in Company H. According to the record, Mead stood five feet nine and a half inches tall and had a fair complexion, blue eyes, and brown hair.

Frank Mead

Though Mead was made a corporal—perhaps through his relationship with Adams—his service records show that he was reduced to a private by court-martial on September 20, 1861. At Bull Run the Union army was soundly beaten, and many of the unproven soldiers fled in panic. Alonzo Heard, also of Company H, notes in a statement dated September 21, 1861, that Mead left the field without a gun before the order to retreat had been sounded. Mead's actions during the battle may have been the reason for his demotion.

Mead was slightly wounded at Fair Oaks on March 31, 1862. Later, he was stricken with camp fever (malarial poisoning) during the Peninsula Campaign. He was transferred by written order of Col. Sully to Company B on May 17 and on July 23, while recovering from fever, was detailed as a printer to Gen. McClellan's headquarters in Harrison's Landing, where he continued on detached service for the remainder of his enlistment.

Three of the Berryville printers, Frank Mead, Henry Lindergreen, and Ole Nelson (who died September 8, 1862), suffered from the effects of malaria ("swamp fever") and/or diarrhea. During the Peninsula Campaign, the army stayed on the battlefield and used the

Henry Ghostley Jr. was assigned to Company C on February 10, 1862. His older brother, Jim, had enlisted in Company H on June 2, 1861, and had been severely wounded at the Battle of Bull Run. Henry was seventeen, and Jim was twenty-two.

Henry was wounded at Bristoe Station. He was knocked unconscious by a partially spent ball and  left for dead on the field, but he recovered. He was promoted to the rank of corporal on July 4, 1863, after the Battle of Gettysburg. When the men of the First Minnesota were mustered out at the end of their three years of service, Henry was transferred to the First Battalion. He was promoted to the rank of sergeant and placed in Company A. Henry was mustered out on December 29, 1864, at the expiration of his three-year term of enlistment.

Pvt. Henry Ghostley

James Tucker Ghostley was born in Moorend Farm, Slimbridge, Gloucester, England, on June 6, 1839. He was the oldest of nine children born to Henry and Ann (Parslow) Ghostley. When they immigrated to America, the travel by ship was very rough. It probably took place during the winter of 1854–55. Ann was seasick most of the time. Henry Sr. spent some time helping the sailors handle the ship in the rough seas. In thanks for this, they insisted that he be served a ration of their grog. The family traveled through Chicago. When local people learned that Henry Sr. and James (Jim), were both masons by trade, they tried to encourage the family to stay. However, Ann wanted to go on to the land they had heard about in Minnesota.

The family arrived in Minnesota in the spring of 1855. Henry Sr., eventually staked a claim to some farmland in Hassan Township near Anoka. It was a developing community made up of many other people from England. There, they built a log house that contained a loft and two rooms downstairs. Henry Sr. used his experience as a mason to build a good fireplace and chimney. Even with this, it was still cold in Minnesota that first winter, so much so that Ann would get up at night and check on her children to make sure that none were freezing to death. She also feared Indians and wild animals and insisted that, when the house was built, the windows would be small and high in the walls so that the "varmints" would have difficulty getting in.

Jim and his father often walked the twenty miles to Minneapolis to work as masons, building chimneys. They would stay there for a few days or weeks and then walk home carrying on their backs supplies for the family.

When the war broke out, Jim enlisted in Company H of the First Minnesota. As mentioned, he was mustered in as a private on June 2, 1861.

At the Battle of Bull Run, Jim was seriously wounded in the shoulder. He was taken by ambulance to a hospital in Washington, DC, and subsequently to one in Annapolis, Maryland. He was in Annapolis through at least September. While he recovered, the bullet was not removed, and he carried it for the rest of his life.

Jim's brother Henry joined him in the First Minnesota when he enlisted in December 1861. In a newspaper article in September 1863, it is noted that Jim served as a bugler in Company H. He was mustered out on May 5, 1864, at the expiration of their three years of service.

His Second Corps badge appears to have been used as a watch fob. Its engraving reads, "J T Ghostly, Mail Agent, 2nd Div, 2nd Corps." Notes indicate that he served in this capacity as of February 23, 1863. Jim did not participate in the Battle of Gettysburg, being detached as a mail agent at the time.

The following excerpts are from his diaries, which cover the years 1862 and 1864:

July 21, 1862—One year since I commenced to carry a musket ball in my shoulder.

Sept 29, 1862—Fine day. On duty as Regt Bugler. Col Sully appointed Brig Gen.

Dec 31, 1862—Cold and windy. Was detailed to assist as clerk in AAGs office, nothing of importance. It is as dull as if there was no such thing as old or new year.

Jim Ghostley's position as the regimental mail agent was to receive and deliver mail. This is the type of wagon out of which he and his colleagues worked. The men in the picture are unidentified.

March 25, 1864—Here we are at Ft Snelling again. What a change in its appearance since we left nearly three years ago, what they are going to do with us I cannot tell. I suppose keep us here until we re-enlist or our term of service expires.

Shortly after the war, the *Minneapolis Directory* listed him as a mason living at the corner of Third and Itasca. In 1866 he and his family built a large frame home, probably to replace their older, original farm home. On February 15, 1866, a tragedy accompanied the building of their new home when Jim lost his life. He was smothered by blackdamp while at the bottom of a well being dug near the house. He was only twenty-six years old. It had such an effect on the family that for years no effort was made to sink a well near the house. He was buried at the St. John Episcopal Church Cemetery in Hassan.

The *Hastings Independent* wrote an article in tribute to him. It may have been written by Frank Mead, who was a printer by trade and worked for the *Independent* for a while after the war:

Many that were members of the old First Minnesota regiment will mourn the loss of their old comrade, James T Ghostly. His many excellent qualities as a gentleman and a soldier, made him a favorite with us at home as well as in the field. He was wounded at Bull Run, sufficient to unfit him for carrying arms, and was offered his discharge papers, but his patriotism bid him continue in the service of the Government. He was mail carrier of the Brigade for some time, and many hearts were made glad by his visits to the camp, bringing messages from loved ones far away in distant homes. He has left his friends and associates of the mystic tie on earth to be received a member of the Grand Lodge above. Peace to his memory.

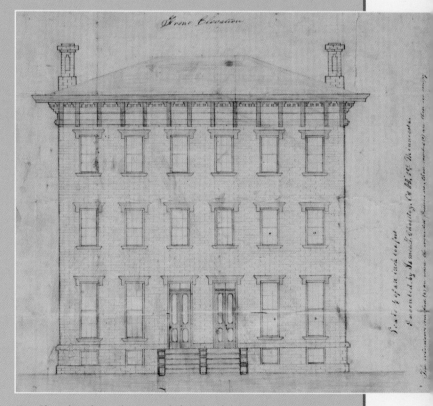

Jim Ghostley drew this pencil sketch of the building in which he was housed in Washington, DC, after being wounded at Bull Run. His notes on the side indicate that he and other wounded Union soldiers were housed behind the two windows on the right side of the second level while some wounded Rebel prisoners were being cared for directly beneath them on the first level.

Jim Ghostley's corps badge

available surface water during the hot month of June 1862. This water is believed to have been contaminated by the rotting corpses of men and horses, and thus, men fell sick. Continuing to suffer from fever and, subsequently, heart disease, Mead was discharged for disability on December 27, 1862, near Falmouth, Virginia.

After his discharge Mead stayed at camp and acted as a correspondent for newspapers in Minnesota. A writer known as Quill Driver mentions Mead in a letter published in the *St. Paul Daily Union* on January 1, 1863:

> He is a tip-top printer, a "bully" soldier, and a perfect gentleman—independent in his views, upright in his dealings, with a good education and a fund of humor; he will make his mark in the world. He was well known as a correspondent, writing over the various nom de plumes of "Shooting Stick," "Plebe," "Howitzer," etc., but more recently as "Handell" of the State Atlas. King [the publisher of the *State Atlas* newspaper] has lost a good correspondent.

Another friend and fellow correspondent, John Mars, describes him as "fearless, independent and outspoken; a good friend and jovial."

Mead returned to Hastings and on August 19, 1864, again joining Lt. Col. Adams, enlisted as a private in Company F of Hatch's Battalion, which was being raised in the Hastings area. On September 1, 1864, Mead was promoted to second lieutenant, likely through Adams' influence. Shortly thereafter, the company left Hastings to join the rest of the battalion. Mead served as its second lieutenant until he was discharged on March 5, 1866.

After the war Mead worked as a traveling correspondent, living in Hastings until 1866, in Farmington from 1868 to 1870, and in Minneapolis from 1872 to 1879. There, he served as the city clerk from 1874 to 1878. He lived in Mandan in Dakota Territory from 1879 to 1886, where he attempted the real estate and insurance businesses. Unsuccessful, he returned to Minneapolis, where he lived from 1887 to 1901.

In 1886 Mead, back from his failed ventures in Mandan, shot and killed a friend during a drunken argument. On September 7, while staying at the Merchant's Hotel in St. Paul, he met Allen Farnsworth, an old friend from Mandan and from their days together in Hatch's Battalion. He had been drinking heavily before meeting Farnsworth. They went out, though, and when they returned to the hotel, Mead turned

2nd Lt. Frank Mead and his first wife, Sarah, whom he married before leaving with the regiment in June 1861. This picture was taken some time after September 1864.

angry and began shouting at him. In a drunken rage, he pulled out a .38-caliber Smith and Wesson and shot Farnsworth in the stomach. One witness said that, when shot, Farnsworth immediately placed both hands on his stomach and cried, "Oh, my God! I'm shot in the stomach! My poor little ones, what will they do!" Farnsworth was quickly carried to a room upstairs and attended by two physicians. Despite their best efforts, he died a day later. Mead was later tried on the charge of murder and acquitted. At the time some people speculated that the decision was made with the help of some Masonic friends.

On August 26, 1887, Mead joined the George N. Morgan GAR post in Minneapolis. He transferred his membership to another post in 1896. He was an active member and participant in the reunions of the First Minnesota Association. He lived in New York City from 1901 to 1906, where he worked as an editorial writer for the *New York Post*. From there, he moved to Boston in 1907 and then back to Minneapolis when his health began to fail. When one document asked his occupation, he wrote, "veteran journalist." Frank Mead died in Minneapolis on November 29, 1908, at the age of sixty-nine.

sent to the field hospital. I have seen thousands of arms and legs thrown in piles outside. I cannot think of it without shuddering. I went into the war with fair hair, but returned with dark hair. While I lay at the hospital all my hair fell off, and when it grew back it was of another color.[1]

Nelson was with the regiment at Gettysburg and was one of the few to avoid being wounded.

On May 7, 1864, almost immediately after the First Minnesota was mustered out, Nelson married Anne Marie Dalemoe. He then transferred to the First Battalion to complete his three-year term of enlistment and was placed in Company B. From June 21 to 23, 1864, Nelson was at the Battle of Jerusalem Plank Road, also known as Weldon Railroad, of which he writes:

> At Weldon Railroad we were surprised by the enemy while we were destroying the railroad tracks. My tentmate, Peder Baardsen [who was also from Trøndelag] was taken prisoner and later starved to death.[2]

Nelson also was with the First Battalion at the Battle of Ream's Station on August 25, 1864. Later in the war, he served as a stretcher-bearer; the September–October 1864 muster roll lists him as on detached service with the Ambulance Corps, Second Division, Second Army Corps.

He was discharged on February 11, 1865, near Petersburg, Virginia, at the expiration of his original three-year term. His military pension in 1880 was four dollars per month for the loss of his thumb. John Nelson died on November 9, 1920, at his farm in Arlington, South Dakota.

Jonas Nelson

b. January 31, 1839; d. November 9, 1920

Jonas Nelson was born in Meråker in Trøndelag, Norway, to Nils and Susanna Iverson. His family, including siblings Iver, Nels, and Anna, came to America in the spring of 1854, and soon after, he began going by John Nelson. As per Norwegian patrilineal naming tradition, his last name became Nilson or, as it was often rendered in the United States, Nelson. The family eventually settled near the little town of Wanamingo near Red Wing.

John enlisted in Red Wing on February 14, 1862. He was twenty-three when, on February 28, he was mustered and placed in Company H. He stood five feet eleven inches tall and, perhaps unsurprisingly, had blue eyes, light hair, and a fair complexion. On October 10, 1862, he was admitted to the Ft. Schuyler Hospital in New York City because of a bullet wound to his thumb received at Antietam. He later wrote:

> At the battle of Antietam my left thumb was shot off, and my right eyebrow too, so I was

William Henry Wikoff

b. June 20, 1835; d. July 2, 1863

William Wikoff was born in Pennsylvania, probably in the town of Easton. He came to Mankato, Minnesota, around 1858 and in late 1860 was elected deputy county registrar, working under a J. B. Hubbell. The 1860 census states that Wikoff roomed with Richard Parry, a banker. Parry moved to Philadelphia early in the war, during which the two men carried on a correspondence.

Wikoff was twenty-six when he enlisted with other

William
Henry
Wikoff

Prior to Bull Run, Wikoff had been very ill and later wrote:

> When we left Centerville for the battlefield I was not in condition to fight. My Captain wanted me to remain there, but go I would and go I did—stood it much better than expected. Had it not been for the marching "double quick" for two or three miles on going to the battlefield our troops would have done better fighting. It told upon me pretty severely. . . . During the retreat the utmost confusion prevailed. The Army was completely panic stricken. Had the enemy followed up the retreat Washington it would have been theirs. I did not reach Washington till 3 days after the fight. Was numbered among the killed. My obituary notice was published in the "Independent" did you see it? Fortunate man what can read his own obituary?[4]

As sick as he was, though, Wikoff helped both James Cannon and Dennis Crandall off the field. After the battle he was sent to a hospital in Georgetown and, later, to a hospital in Annapolis. He remained there until late October, when he rejoined the regiment after an absence of almost three months. Before leaving the hospital, he was offered a medical discharge, but he refused it and returned to the front lines.

On March 9, 1862, while anticipating battle, he wrote:

> They may give us a hell of a fight at Winchester— a few days will tell the tale. When some will "sleep the sleep that knows no waking," beneath the cold green sod of Virginia. If it should be my lot to die on the battlefield it will be a consolation to my friends to know that I died serving my country in the darkest hour of its history.[5]

During the July 2 charge at Gettysburg, Company H and Sgt. Wikoff were on the regiment's far-left flank. The rest of the regiment was to their right as they moved toward the enemy. During the ensuing fight, he was shot through the heart and died instantly.

Wikoff was buried by his comrades on the field at Gettysburg. In October 1863 his remains were removed and on October 24 were reinterred in a family vault in Easton Cemetery in Easton, Pennsylvania.

men from the Mankato area, including Charles Mansfield, George Pfeffer, Frederick Diehr, Benjamin Dewy, James Cannon, W. A. Coy, Ed Casey, and Charles Andrus. The enrolling clerk must have spelled his last name incorrectly, using a *c* instead of a *k,* and thus, he was forever on the military rolls as Henry Wicoff.

His friends knew him, however, as Hank. One in particular, John E. Harrison, had been the county surveyor and sent letters back to the *Mankato Semi-Weekly.* John states that when Hank was ill, he was sorely missed. He also offers the following tongue-in-cheek explanation for Wikoff's promotion to sergeant:

> Capt [Adams] is a tip top officer, the best looking man in the regiment. . . . The Captain told us he wanted to appoint one of us to a non-commissioned office, and wished us to select the one ourselves. Not wishing that all the good looking men should be taken out of the ranks, we selected W H Wikoff, and the said Wikoff was duly appointed 5th sergeant.[3]

12

COMPANY I
THE WABASHA VOLUNTEERS

THE MEN FROM THE WABASHA AND LAKE CITY AREA, located along the Mississippi River, became the nucleus of Company I. They trained at Ft. Snelling during May and June 1861. Ordered to Washington, the First Minnesota embarked at St. Paul on the *War Eagle* and the *Northern Belle*. On the way the steamers stopped at the river ports, and friends and family said good-bye to their soldier sons. The troops traveled past Maiden Rock near Lake City on their way to La Crosse, where they boarded a train and headed to Chicago and, eventually, Baltimore.

Nestled on the Mississippi River between Red Wing and Winona were the communities of Wabasha and Reed's Landing. Men from this area formed the nucleus of Company I.

Philander Coburn Ellis

b. January 28, 1833; d. July 2, 1863

Born in Mayfield, Maine, Philander Ellis moved to Pennsylvania with his family in 1841, eventually settling in Crawford County. At some point, he moved to Minnesota, and on April 29, 1861, he mustered into the First Minnesota as a member of Company I. Called "Cobe" by his family—and "Philo" by his comrades in the First—he was one son among a family of three sisters and seven brothers, four of whom, including Philo, served during the Civil War. Brothers Benjamin and Enoch were in Company K of the 150th Pennsylvania Infantry and served in President Lincoln's bodyguard, and brother Nathan served with Company G of the Second Michigan Cavalry.

Ellis was wounded at Bull Run, and like several of the regiment's wounded, he was captured after the battle. He was sent first to Ligon's tobacco warehouse in Richmond and then to Tuscaloosa, Alabama, along with several other Minnesotans. Later, he was moved to Jefferson Barracks in St. Louis, where he was paroled. Ellis returned to his regiment on December 22, 1862, more than a year after his capture.

Ellis was killed during the July 2 charge at Gettysburg. Ellis' tentmate, Samuel Seymour, wrote the following to Philo's mother:

Camp near Hagerstown, Md.
July 11, 1863
Mrs S A Ellis
Hartstown, Pa
Dear Madam,

P C Ellis was fighting for his country and doing his duty like a good soldier and an honorable man. He was my tent mate ever since he came back to the army, and a better man or a kinder-hearted, quiet, good companion I never expect to find. He was shot through the head on the charge made by our regiment on the enemy's line on the evening of the 2nd of July near Gettysburg, Pa. He never knew he was hurt. Our losses were severe . . . and three companies were not in the fight, only 92 left after the fight. I found him on the way back to the lines a short time after the charge but he was dead. He was my dearest friend. I felt lonely. We buried him decently and marked his grave. He was the first one laid in one large grave next to a large oak tree on the field. I saved his wallet and some few papers. All the rest were lost. I lost all my things while attending to the wounded, and have had no chance to write since, for we have been following the enemy and are now before them, in line of battle. We expect a hard battle tonight or in the morning. There were only five men and one sergeant left in our company that went into the battle on the 2nd of July. How many will be left after this fight who can tell, but we fight in a just and good cause, and feel willing to die like men if that be our fate, or bear with the pain of wounds if wounded.

We have had some very hard marches since the battles near Gettysburg and I almost wish sometimes I had poor Philo's place. Then all would be at peace. Daniel Weaver, our other tent mate, was wounded in the right knee but not dangerously. I expect he has written to some of Ellis's friends. I opened this letter to get your address and this is all the paper I have or can get now. The first opportunity I will give you more particulars. Ellis fought like a man, always did his duty, and died as a soldier wishes to die when his time comes, with his face to the foe and a smile on his face as though all is well. We checked the enemy then and whipped them the next day handsomely. Took many prisoners. All we regretted was that our companions were not there to share our victories. It must be hard for a mother to lose such a son as Philo, but such is the fortune of war. May he enjoy all the blessings of the next life. He deserves it if anyone does. I do not know how I can send this but will try. I knew Ellis for the last few years at Minneiska, Minn.

Yours respectfully and sincerely,
S. O. Seymour[1]

Ellis' body may have been reinterred at the Gettysburg National Cemetery and placed in one of the graves marked "Unknown."

Levi Emery

b. May 18, 1834; September 18, 1895

Born in New York City, Levi Emery and his family settled in Highland Township in Wabasha County, Minnesota. News of Ft. Sumter's bombardment reached Emery via a messenger's arrival at the family's farm. Stirred by the report, he enlisted—the first man to do so from Highland Township—and was mustered on May 26, 1861.

A few days before the First Minnesota's arrival in Baltimore, the Sixth Massachusetts had been attacked by a mob and several of the soldiers killed. Hearing of this, Col. Gorman readied to meet possible trouble, ordering the companies to load muskets and fix bayonets. The band was sent to the rear, and leading the regiment, Col. Gorman started for the other train depot. Emery remembers "some black looks on the faces of the crowd."

Finally, one fellow insolently asked, "Where's your music?"

Col. Gorman, tapping a soldier's musket, replied, "In our gun-barrels." No further problems arose.

July 21, 1861, started out as a hot Sunday morning. The men listened and watched the Union and the Confederate artillery batteries duel each other, ducking as Rebel shells screeched overhead. Some men joked as they noted sudden movements on the part of their comrades: "Look at Jim or Tom or Charlie dodge." But not all the shells went overhead. Emery saw one of the artillery horses get hit. He watched as the artillerymen quickly cut its traces, pulled the horse out of the way, and put another horse in its place.

During the battle Emery felt something strike his

Levi Emery

pant leg. He looked down and saw blood. At first he thought he must have been hit in the leg, but then he noticed a finger from his left hand dangling. He tied it up and went on with the rest of the men until the Rebels, in increased numbers, charged at them again. Levi turned with the rest, but a comrade who was down begged, "O, Emery, you're not going to leave us are you?" So he set his musket against an oak tree and began carrying water for the wounded men. Soon, a body of Confederate cavalry came upon them and took them captive.

He and the other captured Minnesotans who could do so were compelled to walk to Manassas Junction. There, they were put aboard freight cars destined for Richmond, Virginia. Levi had just lain down and dozed off when, at about nine o'clock, he was awakened by a commotion. The guards had thrown a bushel basket of bread to the prisoners. These men had not eaten since early morning and were famished. Seeing a fellow prisoner with a piece of bread about the size of two fists, Emery asked him for a bit of it. The fellow broke it in half and gave it to him. Emery wished he had asked the man's name so that he could have repaid the favor somehow, someday.

After the Union prisoners reached Richmond, the Confederates were confronted with the problem of finding a place to keep them. A large tobacco warehouse was emptied and used as their lodging place. It was later known as Libby Prison.

Meanwhile, the wounded were looked after by both Southern surgeons and Dr. Stewart of the First Minnesota, who had stayed with the wounded and also been captured. It appears, however, that a Confederate surgeon attended to Emery's wound, and he always spoke highly of his treatment. The ring finger of the left hand was removed and the bullet extracted from his hand. Emery writes that he intended to keep the bullet, but one of the two surgeons "wanted to show it to a friend"—and that was the last he saw of it.

Though he was not as severe as some in his condemnation of prisoners' treatment at Libby, particularly those incarcerated later in the war, he did witness a man's thumbs tied together and hooked over a peg as high as he could reach. Emery also admitted that the food could have been better. The cornbread was made from meal that was cob-and-all ground together, and sometimes it got wormy, as well.

At first he had some difficulty getting in touch with friends and relatives in the North, but eventually, his letters went through. One he wrote to his mother on August 4, 1861, undoubtedly not wishing to worry her, states: "I am wounded in the left hand and am in the hospital receiving good medical attention. I have a very comfortable bed and plenty to eat and drink. There are two hundred and eighty wounded Federal soldiers, I understand, in this hospital. I occupy a considerable [amount] of my time doing what I can for some of them."

The question of exchanging prisoners at first stumped federal officials; they feared doing so would acknowledge the Confederacy as a nation. They later invented a workaround, recognizing the Rebels as belligerents, not as a sovereign power, and began a prisoner exchange. On January 19, 1862, Emery left Libby Prison, having been paroled upon his word of honor not to take up arms against the Confederacy unless and until duly exchanged. From Richmond he was sent to Tuscaloosa, Alabama, where he officially was paroled. On April 18, 1862, he was discharged for disability for the wound he received at the Battle of Bull Run.

Emery returned to Highland and the life of a farmer, marrying Ursula Metcalf in January 1863 at Whitewater, Minnesota. He returned to the service, however, when he was drafted on May 26, 1864. On July 6 he wrote the following to his wife from Ft. Snelling:

I took the "Mankato" late yesterday afternoon and we came as far as Red Wing when we changed, taking a smaller boat and arrived here about three o'clock this P.M. I was pretty well examined and passed muster. When he was performing with my arms, (I do not know but he would have discovered my wounded hand) but I guess he did not think it was very serious. I did not electioneer one way or the other. To be drafted is not like volunteering, but candidly, Ursula, I am in fine spirits.

Emery was mustered into service on July 7, 1864. Eventually, he was assigned to the Third Minnesota. On July 21, 1864, he was sent to Arkansas, where the Third was stationed. He was assigned to Company G and did garrison duty with the regiment for over a year. He considered the Third a conscript regiment. Emery was mustered out of military service at Duvall's Bluff, Arkansas, on September 2, 1865, and discharged at Ft. Snelling on September 16, 1865. Although a member of two regiments, he always considered the First Minnesota his regiment. It was the regiment in which he first served and where he got his military training and first and last battle experience.

Ernst L. F. Miller
b. circa 1833; d. April 10, 1883

Ernst Miller emigrated from Saxony, Germany, and settled at Winsted Lake in McLeod County, Minnesota. Originally a farmhand in Germany, for the two years prior to his enlistment he lived in St. Paul, where he was, by trade, a sawyer, or one who cuts logs into lumber. When mustered on May 31, 1861, he was twenty-seven years old and listed as five feet nine and a half inches tall, with a fair complexion, light eyes, and dark hair.

In August 1861 the regiment was bivouacked at what they affectionately called Camp Stone at Edwards Ferry, Virginia, where Miller received his first wound. While Miller was acting as corporal of the picket guard and all were marching to their posts, the soldier in front of him was carrying his rifle too low. He carried it on his shoulder at a more horizontal than an appropriately vertical angle. When he suddenly turned around, the bayonet end of the lowered rifle poked Miller in the right eye, puncturing his cornea. He was hospitalized for two weeks before returning to

several other men of the First were recovering. While recuperating, Miller traveled into town and visited the J. R. Laughlin Photo Studio at the northwest corner of Twelfth and Market streets, where his photograph (at left) was taken. He is seen in a newly received replacement uniform that does not have corporals' stripes. He remained in the hospital for the rest of his term of enlistment. On June 1, 1864, while still in the hospital, he was discharged for disability.

William Henry Worthington

b. October 17, 1820; d. July 5, 1881

William Worthington was born in East Brookfield in Worcester County, Massachusetts. His twin brother, Henry William, died on November 17, 1825. William Henry, also known as "Duke," was a veteran of the U.S.–Mexican War. He served under Gen. Winfield Scott and fought in ten battles from 1846 to 1848. At the time he was listed as five feet six inches tall, with a light complexion and blue eyes.

The outbreak of the Civil War found Worthington living in Wabasha, Minnesota. He volunteered to put down the rebellion in the South and was mustered in on April 29, 1861. He was forty years old at the time and one of the older men in the company. He was respected because of his service in the U.S.–Mexican War.

Prior to moving to Minnesota, Worthington had lived in Huntingdon, Pennsylvania, and when the First Minnesota traveled from Ft. Snelling to Washington, DC, in 1861, they stopped there. The ladies of the town brought out coffee, sandwiches, and other eatables, for which the troops were grateful.

Perhaps because of his war experience, he was, for a brief time, made a sergeant in the company. John Hoblitt of Company D sent many letters home, and in one he mentions a confrontation between Worthington and James Victory, a sergeant in another company.

Ernst L. F. Miller

duty. Later in life, he completely lost his sight in his right eye as the cornea became opaque.

On July 2 during the unit's charge at Gettysburg, Ernst was severely wounded by a bullet that hit him in the front of his right thigh, above the knee. He was sent to the field hospital for initial treatment and later transferred to a hospital, which was located at the Granite Schoolhouse. After staying there for over a week, he was transferred to the Second Corps' hospital along Rock Creek on the Jacob Schwartz farm.

From Rock Creek he was transferred to Gettysburg's large Camp Letterman field hospital and, finally, to Chestnut Hill Hospital in Philadelphia, where

This stencil belonged to Miller and was found at the site of the Second Corps' hospital at Rock Creek, where Miller was taken after being wounded at Gettysburg.

William Henry Worthington

The incident led to a court-martial on August 1, 1861, and these two U.S.–Mexican War vets lost their sergeant's stripes and were reduced to the ranks. The formal charge was being drunk while marching through Washington, DC. Hoblitt thought that this action was best, since both "were rough characters generally." In being found guilty, Worthington also was fined five dollars.

James Kirkman had started in Company I before becoming a hospital steward for the regiment. He mentions Worthington in a letter home written on April 20, 1862, from the regiment's camp near Yorktown, Virginia:

> The Regiment is in good health and most of the
> sick that we left behind at the hospitals have
> joined us in good health. William Worthington,
> known in Wabasha by the name of "Duke,"
> is the sickest man we have. His complaint is
> pneumonia, we have sent him to Shipping
> Point, and he is recovering but will not be able

to take part in the coming battle, which he will regret very much as he is a good soldier.[2]

Three weeks later, on May 14, 1862, the *Wabasha Herald* printed the following:

RETURNED SOLDIER—William Worthington, familiarly known as "The Duke," very unexpectedly arrived here yesterday by the NORTHERN LIGHT [a river boat]. Mr. W is a member of Company I and had a prominent part in the Battle of Bull Run. He is a veteran soldier, of iron constitution, but even he was compelled to succumb to disease contracted in the trenches of Yorktown. He lay at the point of death for several days, but finally a strong constitution triumphed. He looks pale and thin, but is gaining rapidly, and will start to join his regiment again soon.[3]

Worthington was in the following battles: First Bull Run, Ball's Bluff, the Siege of Yorktown, Fair Oaks, Savage Station, Gaines' Mill, Mechanicsville, White Oak Swamp, Chapman's Farm, Malvern Hill, Second Bull Run, Antietam, Sharpsburg, Fredericksburg, Chancellorsville, Gettysburg, Brandy Station, and Thoroughfare Gap. At Fredericksburg a correspondent, after crossing the river from town and back toward the Union headquarters, reported, "The 'Duke' and others have just brought some prisoners over, captured in town."

It is believed that Worthington may have been a member of the twenty-man detail sent on the morning of July 2, 1863, to help at the Second Corps' hospital and, thus, was not in the charge at Gettysburg. On September 20, 1863, he became the orderly for Capt. Duffy in Company I.

He was mustered out with the regiment on May 5, 1864. William Worthington had lived a soldier's life during two wars, spanning a period of five years of active service, and had fought in a total of eighteen battles. After the war he returned to Wabasha. He died on July 5, 1881, at the age of sixty-two.

13

COMPANY K
THE WINONA VOLUNTEERS

AS NEWS OF THE PRESIDENT'S CALL TO ARMS spread, many citizens in Winona gathered for a patriotic rally. In fact, so many people arrived that the hall could not hold them all. Henry Lester, a prominent citizen and the future captain of Company K, urged the adoption of the following document, which was signed by many men that day:

We the undersigned, mutually agree to unite ourselves together as the Winona Volunteer Company and tender our services to the state adjutant-general for the purpose of sustaining the government of the United States in pursuance of the government; the details of subsequent action to be arranged upon receipt of proper instructions from the adjutant-general's office at St Paul.

The *Winona Daily Republican* reported the event on April 26, 1861:

The Winona Company—This volunteer company has received its full complement and stands ready to proceed to the rendezvous at Fort Snelling, whence the Minnesota regiment will march as the Government may direct. The company met this morning, at their drill room

Winona, located in the southeast, was the state's connection east through the railroad in La Crosse and south down the Mississippi River. This view looks southwest, with the river bluffs in the background.

in Sanborn Hall, and elected the following officers: H. C. Lester, Captain; G. Holzborn, first lieutenant, Joseph Periam, second lieutenant; John Ball, sergeant; H. S. Bungham, second sergeant; E. Z. Moore, fourth sergeant; J. W. Morgan, H. A. Brink, S. E. Stebbins, and William Furlong, corporals. These are all excellent selections. Uniforms are being manufactured in this city for the company.

Subsequently, the citizens of Winona presented the company with a U.S. flag and each man with an impressive gray uniform. The only known photograph of this gray uniform is of Color Sgt. George Burgess (see p. 219).

Balthasar Best

b. March 7, 1838; d. April 29, 1911

Balthasar Best was born in Darmstadt, Sterkenburg, in the state of Hessen, Germany, to a family of eight children, four boys and four girls. His father, Jacob, was a doctor, and Jacob's friend, a doctor who had immigrated to America, encouraged him to do the same. In 1850 Best's father packed up the entire family and sailed to America.

They took a steamer, named the *Griffith,* and traveled across Lake Erie from Buffalo, New York, intending to locate in Toledo, Ohio. During the crossing, however, near Cleveland, their boat caught fire and was soon a mass of flames. Balthasar's mother, father, four sisters, and three brothers were all lost. He made it to shore by holding a piece of floating debris and with the help of a man in a boat. Best nearly died, though, from grief and exposure. Later in life in an affidavit dated April 27, 1908, Best would state:

> I beg to report that I am not in possession of the records pertaining to my birth; that on June 17th, 1850, while crossing Lake Erie with my father and mother and other members of my family, our ship was wrecked, my parents and brothers and sisters were all drowned, I being the sole survivor of the family. Everything that we possessed was lost, including the family Bible, wherein the record of my birth was recorded. I was twelve years old, when the disaster occurred, and distinctly remember having seen my name recorded in our family Bible before we sailed from Germany.[1]

Balthasar Best

A German family took him in, and he lived with them for a while. But they treated him cruelly, forcing him to sleep in the basement cellar. One day while the family was gone, he was outside in the yard crying when another young boy came by. He too spoke German, and when Best related how poorly he was being treated, the other boy encouraged him to come to their house. Best left with the boy and was adopted by this new family. Their name was Kleinschmidt. They treated him well, and he came to love them as his own.

At some time, perhaps around 1856, he moved to Prairie du Chien, Wisconsin, where he learned the trade of cabinetmaking. In 1859 he moved to nearby Winona. He lived on Fourth Street, about a block away from Mathias Kinnen, who would later become a comrade and lifelong friend, the result of their war experiences together. In Winona, Best learned the trade of sash (window) and door making.

He was twenty-three years old when he enlisted. At the time of his muster he was five feet eight inches tall and had a light complexion, gray eyes, and brown hair.

Family oral history records that his childhood friend also enlisted in the Union army. When he learned that his friend had been killed, Best felt very bad and said that it should have been him who died. Best reasoned that he was an orphan with no natural family, and here, a good man with a family died instead, leaving those at home to weep. The Kleinschmidts let him know that they felt it was not his fault and told him not to blame himself. This friend who died was probably Cpl. Jacob A. Kleinschmidt. He had enlisted in Company A of the Thirty-seventh Ohio Infantry on September 6, 1861, and was killed at Princeton, West Virginia, on May 17, 1862.

Best kept a diary written in German. At one point during the Battle of Gettysburg, he had his rifle shot out from his hands. His stoic comment is only, "Whole day dirty." Many of the men who were recent immigrants were able to learn the English military commands, but when they had free time, they commonly reverted to their native language when writing or when speaking to others.

Some records indicate that Best was wounded at Bristoe Station on October 14, 1863. He is listed on the U.S. Army's list of casualties for that date. He never mentioned it in his pension application, however, so the wound may have been slight. Best was mustered out with the regiment on May 5, 1864. The stoic German with a tragic childhood grew to manhood and defended his newly adopted country. He participated in twenty battles during his three years of service, including Chancellorsville, Gettysburg, and Bristoe Station.

Horatio Bingham

b. August 31, 1837; d. December 6, 1866

Canadian by birth, Horatio Bingham was twenty-three and living in Winona when the war began. He enlisted and was mustered in as the second sergeant of Company K on April 29, 1861. He fell and was discharged for disability on October 2, 1862.

On January 4, 1864, he accepted a commission as the captain of Company L in the Second Minnesota Cavalry. In February 1865, he took over the job of ordnance officer for the District of Minnesota. He was mustered out of the volunteer army on April 19, 1866. He was given a commission as a second lieutenant in the Second U.S. Cavalry, dating February 23, 1866. His photograph was taken while he was a captain in the Second Minnesota Cavalry.

Horatio Bingham

In 1866 forts were being constructed along the Bozeman Trail to protect wagon trains from hostile Indian attacks. Ft. Phil Kearny, located in what is now Wyoming but was then part of Dakota Territory and under the command of Col. Henry Carrington, was being built at the time. Wanting the white men out of their homeland, Indians constantly harassed the wood details when they went out to gather building materials. Into this uneasiness came reinforcements, including Lt. Horatio S. Bingham's Company C of the Second U.S. Cavalry and infantry captains James Powell and William J. Fetterman.

Most of Ft. Phil Kearny was completed by December 1866. On the morning of December 6, the wood train was attacked once again, and the lookouts on nearby Pilot Hill signaled the fort. Col. Carrington sent army captain Fetterman, Lt. Bingham, and about thirty cavalrymen under Bingham's immediate command to relieve the train and drive the Indians north across Big Piney Creek. Col. Carrington, Lt. Grummond, and about twenty-five mounted infantrymen also rode out from the fort. They intended to circle around Lodge Trail Ridge and cut off the retreating Indians in the Peno Valley.

Initially, things went well for the soldiers. Capt. Fetterman took his group of cavalrymen straight to the wood train, where they found the Indians, who, upon their approach, retired a short distance away. The Indians were followed for some distance before they turned and counterattacked the soldiers. Bingham's cavalrymen became strung out during the pursuit, and many panicked when the Indians turned and attacked. Lt. Bingham and fourteen men fell back to the right and rear, taking the direction of where Col. Carrington's party was supposed to be.

The Indians finally fled before Capt. Fetterman. Col. Carrington's party eventually arrived and went a short distance up Big Horn road. Men straggled and became scattered and no fight occurred, save an occasional shot here and there. Lt. Bingham's men then joined Col. Carrington's party. From there, lieutenants Bingham and Grummond detached themselves and, with four or five enlisted men, gave chase to a few scattering Indians who appeared on their right.

They chased one or two some two miles and, finally, came upon one dismounted Indian, and they endeavored to cut him down with their sabers because their arms had not been reloaded. Suddenly, they discovered themselves surrounded by approximately 150 Indians. They attempted to reach the nearest hill. Lt. Bingham, in going around a ravine, was attacked and quickly felled by arrows. The unit's senior cavalry officer died instantly.

Lt. Grummond was able to return in one piece after slashing his way through the Indians with his saber. Only Lt. Bingham and a Sgt. Bowers died in the December 6 action. Five other soldiers were wounded. Col. Carrington recovered the bodies and returned to the post at four o'clock. When they recovered Lt. Bingham's body, he reportedly had fifty arrows in him, an obvious act of anger meant as a message to the soldiers.

The Indians were no doubt encouraged by the actions that day. Years later, some of them indicated that the December 6 skirmish had convinced them that they could overpower and destroy any force of soldiers sent out from the fort. It also may have convinced them that the decoy tactic might work again at Ft. Phil Kearney. Two weeks later, on December 21, 1866, Capt. Fetterman led a rescue mission out from the fort and was completely surprised by the Indian's

trap. He and all eighty men assigned to him were killed in what became known as the Fetterman Massacre. It was the largest loss of U.S. soldiers in battle against Indians until Custer's fight ten years later.

Eventually, the army gave up the idea of building a string of forts along the Bozeman Trail. Red Cloud and his Cheyenne had won. (Also in that group were many Lakota, one of whom was the young Crazy Horse.) The troops were withdrawn, and the Indians set fire to the forts.

Horatio Bingham was twenty-nine years when he died. He undoubtedly was buried at the fort, but today, the location of his grave is unknown.

Alfred Patrick Carpenter
b. October 29, 1835; d. September 18, 1864

Born in Ashford, Connecticut, in 1852 Alfred Carpenter moved to Minnesota with his parents, Palmer and Martha, and his siblings, Martha and Loren. They left their home in Eastford, Connecticut, and settled in St. Charles Township. Alfred worked on his father's farm and, when the war began, was teaching, as well. He had attended Brown University and taught in an elementary school in Madison, Wisconsin, where he lived with his brother. During the summer months, he returned home to work on his father's farm.

He was mustered into Company K on May 23, 1861, and was known by the men as "Alf" or "Carp." Mathew

Alfred Patrick Carpenter

Marvin was a close friend in the company. Carp was wounded on September 17, 1862, at Antietam. He was promoted to corporal before the Battle of Gettysburg, where he was wounded twice during the July 2 charge. He was sent to a hospital to recuperate.

Regarding Gettysburg, Sgt. Carpenter later recalled:

The sun had gone down and in the darkness we hurried, stumbled over the field in search of our fallen companions, and when the living were cared for, laid down on the ground to gain a little rest, for the morrow bid fair for more stern and bloody work, the living sleeping side by side with the dead. Thousands had fallen, and on the morrow, they would be followed to their long home by thousands more.[2]

On September 23, 1863, when he was well enough to leave, he accepted a commission as lieutenant and transferred soon after to command a company of the Second U.S. Colored Infantry stationed in Key West, Florida. He died of yellow fever on September 18, 1864. He was twenty-eight years old. Today, his name is inscribed on the monument in Washington, DC, dedicated to the U.S. Colored Troops who served the Union's cause during the war.

David Dudley

b. circa 1838; d. October 6, 1862

David Dudley was born in Candia, New Hampshire, in 1838, the youngest of three sons. He came to Minnesota shortly before the outbreak of the war and volunteered along with others from the Winona area. He was twenty-three years old. On April 29, 1861, he was mustered into service as a corporal and assigned to Company K.

After Bull Run he was promoted to the rank of sergeant and on November 15, 1861, was promoted to first sergeant of the company. Dudley fought in the battles of Bull Run, Balls Bluff, and Antietam. Unfortunately, he was severely wounded at Antietam and subsequently died from those wounds on October 6 in Frederick, Maryland.

After the war a GAR post was established in Candia and named the David B. Dudley Post #79 in his honor.

While still living in New Hampshire, Dudley had developed a close relationship with a young woman named Angie Towle. They wrote to each other regu-

David Dudley

larly. In at least one of these letters, he must have mentioned his friend Mathew Marvin because on March 16, 1863, she wrote to Mathew inquiring about David, disclosing that she had not heard from him. Marvin related the sad news of David's death the previous October. She wrote back and thanked him for letting her know David's fate. Mathew and Angie continued to correspond, which began a romance through the mail. They eventually married in 1867.

Chester Durfee

b. September 14, 1845; d. August 3, 1929

Chester Durfee was born at Cook Town in Rock County, Wisconsin. His parents were Hiram and Salome Durfee. He had one sister, Mary, and four brothers, George, Jason, Edward, and Franklin. During the summer of 1850, the family lived in Milwaukee. In 1856 Chester and his family moved to Rollingstone in southeastern Minnesota, near Winona.

When the war began, his twin brothers, George and Jason, went off to join the First Minnesota to help put down the rebellion. Jason was killed at the Battle of Bull Run. Being under seventeen years of age, Chester needed his parents' permission to join George in the First. He got it, was mustered on August 26, 1861, and was placed in Company K along with his brother George. Chester was five feet eight and a half inches

Chester Durfee

tall and had a light complexion, gray eyes, and light-colored hair. He was one of the youngest men in the regiment. Chester enjoyed saying that he was only fifteen years four months old the day he enlisted.

Chester received a shell wound in the left leg, below the knee, on July 3, 1863, during the repulse of Pickett's Charge. Both bones were fractured. Years later, he took a photograph of the large boulder he had tried to hide behind and wrote on the back of the picture:

This large boulder lay about 30 feet from where I was wounded & as I bent over to pick up my cap that was knocked off by a Confederate I also picked up a small piece of our flag that was shot away. I then tried to get refuge behind this

This is the boulder behind which Chester Durfee tried to take refuge during the battle. Seen here at the 1913 fiftieth anniversary of the battle are Medal of Honor recipient Alonzo Pickle of Company K and Confederate veteran Edward S. Duffy, who served in Parker's Battery of Light Artillery at Gettysburg.

The inscribed Second Corps badge worn by Durfee during the war

George Durfee was a bit of an artist and spent part of his time sketching what he saw of the war. Seen here is a view of Fredericksburg, done in the fall of 1862. In it he has pictured his brother, whom he calls "Chet," walking downhill toward the river and the city beyond. He titled it *View of Fredericksburg MD from Our Picket Lines up the River Near Dam No 1.*

boulder but there were too many [wounded men] around it so I hobbled away to Meade's Headquarters.

After lying on the ground for several days, Durfee was taken to the railroad depot with others of his company. They were put into stock cars, and he eventually was taken to Ft. Schuyler Hospital in New York City to recover. Gangrene set in, and three times he had to fight with the doctors about taking his leg. He was there from July 1863 until February 1864. He convalesced in several hospitals until he was discharged for disability on March 9, 1865, at Camp Douglas, Illinois. Durfee did eventually recover but was bothered by the wound for the rest of his life.

Pvt. George Durfee was Chester's older brother.

Charles Ely

b. October 16, 1844; d. August 19, 1916

Charles Ely was born in Lancaster, Ohio, and his family moved to Wabasha Prairie on May 4, 1852. Charles' father, Elder Edward Ely, worked there as a teacher, businessman, and minister. Charles is credited with being the first white boy to come to Winona.

He was a sixteen-year-old store clerk at the time the war broke out, and he enlisted on April 29, 1861. He stood five feet six inches tall and had a dark complexion, hazel eyes, and brown hair. He joined other men from the Winona area in Company K, including his good friend Charlie Goddard.

As the regiment began to move forward during the July 2 charge at Gettysburg, Ely was shot in the side of his right chest, the ball exiting near his spine. After the battle he was found and carried to a nearby field hospital. There, he lay on the ground for four days before he was seen. He lay wrapped in a blanket; his pants, soaked with blood from his wound, were discarded. At one point, 1st Sgt. Mathew Marvin saw a surgeon run a handkerchief through the hole in Ely's body that the minié ball had created. The surgeon then declared that he could not survive such a wound. Nonetheless, they decided to move him to a hospital in the rear in case he might recover.

Ely did survive. Both he and 1st Sgt. Marvin were sent to Cherry Street Hospital in Philadelphia, Ely arriving on July 15. Fourteen of the men from the regiment were on the third floor. While there, he was visited by his mother. Mrs. Ely and Mrs. Goddard had come to visit their wounded sons on July 27. Mrs. Ely stayed until late October, caring for her boy. On December 18, 1863, Ely returned to the regiment. At some point after Gettysburg, he was promoted to the rank of corporal. He was mustered out with the regiment on May 5, 1864.

Ely's war wound bothered him for many years, often opening to expel bits of bone and other matter. In August 1865 his wound reopened, and Ely pulled out a piece of India rubber, the waterproofing material used in a soldier's ground cloth. Going into battle, he must have rolled up his rubber ground cloth and wool blanket and slung them across his shoulder. Hanging from his left shoulder and tied together near his right hip, it was penetrated by the ball before it entered his chest, part of the blanket entering his body along with the bullet. The surgeon removed the bullet and, not looking for anything else, apparently did not see the fabric. In 1866 the wound opened again, and Ely removed a piece of bone. In 1871 his wound became sore, painful, and swollen. A doctor opened the wound and removed another piece of bone. This wound that never healed weakened him and prevented him from meaningful manual labor. He died at Battle Mountain Sanatorium in De Smet, South Dakota, on August 19, 1916, at the age of seventy-two. Initially buried in De Smet, a year later his body was removed and buried at Woodlawn Cemetery in Winona.

Charles E. Goddard

b. May 14, 1845; d. December 9, 1868

Charles Goddard, born in Pennsylvania, faced an unfortunate amount of death as a child. His father, Abner S. Goddard, died on September 11, 1852, at the age of forty-three. The family had moved to Winona, on May 12, 1852, just four months earlier. Ten children were born into the family, and all but Charles died in early childhood. In 1854 his mother, Catherine, married Alexander B. Smith, but Catherine and Alexander were not together for long. It was believed that Alexander drowned in the nearby Mississippi River in 1856.

Goddard wanted to go to war so badly that he lied about his age, claiming to be eighteen, the minimum age for enlistment. One could enlist, however, at the

Charles E. Goddard

age of seventeen with a parent's permission. When Goddard enlisted, he was actually only fifteen years old, and he definitely did not have his mother's permission. His mother, Catherine, worried about him and encouraged him to desert, but her plea fell on deaf ears. He stayed with the First Minnesota and went off to war.

Like many men of the regiment, he wrote many letters home telling of life in the unit. Apparently, Goddard was sickly before he left to join the army, and life as a soldier made things only worse for him. He was sick with dysentery at the beginning of the war and missed their first battle, at Bull Run. He was in the hospital at least once in 1862. The following is a letter he wrote to his mother from West Point, Virginia, on his seventeenth birthday, May 14, 1862:

You requested me in your letter to keep my discharge as a [relic]. I will send it to you and you can do as you have a mind with it. If I keep it with me it runs a good chance of being lost . . . I will tell you how I [happened] to get my discharge papers. I was lying on the bed with my clothes on & there was a doctor come in, one that did not belong to my ward. He asked me how old I was. I supposed he only wanted to

know to satisfy himself so I told him I was 17 years. He did not say anything but continues to make his rounds from room to room and the first thing I knew he handed me a discharge. I took it and saw what it was. I said nothing but [made] for the Regiment and told Capt. H C Lester I did not want a discharge. He told me I need not take it unless I wanted to. This is the way things was arranged.

By the fall of 1862, morale was very low within the ranks of the First Minnesota. As the cavalry and artillery corps were increasing their ranks they were permitted by the War Department to recruit from the ranks of the infantry. Many from the First took this opportunity, hoping they would have a better life on a horse or shooting a cannon. Goddard wrote home on December 4, 1862, and mentioned this issue among other personal tidbits:

Sam Stebbins was going to get his discharge. I do hope that he may, for I don't think he can stand the fatiguing marches the army has to undergo; besides, Sam is a newly married man, and I have no doubt he is very anxious to get home. Ely is in fine health and spirits; but is nearly as dark as an Indian: Charlie North is in good health, and often wishes for a meal at Mrs. Smith's. John Lynn has enlisted in the 1st Regular Cavalry for the remainder of his three years. Hiram Brink is well also. At one time, when we were at Bolivar, nearly the whole Regiment was going to enlist in the 1st Cavalry, but they stopped recruiting, and that was the only thing that saved our Regiment from being scattered through the different cavalry and artillery regiments. Lieut. John Ball is assigned to Co. F, of this regiment, and is 1st Lieutenant. He was our Orderly Sergeant at Camp Stone, Md. Joseph Periam is our Captain; we like him much better than we did when we first came into the service.

At Gettysburg, Goddard was wounded in his left shoulder and his left thigh during the regiment's heroic charge on July 2. Capt. Periam died from a mortal head wound received during the charge.

After the battle Goddard was treated by the army surgeons and sent to the Cherry Street Hospital in Philadelphia to recover. The wound in his thigh was so near the main artery that too much exertion might cause it to bleed, and if he was away from the hospital, he might bleed to death. While in the hospital, his mother came to visit him, accompanied by Charles Ely's mother. Goddard recovered and returned to the regiment. His wound, however, never healed properly. He persevered and served his full three-year enlistment, mustering out on May 5, 1864.

After his discharge Goddard returned to Winona, where he lived with his mother. She ran a boardinghouse, and he helped her with his labor and provided some financial support for her, as well. He also worked for the first six months in a lumberyard in Winona. Immediately after that, he managed a lumberyard in the city of St. Charles in Winona County for about a year. Then, he was employed for about a year and a half in an abstract office by John Ball, who had commanded Company K before eventually serving as a major in the Eleventh Minnesota.

Besides the pain of the physical wounds he received at Gettysburg while still just a teenager, he apparently suffered from psychological trauma, as well, as his itinerant work history might suggest. He ran for county clerk and won, perhaps based on his war record. Before he could serve, however, he died of consumption (tuberculosis), undoubtedly a result of his wounds and perhaps compounded by the mental stress he never overcame. The worn-out Civil War veteran died at the young age of twenty-three on December 9, 1868. He was buried at Woodlawn Cemetery in Winona. Mathew Marvin, his comrade in arms in the First Minnesota, was the caretaker of the cemetery. No doubt it was a sad farewell that Marvin gave to his friend Charles.

Henry Clay Lester

b. November 1831; d. April 5, 1902

Henry Clay Lester was born in Williamsburg near Buffalo, New York, in November 1831. He graduated with honor in the class of 1850 from Hamilton College in Clinton, New York. He read law and was admitted to the bar but never practiced his profession.

He was a prominent real estate broker and clerk of the court when he was elected captain of the Winona Volunteers in April 1861. He distinguished himself at the Battle of Bull Run. He was made the brigade adjutant and shortly thereafter was appointed colonel of the Third Minnesota Infantry by Minnesota's Governor Ramsey.

Henry Clay Lester

Dr. Daniel Hand, assistant surgeon of the First Minnesota, later wrote about Henry's promotion:

One officer in particular I much admired [was] Captain H. C. Lester, of Winona. He was a gentle, scholarly man, thoroughly conscientious in performing his duty, and withal not ambitious. When news came of his appointment as colonel of the Third Regiment he was surprised and stunned. He hesitated what to do, and it was only on my urgent advice that he decided to accept. I have been sorry since I gave it. He knew himself better than I did,—knew the fatal indecision that was his, and so came disaster. He was never a coward, but when the supreme moment of his life came was not prepared for it.[3]

Colonel Lester drilled the men well, and the Third Minnesota was regarded as a fine regiment. The men respected their commander and presented him with a beautiful Tiffany presentation sword. The first test of the regiment came at Murfreesboro in July 12, 1862. Nathan Bedford Forrest, the feared Confederate cav-

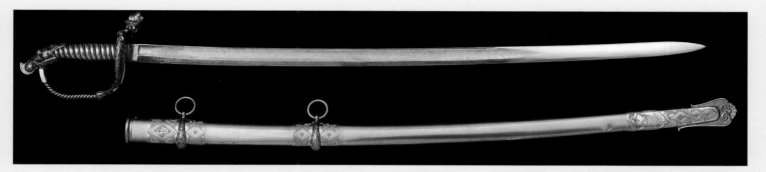

This is a Tiffany and Company adaptation of a U.S. Army Model 1850 Staff and Field Officer's Sword. The sword was presented to commanding officer Col. Henry C. Lester of the Third Minnesota Regiment by his line officers on April 14, 1862. The sword is presentation grade and nonregulation and was made by Tiffany and Company in New York and by Collins and Company in Hartford, Connecticut.

alry commander, captured 1,000 Union troops, including Col. W. W. Dudfield of the Ninth Michigan, who commanded the brigade and was wounded and surrendered with his regiment by Lt. Col. J. G. Parkhurst. The Third Minnesota and Hewitt's Battery of Kentucky Light Artillery held out, resisting two cavalry charges and further skirmishing. The camp of the Third was taken only after three attacks, the last led by Forrest in person, against the sick, the teamsters, and the camp guards, who fought bravely. Later that afternoon, Brigade Adjutant Henry W. Dudfield rode to Lester's position under flag of truce and Forrest's escort to "request" that Lester come talk with Col. Dudfield. It is important to remember that in his after-action report Col. Forrest noted that Dudfield surrendered "the infantry and the artillery" and that the artillery was attached to Lester's command. It is most likely that, unable to defeat the Third Minnesota, Forrest wanted Lester ordered by Dudfield to surrender his command. This would explain Lester's changed personality and behavior upon returning to camp.

Forrest tricked Lester into thinking Forrest had a vastly superior force. He did this by having the Confederate cavalrymen positioned along the road as Lester and his group rode to and from the meeting place. As the group would pass, the cavalrymen were pulled away, circled around, and placed again in line farther down the path so that there appeared to be more troops as Lester and his entourage passed the new lo-

cation. Lester believed and was told by Col. Dudfield that the Third had little chance for survival.

Back at camp he called for a vote of his officers, with Adj. Henry Dudfield an active participant advocating for surrender. Initially, the vote was to stand and fight. A few of the officers left to tell their men of the vote and to prepare for the pending battle. However, a new vote was taken, and with the departure of the officers who had voted to stay and fight, the decision was made to surrender the regiment. Those officers who had left were furious. It has been suggested that perhaps Col. Lester cared too much for his men and feared seeing them die. It may also have been that he was ordered to surrender and to do it in this fashion, which effectively removed attention from two higher-ranking officers: Gen. T. T. Crittenden, the new post commander, who had been captured, and Col. Dudfield, who had surrendered the Ninth Michigan and the Twenty-Third Brigade. Lester seemingly could have tried to free them, but setting him up to surrender would have made him look like the weak link in the chain of events and diverted attention away from Crittenden and Dudfield. In any event, the Third Minnesota Infantry was surrendered after hardly giving battle.

The officers were sent to prison. The men were

involved in a prisoner exchange and in less than two months returned to Minnesota in time to fight at the Battle of Wood Lake. This was the last major battle of the Dakota War. The officers were eventually exchanged, as well.

The decision to surrender did not go well with army leadership. Crittenden and Dudfield made reports directly to the White House. Lester and some of the other officers were dismissed upon the verbal orders of the President. There was no court martial or even a court of inquiry. His many friends thought he may have been done an injustice, believing that he may have been overcautious and concerned for the lives of his men but not that he was a coward. The fact that an officer from another unit, Adj. Henry Dudfield, attended and participated in the officers' council adds to the suspicion that Col. Lester had been ordered by his superior officer to get his men to surrender, making Lester the scapegoat, and that is why he had to call for another vote to get the surrender authorization needed from his officers.

Col. Lester never returned to Winona after his dismissal from the army. The humiliation that resulted from his having surrendered his command may have driven him to leave Minnesota and return to his native state of New York, where he spent the rest of his life and apparently never spoke of his military service. Whereas most veterans' service records were mentioned in their obituaries, there was no such mention in Col. Lester's.

He was married in 1868 at Flushing, Long Island, to Recta Mills. He worked as a civil engineer in New York City and taught the romance languages at Hamilton College. He worked as a clerk of the court for several communities. In 1880 he was living at 83 Main in Mt. Morris in Livingston County. In 1887 he moved to Geneseo, also in Livingston County, where he spent the last fifteen years of his life. He taught at the State University of New York in Geneseo. In 1894 his residence was recorded as 220 Center, and he was listed as a lawyer in the city directory. He also was a vestryman at St. Michael's church.

He ended his days as a piano teacher in Geneseo and died there on May 5, 1902, of heart failure. He was seventy years old. The funeral was at the home of Mrs. Ephraim Curtis, with whom Mr. and Mrs. Lester had lived for the past several years. His body was buried at the Temple Hill Cemetery in Geneseo. His wife, Recta, went to live with her son from her first marriage. When she died in 1905, she was buried next to Henry.

Mathew Marvin

b. September 21, 1838; d. July 25, 1903

Born in Madison County, New York, Mathew Marvin moved to Winona in 1859, where he worked as a clerk at J. J. Randall and Company, a leather goods store. He volunteered at the first call for troops and, at the age of twenty-two, was mustered into Company K. The record shows that he had a fair complexion, brown hair, and blue eyes, and at five feet five and a half inches tall, he was one of the shorter men in the regiment. Men stood in the ranks based on height, the tallest privates standing on the right side as they faced their officer, and thus, Mathew would have stood on the far left as long as he was a private.

Marvin's pay in 1862 was thirteen dollars a month, of which he sent eight home to his mother. He was a good soldier who was promoted to corporal and, eventually, first sergeant during his service. He was wounded in the foot at Bull Run, the thigh at Harrison's Landing, and the foot again at Gettysburg.

After the war he wrote the following thoughts about the Battle of Bull Run:

At Bull Run, our first experience, the regiment was just as courageous. The first shell fired at

This is the canteen used by Mathew Marvin. Note the date "1861" on his canteen's cover.

At Gettysburg, Marvin was Company K's first sergeant. On the morning of July 2, he wrote in his diary, "This is to be the battle of the Civil War." Fearing what could happen, he penciled the following notation on the back cover of his diary:

Should any person find this on the body of a soldier on the field of battle or by the roadside they will confer favor on the parents of its owner by sending the book and pocket piece & silver finger ring on the left hand. Taking their pay for trouble of the greenbacks herein enclosed.

During the charge he was shot in the foot. The ball entered the front of his foot and traveled the length of it, exiting near the heel. The injury caused him considerable suffering for the rest of his life. Recalling that day later in life, he wrote:

Yes, I remember distinctly the particulars of the battle of Gettysburg. Hancock came riding along and stopped about sixty feet from where I stood. He said, "What regiment is this?" "The First Minnesota." "Who is in command?" "Colonel Colville." "Charge," and before Colville could give his command the men were making preparation. 262 against six or seven thousand. The First Minnesota began firing and stopped the advance of the first line of rebels. Those in the rear of the rebel line rushed forward falling over their own men. They were pushed together into a solid mass so that every shot fired by the First did its work. The First was lying down, so much of the shot fired at us went over our heads. We could hear the steady tramp of feet in the rear and the rattling of tin cups as reenforcements came up.

The following is from the diary he kept throughout his service:

The two armies were not 500 yards apart. We had not fired a musket & the rebs were firing rappedly. I dropped to the ground with a wound some whar. I picked my self up as quickly as possible when I saw blood on my shoe the heel of which was tore out. I thought it was a slight one. . . . I had just ketched up again when I fell a second time to Faint to get

us came so close that I dropped on one knee. When the bullet struck me I started to fall forward but swayed so I fell on my left arm, then rolled over on my back. Bullets were so thick on the ground that they almost touched. A handful were under my cartridge box.

On August 9, 1862, he was wounded while in camp at Harrison's Landing. An unknown soldier in a nearby camp of the Fifth New Hampshire discharged his gun, and the ball traveled through Mathew's tent, hitting him in the left thigh, near the groin. Stephen Martin was a tentmate of Marvin's and next to him when he was hit. Marvin was sent to the regimental hospital and from there to Coney Island General Hospital in New York. He returned to the regiment on November 8, 1862, three months after he had been accidentally shot.

The Battle of Fredericksburg was another tough time for the Union army. He wrote a brief note about the battle on December 24, 1862: "We lay under the fire of the rebs . . . the missles of death were whistling their song close to our ears . . . if ever I dug a hole in the ground with my nose it was that day."

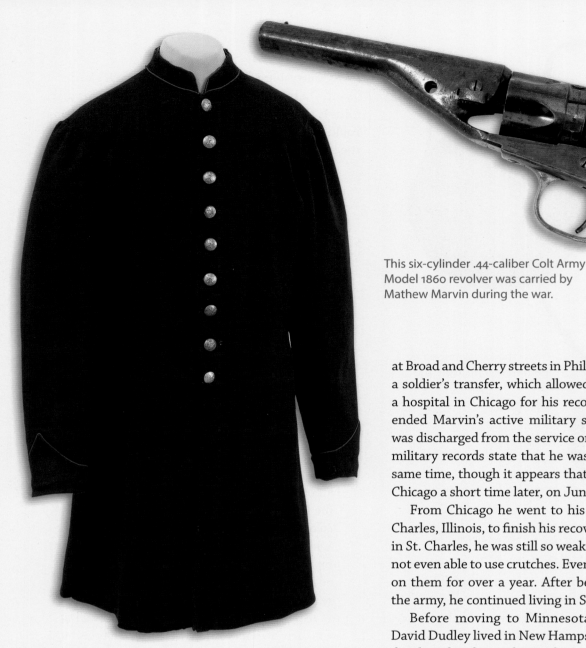

This six-cylinder .44-caliber Colt Army Model 1860 revolver was carried by Mathew Marvin during the war.

The nine-button frock coat was the dress uniform of the men of the First Minnesota. This one was worn by Marvin during the war.

up. I drank some water & put some on my head and wrists then I tried to walk to the rear was to week for that so after resting again I tried the hands and knees.

By crawling on his hands and knees, he was able to get back to where the regiment had started their charge. There his friend Charley North helped him back to the hastily established field hospital near the Union lines. He later wrote: "I got to the rear of our batteries when I divested myself of Gun & Equipment & Knapsack. . . . I have got about all the pain I can stand."

He and several other wounded men from the First were sent to recover at the U.S. general hospital located at Broad and Cherry streets in Philadelphia. He obtained a soldier's transfer, which allowed him to be moved to a hospital in Chicago for his recovery. Gettysburg had ended Marvin's active military service. The regiment was discharged from the service on May 5, 1864, and his military records state that he was mustered out at the same time, though it appears that he was discharged in Chicago a short time later, on June 9, 1864.

From Chicago he went to his family's home in St. Charles, Illinois, to finish his recovery. When he arrived in St. Charles, he was still so weak and lame that he was not even able to use crutches. Eventually, he did, relying on them for over a year. After being discharged from the army, he continued living in St. Charles.

Before moving to Minnesota, Marvin's comrade David Dudley lived in New Hampshire. While there, he developed a close relationship with a woman named Angie Towle, and they regularly wrote to each other. In at least one of these letters he must have mentioned his friend Marvin because on March 16, 1863, she wrote to Marvin inquiring about David, remarking that she had not heard from him. Marvin wrote back to her and related the sad news of David's death the previous October. She wrote back thanking him for the news of David's fate. Mathew and Angie continued their correspondence, and on August 29, 1867, they were married. They lived in St. Charles until 1871, when they moved to Winona.

In Winona, Marvin started a harness business but, on account of his poor health, sold it to his partner. In 1873 he was appointed the caretaker of Woodlawn Cemetery in Winona. Matt, Angie, and their family lived in the house on the cemetery's grounds, which was provided for the superintendent. He retired in 1899.

Mathew and Angie had three children, two boys and one girl. Their daughter, Mabel Lucy Marvin, was born on May 30, 1876. Mathew and his daughter were active in the First Minnesota Veterans Association, Mabel accompanying him on visits to Gettysburg. After his death she continued to be active in the unit, helping whenever she was needed. She often served as secretary of the thinning group and kept the minutes of their meetings. On July 2, 1897, she gave a reading at the dedication of the First Minnesota monument.

Mathew Marvin was sixty-four years old when he died on July 25, 1903. Angie died in 1924. They were buried next to each other in Woodlawn Cemetery, which they knew so well. Their daughter, Mabel, died in 1955 and was buried next to them.

John G. Merritt

b. October 31, 1837; d. December 17, 1892

John Merritt, born in New York City, was twenty-three when he enlisted and made a third sergeant in Company K. A strong man, he stood six feet tall and had a light complexion, brown hair, and blue eyes. He was slightly wounded at the First Battle of Bull Run, where he was shot in the left leg below the knee. He was awarded the Medal of Honor for his gallantry during the battle. As he writes:

John G. Merritt

> I was a sergeant in Co K, First Minnesota Volunteers. . . .
>
> John Ball, the orderly sergeant of Co K, was sick and I was acting as orderly sergeant. As sick as Ball was, he came on the field, and I saw him standing near the regiment while they were engaged, with his arms folded, apparently the most unconcerned person of the lot; he was a brave and fearless man. . . .
>
> . . . Being desirous of obtaining military distinction, I applied to Lieutenant Holtzborn, of my company, for the privilege of selecting four men for the purpose of capturing the first Confederate flag we could get. The lieutenant told me it was a hazardous undertaking, but said, after consultation with Captain Lester, I had permission. Sergeant [David] Dudley, Privates [Jason] Durfee, [Fritz] Grim and one other, whose name I have forgotten, readily consented to my proposal, and all agreed to follow me and to stick to one another under any circumstances.

> Before going into action, the whole regiment divested themselves of knapsacks, haversacks and blankets, and piled them in one large heap beside the road, thinking of course we would be back in a couple of hours—as soon as we had "crushed the Rebellion." I and my four men in particular carried with us but our ammunition and guns. After we supplied ourselves with water, and everything now being ready, orders were given to "Forward!" and we immediately filed through a cluster of trees, where the dying and wounded were being brought on stretchers and blankets. . . .
>
> I never shall forget the first sight of dead, wounded and dying. Pity and sympathy, mingled with a feeling of fear, made me realize in an instant we were approaching death. But the feeling passed away as soon as it came. . . .
>
> It was now about half past one o'clock. We were soon ordered forward, and as we advanced rapidly to the brow of a plateau we knew we were soon to meet the enemy, face to face, at

short range. Just before we got to the top of the plateau the bugle sounded "lie down." With fixed bayonets and loaded rifles we were ready and anxious for business. In about a couple of minutes the bugle sounded "stand up"; no sooner had we done so and were well in line when the command "Forward!" was given. That brought us directly in plain sight and directly in front of "Rebs." We were not more than thirty or thirty five yards apart; in fact we were so close that for a minute we did not know who they were . . . . We saw their colors and all fired immediately; in less than half a minute they gave us a round. We were ordered to lie down and load; then we were ordered to stand up and fire. We had given them three or four rounds and they were slowly falling back, a little confused. When the smoke and dust would break away we could see them and their colors as plain as you can see a man across the street. Just at this time a single gun from Rickett's Battery came directly to the rear of K Company, unlimbered, and in less than half a minute gave them a round of grape and canister. The artillerymen immediately reloaded and gave them another dose of the same medicine. The second round threw them into utter confusion, and it was at about that time myself and the men named above advanced double-quick on the Rebel color-bearer. We had no trouble in reaching him, as the smoke and dust had not risen, and from his actions I thought he was under the impression he had been captured.

The man who carried the colors was about five feet ten or eleven inches, dark complexioned, with black hair, slight mustache and black eyes; he with the others around him, wore gray clothes and black slouch hats; someone was trying to form them. The color-bearer had his coat unbuttoned, with his hat on the back of his head. As I got within a couple of feet of him I commanded him in a peremptory manner to surrender, and at the same time Dudley, Durfee and myself cocked our guns. I grabbed the colors out of his hand; he and one or two more said, "Don't shoot! Don't shoot!"

The flag was a red one with a white stripe running through the middle of it, with blue in one corner and some stars on it. As soon as I grabbed the colors out of the Johnnie's hands I told him to follow me quick, and at the same time told my men to get back to the regiment as soon as possible. Dudley, Grim and myself were laughing at the easy thing we had done, and all of us running for the regiment as fast as we could go, when—bang! bang! bang! came a volley after us, killing Grim and the comrade whose name I have forgotten, and at the same time a dozen or more of the Rebs ran after us, some of them hollering "Kill the d—d black abolition, red shirt Yankee. . . ." and at the same time gave us another round. From the sound it seemed as if a regiment was firing at us. That was the shot that killed young Durfee and wounded me in the leg; another bullet went through the breast-pocket of my shirt and shivered my pipe in pieces. I dropped my gun but held on to the flag, and was going about as fast on one leg as most men generally go on two; but before I had gone ten feet I was hit over the head with what I thought was the stock of a musket. It knocked me down but did not knock me senseless. They immediately pulled the flag out of my hands and fell back on the run.

As they did so, Dudley came back to me (he had run ahead some little distance), helped me up and assisted me along as fast as I could go. How Dudley and I escaped with our lives seems almost incredible, and looks now as if we had been hedged about with some halo of good luck.

. . . What we did, we did quick and without ceremony, and if we could have kept them off from us half a minute longer we would have been safe. As soon as we got back to the regiment and I realized the fact that I could not walk and was bleeding very fast, I took my suspenders off and tied them as tight as I could above the wound, to keep from bleeding to death; and at the same time asked Lieutenant Holtzburn, who happened to see me, to have some one assist me to the rear. This was during some change of position of the regiment.

He ordered Sergeant Dudley and Private [George] Durfee, a twin brother of the one who had just been killed, to carry me off. I put an arm round each of their necks and held on to them as they hurriedly walked along.

As soon as we got to the foot of the hill I feinted away on a spot where some horses had been standing. I was brought to by Dudley throwing some dirty water in my face. This immediately straightened me up, and taking hold of them as before we hurriedly moved off. By the time they got me to a house, which being used as a temporary hospital, I began feeling sick at my stomach and very feint. Surgeons were dressing the wounds of some of Ellsworth's Zouaves, Michigan and Massachusetts men, and giving them stimulants. They gave me two or three swallows, which settled my stomach and made me feel better. The next things I knew I was being pulled up and yanked along as fast as we could go. All commenced to move at a break-neck gait. The retreat had commenced. And of all the helter-skelter, pell-mell, devil-take-the-hind-most gang I ever saw, or heard tell of, or ever read about, that crazy crowd beat them all. They all went as if a cyclone had struck them. All was confusion, all disorder and every one acted as if the Johnnies were determined to have a Yankee apiece for supper; and some of them would pass by and look at the wounded that were being car-ried and helped off, as much as to say, "They can have you, but by golly they shan't catch me!" I don't believe there ever was a greater stampede of troops than there was between that house and the bridge. Dudley and Durfee saved my life without a doubt. Durfee would have abandoned me to Dudley's charge some time before if I had told him the truth about his brother, about whom he was constantly inquiring. And here was an instance where "evasion" seemed better than telling the truth. His brother, as brave and daring a fellow as ever shouldered a musket, and very quiet and modest at all times, made a remark just before I grabbed the colors out of the color-bearer's hands that I shall never for-get. "Sergeant," said he, "when you take it, hold on to it," and in less than a minute he was shot dead. Had I told his brother he had been killed or wounded, he would have returned to his as-sistance immediately, and that would have been the last of me.

I was the only one of the three that had any money, and we finally succeeded, after several attempts, in persuading a teamster, with a four-horse wagon, to let them put me on the off-wheel horse, by giving him four one-dollar gold pieces and some sutler's tickets. Dudley remarked, "Give him all you got, as we might as well go broke here as anywhere." Riding the off-wheel horse brought my wounded leg between

the two horses and on top of the wagon tongue; this caused me so much pain, I had to turn round on the horse so as not to have my leg hurt between the two horses. With one hand holding on to the root of his tail, and the other hand behind me grasping the end of the hanes, bare-headed, with a heavy red woolen shirt on . . . , all open at the collar and the sleeves rolled up, my face covered with blood and dirt, hair sticking straight up and matted full of old leaves and grass and "sacred soil," and with the worst looking wounded leg you ever saw, you can imagine what a pitiful but ludicrous sight I must have presented. . . . I am sure I have not half described my appearance on that horse.

We arrived at Centerville about nine o'clock at night. I was helped off the horse by a regi-mental surgeon under some trees. . . . Surgeons were taking care of the wounded. They looked at my wound and told me I had better have my leg amputated at once, but I would not consent to it. I was suffering very much from pain, and was nearly exhausted from loss of blood; noth-ing in the world kept me up but excitement. A four-horse wagon drove up and the soldiers that were being cared for were helped in. The confu-sion and hurry was still great. I begged them to let me get in the wagon, but an officer refused, saying there was no room for me. I crawled to the wagon and got in over the wheel while oth-ers were being helped in the back end. I stayed in the wagon, although I was ordered out two or three times; they were in too big a hurry to put me out. Off they drove as fast as they could get along. There were seven of us in the wagon, all badly wounded; the driver and the soldier on the seat with him were not wounded: one drove and hollered, while the other whipped and cursed. It was very dark and I think it was raining. The road was still full of wagons, ambulances and straggling troops. We would go very fast at times, and then would stop for a few minutes until the teams ahead of us moved on. I think the driver was the worst scared of all of us, for he tried to drive by, and drive over, everything, uphill and down, over stumps, logs and rocks; we were continually being thrown or tossed from one side of the wagon to the other.

We arrived at Fairfax Courthouse about midnight. I laid my head on a big fat fellow who had sprawled out at full length on the bottom of the wagon. We had been quarrelling all night about interfering with one another's wounds. I supposed the fat fellow had gone to sleep, and taking advantage of his position I laid my head on his stomach and immediately went to sleep myself. I thought it was the softest pillow I ever used. I don't know how long I laid there—perhaps half an hour; we all went to sleep. We were awakened by being jolted about in the wagon, which was going downhill at a lively gait; all were complaining about our wounds; two or three were groaning and whining. When the team would walk we would all go to sleep again—two or three of us using the fat man as a pillow as before. I had a dispute with one of the men about my place on the fat man's stomach and made him move his head along and I resumed my former place. We laid as best we could in that position until daylight, when we discovered we had been using a dead man for a pillow; the poor fellow had died about the time we left Fairfax, as he was very quiet at that place.[4]

Sgt. Merritt survived his ordeal at Bull Run and was sent to the E Street Hospital. The doctors once again wanted to amputate his leg, debating whether to take it off above or below the knee. Merritt continued to vociferously argue against amputation, and finally, the doctors relented. Merritt gradually recovered and was able to walk again. Thirty days later, he was back with the regiment.

He was not, however, with the regiment when they fought at Gettysburg. He had been detailed to the office of the Second Brigade's quartermaster in September 1862, where he served until January 1864. He was mustered out with the regiment in May. James Wright of Company F mentions Merritt in a description of the regiment's send-off banquet:

The return of Col. Colvill to the regiment for the first time since Gettysburg was one of the events of the evening. Most men in his condition would have felt it impossible to be present. He could not walk or stand and was carried in by two of the stalwart members of the regiment, Captain Tom Sinclair and Sergeant Johnny Merritt.[5]

Long after the war, Merritt received the Medal of Honor with the following enclosed letter:

War Department, Washington, April 1, 1880.
Sir:

I transmit to you the enclosed Medal of Honor, which as the inscription shows, is from "The Congress to Sergeant John G Merritt, Co K, 1st Minnesota Volunteers."

This medal is awarded to you under the provisions of law for gallantry at the battle of Bull Run, in July, 1861, where you were wounded while in advance of your regiment.

In connection with this award I find occasion to remember with renewed pleasure and gratitude the patriotism of Minnesota's citizens, who in answer to my call as governor, at the first dawn of the war period, valiantly responded with cheers, the trumpets and the drums of the First Minnesota Regiment, of which you were a member.

Alexander Ramsey, Secretary of War.[6]

Merritt married Mary A. Hoddinoth on March 4, 1863, at the Metropolitan Hotel in New York City. They moved to Washington, DC, in 1867, where he found an interesting line of work serving as the sergeant at arms in the U.S. Senate. Merritt died on December 17, 1892, at the age of fifty-five. He was buried in the congressional section of Arlington National Cemetery.

Joseph Periam
b. August 31, 1831; d. July 7, 1863

Joseph Periam was a real estate investor prior to the war and thought to be the second-richest man in Winona, with a net worth of $15,000. Periam enlisted on April 29, 1861, and received a commission as a second lieutenant in Company K. In November he was promoted to first lieutenant and later, on September 17, 1862, became the company's captain—its third since the war's start.

Beginning in July 1862, Periam suffered from gastrointestinal problems, a symptom of what was commonly called *camp fever* or *typhomalarial fever* (a nonexistent diagnosis in today's medicine). His pain and irritation were, however, quite real, and he received a leave of absence to recover, which eventually had to be extended.

Three months later, Capt. Periam and the First Minnesota found themselves on the fields outside Gettysburg. Down the slope they charged. About a hundred feet from the brook, he was hit. Lt. Lochren of Company K was next to him and saw him fall with a

Joseph Periam

bullet hole in the side of his head. Assuming the captain was dead, he continued his charge.

Company K's first sergeant, Mathew Marvin, a good friend of Periam's, writes about caring for Periam after he had been shot and they both had been taken to a temporary field hospital:

> I was laying by my Capt (Periam) who was wounded in the head, the ball entering at the nose & came out back of the left ear. In taking care of him I got pretty well covered with blood as he bled a good deal. He wanted to go back to the front so I had to hold him most of the time. . . . The ambulances soon came & took us about 2 miles to the rear where they had established the hospital in a hollow near a creek . . . we were all right at last.

From Marvin's papers we know that Lt. Chris Heffelfinger, who commanded Company D, was the first to reach Periam after the charge. He removed the captain's belongings but failed to find a tobacco box that his sister asked for in a later letter.

Howard Stansbury had been the regiment's first color-bearer until he was given a commission in the regular army in June 1861. His father had also been an army officer. Stansbury gave his father's Model 1839 Topographical Engineer's Sword to Periam probably around March 1863. It is a beautiful and rare example of this type of sword. The presentation reads, "Capt J. Periam presented by Lieut. Howard Stansbury." On either side are found a list of the battles in which Periam had participated, from Bull Run up to their most recent fight at Fredericksburg. He died from a wound received at their next battle, Gettysburg.

On Periam's hospitalization and death, a note in his National Archives file states:

> Captain Joseph Periam Co K 1st Minnesota Volunteers was wounded at the battle of Gettysburg, Pennsylvania, July 1–3, 1863 by a gunshot missile which entered the nose and emerged back of the ear. He was admitted into Seminary Hospital, Gettysburg, where simple dressings were applied. Death occurred on July 6, 1863.

As conveyed in the *Winona Republican*, "[Charles] Goddard reported that Periam spent his last few days in 'semi-conscious delirium,' ordering his men to stand & asking about the outcome of the battle."

On August 5, 1863, the *Winona Republican* printed the following article, which includes an extract from Periam's papers, in which he foretells his fate:

> The Late Capt. Periam.—Among the papers of the late Capt. Joseph Periam, left in the hands of his agent here, was recently discovered the following, which bore date May 20, 1861. It appears that upon entering the service of the Republic—which he was among the very first to do—Mr. Periam was strongly impressed with the idea he would not survive the war. This presentiment of death clung to him through all his two years [of] dangerous and difficult campaigning in Virginia and Maryland. A few months ago, while on a brief visit to Winona, he stated in a conversation with the writer of this paragraph that he never expected to return—a remark which we attributed to the feeling of uncertainty which must be engendered to the minds of all who are exposed to danger, rather than to the fixed and unconquerable foreboding from which it sprang. The extract from his papers is as follows:
>
>> I am fully content that I shall never return from this war, and I am entering the lists with this conviction fully impressed upon my mind. I am indeed proud of the privilege afforded me of offering up my life in defense of my beloved country.
>> Joseph Periam

Capt. Joseph Periam was dead at the age of thirty. He was buried with his comrades at Gettysburg National Cemetery, section B, grave no. 9.

Alonzo H. Pickle
b. July 2, 1843; d. May 24, 1925

Alonzo Pickle was born in Farnham, Quebec, and in 1857 his family moved to Wisconsin and then to a farm two miles from Dover, near Rochester, Minnesota. On August 14, 1862, at nineteen years of age, he was mustered into the service. He stood six feet tall and had a light complexion, blue eyes, and blond hair.

He saw his first action at Fredericksburg and fought at Gettysburg, where he was wounded in the leg during the July 2 charge, which fell on his twentieth birthday. He hobbled back toward Gen. Meade's headquarters and lay down. For him the battle was over.

Pickle was promoted to corporal on February 1, 1864, and sent back to Minnesota on recruiting service. When the regiment was mustered out on May 5, 1864, he was transferred to the First Battalion to finish out his three-year enlistment and promoted to sergeant.

On August 14, 1864, the battalion was engaged at Deep Bottom, Virginia. In the early afternoon it was ordered to attack the enemy's breastworks. The battalion assaulted the enemy's lines but was unable to carry them. At the height of the battle, Lt. Henry O'Brien was shot in the chest. Most of the men had fallen back, but Pickle stayed, picked up O'Brien, and carried him off the field to the protection of a ravine. It was an exceptionally brave act and later earned him the Medal of Honor, which he was awarded on June 5, 1895. His commendation reads:

To Sergeant Alonzo Pickle, for most distinguished gallantry in action at Deep Bottom, Va, Aug, 14, 1864, when at the risk of his own life he went to the assistance of a wounded officer lying close to the enemy's lines, and, under fire, carried him to a place of safety.

Wounds or capture often were the causes for promotion. First Sgt. William Churchill was captured at Ream's Station, Virginia, on August 25, 1864. James Bryant became Company K's first sergeant until he was commissioned as a first lieutenant on March 16, 1865. On May 30, 1865, Pickle was promoted to first sergeant to fill Bryant's spot.

Pickle was present at Appomattox. The battalion was on picket duty at the time, and he watched as many beaten Rebel soldiers crossed Union lines and surrendered their arms. First Sgt. Alonzo Pickle was discharged at Bailey's Cross Roads, Virginia, on June 7, 1865.

Jasper Newton Searles

Jasper Newton Searles

b. November 9, 1840; d. April 25, 1927

Born in North Royalton, Ohio, Jasper Searles was Jonathon D. and Harriet C. Searles' second of three children. The family moved to Hastings in 1855, and when the war broke out, Jasper was twenty years old and working as drug store clerk and schoolteacher in Hastings.

He enlisted in Hastings and was mustered as a private in Company H on April 29, 1861. One of the smaller men in the regiment, he stood only five feet two and a half inches tall. He had a light complexion, blue eyes, and blond hair.

While working in the drug store, he had some contact with the use and applications of medicines, and he parlayed this rudimentary medical training into a brief stint as a hospital steward in the regiment. During the First Battle of Bull Run, Searles drove an ambulance wagon for the wounded being shuttled off the field. In a letter from Washington, DC, dated July 25, 1861, he writes the following about the battle:

What a sight! About a mile and a quarter on our left, as we emerged from the woods, were the enemy in their entrenchments, playing upon us with their artillery, but their shots all went too far over us. . . .

Well we moved up into position and beheld directly in front a large body of men who were

dressed very nearly like some of our men—gray clothes—and as we halted and brought ourselves into line they waved their hands in token of friendship, and exclaimed "Don't fire We are friends." And we did not fire, although the men all knew they were our enemies, and the Adjutant, Lieut. Col., Maj. and Serg. Maj. all exclaimed to the Col. that they were our enemies.

But he was soon undeceived for they suddenly gave us a volley that they not fired too high, would have brought down two thirds of the Regt.

After firing five volleys and being broken up by our cavalry, we were compelled to retreat down the hill and collect our forces. . . . During the action I was directly behind the men dressing their wounds and sending them off the field, and when we retreated I allowed them to pass and then followed slowly behind to pick up any wounded. During the action I lost Doct Le Boutillier and the other steward; and have not seen them since.

The 1st Minn. and NY Zouaves were placed in the most dangerous position on the field and stood the fire *better than any of the other regts*. We were commanded to retreat three times before we obeyed and then Gen'l McDowell's aid was compelled to drive us off by such expressions as "retreat!" "God damn you!" "Retreat!" "What do you stand there for!" "I never saw such men fight!" AND INDEED WE DID FIGHT! The regulars even retreated before we did.

On January 8, 1862, Searles was discharged to accept a commission as a second lieutenant in Company H, replacing Lt. Henry Hoover, who had resigned. Searles served as acting regimental quartermaster from February 23 to May 28, 1862, during which time he was also temporarily absent while on duty with the regimental wagon train.

Searles received a promotion to first lieutenant on September 20, 1862, and was transferred to Company K. In November he was again on detached service, this time with the Second Corps' ambulance train. Perhaps owing to his previous medical and hospital steward experience, he was placed in charge of the Second Division's ambulance train.

He did not participate in the July 2 charge at Gettysburg. He and his ambulances arrived late in the day, in time to help carry the wounded to field hospitals. Records indicate that he had men from the First Minnesota driving some of the ambulances. Those known to be in his detail were Theodore Brown (Co. D), Melville Fuller (Co. A), Gates Gibbs (Co. D), Mathias Kinnen (Co. K), Henry Low (Co. H), Neri Reed (Co. G), and Sam Smith (Co. K). Some of these men may have returned to replenish the depleted ranks and fight on July 3. Mathias Kinnen returned and was wounded.

After the battle many of the line officers had been either killed or wounded, and the vacancies they left needed to be filled. On August 16, 1863, Searles was transferred to the command of Company G. On October 3, 1863, he was made captain of Company C to fill the hole left by the death of Capt. Farrell, who like Capt. Periam had also been killed at Gettysburg. Company C had been without a captain for the three months since the battle. He did not stay with the company for long, however, and by November 2, he was back on detached service with the ambulance corps. He returned to the regiment on February 5, 1864, as it prepared to return to Minnesota. Searles was mustered out on May 5, 1864.

On March 17, 1865, he received an appointment

This photo of 6' 2¾" Maj. Mark Downie and 5' 2½" Capt. Searles was taken in Whitney's gallery in St. Paul, probably in February or March 1864, while the regiment was waiting at Ft. Snelling to be discharged in May. They are wearing officers' winter capes.

via Special Order No. 55 from the Department of the Northwest detailing him as a trader with the Indians in camp at Ft. Wadsworth.

Searles married Sarah Lewis Tozer on October 18, 1866. They lived for two years at Ft. Wadsworth (now Sisseton) in Dakota Territory, returning to live in Hastings, where he eventually set up a law practice. He died in Hastings on April 25, 1927, at the age of eighty-six.

14

COMPANY L
THE SECOND COMPANY OF
MINNESOTA SHARPSHOOTERS

HIRAM BERDAN WAS NATIONALLY FAMOUS for being one of the best marksmen in the country. He petitioned President Lincoln and Congress to develop a regiment of sharpshooters from all over the United States. Each company of about a hundred soldiers would be from a different state, making it one of the first national volunteer regiments. Berdan wanted his regiment to be unique, so he designed a uniform that hinted at an attempt at camouflage. The first uniforms had light blue trousers and hunter-green frock coats and caps. The buttons were made of a hard rubber and did not shine like brass buttons. Later versions of this uniform added green trousers and brown leather leggings.

In 1861 a recruitment advertisement appeared in numerous Minnesota newspapers that asked for men who had special skills with a rifle. The advertisement stated that the men who enlisted had to "bring a certificate from a J.P. [justice of the peace] or other county official that they have made a string of 50 inches in consecutive shots at 200 yards, with globe or telescope sights from a rest." The ad closed with the notation that men "will use Sharps Improved Breech Loading Rifles." The recruitment period, which resulted in the formation of two units of sharpshooters, took place between November 2, 1861, and March 17, 1862.

Some of the volunteers who qualified were mustered into the Second Company of Minnesota Sharpshooters on December 22, 1861, though the unit was not officially accepted into the service of the federal government until March 20, 1862. The unit consisted of one hundred enlisted men and three officers, led by Capt. William Russell. On April 21, 1862, they left St. Paul and traveled to Washington, DC, and on May 3 they moved to the area of Yorktown, Virginia. There, the Army of the Potomac was already engaged in the Peninsula Campaign. On May 7 the unit was assigned to the first

of two regiments of sharpshooters commanded by Col. Hiram Berdan, the First U.S. Sharpshooters.

On the afternoon of May 8, 1862, the company received their arms, the Sharps .54-caliber breech-loading rifle. This rifle enabled a soldier to load the rifle from the breech instead of down the muzzle and do so lying down or on the move. The Sharps also gave a soldier a greater rate of fire than did most muzzle-loading rifles or muskets. On May 12, 1862, they received their first lessons in company movements and in skirmishing from Capt. Edward Drew of the First U.S. Sharpshooters. To skirmish is to go out well in front of the main body of troops to engage the enemy, scout its positions, and test its strength. The sharpshooters also would be used as snipers to harass artillery positions and enemy pickets and to slow the enemy's advance.

Their first test was at Hanover Courthouse on May 27, 1862. That year, they participated with the Army of the Potomac in all the major battles out east: Fair Oaks, the Siege of Richmond, Peach Orchard, Savage Station, White Oak Swamp, Nelson's Farm, Malvern Hill, South Mountain, and Antietam.

On May 30, 1862, the company was assigned to

the First Minnesota and thus was detached from the First U.S. Sharpshooters. The First Minnesota already had the required ten companies, so being the eleventh company, it became known as Company L, this assignment occurring on the first day of the Battle of Fair Oaks. From May 30, 1862, until November 23, 1863, the company was attached to the First Minnesota, though at times was pulled away for service elsewhere, such as during the Battle of Gettysburg.

In November 1863 they were detailed as provost guard and never returned to service with the First. The unit saw hard service. When formally mustered out on March 19, 1865, there were only thirty men left in the company. Eighteen men reenlisted and were transferred to companies A and C of the First Battalion.

Berdan's two regiments had done excellent service for the Union. The men of the Second Company of Minnesota Sharpshooters had the honor of serving with two fine fighting units, both Berdan's Sharpshooters and the First Minnesota.

Wilber M. Coleman

b. January 19, 1845; d. December 7, 1915

Wilber Coleman's family moved from Greene Township in Trumbull County, Ohio, in October 1855 and settled in the village of Tamarak, located near Long Lake Township in Hennepin County, Minnesota. There, his father taught school, where the boys undoubtedly attended.

When the war began, Coleman's older brother, Selden, age twenty-three, immediately volunteered and joined the First Minnesota. When the term of enlistment was changed from three months to three years, however, Selden headed back home. A few months later, in October 1861, he joined the Third Minnesota and served for three years. Along with Selden, Coleman's three other brothers enlisted: John, eighteen, and Addison and Madison, both twenty-one. When the four older Coleman boys enlisted, a newspaper story referred to Wilber, reporting, "Mr. Coleman, with difficulty, restrained a lad of sixteen—the only son left—from accompanying his brothers."

Wilber's name was misspelled by the enrolling clerk as Wilbur, and he is carried as such on all the muster rolls.

During the war the minimum age for volunteers was eighteen—seventeen with a parent's permission. Coleman was sixteen years and ten months old when

Wilber M. Coleman

he entered the service on December 18, 1861. He must have lied about his age to the recruiting clerk, and perhaps, he was challenged later, because his father sent the following in March 1862:

I, John H Coleman, do certify that I am the father of Wilber Coleman; that the said Wilber Coleman is 18 years of age, and I do hereby freely give my consent to his enlisting as a soldier of the Army of the United States for the term of three years or during the war. Tamarak, MN, March 11th, 1862.

John A Coleman[1]

At Antietam on September 17, 1862, Coleman was badly wounded in his left leg. A musket ball entered in front of the middle of his leg, just to the outer side of the crest of the tibia, carrying away a small portion of bone and fracturing the fibula. It then passed out the back and outer side of his leg, about three-quarter inches below where it had entered. The damage was severe and was later given the description: "as though you had scooped out all the muscles of the outer side of the leg." Coleman was sent to recover at Ladies' Home Hospital in New York City and did not rejoin his unit until four months later in February 1863.

Coleman returned to duty only to be wounded again five months later at Gettysburg on July 3, suffering a severe wound to the right side of his head from a burst artillery shell. He was sent to Chestnut Hill Hospital in Philadelphia, arriving there on July 7. The following doctor's report, written later in his life, details the seriousness of his wound:

> Right parietal bone of the skull fractured on its outer side an inch behind the frontal bone; there is a jagged irregular indentation an inch or two in length from ¼ to ½ inch in depth. Piece of skull came away at time of wd. probably leaving mem. of brain exposed.

Years later, in 1877, an examining doctor estimated the size of the piece of skull blown away as one inch by two inches. Coleman recovered and, despite the severity of his wound, rejoined his company four months later on October 30, 1863. By that time the unit was serving as provost guard and no longer attached to the First Minnesota.

In the spring of 1864, they participated in the battles of the Wilderness, Spotsylvania Courthouse, Hanover Church, and Cold Harbor. On June 21, 1864, he was placed "on detached service with Sharpshooters at Headquarters 1st Brigade, 2nd Army Corps." Coleman was discharged on December 22, 1864, when his three-year term of service ended. At the time his unit was located at Petersburg, Virginia.

He returned home and, on March 22, 1865, with his brother Addison, enlisted for one year in the U.S. Veteran Volunteers. They were placed in Company A of the Ninth Regiment of Veteran Volunteers. They were mustered in at St. Paul on March 28, and each was paid one-third of a $100 bounty (their enlistment may have been motivated by the bounty). The remaining two-thirds of the bounty was to be paid at a later date. His enlistment record states that he was five feet seven and a half inches tall with gray eyes and light (reddish) hair. By May 15 the brothers were at Camp Stoneman in Maryland. On May 18, 1865, they were each paid the rest of their $300 bounty.

Wilber and Addison were transferred to Burnside Barracks near Indianapolis, and then on October 14, 1865, he received a special order that detached him to serve as an orderly at general headquarters. Wilber was discharged from the service in Indianapolis on March 21, 1866. He entered the service as a private and served as such for his entire military career.

Coleman later moved to Glendive, Montana. In 1897 he returned to Minnesota to take part in the First Minnesota veterans' excursion to Gettysburg for the dedication of the Minnesota monument. In 1952 a niece of one of Wilber's comrades in arms wrote the following remembrance:

> Uncle Elbridge Barnes was born on March 8, 1845, and enlisted at Fort Snelling in the Second Company Sharpshooters consisting of 100 men picked for their expert marksmanship. Captain Mahlon Black of their company called David Archibald, Wilber Coleman and uncle Elbridge his "three boys" as they were the youngest and I always understood that they were the same age; 16 years. The Sharp Shooters did not go into battle in the same formation but were snipers who picked off individual targets from whatever point they could find. In 1897, when the State of Minnesota sent the First Minnesota back to Gettysburg, my father and I saw uncle Elbridge off from the Great Northern station in Minneapolis. Capt. Black and his three "boys" walking around with their arms entwined most of the time for an hour or so that the regiment, or what was left of it after the bloody charge at Gettysburg and after the lapse of 34 years, were still milling about the large waiting room of the old depot across the bridge from where the present depot now stands—renewing their old war born friendships and calling each other by fantastic nicknames they had used for each other during their war experience.

Coleman suffered greatly from the residual pain of his wound for the rest of his life. Though he received a veteran's pension, it could not make up for the pain he endured. In addition to periodic headaches, at some point his right arm became paralyzed, as well. Coleman died at Washington State Soldiers Home on December 7, 1915.

Fingal Fingalson
b. October 1, 1842; d. November 16, 1930

Fingal Fingalson was born in Hallingdal, Norway, his family coming to America when he was two years old and settling near Beloit, Wisconsin. When he was nine, both of his parents fell victim to a cholera epidemic and died within a few hours of each other. At thirteen Fingalson began making his own way by learning the

Capt. Mahlon Black

Mahlon Black was born in Hamilton County, Ohio, on October 4, 1820. He came to Stillwater in 1847 and engaged in surveying and lumbering. He was a representative in the territorial legislature in 1849, 1852, and 1857. He was the postmaster of Stillwater from 1857 to 1861 and mayor from 1860 to 1861.

Black was forty-one years old when he entered the service. On January 2, 1862, he was mustered into the Second Company of Minnesota Sharpshooters. The company was raised in St. Paul to become a part of Berdan's Corps of U.S. Sharpshooters. It began service on March 20, 1862, with one hundred men and three officers. Black began his service as the company's first sergeant. On February 20, 1863, he was discharged to accept a promotion to second lieutenant and acted in that capacity at Gettysburg. He was promoted to first lieutenant on July 14, 1863, and, later, to captain.

The unit saw hard service. Eighteen men reenlisted and were transferred to companies A and C of the First Battalion. Black was one of the eighteen who reenlisted and was transferred. He was mustered out with the battalion on January 3, 1865.

Capt. Black wore this emblem on the front of his Hardee hat. It stands for Minnesota Volunteer Militia.

This is the hat emblem that Capt. Mahlon Black wore on the side of his tall, dark dress hat, often called a Hardee hat after its creator, William Hardee. Hardee was a career army officer and the commandant of cadets at West Point (1856–60) and wrote a drill manual known as *Hardee's Tactics.*

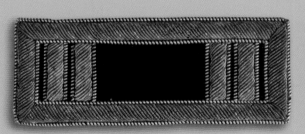

This is one of Capt. Black's shoulder straps, which shows his designation as an officer, the two bars on each side signifying the rank of captain.

This Sharps carbine in the Minnesota Historical Society archives is attributed to Capt. Mahlon Black. Though the three-band Sharps rifle was the weapon issued to the sharpshooters, it is possible that as the ranking officer in the company, Black chose to use this carbine as his weapon. He may have also acquired it after the war.

Fingal Fingalson

He was sent to the Patent Office Hospital in Washington, DC. This former federal building, which housed the country's patent records and models of patented items, had been converted to be used as a hospital. On October 5, 1862, he was sent to the Ladies' Home Hospital in New York City. He spent nine months recovering and was not a participant at the Battle of Gettysburg. Once healthy, though, he reported back for duty. He reenlisted and served until the war ended, and he was mustered out on April 27, 1865.

While in Virginia, he met a young Southern girl who made him a gift of an old twenty-five-cent piece when he offered her a greenback (a Union one-dollar bill) for it. He later flattened the coin into a smooth surface and filed it to make it look like a three-leaf clover. On this badge he had his name, rank, company, and regiment inscribed. It became very precious to him. Twice he lost his little coined corps badge, and twice he miraculously found it again.

Fingalson returned to Northfield and married his prewar sweetheart, Maline, on July 14, 1865. They had twelve children. She died giving birth to their twelfth child, who also died. Both she and the baby were buried together. Maline was forty-five years old. Fingalson died on November 16, 1930, at the age of eighty-eight.

Andrew Lockrem

b. December 22, 1838; d. July 20, 1910

Andrew Lockrem was born in Norway on December 22, 1838, and moved to America with his family in 1848. His family homesteaded six miles south of Northfield in an area known as Valley Grove.

On January 20, 1861, Lockrem answered a recruiting broadside in the *Northfield Telegraph* requesting superior marksmen to try out for an elite group of sharpshooters. Capt. Russell sent a Northfield native, Cpl. C. R. Eldridge, to test many men in the area to see if they could pass the exacting test of hitting ten consecutive shots in a red target twenty inches in diameter placed at two hundred yards. Lockrem passed this test with his two friends and neighbors Halvor Quie and Fingal Fingalson, and all three enlisted. Lockrem stood five feet ten inches tall. He had a light complexion, brown eyes, and light-colored hair.

In September 1862 Gen. Lee's Confederate army invaded Maryland in the hopes of drawing the Union army out of Washington, destroying it, and forcing the Northern states to sue for peace. The Union's forces

carpenter's trade. He followed his brothers and sisters to Minnesota and settled in Rice County. At eighteen he fell in love with and became engaged to Maline Lockrem. The war was beginning, however, and their marriage had to wait.

Fingalson enlisted in the Second Company of Minnesota Sharpshooters on January 20, 1862, along with his friends Endre (Andrew) Lockrem and Halvor Quie. Fingalson was the youngest of three at nineteen. Quie was twenty-seven, and Lockrem, Maline's older brother, was twenty-five.

Fingalson was wounded several times during the war, once at Hanover Courthouse on May 17, 1862, and again a few other times, though only seriously at the Battle of Antietam. During that battle the regiment was at one point outflanked by the enemy, and a bullet struck him from the side. He dropped his rifle, his arm now hanging uselessly. Making his way back from the line of battle and moving to the rear, he met Capt. Russell. Russell ordered him back into line, but Fingalson raised the torn and bleeding arm with his one good hand and said, "You take my place now Captain."

"Humph," snorted the Captain, "you better go and report to the sick squad!"

"Exactly where I am headed for," was Fingalson's answer.[2]

Andrew Lockrem

the field. The pleas of the wounded begging for water or asking not be stepped on filled their ears. Groups of exhausted Union troops from the morning's battle cheered on the Union advance.

As they crossed the field the Union line started to experience the first artillery barrage of solid and canister shot. The Confederate forces under Gen. Thomas "Stonewall" Jackson opened fire on the advancing Union troops from a grove of trees called the West Woods. The Union line entered the woods and exchanged fire with Jackson's men for about an hour. Gen. Sumner was confident that his Second Corps could merely sweep around the Confederate's left and encircle these troops. He was surprised when the Confederate army flanked his left and poured fire into his line, starting a massive panic and a retreat of the Union's forces.

When the regiment to the left of Company L gave way, Capt. Russell thought there was a general order to retreat and ordered his men to withdraw from the line. When he was told to return, he ordered his men to do so, and they coolly returned to their untenable position and resumed fire. At this point in the battle, the company suffered almost 50 percent casualties. Lockrem's friends and neighbors went down around him. Halvor Quie was shot through the left heel and was forced to limp from the field. Fingal Fingalson was shot very seriously in the left arm, forcing his arm to hang uselessly.

Lockrem was shot twice in the left thigh. One bullet went clean through, but the other lodged in his flesh. He went down and could not get up. He watched helplessly as Col. Sully finally ordered the gallant First Minnesota to withdraw from the field. Following their departure, Lockrem was captured and taken prisoner by the Confederate forces.

One can only imagine the nightmare of a Confederate field hospital during and after the Battle of Antietam. The Battle of Antietam was the single-bloodiest day of fighting in American history. One might say that it was a miracle that Lockrem survived the experience with his leg intact.

He was freed in a prisoner exchange a few days after the battle when Lee and the Confederate army retreated across the Potomac River to Virginia. On October 11, 1862, Lockrem was paroled at Schoolhouse Hospital in Chambersburg, Pennsylvania. While there, he received a letter from his fiancée, Anna Halverson. In the letter she had placed a lock of her hair fashioned into a watch fob. Lockrem was discharged for disability and mustered out of the army on February 20, 1863.

caught up with the invading Confederates at Sharpsburg, Maryland, near a creek called Antietam.

On September 17, 1862, around 4:00 A.M., Lockrem, Company L, and the First Minnesota coffeed up and from a farm watched the Union and Confederate forces slam into each other at a place called the Cornfield. Around 7:00 A.M., the Second Corps under Gen. Sumner was called to attack. The men crossed Antietam Creek, and the five thousand men of Gen. Sedgwick's division formed into three lines, with a brigade in each line. The First Minnesota was placed in Gen. Gorman's front line on the right flank. Company L was on the left of the First Minnesota. As they passed a grove of trees called the East Woods they were greeted with a horrific sight. Thousands of Confederate and Union dead and wounded were lying on the field so thick it was hard to march without stepping on the victims of the morning's slaughter. The Cornfield was so shot up that the cornstalks looked as though they had been cut with a knife. The ground was soaked with blood and formed a foul mud on the shoes of Lockrem and the men who marched shoulder to shoulder across

COLOR-BEARERS

URING THE WAR CARRYING A REGIMENT'S flag, or colors, into battle was an honor and a privilege. Many stirring battle paintings show the colors and their intrepid bearers in the forefront of the fight or as a rallying point in a retreat. The colors of a Civil War regiment embodied its honor, and the men chosen to bear them or serve in the color guard did so proudly. Courage was required to carry a flag into combat as the color and its carrier naturally drew the earnest attention of enemy riflemen. It was a very dangerous job that would likely get a man maimed or killed. Four of the five men who carried the national color of the First Minnesota were seriously wounded during their service as color sergeants. Two were killed in action; one was wounded and, after a leg was amputated, discharged for disability; and one was wounded but eventually returned to the regiment. The fifth was offered a commission as an officer in the regular army and left shortly after enlisting in 1861.

A full regiment was made up of ten companies of one hundred men each, with the battle line made up of two lines of approximately five hundred men each. The color guard, comprising eight corporals and one sergeant, as specified in *Casey's Infantry Tactics,* was positioned in the center, with five companies on each side. As the regiment went into battle the position of the national color sometimes was a soldier's only visible indication of a battlefield movement's success or failure. Undoubtedly, the men in the ranks kept careful watch on its position. The flag was considered the symbol of a regiment's valor, and apart from surrender, its loss was the ultimate disgrace. Men routinely sacrificed their lives to save their regiment's flag.

The following regulations regarding regimental flags are found in *The Revised Regulations of the Army of the United States*:

Each regiment of Infantry shall have two silken colors.

The first, or the national color, of stars and stripes, as described for the garrison flag; the number and name of the regiment to be em-

broidered with silver on the center stripe. It shall have thirteen horizontal stripes of equal breadth, alternately red and white, beginning with the red. In the upper quarter, next to the staff, is the Union, composed of a number of white or gold stars, equal to the number of the States, on a blue field, one-third the length of the flag, extending to the lower edge of the fourth red stripe from the top.

The second, or regimental color, to be blue, with the arms of the United States embroidered in silk on the center. The name of the regiment in a scroll, underneath the eagle. The size of each color to be six feet six inches long, and shall have a hoist of six feet on the pike. The length of the pike, including the spear and ferrule, to be nine feet ten inches. The fringe shall be yellow; cords and tassels of blue and white silk intermixed.

Through its three years of service, the First Minnesota carried a number of national and regimental/state colors. As one was damaged by wear and tear, bullets and shrapnel, another was ordered to replace it. At the beginning of the war, some companies also carried national colors. At least three companies, D, G, and I, are known to have carried their own flags at the Battle of Bull Run. This practice of allowing company flags on the field caused some confusion by potentially placing too many flags on the field, and it was disallowed shortly after Bull Run.

On May 24, 1861, when the regiment had been filled to its maximum size, it traveled to St. Paul from Ft. Snelling and, at the eastern front of the capitol, received its first regimental color. It had been purchased by the ladies of St. Paul and was presented to the regiment by Anna Ramsey, the governor's wife. One soldier described it as "beautiful as a dream in red, white and blue silk." After Col. Gorman accepted the flag, he handed it to Sgt. Howard Stansbury of Company A, ordering him to bear it aloft and requesting that if he should "fall in defense of it," his last words would be, "Save the colors of the First Regiment."

That same day, Governor Ramsey bestowed commissions on the three highest-ranking officers in the regiment. As he presented each man his commission he laid special stress on each to return the flag wrought by the ladies "with honor to the state and without a stain upon it." Both Col. Gorman and Lt. Col. Stephen Miller were lawyers and used to public speaking, and each gave an eloquent response promising to return the flag to the state "without a mark of dishonor upon it." Maj. William Dike, a banker from Faribault, was not as gifted a rhetorician, but he had a good sense of humor. After the governor bestowed the third commission upon him, with the same request, Maj. Dike, thinking the whole performance a bit over-done, slipped it into his side pocket, glanced over the audience, and quietly remarked:

Much obliged governor. But, by the way, as you seem to have a great deal of anxiety about the flag, how would it do to

leave that one here in Minnesota, under your individual protection, where we know it would be safe, and carry with us one of less value![1]

The ensuing hilarity lingered in veterans' memories for years afterward.

Though regimental (state) flags were allowed, they were generally carried during formal parades and seldom carried into battle.

The first national color was presented to the regiment by Capt. H. C. Lester of Company K, a gift from the ladies of Winona. Cpl. Burgess of Company K carried the national color into the Battle of Bull Run and it was decimated after just one battle. It was so badly damaged that it was returned to the state for historic preservation, and a new one was requested. Upon receipt of the flag in St. Paul, Governor Ramsey sent the following message to Col. Gorman:

The flag of the First Minnesota, dispatched by you on the thirty first ultimo, was duly received and is deposited in the executive chamber of the Capitol, where our people throng to behold with almost tearful veneration, this dumb witness of valor of our citizen soldiers when defending in the action of the twenty-first the national existence of which it is the national emblem.

The future will no doubt see other flags borne by Minnesota regiments into positions where ball and shell and buck-shot will riddle

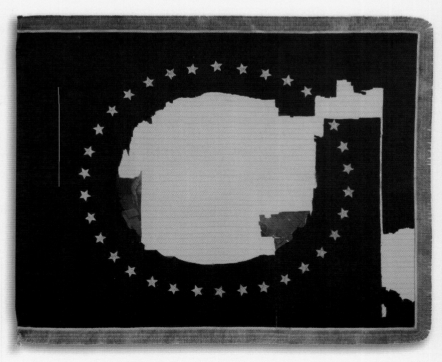

This was the unit's first regimental color. It was presented by the ladies of St. Paul to the First Minnesota on May 24, 1861

This is probably the regiment's first national color presented to the regiment at Ft. Snelling by Capt. Lester of Company K as a gift from the women of Winona. It measures 78 by 78 inches. Carried during the Battle of Bull Run, it was so damaged that, three months after its presentation, it was returned to the state for preservation as a historic artifact. It may be, however, the flag ordered from Horstman in Philadephia by Governor Ramsey on August 10, 1861, to replace the Company K flag. Ramsey gave specific instructions as to what the replacement should look like, which may have been an effort to replicate the looks of the original Company K flag, the first national flag carried by the regiment in battle.

their folds as this one has been; but none of them will be cherished by our people with more fondness and pride when returned from the field that will ever be this, the virgin battle flag of our Northern Light of the American Union.

While the regiment waited for the new flag to arrive, the Company I flag became its national color, measuring 59 by 82 inches. It was distinctive in that the blue canton consisted of thirty-four stars surrounding a gilt eagle. Beneath the eagle was a gold ribbon on which was printed, "MAY GOD PROTECT THE RIGHT."

On August 10, 1861, Governor Ramsey sent the following order to W. H. Horstmann and Son in Philadelphia:

> The Regimental Flag of the 1st Regt of Minnesota Volunteers having been damaged in the action of the 21st and returned to the State you are hereby

requested to prepare immediately a similar Regimental Silk Flag (Star and Stripes) to be of regulation size, trimmings and staff, with the words "1stMinnesota" painted in guilt Capital Letters on the 4th red stripe from the top. When finished the flag should be forwarded in secure package by Express to Washington City, directed to "Colonel Gorman, 1st Minnesota Volunteers care of U.S. Quartermaster Dept.," with the words "Regimental Flag" distinctly marked on the packages.[2]

The Company I flag

Howard Stansbury

b. circa 1839; d. January 27, 1893

Howard Stansbury was mustered in on April 29, 1861, and was given charge of the regimental flag at the presentation ceremony in St. Paul.

The following story was recounted by Jane Grey Swisshelm, a woman who witnessed the dress parade at Ft. Snelling:

> Soon they were all on the parade ground. By slow degrees it became known that the object of the mystery was to permit an artist to take photographic views of the regiment. These were taken first in line-of-battle order, or standing side by side two deep, one rank behind the other. Col. Gorman and staff in the centre, and behind far enough to command a view of the entire line, Col. Miller to his right and Major Dyke to the left. The standard bearer, young [Howard Stansbury], a slight fiery youth, held aloft the magnificent flag presented by Mrs. Ramsey and the ladies of St. Paul. It is of heavy silk, dark blue, the Minnesota coat of arms exquisitely painted in the

> centre of one side and a Union motto on the other and edged with heavy gold fringe. This is the parade flag. The battle flag is the National ensign of rich silk. A second picture was taken, every company standing in single file, one behind the other, and about twenty rods apart.—Col. Gorman and staff in the centre, between the lines. Col. Miller near the front and Major Dyke in the rear. They presented a fine appearance. The two rear companies under Major Dyke had been uniformed at Fort Ridgely in the U.S. uniform of dark blue frock coats with brass shoulder pieces. The others were all in bright red shirts with dark blue pants like the others.[3]

Stansbury did not remain with the regiment for long, however, and never carried a flag into battle for the regiment. On June 6, 1861, he was discharged to accept a commission as a lieutenant in the Nineteenth U.S. Infantry. With Sgt. Stansbury's departure in June, it appears that the regiment may have gone into the Battle of Bull Run with eight corporals in the color guard.

Nathaniel George Burgess

b. February 22, 1837; d. June 29, 1862

Nathaniel Burgess was twenty-four years old when he enlisted in Minneapolis. He was mustered on April 29, 1861, and placed in Company K with the rank of corporal. The ladies of Winona ordered a national flag from the East and donated it to the regiment. It is reasonable to believe that Burgess was the first color-bearer of the national color. It would have been an honor for a soldier from Winona to carry Winona's flag. He distinguished himself on the battlefield at Bull Run, and afterward, Col. Gorman mentioned Burgess in his report to Gen. Franklin, who commanded their brigade:

> The First Minnesota's national color was a natural aiming point for the Confederates who overwhelmed the Regiment. Corporal Burgess of this company, regimental color-bearer, acted bravely. He stood up waved the banner defiantly at the enemy through all the exhausting hours of the fight, and never dodged or budged an inch though musket balls, grape and canister fell in a storm of death around him, and the

Nathaniel George Burgess proudly wears one of the gray uniforms presented by the ladies of Winona to Company K at the start of the war. This is the only known photograph of one of these uniforms.

beautiful flag received seventeen balls and the staff was shattered in his hand.

In August 1861 Burgess was promoted to third sergeant in his company and acted as color sergeant in the color guard. He was the color-bearer for the next eleven months. On June 29, 1862, while carrying the colors at the Battle of Savage Station, he was shot through the lungs by a minié ball and died instantly. Later, Sgt. William Harmon of Company D noted that "he was a fine fellow as well as brave. Every man in the regiment was his friend."

As Sam Bloomer, who was a corporal in the color guard, relates the story of Burgess' death:

Shortly after the battle had opened, our Regiment took ground to the left; this position which brought our center into the road . . . and the left wing into the woods south of it. The fire down the road was such that nothing living could stand it a minute.

Then occurred a temporary opening, or gap, in the line across the road. The colors and a portion of the guard remaining at the right of the left wing. Shortly after this, a regiment of the Vermont Brigade came up behind us, and were allowed to pass thru our line, and they formed in front of us. The command forward being given by the Col. of the Vermont Regiment, Sergeant Burgess, thinking the order meant us, with three of his guards advanced with the Vermont boys thus leaving our regiment without its colors.

This was about 4:50 or 5 o'clock in the afternoon. We had advanced about fifty yards when [Burgess'] attention was called to the fact that we were not with our Regiment. He then, for the first time noticed that we were among strangers; instantly he about faced and ran to the rear with the intention of rejoining our own Regiment. Having arrived as he thought, where the Regiment ought to be, and not finding it, it having changed position, he again about faced intending to join the Vermont Regiment. In these retrograde movements George L Smith, Co C, one of the three color guards was either killed or wounded leaving only Geo. Burgess, Frank Walden and the writer. On again arriving as we supposed where we had left the Vermont Regiment Burgess was killed almost instantly. It was then that Bloomer got the colors. We then started on a run under a brisk fire, as we supposed after the Vermont boys, but instead of finding them we found, and run direct into a line of Rebel Infantry in a small open place or a small dry pond. To say that we were surprised, as also were the Johnnies would be putting it mild. Taking in the situation at a glance we made quick tracks out of that unearthly locality. We did not stand on the order of going, but went, and as we went thru woods and brush we could hear the Rebel invitation for us to "surrender Yanks;" and the hissing of the bullets. I do not think that the tall running Frank Walden and the writer did on that occasion was ever outdone during the war.[4]

Bloomer and Walden eventually made it back to their regiment but without two of their comrades, Pvt. George Smith and Sgt. George Burgess.

his cousin Adam were members of the Wide Awakes, a political group that supported Lincoln in the summer and fall of the 1860 election. Each of the thirty-six Republican members wore an oilcloth cape and a cap and carried a tin lamp on a pole.

Bloomer was mustered into the service as a corporal on April 29, 1861. He was slightly wounded in the head at Bull Run on July 21, 1861. On June 3, 1862, after the Battle of Fair Oaks, he was detailed to serve as one of the color guards. He was promoted from corporal to sergeant and carried the colors through the following engagements: Savage Station, Glendale, White Oak Swamp, Malvern Hill, South Mountain, and Antietam. At Antietam he was severely wounded by a gunshot through his knee.

At South Mountain parts of the flag were literally falling off. Bloomer retained them by taking them from the flag and stuffing them in his blouse (uniform jacket) rather than have them fall off and be lost.

Samuel Bloomer

b. November 30, 1835; d. October 4, 1917

Samuel Bloomer was born in Engi in Glarus, Switzerland. His mother, Anna, died when he was five years old. In 1846, when he was about ten, he came to the United States with his grandparents and his cousins, six-year-old Adam Marty and Adam's three-year-old brother, Fridolin Marty. They settled in St. Louis, where they resided for two years. In October 1848, they moved to Stillwater.

The 1860 census lists Bloomer as a twenty-four-year-old carpenter living in Stillwater. Both he and

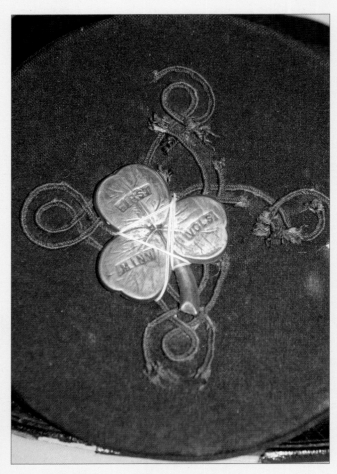

After his discharge from the First Minnesota, Sam Bloomer was given a commission in the Veteran Reserve Corps. This is the officer's cap that he wore from 1863 to 1866. After the war he stitched a metal Second Corps badge to the crown.

These are portions of the national battle flag carried by Color Sgt. Bloomer. This flag is presumed to be the fourth national color carried by the regiment, which was purchased by the people of Minnesota and delivered to the regiment by Maj. William H. Dike in the fall of 1861.

In the following article from the April 1909 issue of *Confederate Veteran* magazine, Bloomer recalls his experience at the Battle of Antietam:

A Wounded Federal Color Bearer—From a report of His Experiences—Sam Bloomer

The battle of Antietam, or Sharpsburg, "one of the deadliest of the Civil war," was fought September 17, 1862. Sharpsburg, a small town, is on Antietam creek, near which the Confederate army was posted before the battle. Gen. R. E. Lee commanded the Southern army, and the Union forces were under the command of Gen. George B. McClellan. General Lee's forces were "outnumbered at least two to one." The loss in killed, wounded, and prisoners aggregated not far from 25,000 men, about equally divided.

The 1st Minnesota Regiment was in the thickest of the fight all day. It was located at the extreme right. Sam Bloomer was the color bearer of the regiment and early in the forenoon while he was resting the flagstaff on a fence in front of him a Minnie ball struck his right leg below the kneecap, passing straight through. At the place of the egress, the bullet left a ghastly wound. About that time, our line was broken, leaving its faithful color bearer to his fate. Sam crawled to the foot of a big oak

tree for protection against the Confederate fire; but as our men fell back and the Confederates occupied the place, he found a change of base desirable. He crawled painfully and slowly around the tree to avoid the fire from his friends. Sam had ripped away his clothing, dressed the wound as best he could, and kept it bathed with water from his canteen, and then bound his leg above the knee with a strip from his blanket to prevent a fatal loss of blood. Several days thereafter when the injured leg was amputated the strip was out of sight, enveloped in the swollen flesh on either side.

"Not far from noon" says Sam, "a Confederate soldier, whom long afterwards I learned was W. H. Andrews, first sergeant of Company M, 1st Regiment Georgia Regulars, came up; and learning of my condition and the fact that I was between two fires, he and some of his comrades piled cord wood around me to protect me from the shots. I have no doubt that more than a hundred bullets struck that barricade during the day. Early in the evening Stonewall Jackson came riding by. He halted a moment, spoke kindly to me, asked to what regiment I belonged, and ordered the men who had charge of a lot of Union prisoners to supply my wants and make me as comfortable as possible. A captain of a North Carolina regiment a little later stopped and chatted with me, gave me a drink from his canteen, and spoke kindly and encouragingly. He rode away, but returned during the night and replenished my canteen with cool water. Previous to this a Confederate officer appeared whose conduct was unlike that of General Jackson and the North Carolina captain. He reviled me with bitter words, called me a nigger thief, etc. I had a revolver and a short sword under my rubber blanket on which I lay, and in my rage I attempted to get at the revolver, intending to shoot the fellow but he had his eyes on me and shouted: 'Disarm that man!' The soldiers of course obeyed, although with a show of reluctance, and all that I could do was protest indignantly. I hated to part with the sword, as it was a present from Capt. Louis Muller. I asked the officer to let me retain the weapon; but he was inexorable, and I never saw the sword again. This was long ago, and time softens our animosities, and I don't know that I would harm that fellow if I should meet him."

Sam lay there on the ground until the evening of Thursday, the 18th, when the Confederates carried him on a stretcher to a little barn surrounded by straw stacks, where he lay another night. He was not alone, for there were more than one hundred other prisoners in the hands of the Confederates, whom it was their intention to parole.

Sam sent word to the officers of his company by Minnesota troops telling of his sad condition. He and three others of the wounded men were conveyed by ambulance to the Hoffman barn. Sam was obliged to sleep on the ground another night, as there were hundreds of others ahead of him awaiting treatment by the surgeon. The next day Dr. Pugsley amputated the injured leg.

The following are his entries for the day of Antietam and for his subsequent days of recovery:

Wednesday Sept 17th

We were up very early then got our coffee & about 7 o'clock we fell in line, forded Antietam Creek, marched about 1 mile, formed in line of battle & advanced through fields, woods & over fences & over the field where the Battle commenced early in the morning & which field was covered with dead & wounded of both sides. At last we halted at the edge of a cornfield by a rail fence but still we were in the woods. Had not been at the fence more than 15 minutes before a most terrific fire was poured into the left of our brigade from the rear & front & which fire came quickly down the line to the right where we were. The firing was very light for a time but I knew I had to go to the rear for I was shot in my leg just below the knee. I had just got behind a large tree when the whole line was ordered to fall back, which they did leaving me behind. The advance of the secesh soon made their appearance & passed by me but did not go a great ways further but formed their picket line about 40 rods in front of me & shortly their line came up & formed just where our line had stood, which left me about 40 rods in front of their line. A wounded prisoner, I was left on the field all day & the shot & shells of both armies play-

ing in or about there all day cutting off limbs of trees & tearing up the ground all around me & which made it a very dangerous place. But as luck would have it, I got through safe. By that fence my pardner Oscar Cornman was killed & one of Co A, likewise some were wounded & all the while the battle was raging terribly on our left. Secesh were quite gentlemanly toward me, but they took from me my sword which was a present to me from Lieut Muller, likewise two revolvers for which I did not care so much.

Since he refers to him as his "pardner," Oscar Cornman likely was Bloomer's tentmate and partner in cooking, and as such, they would generally watch out for each other.

Sept 18th

During the night I slept considerable & woke at day break by a noise at my head & found a secesh pulling at my canteen stopper which he wished to take. Laid on the same spot all day & my pardners dead body lay in my sight all the time. About 6 PM 4 secesh came with a stretcher & took me up to a barn where there were about 100 more of our men & there took our names intending to parrol us in the morning.

Sept. 19th

I for one slept but little last night for pain. During the night the secesh skedaddled [off] for [parts] unknown to us by the barn to be taken care of by our men who soon made their appearance. The first man of our regiment I saw was [David] Coflin of Co I, then Capt [John H.] Pell & gave me some breakfast, & soon my dear Cousin [Adam Marty from Company B] came to see me. About noon I was put in an ambulance & taken to Hoffmans barn Hospital & laid in the yard on the ground where I lay all night with most dreadful pain. There were in around this barn some 5 or 600 wounded soldiers.

Sept. 20th

This day will long be remembered by me, for about 8 o'clock AM the doctors put me up on the table & amputated my right leg above my knee. And from then the suffering commenced in earnest.

Bloomer made no entries in his diary between September 20 and October 29, when he wrote:

Oct. 29th Smoketown Hospital.
Today I got up & stood on my one leg for the first time. But I was very weak & had to have the assistance of my nurse to hold me up & keep me from falling.

Bloomer was discharged for disability on December 2 at Smoketown, Maryland, and arrived home in Stillwater on December 11. Through the rest of the war, he kept up a regular correspondence with his cousin Adam. After the war he also kept up a correspondence with W. H. Andrews, the first sergeant of the First Georgia Infantry who befriended him as he lay at the Dunker Church at Antietam.

Hard as it may be to believe, on August 25, 1863, despite the loss of a leg, Bloomer was given a commission as a lieutenant in the Veteran Reserve Corps. The *Stillwater Messenger* reported on December 26, 1865, the following: "Personal—Lieut. Sam Bloomer of the VRC arrived home from Fort Knox, Maine, a few days since and is awaiting orders for another field of duty." He served faithfully until being mustered out on September 19, 1866.

He became a U.S. citizen on November 18, 1881. His first marriage had ended in divorce. His second and final marriage was to thirty-four-year-old Ellen "Nellie" Pressnell, the ceremony being held on October 7, 1882, in Stillwater. Born in 1846, she was the sister of his First Minnesota comrade Thomas Pressnell, who had served in Company C. In 1861 she had made patriotic red, white, and blue rosettes for the soldiers to wear when they first enlisted. At some point she was probably introduced to Bloomer by her brother.

Bloomer was greatly involved with veterans' affairs through the First Minnesota and his local GAR post. In 1881 he was named assistant adjutant general for the Minnesota Department of the GAR by his cousin Adam, who was the department's commander. Bloomer held a number of civic posts in Stillwater, and he was a familiar sight at the county courthouse. In 1888 he was elected Washington County's treasurer and served for three terms (six years). He constantly kept busy; the loss of a leg did not slow this energetic man.

On June 14, 1905, in a formal parade and ceremony, veterans of the Civil War carried their battle flags as they were transferred from their place of honor in the old capitol to the new capitol building. Bloomer was undoubtedly proud of the honor bestowed on him when he was asked to carry the tattered flag of the First Minnesota.

By 1915 he needed the aid of two canes to help him walk. He died at his home in Mahtomedi on Thursday, October 4, 1917. He was buried in Fairview Cemetery in Stillwater, where many comrades from Company B had also been laid to rest.

Sam Bloomer had been a member of the Last Man's Club. His wife, Nellie, attended the club's final meeting, in Stillwater on July 21, 1930, with Charles Lockwood, the last survivor of Company B, who died in 1935. Nellie died on August 30, 1936.

Ellet Parcher Perkins
b. July 24, 1836; d. September 7, 1903

Ellet Perkins was born in Stowe, Vermont, and came to Minnesota in 1855, settling in the little township of Clearwater. When the war began, Perkins, a twenty-four-year-old teacher in the township, responded to the first call for volunteers and was promoted to corporal in Company D. Records indicate he stood five feet eight and three-quarter inches tall and had a light complexion.

A member of the color guard when Sam Bloomer was seriously wounded at Antietam, Perkins was appointed to the position of regimental color sergeant. Perkins carried the national flag in the unit's subsequent battles, including Chancellorsville, Fredericksburg, and Gettysburg.

On July 2, after receiving his orders from Gen. Hancock, Col. Colvill prepared the regiment. The color guard stepped forward, and the rest of the regiment followed, dressing its line on the color. The guard consisted of only four men that day, Sgt. Ellet Perkins and corporals Tom Nason, John Stevens, and John Dehn.

At this time, the men probably fixed their bayonets to their rifles.[5] That done, they began the charge at the right shoulder shift position, meaning that they held the butts of their rifles at their chests with their right hands, the muzzles resting against their right shoulders and pointed in the air and slightly to the rear. They began the charge at a fast pace known as "double-quick." Afterward, some members said that Colvill halted the charge for a moment after it had begun before proceeding again. This may have been to dress the line before beginning their final charge into the enemy.

It was common practice during the war for enemies to concentrate some fire at the color-bearer. The thought was that men rallied to protect their flag and

Ellet Parcher Perkins

while also shattering the flagstaff, breaking it in two. As Dehn was wounded and went down Cpl. O'Brien grabbed the upper part of the flagstaff and led the remnants of the regiment into their second charge in two days. O'Brien carried the colors forward and into the Confederate masses, almost forcing his comrades to follow to protect their flag. During the ensuing fight, O'Brien was wounded twice. Cpl. Irvine then grabbed the flag and held it to the end of the fight that day.

Another man may have carried the flag on July 2. John Densmore had been a corporal in the color guard until promoted to sergeant in April 1863. He later claimed that he too carried the flag at Gettysburg.[6] During the fight and from his place in Company B, he may have seen the flag fall and rushed to save and carry it. His simultaneous and multiple wounds would support the theory. When he was hit, one bullet virtually tore off his thumb. Another went through the right side of his chest, entering an inch above the right nipple and exiting just below his shoulder blade. Still another hit him in the left thigh, entering about an inch below the groin and exiting through his buttocks. He was on his way down when a fourth bullet hit him in the mouth, ripping away most of his jaw. As he later described his final wound, it was "a gunshot wound in the head, the ball entering about three fourths of an inch below the left corner of the mouth, passing onward and carrying away a large portion of the under jaw and lodging below the mouth on the right side of the face near the windpipe."

Densmore was brought to a field hospital. He was not sent to the corps hospital, because he was too weak to move and was expected to die there. Lieutenant and adjutant William Lochren (Co. K) listed Densmore as mortally wounded. He was left in Gettysburg with others who were also expected to die, and most of them did. Incredibly, however, he survived. He was placed in a Gettysburg hospital, where his thumb was amputated below the second joint. On December 1, 1863, he was moved to an army hospital in York, Pennsylvania. There, on January 7, 1864, the conical ball was extracted from beneath the angle of his jaw on the right side.

After the fight on July 3, Dehn was taken to a hospital in Baltimore known as McKim's Mansion. The bullet that had lodged itself against his wrist joint caused a severe enough wound that his arm had to be amputated four inches below the elbow. He must have been right handed because from then on, whenever

that if it fell, the progress of the regiment might be slowed. Not surprisingly, Sgt. Perkins was hit fairly early in the charge. Corporals Nason and Stevens each had a turn carrying the flag until they also fell, Nason with gunshots in the chest and arm and Stevens with wounds to his chest. John Dehn was the last to carry the flag and brought it back to the hill from which they had started less than half an hour earlier.

The next day, a new color guard was hastily chosen from the few survivors left on the field. They were corporals Henry O'Brien (Co. E) and William "Newt" Irvine (Co. D). Cpl. Dehn held the flag as Pickett's Charge began. As the Rebels closed in and the firing intensified on both sides Dehn was shot. A bullet entered his right hand and lodged against his wrist joint,

his signature was required, all he could do was mark an X. He was not judged capable of serving in the Veteran Reserve Corps and was discharged from military service at the army hospital in Baltimore on November 19, 1863.

Most of the wounded were taken to field hospitals, where there was hope for clean water to bathe their wounds. For most that was a dream that went unfulfilled. Sgt. Perkins and corporals Nason and Stevens lay on the field until picked up and taken to the Second Corps field hospital located at Rock Creek. All three survived their serious wounds and were eventually taken to Chestnut Hill General Hospital on Broad and Cherry streets in Philadelphia. Several other men from the First were sent to the same place, and thirteen ended up in the same ward on the third floor.

Mathew Marvin of Company K mentions Perkins in a letter to Lt. Lochren:

Gen Hospital-Brawd and Cherry.
Philadelphia, Penn.
July 16th, 1863
Lt William Lochren,
Sir:

I have the honor to inform you that I still exist. My wound appears to be doing well, though today it is most dam painfull. . . . Sergt. Perkins is in the bunk next to me and says that he has a peculiar disgust for hard-bread soldiers. His leg is doing first rate. Please give my best respects to the Old Vets of the company. Please accept this from your old companion in the army.

Sgt. M. Marvin.

The bullet had entered the inner part of Perkins' left leg, injured the leg bone, and exited through the right side. His injured leg bone and damaged muscle slowly recovered, and on December 18, 1863, he was discharged

This is the largest-known fragment of the Gettysburg flag carried by Color Sgt. Ellet Perkins. It measures approximately nine by thirteen inches and contains three painted gold stars on a silk background.

from the hospital. On January 26, 1864, he was commissioned as the first lieutenant of Company D, filling one of the many holes in leadership left by Gettysburg.

When the regiment was mustered out, he reenlisted and was mustered into the First Battalion as the captain of Company B. He served from May 5 to October 13, 1864, when he was discharged for disability due to his previous wounds.

After the war Perkins returned to Minnesota. He farmed and later worked for the U.S. Mail Service. In early September 1903, Perkins was stricken with paralysis, probably having suffered a heart attack. As he lay dying in his Minneapolis home, he whispered a request to friends at his side.

"The flag," he said.

Someone was sent to contact Governor Samuel Van Sant, who like Perkins was a Civil War veteran. The governor himself brought the flag of the First Minnesota from its place of honor at the state capitol. These were the colors Perkins had carried at Gettysburg. Given the colors to hold once again, Perkins kissed the tattered flag and held it as he died.

William Newell Irvine

b. circa 1839; d. June 28, 1864

William Irvine came to Minnesota in the late 1850s, settling in Monticello, where he worked on his father's farm. When the Civil War broke out, he traveled to Ft. Snelling and, on May 21, 1861, was mustered into Company D. He proved a competent soldier and was promoted to corporal on September 17, 1862. His younger brother, Theodore, enlisted in December 1861 and was placed in Company C. Both brothers were better known by their middle names, Newell and Alonzo.

At the Battle of Fredericksburg, Col. Morgan received orders to establish a new line as close to the enemy as possible. On the evening of December 14, 1862, the regiment was carefully trying to establish this close line when it found itself in a precarious position. Some of the men heard shoveling noises in front of them. Lt. Chris Heffelfinger and Cpl. Irvine crept out to check out the activity. In doing so, they alerted the Confederates. Heffelfinger made it back, but Irvine was captured. He was later released on parole.

On July 3 during the repulse of Pickett's Charge, Irvine took charge of the flag after Cpl. O'Brien was shot. Irvine's Gettysburg photograph shows him holding the First Minnesota's tattered flag, with its broken

William Newell Irvine

staff. The photo was taken in Alexandria, Virginia, a short time after the battle. As 1st Sgt. James Wright, of Company F, writes about the incident:

Captain Messick was in command, and Corporal John Dehn carried the flag—he being the only one of the color guard of the day before able to be on his feet at the close of fighting the evening of the 2nd—a new detail being necessary. In the "mix-up" with Pickett's men he was shot through the hand, and the same shot splintered the flagstaff so that it broke in two pieces. Corporal Henry D. O'Brien then took the piece with the flag on and kept it until twice wounded, when it passed to the hands of Corporal William N Irvine, who carried it through the fighting. The flag of the 28th Virginia was captured by Marshall Sherman. A portion of this staff was used to replace the broken portion of ours. The splice made in the field by a little rough whittling and bound with a knapsack strap and was carried afterwards until the regiment returned to the state the following February.

Irvine carried the colors from July 3, 1863, until the end of the regiment's three-year enlistment. When the regiment was mustered out, Irvine chose to reenlist and was mustered as a sergeant in Company B of the First Battalion.

On June 18, 1864, the battalion was engaged in a fight during the Battle of Petersburg. While carrying the flag forward, Irvine was shot in the forehead. He was immediately brought to the Second Division's hospital. The bullet had created a one-inch hole in his head and had entered his brain. On June 22 he was conveyed to Carver Hospital in Washington, DC. Initially, he responded favorably to an operation. He became delirious, however, and on June 28 died, ten days after having been wounded. Sgt. William Newell Irvine was buried in Arlington National Cemetery.

Company Flags of the First Minnesota

At the beginning of the war, besides carrying the national colors and, perhaps, a state flag, many regiments allowed each company to carry its own flag. These oftentimes had been presented to the men of the company from the citizens of their communities as a sign of appreciation and to give them a constant reminder of the cause for which they fought. At Bull Run many of these company flags were seen flying along with the regimental flags. The government took note that, while patriotic, it was not practical and ordered that only regimental flags would be used thereafter. Company flags then were usually sent home, with the appreciation of the companies to the citizens who had made the gift.

At least five flags were carried by the companies of the First Minnesota early in the war. They were presented by the ladies of each city to its soldier volunteers. Col. Gorman directed that the maximum size of a company flag would be three by four feet. It is possible that most if not all the ten companies carried flags at the beginning of the war. The companies known to have had a flag were B, D, E, G, and I.

Company B

As volunteers were starting to enlist, a subscription was begun to raise funds to pay for a flag. A flag was made, and on April 27 it was presented to the men in front of the Minnesota House in Stillwater by Mrs. A. J. Van Vorhes. Her husband was editor of the town newspaper, the *Stillwater Messenger,* and her son, Henry, was among the volunteers.

The Minnesota House, where the men of Company B were presented with their flag. Note the spelling on the sign.

The company carried it with them to Ft. Snelling, where they were mustered into service two days later. On or before June 20, however, when the regiment boarded steamboats to leave for the war, the flag was returned to Stillwater and placed in storage. Col. Gorman required company flags be three by four feet, and the national color was six by six and a half feet. The Company B flag was closer in size to the national color and was sent back in order to avoid confusion.

It remained in storage until September 1885, when the Company B Veterans Association was formed. The flag was brought out and adopted as the banner of the company. It was placed in the custody of Sam Bloomer, who had been chosen to be treasurer of the association. Adam Marty wrote *History of the Company B Flag*. A portion of the flag can be seen on the wall behind Charles Lockwood at the last meeting of the Last Man's Club (as seen in the photo at the end of chapter 5). Unfortunately, the location of the flag, as of the printing of this book, is unknown.

Company D

Companies D and E received their flags from the ladies of Minneapolis and St. Anthony during a presentation at Ft. Snelling on Thursday May 9, 1861. As the *State Atlas* reported the event on May 11:

Thursday last was a grand gala day at Fort Snelling, and one that was especially grateful to the men of our home companies. The patriotic ladies of St. Anthony and Minneapolis had been active for a week in preparing a beautiful silk flag for each of the companies from the Falls, and Thursday was selected for the presentation.

Early in the morning carriages went streaming towards Minnehaha and the Fort, each laden with ladies and gentlemen and baskets crowded with good things for the tables of the "boys."

At 3 o'clock the whole regiment was drawn

The flag (also known as the "color") of Company D, seen on the following page, was presented by the ladies of Minneapolis on May 9, 1861, just twelve days before this photograph was taken on May 21. The color in this photograph appears, however, to be a larger national color of the size used by the regiment, the dimensions of which would have been 78 inches by 72 inches on a nine-foot-ten-inch flagstaff. Col. Gorman had specified that company colors were to be of a smaller size. If Company D was acting as the color company that day, that may explain why they appear to be carrying the regiment's national color and not their smaller company color.

This is a pieced-silk U.S. flag with thirty-four white silk stars sewn into the canton. The thirty-fourth star appears to have been cut away or removed. The flag is accompanied by a brass plaque that reads: "Flag presented by the ladies of Minneapolis to the First Company of Volunteers for the War of the Rebellion—April 1861."

up in a hollow square to witness the presentation of the flags.

Miss M. L. Knight on behalf of the ladies of Minneapolis presented the flag to company D, with the following brief speech:

"Gentlemen of the Lincoln Guards:—I have the honor of presenting this flag as a token of regard, from the ladies of Minneapolis. Be assured while you are nobly defending these Stars and Stripes, you have our prayers, our sympathies and our gratitude. May God protect the right."

Capt. Putnam received it and, in a few words, thanked the ladies for their beautiful present, their sympathy, and their prayers.

When the government ruled that only regimental flags would be allowed, the flag was returned to the city. It hung for many years in the Minneapolis Library. Today, the flag, which measures 39 by 61 inches, is in the care of the Minnesota Historical Society.

Company E

The ladies of St. Anthony made the flag pictured on the following page for the men of Company E. The flags were presented to companies D and E on May 9, 1861. It was made of pieced silk with thirty-four stars applied to the canton in gold paint. The canton has one large star in the circle, which is encircled by the thirty-four smaller stars. Gold braid is stitched to the border of the flag. It measures fifty-four by seventy-two inches. The flag was later hung in the Wilcox House in Minneapolis. Note the single large star in the field of blue, possibly signifying Minnesota as the North Star State. Today, it is in the care of the Minnesota Historical Society.

Company G

Ed Needham, in the following letter to his future wife, describes a piece of the Company G flag's history:

Dear Georgia,

When I first heard the fire I was bewildered for an instant, the roar was so terrific & conse-

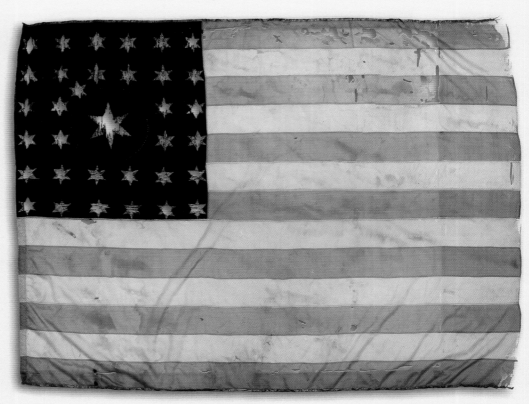

The Company E flag

quently didn't drop as quick as the rest of our men did, but looked around to see what was going on. It did not take me long to find out & I drawed up my gun & was going to fire when I remembered that we had strict orders not to fire till we had orders to do so. So I did not fire but laid down as quick as possible.

I heard somebody yell "fire" so I raised up & fired into the thicket & laid down & loaded as quick as possible & fired again. By this time the boys finding it too hot for them had all gone back over the knoll that I spoke about, but myself & a few others. I saw it was no use for me to stay there as it was sure death as it was a crossfire of our own men & the enemy so I got up to leave & had got a rod or so when I saw our flag bearer fall, a shot having broken his leg. (The Asa Miller that you spoke about had it.) When he fell he raised the flag again & motioned to the boys to get it. I sprang forward & grabbed it & then retreated to the rest of the company where I found our Captain shot dead & some of the boys carrying him off. I followed our Lieutenant [Messick] back down into a hollow & left the flag & then we all rushed forward up onto the hill again & at the rebels.[7]

The August 7, 1861, evening edition of the *Faribault Central Republican* carried an article about the flag at Bull Run, with information provided by one of the soldiers and sent home:

Our Company Flag

The presentation, of which to Company "G" we will not soon forget as I had occasioned before to remind, is preserved, but the particulars of its rescue I did not learn until recently. After the brave Asa Miller was shot down, E. Z. Needham, of Northfield, took it and by command of our Lieutenant stood it by a tree, while he, Needham, made good use of his gun. The next that was seen of it, one of the Company "B" had it and E. Hollister took it from him, and carried it, when Lieut. Messick came up and told Hollister he would not be able to carry it through. Hollister replied that he would not leave it then, and was about to tear it down from the staff when the gallant Lieut. said that he would do it, and do it he did; and thus it was that our colors were saved, after having [received] eight musket balls.

It may have been given by Messick to Needham for safekeeping and perhaps was sent home at that time.

The flag of Company G was carried into the Battle of Bull Run by Pvt. Asa Miller.

According to text written for a fiftieth-anniversary display of Needham's gear, including the Company G flag, he was, as of June 28, 1903, still in possession of the flag.

The flag was donated by a family member to the University of Oklahoma. The photograph seen here was taken while it was there. Other family members withdrew the flag in 1994, and today, its whereabouts are not known.

Company I

In June 1861 the regiment boarded two paddleboats and headed downriver, taking the men on the first leg of the journey to the East Coast. The boats made stops along the way at the river towns, allowing the men of the county to get off and greet their loved ones one last time before leaving for the war. The ladies of Wabasha and Lake City had purchased a beautiful silk flag and, at this time, presented it to the men of Company I. Capt. John Pell from the town of Elgin received it on behalf of the men and thanked the citizens for their patriotic gift. The company carried it in the Battle of Bull Run and also at the skirmish at Edwards Ferry in October.

Later in life, William Colvill recalled seeing the Company I flag during Bull Run:

We came down and found our brave Col. Miller hotly engaged with his independent command. His position was disadvantageous, being outside of the woods, while the enemy, less in numbers, were covered. His command were disheartened and though the Colonel "rallied" incessantly at the top of his voice, they were

fast stealing away. Someone thought of the flag. Capt Pell was also "rallying" with the greatest vigor some distance down to the left and we observed the colors of his company and called the bearer to us, and advanced it toward the wood, getting in line for a moment and pushing the enemy back. The brave Sergeant Knight behaved most gallantly. This flag under which the last stand was made and the last fighting done the first day is preserved at Wabasha, and should be among the collections of our State Historical Society. To return, it was useless, before we realized it, the men were mostly gone, and the Colonel with reluctance fell back with the flag.[8]

This flag became the regiment's second national flag when the Bull Run flag was returned to St. Paul and a temporary replacement was needed until a new one arrived. Perhaps because of the bold and daring eagle in its blue canton, the flag of Company I was chosen. The replacement flag arrived in November 1861, at which time, on November 30, Capt. Pell wrote the following letter to Governor Ramsey:

Governor,

The flag that was presented to my company by the ladies of Wabasha and Lake City now bears honorable marks of service and has become unfit for longer service in the field.

As this and the Regimental flag floated near together on the battle field it is the wish of my company that they again be placed together in the Capital of our State.

This is the last American flag that floated over the spot where many of our Regiment fell.

Trusting that it has been borne in a manner worthy of our cause of our state and of the donor I have the honor to present this flag from my company to the State of Minnesota.

Very Respectfully,

John H Pell

Capt

1 Minn Vol

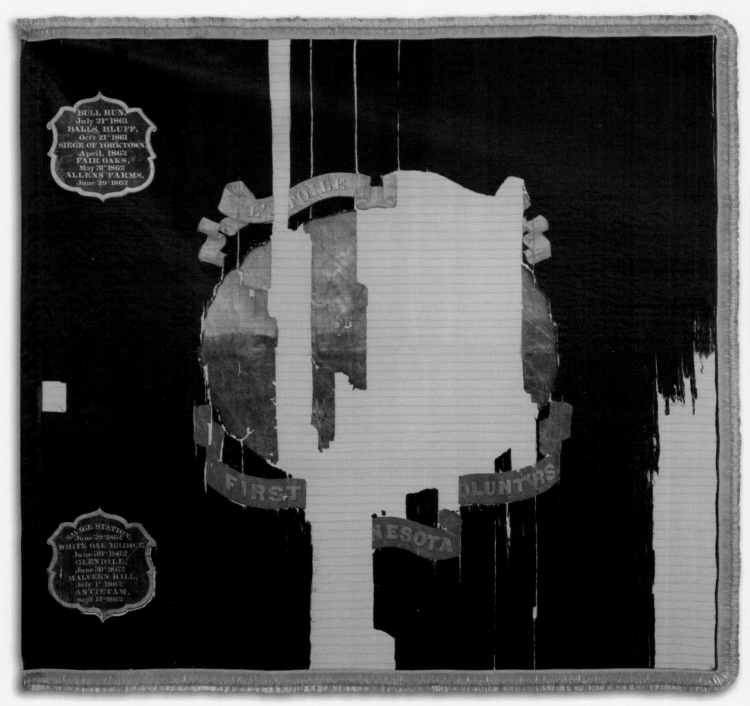

BULL RUN,
July 21st 1861
BALLS BLUFF,
Octr 21st 1861
SIEGE OF YORKTOWN,
April, 1862
FAIR OAKS,
May 31st 1862
ALLENS FARMS,
June 29th 1862

SAVAGE STATION,
June 29th 1862
WHITE OAK BRIDGE,
June 30th 1862
GLENDALE,
June 30th 1862
MALVERN HILL,
July 1st 1862
ANTIETAM,
Sept 17th 1862

The third regimental color was purchased from Horstmann in Philadelphia and paid for by a subscription of the citizens of St. Paul. It was delivered in April 1863 by Governor Ramsey to the regiment in the field. It can be distinguished by its two shields, which contain the regiment's battle honors, the names of the battles in which it had participated up to that time.

MUSICIANS AND BAND

MUSIC WAS AN IMPORTANT part of life in the 1860s. Bands played patriotic tunes at recruiting rallies and helped set the mood for the eager volunteers.

Each company was authorized to have one drummer and one fifer, and at the beginning of the war, many regiments also traveled with a full band. The First Minnesota's was made up of several talented musicians who rallied to the cause. They played while the regiment marched and while it was in camp, entertaining the men at night, taking their minds off the business of war. During battle they pitched in as stretcher-bearers, and when in camp, their tents were placed next to the regimental hospital.

Not being a company of soldiers, they did not have a captain. Instead, they reported to the regiment's adjutant. Initially, Lt. William Leach was the regiment's adjutant and their commander, and while at camp at Harrison's Landing, it was Lt. John Peller.

On August 15, 1861, the *St. Paul Pioneer and Democrat* reported how the band lost their instruments at Bull Run.

This saxhorn was used by a member of the First Minnesota Regimental Band. It is one of the instruments purchased to replace the instruments lost at Bull Run. It measures thirty by seven by three inches. The saxhorn is a valved brass instrument developed during the 1830s. The backward-facing bell version became the most common brass instrument in Civil War bands because troops marching behind the band could hear the music.

We are informed that the band of the First Regiment did not throw away their instruments at the Bully Run. The men were detailed to take care of the wounded, and their instruments were destroyed by being crushed in a wagon load of muskets.

Ed Basset writes:

The boys are getting up a subscription to replace the band instruments we lost at Bull Run. The State of Minnesota gave $500.00 and with what we can raise, we should have as good a band as any Regiment. The boys threw in and bought a violin [Oliver] Graham plays it in the evening and we have a regular tear down.

With so many volunteer regiments bringing their own bands, having so many started to become unwieldy. In the fall of 1862, the government decided to discontinue the use of regimental bands in the army and consolidated some of the musicians into brigade bands. Musicians were allowed to remain with their regiments and serve in the ranks, but most were discharged and sent home. The First Minnesota's band was discharged from service on August 8, 1862, while at Harrison's Landing. Only Ernst Meyer stayed with the regiment, where he served as the regimental bugler.

The following men served in the band: George Atkinson, 23; George Collins, 31; W. H. Colling, 42 (band leader); Charles Durand, 39; William Edson; Oliver Graham, 21; Benjamin Hazen, 23; Chauncey C. Hoffman, 32; Peter Hoffman, 24; Edgar Huntley, 25; Nathaniel Ingalls, 38; J. H. Jones, 46; Marcus Kellogg, 34; George Lovejoy, 23; Augustus Morgan, 34; Ernst Meyer, 30; Fletcher Rowell, 42; Stephen Sherman, 25; Montcalm Stimson, 26; Herman Tyner, 19; and William Woodman, 20.

Henry Fifield

b. August 7, 1841; d. January 13, 1920

Henry Fifield

Henry Fifield was born in Corinna, Maine, and was living in Prescott, Wisconsin, and working as a printer when war was declared. The twenty-one-year-old was mustered in as a drummer for Company C on May 20, 1861. He was five feet seven and a half inches tall and had a fair complexion, hazel eyes, and brown hair.

He was injured on June 10, 1862, while the regiment was fighting at Fair Oaks, Virginia. He was sitting behind a barricade at a field hospital while the enemy was shelling the area when a cannonball struck the barricade's upper logs. The cannonball bounced off the barricade between Fifield and Augustus Ellingson of Company G. The shell hit with such force that Ellingson, whose head was against the log, was killed instantly. Fifield was also struck on the head and was thrown forward several feet and knocked unconscious. His tongue was badly cut by his teeth, and the back of his head and neck were severely bruised.

He was taken to the field hospital, and while he laid there, the cords of his neck swelled to a great size. He was unable to turn his head for two weeks. After several weeks he recovered and returned to duty during the Seven Day's Battles. He felt the pain of that concussion for the rest of his life, suffering from headaches and stiffness in his neck, especially in damp and rainy weather.

Fifield was promoted to principal musician, or drum major, on August 16, 1863. This role placed him in charge of the drummers and fifers. During parades or reviews, he led the group as they marched with the regiment and directed where and when the unit was to march. He continued in this position for the rest of the regiment's service, until it was mustered out on May 5, 1864.

The drum Henry Fifield used during the war

S. Morton Robinson

b. September 17, 1843; d. July 22, 1864

Shannon "Mort" Robinson was born in Prospect, Pennsylvania. At some point his family moved to Minnesota, where his father, George, ran a small harness shop on Washington Avenue in Minneapolis.

On June 6, 1861, Robinson attended a recruiting rally, and Capt. Henry Putnam of Company D enrolled and mustered Robinson that same day. Robinson claimed to be eighteen years old at the time of his enlistment but was actually seventeen. Probably because of his youth and size, he was given the position of company drummer. He was a small young man, standing only five feet four inches tall. He had a light complexion, gray eyes, and light hair. Robinson became ill shortly after Bull Run. His captain, DeWitt Smith, mentions him in a September letter, writing, "Little Mort Robinson is quite sick with measles."

The regiment was mustered out of the service on May 5, 1864, and Mort received the $100 bounty due to him for his service. He took the money to his parents, living in Crystal Lake in Minneapolis, and gave it to his invalid father, saying, "Here Pap. I'll make you a present of this." Robinson still had a short amount of

William Nixon

b. February 15, 1847; d. December 26, 1915

William "Billy" Nixon was born in Wales. When the war began, the young boy was working as a broom maker. When he enlisted, he claimed to be eighteen but was actually only fourteen years old. He has the distinction of being the youngest member of the First Minnesota. He served as the company's drummer for his three years of service and was with the regiment at Gettysburg on July 2. Being a drummer, he was held in reserve in the rear at the time of the charge.

time owed on his three-year enlistment, so he headed back east with the First Battalion.

First Lt. Seth Hammon of Company D, who married Mort's sister Augusta after the war, describes Mort's service as follows:

> While in the line of duty as a soldier [Mort Robinson] was taken sick, with Chronic Diarrhea, at Edward's Ferry, Maryland, sometime in October 1861. He was rendered very low with same disease and in a few weeks, as soon as well enough, he was sent to Ft. Snelling, Minnesota, on a sick leave. He was at said Ft. Snelling Hospital sick with said disease, for about six months, when his health was better, though it was greatly impaired. He was sent to his regiment. He served out his term, but never recovered his health. He was unfit for duty a good deal of the time while he was serving out the remainder of his term by reason of said disease. He was in very poor health when discharged and continued so, unable to do any but light work and but little of that until his death. At the time of his death he was in the employ of the Sanitary Commission at Cliffburne Barracks Hosp. Washington D. C. I was at Washington on duty as Lt. in 7th Reg. Vet. R. C. He died on or about the 22nd of July 1864. He had been sick about three weeks previous to his death, so as to be confined to his bed with said Chronic Diarrhea, and died with said disease as above states at said Cliffburne Hospital. He was in good health—strong and robust—when he entered the service June 6, 1861 and continued so until taken as above described with Chronic Diarrhea and his health was always good during my acquaintance with him prior to his enlisting in the service.
>
> I enlisted with said Co. D. and was 1st Lt. in said Co. and with said soldier when he was first taken with said disease and was with him while he was sick at Ft. Snelling Minn. and frequently saw him during his last sickness at Washington. He was a good soldier temperate and moral and free from bad habits.[1]

After his discharge Robinson was too weak to return home, so he took a position with the Sanitary Commission at Cliffburne Barracks. As mentioned by Hammon, his health deteriorated rapidly, and he died on July 22, 1864. He was buried in Arlington National Cemetery.

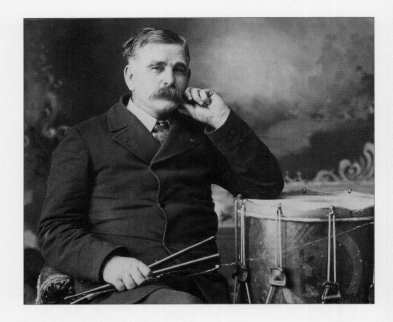

Peter Joseph Hoffman
b. March 25, 1837; d. June 23, 1903

Peter Hoffman was born on March 25, 1837, in New York City. His parents were of Prussian background, and his mother died from cholera in 1848, when Peter was still a boy. On April 4, 1850, when he was thirteen, he enlisted in the regular army as a drummer boy for three years and a bugler for two. He served in Capt. T. W. Sherman's Light Company E of the Third U.S. Artillery. His first year was spent at Governor's Island in New York City. The next two were at Newport, Rhode Island. For his last two years, he was stationed at Ft. Snelling.

After being discharged on April 4, 1855, it appears that he stayed in Minnesota and, for two or three years, starting around 1857, worked for the St. Paul National Bank. He also worked as a liveryman and a musician. In 1860 he was working as a clerk and living at the Superior Hotel in St. Paul.

In the spring of that year, he helped organize the Great Western Band and was considered one of the best players in Minnesota. The band was formed in time for the great combat of the 1860 presidential campaign, playing at rallies for the Wide Awakes and the Little Giants, two political parties of the day. The band also played at the first state fair, held that fall at Ft. Snelling. Little did Hoffman know that he would be returning to the fort next spring to reenter the service. William Bircher, who later served as a drummer in the Second Minnesota, remarked that he met Hoffman before the war and that Hoffman taught him how to beat a drum.

Hoffman was twenty-four when, on May 31, 1861, he was mustered as a drummer in the First Minnesota's band at the rank of musician first class. He served with the First until all bands were dismissed by government order. He was with the regiment at Bull Run, Edwards Ferry, Yorktown, Fair Oaks, Savage Station, and Malvern Hill. He was discharged at Harrison's Landing on August 8, 1862.

He returned to St. Paul, where he became an agent for the Minnesota Stage Company until the spring of 1867. He then moved to the town of Westport in Pope County. He homesteaded a farm there, where he lived for the rest of his life. He became a member of the GAR and also was in the Masonic fraternity. In the 1880s he is recorded as having lived in several communities in Pope County.

An article in the *St. Paul Dispatch* on June 2, 1896, mentions Hoffman playing his drum during the twenty-ninth reunion of the First Minnesota's veterans.

Vets of Old First Celebrate Twenty-Ninth Reunion Today By A Trip On The River From St Paul to Winona.

The veterans seemed to be pleased without exception, with the fact that the same drummer beat the same drum to the music of which the War Eagle pulled out thirty five years ago.

Peter Hoffman, residing at Villard, Minn., who is now a man with an iron gray beard and well along in years, was the favorite drummer of the regiment, and it was remarked that he beat the instrument with more correctness and vehemence this morning, if possible, than he did when he was a boy. Each of the veterans seemed to be of the opinion that his duty was unperformed in some degree until he mounted to the upper deck and given "Drummer Pete's" hand a good shake and congratulated him upon the good work he was doing. Ernst Meyer, the fife player who accompanied Hoffman, was sadly missed by all the veterans, all of whom declared that it was hard to find the equal to the pair when they played together. It will be remembered that Meyer died at Stillwater only about two weeks ago. The fife player of Camp No. 1, Sons of Veterans, supplied the vacant place, the same camp having charge of the cannon, which threateningly points from the deck. This cannon is to be used to salute the different towns just before they are reached, and is really the only instrument of warfare to be seen aboard the Henrietta.

Peter Hoffman died in Westport, Minnesota, on January 23, 1903. He was sixty-five years old.

Peter Hoffman's drum was made by W. R. Tompkins of Yonkers. The metal stamp reads: "Presented to P Hoffman by Hon H M Rice, Col Gorman and officers of the 1st Minn Vols at Alexandria, Va July 15, 1861. Engagements: 1st Bull Run, Edwards Ferry, Fair Oaks, Seven Day fight under Little MC (McClellan)." One can see the wear on the wooden rim, a result of his tenacity as a drummer.

Ernst Meyer

b. March 15, 1827; d. May 7, 1896

Ernst Meyer was born at Lauterbach in Hanover, Prussia. By 1853 he was living in Dubuque, Iowa, and at about that time, he married Henrietta Hoelserhoff. He traveled by boat to St. Paul, looking for land on which to build a house, and bought a piece in Ramsey County. He and Henrietta lived there until 1856, when they moved to St. Peter. In February 1857, while pregnant with their second child, she was taken sick, and

sadly, she and the unborn child died. Later that same year, Meyer was engaged for three weeks in fighting Indians. He served under Capt. Dodds in a local St. Peter militia unit. From 1859 until early 1861, he worked in town as a bank clerk.

Meyer was thirty-four years old when he enlisted as a musician in the First Minnesota. On April 29, 1861, he was mustered into Company A. At that time, or shortly thereafter, he was placed in the regimental band as a musician first class. Meyer was five feet eight and a half inches tall and had a light complexion, blond hair, and blue eyes. He served as a member of the band until August 8, 1862, when all bands were dismissed by government order.

At some early point in his service, he was appointed the regimental bugler. During the Battle of Bull Run, he had his bugle shot away from his hand. A collection was taken, and band leader N. P. Ingalls was sent to New York City in September to purchase new instruments. When the shipment arrived in October, Meyer was surprised and felt honored to receive a new bugle. It was complete with a nice engraving: "Presented to Ernst Meyer by Co. A, 1st Minn. Vols." After the band got their new instruments, for two evenings in a row, they entertained visitors from Stillwater by playing waltzes, polkas, and quadrilles.

During the Peninsula Campaign of April 1862, while camped at Yorktown, Meyer developed problems that haunted him for the rest of his life. Dr. Hand sent him to the hospital for treatment, since he had developed chronic diarrhea and bronchitis and frequently kept everyone in his tent awake with his nighttime hacking cough spells. His illness eventually left him incapable of working at full strength. He and Joseph Lincoln, who was recovering from a case of the mumps, nursed each other for about three or four weeks. During this time they lived in a little shanty, and the rest of the world went on about its business. After this time they caught up with the regiment, which by now had moved about fifty miles away.

After his discharge he returned to St. Peter. He was weak and suffered continually from chronic diarrhea and cramps in his stomach and bowels. He still managed to work, though, and returned to his job at the bank. He was even elected county treasurer. On January 27, 1867, he was married, and that year, he settled on a farm in Oshawa, near St. Peter. By 1869 Meyer was incapable of working the farm, and he rented the

The inscription reads, "Presented to Ernst Meyer by Co A 1st Minn Vols."

land to a James Linquist, who lived on the farm until 1875 and many times was sent to get the doctor to come out and care for Meyer.

In Ernst's final years the doctor prescribed powders containing morphine, which was used to control his severe pain. He once said of the powders, "When they give me that stuff it makes me kind of wild." His mind faded and the pain grew, and on May 7, 1896, Ernst Meyer died as the result of a self-inflicted gunshot wound. His suicide was directly brought about by his pain and perhaps aided by the effects of the heavy doses of morphine. He was sixty-nine years old.

David Archibald

b. October 13, 1845; d. December 9, 1924

David Archibald was born in Musquoduboit, Nova Scotia, and in 1852 his family settled in Tamarack, located in western Hennepin County. The town changed its name to Long Lake in 1869.

Archibald, Wilbur Coleman, and Elbridge Barns, all from the Lake Minnetonka area, went off to war at the same time. David, from Medina, was only sixteen but told the recruiting officer he was seventeen, and his parents gave their written permission for him to enlist. On Christmas Eve 1861 at Ft. Snelling, he became a member of the Second Company of Minnesota Sharpshooters. He had dark hair, dark eyes, and a dark complexion and was only five feet four and half inches tall. He was mustered in as the company's drummer.

Archibald participated in every battle in which the unit was engaged, including Gettysburg. He was severely wounded by a gunshot to his left thigh during battle at Cold Harbor, Virginia, on June 4, 1864. The minié ball passed through the fleshy part of his inner thigh, cut through muscle, and exited through the rear. The wound left him lame for the rest of his life, though he walked without the need of a cane. Archibald was taken to the hospital and remained there until December 30, 1864, at which time he was honorably discharged. After the war he returned to Long Lake. The young man who once stood under five and a half feet tall had grown to a sturdy six feet.

Appendix A

ARTIFACTS

The men are gone, but the artifacts they used during the war remain. Many are shown elsewhere in this book with their related stories. Pictured here are additional items worn and used by the men of the First Minnesota.

In Litchfield, Minnesota, stands a jewel of a museum. The building was a GAR Hall in its day. It is one of only three former GAR Halls in existence in the entire country. Today, the Litchfield Hall is a museum dedicated to the veterans of the war. Inside are many interesting relics of the past, and one of these is worthy of note here.

On July 2, 1863, Cpl. James Bryant of Company D was with the rest of his company on the left side of the regiment as they stood two deep in their line of battle. When ordered, they made the charge that left most of them on the ground either dead or wounded. During the fighting, Bryant was wounded in the left thigh and, at some point, lost his wallet. It may have been during the charge or after he had been wounded, perhaps as he struggled to find something to care for his wound. He had purchased this wallet just prior to the regiment's arrival at Gettysburg. He clearly marked it so there was no doubt as to the owner, "James Bryant, Company D, 1st Regiment Minnesota Volunteers." Perhaps within moments of its loss, the wallet was spotted and picked up by Confederate soldier David Morgan Rise. He carried his trophy with him throughout the rest of the war. At some point it was placed in a trunk and remained there until 2005, when it was discovered by a family member in Michigan who wanted to return it to the Bryant family. A search was made, and a descendent of Bryant's was found who, in turn, gifted the wallet to the GAR Hall in Litchfield in 2007, where it now is proudly displayed in a beautiful wood display case.

Faintly seen at the top of the inner flap of his wallet is James Bryant's name and regiment. That identification led to it being returned to Minnesota almost 150 years after it was lost during the Battle of Gettysburg.

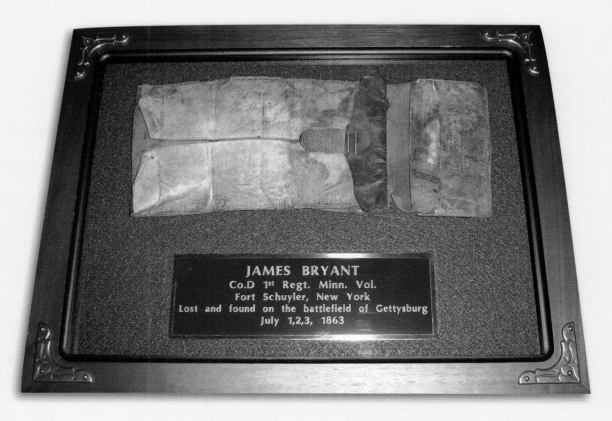

JAMES BRYANT
Co.D 1st Regt. Minn. Vol.
Fort Schuyler, New York
Lost and found on the battlefield of Gettysburg
July 1,2,3, 1863

This Bible was used by Pvt. Azariah W. Darling (Co. D) during the Civil War. After the war this case was made to protect his valued wartime possession, which he gave to his daughter Zoe after carving her initials on the top.

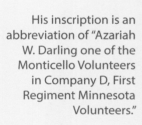

His inscription is an abbreviation of "Azariah W. Darling one of the Monticello Volunteers in Company D, First Regiment Minnesota Volunteers."

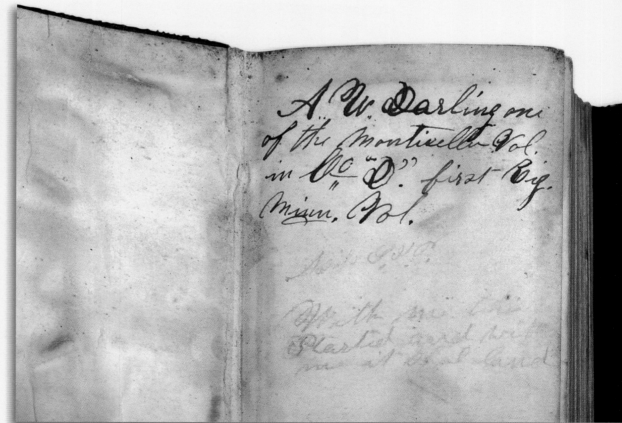

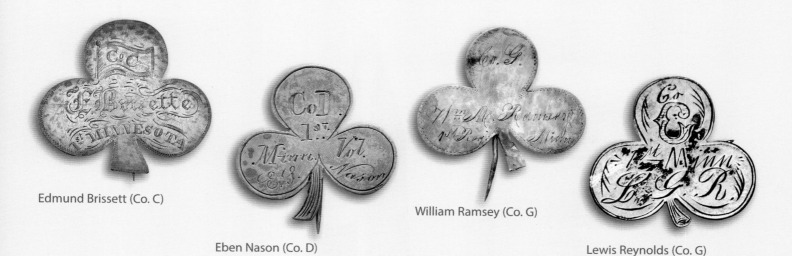

Edmund Brissett (Co. C)

Eben Nason (Co. D)

William Ramsey (Co. G)

Lewis Reynolds (Co. G)

Introduced in early 1863, the corps' badge was created to identify one similar-looking group of soldiers from another. The badge quickly became a thing of pride as men proudly wore the emblem that linked them to their comrades in arms. The "white clubs" of the First Minnesota were well known to the men in the Army of Northern Virginia.

Martin Maginnis (*top*) and Mark Downie (*bottom*) were friends during their service in the First Minnesota. Both men appear to have purchased a beautiful decorative badge celebrating their service in the Army of the Potomac's Second Corps with the First Minnesota. Maginnis is shown wearing his badge, and Downie's is pictured on the right.

Maj. Mark Downie's badge

In his portrait (*left*) William Abell (Co. K) is seen probably wearing this cartridge box (*below*). He spent much of his service as a teamster. At Gettysburg it appears that he was detailed as part of the twenty-man detail that helped take care of the wounded at the Second Corps field hospital at Rock Creek.

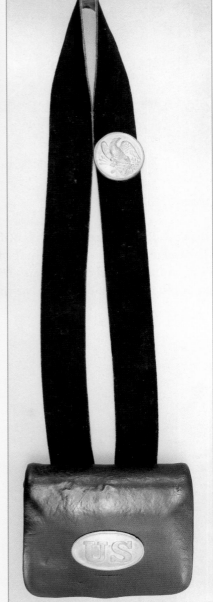

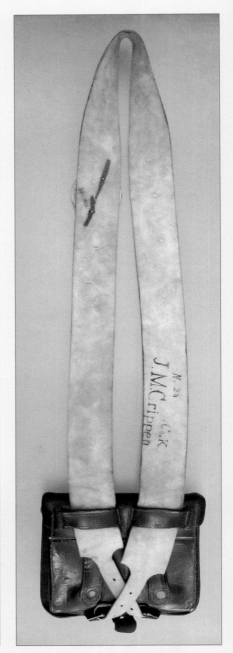

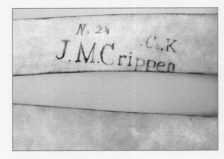

This cartridge box was carried by Pvt. Joseph Crippen (Co. K) during his service with the First Minnesota. The eagle breastplate worn on the front of the leather strap had two iron loops on its back. They were inserted through slits cut in the leather. The plate was held in place by inserting a leather thong through the loops.

William Abell's cartridge box

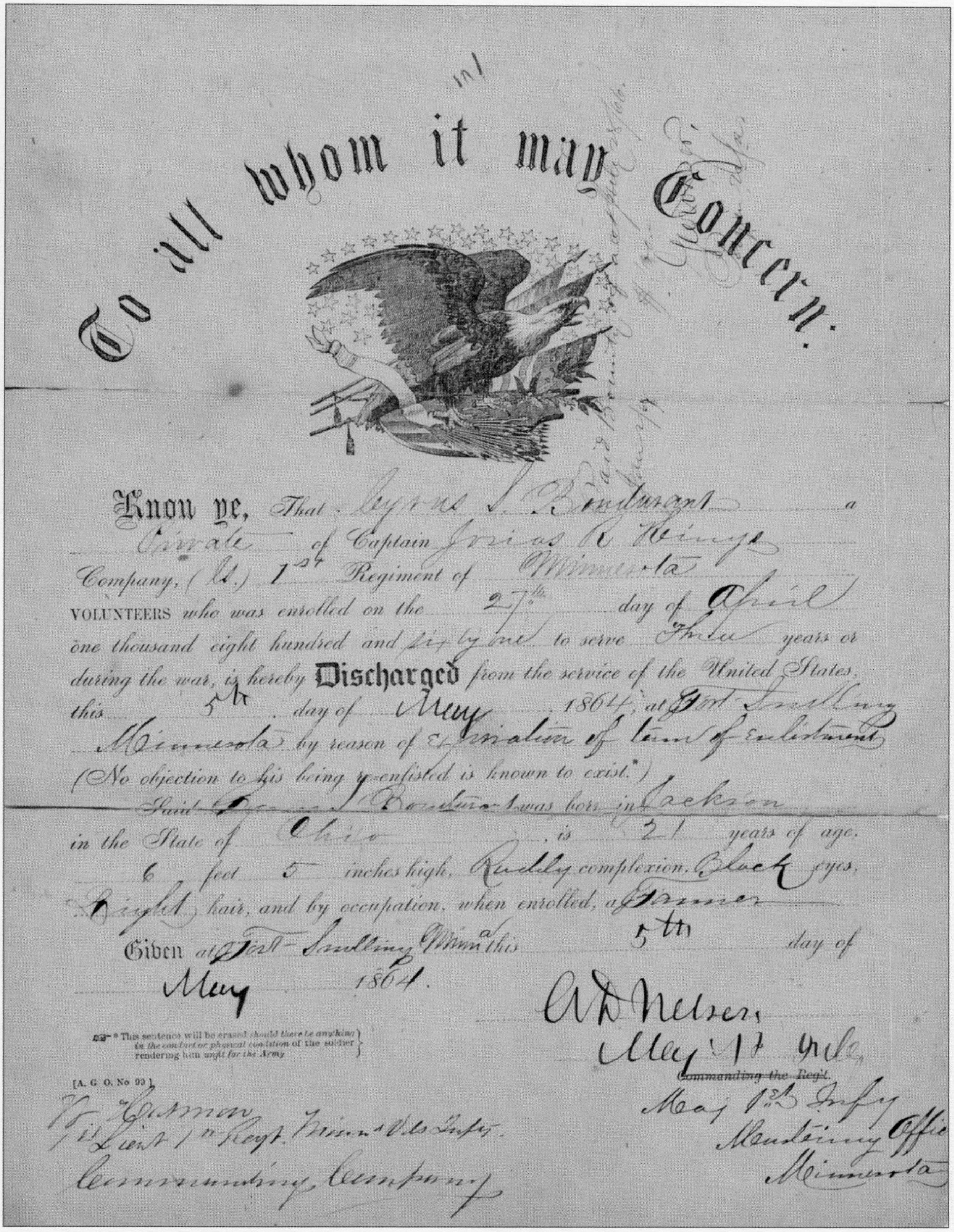

To all whom it may Concern.

Know ye, That _Cyrus S Bondurant_ a _Private_ of Captain _Josias R Kings_ Company, (_G._) 1st Regiment of _Minnesota_ VOLUNTEERS who was enrolled on the _27th_ day of _April_ one thousand eight hundred and _sixty one_ to serve _Three_ years or during the war, is hereby **Discharged** from the service of the United States, this _5th_ day of _May_ 1864, at _Fort Snelling Minnesota_ by reason of _Expiration of term of Enlistment_

(No objection to his being re-enlisted is known to exist.)

Said Cyrus S Bondurant was born in Jackson in the State of _Ohio_, is _21_ years of age, _6_ feet _5_ inches high, _Ruddy_ complexion, _Black_ eyes, _Light_ hair, and by occupation, when enrolled, a _Farmer_

Given at _Fort Snelling Minn_ this _5th_ day of _May_ 1864.

☞ *This sentence will be erased should there be anything in the conduct or physical condition of the soldier rendering him unfit for the Army

[A. G O. No 99].

W. Harmon
1st Lieut 1 Regt Minn Vols Infy.
Commanding Company

A D Nelson
Maj 1 Infy
Commanding the Regt.

Maj 1st Infy
Mustering Officer
Minnesota

This is Pvt. Cyrus S. Bondurant's (Co. G) discharge certificate. He served from April 29, 1861, to May 5, 1864.

Diaries were one of the most common nonregulation items carried by soldiers during the war. Many have survived to this day and give us invaluable insight into the men who served in the First Minnesota. They were commonly about four by five inches with a pebble-finished black cover and made from pressed paper, which gave them some stiffness and rigidity while still remaining pliable. Though others certainly exist, the following soldiers' diaries were used in my research: Balthasar Best, Samuel Bloomer, Thomas Dwelle, James Ghostley, William Lochren, Mathew Marvin, Edward Needham, Jasper Searles, Myron Shepard, Isaac Taylor, Patrick H. Taylor, and Joseph Trevor.

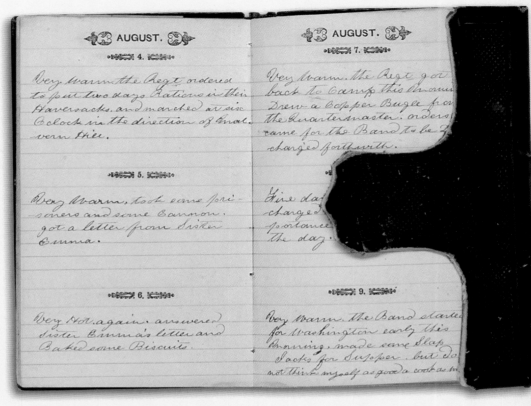

James Ghostley's diary (Col. H)

Hardtack is a biscuit made from flour, water, and salt. Inexpensive to make and, when properly stored, lasting for years, it was a staple of the Civil War soldier's diet. The crackers were very hard and tasted better if fried in bacon grease to make a tasty dish called *skilly gally*. Hardtack biscuits were sent to the troops in boxes marked "2,000 BC," meaning "2,000 biscuit crackers." The troops however felt "2,000 BC" more likely indicated the date the crackers had been made.

The straight-edge razor of the Civil War period tended to have a shorter and wider blade than those used later in the century. Chesley Tirrell (Co. C) used this one during the war.

This piece of hardtack was issued to Richard Gorman during the war. He kept it as a souvenir.

Musician Noah Van Valkenberg (Co. H) served from May 18, 1861, to December 9, 1861. He undoubtedly carried this drum at Bull Run; he brought it home when he was discharged for disability. This metal drum measures sixteen inches high and seventeen inches in diameter.

This drum was used by Pvt. Andrew Wayman, Co. C, First Battalion of Minnesota Infantry, who served during the last months of the war.[1]

Stencils were used by soldiers to mark their gear because it was often difficult to tell one soldier's items from another's.

Pvt. Ole Gilberson (Co. F)

Pvt. George Hooker (Co. B)

Pvt. Samuel Nicklin (Co. K)

Pvt. Milo Whitcomb (Co. I)

Albert Davis rose from the ranks of a private to become the sergeant major of the regiment and later received a commission as a first lieutenant in Company A. Shown here are two sets of shoulder straps. The light blue straps with the single gold bar are the designations for a first lieutenant of infantry. The ones with the black background indicate a first lieutenant in a staff position. Shown additionally are two corps badges he owned. One is of silver and has a cut-out center that allowed the owner to put in the appropriate color for his division. Division colors were in patriotic order: first divisions' were red; second divisions' were white; and third divisions' were blue. The First Minnesota was in the Second Division of the Second Army Corps, whose symbol was the trefoil or clover, hence the white trefoils seen on the men's uniforms. Perhaps he purchased the multicolored corps badge to have all the divisions covered and be a bit patriotic.

The knapsack was the soldier's suitcase, in which he kept his extra clothes. Joseph Holt (Co. D) served for a year with the First Minnesota, from November 11, 1861, to October 22, 1862. He was discharged for disability and then sent home. When discharged, he may have let the government charge him for the cost of his knapsack, and by doing so, he was able to head home with his "suitcase."

This is the only known example of a knapsack identified as having been used by a member of the First Minnesota. On the front strap Holt carved his name and regiment, "J. B. Holt 1st Minn."

This identification disk was worn by Pvt. Chester Durfee (Co. K), who was from Minnesota City in Winona County. A hole was punched into the disk through which a string was attached and then hung around the soldier's neck. This is the early version of what is today called a dog tag. It is a copper disk approximately one inch round. The obverse side (*left*) reads, "Against Rebelion 1861." The reverse reads, "C. P. Durfee, Co. K 1st Reg, Minn. Vol., Minn. City."

Identification tag belonging to Pvt. Lafayette Snow (Co. B)

Cpl. Orange S. King (Co. D) was wounded in the eye by a bayonet thrust from the enemy at Bull Run on July 21, 1861. Though assisted off the field by musician George Fuller, King was later captured and sent to Richmond. He spent several months in Libby Prison and at Salisbury Prison in Salisbury, North Carolina. While in prison, he made this set of clothes for himself. He was subsequently involved in a prisoner exchange and discharged for disability on January 1, 1862.

Patriotic envelopes added some fun to letters. The back of this one, brought back from the war by Pvt. James Brakey (Co. E), shows an engraving of the regiment's first winter quarters at Camp Stone, Maryland.

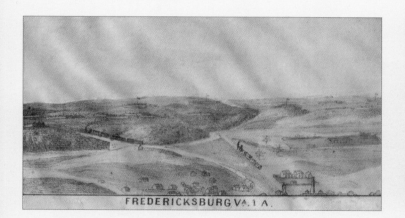

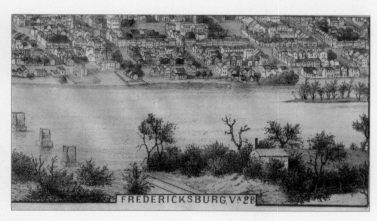

This group of four envelopes, also brought back by Brakey, depict the city of Fredericksburg.

John Chase (Co. H) used this folding mirror (*top*) for his personal grooming. Note his name and the "1st Minnesota" identification. He carried this 1862 U.S. infantry tactics manual (*bottom*) to help him with his duties as an officer.

Musician Henry Fifield's postwar ladder badge

This reunion pin in the shape of a Second Corps badge was worn by Pvt. Harvey Scott of Company E.

In 1913 the veterans of the First who attended the fiftieth anniversary of the Battle of Gettysburg received one of these to wear.

In later years the First Minnesota Association printed rosters of surviving veterans and included their last-known addresses. John Churchill kept two of these, along with his GAR membership ribbon and a ladder badge he purchased that shows he was a member of Company I.

After the war several companies created artistic records for their soldiers. These soldiers' memorials recorded the names of men in a specific company and whether they were wounded, captured, or killed. This memorial was made for Company F and was owned by Charles Berdan, providing him with a memory of the men with whom he had served his country.

Henry O'Brien's Medal of Honor

Appendix B

REGIMENTAL AND BATTALION PHOTO GALLERY

Presented here are pictures of the men who served in the First Regiment of Minnesota Volunteer Infantry during the period from 1861 to 1864. Included are their names, dates of service with the regiment or battalion, and the battle or battles in which, if applicable, they were wounded or killed. If a man served in either the First Minnesota or the Second Company of Sharpshooters (Co. L) and also served in the battalion, his picture is shown only once. If a soldier was enrolled under a last name different from his family name, then the military name, by which he can be found in the rosters, is in parentheses.

The First Regiment of Minnesota Volunteer Infantry

William H. Abell
5/22/61–7/16/65

William H. Acker
4/29/61–8/8/61
Killed at Shiloh

Charles P. Adams
4/29/61–5/5/64
Wounded 6 times in 3 battles

Edward C. Agnew
4/29/61–5/5/64

James Akers (Ackers)
4/29/61–7/2/63
Killed at Gettysburg

Levi J. Allred
4/29/61–5/5/64

Minor Atherton
4/29/61–12/13/63
Gettysburg

Francis Baasen
4/29/61–5/5/64

Charles E. Baker
5/29/61–7/2/63
Killed at Gettysburg

John Ball
4/29/61–5/5/64
Bristoe Station

The First Regiment of Minnesota Volunteer Infantry

Edward H. Bassett
4/29/61–5/5/64
Bristoe Station

William H. Bassett
4/29/61–5/5/64

William D. Bennett
4/29/61–2/4/63
Savage Station

Charles M. Benson
5/22/61–5/5/64
Bristoe Station

Charles A. Berdan
10/29/61–11/17/64
Fredericksburg &
Bristoe Station

Peter Bergh
2/11/62–7/12/65
Captured at Petersburg

Balthasar Best
4/29/61–5/5/64
Bristoe Station

Horatio S. Bingham
4/29/61–10/2/62
Died in Indian Territory

John Blesi
4/29/61–11/16/63
Bull Run

Samuel Bloomer
4/29/61–12/6/62
Antietam

Charles B. Boardman
5/22/61–5/4/64
Fredericksburg

Fridelin Boll
5/23/61–5/5/64

Daniel Bond
8/22/62–7/15/65
Fredericksburg,
Captured at Petersburg

Hezekiah Bond
8/14/62–10/26/64
Died at Salisbury Prison

Cyrus S. Bondurant
4/29/61–5/5/64
Gettysburg

George Boyd
4/29/61–5/5/64
Gettysburg

Henry C. Bradley
5/23/61–5/5/64
Gettysburg & Savage
Station

Hiram A. Brink
4/29/61–7/15/65

Carlisle A. Bromley
4/29/61–7/15/62

Cyrus A. Brooks
5/22/61–6/12/63

The First Regiment of Minnesota Volunteer Infantry

John Brown
5/16/61–5/5/64

William W. Brown
9/12/61–9/12/64
Gettysburg

Hezekiah Bruce
4/29/61–5/5/64

Adelbert Bryant
5/21/61–1/28/63

George R. Buckman
5/23/61–5/5/64

**Daniel C. Buswell
(Boswell)**
4/29/61–8/26/62

Stephen F. Bunker
4/29/61–12/10/61
Bull Run

N. George Burgess
4/29/61–6/30/62
Killed at Savage Station

Samuel W. Burgess
11/11/61–1/27/63
Antietam

Henry Burritt
4/29/61–10/24/62
Savage Station

Alfred P. Carpenter
5/23/61–9/24/63
Antietam & Gettysburg

Merritt B. Case
5/23/61–12/22/63
Bull Run

Andrew J. Chase
12/26/61–11/8/62

John N. Chase
4/29/61–5/5/64

Henry R. Childs
5/31/61–5/5/64
Bull Run

William H. Churchill
10/24/61–7/15/65
Captured at Vienna &
Ream's Station

George B. Clark
5/17/61–7/14/65
Captured at Antietam &
Petersburg

Charles I. Clark
6/22/61–6/18/64
Bull Run, Killed at
Petersburg

John Clater (Cleator)
5/22/61–2/7/63
Antietam

James Cleary
4/29/61–5/5/64

The First Regiment of Minnesota Volunteer Infantry

Carroll H. Clifford
5/21/61–5/5/64

Henry C. Coates
4/29/61–5/5/64

David A. Coflin
4/29/61–5/5/64

William Colvill Jr.
4/29/61–5/5/64
Glendale & Gettysburg
(2x)

Napoleon J. T. Dana
10/2/61–2/3/62
Antietam

Albert S. Davis
4/29/61–5/3/64
Bull Run

Charles C. Davis
4/29/61–5/5/64

C. Edward Davis
4/29/61–5/5/64

Jonas P. Davis
4/29/61–5/5/64
Savage Station

James DeGray
4/29/61–3/15/64
Bristoe Station &
Gettysburg

David B. Demerest
4/29/61–7/30/63
Died of wounds from
Gettysburg

Thomas L. Doble
5/26/61–5/3/64

William H. Dooley
4/29/61–11/7/63
Bull Run & Gettysburg

Nelson Doran
4/29/61–11/22/64
Died at Salisbury Prison

Mark Downie
4/29/61–5/5/64
Bull Run & Gettysburg
(3x)

David B. Dudley
4/29/61–10/6/62
Died of wounds from
Antietam

Phineas L. Dunham
4/29/61–7/17/63
Died of wounds from
Gettysburg

**James F. Dunsmore
(Dunsmoor)**
5/23/61–8/1/61
Bull Run

Chester H. Durfee
8/28/61–7/15/65
Gettysburg

George H. Durfee
5/23/61–5/4/64

The First Regiment of Minnesota Volunteer Infantry

Thomas L. Dwelle
9/10/61–2/6/63
Edwards Ferry

Joshua Dyer
11/5/61–3/29/65
Captured at Petersburg,
drowned at sea

Joseph S. Eaton
5/22/61–5/5/64
Bull Run & Gettysburg

Philander Ellis
4/29/61–7/2/63
Bull Run, Killed at
Gettysburg

Charles Ely
4/29/61–5/5/64
Gettysburg

Levi Emery
5/26/61–4/18/62
Bull Run

Wilson B. Farrell
4/29/61–7/4/63
Died of wounds from
Gettysburg

James Farwell
5/17/61–2/27/65

Henry O. Fifield
5/20/61–5/5/64

Van Hayden Fisk
9/14/61–2/16/63

Jay Foss
9/3/61–4/30/63

John French
4/29/61–5/5/64

Joseph P. Garrison
4/29/61–8/10/61
Died of wounds from
Bull Run

William H. Garvey
5/16/61–4/10/63

Jacob George
6/1/61–7/14/65
Bull Run

Henry Ghostley
12/25/61–12/29/64
Bristoe Station

Frances Gibson
5/23/61–12/16/61

Ole Gilberson
5/16/61–5/5/64

James B. Gilman
4/29/61–5/5/64
Bull Run

Charles E. Goddard
4/29/61–5/5/64
Gettysburg

The First Regiment of Minnesota Volunteer Infantry

Jonathan Goodrich
5/23/61–5/5/64
Gettysburg

Hanford L. Gordon
5/21/61–12/1/61

William Gordon
4/29/61–8/20/62

Richard L. Gorman
4/29/61–12/31/61

Willis A. Gorman
4/29/61–10/1/61
Promoted to Brigadier
General

George W. Goulding
5/24/61–5/5/64

William W. Goundry
5/23/61–5/4/64

Emil Graf
4/29/61–4/29/64

Aaron Greenwald
4/29/61 – 7/5/63
Died of wounds from
Gettysburg

Philo Hall
4/29/61–5/5/64
Gettysburg

Philip R. Hamlin
4/29/61–7/3/63
Killed at Gettysburg

Dr. Daniel W. Hand
7/23/61–10/5/61

Hiram Harding
4/29/61–8/2/61
Bull Run

William Harmon
4/29/61–5/5/64
Gettysburg

Charles N. Harris
4/29/61–12/5/62
Bull Run

Charles W. Haskell
4/29/61–3/8/63
Glendale, Died of
disease

Cyrus M. Hatch
4/29/61–12/5/62
Antietam

Charles F. Hausdorf
4/29/61–7/14/65
Gettysburg

Alonzo C. Hayden
4/29/61–7/3/63
Died of wounds from
Gettysburg

Anson R. Hayden
5/24/61–5/5/64
Bull Run & Gettysburg

The First Regiment of Minnesota Volunteer Infantry

Orrin T. Hayes
4/29/61–7/29/61

Christopher Heffelfinger
4/29/61–5/5/64
Gettysburg

Marcus L. Hendricks
4/29/61–10/24/62

Elvin G. Hill
5/23/61–5/5/64

Jonas R. Hill
9/14/61–9/14/64
Gettysburg

Joseph S. Hill
5/22/61–5/5/64

Alonzo Holland
11/18/61–11/18/64
Petersburg

George J. Hopkins
5/28/61–6/9/64
Gettysburg (2x)

Adolphus C. Hospes
5/20/61–5/5/64
Captured at Antietam

Mark A. Hoyt
4/29/61–7/18/62

Javan B. Irvine
9/3/61–12/15/61

William N. Irvine
5/21/61–6/28/64
Fredericksburg, Killed at Petersburg

Rufus R. Jefferson
6/22/61–10/24/62
Bull Run

Albert Johnson
4/29/61–5/5/64
Chancellorsville

Ole Johnson
4/29/61–5/5/64

William A. Joy
3/15/62–7/15/65

Julian J. Kendall
4/29/61–5/4/64
Savage Station

Charles H. King
4/29/61–2/4/62

Josias King
4/29/61–5/5/64

Orange S. King
4/29/61–1/5/62
Bull Run

The First Regiment of Minnesota Volunteer Infantry

William H. Kinyon
5/22/61–5/5/64
Gettysburg

James Kirkman
4/29/61–4/1/62

Edwin M. Knight
12/17/61–1/14/63

Jacob W. Kouts
5/20/61–5/5/64
Gettysburg

Origin R. Lacy
4/29/61–3/8/62

Adin A. Laflin
5/17/61–5/5/64

William L. Larned
4/29/61–12/15/62
Bull Run

William B. Leach
4/29/61–2/23/62

John B. LeBlond
5/25/62–5/5/64

Maurice Leonard
11/18/61–7/7/65
Captured at Petersburg

Henry C. Lester
4/29/61–11/15/61

Andrew Levering
4/29/61–3/27/63
Died of illness

George L. Lewis
4/29/61–8/8/63

Samuel Lilly
5/23/61–5/5/64
Gettysburg

Charles E. Lincoln
4/29/61–5/24/62
Captured at Bull Run

Joseph Lincoln
11/18/61–9/6/62
Bull Run

Henry W. Lindergreen
4/29/61–7/23/62

William Lochren
4/29/61–12/30/63

Harrison Lyons
5/25/61–5/5/64
Gettysburg, Savage
Station

Stephen Lyons
4/29/61–5/5/64
Gettysburg

The First Regiment of Minnesota Volunteer Infantry

George Maddock
4/29/61–5/5/64
Bull Run

George Magee
5/23/61–5/5/64
Gettysburg

Martin Maginnis
4/29/61–5/5/64
Savage Station

**John Mannings
(Manning)**
5/23/61–5/5/64
Antietam

Stephen E. Martin
5/22/61–5/5/64

Adam Marty
4/29/61–5/5/64
Gettysburg

Mathew Marvin
4/29/61–5/5/64
Bull Run & Gettysburg

Charles F. Mason
5/23/61–5/5/64
Bull Run, Gettysburg

Charles H. Mason
4/29/61–8/18/63
Died of wounds from
Gettysburg

John S. May
4/29/61–7/14/65
Captured at Petersburg

William M. May
4/29/61–5/5/64
Gettysburg

John J. McCallum
4/29/61–7/28/63
Fredericksburg

Joseph McDonald
4/29/61–4/1/65
Savage Station

Lewis McKune
4/29/61–7/21/61
Killed at Bull Run

Freeman McKusick
5/20/61–5/5/64

**Maxwell A. McLane
(McLean)**
5/27/61–5/5/64

Frank J. Mead
5/24/61–12/27/62
Fair Oaks

Charles W. Merritt
4/29/61–5/5/64
Bull Run

John G. Merritt
4/29/61–5/5/64
Bull Run

Nathan S. Messick
4/29/61–7/3/63
Died of wounds from
Gettysburg

The First Regiment of Minnesota Volunteer Infantry

Ernst Meyer
4/29/61–8/8/62

Ernst L. F. Miller
5/30/61–6/1/64
Gettysburg

Stephen Miller
4/29/61–9/16/62

William D. Mitchell
5/23/61–11/1/63

John Moore
5/22/61–2/7/63

Oliver Moore
5/23/61–10/24/62

Samuel Morford
5/23/61–5/5/64
Gettysburg

George N. Morgan
4/29/61–5/5/63
Promoted to brigadier
general

Ludwell J. Mosher
5/23/61–5/5/64
Antietam & Gettysburg

Charles Muller
4/29/61–5/5/64
Gettysburg

Louis Muller
4/29/61–7/2/63
Killed at Gettysburg

Thomas B. Nason
5/28/61–5/5/64
Antietam & Gettysburg
(2x)

Charles Nassig
5/29/61–1/30/63
Antietam

Joseph B. F. Navarre
4/29/61–10/24/62
Fair Oaks

Edward Z. Needham
4/29/61–5/5/64

Edward D. Neill
4/29/61–7/13/62
Became Lincoln's
personal secretary

Jonas (John) Nelson
2/14/62–7/14/64
Antietam

William Nixon
4/29/61–5/5/64

Charles F. North
4/29/61–5/5/64
Gettysburg

Anson Northrup
4/29/61–3/1/62

The First Regiment of Minnesota Volunteer Infantry

Henry D. O'Brien
9/28/61–7/15/65
Deep Bottom,
Gettysburg (3x)

Freeman Orcutt
5/26/61–5/10/64

Henry Orcutt
5/26/61–5/5/64

Charles C. Parker
4/29/61–7/15/65

Edmund F. Parker
9/28/61–4/18/65
Captured at Petersburg

Edward Past
4/29/61–12/1/62
Antietam

John H. Pell
4/29/61–3/26/63
Antietam

John Peller
4/29/61–5/5/64
Gettysburg

Joseph Periam
4/29/61–7/7/63
Died of wounds from
Gettysburg

Daniel Perkins
12/16/61–6/29/65
Captured at Petersburg

Ellet P. Perkins
4/29/61–10/13/64
Gettysburg

Alonzo H. Pickle
8/14/62–6/25/65
Gettysburg

John W. Plummer
4/29/61–5/5/64

Robert A. Plummer
4/29/61–5/5/64

George Pomeroy
4/29/61–9/22/62
Antietam

Thomas Pressnell
4/29/61–7/15 65
Wounded 5 times in 5
battles

Turner Pribble
11/15/61–7/24/65
Petersburg, Captured at
Petersburg

John W. Pride
4/29/61–7/15/65
Bristoe Station,
captured at Petersburg

Henry R. Putnam
4/29/61–8/8/61
Bull Run

Andrew P. Quist
4/29/61–1/22/64
Antietam & Gettysburg

The First Regiment of Minnesota Volunteer Infantry

Samuel T. Raguet
4/29/61–7/15/62
Bull Run

William M. Ramsey
5/23/61–5/5/64

Nathaniel Reed
5/20/61–10/22/64
Died of illness at
Washington, DC

Walter S. Reed
5/23/61–7/15/65
Wounded 3x, Captured
at Petersburg

John C. Renshaw
4/29/61–9/9/61
Died of wounds from
Bull Run

John M. Rhorer
4/29/61–5/5/64
Bull Run, Gettysburg

Benjamin Roberts
5/23/61–11/30/64

S. Morton Robinson
6/6/61–5/5/64
Died of illness at
Washington, DC

William J. Roe
4/29/61–4/1/64
Died of wounds from
Gettysburg

Leroy F. Sampson
5/17/61–2/2/63
Antietam

George P. Sawyer
4/29/61–7/2/63
Killed at Gettysburg

Amos G. Scofield
4/29/61–8/18/61
Died of wounds from
Bull Run

David H. Seamans
9/21/61–2/12/63

Jasper N. Searles
5/1/61–5/5/64

John C. Shafer
4/29/61–5/5/64

Myron Shepard
7/20/61–5/5/64

Marshall Sherman
4/29/61–7/24/65
Deep Bottom, leg
amputated

Albert Sieber (Sebers)
3/4/62–11/14/65
Gettysburg (2x)

Thomas Sinclair
4/29/61–5/5/64
Wounded in 4 battles

DeWitt C. Smith
4/29/61–10/7/63
Antietam

The First Regiment of Minnesota Volunteer Infantry

George H. Smith
11/11/61–2/13/63

William Smith
4/29/61–11/17/61

Joseph H. Spencer
4/29/61–5/29/63

Edgar L. Sproat
4/29/61–7/21/62

**Gideon L. Squier
(Squires)**
5/26/61–4/6/64
Gettysburg

Howard Stansbury
4/29/61–6/1/61

Benjamin F. Staples
5/30/61–5/5/64
Antietam & Gettysburg

Samuel E. Stebbins
4/29/61–11/28/62
Bull Run

Charles A. Steen
4/29/61–5/3/64
Gettysburg

Dr. Jacob H. Stewart
4/29/61–10/15/62

Adam C. Stites
9/28/61–9/28/64
Gettysburg

Samuel B. Stites
4/29/61–5/3/64
Gettysburg

Alfred Sully
2/3/62–9/26/62
Promoted to Brigadier
General

Edward Taylor
8/28/61–6/30/62
Died of wounds from
Savage Station

Isaac L. Taylor
8/21/61–7/2/63
Killed at Gettysburg

Patrick Henry Taylor
5/26/61–5/5/64
Bull Run & Savage
Station

Minor T. Thomas
4/29/61–10/18/61
Bull Run

Joseph Trevor
4/29/61–7/2/63
Killed at Gettysburg

Edward Tuman
4/29/61–5/5/64

Henry C. Van Vorhes
4/29/61–7/21/62

The First Regiment of Minnesota Volunteer Infantry

Dietrich Vogelsang
4/29/61–11/30/62
Antietam

James Walsh
4/29/61–5/5/64
Antietam & Gettysburg

Lester Webb
5/15/61–10/24/62
Antietam

Abraham Edward Welch
4/29/61–11/5/61
Bull Run

Thomas N. Whetstone
4/29/61–7/25/65

William H. Wikoff
5/23/61–7/2/63
Bull Run, Killed at Gettysburg

Alexander Wilkin
4/29/61–9/18/61
Killed at Tupelo, MS, in command of 2nd MN

George Williams
4/29/61–5/5/64
Bull Run

John Williams
4/29/61–7/14/63
Antietam

George H. Woods
4/29/61–11/28/61

William Worthington
4/29/61–5/5/64

James A. Wright
4/29/61–5/5/64
Bull Run & Gettysburg

Charles Zierenberg
4/29/61–9/13/62
Died of wounds from Vienna

The Second Company of Minnesota Sharpshooters (Co. L)

David Archibald
12/24/61–1/2/65
Cold Harbor

Ozias Baker
1/6/62–9/27/65
Gettysburg

Mahlon Black
1/4/62–1/3/65

Emil A. Berger
1/1/62–11/23/63

James Chamberlain
2/27/62–3/8/63
Antietam

Josiah B. Chaney
12/16/61–10/22/62

Wilber M. Coleman
12/18/61–3/21/66
Antietam & Gettysburg

Gad Merrill Dwelle
12/17/61–2/28/63
Antietam

Fingal Fingalson
1/20/62–4/27/65
Antietam & Hanover
Court House

Andrew Lockrem
1/20/62–2/25/63
Antietam

Franklin Paine
1/21/62–3/19/63

Luman O. Tanner
2/12/62–2/16/63

The First Battalion of Minnesota Volunteer Infantry

Orville Ames
2/24/64–7/15/64
Died of disease

John H. Blase
3/14/65–7/14/65

Ole Christianson
2/29/64–7/14/65

Robert Dieff (Duff)
3/15/65–7/14/65

John McClay
2/27/64–8/14/64
Deep Bottom

Andrew Nelson
2/29/64–7/14/65

Albert C. Poor
3/14/65–6/15/65

Isaiah Roberts
3/25/65–7/14/65

William Stacy
12/25/63–7/14/65

John Swanson
3/24/64–1865

John Thomas Walker
10/5/61–7/14/65
The Wilderness

The formation of the two companies of the First Battalion began on May 5, 1864. Two captains were chosen on the fifth, and the four lieutenants received their commissions on May 12. First Lt. Chesley Tirrell (Co. A) immediately headed to Michigan, where he was married on May 21. While he was on leave, the other five officers headed to Tuttle's Photographic Studio on Third Street in St Paul. There, they posed for this picture. The officers in this previously unidentified photograph are believed to be as follows: standing, *from left to right,* 1st Lt. Charles Hausdorf (Co. B), 2nd Lt. Henry O'Brien (Co. A), and 2nd Lt. Charles Parker (Co. B); seated, *from left to right,* Capt. Ellet Perkins (Co. B) and Capt. James Farmwell (Co. A).

Appendix C

REUNION PHOTOGRAPHS

Twenty-First
Annual Reunion
— OF —
"The Old First"

ORONO POINT,
LAKE MINNETONKA,
JUNE 27th, 1888.

GUESTS OF GEO. A. BRACKETT.

In 1888, George Brackett hosted the annual reunion of the veterans at his home on Brackett's Point in Wayzata. He is the balding man seated second to the left of the drum. Sitting in the center of the second row are, *from left to right,* Christopher Heffelfinger, William Lochren, Governor Alexander Ramsey, William Colvill, Rev. Edward Neill, William Leach, and Dr. John LeBlond.

Pictured here are some of the officers of the First Minnesota Association for 1888 and 1889 and some important people in the history of the regiment. With their rank at the time of the Battle of Gettysburg, they are, *from left to right,* Sgt. Charles Hausdorf (association secretary, 1888), 1st Sgt. Henry Clay Whitney (association secretary, 1889), Capt. Christopher Hefelfinger (active in the association), Judge William Lochren, Governor Alexander Ramsey, Col. William Colvill, Chaplain Edward Neill, 1st Lt. and Adj. William Leach, Surgeon John LeBlond, and Pvt. John Cannon (association treasurer, 1888 and 1889). Seated is George Brackett, the host of the event. Brackett lived in Minnesota but was not in the military during the war. He provided meat to the Union army and, whenever possible, saw to it that the First Minnesota was treated well. For this care they were ever greatful, thought kindly of him, and after the war made him an honorary member of the association.

Veterans at the dedication of the Minnesota monument at Gettysburg in 1897

The 1902 reunion was held at the soldiers' home in Minneapolis. The veterans gathered for a picture at the Round Tower, one of the main buildings from their days at Ft. Snelling. Col. William Colvill can be seen standing fourth from the left of the flag. The two tall veterans to the right of the flag are Alonzo Pickle, *left,* and Harrison Lyons, *right*.

On July 2, 1913, the veterans met again to celebrate the fiftieth anniversary of the Battle of Gettysburg.

Behind the veterans is the field over which the regiment charged fifty years earlier. The woods, which were not there then, are the site of Plum Run, where the enemy was met. The photographer had asked all the veterans who had participated in the charge to gather at the fence. Many did not hear the instructions, however, and some who should have gotten into the photo did not and some who were not in the charge joined thinking it was another opportunity to have their picture taken. In the back row are, *from left to right,* Alonzo Pickle, Chester Durfee, Charles Merritt, George Mortimer, and Stephen Martin. In the middle row are, *from left to right,* Edmund Soper, John Rhorer, Henry Burgetorf, John French, James Walsh, Charles Berry, Christopher Heffelfinger, Sam Smith, Archibald Curtis, an unidentified veteran, Charles Benson, and Franklin Sheeks. In the front row are, *from left to right,* Jonas Davis, an unidentified veteran, Peter Hall, Samuel Lilly, George Kline, and Enos Grow.

One of the last reunions was held in 1922 in St. Paul at the home of Edward Bassett's son, L. B. Bassett. Previously unidentified, it is believed that the veterans are as follows: back row, *from left to right*, Turner Pribble, Charles Berry, Rufus Jefferson, Harrison Lyons, Dan Sullivan, Cyrus Eddy, Tom Dwelle, Sam Smith, Daniel Drayne, David Archibald, and an unidentified veteran; front row, *from left to right*, James Walsh, John Mannings, John Fleetham, Richard Freer, Chester Durfee, Adam Marty, Alvin Taunt, Isaac Hoblitt, Nathaniel Drew, John Goff, Newton Brown, George Mortimer, and Charles Muller.

First Sgt. James Wright of Company F was the last surviving member of the First Minnesota. He died at his home in Beverly, Massachusetts, on August 25, 1936. He had lived a full life of ninety-five years, eight months, and twenty-eight days. With the encouragement of his comrades from Company F, Wright put together his memories of their years of service. Wright's wonderful manuscript, full of detail about the lives of these men, lay in the archives of the Minnesota Historical Society until it was superbly brought to life by Steven Keillor and published in 2001 as *No More Gallant a Deed*.

Appendix D

REGIMENTAL AND BATTALION ROSTER

Originally published in 1890 in the book *Minnesota in the Civil and Indian Wars,* on the following pages are the rosters for the First Regiment of Minnesota Volunteer Infantry (1861–64), the Second Company of Minnesota Sharpshooters (1861–64), and the First Battalion of Minnesota Infantry (1864–65).

ROSTER OF FIELD AND STAFF OFFICERS OF THE FIRST REGIMENT.

NAMES.	AGE.	MUSTERED IN.	MUSTERED OUT.	REMARKS.
Colonels —				
Willis A. Gorman	46	Apl. 29, '61	Oct. 1, '61	Brig. Gen. 1st Brig., 2d Div., 2d Corps.
Napoleon J. T. Dana	39	Oct. 2, '61	Feb. 3, '62	Brig. Gen. 3d Brig., 2d Div., 2d Corps; wounded at Antietam.
Alfred Sully	......	Feb. 3, '62	Sept. 26, '62	Brig. Gen. 1st Brig., 2d Div., 2d Corps, Brevet Maj. Gen., Brevet Brig. Gen. U. S. A
George N. Morgan	......	Sept. 26, '62	May 5, '63	Capt. Co. E, Maj., Lieut. Col.; resigned; Brevet Brig. Gen.
William Colvill	......	May 6, '63	May 4, '64	Capt. Co. F, Maj., Lt. Col.; wnd. Glendale and Gettysburg; Bvt. Brig. Gen.
Lieutenant Colonels —				
Stephen Miller	45	Apl. 29, '61	Sept. 16, '62	Col. 7th Minn. Vols., Brig. Gen., Gov. of Minnesota.
Charles Powell Adams	......	Sept. 26, '62	May 4, '64	Capt. Co. H, Maj.; wnd. Bull Run, Malvern, Antietam, Gettysburg; Brevet Brig. Gen.
Majors —				
William H. Dike	47	Apl. 29, '61	Oct. 22, '61	Resigned.
Mark W. Downie	25	May 6, '63	May 4, '64	Q. M., 1st Lt. and Capt. Co. B; wnd. Gettysb'g; Lt. Col. 1st Batt.
Adjutants —				
William B. Leach	27	Apl. 29, '61	Feb. 23, '62	1st Lt. Co. H, Capt. and A. A. G. Dana's Brigade.
John N. Chase	26	Oct. 22, '61	....	1st Serg. and 1st Lieut. Co. E, Capt. Co. H.
Josias R. King	29	July 10, '62	....	1st Serg., 2d and 1st Lieut. Co. A, Capt.Co.G.; wnd.Savage Station.
John Peller	31	Jan. 14, '63	May 4, '64	Sergt. Major, 2d Lieut. Co. A; 1st Lieut.; wnd. Gettysburg.
Quartermasters —				
George H. Woods	......	Apl. 29, '61	Aug. 13, '61	Pro. Capt. and C. S.U.S.A.,Lt.Col.and Chf. C.S.Sheridan's Corps.
Mark A. Hoyt	......	Jan. 1, '62	....	Resigned '62.
Francis Baasen	......	July 10, '62	May 4, '64	
Surgeons —				
Jacob H. Stewart	......	Apl. 29, '61	....	Captured at Bull Run; Exam. Surg. at St. Paul.
William H. Morton	......	Feb. 1, '62	June 23, '63	Med. Director 2d Div., 2d Corps; resigned from disability.
John B. Le Blond	......	......	May 4, '64	Asst. Surg., Surg. 1st Battalion.
Assistant Surgeons —				
Chas. W. Le Boutillier	34	Apl. 29, '61	....	Captured at Bull Run; Surg. 9th Minn. Volunteers.
Daniel W. Hand	......	July 23, '61	....	Brigade Surgeon, charge of general hospitals.
Edmund J. Pugsley	......	Aug. 29, '63	Aug. 15, '63	Cashiered.
Peter Gabrielson	......	Feb. 17, '64	May 4, '64	
Chaplains —				
Edward D. Neill	37	Apl. 29, '61	July 13, '62	Resigned; private secretary to Pres. Lincoln and Johnson.
F. A. Conwell	48	Oct. 15, '62	May 4, '64	
Sergeant Majors —				
C. Edward Davis	......	Apl. 29, '61	....	2d Lieut. Co. I, 1st Lieut. Co. A; Capt. Co. E.
Edward S. Past	......	Apl. 29, '61	....	Wounded at Antietam; discharged for disability.
David A. Coffin	......	Apl. 29, '61	....	1st Lieut. Co. A Oct. 7, '63.
Albert S. Davis	......	Apl. 29, '61	....	1st Lieut. Co. A Mch. 4, '64.
John W. Pride	......	Apl. 29, '61	May 4, '64	Re-enlisted in 1st Battalion.
Quartermaster Sergeants —				
William Smith	......	Apl. 29, '61	Nov. 17, '61	Discharged.
Aaron Greenwald	......	Apl. 29, '61	....	Resigned and transferred to Co. C; killed at Gettysburg.
T. A. Wood	......	Apl. 29, '61	May 4, '64	Company F.
Commissary Sergeants —				
J. Mahoney	......	Apl. 29, '61	Feb. '63	Discharged.
Mathew M. Standish	......	Apl. 29, '61	....	Resigned and transferred to Co. D May 8, '63.
Jacob Marty	......	Apl. 29, '61	....	Promoted 1st Lieut. Oct. 3, '63.
Frank Dickinson	......	Apl. 29, '61	May 4, '64	Corp. Co. G.
Hospital Stewards —				
James Kirkman	......	Apl. 29, '61	....	
G. F. Marble	......	Apl. 29, '61	....	Company C.
C. A. Brooks	22	June, '61	June 12, '63	Appointed Hospital Steward U. S. A.
Chas. H. Spear	......	Apl. 29, '61	May 4, 64	Co. L, or 2d Co. Sharpshooters.
Principal Musicians —				
Henry O. Fifield	......	Aug. 16, '63	....	Company C.
Ezra D. Haskins	......	Aug. 16, '63	....	Company G.

4

ROSTER OF COMPANY A.

Names.	Age.	Mustered In.	Mustered Out.	Remarks.
OFFICERS.				
Captains—				
Alexander Wilkin	29	Apl. 29, '61	May 5, '64	Pro. Major 2d Minn. Sept. 18, '61.
Henry C. Coates	28	Sept. 18, '61	May 5, '64	1st Lieut.; commanded regiment 3 months after Gettysburg.
First Lieutenants—				
Charles Zierenberg	28	Sept. 18, '61	May 5, '64	2d Lieut.; died Sept. 13, '62, of wounds at Vienna, Va.
Josias R. King	29	Sept. 14, '62	......	1st Serg., 2d Lieut., Capt. Co. G; on Gen. Sully's staff; wd. S. Sta.
C. Edward Davis	......	Oct. 7, '62	......	Serg. Major, 2d Lieut. Co. I, Capt. Co. E.
David A. Coflin	28	Oct. 7, '63	......	Corp. Co. I, Serg. Major; transferred to Co. K.
Albert S. Davis	......	Mch. 4, '64	Mch. 5, '64	Priv. Co. I, Corp. Co. B, Serg. Major; wounded at Bull Run.
Second Lieutenants—				
John Peller	31	July 19, '62	......	Serg., Serg. Major, Adjutant; wounded at Gettysburg.
Joseph H. Spencer	29	......	......	Transferred to Co. F Oct., '62.
August Kruger	29	......	......	Serg.; drowned Aug. 20, '63, at Alexandria, Va.
ENLISTED MEN.				
Adams, Hiram	24	Apl. 29, '61	......	Killed June 29, '62, at Savage Station.
Adams, Lucius A	27	Apl. 29, '61	......	Wnd. at Savage Station; absent sick on discharge of regiment.
Agnew, Edward C	34	Apl. 29, '61	May 5, '64	Musician.
Alpers, John H. A	24	May 22, '61	......	Re-enlisted 1st Battalion; wounded at Antietam.
Becher, William	26	Apl. 29, '61	Mch. 12, '63	Discharged for disability; wounded at Bull Run.
Biddle, Abel	25	Apl. 29, '61	......	Discharged for disability.
Biesi, John	32	Apl. 29, '61	......	Transferred to V. R. C. Nov. 16, '63.
Brown, Frederick A	37	Apl. 29, '61	......	Wounded at Bull Run.
Brandt, Clark	25	Apl. 29, '61	......	Died July 14, '63, of wounds at Gettysburg.
Canfield, Lucien F	21	May 21, '61	......	Transferred to U. S. Cavalry Oct. 23, '62.
Clark, George B	20	May 17, '61	......	Corp.; wounded at Bristow; re-enlisted in 1st Battalion.
Clark, Charles F	24	May 28, '61	......	Wounded at Bull Run.
Crawley, Timothy	26	Apl. 29, '61	......	Corp.; wounded at Antietam; killed at Gettysburg.
Dehn, John	25	Apl. 29, '61	......	Corp.; discharged for wounds at Gettysburg.
Devlin, Mike	21	Sept. 27, '61	......	Wounded at Gettysburg; re-enlisted 1st Battalion.
Dooley, Wm. H. H	30	Apl. 29, '61	......	Serg.; wounded at Bull Run.
Doran, Nelson	25	Apl. 29, '61	......	Re-enlisted in 1st Minn. Battalion.
Drake, Charles S	21	Apl. 29, '61	......	Wounded at Gettysburg.
Drescher, Ernest	26	May 22, '61	......	Musician; killed at Bull Run.
Edler, Julius	19	Apl. 29, '61	......	Corp.; killed at Gettysburg.
Eichler, Charles	38	Apl. 29, '61	Feb. '3, '63	Discharged for disability.
Farwell, James C	28	May 17, '61	......	Re-enlisted; Capt. Co. A 1st Battalion.
Farquhar, Daniel W	29	Apl. 29, '61	May 4, '64	Wounded at Antietam and Gettysburg.
Farquhar, John	30	Oct. 22, '62	......	Wounded at Antietam and Gettysburg; transferred to 1st Batt.
Fegar, Jacob	31	Apl. 29, '61	May 4, '64	
Foss, Jay B	21	Sept. 3, '61	May 10, '61	Discharged for disability.
Freer, Richard W	20	Apl. 29, '61	......	Corp.; transferred to U. S. Cav. Oct. 23, '62.
Fuller, Melville	21	Apl. 29, '61	May 5, '64	
Gallman, John J	39	Apl. 29, '61	May 3, '64	
Gibbs, Gates	22	Apl. 29, '61	......	Wagoner; re-enlisted in 1st Battalion.
Geiser, Frederick	31	Sept. 3, '62	......	Transferred to 1st Battalion.
Glave, Frederick	23	May 22, '61	......	Died July 10, '63, of wounds received at Gettysburg.
Guntzer, Nicholaus	26	Apl. 29, '61	......	Wounded at Gettysburg; absent on discharge of regiment.
Halsted, John T	44	Apl. 29, '61	Sept. 1, '62	Discharged for disability from wounds at Bull Run.
Hauser, John	30	May 15, '61	......	Killed at Gettysburg.
Hedapp, George	32	Apl. 29, '61	May 3, '64	
Hines, Henry C	23	July 20, '61	......	Regiment postmaster, Aug. 16, '61.
Hoff, Edward C	29	Apl. 29, '61	......	Died Oct. 14, '62, of wounds near Vienna, Va.
Hausdorf, Charles F	20	Apl. 29, '61	......	Corp., Serg., 1st Serg., Lieut. Col. 1st Batt.; wnd. at Gettysburg.
Irvine, Javan B	30	Sept. 3, '61	......	1st Lieut. in 13th U. S. Infantry, Dec. 15, '61.
Jeniesch, William	24	May 15, '61	May 3, '64	
Keyes, James N	......	May 11, '62	......	Corp.; killed at Gettysburg.
Kiefer, Louis	29	May 18, '61	......	Discharged for wounds at Savage Station, '62.
King, Charles	19	Apl. 29, '61	Feb. 4, '62	Discharged per order.
Klingel, Jacob	34	Apl. 29, '61	......	Transferred to U. S. Cav. Oct. 23, '62.
Kraemer William	27	Apl. 29, '61	Feb. 4, '62	Corp.; discharged per order.
Kratka, Chas. A	19	May 17, '61	......	Transferred to U. S. Cav. Oct. 23, '62; killed at Gettysburg.
Latta, Simon E	23	May 17, '61	May 3, '64	
Levering, Andrew	33	May 17, '61	......	2d Lieut. Co. E; died March 27, '63.
Lemmer, Peter	......	Feb. 24, '64	......	Transferred to 1st Battalion.
Lichtenberg, August	......	Feb. 20, '64	......	Transferred to 1st Battalion.
Loomis, Chas. C	19	Apl. 29, '61	......	Killed at Gettysburg.
Lyons, Stephen	22	Apl. 29, '61	May 3, '64	Corp. and Serg.; wounded at Gettysburg.
Lyons, Harrison	19	May 25 '61	......	Wounded at Gettysburg; absent sick on discharge of regiment.
Maloy, James	23	Apl. 29, '61	May 3, '64	Corp.; wounded at Bull Run.
Marks, Peter	29	Apl. 29, '61	......	Corp.; died July 8, '63, from wounds at Gettysburg.
Matheis, Nicholas	20	May 22, '61	May 3, '64	Wounded at Antietam.
Marshall, John J	19	Apl. 29, '61	......	Transferred to Inv. Corps Nov., 1863.
Marshall, James	29	Feb. 11, '62	......	Transferred to 1st Battalion.
Magnussen, Engel A	30	Sept. 3, '61	Aug. 20, '62	Discharged for disability.
McEwen, John	21	Apl. 29, 61	......	Corp., Sergt.; killed at Antietam.
McWilliam, David	25	Apl. 29, '61	......	Re-enlisted in 1st Battalion.
McLean, Maxwell A	19	May 27, '61	Aug. 20, '62	Wounded at Antietam.
Miller, Wm. F	25	May 17, '61	......	Killed at Gettysburg.
Mowry, Rascellas S	20	May 25, '61	May 3, '64	Wounded at Gettysburg.
Morrison, John T	23	Apl. 29, '61	Mch. 12, '62	Corp.; discharged for disability.
Mockwitz, Charles	23	Apl. 29, '61	Jan. 29, '62	Discharged for disability.
Muller, Charles	29	Apl. 29, '61	May 3, '64	Wounded at Gettysburg.
Nelson, Nels E	28	May 17, '61	Nov. 6, '62	Serg.; discharged for disability.
Nelson, Ole	25	Apl. 29, '61	......	Died Sept. 8, '62, at Fort Monroe.
Nickell, Henry	22	Apl. 29, '61	......	Killed at Gettysburg.
Nixon, William	18	Apl. 29, '61	May 3, '64	
Olson, Andrew	35	Apl. 29, '61	Feb. 3, '63	Discharged for disability.

ROSTER OF COMPANY A—*Continued.*

Names.	Age.	Mustered In.	Mustered Out.	Remarks.
Palmer, Eli J	42	Apl. 29, '61	May 3, '64	
Parker, Geo. H	22	Apl. 29, '61	......	Transferred to 3d U. S. Cav., 1862.
Payher, Frank	......	Feb. 27, '64	......	Transferred to 1st Battalion.
Pfeffer, George	24	May 21, '61	Feb. 15, '63	Wounded at Bull Run; discharged for disability.
Pitkin, Samuel J	23	May 18, '61	May 3, '64	Bayonet wound at Bristow.
Rathmann, Hans	36	May 27, '61	Jan. 24, '64	Wounded; prisoner at Bull Run; discharged for disability.
Rohring, John	19	May 22, '61	......	Killed near Warrenton, Va.
Sanders, Benjamin F	29	May 22, '61	May 3, '64	
Sattler, Louis	21	May 22, '61	......	Transferred to U. S. Light Artillery Oct. 27, '62.
Schooley, David	35	May 21, '61	......	Wounded at Bull Run.
Schmucker, Joseph	27	Apl. 29, '61	......	Wounded at Gettysburg.
Schmidter, William	22	Apl. 29, '61	May 3, '64	
Simonson, Hans M	21	May 26, '61	......	Died of wounds at Gettysburg.
Smoot, George W	21	Apl. 29, '61	Aug. 1, '61	Discharged per order.
Sonderman, John G	31	Apl. 29, '61	May 3, '64	Corporal.
Sproat, Edgar L	28	Apl. 29, '61	July 31, '63	Pro. 1st Lieut. and Q. M. 32d N. Y.
Stevens, Robert	28	Apl. 29, '61	......	Wounded at Bull Run; arm amputated.
Stoll, Andrew	32	Apl. 29, '61	Sept. 9, '62	Discharged for disability.
Stoll, Jacob	30	Apl. 29, '61	Feb 27, '63	Discharged for disability.
Stansbury, Howard	22	Apl. 29, '61	June, '61	Color Sergt.; appointed 2d Lieut. in U. S. Army.
Steffes, Matthias	27	Apl. 29, '61	......	Corp., Serg.; wounded at Antietam.
Steen, Charles	23	Apl. 29, '61	......	Serg., 1st Serg.; lost leg at Gettysburg.
Streit, Nicholas	29	May 15, '61	Feb. 3, '63	Discharged for disability.
Theissen, Matthias	27	Apl. 29, '61	May 3, '64	
Thiem, Joseph	30	May 27, '61	May 3, '64	Wounded at Gettysburg.
Tinker, Herbert E	25	May 23, '61	......	Discharged for disability.
Van Woert, Wm. T	23	May 21, '61	Mch. 3, '63	Discharged for disability.
Vogelsang, Deitrich	31	Apl. 29, '61	......	Wounded at Antietam; leg amputated; discharged.
Wagner, Warren	21	May 27, '61	......	Killed at Gettysburg.
Weld, Charles P	37	Apl. 29, '61	May 3, '64	Corporal.
Wells, George A	40	May 18, '61	......	Died Oct., '62.
Wentworth, Hiram	32	Aug. 21, '61	Mch. 3, '62	Discharged for disability.
Wilson, John	21	Sept. 25, '61	......	Killed at Gettysburg.
Wright, Henry C	29	May 17, '61	......	Serg.; wounded at Bull Run; killed at Gettysburg.

ROSTER OF COMPANY B.

Names.	Age.	Mustered In.	Mustered Out.	Remarks.
OFFICERS.				
Captains—				
Carlisle A. Bromley	31	Apl. 29, '61	......	Resigned July 15, '62.
Mark W. Downie	25	July 16, '61	......	1st Lieut.; pro. Maj. May 6, '63; wnd. Bull Run and Gettysburg.
Thomas Sinclair	......	May 7, '63	May 5, '64	Serg., 2d and 1st Lieut.; wnd. Bull Run, Gettysburg and Bristow.
First Lieutenants—				
Minor T. Thomas	30	......	......	2d Lieut.; wnd. at Bull Run; pro. Lieut. Col. 4th Minn. Oct. 18, '61.
Louis Muller	26	Nov. 18, '61	......	Serg., 1st Serg., 2d Lieut.; pro. Capt. Co. E Sept. 17, '62; wnd. at Bull Run; killed at Gettysburg.
William M. May	30	Sept. 10, '63	May 5, '64	Serg., 1st Serg., 2d Lieut.; wounded at Gettysburg.
ENLISTED MEN.				
Allen, Lorenzo D	30	May 20, '61	......	Wagoner.
Anderson, John	27	Apl. 29, '61	May 5, '64	
Arnold, George	23	Apl. 29, '61	May 5, '64	Wounded at Gettysburg.
Aucker, Wm. H	21	Feb. 28, '62	......	Wounded at Gettysburg; transferred to 1st Battalion.
Bates, Wm. F	......	......	......	Killed at Gettysburg.
Bernds, Frederick L	28	Apl. 29, '61	May 5, '64	Wounded at Bristow.
Binns, Zebulon E	33	Apl. 29, '61	Jan. 17, '62	Serg.; wounded at Bull Run; discharged for disability.
Blanchard, Rufus G	26	Apl. 29, '61	May 5, '64	Corp.; wounded at Gettysburg.
Boswell, Daniel C	25	Apl. 29, '61	......	Promoted Capt. 9th N. H. Vols. Aug. 26, '62.
Brown, Thomas	25	Apl. 29, '61	Aug. 4, '62	Discharged for disability.
Bloomer, Samuel	22	Apl. 29, '61	Dec. 6, '62	Corp., Color Serg.; wnd. at Bull Run, Antietam; dis.; loss of leg.
Butler, Daniel	......	......	......	
Caplazi, Albert	31	Apl. 29, '61	May 5, '64	Wounded at Gettysburg.
Cathoman, Louis	33	May 20, '61	......	Wounded at Bull Run.
Carriegiet Bartholomew	......	......	......	Transferred from Co. I; wounded at Gettysburg.
Capron, Alonzo A	28	Apl. 29, '61	......	Serg.; wounded at Bull Run.
Clearey, James	18	Apl. 29, '61	May 5, '64	
Connolly, Andrew	18	May 17, '61	May 5, '64	Musician.
Cornman, Oscar L	20	Apl. 29, '61	......	Corp.; killed at Antietam.
Crome, Frederick	24	May 20, '61	May 5, '64	Corp. and Serg.; wounded at Gettysburg.
Davis, Albert S	......	......	......	Serg., Serg. Maj., 1st Lieut. Co. A.
Darms, John M	44	Apl. 29, '61	Feb. 8, '63	Wounded at Fredericksburg; discharged for disability.
Darms, John N	19	Apl. 29, '61	May 5, '64	
Densmore, John D	20	May 22, '61	......	Corp., Serg.; wounded at Gettysburg.
Dittmer, August	26	Apl. 29, '61	Aug. 9, '61	Discharged per order.
Dotts, Charles J	22	Apl. 29, '61	May 5, '64	Corporal.
Durich, William	37	Apl. 29, '61	Oct. 13, '61	Discharged per order.
Ehrhardt, Morritz	18	Apl. 29, '61	......	Wounded at Gettysburg.
Eppenberger, Adam	40	Apl. 29, '61	Aug., '62	Discharged for disability.
Everson, Peter	24	May 20, '61	......	Wounded at Gettysburg.
Fallihee, Patrick	30	Apl. 29, '61	May 5, '64	Corporal.

Roster of Company B—*Continued.*

Names.	Age.	Mustered In.	Mustered Out.	Remarks.
Foreman, Noah	25	Apl. 29, '61	Jan. 8, '62	Discharged for disability.
French, Henry C.	20	Apl. 29, '61	Nov. 19, '61	Discharged for disability.
Goundry, John E.	24	Apl. 29, '61		Killed at Antietam.
Goff, John S.	18	Apl. 29, '61	May 5, '64	Wounded at Savage Station.
Gove, Charles H.	22	Apl. 29, '61		Died of wounds received at Gettysburg.
Goodman, Henry	28	May 20, '61	May 5, '64	
Grandstrand, Gustave A.	28	Apl. 29, '61	June 9, '62	Wounded at Bull Run; discharged for disability.
Graf, Emil	22	Apl. 29, '61	Jan. 9, '62	Wounded by accident.
Grusemann, Jacob	28	May 20, '61	Feb. 9, '63	Discharged for disability.
Hall, Peter	23	Apl. 29, '61	May 5, '64	
Hamann, Charles	22	Apl. 29, '61	May 5, '64	Wounded at Gettysburg.
Harvey, James	21	Apl. 29, '61	July, '62	Discharged for disability.
Henry, Martin J.	26	Apl. 29, '61	May 5, '64	Wounded at Gettysburg.
Herrin, Edwin E.	30	Apl. 29, '61	Jan. 29, '63	Discharged for disability.
Hebenstreit, Nicholas	25	Apl. 29, '61		Transferred to Inv. Corps Nov. 18, '63.
Hooker, George	22	Apl. 29, '61	May 5, '64	
Hospes, Adolphus C.	20	May 20, '61	May 5, '64	Corp.; captured at Antietam.
Johnson, Swen	24	Apl. 29, '61	Dec. 14, '62	Wounded at Antietam; discharged for disability.
Johnson, David	22	Apl. 29, '61	Sept. 29, '63	Wounded at Gettysburg; discharged.
Johnson, Samuel	24	Apl. 29, '61	Nov. 17, '61	Discharged for disability.
Johnson, Andrew	22	June 4, '61	Apl. 30, '63	Transferred from Co. I; discharged for disability.
Kelly, William	18	June 4, '61	May 5, '64	
Klasi, Thomas	26	June 4, '61	Sept. 26, '62	Discharged for disability.
Koenig, Augustus	29	May 20, '61		Wounded at Bull Run; killed July 2, '63, at Gettysburg.
Krone, Henry W.	37	Apl. 29, '61		Wounded and captured at Bull Run.
Kunzelman, John	28	May 20, '61	Aug., '62	Discharged for disability.
Lockwood, Charles M.	19	Apl. 29, '61		Corp., Serg., 2d Lieut. 24th Wis. Vols., Aug. 28, '62.
Lord, David	26	Apl. 29, '61	May 5, '64	Corp., Serg. and 1st Serg.; wounded at Gettysburg.
Marty, Jacob	28	Apl. 29, '61		Com. Serg., 1st Lieut. Co. E.
May, John S.	22	Apl. 29, '61	May 5, '64	Corp.; re-enlisted 1st Battalion.
Marty, Adam	24	Apl. 29, '61	May 5, '64	Corp.; wounded at Gettysburg.
Marty, Fridolin	18	May 20, '61		Wounded at Gettysburg.
McLaughlin, Almond C.	21	May 23, '61	Feb. 16, '63	Discharged for disability.
McIntyre, Harlow	30	May 23, '61	Jan. 7, '63	Discharged for disability.
McKusick, Freeman L.	19	May 20, '61	May 5, '64	
McNeill, Geo. C.	30	Apl. 29, '61	Apl. 30, '63	Discharged for disability.
Meyers, Wm. J.	28	Apl. 29, '61		Transferred to Signal Corps August, '61.
Mead, Frank J.			Dec., '62	Transferred from Co. H; discharged for disability.
Morgan, Wm. A.	18	Apl. 29, '61	May 5, '64	Captured at Antietam.
Nelson, Chas. L.	26	May 20, '61	Aug. 2, '61	Discharged per order.
Nickerson, Samuel B.	30	Apl. 29, '61		Serg.; killed at Gettysburg.
Nystedt, Erick	30	Apl. 29, '61	May 5, '64	Wounded at Gettysburg.
Olson, Hocken	35	Apl. 29, '61	Nov. 8, '61	Discharged for disability.
Older, Joseph	19	Apl. 29, '61		Died of disease April 13, '62.
Oliver, George A.	25	Apl. 29, '61	May 5, '64	Serg. and 1st Serg.; wounded at Antietam and Gettysburg.
Peterson, Andrew	25	Apl. 29, '61	Nov. 24, '61	Discharged for disability.
Pierson, Wm. S.	20	Apl. 29, '61		Died of wounds at Bull Run while prisoner.
Pooler, Albert	21	Feb. 21, '62	Feb. 25, '64	Wounded at Gettysburg; discharged for disability.
Quist, Andrew P.	19	Apl. 29, '61		Wounded at Antietam and Gettysburg.
Ricketts, Charles F.	20	May 20, '61	Aug. 14, '62	Wounded at Bull Run; arm amputated.
Reichard, Adolph L.	27	Apl. 29, '61	Aug. 21, '61	Corp.; wounded at Bull Run; 2d Lieut. 98th Penn. Vols.
Robinson, Ebenezer B.	30	Apl. 29, '61		Transferred to Inv. Corps for wounds at Fredericksburg.
Rowley, Charles F.	39	May 20, '61		Died Dec. 8, '62, at Washington, D. C.
Sawtell, John M.	22	May 23, '61		Transferred to U. S. Light Artillery July 16, '62.
Schoenbeck, John P.	35	Apl. 29, '61		Wounded at Antietam and Gettysburg.
Schroeder, Wm. F.	22	Apl. 29, '61	Jan. 7, '63	Discharged for disability.
Seaman, Henry S.	22	Apl. 29, '61		Wounded at Savage Station.
Shepard, Myron	29	July 21, '61		Serg., 2d Lieut. Co. H, and 1st Lieut. Co. F and Co. H.
Sebers, Albert	18	Mch. 4, '62		Wounded at Gettysburg; transferred to 1st Battalion.
Smith, Ralph W.	21	Apl. 29, '61	Dec. 6, '62	Corp.; discharged for disability.
Snow, Lafayette W.	30	Apl. 29, '61		Re-enlisted in 1st Minn. Battalion.
Stevens, John B.	25	Apl. 29, '61	May 5, '64	Corp., Serg.; wounded at Gettysburg.
Steinacker, Frederick	30	Apl. 29, '61	Jan. 14, '63	Discharged per order.
Stevens, Edward A.	23	Apl. 29, '61	Jan. 3, '63	Wounded at Bull Run; discharged per order.
Staples Chas. A.	20	May 23, '61		Deserted Dec. 10, '61, from Camp Stone.
Stirnemann, Frederick	27	Apl. 29, '61	Aug. 7, '61	Musician; discharged for disability.
Tanner, Chas. G.	23	Apl. 29, '61	Sept. 26, '62	Wounded and captured at Bull Run; discharged for disability.
Tanner, Joseph A.	21	May 23, '61		Wounded at Gettysburg.
Thompson, Ole	31	Apl. 29, '61		Wounded at Bull Run; died of wounds received at Gettysburg.
Van Vorhes, Henry A.	22	Apl. 29, '61	Aug. 14, '62	Corp.; discharged for disability.
Van Kuster, Oscar	21	Apl. 29, '61	Dec. 19, '61	Discharged for disability.
Valentine, Chas.	31	May 23, '61	Sept. 8, '62	Discharged for wound at Savage Station.
Walsh, Joseph	23	Apl. 29, '61		Wounded at Haymarket; re-enlisted in 1st Battalion.
Wells, Edwin	19	Apl. 29, '61		Corp.; wounded at Gettysburg.

Roster of Company C.

Names.	Age.	Mustered In.	Mustered Out.	Remarks.
OFFICERS.				
Captains—				
William H. Acker	26	Apl. 29, '61		Wnd. at Bull Run; Capt. 16th U.S. Inf., Aug. 8, '61; killed Shiloh.
Wilson B. Farrell	31	Aug. 8, '61		1st Lieut.; killed at Gettysburg.
Jasper N. Searles	20	Oct. 7, '63	May 4, '64	Pro. from 1st Lieut. Co. K.
First Lieutenants—				
Samuel T. Raguet	23	Aug. 8, '61		2d Lieut.; wounded at Bull Run; transferred to Co. I.
Wilbur F. Duffy	23	Jan. 19, '62		1st Serg., Capt. Co. I, March 26, '63.
William Harmon	25	Mch. 26, '63	May 4, '64	2d Lieut. Co. D; wounded at Gettysburg.
Second Lieutenants—				
Wm. C. Larned	44	Aug. 8, '61		Corp.; wnd. at Bull Run; transferred Dec., '62, to Signal Corps.
Chas. H. Mason	25			Transferred from Co. D; 1st Lieut.; died Aug. 18, '63, of wounds at Gettysburg.
Andrew Levering				Died Dec. 16, '63, at Sioux City, Ia.
ENLISTED MEN.				
Abell, John	21	Jan. 20, '62		Transferred to 1st Battalion.
Arnsdorf, Henry	24	Apl. 29, '61		Killed June 1, '62, on picket at Fair Oaks.
Atherton, Minor	19	Apl. 29, '61		Wounded at Gettysburg; transferred to Inv. Corps Dec. 13, '63.
Barnes, Andrew J.	22	May 21, '61	May 5, '64	
Barton, Wm. H.	26	Sept. 11, '61	Mch. 27, '63	Discharged for disability.
Baldwin, Jerome	18	Mch. 4, '64		Transferred to 1st Battalion.
Blanquest, Charles	38	Apl. 29, '61		Absent as paroled prisoner on discharge of regiment.
Bleaser, Michael	34	May 23, '61	Oct. 6, '62	Discharged for disability.
Blanchard, Chas. C.	22	Nov. 25, '61		Transferred to 1st Battalion.
Boyce, Henry W.	25	May 17, '61	May 5, '64	Corporal.
Brisette, Edmund	44	May 21, '61	Feb. 7, '63	Wounded at Bull Run; discharged for disability.
Brack, Wm. A.	20	May 17, '61	May 5, '64	Serg.; wounded at Savage Station.
Brown, Henry J. W.	33	Sept. 30, '61		Wounded at Savage Station; transferred to 1st Battalion.
Buck, Geo. W.	21	Apl. 29, '61		Wnd. Bull Run and Antietam; absent (prisoner) on dis. of regt.
Burt, Geo.	32	May 26, '61		Wounded Bull Run; re-enlisted Jan. 1, '64; died March 24, '64.
Carpenter, Robert A.	41	May 23, '61	May 5, '64	
Chamberlain, Wesley	21	Apl. 29, '61		Wounded at Antietam; transferred to U. S. Cav. Oct. 24, '62.
Clark, Joseph M.	41	Apl. 29, '61		Transferred to Inv. Corps Sept. 1, '63.
Clark, Chas. I.	30	June 22, '61		Wounded at Bull Run; transferred to 1st Battalion.
Clancy, Daniel	27	Oct. 2, '61		Wounded at Gettysburg; transferred to 1st Battalion.
Coombs, Charles C.	19	May 22, '61		Wounded at Bull Run; transferred to Inv. Corps Oct. 31, '62.
Coombs, William	29	Dec. 30, '61		Re-enlisted; transferred to 1st Battalion.
Coles, John W.	25	Nov. 25, '61		Corp., Serg.; wounded at Antietam.
Collins, Jeremiah	28	Dec. 9, '61		Re-enlisted; transferred to 1st Battalion.
Cunningham, Wm. C.	24	Apl. 29, '61		Wounded at Bull Run, supposed to be mortal.
Demarest, David B.	27	Apl. 29, '61		Serg. and 1st Serg., 2d Lieut. Co. E; wounded at Gettysburg.
Dorathy, Charles H.	22	May 21, '61	May 5, '64	Wounded at Bull Run.
Dubois, Garrett N.	24	Apl. 29, '61	Aug. 13, '61	Discharged for disability.
Eastman, Rufus M.	28	Dec. 16, '61		Missing at Savage Station.
Echoldt, August T.	18	Oct. 2, '61		Wnd. Savage Station; transf. U.S. Cavalry Oct., '62.
Ellsworth, John	20	May 22, '61		Wnd. Savage Station; died Aug. '63 of wnds. at Gettysburg.
Ellingson, Henry	19	Apl. 29, '61	May 5, '64	
Fifield, Henry O.	21	May 20, '61		Musician, Drum Major.
Finical, Benjamin F.	25	May 23, '61	May 5, '64	Wounded at Savage Station.
Finical, Chas. A.	18	Dec. 23, '61		Transferred to U. S. Cavalry Oct. 24, '62.
Foster, Edward H.	18		Nov. 6, '61	Discharged for pro. in 4th Minn. Infantry.
Gard, Samuel D.	23	May 23, '61	Feb. 8, '62	Discharged for disability.
George, Jacob	29	June 1, '61	May 5, '64	Wounded at Bull Run; Corp.; transferred to 1st Battalion.
Gilman, James B.	29	Apl. 29, '61	May 5, '64	Corp.; wounded at Bull Run.
Ghostly, Henry	19	Dec. 25, '61		Corp.; wounded at Bristow; transf. to 1st Battalion.
Gay, Gustave	33	Apl. 29, '61	Aug. 6, '61	Discharged for disability.
Groat, James W.	37	May 23, '61		Transferred to U. S. Cavalry Oct. 24, '62.
Greenwald, Aaron	28	Apl. 29, '61		Corp., Q. M. Serg.; killed at Gettysburg.
Hastie, James	40	Apl. 29, '61	May 5, '64	Wounded at Bull Run.
Haskell, John S.	29	Apl. 29, '61		Wounded at Bull Run, supposed mortally.
Haskell, Chas. W.	21	Apl. 29, '61		Wounded at Glendale; died in hospital Mch. 8, '63.
Harvey, Julius	19	Nov. 11, '62		Transferred to 1st Battalion.
Hamilton, Helon	27	Sept. 14, '61		Died Sept. 1, '62, Point Lookout, Md.
Hayford, Faxon	19	Dec. 16, '61		Re-enlisted; transferred to 1st Battalion.
Henderson, Thos. D.	40			Transferred to 1st Battalion.
Howard, Henry H.	23	Apl. 29, '61		Corp., Serg., 1st Serg.; died of wounds at Gettysburg.
Hough, Chas. H.	24	Apl. 29, '61		Killed at Bull Run.
Hotchkiss, Chas. J.	32	May 26, '61	May 5, '64	Corp. and Serg.
Irvine, Theodore A.	18	Dec. 23, '61		Transferred to 1st Battalion.
Kennedy, Chas. W.	18	May 22, '61	Sept. 3, '61	Discharged per order for non-age.
Klein, Herman	23	May 23, '61	May 5, '64	
Kramer, Sigismond O.	24	Apl. 29, '61		Re-enlisted; transferred to 1st Minn. Battalion.
Krueger, Andrew F.	22	Apl. 29, '61	May 5, '64	Corp., Serg.; wounded at Gettysburg.
Ladd, Austin N.	29	Apl. 29, '61		Wounded at Bull Run; died of wounds Oct., '61.
Leonard, Maurice F.	21	Nov. 18, '61		Re-enlisted; transferred to 1st Battalion.
Little, David M.	22	May 21, '61	June 12, '62	Discharged for disability.
Lloyd, Edward S.	24	Apl. 29, '61	Feb. 6, '63	Discharged for disability.
Linberg, John	18	May 20, '61	May 5, '64	
Lonquist, John	30	May 20, '61		Re-enlisted; transferred to 1st Battalion.
Lufkin, Wade	25	May 20, '61		Serg.; killed at Gettysburg.
Marr, Christopher C.	19	Apl. 29, '61	Feb. 6, '63	Wounded at Bull Run; discharged for wounds.
Mayence, John B.	23	Apl. 29, '61	Feb. 6, '63	Wounded at Bull Run; discharged for wounds.
Marble, Geo. F.	20	May 23, '61		Musician, Hospital Steward; discharged for disability '63.
McDonald, Joseph	25	Apl. 29, '61		Corp.; wnd. Savage Station; re-enlisted in 1st Battalion.
McNelly, James R.	22	Apl. 29, '61	Apl. 23, '63	Wounded three times at Bull Run; discharged for disability.
McMullen, Nathan	19	May 21, '61	Sept. 3, '61	Discharged per order for non-age.
McLean, David	29	May 26, '61	May 5, '64	
McCray, Samuel C.	35	May 28, '61	May 5, '64	

ROSTER OF COMPANY C — *Continued.*

Names.	Age.	Mustered In.	Mustered Out.	Remarks.
McCausland, Andrew	42	Nov. 18, '61	Jan. 8, '63	Wounded at Savage Station; discharged for disability.
McMullen, George	21	Apl. 29, '61		Corp.; killed at Bull Run.
McConkey, John	37	Apl. 29, '61	Feb. 16, '63	Corp.; discharged for disability.
Miller, Samuel L	22	May 21, '61		Died Nov. 8, '61.
Morton, Albert B	18	May 21, '61	Jan. 8, '63	Wounded at Antietam; discharged for disability.
Mortimer, George F	23	Sept. 29, '61		Corp.; transferred to 1st Battalion.
Murphy, James A	21	May 17, '61	Sept. 17, '62	Wounded at Glendale; discharged for disability.
Navarre, Joseph B. F	21	Apl. 29, '61		Corp.; transferred to U. S. Cavalry Oct. 24, '52.
Newell, Phocian P	23	Apl. 29, '61		Corp., Serg.; transferred to Kirby's Battery July 16, '62.
Odell, Joseph H	22	Apl. 29, '61	May 5, '64	
Onermann, Wilhelm	20	Apl. 29, '61	May 5, '64	
Owen, Robert P	30	Apl. 29, '61	May 5, '64	Corp., Serg. and 1st Serg.
Parsons, Tansor S	20	May 17, '61		Transferred to U. S. Cavalry Oct. 24, '62.
Pethybridge, Joshua	24	Apl. 29, '61	May 5, '64	
Perkins, Andrew F	28	Dec. 16, '61		Transferred to U. S. Cavalry.
Perkins, Daniel A	27	Dec. 16, '61		Transferred to 1st Battalion.
Pressnell, Thos. H	18	Sept. 9, '61		Corp.; Capt. in 1st Battalion.
Pribble, Turner	24	Nov. 25, '61		Transferred to 1st Battalion.
Randolph, Wareham G	43	Apl. 29, '61	Jan. 7, '62	Wounded at Bull Run; discharged for disability.
Reynolds, Wm. M	22	May 21, '64		Absent in confinement on discharge of regiment.
Renshaw, John C	23	Apl. 29, '64		Serg.; wounded at Bull Run; died of wounds.
Richardson, Richmond	34	May 17, '64		Wounded at Bull Run.
Roberts, Gustave A	20	Apl. 29, '64		Wounded Savage Station; transferred to U. S. Cavalry.
Robertson, Daniel M	19	May 22, '64		Wounded at Bull Run, supposed to be mortal.
Roach, Wm. C	20	May 22, '61	Oct. 21, '62	Discharged to enlist in U. S. service.
Rosemeyer, George	31	Aug. 22, '62		Transferred to 1st Battalion.
Sernan, John	29	Apl. 29, '61	May 5, '64	
Sherman, Marshall	37	Apl. 29, '61		Took rebel flag at Gettysburg; re-enlisted in 1st Battalion.
Simpson, Robert C	33	Nov. 25, '61		Killed at Antietam.
Sias, G	19			Transferred to 1st Battalion.
Smith, Julius	41	Apl. 29, '61	May 5, '64	Wounded at Bull Run and Antietam.
Smith, Cyrus	29	May 21, '61		Wounded at Bull Run.
Smith, Geo. L	26	May 26, '61		Mortally wounded at Savage Station.
Snow, Leonard	25	Nov. 25, '61	Feb. 17, '62	Wounded at Savage Station; discharged for disability.
Sohns, Charles	41	May 23, '61	Mch. 24, '63	Discharged for disability.
Squiers, Gideon L	29	May 26, '61		Corp.; wounded at Gettysburg.
Staats, Isaac	25	May 22, '61		Deserted while absent sick.
Taylor, Edward	23	Aug. 21, '61		Mortally wounded June 29, '62, at Savage Station.
Thompson, Joseph H	19	Apl. 29, '61		Killed at Bull Run.
Tirrell, Chesley B	23	May 22, '61		Serg.; Lieut. in 1st Battalion.
Townsend, Geo. W	21	Jan. 20, '62	Apl. 18, '62	Discharged for disability.
Townsend, Perry C	22	Dec. 30, '61		Transferred to 1st Battalion.
Tripp, Thomas T	29	May 17, '61		Missing, probably killed at Bull Run.
Treadway, Calvin	23	Apl. 29, '61	May 5, '64	Wagoner.
Twitchell, Isaac L	30	May 23, '61		Wounded at Bull Run
Van Solen, George L	26	Sept. 9, '61	Apl. 18, '62	Discharged for disability.
Victory, James	35	Apl. 29, '61		Serg.; re-enlisted; transferred to 1st Battalion.
Watkins, Wm	30	Sept. 7, '61		Transferred to Kirby's Battery June 16, '62.
Waterhouse, Sewall N	26	Apl. 29, '61		Corp.; killed at Bull Run.
Waltz, William	26	Aug. 21, '61	Nov. 1, '62	Wounded at Bull Run; discharged for disability.
Westlake, Reuben M	23	Apl. 29, '61	May 5, '64	Corp. and Serg.
Whetstone, Thos. N.	27	Aug. 29, '61		Re-enlisted; Capt. in 1st Battalion.
Willey, George	17	Feb. 24, '64		Transferred to 1st Battalion.
Willey, Warner	28	Nov. 18, '61	May 11, '62	Discharged for disability.
Williams, Henry H	23	Aug. 21, '61	Oct. '62	Discharged for disability; captured at Bull Run.
Wilmer, Eugene	26	Apl. 29, '61		Serg.; wounded at Bull Run; died Apl. '62.
Wren, Nicholas	21	Dec. 9, '61		Mortally wounded at Savage Station; died June 30, '62.

ROSTER OF COMPANY D.

Names.	Age.	Mustered In.	Mustered Out.	Remarks.
OFFICERS.				
Captains —				
Henry R. Putnam	29	Apl. 29, '61		Wounded at Bull Run; Capt. 12th U. S. Inf.
Dewitt C. Smith	35	Aug. 8, '61		2d Lieut; wounded at Antietam; transferred to Co. G; Paymaster; killed by guerrillas.
Chris. B. Heffelfinger	26	July 4, '63	May 4, '64	Serg., 1st Serg., 2d and 1st Lieut.; wounded at Gettysburg; Major 1st Heavy Artillery.
First Lieutenants —				
Geo. H. Woods	29	Apl. 29, '61	Nov. 28, '61	Pro. Capt. and C. S., Lieut. Col. and Chief C. S. Cav. Corps, '64.
Seth L. Hammond	26	Nov. 26, '61	Sept. '62	1st Serg., 2d Lieut.; resigned.
Jacob Marty				Transferred to Co. E.
Ellet P. Perkins	24		May 5, '64	Corp., Color Serg.; wounded at Gettysburg; Capt. 1st Battalion.
Second Lieutenants —				
Wm. Harmon	25	Sept. 13, '62		Serg., 1st Serg.; pro. 1st Lieut. Co. C; wounded at Gettysburg.
Chas. H. Mason	25	Sept. 27, '62		Serg.; transferred to Co. C; pro. 1st Lieut; died Aug. 18, '63, of wounds at Gettysburg.
ENLISTED MEN.				
Abraham, Geo. W. F	17	Feb. 20, '64		Transferred to Battalion; died Andersonville Nov. 12, '64.
Allen, William R	24	May 16, '61		Killed at Gettysburg.
Ames, Orville	34	Feb. 25, '64		Transferred to 1st Battalion.
Anderson, Charles	26	May 20, '61	May 5, '64	
Ball, Edward W	19	May 20, '61	May 5, '64	
Bartlett, George W	19	May 29, '61	May 5, '64	Wounded at Gettysburg.

ROSTER OF COMPANY D — *Continued.*

Names.	Age.	Mustered In.	Mustered Out.	Remarks.
Baker, Chas. E	19	May 29, '61		Killed July 2, '63, at Gettysburg.
Bartlett, Ransom A			Oct. 7, '62	Discharged for disability.
Bingenheimer, Henry	19	May 16, '61	May 5, '64	
Blake, Horace K	23	May 22, '61	May 5, '64	
Bryant, Adelbert	20	May 21, '61	Jan. 26, '63	Discharged for disability.
Bryant, James	18	May 29, '61		Corp., Serg.; wounded at Gettysburg; re-enlisted in 1st Batt.
Brown, John	21	May 16, '61	May 5, '64	
Brown, Theodore		July 20, '61		Prisoner at Bull Run; transferred to 1st Battalion.
Carter, Leonard B	26	May 22, '61		Wounded at Antietam and Bristow.
Carpenter, Edson B	21	Mch. 30, '64		Transferred to 1st Battalion.
Chaffee, Jacob W	18	Apl. 29, '61	Apl. 17, '63	Discharged for disability.
Chandler, Enoch H	22	Apl. 29, '61	May 5, '64	
Chase, Henry B			Feb. 2, '63	Wounded at Antietam; discharged.
Clifford, Carroll H	18	May 21, '61	May 5, '64	
Clater, John	31	May 22, '61	Feb. 7, '63	Wounded at Antietam; discharged for disability.
Crown, Henry W	21	May 17, '61		Transferred to Inv. Corps March, '64.
Curtis, Francis I	21	May 26, '61	Dec. 29, '61	Discharged for disability.
Curtis, Archibald	21	Oct., '61		Re-enlisted in 1st Battalion.
Darling, Azariah W	24	May 21, '61	Oct. 16, '62	Discharged for disability.
Devergill, Franklin	35	May 21, '61		Transferred to gunboat service Nov. 16, '63.
Dean, Henry A	24	May 16, '61		Killed at Bull Run.
Dunsmore, S				Discharged for disability, '61.
Donnelly, Stephen	23	May 20, '61	Jan. 7, '62	Discharged for disability.
Drew, Nathaniel	21	May 21, '61		Transferred to gunboat service Nov. 16, '63.
Dunsmore, James F	23	May 23, '61	Aug. 1, '61	Discharged for disability.
Eddy, Cyrus E	23	May 17, '61		Transferred to Inv. Corps Jan. 16, '64.
Ferguson, Ami R	18	Apl. 29, '61	May 5, '64	
Fletcher, Levi	18	May 31, '61	Oct. 25, '61	Discharged for disability.
French, John O	18	Apl. 29, '61		Corporal.
Fuller, Geo. E	23	May 21, '61	May 5, '64	Musician; promoted Corporal.
Garvey, Wm. H	20	May 16, '61	Apl. 10, '63	Discharged for disability April 10, '63.
Geer, Lewis B	21	May 21, '61	May 5, '64	Promoted Corporal; wounded at Gettysburg.
Geer, Chas. W	19	May 21, '61	May 5, '64	Wounded at Gettysburg.
Goeppinger, August A	25	Apl. 29, '61	May 5, '64	Wounded at Gettysburg and Bristow.
Gordon, Wm. A	21	May 21, '61	Oct. 2, '62	Discharged for disability.
Gordon, Hanford L	24	May 21, '61	Dec. 1, '61	Corp.; discharged for disability.
Grandy, George				Corp.; died July 3, '63, of wounds received at Gettysburg.
Hayden, Alonzo C	22	Apl. 29, '61		Killed at Gettysburg.
Hamilton, Emsley I	20	Apl. 29, '61	Nov. 27, '61	Discharged for disability.
Hatch, Cyrus M	28	Apl. 29, '61	Dec. 5, '62	Wounded at Antietam; discharged.
Haner, John H	23	May 21, '61	Dec. 2, '62	Wounded at Antietam; discharged.
Hamilton, E. J				Transferred to Battalion.
Hawks, James		Feb. 29, '64		Transferred to 1st Battalion.
Hamilton, E. M. C				Transferred to Battalion.
Hoblitt, John T	21	Apl. 29, '61		Corp.; died Nov. 20, '61.
Howe, Archibald E	20	Apl. 29, '61	May 5, '64	Wounded at Gettysburg.
Howe, Wm. H	23	Apl. 29, '61	May 5, '64	
Howe, David M			Jan. 6, '63	Discharged for disability.
Hoblitt, Isaac N	20	Apl. 29, '61	July, '61	Discharged for disability.
Holt, Joseph B			Jan. 9, '62	Corp.; discharged for disability.
Hughes, Chas. W	23	Apl. 29, '61	May 5, '64	
Hutchins, Charles A	18	Apl. 29, '61	Dec. 5, '62	Discharged for disability.
Hughes, Thomas			Dec. 20, '61	Discharged for disability.
Hyatt, Alexander H	24	May 21, '61	June 14, '62	Corp.; discharged for disability.
Irvine, William N	22	May 21, '61		Corp.; re-enlisted in 1st Battalion.
Jenkins, David			Aug. 20, '63	Discharged for disability.
Jordon, Amos C	19	Apl. 29, '61		Transferred to Signal Corps Aug. 1, '61; promoted Sergeant.
Kelly, Thomas		Oct., '61	Dec. 18, '62	Wounded at Fredericksburg; discharged.
Kendall, James W	24	Apl. 29, '61	May 5, '64	
King, Orange S	23	Apl. 29, '61		Wounded and captured at Bull Run.
Kouts, Jacob W	19	May 20, '61	May 5, '64	Corp.; wounded at Gettysburg.
Lawrence, Irving	21	Apl. 29, '61		Wounded at Antietam; killed at Gettysburg.
Laflin, George A	24	May 17, '61	Mch. 25, '63	Wounded at Antietam; discharged.
Laflin, Adin A	20	May 17, '61	May 5, '64	
Lambdin, Edwin			Dec. 2, '62	Wounded at Antietam; discharged.
Lancaster, Wm. H	22	May 22, '61	May 5, '64	Wagoner.
Legg, Daniel B	31	May 22, '61	May 5, '64	Wounded at Savage Station.
Leonard, Webster G			Feb. 4, '63	Discharged for disability.
Longfellow, Henry W	23	Apl. 29, '61	May 11, '62	Serg.; discharged for disability.
Martin, Horace M	23	Apl. 29, '61	May 5, '64	Serg.; wounded at Gettysburg.
Maddock, George	28	Apl. 29, '61	May 5, '64	Wounded at Bull Run.
McAllister, Henry A	23	Apl. 29, '61	Feb. 3, '63	Corp.; discharged for disability.
Markham, Charles S	34	May 22, '61	Feb. 27, '63	Discharged for disability.
Meeker, Lewis C	26	Apl. 29, '61	May 5, '64	
Messer, Edward D			Dec. 29, '61	Discharged for disability.
Miller, Wesley F	20	Apl. 29, '61		Lieut. 7th U. S. Inf.; killed at Gettysburg.
Morgan, David L	21	Mch. 30, '64		Transferred to 1st Battalion.
Nason, Thos. B	18	May 28, '61	May 5, '64	Corp.; wounded at Antietam and Gettysburg.
Nason, Eben S			Feb. 15, '63	Discharged for disability.
Newton, Wm. J	21	May 22, '61	Apl. 2, '62	Discharged for disability.
Newton, Francis H	18	May 22, '61		Absent sick on discharge of regiment.
Noel, Benjamin F	18	May 26, '61	May 5, '64	Wounded at Gettysburg.
Over, William	19	May 20, '61	Jan. 1, '63	Enlisted in regular army.
Patten, Geo. W	20	May 21, '61	Apl. 7, '63	Wounded Fair Oaks and Antietam; discharged for disability.
Past, Marcus A				Wounded at Antietam; died of wounds at Gettysburg.
Past, Edward S	20	Apl. 29, '61		Corp., Serg., Serg. Maj.; dis. for wounds at Antietam.
Parker, Raymond J	25	Apl. 29, '61	May 5, '64	Sergeant, 1st Sergeant.

ROSTER OF COMPANY D—*Continued.*

NAMES.	AGE.	MUSTERED IN.	MUSTERED OUT.	REMARKS.
Pendergast, Lloyd G	19	Apl. 16, '61	....	Discharged for disability.
Plummer, Robt. A	19	Apl. 29, '61	May 5, '64	
Plummer, John W	21	Apl. 29, '61	May 5, '64	Corporal, Sergeant.
Plummer, Henry C	24	Apl. 20, '61	May 14, '62	Discharged for disability.
Prime, Joseph H	......	....	....	Killed July 2, '63, at Gettysburg.
Pratt, Job	23	....	....	Transferred to 1st Battalion.
Pratt, M. G	......	....	....	Died April, '64, of smallpox.
Rines, Charles H	19	May 21, '61	May 5, '64	Corp.; wounded at Gettysburg.
Robinson, Calvin D	23	Apl. 29, '61	May 5, '64	Corp., Serg.; wounded at Gettysburg.
Robinson, S. Morton	18	June 6, '61	May 5, '64	Musician.
Rollins, Frank	......	June 30, '63	....	Died Aug. 3, '63, of wounds at Gettysburg.
Sullivan, Daniel	19	Nov. 1, '61	....	Wounded at Gettysburg; transferred to Battalion.
Sampson, Leroy F	18	May 17, '61	Feb. 2, '63	Wounded at Antietam; discharged.
Scherfenberg, Frederick	22	May 20, '61	Oct. 17, '62	Discharged for disability.
Sly, Gilbert E	......	Mch. 1, '64	....	Transferred to 1st Battalion.
Smith, Geo. W	......	....	Feb. 13, '63	Discharged for disability.
Smith, Wm. C	......	June 30, '63	....	Wounded at Gettysburg; transferred to Battalion.
Smith, Chas. W	21	Apl. 27, '61	May 5, '64	
Smithyman, Joseph	32	Apl. 29, '61	May 5, '64	Corp., Serg.; wounded at Gettysburg.
Spaulding, Norris H	21	May 21, '61	Jan. 5, '63	Corporal.
Standish, Mathew M	28	May 21, '61	....	Serg., Com. Serg. Feb. 16, '63.
Savage, Charles W	28	....	....	Corp., Serg.; wounded at Fredericksburg.
Taunt, Alvin B	21	Apl. 20, '61	Feb. 8, '62	Discharged for disability.
Titus, Platt S	24	May 21, '61	May 5, '64	Corporal.
Walsh, James W	24	Apl. 29, '61	May 5, '64	Wounded at Antietam and Gettysburg.
Walker, Edward A	22	May 21, '61	May 5, '64	Corporal.
Wetmur, David G	29	Apl. 29, '61	May 5, '64	
Welsh, Henry P	20	May 20, '61	May 11, '62	Discharged for disability.
Whittemore, John D	18	May 23, '61	....	Died of wounds, near Vienna, Va., Sept., '62.
Wilgus, Henry N	36	Apl. 29, '61	....	Transferred to gunboat service Nov. 16, '63.
Woodworth, Chas. M	22	May 21, '61	....	Died Sept. 28, '61, at Camp Stone.
Young, Joseph J	34	Apl. 29, '61	Jan. 3, '63	Corp.; wounded at Antietam; discharged.

ROSTER OF COMPANY E.

NAMES.	AGE.	MUSTERED IN.	MUSTERED OUT.	REMARKS.
OFFICERS.				
Captains—				
George N. Morgan	35	Apl. 29, '61	....	Major, Lieutenant Colonel, Colonel, Brev. Brigadier General.
George Pomeroy	25	Oct. 22, '61	Sept. 19, '62	2d Lieut.; wounded at Antietam; Lieut. Col. 146th N. Y.; Paymaster U. S. A.
Louis Muller	26	Sept., '62	....	1st Lieut. Co. B.; killed at Gettysburg.
C. Edward Davis	......	July 3, '63	May 4, '64	1st Lieut. Co. A, 2d Lieut. Co. I, Serg. Maj.
First Lieutenants—				
James Hollister	25	Apl. 29, '61	Oct. 22, '61	Resigned.
John N. Chase	26	Oct. 22, '61	....	1st Serg., Capt. Co. H, Sept. 26, '62.
Samuel T. Raguet	23	Aug. 8, '61	....	Transferred from Co. I, A. D. C., to Gen. Gorman.
David B. Demerest	27	Sept. 26, '62	....	Serg. Co. C, 2d Lieut. Co. E; died July 30, '63, of wounds at Gettysburg.
Wm. Lochren	29	July 3, '63	Dec. 30, '63	Serg. Co. E, 2d Lieut. Co. K; resigned on certificate of disability.
Jacob Marty	......	Oct. 7, '63	May 4, '64	Transferred from Co. D Jan. '64.
Second Lieutenants—				
James H Shepley	26	Oct. 22, '61	....	Serg.; wounded at Antietam; 1st Lieut. Co. G, July 19, '62,
George Boyd	30	July, '62	....	Serg., 1st Serg., 2d Lieut. Co. H, 1st Lieut. Co. I.
ENLISTED MEN.				
Abbott, Asa T	20	Apl. 29, '61	....	Trans. to Sig. Cor. Aug., '61; Lieut.; wnd.; Lieut. Reg. Army.
Adams, Daniel	21	May 23, '61	May 3, '64	
Adams, George M	19	May 23, '61	May 3, '64	Wounded at Gettysburg.
Aldrich, Bradley B	26	May 23, '61	May 3, '64	Corporal.
Austin, Edward A	22	May 26, '61	May 3, '64	Corporal; wounded at Gettysburg.
Barnard, John F	25	Apl. 29, '61	July 31, '61	Discharged for disability.
Bassett, Wm. H	20	Apl. 29, '61	May 3, '64	Corporal.
Berry, Amos O	27	May 23, '61	May 3, '64	Wounded at Gettysburg.
Berry, Charles A	19	Apl. 29, '61	....	Wounded at Antietam and Gettysburg.
Brower, James S	22	May 26, '61	May 3, '64	Corporal; wounded at Gettysburg.
Brakey, James	22	May 20, '61	May 3, '64	
Bofferding, W	......	....	....	
Bradley, Henry C	28	May 23, '61	May 3, '64	Corp., Serg.; wounded at Savage Station and Gettysburg.
Brenchley, Philip	22	Feb. 18, '64	....	Transferred to 1st Battalion.
Brown, Edward F	17	Feb. 20, '64	....	Transferred to 1st Battalion.
Butler, David	26	May 24, '61	....	
Burgan, John M	25	May 26, '61	....	Discharged for disability '62.
Buck, Philip A	18	Feb. 27, '64	....	Transferred to 1st Battalion.
Cassedy, Hugh G	30	May 23, '61	....	Serg.; died of wounds at Savage Station.
Carlton, David	28	Feb. 26, '63	....	Transferred to 1st Battalion.
Carter, John H	28	May 20, '61	....	
Camp, Abner W	25	May 23, '61	Dec. 5, '61	Discharged for disability.
Churchill, Henry	22	Apl. 29, '61	....	Wounded at Antietam.
Connick, Bryce	29	May 23, '61	Jan. 20, '63	Wounded at Antietam; discharged for disability.
Cook, Charles H	20	Apl. 29, '61	Dec. 29, '62	Discharged for disability.
Coombs, Albert B	18	Apl. 29, '61	....	Transferred to U. S. Engineers Oct. 24, '62.
Curry, John	25	May 26, '61	May 3, '64	Wounded at Gettysburg.

ROSTER OF COMPANY E—*Continued.*

NAMES.	AGE.	MUSTERED IN.	MUSTERED OUT.	REMARKS.
Cundy, Wm. E	22	May 23, '61	May 3, '64	
Davenport, Wm. H	19	Apl. 29, '61	Sept. 26, '61	Musician; discharged per order.
Day Henry, M	21	Apl. 29, '61	....	Discharged for promotion in colored regiment.
Davis, John W	23	Apl. 29, '61	....	Killed at Gettysburg.
Dow, Lloyd U	26	Apl. 29, '61	....	Wounded at Antietam; discharged for disability, '63.
Doble, Thomas L	28	May 26, '61	May 3, '64	Wounded.
Drake, Hiram	24	May 18, '61	May 3, '64	Wounded at Gettysburg.
Elliott, John	22	May 23, '61	....	Wounded at Bull Run and Malv. Hill; trans. to U. S. Cav.
Ewart, James T	22	May 23, '61	....	Deserted March, '64.
Farrington, William	18	Feb. 19, '64	....	Transferred to 1st Battalion.
Fenton, Benjamin	22	May 29, '61	May 3, '64	Wounded at Gettysburg.
Fleetham, John	22	May 23, '61	Mar. 25, '63	Wounded at Bull Run and Antietam; discharged for disability.
Fisher, Henry I	21	May 23, '61	....	Wounded at Gettysburg; re-enlisted in 1st Battalion.
Ford, Lucius	31	May 26, '61	May 3, '64	
Fowler, Norman	26	Apl. 29, '61	....	Killed at Gettysburg.
Fullerton, William E	18	May 20, '61	....	Transferred to gunboat service Nov. 16, '61.
Goulding, George W	20	May 24, '61	May 3, '64	Corporal and Sergeant.
Goundry, Wm. W	25	May 23, '61	....	Absent sick on discharge of regiment.
Holden, Wm. W	23	Feb. 26, '63	....	Wounded at Gettysburg; transferred to Battalion.
Hollister, Geo. N	18	Apl. 29, '61	....	Transferred to 4th U. S. Cav., Oct. 27, '62.
Hanscome, James	27	May 23, '61	....	Killed at Antietam.
Harrington, John	27	May 23, '61	....	Wounded at Bull Run; transferred to 4th U. S. Cav.
Hanley, John	23	May 26, '61	....	Wounded at Bull Run.
Hill, Jonas R	30	Sept. 14, '61	....	Wounded at Gettysburg; transferred to 1st Battalion.
Hill, Elvin G	28	May 23, '61	....	Corporal.
Hobson, Albion T	29	Apl. 29, '61	....	Corporal; killed at Bull Run.
Jackins, Israel	18	Apl. 29, '61	....	Killed at Gettysburg.
Jewett, Chas. H	17	May 23, '61	....	Corp., Serg.; discharged for promotion Sept. 21, '63.
Jefferson, Ernest	18	May 23, '61	....	Lost leg by wound at Gettysburg.
Johnson, Wm. R	22	May 23, '61	Mar. 25, '63	Wounded at Antietam; discharged for disability.
Jefferson, Rufus H	......	....	....	Wounded at Bull Run; transferred to 4th U. S. Cav.
Keen, Edwin	18	Apl. 29, '61	....	Transferred to gunboat service Nov. 16, '61.
Kelsey, George B	20	May 23, '61	....	Wounded at Bull Run; transferred to 4th U. S. Cav.
Kittel, Francis	37	Apl. 29, '61	Dec. 21, '63	Corp., Serg., Drum Major; discharged for disability.
Knowlton, Geo. W	18	Feb. 13, '64	....	Transferred to 1st Battalion.
Leyde, Samuel F	30	May 23, '61	....	Wounded at Bull Run; transferred to gunboat service.
Leighton, Ephraim F	......	....	....	Wounded at Antietam.
Lowell, Edwin B	28	May 23, '61	May 3, '64	Wounded at Bristow.
Losee, Wm. H	25	May 23, '61	....	Wounded at Bull Run and Gettysburg; trans. to Inv. Corps.
Mayo, Reuben M	26	May 23, '61	....	Wounded at Vienna.
McKenzie, John	24	May 23, '61	....	Died Aug. 4, '63, from wounds at Gettysburg.
McDonald, Chas	44	....	....	Transferred to U. S. Cav. Oct. 26, '62.
McDonald, Chas. Jr	19	Apl. 29, '61	....	
Mitchell, Wm. D	25	May 23, '61	....	Transferred to Inv. Corps Nov., '63.
Middlestadt, Vincent	20	May 24, '61	....	Wounded at Gettysburg.
Moss, James R	27	May 18, '61	....	Killed July, Bull Run.
Mulvy, Booth C	28	Apl. 29, '61	....	Corporal.
Northup, Geo. W	18	Apl. 29, '61	....	Transferred to 6th U. S. Cav, Oct. 27, '62.
Northup, Charles	25	Apl. 29, '61	....	Wagonmaster.
O'Brien, Henry D	......	....	....	Corp.; wounded at Gettysburg; Major in 1st Battalion.
Pattison, Murdock	27	May 26, '61	Oct., '62	Wounded at Savage Station; discharged for disability.
Patterson, James	26	May 23, '61	....	Deserted Nov., '62.
Pride, John W	22	Apl. 29, '61	....	Serg., Serg. Maj.; wounded at Bristow; transferred to 1st Batt.
Randall, Horace	23	May 23, '61	....	Musician; deserted '62.
Ray, Francis	28	May 24, '61	May 3, '64	
Russell, Obed	27	Apl. 29, '61	Dec. 31, '62	Discharged for disability.
Schumacher, Wm. E	26	Apl. 29, '61	....	Wounded at Bull Run, re-enlisted 1st Battalion.
Scott, Harvey E	34	May 20, '61	....	Wounded at Savage Station.
Sears, Oscar Wilson	20	Apl. 29, '61	....	Captured at Bull Run; transferred to Inv. Corps.
Sherbrook, Calvin	......	....	....	Wounded at Savage Station.
Sherman, Henry	25	May 20, '61	Oct. 26, '63	Wounded at Gettysburg and Antietam; discharged for disability.
Smith, Martin	21	Apl. 29, '61	Jan. 7, '63	Wounded at Antietam; discharged for disability.
Smiley, Wm. W	26	May 23, '61	....	Corp.; transferred to gunboat service Nov. 16, '61.
Stites, Samuel B	24	Apl. 29, '61	May 3, '64	Corp. and Serg.; wounded at Gettysburg.
Staples, Benjamin F	25	May 30, '61	May 3, '64	Corp. and Serg.; wounded at Antietam and Gettysburg.
Stealson, Thomas	23	Apl. 29, '61	Feb. 16, '64	Wounded at Gettysburg; discharged for disability.
Stites, Adam C	18	Sept. 28, '61	....	Wounded at Gettysburg; transferred to Battalion.
Stewart, Geo. E	33	May 23, '61	May 3, '64	
Sutton, Stephen B	35	Apl. 29, '61	May 3, '64	
Taylor, Patrick H	22	May 24, '61	May 3, '64	Corp., Serg., 1st Serg.; wounded at Savage Station
Taylor, Mathew F	25	Aug. 21, '61	May 3, '64	Corp.; wounded at Gettysburg.
Taylor, W. O	......	....	....	Killed at Antietam.
Taylor, Isaac L	......	....	....	Killed July 2, '63, at Gettysburg.
Thatcher, Orville D	22	Apl. 29, '61	May 3, '64	Corp.; wounded at Bull Run.
Trevor, Joseph G	27	Apl. 29, '61	....	Corp., Serg.; killed July, 2, '63, at Gettysburg.
Wakefield, Wm. L	27	May 23, '61	Jan. 4, '64	Discharged for disability.
Wardwell, John	28	....	Aug. 7, '61	Discharged for disability.
Waite, Daniel H	23	May 26, '61	....	Wounded at Gettysburg.
Weaver Joseph	18	....	....	
Weaver, James E	20	....	....	Re-enlisted in 1st Battalion.
Weaver, Elijah	31	May 23, '61	May 3, '64	Wounded at Gettysburg.
Welin, Peter	30	May 23, '61	....	Wounded at Bull Run; died July 6, '63, of wounds at Gettysburg
White, John D	23	May 26, '61	Jan. 9, '62	Discharged for disability.
Winants, George H	18	Apl. 29, '61	Dec. 25, '61	Discharged for disability.
Wilson, Wm. W	25	Apl. 29, '61	July 23, '62	Discharged for disability.

ROSTER OF COMPANY F.

NAMES.	AGE.	MUSTERED IN.	MUSTERED OUT.	REMARKS.
OFFICERS.				
Captains —				
William Colvill, Jr.	30	Apl. 29, '61		Maj., Lt. Col., Col., Bvt. Brig. Gen.; wd. Glendale & Gettysburg.
John J. McCallum	40	Aug. 29, '62		Serg. & 1st Lt. Co. G; wd. Fredericksburg; trans. to Inv. Corps.
John Ball		May 6, '63	May 4, '64	1st Lieut., 1st Serg. and 2d Lieut. Co. K; wounded at Bristow.
First Lieutenants —				
A. Edward Welch	22	Apl. 29, '61		Wounded and captured at Bull Run; Major 4th Minn. Vols.
Mark A. Hoyt	23	Jan. 8, '62	July 18, '62	2d Lieut.; resigned; Inv. Corps.
Myron Shepard			May 4, '64	Transferred from and to Co. H.
Hezekiah Bruce	27	Sept. 26, '63	May 4, '64	Sergeant, 1st Sergeant, 2d Lieutenant.
Second Lieutenants —				
Martin Maginnis	20	Jan. 8, '62		1st Serg. Co. F, 1st Lieut. Co. H, Capt. Co. K.
Joseph H. Spencer	21	Aug., '61		1st Serg. and 2d Lieut. Co. G; transferred to Sig. Corps; Major.
ENLISTED MEN.				
Abbott, Marion	25	Apl. 29, '61	Nov. 1, '63	Wounded at Gettysburg; discharged for disability.
Abbott, David P	23	May 18, '61		Killed at Antietam.
Adams, Charles E	18	Apl. 29, '61		Died May 27, '63, at Washington, D. C.
Alley, John				Transferred to Inv. Corps Nov. 2, '63.
Barrow, John	30	Apl. 29, '61	Feb. 14, '63	Corp.; wounded at Bull Run; discharged for disability.
Baker, Abraham P	25	Apl. 29, '61	May 5, '64	
Bambor, Archibald	18	Apl. 29, '61	May 5, '64	
Barber, Horatio N	30	May 24, '61	May 5, '64	Corp.; wounded at Gettysburg.
Bachelor, James F	22	Apl. 29, '61	May 5, '64	Wounded at Gettysburg.
Barnes, Rudolph C	24	Apl. 29, '61	May 5, '64	Wounded at Antietam.
Bayer, Andrew	29	May 15, '61	May 5, '64	Corp.; wounded at Flint Hill.
Borgh, Peter		Feb. 11, '62		Re-enlisted 1st Battalion.
Bevans, Henry T	22	Apl. 29, '61	Sept. 9, '63	Serg.; discharged for promotion.
Bennett, Wm. D	19	Apl. 29, '61	Feb. 4, '63	Corp.; discharged for disability.
Bevans, Milton L	18	May 22, '61	May 5, '64	Musician.
Berdan, Charles A	24	Oct. 29, '61		Wounded at Bristow and Fredericksburg; trans. to 1st Batt.
Blackwell, Henry	32	Mch. 28, '64		Transferred to 1st Battalion.
Bofferding, Peter G	32	Feb. 18, '64		Transferred to 1st Battalion.
Benner, Jefferson	26	Apl. 29, '61	May 5, '64	Corp. and Serg.
Bond, Daniel		Aug. 22, '62		Transferred to 1st Battalion; wounded at Fredericksburg.
Bondurant, Cyrus S	21	Apl. 29, '61		Transferred from Co. G.
Bond, Hezekiah	27	Aug. 14, '62		Transferred to Battalion.
Broffee, James	22	May 24, '61		Transferred to Kirby's Battery July 16, '62.
Brooks, Cyrus A	29	May 22, '61		Hospital Steward May 14, '63.
Burritt, Henry	21	Apl. 29, '61		Transferred to U. S. Cav. Oct. 24, '62; killed in Wilderness.
Burgetorf, Henry	19	May 13, '61	May 5, '64	Wounded at Bull Run and Gettysburg.
Brown, John H	20	Apl. 29, '61	May 5, '64	Wagoner; wounded at Bull Run; Wagonmaster.
Cannon, Lewis	35	Apl. 29, '61	Dec. 18, '61	Discharged for disability.
Childs, Henry R	24	May 31, '61	May 5, '64	Corp., Serg.; wounded at Bull Run.
Clark, Calvin P	24	Apl. 29, '61	May 5, '64	Serg.; wounded and captured at Savage Station.
Clausen, John	27	May 15, '61	Feb. 10, '63	Discharged for disability.
Clifton, Edward	29	Feb. 26, '64		Transferred to 1st Battalion.
Clark, John	33	Feb. 29, '64		Transferred to 1st Battalion.
Cox, Edwin	19	May 22, '61		Corp.; killed at Antietam.
Davis, Edward E	25	May 29, '61		Died Aug. 31, '62, of wounds at Savage Station.
Davis, Edward L	23	Apl. 29, '61	July 6, '62	Discharged for disability.
Davis, Jonas P	21	Apl. 29, '61	May 5, '64	Wounded and captured at Savage Station.
Davis, Almeron	18	May 22, '61		Wounded at Fredericksburg, Flint Hill and Gettysburg.
Daucher, George F	35	May 15, '61		Corp.; transferred to Inv. Corps Dec. 1, '63.
Decker, Artemus L. M		Sept. 16, '61		Wounded at Gettysburg; transferred to 1st Battalion.
Duling, William	23	Apl. 29, '61		Transferred to Kirby's Battery.
Eastman, Christopher	25	Apl. 29, '61		Transferred to U. S. Cav. Oct. 24, '62.
Eastman, Alva H	43	May 29, '61	June 29, '62	Discharged for disability.
Frary, Edrick J	28	Dec. 17, '61		Wounded at Bristow; transferred to 1st Battalion.
Flynn, Jonathan		Sept. 12, '61		Transferred to Inv. Corps June, '64.
Garrison, Wm. H	23	May 16, '61		
Garrison, Joseph P				Died Aug. 10, '61, of wounds at Bull Run.
Gilberson, Ole	25	May 16, '61	May 5, '64	
Glazier, Aaron	28	Apl. 29, '61		Re-enlisted in 1st Battalion.
Gordon, Wm	43	Apl. 29, '61	Aug. 20, '62	Discharged for disability.
Grinnell, Geo. W	21	May 24, '61		Transferred to U. S. Cav. Oct. 24, '62.
Grow, Enos F	18	Apl. 29, '61	May 5, '64	Corp.; wounded at Savage Station.
Harris, Charles N	22	Apl. 29, '61	Dec., '62	Serg.; wounded at Bull Run; discharged for disability.
Hamlin, Philip	20	Apl. 29, '61		Corp., Serg., 1st Serg.; killed at Gettysburg.
Halsted, Hans	35	Apl. 29, '61	Aug. 31, '61	Captured at Bull Run; discharged for disability.
Hammer, Nicholas	31	May 15, '61		Killed at Fair Oaks.
Herbert, Wm. M	21	May 22, '61		Wounded at Fredericksburg; trans. to Inv. Corps Dec. 19, '63.
Howe, Asa	23	Apl. 29, '61		
Hoffstetter, John W	19	May 23, '61		
Hubbs, Charles L	18	May 29, '61	May 5, '64	Wounded at Bull Run and Gettysburg.
Hoyt, William H	20	Sept. 9, '61		Transferred to 1st Battalion.
Hudson, Charles E	22	Apl. 29, '61		Wounded at Bull Run; deserted Sept. 17, '62.
Imeson, James W	18	June 20, '61	June 20, '64	Captured at Bull Run; transferred to 1st Battalion.
Jackson, Elisha O	19	Apl. 29, '61	Aug. 1, '61	Discharged for disability.
Jacobs, Romulus E	21	Apl. 29, '61		Wounded at Gettysburg.
Jenkins, Erastus		Mch. 28, '64		Transferred to 1st Battalion.
Johnson, Ole	24	Apl 29, '61	May 5, '64	
Johnson, Ferris	26	Apl. 29, '61		Corp.; killed June 29, '62, at Savage Station.
King, Levi	24	Apl. 29, '61		Wounded at Gettysburg; transferred to Inv. Corps.
Leeson, Robert W	23	Apl. 29, '61		Killed at Glendale.
Leighton, Gardner D	30	Apl. 29, '61	Mch 10, '63	Wounded at Bull Run; discharged for disability.
Lee, John M	18	May 24, '61		Wounded at Bull Run.
Lewis, Geo. L	20	Apl. 29, '61		Transferred to Signal Corps Aug. 18, '63.
Leamans, David H			Feb. 13, '62	Discharged for disability.

ROSTER OF COMPANY F — *Continued.*

NAMES.	AGE.	MUSTERED IN.	MUSTERED OUT.	REMARKS.
Lindquist, John	26	Apl. 29, '61	Aug. 31, '62	Discharged for disability.
Lindergreen, John			Aug. 31, '62	Discharged for disability.
Ludden, Otis W	16	Apl. 29, '61	Aug. 1, '61	Musician; discharged for disability.
Marshall, David	22	Apl. 29, '61	July 6, '62	Discharged for disability.
McLenathan, Ira C	32	Apl. 29, '61		Transferred to gunboat service Nov. 16, '61.
McGee, Richard	18	Apl. 29, '61		Re-enlisted and transferred to 1st Battalion.
McKinley, George	23	May 23, '61		Mortally wounded at Bull Run.
McGuire, Hugh G	32	Mch. 24, '64		Transferred to 1st Battalion.
Metselder, Dirk	21	Apl. 29, '61	May 5, '64	Wounded at Savage Station.
Merritt, Charles W	23	Apl. 29, '61	May 5, '64	Musician, Corp.; wounded at Bull Run.
Miller, Frederick E	18	Apl. 29, '61		Corp.; captured at Bull Run; officer of colored regiment.
Milliken, Marcello B	21	Apl. 29, '61		Killed at Antietam.
Mills, Charles W	28	Apl. 29, '61	Feb. 20, '63	Discharged for disability.
Mott, Ransom	21	May 27, '61	Feb. 17, '63	Dis. for disability; wnd. at Savage Station; arm amputated.
Nelson, Paul				
Olsen, Butler	21	Apl. 29, '61		Transferred to U. S. Cav. Oct. 24, '62.
Oscar, Ole	25	May 29, '61	May 12, '63	Wounded at Savage Station; discharged for disability.
Parker, Edmond F		Sept. 26, '61		Transferred to 1st Battalion.
Peterson, Thomas	36	May 29, '61	May 5, '64	Wounded at Savage Station.
Peterson, Hans		Feb. 14, '62		Wounded at Savage Station; killed at Bristow.
Pitcher, Eli F	21	Apl. 29, '61		Wounded; transferred to U. S. Cav. Oct. 24, '62.
Richardson, Josiah	31	May 24, '61	May 5, '64	Wounded at Fredericksburg.
Riddle, Wm. C	19	Apl. 29, '61		Re-enlisted in 1st Battalion.
Rush, Hiram I	23	Apl. 29, '61		Killed at Bull Run.
Sallee, James F	25	May 22, '61		Killed at Bull Run.
Season, Edwin	23	May 23, '61	May 5, '64	
Schweiger, David	18	Apl. 29, '61	May 5, '64	
Seamans, Daniel H		Sept. 21, '61	Jan., '63	Discharged for disability.
Scofield, Amos G	24			Corp.; died Aug. 18, '61, of wounds at Bull Run.
Scurry, James	25	May 24, '61		Transferred to Cavalry; re-enlisted in 1st Battalion.
Shay, Michael	18	May 24, '61		Transferred to Cavalry; re-enlisted in 1st Battalion.
Shadinger, Wm			Mch. 25, '63	Discharged for wounds at Vienna.
Skinner, Hiram A	19	May 29, '61		Died at Fair Oaks June, '62.
Skinner, Wm. J				Died July 5, '62, of disease.
Smith, John H	21	Apl. 29, '61	Oct. 2, '61	Discharged for disability.
Smith, Francis	27	Mch. 30, '64		Transferred to 1st Battalion.
Squire, Leonard J	24	Apl. 29, '61		Killed at Gettysburg.
Standish, Merritt G				Corp.; transferred to U. S. Cav. Oct. 24, '62.
Steinberg, Adam		Mch. 29, '64		Transferred to 1st Battalion.
Syverson, Amos	21	May 17, '61		Wounded at Savage Station; trans. to U. S. Cav. Oct. 24, '62.
Smith, Josiah R	39	Jan. 1, '62		Transferred to 1st Battalion.
Thomas, Elijah F	21	Apl. 29, '61		Died Sept. 6, '61, from wounds at Bull Run.
Underwood, James M	22	Apl. 29, '61		Killed at Bull Run.
Webb, Lester A	18	May 15, '61		Transferred to U. S. Cav. Oct. 24, '62.
Williams, John	27	Apl. 29, '61		Corp.; wounded at Antietam; discharged from general hospital.
Willman, Martin	30	May 15, '61		Corp.; killed June 29, '62, at Savage Station.
Williams, E. Oscar	18	Apl. 29, '61		Serg.; transferred to U. S. Cav. Oct. 24, '62.
Wood, Theodore A	25	Apl. 29, '61	May 5, '64	Corp., Serg.; detailed with Division Quartermaster.
Wright, James A	22	Apl. 29, '61		Corp., Serg., 1st Serg.; wnd. at Gettysburg; Lieut. 1st Batt.

ROSTER OF COMPANY G.

NAMES.	AGE.	MUSTERED IN.	MUSTERED OUT.	REMARKS.
OFFICERS.				
Captains —				
Lewis McKune	39	Apl. 29, '61		Killed July 21, '61, at Bull Run.
Nathan S. Messick	34	July 29, '61		1st Lieut.; killed July 3, '63, at Gettysburg.
Dewitt C. Smith	35	Aug. 8, '61		Trans. from Co. D; resigned Oct, 7, '63; Paymaster; killed by guerrillas.
Josias R. King	29	Oct. 19, '63	May 4, '64	1st Lieut. Co. A and G.
First Lieutenants —				
John J. McCallum	40	July 29, '61		Serg., Capt. Co. F; wounded at Fredericksburg; trans. Inv. Corps; Bvt. Maj.
James H. Shepley	26	July 19, '62	Jan. 13, '63	2d Lieut. Co. E.; resigned.
James De Gray	21	July 2, '63		Corp., 2d Lt.; wd. at Gettysburg and Bristow; trf. to Inv. Corps.
Second Lieutenants —				
William E. Smith	27	Apl. 29, '61	July 31, '61	Resigned.
Joseph H. Spencer	26	July 31, '61		1st Serg.; trans. to Co. F.; trans. to Signal Corps.
ENLISTED MEN.				
Areman, Adam	28	May 16, '61	May 5, '64	Wounded at Gettysburg.
Andress, Marvin D	20	May 23, '61	Oct. 9, '62	Discharged for disability.
Bassett, Edward H	19	Apl. 29, '61	May 5, '64	
Barton, Dana S	29	Apl. 29, '61	May 5, '64	Wounded at Gettysburg.
Barron, Norman B	26	May 23, '61	May 5, '64	
Baker, Jefferson G	20	May 23, '61		Transferred to 1st Battalion.
Babcock, James M	18	Mch. 24, '64		Transferred to 1st Battalion.
Belote, James	24	May 23, '61		Transferred to 6th U. S. Cav. Oct. 24, '62.
Benson, Chas. M	24	May 22, '61	May 5, '64	Corporal.
Bemis, Joseph G	18	May 23, '61		Transferred to 6th U. S. Cav. Oct. 24, '62.

ROSTER OF COMPANY G—*Continued.*

NAMES.	AGE.	MUSTERED IN	MUSTERED OUT.	REMARKS.
Bennett, Wm. D.			Feb. 4, '63	Discharged for disability.
Borchert, Henry	22	Apl. 29, '61		Transferred to U. S. Cav. Oct. 25, '62.
Boll, Fridelin	22	May 23, '61	May 5, '64	
Bondurant, Cyrus S.	21	Apl. 29, '61		Trans. Sept. 10, '61 to Co. F; wounded at Gettysburg.
Brook, Wm. A.	21		Feb. 4, '63	Discharged for disability.
Brown, Wm. W	21	Sept. 18, '61		Transferred to 1st Battalion; wounded at Gettysburg.
Buckman, George R	28	May 23, '61	May 5, '64	Corporal, Sergeant.
Case, Merritt B	22	May 23, '61		Wnd. at Bull Run; dis. for prom. Maj. of colored regiment.
Carney, James H.				Wnd. at Gettysburg; 1st Lieut. Heavy Artillery.
Card, William	18	May 23, '61		Died June 2, '62, at Fair Oaks.
Coombs, Charles A.				Wounded at Gettysburg.
Coen, Wm. G	21	Apl. 29, '61	May 5, '61	Wounded at Antietam and Gettysburg.
Crooker, Geo. W	20	May 28, '61	Aug. 8, '61	Wounded at Bull Run; discharged for disability.
Curtis, M. M	25	Aug. 22, '61	Jan. 26, '62	Discharged for disability.
Davison, Charles E.	27	Apl. 29, '61		Wounded at Bull Run; died Nov. 6, '62, at New York.
Davis, Chas. C	26	Apl. 29, '61	May 5, '64	
Dickinson, Frank	18	Apl. 29, '61	May 5, '64	Corp.; Com. Serg.
Dunham, Phineas L	20	Apl. 29, '61		Killed at Gettysburg.
Dubois, James L.	24	Apl. 29, '61	Feb. 6, '63	Wnd. at Bull Run; discharged for disability July 6, '63.
Ernst, Anthony W	22	May 23, '61		Died Aug. 5, '63, of wounds at Gettysburg.
Farnsworth, Jerome	18	May 23, '61		Died July 5, '63, of wounds at Gettysburg.
Ferguson, Stephen E.	28	May 23, '61	May 5, '64	Wounded at Bull Run
Gatzke, John	22	Apl. 29, '61	May 5, '64	Wounded at Antietam and Gettysburg.
Gibson, Francis	25	May 23, '61	Dec. 16, '61	Wagoner; discharged for disability.
Gifford, Samuel S.	22	Mch. 30, '64		Transferred to 1st Battalion.
Goodrich, Jonathan	21	May 23, '61	May 5, '64	Wounded at Gettysburg.
Gregg, Robert	21	May 15, '61	May 5, '64	
Gross, Oscar	25	May 28, '61		Discharged; wounded at Bull Run.
Graves, David	18	Aug. 26, '61	Jan. 20, '63	Discharged for disability.
Hall, Philo	19	Apl. 29, '61	May 5, '64	Corp.; Serg.; wounded at Gettysburg.
Haskell, Merritt	20	Mch. 30, '64		Transferred to 1st Battalion.
Hanneman, Louis E.	20	Apl. 29, '61	Dec. 23, '61	Musician; discharged.
Haskins, Ezra D.	20	Apl. 29, '61	May 5, '64	Bugler and Principal Musician.
Hausauer, Michael	19	May 28, '61	May 5, '64	
Healey, Martin	38	May 28, '61	Aug. 3, '63	Discharged for disability.
Hess, Charles E.	23	Apl. 29, '61	Aug. 3, '61	Corp.; wounded at Bull Run; discharged for disability.
Hollister, Edward	28	Apl. 29, '61	Aug. 3, '61	Corp.; wounded at Bull Run; discharged for disability.
House, Joseph L.	26	Apl. 29, '61	Apl. 2, '63	Discharged for disability.
Holther, John	30	Apl. 29, '61		Transferred to U. S Artillery.
Hopkins, George J	18	May 28, '61		Wounded at Gettysburg.
Jackson, Caleb B.	19	Apl. 29, '61	May 5, '64	Corporal.
Jewell, Benjamin H.	19	Apl. 29, '61		Transferred to 6th U. S. Cav. Oct. 24, '62.
Johnson, Albert	19	Apl. 29, '61	May 5, '64	Corporal.
Jones, Anthony	25	May 15, '61	Jan. 4, '64	Wounded at Bull Run and Gettysburg; discharged for disab.
Johnson, Stephen H.	23	May 23, '61	Dec. 8, '61	Discharged for disability.
Kenney, George A.	22	Apl. 29, '61		Wounded at Haymarket and Antietam; trans to Inv. Corps.
Knight, Edwin M.	18	Dec. 17, '61	Jan. 14, '64	Wounded at Gettysburg; discharged for disability.
Laird, Samuel	22	May 18, '61		Died Aug. 22; '62.
Livingston, Francis F.	24	May 23, '61	May 5, '64	Division Wagonmaster.
Lilly, Samuel	20	May 23, '61	May 5, '64	Wounded at Gettysburg.
Logan, John D.	22	Apl. 29, '61		Corp.; wounded on picket.
Magee, George	21	May 23, '61	May 5, '64	Wounded at Gettysburg.
McKinstry, John	21	May 28, '61		Died Aug. 22, '63, of wounds at Gettysburg.
McCulloch, Jonas G.	18	Mch. 22, '64		Transferred to 1st Battalion.
Meyers, William	26	May 23, '61	May 5, '64	
Miller, Asa	22	Apl. 29, '61		Killed at Bull Run.
Mosher, Ludwell J.	22	May 23, '61	May 5, '64	Wounded at Antietam and Gettysburg.
Mollison, Allen	23	May 23, '61		Corp.; transferred to U. S. Cav. Oct. 24, '62.
Morford, Samuel D.	19	May 23, '61		Wounded at Gettysburg; absent, sick, at disch. of regiment.
Needham, Edward Z.	18	Apl. 29, '61	May 5, '64	Corporal.
Nichols, James L.	19	Apl. 29, '61		Absent, paroled prisoner, at discharge of regiment.
Northrup, Irvine W.	23	May 23, '61		Serg.; died July 14, '62, of disease.
Olmsted, Geo. W.	20	May 23, '61		Transferred to U S. Engineers Oct. 25, '62.
Parker, Chas. C.	24	Apl. 29, '61	May 5, '64	Serg.; Capt. in 1st Battalion.
Patton, Merritt B.	25	May 23, '61		Killed at Bull Run.
Patterson, Martin	27	Aug. 22, '61	Jan. 7, '63	Discharged for disability.
Pearl, S. J.	23	Sept. 10, '61		Died Aug. 21, '62.
Peasley, Joseph W.	18	Mch. 24, '64		Transferred to 1st Battalion.
Phelps, Alvin	19	May 22, '61	Jan. 10, '63	Discharged for disability.
Phillips, Edward P.	21	May 22, '61		Corporal.
Potter, Edward	20	Apl. 29, '61	Aug. 3, '61	Wounded at Bull Run; discharged for disability.
Potter, William	23	Apl. 29, '61	Aug. 13, '61	Discharged for wounds at Bull Run.
Ramsey, William	22	May 23, '61	May 5, '64	Corporal.
Ramsdell, Peter W.	41	Apl. 29, '61	Jan. 26, '62	Discharged for disability.
Reed, Walter S.	22	May 23, '61		Wounded at Bull Run and Gettysburg; re-enlisted 1st Batt.
Reed, Neri	21	May 23, '61	May 5, '64	Wounded at Bull Run.
Reed, Nathaniel	21	May 20, '61		Re-enlisted 1st Battalion.
Rhorer, John M.	20	Apl. 29, '61	May 5, '64	Wounded at Gettysburg.
Reynolds, Samuel	21	Apl. 29, '61	May 5, '64	
Reynolds, Lewis G.	20	Apl. 29, '61	Feb. 6, '63	Wounded at Bull Run; discharged for disability.
Roberts, Benjamin	19	May 23, '61		Re-enlisted 1st Battalion.
Rooks, Wm. A.	19	Apl. 29, '61	Jan. 19, '63	Discharged for disability.
Russell, James E.	22	Apl. 29, '61	Feb. 14, '63	Wounded at Fredericksburg; discharged for disability.
Sawyer, George P.	22	Apl. 29, '61		Killed at Gettysburg.
Sawyer, James T.	25	May 23, '61		Wounded at Antietam.
Schultz, Julius	29	Apl. 29, '61	Jan. 10, '62	Wounded at Bull Run; discharged for disability.
Sissler, Joseph	28	Aug. 29, '61		Killed at Gettysburg.

ROSTER OF COMPANY G—*Continued.*

NAMES.	AGE.	MUSTERED IN.	MUSTERED OUT.	REMARKS.
Soule, Battus K.	31	Apl. 29, '61	Feb. 17, '63	Wounded at Fredericksburg and Antietam; disch. for disab'ty.
Squiers, Chauncey	25	Apl. 29, '61		Wounded at Bull Run.
Strickland, Almond C.	23	May 23, '61	Aug. 3, '61	Wounded at Bull Run; discharged for disability.
Strothman, John E.	28	May 15, '61		Musician, Corp.; killed at Gettysburg.
Taylor, Charles E.	36	Feb. 28, '64		Transferred to 1st Battalion.
Tiffany, Edgar	22	May 23, '61	May 5, '64	Musician.
Thom, George	24	May 23, '61	May 5, '64	
Tuman, Edward	27	Apl. 29, '61	May 5, '64	Corporal, Sergeant.
Wattles, Richard M.	20	Apl. 29, '61	Jan. 3, '63	Wounded at Bull Run; discharged for disability.
Wattles, Leander	18	Aug. 26, '61	Jan. 15, '63	Discharged for disability.
Welles, Henry G.	22	Apl. 29, '61	Nov. 28, '62	Wounded at Savage Station; discharged for disability.
Webster, Chas. E.	21	May 23, '61	Dec. 1, '62	Wounded at Antietam; discharged for disability.
Whitney, Henry Clay	23	Apl. 29, '61	May 5, '64	Sergeant, 1st Sergeant.
Williams, Theodore	22	May 23, '61		Died Sept. 24, '62.
Winchell, Nathaniel	20	May 23, '61	May 5, '64	
Williams, Geo. A.	24	Apl. 29, '61	May 5, '64	Sergeant.
Wood, Luman S.	23	May 23, '61	May 5, '64	Corporal.
Wood, David	26	Apl. 29, '61	May 5, '64	
Verplank, Edward E.	25	Apl. 29, '61	July 31, '61	Wounded at Bull Run; discharged for disability.

ROSTER OF COMPANY H.

NAMES.	AGE.	MUSTERED IN.	MUSTERED OUT.	REMARKS.
OFFICERS.				
Captains—				
Chas. P. Adams	29	Apl. 30, '61		Maj., Lt. Col., Bvt. Brig. Gen.; wnd. Bull Run, Malvern, Antietam and Gettysburg.
John N. Chase	26	Sept. 26, '62	May 4, '64	1st Lieut. and 1st Serg. Company E.
First Lieutenants—				
Orrin T. Hayes	33	Apl. 30, '61	July 29, '61	Resigned.
Wm. B. Leach	27	July 29, '61		2d Lieut., Adjt., Capt. and A. A. G. to Gen. Dana, Feb, 23, '62.
Francis Baasen		Feb. 24, '62		Priv.; appointed Q. M. July 10, '62.
Martin Maginnis	20	Sept. 17, '62		2d Lieut. Co. F.; Capt. Co. K July 28, '63.
Myron Shepard		July 4, '63		Serg. Co. B.; 2d Lieut. Co. H.; transf. to and from Co. F.
Second Lieutenants—				
Henry Hoover	30	July 29, '61	Jan. 8, '62	1st Serg.; resigned.
Jasper N. Searles	20	Jan. 10, '62		Priv.; 1st Lieut. Co. K; Capt. Co. G.
George Boyd				Transferred to Co. E Jan. 23, '63; 1st Lieut. Co. I.
ENLISTED MEN.				
Ackers, James	24	Apl. 29, '61		Serg.; killed at Gettysburg.
Arnsden, Albert	23	Apl. 29, '61		Deserted while absent, sick.
Bates, William	27	Apl. 29, '61	Dec. 21, '61	Discharged for disability.
Baker, Allen	19	May 22, '61	Aug. 5, '61	Discharged for disability.
Bauman, Franklin	18	Apl. 29, '61	May 5, '64	Wounded at Bull Run.
Berkman, William	22		Dec. 23, '62	Discharged for disability.
Bitke, Christian	36		May 5, '64	Wounded at Bull Run.
Boyce, Geo. E.				Killed at Antietam.
Bradbury, Geo. W.	23		May 5, '64	
Brown, David W	21	May 15, '61		Transferred to Inv. Corps Aug., '63.
Brock, Andrew J.	18	May 23, '61		Transferred to U. S. Cav. Oct. 24, '62.
Brock, Columbus	19	May 23, '61		Killed at Bull Run.
Brown, Newton	18	May 23, '61	Dec. 24, '61	Wounded at Bull Run; discharged for disability.
Bunker, Stephen F.	18		Dec. 15, '61	Wounded at Bull Run; discharged for disability.
Cady, Henry C.	19	Apl. 29, '61	Feb. 6, '63	Discharged for disability.
Canfield, Mortimer	23	Apl. 29, '61	May 5, '64	
Cagger, Wilson	26	Apl. 29, '61		Killed at Antietam.
Caniff, J	25	Mch. 24, '64		Transferred to 1st Battalion.
Chase, Andrew J.	24	Dec. 26, '61	Nov. 8, '62	Discharged for disability.
Clausen, John	22	Apl. 29, '61	May 5, '64	Wounded at Bull Run and Gettysburg.
Clutch, David P	23	May 23, '61	May 23, '63	Discharged for disability.
Clifford, Jeremiah	19	Nov. 6, '61		Transferred to U. S. Cavalry Oct. 24, '62.
Conley, Wm. I.	18	May 23, '61		Killed at Bull Run.
Collins, Peter	35	Mch. 24, '64		Transferred to 1st Battalion.
Crandall, Dennis	28	May 15, '61	Feb. 3, '63	Wounded at Bull Run; discharged for disability.
Cronkhite, Samuel S.	29	May 22, '61		Wounded at Gettysburg.
Cross, David C.	31	May 23, '61	Jan. 7, '62	Discharged for disability.
Cummings, Wm. W.	26	Apl. 29, '61		Serg.; wounded Bull Run; killed Oct. 27, '61, accid. dis. of gun.
Dayton, Samuel	43	May 22, '61	Aug. 12, '61	Wagoner; discharged for disability.
Dewey, Benjamin P.	26	May 23, '61	May 1, '63	Discharged for promotion in regular army.
Downs, Thomas	30	May 23, '61	Sept. '62	Discharged for disability.
Drondt, Kellian	26	Apl. 29, '61	May 5, '64	Wounded at Bull Run.
Dyer, Joshua	22	Nov. 5, '61		Corp. and Serg.; transferred to 1st Battalion.
Eaton, William	18	May 22, '61		Transferred to U. S. Cavalry Oct. 24, '62.
Einson, Sear	46	May 23, '61		Killed at Bull Run.
Ellis, Aaron G.	22	May 20, '61	Jan. 23, '63	Discharged for disability.
Erdman, Geo. A.	29	Apl. 29, '61	Feb. 14, '63	Corp.; wounded at Bull Run; discharged for disability.
Estes, Israel H.	24	Apl. 29, '61		Transferred to U. S. Cavalry Oct. 24, '62.

ROSTER OF COMPANY H — *Continued.*

NAMES.	AGE.	MUSTERED IN.	MUSTERED OUT.	REMARKS.
Essencey, John H	26	Apl. 29, '61		Wounded at Antietam; killed at Gettysburg.
Everts, Wm. W	23	Apl. 29, '61		Wounded at Antietam; transferred to U. S. Cavalry Oct. 24, '62.
Farnsworth, Allen C	42	Nov. 5, '61	Jan. 9, '62	Discharged for disability.
Flanagan, John	18	May 22, '61		Deserted June 20, '61, at Fort Snelling, Minn.
Fritz, Alvis	39	May 22, '61		
Galvin, Thomas	25	Apl. 29, '61		Killed in battle.
Geering, Robert	32	Apl. 29, '61	Nov. 2, '62	Discharged for disability.
Getchell, Daniel W	18	Apl. 29, '61	Jan. 2, '62	Discharged for disability.
Ghostly, James T	22	June 2, '61	May 5, '64	Wounded at Bull Run.
Giles, James A	26	Feb. 27, '64		Transferred to 1st Battalion.
Harris, John	19	Apl. 29, '61	Jan. 26, '62	Wounded at Bull Run; discharged for disability.
Harrown, Geo. T	18	Apl. 29, '61		Transferred to U. S. Cavalry Oct. 24, '62.
Harrison, John E	37	May 23, '61	Mch. 17, '63	Discharged for disability.
Harmon, Ransom	27	Apl. 29, '61	May 5, '64	
Hainlin, Ernst	21	Apl. 29, '61	July 5, '62	Discharged for disability.
Henry, James T	22	Apl. 29, '61		Died July 6, '62, of disease.
Helmer, Jeremiah	19	Apl. 29, '61	Feb. 20, '63	Wounded at Bull Run and Antietam; discharged for disab.
Hess, Greenhalt	26	Apl. 29, '61	May 5, '64	Wounded at Antietam.
Heard, Alonzo R	22	May 15, '61		Transferred to Signal Corps Aug. 12, '61.
Hoag, Charles M	26	Apl. 29, '61	Nov. 2, '62	Corp.; discharged for disability.
Hoag, F. W	18	Mch. 28, '64		Transferred to 1st Battalion.
Hunnybun, Thomas	43	Apl. 29, '61	Dec. 17, '61	Wounded at Bull Run; discharged for disability.
Hubbard, Henry A	20	Apl. 29, '61	Dec. 15, '61	Wounded at Bull Run; discharged for disability.
Johnson, Samuel	18	Mch. 10, '64		Transferred to 1st Battalion.
Keating, Robert	18	Apl. 29, '61	June 19, '61	Discharged by writ of habeas corpus.
Kendall, Julien	20	Apl. 29, '61		Discharged for disability.
Keating, Lawrence	28	May 22, '61	May 5, '64	Wounded at Antietam.
Keelty, John K	24	May 23, '61	Mch. 26, '62	Discharged for disability.
Kreitler, John	35	Nov. 5, '61		Transferred to Inv. Corps Sept. 11, '63.
Lawton, Wesley	20	May 22, '61		Musician.
Leathers, Charles	24	Apl. 29, '61	May 5, '64	Wounded at Bristow.
Lindergreen, H. W	25	Apl. 29, '61	July 23, '62	Discharged for disability.
Lowe, Henry A	29	Apl. 29, '61	May 5, '64	Corp.; Serg.; wounded at Bristow.
Mahoney, James	35	Apl. 29, '61	June, '63	Discharged for disability.
Mathews, Adolph	38	May 18, '61	Aug. 5, '61	Discharged for disability.
Macar, John	31	May 23, '61		
Mansfield, Charles	32	May 23, '61	May 5, '64	Wounded at Bull Run.
Mars, John R	27	May 16, '61	May 5, '64	Corporal, 1st Sergeant.
Mead, Frank J	22	May 24, '61		Corp.; transferred to Company B May 17, '62.
Meyer, John	35	May 23, '61		Transferred to Inv. Corps July, '63.
Mosburger, Jacob	19	May 15, '61	Feb. 14, '63	Wounded at Bull Run; discharged for disability.
Munson, M. C	26	Feb. 29, '64		Transferred to 1st Battalion.
Myers, Frederick	19	Apl. 29, '61		Transferred to U. S. Cavalry Oct, 24, '62.
O'Neil, Charles C	20	May 23, '61	Dec. 3, '62	Discharged for disability.
Owen, Apollus E	19	Apl. 29, '61	Nov. 5, '62	Wounded at Antietam; discharged for disability.
Owen, Earl P	25	Oct. 11, '61	Mch. 21, '63	Wounded at Bull Run; discharged for disability.
Panehalt, Geo. F	21	May 23, '61		Killed at Antietam.
Preston, Wallace M	18	Nov. 6, '62	Mch. 10, '63	Discharged for disability.
Pusey Joseph F	27	May 23, '61	Dec. 1, '62	Discharged for disability.
Raymond, Frederick W	19	Apl. 29, '61		Wounded at Gettysburg.
Ratch, William	34	Apl. 29, '61		Absent, sick, on discharge of regiment.
Ragey, Robert	38	Apl. 29, '61		Died Sept. 18, at Alexandria, Va.
Ridge, Joseph	23	May 20, '61	May 5, '64	
Roundtree, James	29	Apl. 29, '61		Transferred to U. S. Cavalry Oct. 24, '64.
Ryan, Patrick	19	May 31, '61	May 5, '64	
Rye, Charles	35	Feb. 27, '64		Transferred to 1st Battalion.
Sastrow, Walter	24	Apl. 29, '61	May 5, '64	
Schultz, Peter	25	Feb. 19 '64		Transferred to 1st Battalion.
Shetts, Charles	22	Apl. 29, '61		Corp., Serg.; transferred to U. S. Cavalry Oct. 24, '62.
Shafer, John C	18	Apl. 29, '61	May 5, '64	
Sholl, John	32	Nov. 5, '61		Killed at Antietam.
Simons, Edwin B	24	Apl. 29, '61		Wounded at Bull Run and Antietam.
Snitsinger, Jabez	22	May 23, '61		Killed at Bull Run.
Starckloffe Herman	29	Mch. 28, '64		Transferred to 1st Battalion.
Sunbay, G. G	27	Feb. 27, '64		Transferred to 1st Battalion.
Truax, Robt. J	18	Apl. 29, '61	June 17, '61	Discharged by writ of habeas corpus.
Tucker, Charles M	23	Apl. 29, '61	Dec. 8, '62	Corp., Serg.; wnd. Fair Oaks; discharged for disab.
Twiggs, David	25	May 20, '61	Aug. 5, '61	Discharged for disability.
Twitchell, Newton H	18	May 20, '61	July 25, '62	Discharged for disability.
Vace, H P			Feb. 11, '63	Discharged for disability.
VanValkenberg, Noah	18	May 18, '61	Dec. 9, '61	Musician; discharged for disability.
Webster, Solon	33	May 22, '61	Aug. 9, '92	Discharged for disability.
White, John	29	Apl. 29, '61		Absent, sick, on discharge of regiment.
Whalen, Martin S	37	Feb. 25, '61		Transferred to 1st Battalion.
Wicoff, Wm: H	26	May 28, '64		Serg.; killed at Gettysburg.
Wixon, John W	21	May 22, '61	Aug. 8, '62	Discharged for disability.
Wingett, Oliver	21	Feb. 21, '62		Died Aug. 5, '62, of disease in Virginia.
Wood, Edward L	18	Apl. 29, '61		Sergeant.
Young, Alonzo I	36	Apl. 29, '61		Serg.; discharged for disability.
Youmans, Michael	19	Apl. 29, '61		Wounded at Bull Run.

ROSTER OF COMPANY I.

NAMES.	AGE.	MUSTERED IN.	MUSTERED OUT.	REMARKS.
OFFICERS.				
Captains—				
John H. Pell	30	Apl. 29, '61	Mch. 26, '63	Resigned.
Wilbur F. Duffy	23	Mch. 26, '63	May 4, '64	1st Lieutenant Co. C.
First Lieutenants—				
Joseph Harley		Apl. 30, '61		Wounded at Bull Run; resigned July 31, '61.
Samuel T. Raguet		Aug. 8, '61		Transferred from Co. C and to Co. E.
George Boyd			May 4, '64	2d Lieut. Cos. E and H.
Second Lieutenants—				
Charles B. Halsey		Apl. 30, '61	Nov. 15, '61	Resigned.
C. Edward Davis		Nov. 18, '61		Promoted Capt. Co. E July 3, '63.
Waldo Farrar				1st Serg.; killed at Gettysburg.
ENLISTED MEN.				
Abbott Henry	18	May 22, '61	May 5, '64	
Baker, Nahum C	18	May 26, '61	Aug. 1, '61	Discharged for disability.
Bartlett, Ransom A	24	Apl. 29, '61		Transferred to Co. G.
Bledin, Nathan S	18	May 24, '61		Transferred to 4th U. S. Cav. Oct. 23, '62.
Boyd, Jehial W	26	May 24, '61		Deserted June, '61, at Fort Snelling.
Brown, Frank S	18	Sept. 28, '61	Dec. 16, '61	Discharged for disability.
Burnham, Rollin M	18	May 26, '61		
Coffin, David A	35	Apl. 29, '61		Corp., Serg., Serg. Major, 1st Lieut. in Co. A.
Carlson, Carl M	30	May 28, '61	May 5, '64	Musician.
Canfield, Wm. O	23	Apl. 29, '61	May 5, '64	Corporal.
Cannon, James	42	Apl. 29, '61	Nov. 27, '62	Wounded at Bull Run and Fair Oaks; discharged for wounds.
Carroll, Thomas	20	Apl. 29, '61	Dec. 15, '63	Discharged per order.
Cariguet, Bartholomew	29	Apl. 29, '61		Transferred to Co. B Feb. 21, '62.
Canfield, Amos	33	Apl. 29, '61	Feb. 15, '63	Discharged for disability.
Churchill, John M	25	Apl. 29, '61	May 5, '64	Corporal.
Clark, Levi	30	Sept. 10, '61		Transferred to 1st Battalion.
Colyer, Andrew H	18	Apl. 29, '61		Killed at Bull Run.
Coleman, James	24	Apl. 29, '61		Transferred to 4th U. S. Cav. Oct. 23, '62.
Conner, Thomas	23	Sept. 14, '61		Transferred to 4th U. S. Cav. Oct. 23, '62.
Coleman, Henry	35	Mch. 29, '64		Transferred to 1st Battalion.
Cooper, John	40	Mch. 29, '64		Transferred to 1st Battalion.
Crandall, Dennis			Feb. 4, '63	Discharged for disability.
Cureneff, Patrick S	18	Apl. 29, '61		Killed at Bull Run.
Davis, Albert S	27	May 24, '61		Wnd. at Bull Run; trans. to Co. B; Corp. and Serg. Major; 1st Lieut. Co. A.
Dechanette, Alfred	22	Apl. 29, '61	May 5, '64	
Dilly, Stephen B	22	Apl. 29, '61	Mch. 5, '63	Serg.; discharged for disability.
Donevan, Jeremiah	18	May 23, '61	May 5, '64	Wounded at Bull Run and Gettysburg.
Dwelle, Thomas M	21	Sept. 10, '61	Feb. 7, '63	Discharged for disability.
Ellison, Augustus	22	Apl. 29, '61		Wounded at Bull Run; killed June 13, '62, near Fair Oaks.
Ellis Philander C	28	Apl. 29, '61		Wounded at Bull Run; killed at Gettysburg.
Enery, Levi	27	May 26, '61	Apl. 18, '62	Discharged for wounds at Bull Run.
Erwin, Alexander		Dec. 18, '61	Jan. 27, '63	Discharged for disability.
Ferris, Myron I	19	May 26, '61		Transferred to 4th U. S. Cav. Oct. 23, '62.
Fisher, Chas. K	23	Sept. 28, '61		Transferred to 1st Battalion.
Fisk, Van H	21	Sept. 14, '61	Feb. 16, '63	Discharged for disability.
Fox, John	28	May 30, '61	May 5, '64	
Fernirod, Francis	33	Apl. 29, '61	May 5, '64	Corp.; wounded at Bull Run.
Freeze, Jacob F	23	Apl. 29, '61		Died Aug. 2, '63, of wounds at Gettysburg.
Frey, Joseph	32	May 30, '61		Wounded at Bull Run; killed at Gettysburg.
Gorman, Richard L	24	Apl. 29, '61		Discharged for promotion 1st Lieut. in 34th N. Y. Vols.
Hancock, Allen H	18	Apl. 29, '61		Wounded at Bull Run.
Harris, Wesley	18	May 24, '61		Died April, '64.
Hayden, Anson R	25	May 24, '61	May 5, '64	Corp., Serg.; wounded at Bull Run.
Hale, Edward P	22	Sept. 28, '61		Died of wounds received at Gettysburg Sept. 12, '63.
Hendricks, Marcus L	21	Apl. 29, '61		Transferred to 4th U. S. Cav. Oct. 23, '62.
Hetherington, James W	19	May 24, '61		Deserted June 9, '61, at Fort Snelling.
Hendricks, F. M	24	Dec. 27, '61		Died July 22, '62.
Hickey, John	29	May 22, '61		Deserted Sept. 6, '63, at Brooklyn, N. Y.
Hitt, Thadeus N	43	Dec. 17, '61	May 16, '63	Discharged for disability.
Howell, Wm. D	22	May 24, '61		Wounded at Gettysburg.
Hutchins, Daniel	26	May 30, '61		Wounded at Gettysburg.
Jackson, Benjamin	29	Sept. 28, '61		Wounded at Gettysburg; transferred to 1st Battalion.
Johnson, Andrew	22	June 4, '61		Transferred to Co. H Feb. 1, '62.
Johnson, Nelson	21	May 23, '61		Transferred to 4th U. S. Cav. Oct. 23, '62.
Johnson, John A	19	May 31, '61		Transferred to 4th U. S. Cav. Oct. 23, '62.
Jones, Ambrose	28	Sept. 28, '61		Transferred to 1st Battalion.
Keeler, George S	18	Apl. 29, '61	May 5, '64	
Keis, Daniel	25	Apl. 29, '61	May 5, '64	
Kerrott, Edwin M	18	May 24, '61	Dec. 3, '61	Wounded at Bull Run; discharged for disability.
Kenney, Mark	19	May 23, '61	May 5, '64	Wounded.
Ketchum, George W	23	Sept. 28, '61		Wounded at Antietam; transferred to 1st Battalion.
Kline, George	22	May 24, '61	Feb. 7, '63	Wounded at Bull Run; discharged for disability.
Knight, Oliver M	23	Apl. 29, '61	Oct. 2, '63	Serg.; wnd. at Gettysburg; dis. for pro. Prov. Marshal 1st Div. 25th Corps.
Lawson, Herman	20	Apl. 29, '61	May 5, '64	Corp.; wounded at Bull Run and Gettysburg.
Lavercombe, John	29	Mch. 30, '64		Transferred to 1st Battalion.
Lessing, Ferdinand	24	Apl. 29, '61		Absent on detached service on discharge of regiment.
Lent, Benjamin	23	Apl. 29, '61	Nov. 16, '63	Wounded; discharged per order.
Mason, Charles F	19	May 23, '61	May 5, '64	Wounded at Bull Run.
McKey, John H	18	May 22, '61	May 5, '64	
McClay, John	24	Feb. 26, '64		Transferred to 1st Battalion.
Miller, George	20	Apl. 29, '61		Transferred to 4th U. S. Cav. Oct. 23, '62.
Miller, Frederick	18	May 24, '61	Dec. 28, '63	Discharged per order.
Milliken, George A	19	Apl. 29, '61	Dec. 15, '63	Wounded at Gettysburg; discharged for disability.

Roster of Company I — *Continued.*

Names.	Age.	Mustered In.	Mustered Out.	Remarks.
Miller, Ernst L. F	27	May 30, '61		Wounded at Gettysburg.
Milne, John O	23	June 1, '61	Dec. 16, '61	Wounded at Bull Run; discharged for disability.
Mitchell, Lewis F	27	June 2, '61		Killed Oct. 22, '61, on skirmish at Edwards' Ferry.
Murray, John W	31	June 3, '61	Dec. 7, '61	Wounded at Bull Run; discharged for disability.
Nassig, Charles	38	May 29, '61	Jan. 30, '63	Wounded at Antietam; discharged for disability.
Noonan, Patrick	35	Mch. 14, '64		Transferred to 1st Battalion.
O'Neil, James	21	Apl. 29, '61		Corp., Serg., 1st Serg.; wounded at Bull Run and Gettysburg.
Orcutt, Henry C	20	May 26, '61	May 5, '64	
Orcutt, Freeman	18	May 26, '61		Absent on detached service.
Organ, George A	26	May 30, '61		Corp., Serg.; died Feb. 3, '63, of disease.
Paul, Wm. L	19	Apl. 29, '61		Transferred to U. S. Cav. Oct. 23, '62.
Paul, Edwin	21	May 26, '61		Died July 14, '63, of wounds at Gettysburg.
Parsons, Henry	21	May 24, '61		Transferred to 4th U. S. Cav. Oct. 23, '62.
Peck, Wm. N	21	May 29, '61		Died July 4, '63, of wounds at Gettysburg.
Pendergast, Lloyd G	19	May 4, '61		Transferred to 4th U. S. Cav. Oct. 23, '62.
Philbrook, Wm. B	20	May 24, '61	May 5, '64	
Pickett, Corwin	21	Apl. 29, '61		Died June 13, '62.
Pittenger, James Q	19	May 22, '61		Wounded at Bull Run; died Nov. 4, '62, at Harper's Ferry.
Pickett, Thomas C				Died July 22, '62.
Price, Edward B	41	May 22, '61	May 5, '64	Serg.; wounded at Gettysburg.
Putnam, Wm A	27	Apl. 29, '61	Mch. 27, '63	Discharged for disability.
Rabaca, Herman	21	Apl. 29, '61	May 5, '64	
Richards, Wm. K	27	June 3, '61	May 5, '64	Corp., Serg.; wounded at Gettysburg.
Roe, Wm J	31	Apl. 29, '61		Corp., Serg.; died of wounds received at Gettysburg.
Schweizer, Michael	27	May 30, '61	May 5, '64	Wounded.
Schimeck, Anton E	33	May 24, '61		Killed at Bull Run.
Scurry, James		Feb. 27, '64		Transferred to 1st Battalion.
Schweigert, William		Mch. 23, '64		Transferred to 1st Battalion.
Seymour, Samuel O. K	37	Apl. 29, '61	May 5, '64	Wounded at Bull Run and Gettysburg.
Shook, Norman		Mch. 30, '64		Transferred to Battalion.
Smith, George M	19	May 24, '61		
Soper, Palmer	43	May 26, '61	Dec. 15, '61	Discharged for disability.
Soper, Edmund	18	May 26, '61	May 5, '64	
Strandt, Sivert	25	May 31, '61	Feb. 10, '63	Discharged for disability.
Stull, William	21	May 22, '61		Transferred to U. S. Cav. Oct. 23, '63.
Sutliff, Omar H	24	May 24, '61	May 5, '64	Wounded at Gettysburg.
Sullivan, John	44	May 28, '61	May 5, '64	
Veon, Edmund	23	Sept. 28, '64		Transferred to 1st Battalion.
Weaver, Daniel S	26	Apl. 29, '61	May 5, '64	Corporal.
Wells, Henry G	22	Apl. 29, '61		Corp.; transferred to Co. G.
Welch, Byron	23	Apl. 29, '61		Wagoner; killed at Gettysburg.
Weaver, George	28	Apl. 29, '61	May 5, '64	
Whitcomb, Milo S	23	May 23, '61	Feb. 14, '63	Wounded at Antietam; discharged for disability.
Widger, Henry	23	May 22, '61	Jan. 20, '64	Discharged for disability.
Winkelman, Edward E	38	Apl. 29, '61		Absent on detached service.
Woodard, Oscar	18	May 24, '61		Killed at Gettysburg.
Worthington, Wm H	41	Apl. 29, '61	May 5, '64	Serg.; wounded at Gettysburg.
Wellman, William F	18	May 26, '61		Died Aug. 27, '63, of wounds at Gettysburg.

ROSTER OF COMPANY K.

Names.	Age.	Mustered In.	Mustered Out.	Remarks.
OFFICERS.				
Captains —				
Henry C. Lester	29	Apl. 30, '61	Nov. 15, '61	Pro. Col. 3d Minn. Inf.
Gustavus A. Holtzborn	32	Nov. 15, '61		1st Lieut.; killed Sept. 17, '62, at Antietam.
Joseph Periam		Sept. 17, '62		1st and 2d Lieut.; died July 7, '63, at Gettysburg, of wounds.
Martin Maginnis		July 8, '63	May 4, '64	1st Lieut. Co. H., 2d Lieut. and 1st Serg. Co. F.
First Lieutenants —				
Jasper N. Searles				2d Lieut. and Priv. Co. H; Capt. Co. G.
David A. Coflin			May 4, '64	Transferred from Co. A.
Second Lieutenants —				
John Ball	25	Nov. 15, '61		1st Serg., 1st Lieut. and Capt. Co. F; wounded at Bristow; Lieut. Col. 11th Minn.
William Lochren	29	Sept. 22, '62		Serg. and 1st Lieut. Co. E.
ENLISTED MEN.				
Abell, William H	21	May 22, '61		Re-enlisted in 1st Battalion.
Alderson, John	21	May 22, '61	Mch. 26, '62	Wounded and captured at Bull Run; discharged for disability.
Allred, Levi J	31	Apl. 29, '61	May 5, '64	Corp., Serg., Lieut. 1st Heavy Artillery.
Andrus, Charles H	26	May 22, '61	Aug. 10, '61	Discharged for disability.
Badgely, John J	21	May 23, '61	Nov. 25, '61	Discharged for disability.
Babcock, James M	23	May 22, '61		Transferred to Inv. Corps Dec. 1, '63.
Barton, Wm. J	18	Apl. 29, '61		Wounded at Bull Run.
Best, Baltasar	23	Apl. 29, '61	May 5, '64	Wounded at Bristow.
Behr, Chas	23	Apl. 29, '61		Wounded at Gettysburg.
Beals, William	24	May 22, '61	May 5, '64	
Berry, Noah F	23	May 22, '61		Transferred to Inv. Corps Dec. 1, '63.
Bingham, Horatio S	23	Apl. 29, '61	Oct. 2, '62	Serg.; discharged per order; Capt. 2d Cav.
Boyson, Henry	23	Apl. 29, '61	May 5, '64	
Bourne, Chardon	27	May 22, '61	May 5, '64	

Roster of Company K — *Continued.*

Names.	Age.	Mustered In.	Mustered Out.	Remarks.
Boardman, Charles B	26	May 22, '61	May 5, '64	Wounded at Fredericksburg.
Brockway, Stephen R	22	May 22, '61	Nov. 10, '61	Wounded at Bull Run; discharged for disability.
Brink, Hiram A	31	Apl. 29, '61		Serg.; re-enlisted in 1st Battalion.
Burgess, George N	24	Apl. 29, '61		Corp., Color Serg.; killed at Savage Station.
Burton, Ephraim P	22	Apl. 29, '61		Killed at Bull Run.
Burgess, Samuel M	21	Nov. 11, '61	Jan. 27, '63	Wounded at Antietam; discharged for disability.
Carpenter, Alfred P	24	May 23, '61	Sept. 24, '63	Corp., Serg.; wnd. at Antietam and Gettysburg; Lt in col'd regt.
Casey, Edward	20	May 23, '61		Transferred to U. S. Light Art. Oct. 24, '62.
Caulkin, Gavin E	36	Feb. 27, '61		Transferred to 1st Battalion.
Chapman, Edgar	23	Apl. 29, '61	May 5, '64	Sergeant.
Chase, Wm. B	22	May 23, '61		Transferred to U. S. Light Art. Oct. 24, '62.
Churchill, Wm. H	20	Oct. 4, '61		Captured; transferred to 1st Battalion.
Chandler, Joseph C				Wounded at Gettysburg.
Countryman, Chas. C	22	May 22, '61		Wounded at Antietam; transferred to 7th U. S. Inf.
Coy, Wm. A	21	May 22, '61	Feb. 18, '63	Wounded at Antietam; discharged for disability.
Colburn, Alfred	27	Nov. 4, '61	Aug. 23, '62	Discharged for disability.
Crippen, Joseph M	24	May 22, '61		Transferred to U. S. Cav. Oct. 24, '62.
Day, John	29	Apl. 29, '61		Transferred to U. S. Cav. Oct. 24, '62.
Dribblebiss, John	33	Apl. 29, '61	Apl. 10, '63	Wagoner; discharged for disability.
Drayne, Daniel	24	Apl. 29, '61	May 5, '64	
Dudley, David B	23	Apl. 29, '61		Corp., Serg., 1st Serg.; died Oct. 6, '62, of wounds, at Antietam.
Durfee, George H	22	May 23, '61	May 5, '64	
Durfee, Jason	20	May 23, '61		Wounded at Bull Run; died at Richmond.
Durfee, Chester H	18	Aug. 26, '61		Wounded at Gettysburg; transferred to 1st Battalion.
Durr. Israel	21	Jan. 25, '62		Died of wounds at Gettysburg.
Eaton, Joseph S	29	May 22, '61		Wounded at Bull Run and Gettysburg.
Einfeldt, John	23	Apl. 29, '61	May 5, '64	Corp., Serg.; wounded at Gettysburg.
Ely, Charles E	18	Apl. 29, '61	May 5, '64	Corp.; wounded at Gettysburg.
Evans, John J	24	Apl. 29, '62	Nov. 28, '62	Serg.; discharged for disability.
Fajans, Julius	24	May 22, '61	May 4, '62	Corp.; discharged for promotion as Hospital Steward.
Flemming, W H	22	May 22, '61	July 13, '61	Discharged for disability.
French, James H	21	Apl. 29, '61		Deserted June, '62.
George, Andrew	23	May 20, '61		Deserted July 27, '61, at Washington, D. C.
Geisreiter, Jacob	23	May 22, '61		Killed at Gettysburg.
Goddard, Charles E	18	Apl. 29, '61	May 5, '64	Corp.; wounded at Gettysburg.
Gore, Leslie P	19	May 22, '61		Corp.; killed at Gettysburg.
Grimm, Fritz	22	Apl. 29, '61		Killed at Bull Run.
Harding, Hiram	23	Apl. 29, '61	Aug. 2, '61	Wounded at Bull Run; discharged for promotion.
Hanson, Lewis	21	Dec. 16, '61		Wounded at Gettysburg.
Hill, Joseph S	22	May 22, '61	May 5, '64	
Holland, Alonzo	23	Nov. 18, '61		Transferred to 1st Battalion.
Iverson, Erick	21	May 22, '61	May 5, '64	Musician.
Johnson, Geo. F	20	Mch. 18, '64		Transferred to 1st Battalion.
Keiley, Timothy	21	Apl. 29, '61		Corp.; wounded at Gettysburg.
Kennedy, Mack J	28	Apl. 29, '61	Nov. 13, '62	Discharged per order.
Kenniston, Alfred	34	Nov. 26, '61	Aug. 14, '62	Discharged for disability.
Ketchum, Cornelius	23	Nov. 18, '61		Sent to general hospital Mch. 28, '62.
Kinnen, Mathias	24	May 22, '61	May 5, '64	Musician.
Kinyon, Wm H	21	May 22, '61	May 5, '64	Wounded at Gettysburg.
Knapp, Byron C	21	May 22, '61	Nov. 27, '61	Discharged for disability.
Lacy, Origen R	20	Apl. 29, '61		Sent to general hospital; trans. to 9th Minn. Vols.
Lincoln, Charles E	21	Apl. 29, '61		Discharged per order.
Lincoln, Joseph	23	Nov. 18, '61	Sept. 6, '62	Discharged for disability.
Lynn, John	28	Apl. 29, '61		Transferred to U. S. Cavalry Oct. 21, '62.
Martin, Wm A	21	May 22, '61		Killed at Antietam.
Manning, John	20	May 23, '61	May 5, '64	Wounded at Antietam.
Marvin, Mathew	22	Apl. 29, '61		Corp., Serg., 1st Serg.; wounded at Bull Run, Harrison's Landing and Gettysburg.
Martin, Stephen E	19	May 22, '61	May 5, '64	Corporal.
McIntyre, Malcolm	29	Apl. 26, '61	May 5, '64	
McDonnell, Allen	22	May 23, '61	Jan. 8, '62	Discharged per order.
Merritt, John G	23	Apl. 29, '61	May 5, '64	Serg.; wounded at Bull Run.
Moore, Zuar E.	26	Apl. 29, '61		Serg.; killed at Bull Run.
Moore, Oliver W	30	May 23, '61		Corp.; transferred to U. S. Light Artillery Oct. 24, '62.
Moore, John	22	May 22, '61	Feb. 7, '63	Discharged for disability.
Morton, Henry	18	May 23, '61		Killed at Bull Run.
Nicklin, Samuel	25	May 23, '61	Dec. 18, '62	Wounded at Bull Run; discharged for disability.
North, Charles	21	Apl. 29, '61		Corp., Serg., 1st Serg.; wounded at Gettysburg.
Palmer, John W	19	Apl. 29, '61	Apl. 5, '64	Discharged per order.
Patton, William	22	May 22, '61		Wounded at Bull Run; sent to general hospital Oct. '62.
Pfund, William	29	Apl. 29, '61	Aug. 25, '61	Discharged for disability.
Pickle, Alonzo	19	Aug. 14, '62		Transferred to Battalion.
Raymond, George	22	Apl. 29, '61	Aug. 1, '61	Discharged for disability.
Raig, W. R	18	Feb. 9, '64		
Reynolds, James J	19	Apl. 29, '61		Transferred to U. S. Cav. Oct. '62.
Remore, Elijah	25	Apl. 29, '61		Transferred to Inv. Corps.
Richardson, James O	21	May 23, '61	May 5, '64	
Rowley, Edward A	19	May 22, '61		Wounded and captured at Bull Run.
Sargent, Wm G	18	May 22, '61	May 5, '64	Corp.; discharged per order.
Seeley, James A	23	Apl. 29, '61		Corp.; transferred to U. S. Light Artillery Oct. 24, '62.
Shaw, Alexander	20	May 23, '61	May 5, '64	Wounded at Fair Oaks and Fredericksburg.
Sheeks, Franklin	20	May 23, '61	May 5, '64	
Sherman, Wm M	18	Dec. 2, '61		Wounded at Antietam; transferred to U. S. Cav. Oct. 27, '62.
Smith, Elbridge	19	Apl. 29, '61	Jan. 15, '63	Discharged for promotion U. S. Top. Eng. Corps.
Smith, Geo. C	29	Apl. 29, '61	Dec. 21, '61	Discharged for disability.
Smith, Samuel	21	Apl. 29, '61	Dec. 22, '61	Wounded at Bull Run; discharged for disability.
Smith, Augustus H	22	Nov. 25, '61		Killed at Gettysburg.

5

THE FIRST REGIMENT AND BATTALION.

ROSTER OF COMPANY K—Continued.

NAMES.	AGE.	MUSTERED IN.	MUSTERED OUT.	REMARKS.
Smith, Wm.	25	Apl. 29, '61		Corp.; killed at Antietam.
Southmayd, John A.	24	May 23, '61		Discharged in hospital.
Stebbins, Samuel E.	31		Nov. 28, '62	Corp.; wounded at Bull Run; discharged for disability.
Sully, John W.	18	Nov. 20, '62		Transferred to U.S. Cav. Oct. 24, '62.
Taylor, David	24	May 23, '61		Killed at Gettysburg.
Tallman, S. F.	21	Mch. 30, '64		Transferred to 1st Battalion.
Teeter, Moses J.	24	May 23, '61	Aug. 3, '61	Discharged per disability.
Terrl, Israel M.	28	May 23, '61		Discharged for disability.
Tomlison, Reuben	21	Dec. 16, '61		Discharged from hospital.
Thompson, Aaron J.	18	Apl. 29, '61		Transferred to U.S. Cav. Oct. 24, '62.
Thorp, John	21	Mch. 31, '64	May 5, '64	Wounded at Bristow.
Tolby, Ed.	21			Transferred to 1st Battalion.
Tenney, Samuel S.	17			Wounded at Gettysburg; transferred to 1st Battalion.
Truesdale, Andrew J.	23	Dec. 24, '61	Nov. 28, '62	Wounded at Fair Oaks; discharged for disability.
Towner, James	23			Wounded at Gettysburg.
Vosz, Peter	38	May 22, '61		Killed at Gettysburg.
Warner, Warren	27	May 22, '61	Oct. 14, '63	Wounded at Vienna; discharged for disability.
Walden, Lucius F.	20	Feb. 15, '64		Corp.; transferred to U.S. Cav. Oct. 24, '62.
Wentworth, Wm B.	23	May 22, '61		Transferred to 1st Battalion.
Winchell, Wm B.	28	May 22, '61		Killed Sept. 1, '62, in action near Flint Hill.
Winters, Henry C.	29	May 22, '61		Wounded at Antietam; killed at Gettysburg.
Woodward, Frank	30	Apl. 29, '61	Nov. 27, '61	Discharged for disability.
Wright, Randolph	20	May 22, '61		Corp.; killed at Gettysburg.
Zimmerman, Chris.	28	Apl. 29, '61	May 5, '64	Wounded at Bull Run.

FIELD AND STAFF OFFICERS OF THE FIRST BATTALION.

NAMES.	AGE.	MUSTERED IN.	MUSTERED OUT.	REMARKS.
Lieutenant Colonel.				
Mark W. Downie.	29	Apl. 6, '65	July 14, '65	Maj. 1st Minn.; com. Col. of Battalion.
Major.				
Charles F. Hausdorf.		May 2, '65	July 14, '65	Vet.; 1st Lieut. and Capt. Co. B; com. Lieut. Col. of Battalion.
Adjutant.				
James H. Plane.	32	July 1, '65	July 14, '65	Priv. Co. D; Serg. Maj.
Quartermaster.				
John W. Pride.	26	July 1, '65	July 14, '65	Vet., Serg. Maj.
Surgeon.				
John B. Le Blond.		May 17, '65	July 14, '65	Surg. 1st Minnesota.
Assistant Surgeon.				
Charles H. Spear		July 1, '65	July 14, '65	Vet. Co. B, Minn. Sharpshooters; Hospital Steward.
Sergeant Major.				
Hugo Reed.	21	Mch. 14, '65	July 14, '65	Priv. Co. I.
Quartermaster Sergeant.				
David L. Morgan.	18	Apl. 1, '64	July 14, '65	Priv. Co. D; transferred to Co. F.
Commissary Sergeant.				
Quinton Bunch.		Mch. 15, '65		Vet., Priv. Co. B July 1, '65.
Hospital Steward.				
Albert Little.	30	Dec. 21, '63	July 14, '65	Veteran.

ROSTER OF COMPANY A.

NAMES.	AGE.	MUSTERED IN.	MUSTERED OUT.	REMARKS.
OFFICERS.				
Captains.				
James C. Farwell.	31	May 5, '64	Dec. 7, '64	Vet.; discharged per order; Brevet Maj.
Henry D. O'Brien.	22	Apl. 10, '65	July 14, '65	Vet.; wnd. Deep Bottom Aug. 14, '64; 2d Lt. Co. B; com. Maj.
First Lieutenants.				
Chesley C. Tirrell.	26	May 12, '64	Dec. 15, '64	Vet.; discharged for wounds received Petersburg June 18, '64.
Charles C. Parker.	27	Dec. 26, '64		Vet., 2d Lieut., Capt. Co. C.
Thomas H. Pressnell.	21	Apl. 1, '65		Vet., 1st Serg., 2d Lieut., Capt. Co. B.
Second Lieutenant.				
John W. Pride.		Apl. 24, '65	July 14, '65	Veteran.
ENLISTED MEN.				
Abel, John.	20	Jan. 1, '62	Dec. 31, '64	
Abbott, Elza S.	22	Mch. 9, '65	July 14, '65	
Adams, William	19	Apl. 1, '64		Died Sept. 1, '64, at White Hall, Pa.
Allyn, J. H. A.	27	Mch. 24, '64		Vet., Corp., Serg.; pris. of war; absent on dis. of battalion.
Allyn, Joshua	33	Mch. 8, '65	July 14, '65	
Baker, Charles B.	24	Jan. 9, '64	Aug. 4, '65	Vet.; captured near Petersburg; paroled; dis. per order.
Baker, Jefferson G.	20	Apl. 5, '64		Vet.; died in rebel prison.
Babcock, James M.	18	Mch. 25, '63	July 14, '65	Vet.; Corp.; wounded June 22, '64, Petersburg.

ROSTER OF COMPANY A—Continued.

NAMES.	AGE.	MUSTERED IN.	MUSTERED OUT.	REMARKS.
Baldwin, Jerome.	18	Mch. 4, '64		Vet.; died Aug. 11, '64, at David's Island, N.Y. Harbor.
Bennett, Theodore A.	20	Dec. 25, '61		Vet.; missing at Hatcher's Run.
Bennett, Wm. P.	39	Mch. 6, '65	Aug. 10, '65	Discharged per order.
Benson, Halver	24	Feb. 29, '64	June 9, '65	Corp.; wounded at Reams' Station Aug. 25, '64.
Bertram, James		Apl. 2, '62		Transf. from A, 2d Sharpshooters; transf. to V.R.C. May 27, '65; vet.
Blanchard, Chas. C.	22	Nov. 16, '61	Nov. 26, '64	Veteran.
Blackwell, Henry	27	Mch. 30, '63		Absent on discharge of battalion.
Blake, George	24	Dec. 25, '63		Transf. from A, 2d S.S., Jan.30,'65; missing battle May 6,'64; vet.
Blakely, Wm.	17	Mch. 6, '65		Died May 5, '65, in A.C. hospital.
Boney, Sylvester		Apl. 1, '64		Captured in battle Aug. 25, '64.
Botterding, Peter G.		Feb. 20, '64	June 8, '65	Discharged per order.
Boan, Dudley A.		Mch. 30, '65	July 14, '65	Vet.; transf. from A, 2d Sharpshooters, Jan. 30, '65.
Brown, Wm. J. W.	35	Sept. 30, '61	Oct. 31, '64	Veteran.
Brown, Wm. W.	22	Sept. 13, '61	Sept. 14, '64	Vet.; absent sick on dis. of company; dis. per order.
Brady, Thomas.	35	Mch. 11, '65	July 14, '65	Vet., Corp.
Brown, Frederick A.	40	Feb. 27, '64	July 14, '65	Corp.; wnd. Nov. 5, '64; dis. for pro. in 1st Heavy Art.
Brown, John J.	23	Mch. 6, '65	Jan. 24, '65	Vet.; captured at Petersburg; dis. per order.
Carney, James H.	23	Apl. 1, '64	July 14, '65	
Carpenter, Edson.	34	Feb. 29, '64	July 14, '65	
Christianson, Ole	31	Mch. 6, '65	July 14, '65	
Chisholm, Daniel	29	Feb. 28, '64		Killed June 18, '64, near Petersburg, Va.
Clen, Jacob	29	Mch. 24, '64	July 14, '65	Corp., Serg.
Clark, George B.	30	Oct. 2, '61		Vet.; transferred to V.R.C. May 19, '65.
Clancy, Daniel	30	Feb. 27, '61		Vet.; wnd. June 22, '64, Petersburg, transf. to V.R.C.
Clifton, Edward		July 20, '61		Vet.; killed June 18, '64, near Petersburg.
Clark, Charles I.	33	Sept. 18, '61		Vet.; wnd. June 18, '64, near Petersburg.
Clark, Levi		Mch. 8, '61		Vet., Corp.; discharged per order.
Close, Theodore A.	18	Feb. 1, '64		Veteran.
Cook, William H.	38	Jan. 1, '64		Veteran.
Collins, Jeremiah		June 27, '61		Veteran.
Coombs, William		July 20, '64		
Coonus, Charles A.	35	Sept. 16, '61		Vet.; died April 1, '65, at Benton Barracks, Mo.
Crist, John J	23	Sept. 16, '61		Vet.; died in rebel prison.
Devlin, Michael	23	Apl. 8, '62	Apl. 26, '65	Vet.; transf. from A, 2d S.S., Jan. 30, '65; killed in battle Mch. 13, '65.
Doran, Nelson	20	Mch. 31, '64	Dec. 18, '64	Veteran.
Doughty, Asa B.	21	Feb. 19, '64	July 11, '65	Vet.; transf. 2d S.S., Jan. 30, '65; killed in battle Mch. 13, '65.
Doolan, Thomas.	18	Mch. 2, '65	Dec. 18, '64	In hospital.
Eastman, Rufus M.	18	Feb. 19, '64	July 11, '65	Corp.; wounded June 22, '64, near Petersburg.
Ellsworth, Charles B.	36	Feb. 29, '64	July 14, '65	Wounded June 22, '64, near Petersburg.
Erickson, Edward	22	Feb. 19, '64	June 8, '65	Wounded June 18, '64, near Petersburg.
Evanston, Andrew	83	Aug. 12, '62	July 14, '65	Corp.; discharged per order.
Farrington, William F.	18	Sept. 28, '61		
Farnand, John	44	Jan. 4, '64	June 26, '65	Vet.; killed Aug. 14, '64, at Deep Bottom, Va.
Farnand, Frank J.	32	Mch. 6, '65	July 14, '65	Vet.; transf. from I, 1st U.S.S.S., Jan. 30, '65; dis. per order.
Fisher, Charles K.	84	Sept. 2, '61		Vet., Serg.
Fisher, Jacob	30	Dec. 29, '64	Dec. 29, '64	Vet.; died Aug. 15, '64, at Deep Bottom of wounds.
Fuller, Lyman R.	25	Mch. 31, '64		Vet., Serg.
Geiser, Frederick	34	Apl. 4, '64	July 14, '65	Vet., Wagoner.
George, Jacob	18	July 29, '61		Died Oct. 20, '64, in rebel prison.
Gibbs, Gates.	83	Feb. 29, '61	July 14, '65	
Gifford, Samuel S.	83	Mch. 20, '64	June 26, '65	Corporal.
Gould, Aaron	24	Jan. 4, '64	July 14, '65	
Gunnaison, Hans.		Apl. 4, '64	July 17, '65	
Gunderson, Ole.		Sept. 2, '62	Dec. 29, '64	
Graffham, Francis.	80	Dec. 31, '64		
Hanson, Charles W.		Apl. 1, '64	July 14, '65	
Hayford, Faxon.		July 29, '64	July 14, '65	
Harvey, Julius	18	Sept. 27, '61	Sept. 27, '64	
Haskell, Merritt.	24	Feb. 17, '65	July 14, '65	
Henderson, Thomas D.	42	Mch. 9, '65	July 14, '65	
Herrick, John G.		Mch. 9, '65	July 14, '65	
Irvine, Theodore A.	18	Dec. 30, '61		Vet.; wounded June 22, '64, Petersburg.
Jackson, Benjamin	37	Sept. 28, '61	Sept. 27, '64	
Jacobson, Martin	26	Mch. 9, '65	July 14, '65	Veteran.
Jenkins, Erastus.		Sept. 28, '61	Sept. 27, '64	
Jennings, Frank M	27	Mch. 9, '65	July 14, '65	
Johnson, John	23	Mch. 9, '65	July 14, '65	
Jones, Ambrose	23	Sept. 28, '61	July 14, '65	Vet., Corp., Serg., 2d Lieut. Co. C.
Jones, Henry.	36	Mch. 31, '64	July 14, '65	
Johnson, Soren.	22	Mch. 9, '65	July 14, '65	
Joy, Wm. A.	23	Apl. 27, '64	May 27, '65	Transferred to V.R.C. May 27, '65; Musician.
Johnson, Wm. H.	21	Mch. 24, '64	July 14, '65	Vet., Corp.
Johnson, Geo. F.	23	Aug. 12, '62		Transf. from A, 2d Sharpshooters; missing in battle May 13, '64.
Kerr, John.	22	Sept. 28, '61	July 14, '65	Vet.; captured at Reams' Station.
Ketchum, George W.	23	Jan. 1, '64	July 14, '65	
Kuhn, George M.	23	Mch. 9, '65	July 14, '65	
Latourell, Reuben O.	24	Jan. 1, '64	June 8, '65	Died Jan. 9, '65; wnd. Reams' Station Aug. 25, '64.
Lacher, John J	25	Mch. 24, '64	June 8, '65	Vet.; transf. from Co. A, 2d U.S. Sharpshooters; dis. per order.
Lang, James		Sept. 2, '64	Jan. 22, '65	Discharged for disability.
Leamier, Peter	23	Feb. 24, '64	June 8, '65	
Leonard, Maurice F	35	Mch. 8, '65	July 14, '65	
Lewis, Asa B.		Mch. 8, '65	July 14, '65	Vet., Corp.; captured at Petersburg.
Little, Albert	30	Dec. 25, '63		Trans. from A, 2d Sharpshooters; trans. to V.R.C. May 27, '65.

Roster of Company A — *Continued.*

Names.	Age.	Mustered In.	Mustered Out.	Remarks.
Litchenberg, August	30	July 20, '64		Vet.; wounded June 22, '64, Petersburg.
Lonquist, John	30	Jan. 1, '64		Killed June 22, '64, near Petersburg.
May, John S.	22	Mch. 24, '64	July 14, '65	Vet., Corp., Serg.
Marshall, James	24	Feb. 11, '62		Vet.; died June 28, '64, of wounds June 23, '64, at Petersburg.
Mattison, Mathias	19	Mch. 9, '65	July 14, '65	
Maricle, Abraham	37	Dec. 25, '63	July 14, '65	Vet.; transferred from A, 2d Sharpshooters.
Martell, Nelson	35	Aug. 16, '64	June 8, '65	Vet.; transferred from A, 2d Sharpshooters; dis. per order.
McDonald, Joseph	28	Jan. 1, '64		Vet., Serg.; died April 1, '65, in Minnesota.
McWilliams, David	28	Mch. 31, '64	July 14, '65	Veteran.
McKillup, Geo. W	38	Jan. 20, '64	Aug. 31, '65	Vet.; trans. from A, 2d Sharpshooters; discharged per order.
McCulloch, Jonas G.	18	Mch. 24, '64		Vet.; died Aug. 13, '64, in De Camp General Hospital, N. Y.
Merritt, Lorenzo		Apl. 1, '64	July 15, '65	Wounded at Petersburg; discharged in hospital.
Metz, Peter		Mch. 24, '64		Killed near Petersburg June 22, '64.
Mortimer, Geo. F.	23	Sept. 9, '61	Sept. 16, '64	Vet., Corp.
Nelson, Andrew	18	Feb. 29, '64	July 14, '65	
Nelson, Evan B.	18	Mch. 9, '65	July 14, '65	
Newel, Erastus W	21	Mch. 8, '65	July 14, '65	
Perkins, Daniel A.	29	Mch. 24, '64	June 19, '65	Discharged per order.
Pettyjohn, Dyer B.	28	Oct. 1, '61		Vet., Serg.; transferred from A, 2d U. S. Sharpshooters.
Peasley, Joseph W	18	Mch. 25, '64	July 14, '65	Musician, Vet.
Phillips, John	39	Mch. 6, '65	July 14, '65	
Pomeroy, Harlan P.	19	Mch. 23, '64		Vet.; absent sick on discharge of company.
Pribble, Turner	24	Nov. 25, '61	July 24, '65	Captured June 22, '64; discharged per order.
Putnam, Clark	32	Jan. 4, '64	July 14, '65	Vet.; prisoner of war.
Rayher, Frank		Feb. 27, '64		Vet.; died Oct. 14, '64, at Fort Schuyler, New York Harbor.
Reed, Nathaniel	18	Feb. 28, '64		Vet.; died Oct. 22, '64, at Philadelphia, Pa.
Reed, Walter S.	25	Apl. 5, '64	June 13, '65	Corp.; discharged per order June 13, '65.
Roberts, Benjamin	22	Mch. 31, '64	Nov. 30, '64	Vet., Serg.; discharged for disability.
Rosemeyer, George	31	Aug. 22, '62		Transferred to V. R. C. Sept. 22, '64.
Rye, Knute T.	24	Feb. 29, '64		Transferred to V. R. C. April 19, '65.
Ryder, Edward A.	25	Dec. 25, '61		Prisoner at Andersonville; discharged July 24, '64.
Scovill, Everett W	29	Dec. 25, '63	July 14, '65	Vet.; transferred from A, 2d Sharpshooters, Jan. 30, '65.
Shepard, Maurice F.	28	Feb. 29, '64	July 14, '65	Vet.; prisoner of war.
Sherman, Marshall	40	Mch. 24, '64		Vet.; lost leg at battle of Deep Bottom, Va., Aug. 14, '64.
Sias, George	21	Mch. 15, '64	July 14, '65	Prisoner at Andersonville.
Smith, Nelson B.	40	Feb. 29, '64	July 14, '65	
Smith, Almon P.	21	Feb. 28, '64		Vet.; transf. from A, 2d Sharpshooters, Jan. 30, '65; dis. per order June 8, '65.
Smith, Francis	27	Apl. 4, '64		Died July 14, '65, of wounds.
Steinberg, Adam		Mch. 30, '64	July 14, '65	
Storkelson, Ole	32	Feb. 29, '64		Died Dec. 9, '64, at Washington, D. C.
Stacy, William H.	24	Dec. 25, '63		Vet.; transf. from A, 2d Sharpshooters, Jan. 30, '65; absent, sick, on discharge of company.
Swartwout, Eugene	21	Mch. 30, '64	July 14, '65	Vet.; transferred from A, 2d Sharpshooters, Jan. 30, '65.
Taylor, Charles E.	36	Feb. 28, '64	July 8, '65	Discharged in hospital per order.
Thomas, Evan	17	Mch. 6, '65	July 8, '65	
Townsend, Perry C.	28	Jan. 1, '64		Wounded near Petersburg; absent on discharge of company.
Tompkins, Elias	30	Mch. 9, '65	July 8, '65	
Veon, Edmund	23	Sept. 28, '61	Sept. 27, '64	Vet.; wounded Jerusalem Plank Road June 21, '64.
Victory, James C.	35	Jan. 1, '64	Sept. 26, '64	Vet., Corp.
Waugh, Joseph B.	25	Mch. 8, '65	July 14, '65	
Weaver, Simon	36	Feb. 20, '64	June 7, '65	Vet.; trans. from A, 2d Sharpshooters, Jan. 30, '65; dis. per order.
Whetstone, Thomas N.	30	Mch. 24, '64		Vet., Serg.; promoted Capt. Co. D March 17, '65.
Whittemore, James A.	21	Feb. 29, '64	June 7, '65	Transferred from A, 2d Sharpshooters, Jan. 30, '65.
Willey, George	17	Feb. 24, '64	June 7, '65	Musician.
Woodworth, Walter C.	26	Mch. 9, '65	June 22, '65	Discharged per order.

ROSTER OF COMPANY B.

Names.	Age.	Mustered In.	Mustered Out.	Remarks.
OFFICERS.				
Captains—				
Ellett P. Perkins	27	May 5, '64	Oct. 13, '64	Vet.; discharged per order.
Charles F. Hausdorf	23	Nov. 26, '64		Vet., 1st Lieut. May 12, '64; Maj. May 2, '65; com. Lieut. Col.
Thos. H. Pressnell	22	June 6, '65	July 14, '65	2d and 1st Lieut. Co. A.
First Lieutenant—				
J. Thomas Walker	23	Jan. 1, '65	July 14, '65	Transferred from Co. A to 2d Sharpshooters.
Second Lieutenant—				
Henry D. O'Brien	22	May 12, '64		Vet., Capt. Co. A, Apl. 10, '65; com. Major.
Wm. W. Holden	23	Apl. 9, '65		Vet., 1st Lieut. Co. H, June 8, '65.
ENLISTED MEN.				
Abraham, Geo. W. F.	17	Apl. 1, '64		Musician; died Nov. 12, '64, in Andersonville, Ga.
Abel, Wm. H.	24	Mch. 24, '64	July 14, '65	Vet., Wagoner.
Adams, David A.	25	Mch. 8, '65	July 14, '65	
Ames, Orville	34	Feb. 27, '64		Supposed to have died July, '64.
Aucker, Wm. H.	21	Feb. 28, '62		Wounded at Gettysburg July 2, '63; absent, sick.
Barton, Wm. F.	18	Apl. 1, '64	July 14, '65	Promoted Corp.
Bergh, Peter	21	Mch. 24, '64		Prisoner at Andersonville 8 mos.; dis. July 24, '65; absent, sick.
Berdan, Charles A.	24	Nov. 15, '61	Nov. 17, '64	Vet.; discharged on expiration of term.

Roster of Company B — *Continued.*

Names.	Age.	Mustered In.	Mustered Out.	Remarks.
Bond, Hezekiah	26	Aug. 22, '62		Wounded near Petersburg; died Oct. 26, '64, at Andersonville.
Bowers, John G	34	Mch. 8, '65	July 14, '64	
Bouler, Theodore	28	Mch. 9, '65	July 14, '65	
Bofferding, Wm.	21	Feb. 20, '64	July 14, '65	
Bond, Daniel	19	Aug. 22, '62	July 24, '65	Vet., Corp.; prisoner at Andersonville 8 months.
Bryant, James	21	Apl. 16, '64		Vet., 1st Serg.; promoted 1st Lieut. Mch. 16, '65.
Brown, Edward F.	17	Feb. 20, '64	July 14, '65	Musician.
Breich, Lewis	19	Mch. 31, '64	July 14, '65	
Brink, Hiram A.	36	Apl. 2, '64		Vet.; discharged '65; absent, sick.
Brenchley, Philip	22	Feb. 20, '64	Dec. 27, '64	Discharged for disability.
Brown, Theodore		July 20, '61	July 20, '64	Vet.; discharged on expiration of term.
Brown, Wm. B.	18	Mch. 8, '65	July 14, '65	
Buck, Philip	18	Mch. 5, '64	July 14, '65	Promoted Corp.; prisoner 6 months.
Carlton, David	38	Feb. 26, '63	July 14, '65	Veteran.
Canniff, John	21	Mch. 24, '64	July 14, '65	Veteran, Corporal.
Caulkin, Gavin E.	36	Feb. 27, '64		Vet., Capt. Co. E, Mch. 21, '65.
Carlson, Carl	34	Mch. 11, '65		Discharged '65; absent.
Churchill, Wm. H.	22	Mch. 24, '64	July 14, '65	Vet., Corp.; promoted Serg., 1st Serg.; prisoner 6 months.
Chandler, J. C.	30	Mch. 24, '64	July 14, '65	Promoted Corp.
Church, Harrison	29	Mch. 8, '65		Died '65.
Collins, Peter		Mch. 24, '64		Vet.; killed July 14, '65, at Deep Bottom, Va.
Coleman, Henry	24	Mch. 30, '64	July 14, '65	
Cooper, John	41	Mch. 30, '64	July 14, '65	Veteran.
Curtis, Archibald	21	Mch. 24, '64	July 14, '65	Veteran, Corporal.
Decker, A. L. M	21	Sept. 10, '61	June 1, '64	Discharged for wounds.
Densmore, Sylvester	24	Mch. 1, '64		Died Nov. 25, '64, at City Point, Va.
Docker, J. H.	19	Feb. 11, '62		Wounded July 2, '63, at Gettysburg; absent since.
Durfee, Chester	18	Aug. 26, '62	Mch. 9, '65	Vet.; discharged for disability.
Dyer, Joshua	24	Mch. 31, '64		Vet., Serg.; pris. at Andersonville 8 mos; supposed dead
Fisher, Henry J.	23	Mch. 24, '64	July 14, '65	Vet.; wounded June 22, '64, at Petersburg.
Frary, Eldrick J.	28	Feb. 21, '62	Feb. 20, '65	Vet.; discharged on expiration of term.
Gilroy, Thomas	32	Mch. 11, '65	July 14, '65	
Gilbert, Richard	44	Mch. 9, '65		Died May 19, '65, at Baltimore, Md.
Giles, James A.	26	Feb. 27, '64	June 17, '65	Vet.; discharged for disability.
Glazier, Aaron	29	Apl. 1, '64		Vet., Corp.; died Sept. 3, '64, wounds Reams' Station Aug. 25, '64.
Gullman, John	19	Feb. 20, '62	Feb. 20, '65	Vet.; discharged on expiration of term.
Hansen, Lewis	21	Dec. 16, '61	Dec. 18, '64	Vet.; discharged on expiration of term.
Hamilton, E. M. C.	30	Apl. 4, '64	June 19, '65	Discharged in hospital.
Hamilton, Elmsley J	22	Mch. 1, '64	June 28, '65	Prisoner at Andersonville 8 months; discharged.
Hawks, James		Mch. 1, '64	July 14, '65	Vet.; wounded June 22, '64, near Petersburg.
Hayes, Charles	17	Mch. 10, '65	June 9, '65	Discharged per order.
Halleck, Joseph	42	Feb. 14, '65	Apl. 4, '65	Discharged per order.
Hamblett, Albert H.	21	Sept. 30, '61		Killed May 6, '64, in battle.
Henderson, Lyman H.	23	Mch. 9, '65	July 14, '65	
Hill, Jonas R.	30	Sept. 14, '61	Sept. 14, '64	Vet.; discharged on expiration of term.
Hill, Corlett	28	Mch. 9, '65	July 14, '65	
Holland, Alonzo	25	Nov. 18, '61	Nov. 18, '64	Vet.; wounded Jerusalem Plank Road, June 21, '64.
Hoyt, Wm. H.	20	Sept. 10, '61	Apl., '65	Vet.; discharged on expiration of term.
Hohage, F. W	43	Mch. 28, '64	July 14, '65	
Irvine, Wm. N.	22	Apl. 8, '64		Vet., Serg.; died June 28, '64, of wounds at Petersburg.
Imeson, James W.	18	June 20, '61	July 20, '64	Vet.; discharged on expiration of term.
Johnson, Samuel		Mch. 10, '64	July 14, '65	Corporal.
Kern, William	35	Mch. 8, '65	July 14, '65	
Knowlton, Geo. W	18	Feb. 13, '64	July 27, '65	Discharged in hospital.
Koenig, Sebastian	24	Mch. 2, '65	Apl. 4, '65	Discharged per order.
Knowles, William	28	Mch. 8, '65	July 14, '65	
Lavercombe, John		Mch. 30, '64		Vet.; died Nov. 19, '64, at Washington, D. C.
Matson, John	35	Mch. 27, '65	July 14, '65	
Magnuson, Magnus	30	Mch. 11, '65	July 14, '65	
McGee, Richard	29	Mch. 24, '64	July 14, '65	Corporal.
McIntyre, Malcolm	21	Mch. 24, '64		Vet., Corp. and Serg. June 8, '65.
McGuire, Hugh G.	32	Mch. 35, '64	July 14, '65	
McClay, John	27	Feb. 27, '64		Wounded at Deep Bottom Aug. 14, '64.
Morgan, David L.	21	Apl. 1, '64		Promoted Q. M. Serg. April 1, '65.
Munson, Madse	18	Mch. 1, '64	July 14, '65	
Nelson, John	23	Feb. 4, '62	Feb. 11, '65	Discharged on expiration of term.
Nelson, Paul	24	June 19, '61	July 4, '64	Vet.; discharged on expiration of term.
Noonan, Patrick	35	Mch. 14, '64		Died Oct. 29, '64, in prison at Salisbury, N. C.
Noble, Charles	35	June 20, '61	July 20, '64	Vet., Serg.; discharged on expiration of term.
Olen, Olof	36	Mch. 8, '65	July 14, '65	
Page, Henry D.	43	Mch. 9, '65	July 14, '65	
Parker, Edmund F.		Sept. 28, '61	Apl. 21, '65	Vet.; discharged on expiration of term.
Peterson, Peter	28	Feb. 11, '62		Died Dec. 15, '64, at Salisbury Prison, N. C.
Peters, John	37	Feb. 29, '65	July 14, '65	
Peterson, Carl	30	Mch. 11, '65	July 14, '65	
Person, Peter	34	Mch. 11, '65	July 14, '65	
Pickle, Alonzo	20	Aug. 14, '62	June 7, '65	Veteran, Corporal; discharged per order.
Piker, Wm. C.	37	Feb. 24, '65	July 14, '65	
Pratt, Job J.	23	Mch. 1, '64	July 14, '65	Wounded June 22, '64, near Petersburg.
Ray, Wm.		Mch. 24, '64	July 14, '65	
Riddle, Wm. C.	32	Apl. 2, '64	July 14, '65	Corporal.
Reb, Stephen	34	Mch. 9, '65	July 14, '65	
Roberts, Isaiah M.	43	Mch. 24, '65	July 14, '65	
Rye, Charles	21	Feb. 27, '64	July 14, '65	
Sampier, Francis	17	Feb. 17, '65	July 14, '65	
Schumacher, Wm. E.	28	Apl. 2, '64	July 14, '65	Veteran, Corporal, Sergeant.
Sebers, Albert	18	Mch. 4, '62		Vet.; wounded at Gettysburg; discharged 1865.

THE FIRST BATTALION.

ROSTER OF COMPANY B—Continued.

NAMES.	AGE	MUSTERED IN.	MUSTERED OUT.	REMARKS.
Scurry, James	27	Feb. 27, '64	....	Vet.; died Aug. 27, '64, of wounds at Deep Bottom Aug. 14, '64.
Stook, Norman	22	Apl. 1, '64	July 14, '65	Captured at Reams' Station.
Schutz, Peter	30	Feb. 1, '64	July 21, '65	Died Sept. 21, '64, in prison at Richmond, Va.
Sly, Gilbert E.	21	Mch. 31, '65	....	Corp., Killed Aug. 14, '64, at Deep Bottom, Va.
Smith, J. Benjamin	21	Jan. 1, '64	July 14, '65	Discharged on expiration of term.
Smith, John H.	39	Aug. 14, '62	June 7, '65	
Snow, Lafayette W.	18	Sept. 28, '61	July 14, '65	Vet.; discharged on expiration of term.
Stites, Adam C.		Aug. 28, '61	Sept. 28, '64	Prisoner at Andersonville 6 months; discharged 1865.
Starckloth, Herman	37	Mch. 8, '65	July 29, '65	Discharged; absent, sick.
Studley, George W.	38	Mch. 8, '65	July 14, '65	
Summers, Elam		Feb. 27, '64	....	Died Dec. 7, '64, of disease got in rebel prison.
Sunbey, Geo. G.	19	Nov. 8, '61	May 18, '65	Vet.; discharged on expiration of term.
Sullivan, Daniel	38	Nov. 8, '61	June 7, '65	Discharged as per order.
Swan, Erickson	30	Mch. 24, '64	June 7, '65	Veteran.
Swoigert, Wm.		Mch. 24, '64	....	Discharged in 1865; absent, sick.
Swanson, John	21	Mch. 24, '64	....	Wounded June 23, '64, at Petersburg; died June 27, '64.
Talby, Edward		Apl. 1, '64	....	Vet.; promoted Com. Serg. July 1, '65.
Tollman, Sylvester	23	Nov. 8, '61	July 14, '65	Vet.; died April 8, '65, of disease contracted in rebel prison.
Walsh, Joseph	23	Mch. 9, '65	July 14, '65	Killed Aug. 14, '64, at Deep Bottom, Va.
Waterburg, Andrew P.	20	Mch. 24, '64	July 14, '65	
Weaver, James E.	20	Mch. 24, '64	....	Veteran.
Weeks, John		Feb. 13, '64	....	Died Aug. 8, '64, in field hospital, Virginia.
Westworth, Walter		Feb. 1, '64	....	Prisoner at Andersonville 8 months; discharged 1865.
Whallon, Martin S.	23	Mch. 24, '64	July 14, '65	Veteran.
Winger, C. Wesley				

ROSTER OF COMPANY C.

NAMES.	AGE	MUSTERED IN.	MUSTERED OUT.	REMARKS.
Captains.				
Charles C. Parker	27	Mch. 14, '65	June 15, '65	Vet., 2d and 1st. Lieut. Co. A; resigned.
James Bryant	22	June 16, '65	July 14, '65	Vet., 1st Serg. Co. B.
First Lieutenant.				
Albert C. Poor	35	Mch. 14, '65	June 15, '65	Resigned.
Second Lieutenant.				
Wm. A. Joy	26	Apl. 1, '65	July 14, '65	Veteran.
ENLISTED MEN.				
Allen, David H.	22	Mch. 8, '65	July 14, '65	
Ballard, Isaac	30	Mch. 11, '65	July 14, '65	Deserted Mch. 19, '65, at La Crosse, Wis.
Bassy, Charles	22	Mch. 8, '65	July 14, '65	
Baldwin, M. W.	22	Mch. 8, '65	July 14, '65	
Baker, Morris G.	16	Mch. 11, '65	July 14, '65	
Barnes, Jonathan	42	Mch. 1, '65	July 14, '65	
Billings, Isaac M.	23	Mch. 8, '65	July 14, '65	
Blankey, Daniel	38	Mch. 8, '65	July 14, '65	
Boldner, Philip	21	Mch. 11, '65	July 14, '65	Died June 26, '65, at Frederick, Md.
Bowman, John W.	31	Mch. 8, '65	July 14, '65	Promoted Corporal.
Brill, Hezekiah	19	Mch. 1, '65	July 14, '65	Deserted Mch. 19, '65, at La Crosse, Wis.
Brennan, John	24	Mch. 1, '65	July 8, '65	Corporal; discharged per order.
Brown, George	22	Feb. 28, '65	June 6, '65	
Chipman, Horace A.	35	Feb. 27, '65	July 14, '65	
Charlson, Frank W.	23	Feb. 1, '65	July 14, '65	
Clow, Malcolm	19	Mch. 1, '65	July 14, '65	
Crandall, Byron F.	35	Mch. 7, '65	July 14, '65	
Crandall, Henry A.	35	Mch. 7, '65	July 14, '65	
Crink, John	38	Feb. 28, '65	July 14, '65	
Custer, Isaac	34	Feb. 28, '65	July 14, '65	Discharged in 1865, in hospital, sick.
Dorn, William	32	Mch. 10, '65	July 14, '65	Deserted Mch. 20, '65, at Chicago, Ill.
Dodge, William	32	Mch. 7, '65	July 14, '65	
Dunham, Abner	30	Mch. 7, '65	July 14, '65	
Dunham, Gabel	17	Mch. 7, '65	July 14, '65	
Dunton, Geo. W.	29	Feb. 24, '65	July 14, '65	
Durland, John	42	Mch. 10, '65	July 14, '65	
Elger, William	33	Mch. 1, '65	Aug. 10, '65	Discharged in hospital.
Flanagan, Lauren	31	Feb. 25, '65	July 14, '65	Sergeant.
Frazier, Julius H.	19	Feb. 23, '65	July 14, '65	

ROSTER OF COMPANY C—Continued.

NAMES.	AGE	MUSTERED IN.	MUSTERED OUT.	REMARKS.
Harris, Charles	42	Mch. 7, '65	July 14, '65	Died June 16, '65, near Munson's Hill, Va.
Hayes, Samuel	37	Mch. 7, '65	July 14, '65	
Harriman, B. W.	34	Mch. 10, '65	July 14, '65	Died at City Point. (No date.)*
Henry, Alexander	31	Mch. 2, '65		Corporal.
Hoff, Abraham M.	22	Mch. 8, '65	July 14, '65	
Hobert, Anton	21	Mch. 8, '65	July 14, '65	
Hovey, Alonzo	20	Mch. 9, '65	July 14, '65	
Hockoff, George A.	19	Mch. 10, '65		Discharged, 1865, from hospital.
Hunt, William	21	Mch. 1, '65		Discharged, 1865, from hospital.
Johnson, Robert	32	Mch. 8, '65	July 14, '65	Discharged in hospital 1865.
Johnson, John	18	Mch. 8, '65	July 14, '65	
Johnson, Wm. H.	18	Mch. 10, '65	July 14, '65	
Jones, George	35	Mch. 8, '65	July 14, '65	Corporal.
Kills, John	26	Mch. 8, '65	July 14, '65	
Krick, Philip	31	Mch. 9, '65	July 14, '65	
Lauerman, Michael	32	Mch. 10, '65	July 14, '65	
Lahr, Peter	28	Mch. 7, '65	July 14, '65	Sergeant.
Lee, Aaron	28	Mch. 1, '65	July 14, '65	Corporal; disabled, absent, sick.
Libby, J. J.	17	Feb. 24, '65	Aug. 8, '65	Sergeant; discharged in hospital.
Lucas, John	27	Mch. 1, '65	Aug. 8, '65	Corporal.
Magoon, Harrison C.	27	Mch. 1, '65		Corporal.
Marlett, Charles	38	Mch. 10, '65	July 14, '65	Died June 3, '65, at Munson's Hill, Va.
McClelland, John	27	Mch. 6, '65		Died April 30, '65, near Burkville, Va.
McLean, William	16	Mch. 10, '65	July 14, '65	
Menske, August	48	Mch. 6, '65	July 14, '65	
Monroe, Bennett	22	Mch. 10, '65	July 14, '65	
Morse, Windsor F.	42	Feb. 1, '65	July 14, '65	
Myers, Julius	41	Mch. 19, '65	July 14, '65	Discharged in hospital.
Newhall, R. B.	29	Aug. 21, '65	June 9, '65	Corporal.
Nickel, Philip	35	Mch. 11, '65	June 9, '65	Discharged per order.
Fakenquist, L. H.	21	Feb. 28, '65	June 8, '65	Discharged per order.
Parmere, W. H.	33	Mch. 11, '65	June 8, '65	Discharged per order.
Paulson, Paul	25	Feb. 20, '65	June 6, '65	Discharged per order.
Pierce, E. W.	37	Mch. 10, '65	May 3, '65	Discharged in hospital.
Priest, John A.	22	Mch. 19, '65	July 14, '65	
Preston, Smith	24	May 8, '65	July 14, '65	
Riley, John	24	Mch. 7, '65	July 14, '65	
Saupe, Frederick	21	Mch. 11, '65	July 14, '65	Corporal; discharged in hospital.
Schaffer, Jacob	35	Feb. 27, '65	July 14, '65	
Sherman, John H.	20	Mch. 13, '65	July 14, '65	
Spooner, John W.	39	Mch. 10, '65	July 14, '65	
Star, Adolph F.	41	May 8, '65	July 14, '65	
Stetson, Lorenzo P.	22	Mch. 11, '65	July 14, '65	
Story, Zachens	30	Mch. 11, '65	July 14, '65	Died June 7, '65, near Munson's Hill, Va.
Stahler, Michael	20	Mch. 11, '65	July 14, '65	
Taylor, George	22	Mch. 7, '65	July 14, '65	
Thrall, W. C.	24	Mch. 8, '65	July 14, '65	Discharged per order.
Thalenhorst, Henry	41	Mch. 11, '65	July 14, '65	Corporal.
Tripp, Nathan	38	Mch. 8, '65	July 14, '65	Corporal.
Utter, Charles S.	24	Feb. 25, '65	July 14, '65	
Van Loon, Lawrence	18	Feb. 28, '65	July 14, '65	
Wayman, Andrew	17	Mch. 8, '65	July 14, '65	

ROSTER OF COMPANY D.

NAMES.	AGE	MUSTERED IN.	MUSTERED OUT.	REMARKS.
OFFICERS.				
Captain.				
Thomas N. Whetstone	30	Mch. 17, '65	July 14, '65	Veteran, Sergeant Co. A.
First Lieutenant.				
Ransom J. Madison	26	Mch. 17, '65	May 29, '65	Resigned.
Second Lieutenant.				
Francis E. Wheeler	25	Apl. 30, '65	May 5, '65	Resigned.
ENLISTED MEN.				
Adams, Andrew J.	25	Mch. 15, '65		Died June 9, '65, near Munson, Va.
Andrews, Wm. H.	44	Mch. 15, '65		Sergeant.
Aughen, Caugh John W.	18	Mch. 14, '65	July 14, '65	Corporal.
Atwater, James P.	22	Mch. 14, '65	July 14, '65	Sergeant.
Bates, L. C.	40	Mch. 14, '65	July 14, '65	
Batzia, Christopher	27	Feb. 28, '65	July 14, '65	
Baumgartner, B.	40	Mch. 13, '65	July 14, '65	

COMPANY E.

ROSTER OF COMPANY D—Continued.

NAMES.	AGE	MUSTERED IN.	MUSTERED OUT.	REMARKS.
Walter, John	29	Mch.15,'65	July 14,'65	
Wheeler, W. H.	22	Mch.15,'65	July 14,'65	
Wheeler, Trueman B.	21	Mch.15,'65	July 14,'65	
Wilson, Nathan	30	Mch.16,'65	June 7,'65	Discharged per order.

ROSTER OF COMPANY E.

NAMES.	AGE	MUSTERED IN.	MUSTERED OUT.	REMARKS.
OFFICERS.				
Captain—				
Gavin E. Caulkin	37	Mch.25,'65	June15,'65	Veteran, Private Co. B; resigned.
First Lieutenant—				
James A. Wright	24	Apl.21,'65	July 14,'65	Veteran.
Second Lieutenants—				
Geo. W. Crooker	29	Apl.21,'65	Apl.27,'65	Resigned.
Lewis J. Bennett		Apl.4,'65	June15,'65	Resigned.
ENLISTED MEN.				
Abbott, J. D.	35	Mch.15,'65	July 14,'65	
Adam, Wm. L.	25	Mch.15,'65	July 14,'65	
Allen, Wm. E.	33	Mch.17,'65	July 14,'65	
Andrews, Theodorus J.	29	Mch.18,'65	July 14,'65	
Arnold, Wm. W.	36	Mch.18,'65	July 14,'65	
Austin, George	33	Mch.17,'65	July 14,'65	Discharged in hospital '65.
Barnard, George	24	Mch.18,'65	July 14,'65	Sergeant.
Bennett, J. G.	24	Mch.18,'65	July 14,'65	Corporal.
Bullard, Samuel	35	Mch.18,'65	July 14,'65	
Buck, Edwin P.	21	Mch.18,'65	July 9,'65	Discharged per order.
Carvey, Stephen	38	Mch.17,'65	July 14,'65	
Chamberlain, H. P.	22	Mch.17,'65	July 14,'65	Corporal, Sergeant.
Churchill, Eben	31	Mch.18,'65	July 14,'65	Corporal.
Chafey, Wm.	40	Mch.15,'65	July 14,'65	
Chambers, George	41	Mch.16,'65	July 14,'65	
Dixon, Wm.	32	Mch.15,'65	July 14,'65	
Doland, Thomas	17	Mch.15,'65	July 14,'65	
Doramus, John F.	28	Mch.15,'65	July 14,'65	
Duncan, John	17	Mch.17,'65	July 14,'65	
Dye, George	28	Mch.8,'65	Aug. 6,'65	Discharged in hospital Aug. 8, '65.
Edwards, Huntington	18	Mch.16,'65	June22,'65	Discharged in hospital.
Ellison, John B.	29	Mch.18,'65	July 14,'65	Sergeant.
Ellsburg, Charles	34	Mch.17,'65	July 14,'65	
Enny, Joseph J.	31	Mch.18,'65	July 14,'65	
Erah, Joseph J.	31	Mch.17,'65	June21,'65	Discharged per order.
Farnham, Hiram	44	Mch.15,'65	June21,'65	Discharged in hospital.
Fligal, Wm.	32	Mch.17,'65	July 14,'65	
Gee, William	89	Mch.16,'65	July 14,'65	
Guttormson, Gull	44	Mch.16,'65	July 19,'65	Discharged in hospital.
Haverson, Halver	30	Mch.17,'65	July 14,'65	Sergeant.
Harris, Wm. A.	23	Mch.18,'65	July 14,'65	
Hewitt, Charles	23	Mch.18,'65	July 14,'65	
Heskett, Geo. E.	37	Mch.18,'65	July 24,'65	Discharged in hospital.
Hickok, Franklin K.	40	Mch.18,'65	July 14,'65	Discharged per order.
Howe, Lafayette	35	Mch.18,'65	June19,'65	Discharged per order.
Hobbs, Daniel F.	30	Mch.17,'65		Died at Washington, D. C.
Houston, Cyrus H.	35	Mch.18,'65	June19,'65	Sergeant.
Higgins, John P.	38	Mch.17,'65	July 14,'65	
Iverson, Lars	24	Mch.17,'65	June 2,'66	Promoted Corporal.
James, John E.	21	Mch.17,'65	July 14,'65	Promoted Corporal.
Johnson, Martin	25	Mch.18,'65	Aug.10,'65	Discharged in hospital.
Johnson, Hernyon A.	39	Mch.17,'65	July 14,'65	
Knowlton, Charles R.	84	Mch.17,'65	July 14,'65	Discharged in hospital.
Larson, Martin	42	Mch.17,'65	Aug. 2,'65	
Lewis, Jacob	84	Mch.17,'65		Died March 26, '65, at Fort Snelling, Minn.
Lovejoy, Luther N.	25	Mch.17,'65	July 26,'65	Discharged in hospital.
McColly, George	88	Mch.18,'65	July 26,'65	
McPeak, Michael	27	Mch.18,'65	July 26,'65	Discharged in hospital.
Miller, Christopher	86	Mch.18,'65		Discharged in hospital.
Miller, C. F.	80	Mch.16,'65	July 14,'65	
Morrison, Daniel R.	37	Mch.16,'65	July 14,'65	Discharged per order.
Neamith, James	22	Mch.16,'65	July 17,'65	
Oleson, Niels	37	Mch.17,'65	June17,'65	
Parker, Newton	87	Mch.17,'65	July 14,'65	
Perry, Zepheniah	44	Mch.16,'65	July 17,'65	Corporal.
Pettengill, James M.	29	Mch.17,'65	July 14,'65	
Phillips, Francis E.	31	Mch.18,'65	July 14,'65	
Pitcher, Wesley W.	21	Mch.17,'65	July 14,'65	
Porter, Lorenzo D.	28	Mch.17,'65	July 14,'65	Corporal.
Rawler, Wm. F.	39	Mch.18,'65	July 14,'65	Sergeant, Corporal.
Ramsay, Nathaniel	34	Mch.17,'65	July 14,'65	
Scott, James	35	Mch.16,'65	July 14,'65	
Shoreson, James				

THE FIRST BATTALION.

ROSTER OF COMPANY D—Continued.

NAMES.	AGE	MUSTERED IN.	MUSTERED OUT.	REMARKS.
Bascombe, Hubert	25	Mch.14,'65	July 14,'65	
Bioestorn, Wm.	22	Mch.14,'65	July 14,'65	
Bisse, John H.	36	Mch.14,'65	July 14,'65	
Bryan, Thomas	35	Mch.14,'65	July 14,'65	
Brut, Wm. P.	37	Mch.14,'65	July 14,'65	
Brown, Wm.	41	Mch.13,'65	July 14,'65	
Burdice, Job W.	34	Feb.27,'65	July 14,'65	
Buhler, John	42	Mch.14,'65	July 14,'65	
Bunch, Quinton	88	Mch.16,'65	July 14,'65	Sergeant.
Campbell, Thomas	88	Mch.17,'65	July 18,'65	Discharged in hospital.
Cahill, Michael	37	Mch.16,'65	Aug.10,'65	Discharged in hospital Aug. 10, '65.
Campbell, John	26	Mch.16,'65	July 14,'65	Sergeant, 1st Sergeant.
Clark, Thomas	43	Mch.7,'65	July 14,'65	
Cole, Leander	21	Mch.7,'65	July 14,'65	
Cole, Elihu	26	Mch.7,'65	July 14,'65	
Cohoes, John	22	Mch.7,'65	July 14,'65	
Cutter, Marshall	28	Mch.15,'65	July 14,'65	Sergeant.
Daloy, John	40	Mch.16,'65	July 14,'65	
Daloy, Leonard B.	37	Mch.16,'65	July 14,'65	
Devine, Thomas	43	Mch.16,'65	July 14,'65	
Deidrich, August	30	Mch.14,'65	July 14,'65	
Dief, Robert	18	Mch.15,'65	July 14,'65	
Dickman, John	24	Mch.16,'65	July 14,'65	
Doyle, John	38	Mch.16,'65	July 14,'65	
Dreager, Ernst	21	Mch.18,'65	July 14,'65	
Dressel, Richard	21	Mch.16,'65	July 14,'65	
Ellis, Wm.	44	Mch.14,'65	July 14,'65	Corporal.
Farnham, Wm. M.	20	Mch.16,'65	July 14,'65	Corporal.
Field, John M.	19	Mch.16,'65	July 14,'65	
Flood, Edward	80	Mch.17,'65	July 14,'65	
Gillett, Albert	35	Mch.16,'65	July 14,'65	Discharged per order.
Green, Joseph M.	87	Mch.8,'65	July 14,'65	
Grewe, Wm.	29	Mch.16,'65	July 14,'65	Discharged per order.
Gunderson, Borge	23	Mch.14,'65	July 14,'65	Discharged per order.
Hamum, Frederick	32	Mch.14,'65	July 14,'65	
Harding, Henry H.	38	Mch.14,'65	July 14,'65	
Halverson, Halver	30	Mch.15,'65	July 14,'65	
Hassler, Swan	44	Mch.16,'65	May 29,'65	
Hanzes, Daniel	20	Mch.16,'65	July 14,'65	
Henderson, Roswell	28	Mch.14,'65	July 14,'65	
Hedges, Allen W.	28	Mch.8,'65	July 14,'65	Corporal.
Heller, Henry	21	Mch.14,'65	July 14,'65	Corporal.
Hosmer, Edwin M.	28	Mch.15,'65	July 14,'65	
Hurley, Theodore F.	18	Mch.13,'65	July 14,'65	
Hurley, Patrick	37	Mch.15,'65	July 14,'65	
Kilmer, Francis A.	20	Mch.16,'65	July 14,'65	
Knoche, Albert	21	Mch.14,'65	July 14,'65	Corporal.
Korfage, Wm.	81	Mch.14,'65	July 14,'65	
Krenbring, John	28	Mch.15,'65	July 14,'65	
Kuntz, Frank	87	Mch.14,'65	July 14,'65	
Linn, Andrew	18	Mch.15,'65	July 14,'65	
Malimson, Mathew	38	Mch.16,'65	July 14,'65	
Meary, John	21	Mch.15,'65	July 14,'65	
Morey, Chauncey	39	Mch.15,'65	July 14,'65	Promoted per order June 7, '65.
Morris, John F.	26	Mch.17,'65	July 14,'65	
Muckingham, John	23	Mch.15,'65	July 14,'65	
Oleson, Ole	38	Mch.15,'65	July 14,'65	Corporal.
Oleson, Erick	17	Mch.15,'65	July 14,'65	
Ostrom, Swan P.	29	Mch.2,'65	July 14,'65	
Parsons, Wm.	28	Mch.15,'65	July 14,'65	
Perkins, Thomas	43	Mch.16,'65	July 14,'65	
Peaslee, Nathaniel D.	36	Mch.16,'65	July 14,'65	Sergeant.
Philbrick, Samuel C.	19	Mch.14,'65	July 14,'65	Sergeant Major.
Place, James H.	82	Mch.8,'65	July 14,'65	
Powers, Augustus W.	37	Mch.14,'65	July 14,'65	
Reese, Isaac	33	Mch.15,'65	July 14,'65	Corporal.
Rhinehart, Oscar	81	Mch.14,'65	July 14,'65	
Ritz, Andrew	42	Mch.15,'65	July 14,'65	
Richardson, L. G.	25	Mch.16,'65	July 14,'65	
Bosch, Jacob	40	Mch.14,'65	July 14,'65	
Rolfing, John	86	Mch.14,'65	July 14,'65	
Schugg, John	87	Mch.15,'65	July 14,'65	
Schaumberg, Fred	20	Mch.14,'65	July 14,'65	
Simonson, Ole	26	Mch.15,'65	July 14,'65	
Smith, Wm.	30	Mch.16,'65	July 14,'65	
Smith, John Y.	41	Mch.16,'65	July 14,'65	
Speakman, Samuel	26	Mch.14,'65	July 14,'65	
Stearns, Levi W.	43	Mch.15,'65	July 14,'65	
Stearns, Peter	44	Mch.14,'65	July 14,'65	Promoted Corporal.
Taylor, John H.	26	Mch.15,'65	July 14,'65	Promoted Corporal; died June 2, '65, near Munson's Hill, Va.
Thompson, Oscar M.	42	Mch.16,'65	July 14,'65	
Thole, Charles	27	Mch.16,'65	July 14,'65	
Thompson, John C.	24	Mch.15,'65	July 14,'65	
Torkelson, Torkel				

ROSTER OF COMPANY E—Continued.

NAMES.	AGE	MUSTERED IN.	MUSTERED OUT.	REMARKS.
Snyder, Conrad	35	Mch. 18, '65	July 14, '65	
Stevens, Lafayette	36	Mch. 18, '65	July 14, '65	Corporal.
St. Claire, John	28	Mch. 17, '65	July 14, '65	
Steinberg, Wm.	22	Mch. 17, '65	July 14, '65	
Thompson, Wm.	38	Mch. 16, '65	July 14, '65	Absent on discharge of company.
Thomas, Lewis	38	Mch. 17, '65	July 14, '65	
Tolefson, Sander	19	Mch. 16, '65	July 14, '65	
Turner, Wilbur	29	Mch. 17, '65	July 14, '65	
Ward, Geo. W.	32	Mch. 16, '65	July 26, '65	Discharged in hospital July 29, '65.
Walker, John W.	32	Mch. 16, '65	July 26, '65	
Wallace, Thomas	37	Mch. 17, '65	July 26, '65	
Weaver, Philip	34	Mch. 18, '65	July 14, '65	
Weaver, John	36	Mch. 15, '65	July 14, '65	
Winters, Peter	38	Mch. 15, '65	July 14, '66	
Wilcox, John	38	Mch. 18, '65	July 14, '65	Discharged per order.
Widrich, John	36	Mch. 18, '65	July 14, '65	
Williamson, Charles M.	32	Mch. 16, '65	July 26, '65	
Wrangham, Wm. B.	24	Mch. 16, '65	July 14, '66	

ROSTER OF COMPANY F.

NAMES.	AGE	MUSTERED IN.	MUSTERED OUT.	REMARKS.
Officers.				
Captain—				
Lafayette Hadley	35	Mch. 31, '65	July 14, '65	
First Lieutenant—				
Thomas H. Kelly	24	May 25, '65	July 14, '65	
Second Lieutenant—				
Clark Andrews	30	Mch. 29, '65	June 15, '65	Resigned.
Enlisted Men.				
Anderson, Silas	34	Mch. 24, '65	July 14, '65	Absent on discharge of company.
Baker, John	36	Mch. 23, '65	July 14, '65	Discharged per order.
Bidwell, Benjamin	38	Mch. 20, '65	July 14, '65	Discharged in hospital.
Bissonet, Lewis	23	Mch. 22, '65	July 14, '65	
Biggerstaff, James	36	Mch. 30, '65	July 14, '65	
Bonham, Amos C.	18	Mch. 27, '65	July 14, '65	
Boyd, John F.	29	Mch. 22, '65	June 8, '65	Discharged per order.
Bunt, Adam	34	Mch. 25, '65	July 14, '65	Discharged per order.
Buck, Sidney	18	Mch. 25, '65	June 8, '65	
Click, Abram	32	Mch. 24, '65	July 14, '65	
Collard, Alfred	37	Mch. 20, '65	July 14, '65	
Cole, James M.	20	Mch. 30, '65	July 14, '65	Discharged per order.
Cripps, Wm.	31	Mch. 25, '65	July 14, '65	Discharged per order.
Dearman, Geo. W.	36	Mch. 27, '65	June 8, '65	Promoted Corporal.
Dorr, John J.	29	Mch. 22, '65	July 14, '65	
Elliott, John W.	19	Mch. 22, '65	July 14, '65	Discharged in hospital '65.
Eels, Mortimer R.	32	Mch. 33, '65	July 14, '65	Discharged per order.
Emidson, Gunder	35	Mch. 22, '65	July 14, '65	
Erickson, Ole	19	Mch. 24, '65	June 8, '65	Sergeant.
Esbaugh, David	22	Mch. 30, '65	July 14, '65	Corporal.
Garland, Wm. H.	81	Mch. 24, '65	July 14, '65	Died, 1865, at Parkersburg, Va.
Gverland, Mads	19	Mch. 24, '65	July 14, '65	
Gilbertson, Gilbert	38	Mch. 20, '65	July 14, '65	Corporal.
Gould, Charles	39	Mch. 27, '65	July 14, '65	
Green, Ezra W.	25	Mch. 22, '65	July 14, '65	Discharged in hospital.
Harvey, Alphonso	24	Mch. 23, '65	July 14, '65	
Hanson, Joseph L.	26	Mch. 22, '65	June 2, '65	Discharged in hospital '65.
Hardy, Wm.	19	Mch. 22, '65	July 14, '65	Discharged per order.
Hall, Leslie	32	Mch. 27, '65	July 14, '65	
Harrison, Wm. W.	33	Mch. 22, '65	July 14, '65	
Hadley, Simon	38	Mch. 22, '65	July 14, '65	Corporal.
Hoople, David	18	Mch. 22, '65	July 14, '65	
Howard, Silas N.	17	Mch. 27, '65	July 14, '65	Corporal.
Ingraham, James	22	Mch. 20, '65	July 14, '65	
Jacobson, John	38	Mch. 25, '65	July 14, '65	
Jenkins, Wm.	41	Mch. 23, '65	July 14, '65	
Johnson, Moses	19	Mch. 27, '65	July 14, '65	Corporal.
Kingston, Wm. D.	19	Mch. 24, '65	July 14, '65	
Koole, Nels	17	Mch. 25, '65	July 14, '65	Corporal.
Larson, Nils	23	Mch. 22, '65	July 14, '65	
Leech, John	28	Mch. 20, '65	July 14, '65	
Lihvig, Daniel A.	37	Mch. 25, '65	June 9, '65	Discharged in hospital.
Loomis, Oliver	37	Mch. 20, '65	July 14, '65	
McGaffey, Oliver	21	Mch. 25, '65	July 14, '65	
McKay, Hugh	27	Mch. 27, '65	July 14, '65	
Mitchell, George	31	Mch. 24, '65	July 14, '65	
Morris, Wm. B.	32	Mch. 22, '65	June 9, '65	Discharged in hospital.

ROSTER OF COMPANY F—Continued.

NAMES.	AGE	MUSTERED IN.	MUSTERED OUT.	REMARKS.
Morse, Henry	19	Mch. 25, '65	July 14, '65	Deserted April 7, '65, at La Crosse, Wis.
Ogden, John	29	Mch. 25, '65	July 14, '65	
Ogden, John R.	32	Mch. 25, '65	July 14, '65	
Oleson, Ole	18	Mch. 22, '65	July 14, '65	
Oleson, Halvar	37	Mch. 25, '65	July 14, '65	
Oleson, Austin	29	Mch. 22, '65	July 14, '65	
Park, Zebadiah	37	Mch. 24, '65	June 8, '65	Discharged per order.
Price, James K.	32	Mch. 16, '65	July 14, '65	
Reed, Joshua	39	Mch. 22, '65	July 14, '65	Corporal.
Reardon, Timothy W	37	Mch. 23, '65	July 14, '65	Died at Washington, D. C., 1865.
Schoen, John A.	33	Mch. 22, '65	July 14, '65	
Simonson, John F	37	Mch. 22, '65	June 6, '65	Discharged per order.
Sidebottom, Wm. D.	43	Mch. 21, '65	July 14, '65	
Smith, Wm. D.	18	Mch. 18, '65	July 14, '65	
Stevens, Chas. L.	24	Mch. 24, '65	July 14, '65	
Stevens, August	18	Mch. 25, '65	July 14, '65	
Swenson, Kittel	18	Mch. 22, '65	July 14, '65	
Thurston, Henry H.	32	Mch. 25, '65	July 14, '65	1st Sergeant.
Vaught, Hans H.	18	Mch. 22, '65	July 14, '65	Sergeant.
Vinton, Winfield	21	Mch. 21, '65	July 14, '65	
Warner, John M.	36	Mch. 20, '65	June 21, '65	Discharged in hospital.
Walk, Charles A	17	Mch. 22, '65	July 14, '65	Sergeant.
Warner, Benjamin	28	Mch. 22, '65	June 21, '65	Corporal; discharged in hospital.
Warner, Harvey G.	29	Mch. 22, '65	July 14, '65	
White, Wm. H.	41	Mch. 22, '65	July 14, '65	Discharged per order.
Wilsey, Charles	26	Mch. 25, '65	June 6, '65	Corporal.
Williams, Julius C	35	Mch. 20, '65	July 14, '65	
Work, Adolphus A	34	Mch. 21, '65	July 14, '65	
Woolf, Theodore.	20	Mch. 20, '65	July 14, '65	Discharged in hospital.
Wolfe, George.	19	Mch. 24, '65	July 14, '65	
Young, Wm. H	22	Mch. 25, '65	July 14, '65	
Zimmer, John	36	Mch. 27, '65	July 14, '65	

ROSTER OF COMPANY G.

NAMES.	AGE	MUSTERED IN.	MUSTERED OUT.	REMARKS.
Officers.				
Captain—				
James N. Dodge	22	Apl. 5, '65	July 14, '65	
First Lieutenant—				
Orlando J. Gardiner	23	Apl. 5, '65	June 15, '65	Resigned.
Second Lieutenant—				
Joseph Halleck	42	Apl. 5, '65	June 4, '65	Resigned.
Enlisted Men.				
Adams, John	30	Mch. 28, '65	July 14, '65	
Allen, Horace B.	28	Mch. 30, '65	June 10, '65	Discharged per order.
Allen, David T.	26	Mch. 30, '65	July 14, '65	Corporal.
Alexander, Geo. J	18	Mch. 28, '65	July 14, '65	
Andrews, Bradford W	41	Mch. 30, '65	July 14, '65	
Arnoldy, Peter	32	Mch. 30, '65	July 14, '65	
Baldwin, Wm.	35	Mch. 30, '65	July 14, '65	Discharged per order.
Bendson, Christian.	44	Mch. 30, '65	July 14, '65	
Billings, Levi.	20	Mch. 30, '65	June 20, '65	
Billings, Geo. W	24	Mch. 30, '65	July 14, '65	
Borden, Lysander	34	Mch. 30, '65	July 14, '65	Discharged per order.
Bren, John	16	Mch. 24, '65	July 14, '65	
Chinnard, Lewis	19	Mch. 30, '65	July 14, '65	Sergeant.
Cook, Fayette	16	Mch. 30, '65	June 8, '65	
Comstock, Wm. H.	39	Mch. 30, '65	July 14, '65	Died July 9, '66, at Jeffersonville, Ind.
Cooper, James H	85	Mch. 30, '65	July 14, '65	
De Grush, Wm. J.	24	Mch. 30, '65	July 14, '65	Corporal.
Dodge, Emerson	17	Mch. 30, '65	July 14, '65	
Drowley, George.	43	Mch. 30, '65	July 14, '65	Sergeant.
Dullard, Michael	23	Mch. 27, '65	July 14, '65	
Eaton, Horace G.	24	Mch. 28, '65	July 14, '65	
Elwiss, Francis	32	Mch. 30, '65	July 14, '65	
Federer, Dominick	34	Mch. 28, '65	July 14, '65	Died May 11, '65, at Washington, D. C.
Felton, John	18	Mch. 30, '65	July 14, '65	
Fiero, Sidney A.	27	Mch. 30, '65	July 14, '65	
Fible, Henry	18	Mch. 30, '65	July 14, '65	
Fogarty, Patrick	23	Mch. 27, '65	July 14, '65	
Gay, Charles H	31	Mch. 23, '65	July 14, '65	
Garrison, Geo. W	26	Mch. 30, '65	July 14, '65	
Gapp, John	32	Mch. 30, '65	Aug. 2, '65	Discharged in hospital Aug. 2, '65.
Gorman, David C.	32	Mch. 27, '65	July 14, '65	
Hanson, Peter.	23	Mch. 25, '65	July 14, '65	
Harvey, Lewis E.	16	Mch. 27, '65	June 9, '65	Died May 5, '65, at City Point, Va.

ROSTER OF COMPANY H—Continued.

NAMES.	AGE.	MUSTERED IN.	MUSTERED OUT.	REMARKS.
Dee, William	27	Apl. 7,'65	July 14,'65	Promoted Corporal.
Degood, Hart B.	22	Apl. 4,'65	July 14,'65	
Denton, Marion G.	18	Mch. 81,'65	July 14,'65	
Durkee, Edwin	29	Mch. 28,'65	July 14,'65	Sergeant.
Eastman, Leander	37	Mch. 31,'65	July 14,'65	
Einfeldt, Henry	19	Apl. 28,'65	July 14,'65	
Ellingson, Hittel	26	Apl. 3,'65	July 14,'65	
Elliot, Simpson	44	Mch. 31,'65	July 14,'65	Corporal.
Erickson, Erick	82	Mch. 28,'65	July 14,'65	Corporal.
Erhmeke, Chas. H	80	Mch. 28,'65	July 14,'65	Discharged per order,
Farrell, Garrett	40	Apl. 4,'65	June 2,'65	Discharged in hospital.
Fisher, Albert	85	Apl. 4,'65	June 24,'65	Corporal.
Fowler, Leonard E.	27	Apl. 1,'65	July 14,'65	
Gessell, Wm	24	Apl. 6,'65	July 14,'65	Discharged per order.
Grinsted, Joseph H.	17	Mch. 28,'65	May 9,'65	
Gunderson, Peter	31	Mch. 29,'65	July 14,'65	
Gulson, Charles	22	Mch. 28,'65	July 14,'65	
Halverson, Seben.	38	Mch. 28,'65	July 14,'65	
Halverson, Christopher.	21	Apl. 3,'65	June 4,'65	Discharged in hospital '65.
Harvey, Geo. K	16	Apl. 3,'65	July 14,'65	Discharged per order.
Hanson, Steen, Jr.	18	Apl. 3,'65	July 14,'65	
Heliker, Samuel C.	43	Mch. 81,'65	June 24,'65	Discharged in hospital.
Isaac, Lewis	26	Mch. 30,'65	July 14,'65	
Janes, Charles	18	Mch. 29,'65	May 16,'65	Discharged per order.
Johnson, Andrew.	18	Apl. 3,'65	July 14,'65	
Johnson, Horace M.	89	Apl. 3,'65	July 14,'65	
Johnson, Abraham	25	Apl. 5,'65	July 14,'65	Corporal.
Kennedy, Thomas E.	19	Apl. 5,'65	July 14,'65	
Kelly, James	21	Mch. 28,'65	July 14,'65	
Kerns, George	25	Apl. 3,'65	July 14,'65	Promoted Sergeant.
Kidney, Chauncey J	19	Apl. 8,'65	July 14,'65	Promoted Sergeant.
Kimber, Albert.	18	Mch. 81,'65	July 14,'65	Discharged in hospital '65.
Larson, Paul	40	Mch. 29,'65	July 14,'65	
Landscho, Jochim	30	Mch. 30,'65	July 14,'65	Discharged per order.
Laplourt, J. B	85	Apl. 3,'65	May 16,'65	
Laird, Andrew, Jr.	20	Apl. 5,'65	July 14,'65	Corporal.
Miller, Edwin B.	21	Apl. 8,'65	July 14,'65	Died May 29,'65, at Alexandria, Va.
Monson, Knudt	18	Apl. 4,'65	July 21,'65	Discharged per order.
Neihart, Charles	19	Mch. 29,'65	July 14,'65	
Oleson, John.	18	Mch. 30,'65	July 14,'65	
Oleson, Lewis	25	Mch. 28,'65	July 14,'65	
Page, Horace.	29	Sept. 28,'65	July 14,'65	
Rohwerder, Claus.	17	Apl. 4,'65	June 5,'65	Discharged in hospital, Aug. 10,'65.
Rolf, Charles H.	26	Apl. 10,'65	June 5,'65	Discharged per order.
Sadler, George.	81	Apl. 5,'65	June 9,'65	Discharged per order.
Seamans, James R.	18	Apl. 6,'65	July 14,'65	
Seamans, Solomon L.	24	Mch. 28,'65	July 14,'65	
Shay, Frank	18	Mch. 28,'65	July 14,'65	Discharged in hospital.
Shay, Martin	19	Apl. 5,'65	July 14,'65	
Stevens, Wm. A.	83	Mch. 31,'65	July 14,'65	
Swanger, Wm.	5	Apl. 5,'65	July 14,'65	Corporal, Sergeant.
Thomas, Azariah.	27	Apl. 5,'65	July 14,'65	
Tarbox, Gonzelo E.	18	Apl. 6,'65	July 14,'65	
Thompson, George G.	22	Apl. 6,'65	July 14,'65	
Tronson, Edwin E.	30	Apl. 4,'65	July 14,'65	
Truesdell, Charles B.	24	Apl. 6,'65	July 14,'65	Died June 2,'65, at Munson's Hill, Va.
Tritscher, Belatus	86	Apl. 10,'65	July 14,'65	
Wells, David.	80	Apl. 10,'65	July 14,'65	
Wheeler, Jewett W.	24	Apl. 4,'65	July 14,'65	Discharged per order June 16,'65.
Whipple, Melvin J.	24	Apl. 16,'65	July 14,'65	
Williams, Peter	28	Mch. 27,'65	July 14,'65	Discharged in hospital '65.
Williams, Lewis	17	Mch. 81,'65	July 14,'65	

ROSTER OF COMPANY I.

NAMES.	AGE.	MUSTERED IN.	MUSTERED OUT.	REMARKS.
OFFICERS.				
Captain—				
John N. Wallingford	31	Apl. 25,'65	July 14,'65	
First Lieutenant—				
Jacob Z. Barncord	22	Apl. 25,'65	July 14,'65	
Second Lieutenant—				
Wm. J. Cornman	29	Apl. 25,'65	July 14,'65	
ENLISTED MEN.				
Ayers, Charles G.	37	Apl. 7,'65	July 14,'65	Discharged per order.
Barnett, Darius	18	Apl. 8,'65	July 14,'65	
Beatty, Daniel	25	Apl. 10,'65	July 14,'65	
Brooks, Israel	18	Apl. 11,'65	July 14,'65	

ROSTER OF COMPANY G—Continued.

NAMES.	AGE.	MUSTERED IN.	MUSTERED OUT.	REMARKS.
Hallett, Abram	18	Mch. 28,'65	July 14,'65	
Heath, Charles E.	17	Mch. 27,'65	July 14,'65	
Horton, Lucius	27	Mch. 27,'65	July 14,'65	
Jose, Horatio L.	43	Mch. 24,'65	July 14,'65	Sergeant.
Kellogg, Judson	25	Mch. 30,'65	June 8,'65	Discharged per order June 8,'65.
Knewel, John	29	Mch. 30,'65	July 14,'65	
Langton, James	26	Mch. 30,'65	July 14,'65	
Lent, Nicholas	19	Mch. 30,'65	July 29,'65	Discharged in hospital,
Livingston, Duncan	19	Mch. 30,'65	May 31,'65	Discharged per order.
Lowell, George	17	Mch. 27,'65	July 14,'65	Discharged in hospital '65,
Mann, James S.	82	Mch. 28,'65	July 14,'65	
McLaughlin, Samuel	28	Mch. 27,'65	July 14,'65	
McGill, Charles	39	Mch. 27,'65	June 8,'65	Discharged per order.
McQueen, Wm. B.	31	Mch. 30,'65	July 14,'65	Corporal.
Metcalf, Milton B.	26	Mch. 30,'65	July 14,'65	
Mills, Milton F.	31	Mch. 9,'65	June 8,'65	Discharged in hospital,'65,
Monson, Joseph	17	Mch. 21,'65	June 8,'65	Discharged in hospital June 8,'65.
Morse, Henry N.	22	Mch. 80,'65	June 8,'65	Discharged in hospital '65.
Nash, Elbert	25	Mch. 22,'65	July 14,'65	
Oleson, Adam	19	Mch. 14,'65	July 14,'65	Corporal.
Ordway, Isaac F.	25	Mch. 14,'65	July 14,'65	
Parsons, Warren	22	Mch. 27,'65	July 14,'65	
Payne, Henry	19	Mch. 29,'65	July 14,'65	Discharged in hospital,'65,
Parks, Geo. L.	16	Mch. 29,'65	June 8,'65	Discharged in hospital June 8,'65.
Pinney, Jerome S.	18	Mch. 27,'65	June 8,'65	Discharged in hospital '65.
Pope, Frentis A.	43	Mch. 30,'65	July 14,'65	
Porter, Cyren O.	20	Mch. 30,'65	July 14,'65	
Prentiss, Worthington S.	23	Mch. 13,'65	July 14,'65	Discharged in hospital.
Pugsley, Lyman	88	Mch. 14,'65	June 12,'65	
Rafferty, John	16	Mch. 14,'65	July 14,'65	Corporal.
Renoll, John	16	Mch. 28,'65	July 14,'65	
Sartwell, Theodorus	18	Mch. 27,'65	July 14,'65	
Schaffer, Oliver F.	38	Mch. 28,'65	July 14,'65	
Slocum, Marvin B.	18	Mch. 28,'65	July 14,'65	Discharged per order.
Stout, Joseph	24	Mch. 24,'65	July 14,'65	
Stocking, Frank	35	Mch. 28,'65	July 14,'65	
Thirll, Charles	18	Mch. 28,'65	June 8,'65	Died May 14,'65, at City Point, Va.
Thompson, Algernon A.	32	Mch. 27,'65	July 14,'65	Discharged in hospital
Vanderwort, Edward H.	18	Mch. 27,'65	July 14,'65	
Walker, Richard W.	18	Mch. 24,'65	July 14,'65	Discharged in hospital.
Webster, John E.	18	Mch. 30,'65	July 14,'65	
Whitcombe, Valentine O.	85	Mch. 30,'65	June 8,'65	Discharged per order.
Whitney, John	87	Mch. 30,'65	July 14,'65	Corporal.
White, John	18	Mch. 28,'65	July 14,'65	Sergeant.
Wickwire, Philander	41	Mch. 30,'65	July 14,'65	
Willis, Wm. W.	24	Mch. 27,'65	July 14,'65	
Woodruff, Geo. E.	24	Mch. 30,'65	July 14,'65	Discharged per order.
Wood, Mason H.	47	Mch. 30,'65	July 14,'65	

ROSTER OF COMPANY H.

NAMES.	AGE.	MUSTERED IN.	MUSTERED OUT.	REMARKS.
OFFICERS.				
Captain—				
John C. Crawford	35	Apl. 14,'65	June 15,'65	Resigned.
First Lieutenant—				
Philander C. Seeley	41	Apl. 10,'65	June 3,'65	Resigned.
Wm. W. Holden	24	June 8,'65	July 14,'65	Veteran.
Second Lieutenant—				
David Richardson	42	Apl. 14,'65	June 15,'65	Resigned.
ENLISTED MEN.				
Baker, Orin	41	Mch. 31,'65	July 14,'65	
Ball, John	25	Mch. 29,'65	July 14,'65	Corporal.
Baker, Benjamin F.	89	Apl. 1,'65	July 14,'65	Discharged in hospital '65.
Bingham, John G.	87	Apl. 1,'65	July 14,'65	
Blood, Milo N.	21	Apl. 6,'65	July 14,'65	
Boie, John	28	Mch. 28,'65	July 14,'65	
Boyd, Isaac D.	28	Mch. 28,'65	July 14,'65	
Bourdon, Peter	18	Mch. 28,'65	July 14,'65	
Burkins, James H.	19	Apl. 6,'65	July 14,'65	Deserted June 1,'65.
Burkhardt, Gottfried	21	Apl. 6,'65	July 14,'65	Promoted 1st Sergeant.
Butler, William	80	Mch. 25,'65	July 14,'65	
Cravath, O'Birney	30	Mch. 81,'65	July 14,'65	Discharged in hospital '65.
Chesroun, George	17	Apl. 7,'65	July 26,'65	Discharged in hospital
Chambers, Olin F.	16	Apl. 8,'65	July 14,'65	Deserted June 1,'65.
Cooper, Charles A.	53	Mch. 81,'65	July 14,'65	
Close, Wm.	33	Apl. 7,'65	July 14,'65	
Davis, Oscar W.	26	Apl. 5,'65	May 16,'65	Discharged per order.

ROSTER OF THE SECOND COMPANY OF MINNESOTA SHARPSHOOTERS.

NAMES.	AGE.	MUSTERED IN.	MUSTERED OUT.	REMARKS.
OFFICERS.				
Captains—				
Wm. F. Russell	30	Nov. 1, '61		Resigned Feb. 20, '63.
Emil A. Burger	29	Jan. 1, '62		Resigned Nov. 23, '63; 1st Lieutenant.
Mahlon Black	41	Jan. 4, '62	Jan. 3, '65	1st Serg.. '62; 2d Lieut. Feb. 20, '63; 1st Lieut. July 14, '63.
First Lieutenants—				
John A. W. Jones	29	Jan. 24, '62		Resigned May 26, '63; 2d Lieutenant.
Louis Fitzsimmons	20	Dec. 20, '61	Mch. 3, '65	Corporal, 1st Sergeant; wounded at Antietam; captured at Ream's Station Aug. 25, '64.
Second Lieutenant—				
Daniel H. Priest	22	Dec. 22, '61		Veteran; promoted Corporal, Sergeant.
ENLISTED MEN.				
Archibald, David	17	Dec. 24, '61		Mus.; wnd. severely in thigh at Cold Harbor, Va., June 4, '64.
Abbot, George	19	Feb. 27, '62		Dis. per Gen. Order, No. 154, Oct. 24, '62, to enlist in U. S. Cav.
Baker, Charles B.	26	Jan. 6, '62		Captured at Savage Station June 29, '62; exchanged; wounded at Bristoe Station Oct. 14, '63; captured at Ream's Station Aug. 25, '64; veteran.
Baker, Ozias B.	19	Jan. 6, '62		Captured at Savage Station June 29, '62; exchanged; wounded at Gettysburg July 3, '63.
Balsley, Sylvanus	26	Feb. 13, '62		Died at Harrison's Landing, Va., July 6, '62, of disease.
Bancroft, Geo. W	19	Dec. 13, '61		Wounded, badly, in shoulder at Antietam Sept. 17, '62; discharged for disability Dec. 7, '62.
Barnes, Elbridge S.	18	Dec. 24, '61		Wounded in shoulder at Fredericksburg, Md., Dec. 13, '62.
Barnes, John C.	22	Feb. 10, '62		Died of fever in Regimental Hosp. at Harper's Ferry Oct. 9, '62.
Barnes, Percival S.	18	Dec. 13, '61		Cap. at Savage Station June 29, '62; exch.; wnd. at Cold Harbor June 3, '64; cap. again at Ream's Station Aug. 25, '64; died in rebel prison.
Beach, Samuel B.	24	Nov. 30, '61		Vet. Jan. 1, '64; disch. to enlist as Hospital Steward in U. S. A.
Beecroft, John	21	Oct. 24, '61		Deserted in '62.
Benton, James H.	24	Mch. 3, '62		Wnd. in hip at Antietam Sept. 17, '62; disch. for dis. Jan. 5, '63.
Biggs, Edward	22	Dec. 6, '61		Dis. for dis. in '62 at St. Paul; did not go with company; left, sick.
Billings, Myron E.	25	Dec. 16, '61		Sergeant; wounded in foot at battle of Antietam Sept. 17, '62; discharged for disability Jan. 7, '63.
Borden, Daniel B.	19	Feb. 24, '62		Captured at Savage Station June 29, '62; exchanged; wounded at Antietam Sept. 17, '62; discharged for dis. June 12, '63.
Brown, Joseph T.	27	Dec. 24, '61		Captured at Savage Station June 29, '62; exchanged; died of fever at Frederick, Md., Sept. 30, 62.
Brown, Joseph L.	24	Feb. 1, '62		Vet. Feb. 1, '64; pro. Corp.; dis. to enlist in U. S. Cav. Feb. 6, '65.
Brown, Sylvester	20	Dec. 3, '61		Captured at Savage Station June 29, '62; exchanged; killed in action July 3, '63, at Gettysburg.
Brown, Wesley	19	Feb. 18, '62		No record.
Bruce, Franklin	25	Dec. 4, '61		Deserted; arrested and escaped from Pro. Marshal at Wash., D.C.
Buttolph, Morris	34	Jan. 3, '62		Musician; died of disease Sept. 5, '62, at Newport News.
Chaney, J. B.	34	Dec. 16, '61		Corp.; dis. for dis. Oct. 22, '62, at Wash., D. C. (Finley Hospital).
Chamberlain, James	24	Feb. 27, '62		Wounded in arm, badly, at Antietam, Sept. 17, '62; discharged for disability March 8, '63.
Chandler, Wm. B.	23	Feb. 17, '62		Captured at SavageStation June 29, '62; dis. for dis. Nov. 20, '62.
Cheney, Oscar F.	31	Jan. 4, '62		No record.
Churchill, Salmon R.	39	Jan. 16, '62		Discharged for disability Sept. 20, '62; cause, sickness.
Coates, John T.	21	Dec. 24, '61		Wnd., badly, at Antietam Sept. 17, '62; dis. for dis. Feb. 18, '63.
Coleman, Wilbur M.	18	Dec. 18, '61		Wounded in leg, badly, at Antietam Sept. 17, '62; wounded in head at Gettysburg July 3, '63.
Connor, Dennis	21	Feb. 16, '62	Feb. 20, '65	Near Petersburg, Va., at expiration of term.
Cook, Wm. H.	38	Feb. 1, '62		Veteran Feb. 1, '64; transf. to Co. A, 1st Bat., Minn. Vol. Inf.
Cutler, Isaac J.	32	Dec. 18, '61		No record.
Curry, Hugh	30	Dec. 31, '61		Corporal; reduced at his own request; captured at Ream's Station, Va., Aug. 25, '64.
Dahle, Jens T.	22	Jan. 20, '62		Wnd. at Antietam Sept. 17, '62; capt. at Ream's Station Aug. 25, '64; mus. out at St. Paul June 29, to take effect April 22, '65.
Day, Wm. B.	31	Jan. 6, '62		Discharged for disability Dec. 4, '62.
Dennison, Alfred	24	Oct. 24, '61		Discharged for disability Nov. 15, '62.
Donely, Upton	21	Jan. 6, '62		Discharged per General Order, No. 154, Oct. 24, '62, to enlist in 6th U. S. Cavalry.
Dwelle, G. Merrill	26	Dec. 17, '61		Corporal; wounded in thigh at Antietam Sept. 17, '62; discharged for promotion Feb. 4, '64.
Eldredge, Charles R.	28	Dec. 31, '61		Corporal; wounded at Antietam, Va., Sept. 17, '62.
Eldred, John	19	Nov. 26, '61		Deserted.
Eldred, Morris	22	Nov. 26, '61		Deserted.
Elphee, Caleb	18	Jan. 29, '62		Discharged for disability Oct. 4, '62, at St. Paul, Minn.
Fallon, Hammond	25	Nov. 30, '61		Wounded at battle of Hanover Court House, Va., May 27, '62; discharged for disability Feb. 16, '63.
Fitzsimmons, Chas	19	Dec. 20, '61		No record.
Fingalson, Fingor	19	Jan. 20, '62		Wounded at Hanover Court House May 27, and again at Antietam Sept. 17, '62; re-enlisted March 31, '64.
Fisher, Jacob	44	Jan. 4, '62		Wagoner; re-enlisted Jan. 5, '64; wounded at Cold Harbor, Va., June 4, '64; captured at Ream's Station Aug. 25, '64; exch.; transferred to Co. A, 1st Battalion Infantry, Jan. 30, '65.
Fingalson, Truls	30	Jan. 20, '62		Discharged for disability Oct. 4, '63.
Fisher, Wm	40	Jan. 8, '62		Veteran; killed in action near Petersburg, Va., June 22, '64, by cannon ball.
Flom, Arthur A.	22	Jan. 22, '62		Promoted Corporal; re-enlisted March 31, '64.
Gaskill, Fred	28	Feb. 27, '62		Vet.; dis. to enlist in U. S. Cav. Feb. 16, '64; re-enl. Feb. 29, '64.
Goodrich, Evans	31	Dec. 24, '61		Sergeant; discharged for disability Feb. 18, '63.
Hanson, Chas. W	33	Jan. 22, '62		Deserted at St. Paul, Minn., March 23, '62.
Hanson, Christopher	23	Jan. 20, '62		Wounded by accidental discharge of his own rifle; discharged for disability Oct. 8, '62.
Hathaway, Charles E.	18	Jan. 30, '62		Discharged per General Order, No. 154, Oct. 22, '62; transferred to Battery C, 4th U. S. Artillery.
Heath, James L.	26	Feb. 13, '62		Transferred to Veteran Reserve Corps Sept. 26, '63.

ROSTER OF THE SECOND COMPANY OF MINNESOTA SHARPSHOOTERS—*Continued.*

NAMES.	AGE.	MUSTERED IN.	MUSTERED OUT.	REMARKS.
Howe, Thompson M.	44	Feb. 11, '62		Captured in hospital at Savage Station June 29, '62; exchanged; discharged for disability Feb. 11, '63.
Hurly, James L.	21	Jan. 26, '62		Discharged for disability Oct. 27, '62 (revolver wound in foot by his own carelessness).
Kellogg, Theodore B.	23	Dec. 19, '61		Promoted Sergeant.
Lawson, Mathew	18	Mch. 1, '62		Died at Washington Dec. 14, '62, of disease.
Lake, Sidney	29	Feb. 27, '62		No record.
Lind, Christen J.	23	Jan. 2, '62		Wounded at Fair Oaks, Va., June 1, '62; lost a finger; discharged for disability Oct. 10, '62.
Lockrem, Andrew	25	Jan. 20, '62		Wounded, badly, in thigh at Antietam Sept. 17, '62, and taken prisoner; exchanged; discharged for disability Feb. 20, '63.
Magoon, Harry	18	Jan. 27, '62		(Harrison C.); Veteran Feb. 29, '64; wounded at Cold Harbor, Va., June 4, '64; pro. Corp.; captured at Ream's Station Aug. 25, '64; exch.; pro. Serg; transf. to Co. C, 1st Battalion Infantry.
McMahon, William	20	Feb. 10, '62		Discharged per order Oct. 24, '62; transf. to 6th U. S. Cavalry.
Miller, James C.	43	Jan. 7, '62		Discharged for disability at camp near Fredericksburgh, Va., Nov. 28, '62, by order of Gen. Couch.
Morrison, Wm. E.	22	Dec. 26, '61		Corporal; promoted Sergeant.
Mosier, Norman	32	Jan. 28, '62		Wounded in hand at battle of Antietam, Va., Sept. 17, '62.
Ousten, Siver	26	Feb. 21, '62		Wnd., severely, in shoulder at battle of Antietam Sept. 17, '62.
Paine, Franklin	19	Jan. 21, '62		Serg.; dis. for pro. March 19, '63 (Capt. Co. B, 11th Minn. Infy).
Perry, Oscar	24	Dec. 5, '61		No record.
Pomeroy, Harlan P.	19	Mch. 4, '62		Vet. March 23, '64; captured at Ream's Station, Va., Aug. 25, '64; exchanged; transferred to Co. A, 1st Battalion Infantry.
Powers, John	32	Jan. 21, '62		Discharged for disability Dec. 28, '62.
Putnam, Clark	32	Jan. 4, '62		Re-enl. Jan. 5, '64; captured at Ream's Station, Va., Aug. 25, '64; exchanged; transf. to Co. A, 1st Battalion Minn. Infantry.
Quie, Halvor H.	27	Jan. 20, '62		Wnd. in heel, badly, at Antietam Sept. 17, '62; dis. for dis. Jan. 8, '63.
Richardson, F. C.	21	Dec. 24, '61		Corporal, Sergeant; discharged per order Oct. 24, '62; transferred to Co. B, 1st U. S. Cavalry, Oct. 24, '62.
Rinhart, Edward D.	25	Jan. 6, '62		Discharged for disability Sept. 26, '64; lost left eye in the affair near Vienna, Va., Sept. 2, '62.
Roe, John W.	30	Nov. 30, '61		Veteran Jan. 1, '64.
Ryan, Dennis	23	Feb. 16, '62		Died of disease July 30, '62, in hospital at Point Lookout, Md.
Ryan, Edward	21	Feb. 16, '62		Died near Frederick, Md., December, '62, of wound in head received at Antietam Sept. 17, '62.
Salt, John	23	Feb. 16, '62		Corporal; discharged for disability.
Scott, William	19	Jan. 21, '62		Wnd., severely, in battle of Antietam Sept. 17, '62; dis. for dis.
Sheopard, Morris F.	28	Feb. 27, '62		Vet. Feb. 29, '64; cap. at Ream's Station, Va., Aug. 25, '64; exch.; transf. to Co. A, 1st Batt., Minn. Inf.; dis. July 26, '65.
Smith, Nelson B.	40	Jan. 28, '62		Veteran Feb. 1, '64; credited to quota 4th Ward, Boston, Mass.; transferred to Co. A, 1st Battalion, Minnesota Infantry.
Smith, Wm. H.	21	Dec. 9, '61		Promoted Sergeant.
Spear, Charles H.	21	Jan. 14, '62		Promoted Hospital Steward 1st Battalion, Minnesota Infantry.
Stowman, Nathan	22	Jan. 7, '62		Re-enlisted Feb. 29, '64.
Strong, Robert J.	18	Feb. 18, '62		Discharged near Stevensburg, Va., Dec. 16, '63, to enlist as Hospital Steward in U. S. A.
Steffes, Anthony	......	July 15, '62		Wounded at Antietam Sept. 17, '62; discharged to enlist in U. S. Cavalry Feb. 16, '63.
Tonnar, George	20	Jan. 23, '62		No record.
Tanner, Luman O.	20	Feb. 12, '62		Discharged to enlist as Hospital Steward Feb. 16, '63.
Taylor, John	35	Dec. 11, '61		Discharged for disability in '62.
Underwood, A. J.	29	Dec. 16, '61		Serg.; wounded in thigh at Antietam Sept. 17, '62; discharged for disability Nov. 1, '62, at hospital in Harrisburg, Pa.
Wheeler, Francis E.	21	Dec. 22, '61		Discharged for disability Dec. 8, '62, at Alexandria, Va.
White, Lawrence	21	Jan. 23, '62		Died of wounds received in the affair near Vienna Sept. 2, '62.
Widstrand, Charles T.	18	Dec. 16, '61		Wounded, severely, in thigh at Antietam, Va., Sept. 17, '62.
Wiley, Edward L.	22	Mch. 17, '62		Deserted at Washington, D. C., April 28, '62.
Wilson, Andrew J.	28	Dec. 24, '61		Wnd. at Antietam Sept. 17, '62; transf. to V. R. C. July 1, '63.
Wilson, Harry H.	21	Jan. 15, '62		Veteran Feb. 29, '64; discharged for promotion April 1, '65; promoted 2d Lieut. Co. K, 1st Heavy Artillery, Minn. Vols.
Woods, Alanson B.	29	Dec. 31, '61		Discharged for disability Sept. 18, '62, at Philadelphia, Pa.

NOTES

1. A Brief History

1. Gertrude W. Ackermann, "Volunteer Guards in Minnesota," *Minnesota History* 16, no. 2 (June 1935), 175; D. R. Farnham, *D. R. Farnham's History of Wright County* (Buffalo, MN: Wright County Historical Society, 1976), 56–57.

2. William F. Fox, *Regimental Losses in the American Civil War, 1861–1865* (Albany, NY: Albany Publishing Company, 1889).

3. *Oxford Mid-weekly,* February 8, 1888.

4. *Duluth Herald,* May 30, 1907.

2. The Battle of Gettysburg

1. Dominic J. Dal Bello, *Parade, Inspection, and Basic Evolutions of the Infantry Battalion: Being a Manual for Company Officers and Non-commissioned Officers of Civil War Living History Units on the Movements of a Battalion of Infantry,* 3rd ed. (Santa Barbara, CA: D. J. Dal Bello, 1996).

2. Letter from William Colvill to John B. Batchelder, June 9, 1866, Batchelder papers, Minnesota Historical Society, St. Paul.

5. Company B

1. Dan L. Thrapp, *Al Sieber: Chief of Scouts* (Norman: University of Oklahoma Press, 1964), 174.

2. Thrapp, Al Sieber, 326.

6. Company C

1. Edward D. Neill, *The History of Minnesota: From the Earliest French Explorations to the Present Time* (Minneapolis: Johnson, Smith, and Harrison, 1878), 679.

2. William C. Oates and Frank A. Haskell, *Gettysburg,* edited and with an introduction by Glenn LaFantasie (New York: Bantam Books, 1992), 200–201.

3. William Harmon, "Co. C at Gettysburg," *Minneapolis Journal,* July 30, 1897.

4. Harmon, "Co. C at Gettysburg."

5. Letter from Marian Verbeke to Capt. DeWitt Smith, July 28, 1863, DeWitt Clinton Smith letter collection, Minnesota Historical Society, St. Paul.

6. Thomas H. Pressnell, "Incidents in the Civil War," chapter 10, page 5, P2135, manuscript notebooks, Minnesota Historical Society, St. Paul.

7. Pressnell, "Incidents in the Civil War," chapter 11, page 3.

8. Pressnell, "Incidents in the Civil War," chapter 12, page 10.

9. Pressnell, "Incidents in the Civil War," chapter 11, pages 9–10.

7. Company D

1. "An Incident," *Monticello (MN) Republican,* May 25, 1861.

2. Lucia L. Peavey Heffelfinger, *Memoirs of Christopher B. Heffelfinger* (Minneapolis, 1922), 34.

3. John Plummer, "Letter from a Soldier of the First Minnesota," *Minneapolis State Atlas,* August 26, 1863.

4. U.S. War Department, *War of the Rebellion: A Compilation of the Official Records of the Union and Confederate Armies,* series 1, vol. 49, part 1 (Washington, DC: Government Printing Office, 1880–1898).

8. Company E

1. "Surprised," *Altoona (PA) Tribune,* August 22, 1861.

2. James A. Wright, *No More Gallant a Deed,* edited by Steven Keillor (St. Paul: Minnesota Historical Society Press, 2001), 313.

3. Letter from Caleb Jackson to the secretary of war, Morehead, MN, December 17, 1889, Edwin Clark papers, Minnesota Historical Society, St. Paul.

4. Diary of Patrick Taylor, July 1 and 2, 1863, Patrick Henry Taylor and Isaac Lyman papers, Minnesota Historical Society, St. Paul.

9. Company F

1. Wright, *No More Gallant a Deed,* 65.

2. Wright, *No More Gallant a Deed,* 52.

3. Wright, *No More Gallant a Deed,* 194.

4. Letter from C. W. Merritt to a comrade, undated, photocopy, private collection.

5. "Letter From Dr. Stewart," *Mantorville (MN) Express,* October 18, 1861.

6. Letter from James H. Croff to the parent and sister of Joseph Garrison, Boston, MA, June 25, 1862, typed transcript, private collection.

7. Wright, *No More Gallant a Deed,* 235.

8. Wright, *No More Gallant a Deed,* 365–66.

9. Mark A. Hoyt's journal, John F. Hoyt and family papers, 1885–1886, Minnesota Historical Society, St. Paul.

10. Charles Merritt, "The Charge of Lieut Bruce," *Red Wing Republican,* August 9, 1905.

11. James A. Wright, "The Story of Company F., First Regiment," page 354, James A. Wright papers, Minnesota Historical Society, St. Paul.

10. Company G

1. Edward H. Bassett, *From Bull Run to Bristow Station*, edited by M. H. Bassett (St. Paul: North Central Publishing, 1962), 24.

2. Richard G. Krom, *The 1st MN: Second to None* (Rochester, MN: Richard G. Krom, 2010), 496–99.

3. Bassett, *From Bull Run to Bristow Station*, 35.

4. *Faribault Central Republican*, August 5, 1863.

5. Krom, *The 1st MN*, 496–99.

6. Letter from Edward Needham to Georgia Holt, July 23, 1861, Edward Needham papers, Minnesota Historical Society, St. Paul.

7. Letter from George Sawyer to Helen, April 24, 1863, private collection.

8. George Buckman deposition, October 9, 1900, Christopher B. Heffelfinger papers, box 2, page 615, Minnesota Historical Society, St. Paul.

9. Edward Needham papers, Minnesota Historical Society, St. Paul.

10. Charles Parker, military service and pension files, National Archives, Washington, DC.

11. Letter from George Sawyer to Helen, May 20, 1862, private collection.

12. Letter from George Sawyer to Helen, March 24, 1863, private collection.

13. Letter from Sgt. Henry C. Whitney to B. C. Sanborn, December 25, 1863, private collection.

11. Company H

1. Martin Ulvestad, *Nordmændene i Amerika: deres historie og rekord*, vol. 1 (Minneapolis: History Book Company's Forlag, 1907), 312.

2. Ulvestad, *Nordmændene i Amerika*, 312.

3. *Mankato Semi-weekly Record*, June 1861–July 18, 1863.

4. *Mankato Semi-weekly Record*, June 1861–July 18, 1863.

5. Letter from W. H. Wikoff to Richard Parry, March 9, 1862, private collection.

12. Company I

1. Letter from S. O. Seymour to Mrs. S. A. Ellis, July 11, 1863, private collection.

2. "From the Minnesota First," *Wabasha County Herald*, May 7, 1862.

3. "Returned Soldiers," *Wabasha County Herald*, May 14, 1862.

13. Company K

1. Balthasar Best, military service and pension files, National Archives, Washington, DC.

2. Letter from Alfred Carpenter, July 30, 1863, Winona County Historical Society, Winona, MN.

3. Daniel Hand, "Glimpses of an Army Surgeon," in *Glimpses of the Nation's Struggle: A Series of Papers Read before the Minnesota Commandry of the Military Order of the Loyal Legion of the United States*, vol. 1 (St. Paul: St. Paul Book and Stationery Company, 1887), 279.

4. Theophilus F. Rodenbough, ed., *Uncle Sam's Medal of Honor: Some of the Noble Deeds for Which the Medal Has Been Awarded, Described by Those Who Have Won It, 1861–1866* (New York: G. P. Putnam's Sons, 1886), 9–20.

5. Wright, *No More Gallant a Deed*, 401.

6. Rodenbough, *Uncle Sam's Medal of Honor*, 19–20.

14. Company L

1. Permission slip to enlist, private collection.

2. Emma Quie Bonhus, "The Old Sergeant Looking Back upon a Life Full of Stirring Events," *The Friend* (a Norwegian Lutheran Church publication), September 1930, 17.

15. Color-bearers

1. Minnesota Historical Society, *Scrapbook on the First Regiment Minnesota Volunteers in the Civil War* (St. Paul: Minnesota Historical Society, 1897–1908), 10.

2. Board of Commissioners, *Minnesota in the Civil and Indian Wars, 1861–1866*, vol. 2 (St. Paul: Pioneer Press Company, 1893), 28–29.

3. Jane Grey Swisshelm, *Crusader and Feminist: Letters of Jane Grey Swisshelm, 1858–1865*, edited and with an introduction and notes by Arthur J. Larsen (St. Paul: Minnesota Historical Society, 1934), 112.

4. *St. Paul Pioneer and Democrat*, July 17, 1862.

5. Henry D. O'Brien, "The First Minnesota at Gettysburg," *National Tribune*, December 1893.

6. A. B. Easton, *History of the St. Croix Valley* (Chicago: H. C. Cooper Jr., 1909), 42.

7. Edward Needham papers, Minnesota Historical Society, St. Paul.

8. William Colvill Jr., *Bull Run: Address of Col. Wm. Colvill at the Re-union of the Survivors of the First Minnesota, June 21, 1877* (Association of the Survivors of the First Minnesota, [1877?]), 6.

16. Musicians and Band

1. Affidavit by Seth Hammon, September 25, 1869, S. Morton Robins, military service and pension files, National Archives, Washington, DC.

Appendix A

1. Accession documents, First Minnesota infantry drum, Minnesota Historical Society, St. Paul.

BIBLIOGRAPHY

Ackermann, Gertrude W. "Volunteer Guards in Minnesota." *Minnesota History* 16, no. 2 (June 1935): 166–77.

Bassett, Edward H. *From Bull Run to Bristow Station.* Edited by M. H. Bassett. St. Paul: North Central Publishing, 1962.

———. Letters. Private collection.

Batchelder papers. Minnesota Historical Society, St. Paul.

Best, Balthasar. Diary. Author's collection.

Board of Commissioners. *Minnesota in the Civil and Indian Wars, 1861–1865.* 2 vols. St. Paul: Pioneer Press Company, 1891–1899.

Bond, Daniel. "Daniel Bond Reminiscences." M165. Microfilm. Manuscript collection. Minnesota Historical Society, St. Paul.

Bromley, Edward. *Minneapolis Portrait of the Past: A Photographic History of the Early Days in Minneapolis.* Minneapolis: Voyageur Press, 1973. First published in 1890 by F. L. Thresher.

Buckman, George R. Diary, 1863–1864. George Buckman Civil War papers. Minnesota Historical Society, St. Paul.

Carley, Kenneth. *The Dakota War of 1862: Minnesota's Other Civil War.* 2nd ed. St. Paul: Minnesota Historical Society Press, 2001.

———. *Minnesota in the Civil War.* Minneapolis, MN: Ross and Haines, 1961.

———. *Minnesota in the Civil War: An Illustrated History.* St. Paul: Minnesota Historical Society Press, 2000.

Carter, Horace D. *Roster: George N. Morgan Post, No. 4, G.A.R., Dept. of Minnesota.* Minneapolis: Wall and Haines, 1903.

Chaney, Josiah B. *History of the Acker Post, No. 21, G.A.R. St. Paul, Minn.: Prepared and Read on Its 20th Anniversary, April 10, 1890.* St. Paul: H. L. Collins Company, [1891 or 1892].

Colvill, William, Jr. *Bull Run: Address of Col. Wm. Colvill at the Re-union of the Survivors of the First Minnesota, June 21, 1877.* Association of the Survivors of the First Minnesota, [1877?].

Dal Bello, Dominic J. *Parade, Inspection, and Basic Evolutions of the Infantry Battalion: Being a Manual for Company Officers and Non-commissioned Officers of Civil War Living History Units on the Movements of a Battalion of Infantry.* 3rd ed. Santa Barbara, CA: D. J. Dal Bello, 1996.

Farnham, D. R. *D. R. Farnham's History of Wright County.* Buffalo, MN: Wright County Historical Society, 1976.

Ferrell, Robert H., ed. *Monterrey Is Ours! The Mexican War Letters of Lieutenant Dana 1845–1847.* Lexington: University Press of Kentucky, 1990.

First Minnesota Volunteer Infantry annual reunion collection, 1888–1930. Minnesota Historical Society, St. Paul.

Fitzharris, Joseph C. "The Crittenden Court of Inquiry and Historical Accuracy: Murfreesboro, TN, July 13, 1862." Presented at the Northern Great Plains History Conference, St. Cloud, MN, October 14–17, 2009.

———. "My Career before Yours, Sir: The Surrender of the Third Minnesota at Murfreesboro, July 13, 1862." Presented at the SMH Conference, Calgary, Alberta, Canada, May 24–27, 2001.

———. "What Can 21st Century Aerospace Officers Learn from 19th Century Infantry Officers?" Presented to the Air War College, February 24, 2003.

Fox, William F. *Regimental Losses in the American Civil War, 1861–1865.* Albany, NY: Albany Publishing Company, 1889.

Graf, Emil. Autobiography. Transcript. Private collection.

Groat, James W. *Pages Clothed in the Plainest of Dress: The Groat Diary.* Anoka, MN: Anoka County Historical Society, 1988.

Hamline University. *History of the Hamline University of Minnesota When Located at Red Wing Minnesota, from 1854 to 1869.* [St. Paul?]: Alumni Association of the College of Liberal Arts of Hamline University, 1907.

Hancock, Joseph Woods. *Goodhue County, Minnesota, Past and Present.* Red Wing, MN: Red Wing Printing Company, 1893.

Hand, Daniel. "Glimpses of an Army Surgeon." In *Glimpses of the Nation's Struggle: A Series of Papers Read before the Minnesota Commandry of the Military Order of the Loyal Legion of the United States.* Vol. 1. St. Paul: St. Paul Book and Stationery Company, 1887.

Heffelfinger, Christopher B., Papers. Minnesota Historical Society, St. Paul.

Heffelfinger, Lucia L. Peavey. *Memoirs of Christopher B. Heffelfinger.* Minneapolis, 1922.

Holcombe, R. I. *History of the First Minnesota Regiment Volunteer Infantry, 1861–1864.* Stillwater, MN: Easton and Masterson, 1916.

Hoyt, John F., and family papers. Minnesota Historical Society, St. Paul.

Johnson, Paul D. *Civil War Cartridge Boxes of the Union Infantryman.* Lincoln, RI: Andrew Mowbray Publishers, 1998.

Krom, Richard G. *The 1st MN: Second to None.* Rochester, MN: Richard G. Krom, 2010.

Lang, Wendell W., Jr. "The 1st Minnesota, So Grand a Body of Men." *North South Trader's Civil War,* July/August 1997.

Leehan, Brian. *Pale Horse at Plum Run.* St. Paul: Minnesota Historical Society Press, 2002.

Lochren, William. Papers. Minnesota Historical Society, St. Paul.

Loehr, Rodney C. "The First Minnesota at Gettysburg." *Gopher Historian* 16, no. 2, 1–5.

Lord, Francis A. *Civil War Collector's Encyclopedia*. Secaucus, NJ: Castle and Company, 1965.

Marty, Adam. "Muster Out Roll of Company B: 1st Minnesota Vols since the War." 1919. Author's collection.

Military service and pension files. National Archives, Washington, DC.

Minnesota Adjutant General's Office. *Minnesota Adjutant General's Report of 1866*. St. Paul: W. R. Marshall, 1866.

Minnesota Historical Society. *Scrapbook on the First Regiment Minnesota Volunteers in the Civil War*. St. Paul: Minnesota Historical Society, 1897–1908.

Minnesota Soldiers Home (Minneapolis). Commandant/administrator subject files. Minnesota Historical Society, St. Paul.

Moe, Richard. *The Last Full Measure*. New York: Henry Holt and Company, 1993.

Needham, Edward. Papers. Minnesota Historical Society, St. Paul.

Neill, Edward D. *History of Hennepin County and the City of Minneapolis*. Minneapolis: North Star Publishing Company, 1881.

———. *The History of Minnesota: From the Earliest French Explorations to the Present Time*. Minneapolis: Johnson, Smith, and Harrison, 1878.

Newsom, T. M. *Pen Pictures of St. Paul, Minnesota, and Biographical Sketches of Old Settlers: From the Earliest Settlement of the City, up to and including the Year 1857*. St. Paul: T. M. Newsom, 1886.

Oates, William C., and Frank A. Haskell. *Gettysburg*. Edited and with an introduction by Glenn LaFantasie. New York: Bantam Books, 1992.

O'Brien, Frank G. *Minnesota Pioneer Sketches: From the Personal Recollections and Observations of a Pioneer Resident*. Minneapolis: H. H. S. Rowell, 1904.

Pressnell, Thomas H. "Incidents in the Civil War." P2135. Manuscript notebooks. Minnesota Historical Society, St. Paul.

Ramsey, Alexander. Papers. Minnesota Historical Society, St. Paul.

Richardson, Antona Hawkins. *Roll of the Dead, 1886–1906: Department of Minnesota, Grand Army of the Republic*. St. Paul: Paduan Press, 2000.

Rodenbough, Theophilus F., ed. *Uncle Sam's Medal of Honor: Some of the Noble Deeds for Which the Medal Has Been Awarded, Described by Those Who Have Won It, 1861–1866*. New York: G. P. Putnam's Sons, 1886.

Smith, DeWitt Clinton. Letter collection. Minnesota Historical Society, St. Paul.

Swisshelm, Jane Grey. *Crusader and Feminist: Letters of Jane Grey Swisshelm, 1858–1865*. Edited and with an introduction and notes by Arthur J. Larsen. St. Paul: Minnesota Historical Society, 1934.

Taylor, Patrick Henry, and Isaac Lyman papers. Minnesota Historical Society, St. Paul.

Thrapp, Dan L. *Al Sieber: Chief of Scouts*. Norman: University of Oklahoma Press, 1964.

Ulvestad, Martin. *Nordmændene i Amerika: deres historie og rekord*. Vol. 1. Minneapolis: History Book Company's Forlag, 1907.

Upham, Warren. *Minnesota Place Names*. St. Paul: Minnesota Historical Society Press, 2001.

U.S. War Department. *War of the Rebellion: A Compilation of the Official Records of the Union and Confederate Armies*. Series 1. Vol. 49. Washington, DC: Government Printing Office, 1880–1898.

Walker, Edward A. Letters. Author's collection.

Wright, James A. *No More Gallant a Deed*. Edited by Steven J. Keillor. St. Paul: Minnesota Historical Society Press, 2001.

———. Papers. Minnesota Historical Society, St. Paul.

ILLUSTRATION CREDITS

About the Photographs
author's collection—xiv (top left and center), xvi (top), xvi (middle)
Richard G. Krom—xiv (top right)
Larry Scherber—xiv (bottom left)
Gettysburg National Military Park Library—xiv (bottom right)
Winona County Old Settlers Association—xv (top left and right)
William and Sandra Shumate—xv (middle left)
Minnesota Historical Society (MHS)—xv (middle center and bottom right)
W. J. Hefferman–Spencer Leader Print—xv (middle right)
Vesterheim Museum, Decorah, IA—xv (bottom left)
Dee Potterfield—xvi (bottom)

Chapter 1
MHS—3, 4 (all), 5 (all), 6 (all), 7 (top), 9, 10, 11, 12, 14, 15 (center left, center right, right), 17, 18
author's collection—7 (bottom), 15 (left)
Glenn Berdan and Julie Berdan Hipple—13

Chapter 2
MHS—23, 26, 27 (center left and center right)
U.S. Army Military History Institute—27 (left)
author's collection—27 (right), 33
Nancy Johnson—34
Gettysburg National Military Park Library—35
Maurice Olson—38 (top)
Michael Cunningham—38 (badge)
Larry Scherber—38 (bottom)

Chapter 3
author's collection—39, 42, 44 (all), 45 (bottom), 46, 53, 55, 57, 58 (top), 59
MHS—41, 43 (all), 45 (top), 47 (left), 49 (bottom), 56, 58 (middle and bottom)
Eugene Buelow—47 (right)
U.S. Army Military History Institute—49 (top)
Dennis Johnson—52 (top)
Pat Pasmore—61 (bottom)

Chapter 4
MHS—63, 64 (all except Richard Gorman), 65, 67, 71

author's collection—64 (Richard Gorman), 66, 69
Mike McAffe—68

Chapter 5
MHS—73, 75, 77 (top), 78, 86 (bottom), 87
Stephen and Wendy Osman—74
author's collection—76, 77 (bottom), 81, 82, 88 (top)
Hennepin History Museum—80
Skippy Davis—83 (all)
Arizona Historical Society—84 (top), 85 (bottom left)
Sharlot Hall Museum—84 (bottom), 85 (top)
True West magazine archives—86 (top)
Washington County Historical Society—88 (bottom)

Chapter 6
MHS—89 (all), 93, 101, 104
author's collection—90, 94, 95, 105
Michael Cunningham—92
Barbara Harmon—96, 97, 99
Hennepin History Museum—100
Stephen and Wendy Osman—106 (left)
U.S. Army Military History Institute—106 (right)

Chapter 7
MHS—107 (all), 109 (right), 111
author's collection—108 (all), 109 (left), 113 (all), 115 (bottom)
Hennepin History Museum—110 (top)
Minneapolis Public Library—112
Gordon Smith—114, 116, 117
Dana and Mary McDill—115 (top)

Chapter 8
author's collection—119, 120 (left), 121 (top right), 126
MHS—120 (right), 121 (top left), 124 (all)
Eugene Buelow—121 (bottom left and right)
Frank Underwood—129 (bottom)
U.S. Army Military History Institute—129 (top)
David Johnson—132

Chapter 9
MHS—133, 134 (top), 135 (Welch), 142, 143, 145, 149, 150, 151
Hamline University—134 (bottom), 135 (Bennett, Garrison, Harris), 137, 139 (left)

Glen Berdan and Julie Berdan Hipple—135 (Berdan), 139 (right)
U.S. Army Military History Institute—135 (Brooks)
Michael Cunningham—135 (Hoyt)
North Dakota State University—135 (Maginnis)
author's collection—135 (Webb), 148
Christopher Herrick—135 (Wright), 153, 155
Denise Bond—146
David Dickenson—156 (top)
Heidi Busse-Hansen—156 (bottom)

Chapter 10
MHS—157, 161, 162, 168 (bottom), 169
Richard G. Krom—159
Michael Cunningham—160 (all), 163
author's collection—158, 164
Mike McAffe—166
University of Oklahoma—167
Maurice Olson—168 (top)
Hennepin History Museum—170

Chapter 11
MHS—171, 172 (bottom), 174
author's collection—173, 175, 178, 177 (all), 180
Champlin Historical Society—176
Donald Nelson—179

Chapter 12
MHS—181
Richard Smith—182
Brian Stephens—183
Mike McAffe—185 (top)
author's collection—185 (bottom)
W. J. Hefferman–Spencer Leader Print—186

Chapter 13
MHS—187, 189, 195, 197, 199, 200 (all), 207
U.S. Army Military History Institute—190, 201
Stephen and Wendy Osman—192 (bottom left)
Janice Pickle Skold—192 (bottom right)
Earl Johnson—193 (top)
David Grant—194
author's collection—198
John Thillmann—205 (bottom)
Brown County Historical Society—260
Neville Public Museum of Brown County—208

INDEX

Page numbers in italics refer to pictures and captions.